The New Complete Treatise on the Arts of Tanning, Currying and Leather Dressing

by Professor H. Dussauce

with an introduction by Roger Chambers

This work contains material that was originally published by the Us Department of Agriculture in 1865.

This publication was created and published for the public benefit, utilizing public funding and is within the Public Domain.

This edition is reprinted for educational purposes and in accordance with all applicable Federal Laws.

Introduction Copyright 2018 by Roger Chambers

Self Reliance Books

Get more historic titles on animal and stock breeding, gardening and old fashioned skills by visiting us at:

http://selfreliancebooks.blogspot.com/

Introduction

I am pleased to present yet another title on Trapping and Tanning.

The work is in the Public Domain and is re-printed here in accordance with Federal Laws.

As with all reprinted books of this age that are intended to perfectly reproduce the original edition, considerable pains and effort had to be undertaken to correct fading and sometimes outright damage to existing proofs of this title. At times, this task is quite monumental, requiring an almost total "rebuilding" of some pages from digital proofs of multiple copies. Despite this, imperfections still sometimes exist in the final proof and may detract from the visual appearance of the text.

I hope you enjoy reading this book as much as I enjoyed making it available to readers again.

Roger Chambers

TO
HON. J. C. G. KENNEDY,
SUPERINTENDENT OF THE CENSUS, WASHINGTON, D. C.

My Dear Sir:

Permit me to offer to you the following work, as a very feeble mark of gratitude for your unvarying friendship, the aid you have extended to me in the preparation of this volume, and a sincere testimonial of the high respect and esteem of,

> My dear sir,
>> Your very obedient servant,
>>> And obliged friend,
>>>> H. DUSSAUCE.

New Lebanon, N. Y., May 1, 1865.

PREFACE.

THE art of tanning has for a long time consisted of a series of empirical operations, notwithstanding the fact that there is no art which is so dependent upon certain fixed principles, and on which chemistry exerts so great an influence. The processes followed in manufactories, in the past, have varied according to their localities; and have been transmitted from father to son, as heirlooms which they have had great scruples in abandoning or even touching. All new innovations were viewed with scorn, and rejected, even without experiment. When a workman had succeeded in producing good work, he believed he had attained the *ne plus ultra* of his art, and he would have believed he was unworthy of this title, if he could have been persuaded that he had yet many things to learn.

Prejudice and routine are, nearly always, the faithful associates of ignorance and pride, principally with those who, accustomed to manual occupations, look upon as useless, and even banish as dangerous, those theories which alone can transform an empirical art into a rational one. For a long time yet, industry will be thus hampered and the benefits of science disregarded, and it is only by degrees that it will verify the arts.

The closing years of the eighteenth century, and those of the nineteenth which have passed, have changed the ideas of manufacturers. Those who, located in the large cities, have been benefited by the help of science, have found imitators, and their innovations have gradually spread over the civilized world.

The art of tanning was one of those of which the theoretical study was the most neglected; the first author who seems to have given his attention to it was M. DESBILLETTES, member of the Académie des Sciences, who in 1708 published a work on tanning, and in 1754 furnished to the celebrated astronomer DELALANDE very good materials for his encyclopedical work on tanning and currying. The researches of M. DELALANDE give exact processes, and a true picture of the method then followed. Guided by these works, several experimenters, amongst whom we may mention MACBRIDE, PFEFFER, and ST. REAL, published processes for the improvement of the art of tanning, which, if they were not completely adopted, at least presented useful views. Such was the position of this art when one of the fellow-laborers of the illustrious LAVOISIER, M. SEGUIN, proposed in 1774 to tan hides in from one to two or three months. The quality of the leather did not, however, correspond with the quickness of the operation. Notwithstanding this failure, the works of this chemist exercised a powerful influence on the progress of the art, principally after his chemical studies of tannin. Several English chemists adopted the ideas of Seguin, while others modified them, and discovered new processes. The art of tanning ceased to be an entirely empirical one, when chemistry began to help it, by the different works and researches of Gettliffe, the father and the son, Monier and Ray, Paillard Vaillant, Grouvelle, Duval Duval, Salleron, Dolphus, Fischerstrœm, Payen, Kartsoff, Didier, J. Smith and J. Thomas, Trempé, Nenory, Tournal, Curaudeau, Conche, Poul, Labarraque, Leprieur, Bagnal,

PREFACE.

Weldon, Dessables, Delbut, Boetger, Boudet, Berlingue, Berendorf, Cox, Beringer, Vauquelin, Ogereau, Spilsburg, Kampfmeyer, Turnbull, Snyder, and others.

We have here given the important facts, and the principles established by these investigators and authors on this subject.

While gladly and fully acknowledging our indebtedness for much matter to Professor Morfit's edition of De Fontenelle and Malepeyre's treatise, prepared some years since for the publisher of this volume, the present publication may lay claim to being a new work, by reason as well of the numerous additions as by the considerable and important changes and improvements we have made throughout it.

We take great pleasure in acknowledging our indebtedness to those who have so kindly assisted us in our researches, and would express our particular obligations to the Hon. J. C. G. Kennedy, Hon. D. P. Holloway, D. Aldrich, Esq., Hatch, the Shaker Society of New Lebanon, etc. We have taken several articles from the two most important industrial publications of this country, the *Shoe and Leather Reporter* and the *Scientific American*, and desire here to acknowledge our obligations to them. We have consulted nearly all foreign and home publications; in a word, we have neglected neither pains nor trouble to make this work a standard one. We trust it will answer the purposes for which it is designed, and our reward will then be found in the services we have rendered to the profession.

CONTENTS.

	PAGE
Introduction	17
Imports of hides at New York for the past sixteen years	21
" " at New York for 1863	22
" " at Boston for 1863	24
" " at Philadelphia	26
" " at Salem, Mass.	26
Leather produced in the United States in 1850 and 1860	27
Origin and Development of the Art of Tanning	31
Parchment Dressing	38

PART I.
CHEMISTRY OF TANNING.

SECTION I.
TAN AND TANNIN.

CHAPTER I.
PURE TANNIN.

Chemical properties, 44.—Composition, 50.—Preparation, 50.

CHAPTER II.
IMPURE TANNIN.

Chemical properties of impure tannin; Preparation; Varieties in the impure tannin, 53.—Preparation of tannin from nutgalls, 55.—Proust's process, 55.—Deyeux's process, 56.—Dize's process, 56.—Merat-Guillot's process, 56.—Bouillon-Legrange's process, 57.—Tromsdorff's process, 57.—Serturner's process, 58.—Varieties of impure tannin, 58.—Tannin of catechu, 59.—Tannin of bark of trees; Sumach; Kino, 59.—Tannin which forms a bluish-black precipitate in solutions of a sesqui-salt of iron, 60.—Tannin which forms a green precipitate in the dissolution of iron, 60.

CONTENTS.

CHAPTER III.
ARTIFICIAL TANNIN.

Properties, 61.—Composition, 62.—First variety, 62.—Second variety, 63.—Third variety, 63.—Preparation of a tannin from turf, 63.

CHAPTER IV.
TANNIN FROM VARIOUS SOURCES, 64.

CHAPTER V.
GALLIC AND ELLAGIC ACIDS.

Gallic acid, 65.—Preparation, 66.—Scheele's process, 66.—Fiedler's process, 66.—Braconnot's process, 66.—Ure's process, 67.—Properties, 68.—Composition, 71.—Ellagic acid, 71.

CHAPTER VI.
EXTRACTIVE, 73.

SECTION II.
TANNING MATERIALS.

CHAPTER VII.
TANNING SAPS—TANNING JUICES—KINO—CATECHU.

Tanning saps, 78.—Sap of the beech tree, 79.—Tanning juices, 80.—Kino, 80.—African kino, 81.—Jamaica kino, 82.—South American, Columbia, or Caraccas kino, 82.—Catechu, 82.—Cake catechu, 84.—Pegu catechu, 84.—Bengal catechu, 84.—Bombay catechu, 84.—Gambir, 84.—Areca catechu, 85.

CHAPTER VIII.
EXCRESCENCES CONTAINING TANNIN.

Nutgalls, 86.

CHAPTER IX.
LEAVES—TEA—FLOWERS AND FRUITS—SEEDS AND BULBS.

Leaves, 88.—List of tanning leaves, 89.—Tea, 90.—Flowers and fruits, 91.—Valonia, 91.—Divi-divi, 93.—Of tanning flowers and flower tops, 94.—Seeds and bulbs suitable for tanning, 95.

CHAPTER X.
WOODS—ROOTS—BARKS.

Woods, 96.—Roots, 96.—Dentelaria, 96.—Malefern, 96.—Rhatany, 97.—Marsh rosemary, 97.—Barks, 98.—Cinnamon, 101.—Sassafras, 102.—Birch bark, 103.—Chestnut bark, 103.—Horse-chestnut, 103.—Beech

CONTENTS.

bark, 103.—Lombardy poplar bark, 103.—Black thorn bark, 103.—Pomegranate bark, 103.—Ash bark, 104.—Elm bark, 104.—Cinchona bark, 104.—Poison oak, 104.—Sumach, 104.—Willow bark, 106.—Tamarisk, 107.—Hemlock bark, 107.

CHAPTER XI.
OAK BARKS.

European oaks, 108.—American oaks, 110.

CHAPTER XII.
BARKING OF THE TREES.

Parts of the bark containing the most tannin, 112.—Age of the trees relatively to the richness of the barks in tannin, 113.—Barking and the most convenient time for it, 113.—Influence of seasons and place at the time of barking on the richness in tannin, 115.—Decrease in weight of smooth bark when exposed to the air, 115.

CHAPTER XIII.
PLANTS CONTAINING TANNIN USED AS SUBSTITUTES FOR OAK BARKS, 117.

CHAPTER XIV.
METHODS OF ESTIMATING THE TANNING POWER OF ASTRINGENT SUBSTANCES.

Examination of barks, 123.—Chemical examination, 123.—R. Warrington's process, 124.—Davy's process, 125.—Bell Stephens' process, 125.—Muller's process, 126.—Method of Dr. D. W. Gerland, 131.—Table of the quantities of tannin contained in the principal tanning substances, 134.—Comparative quantities of different tanning substances necessary to tan an equal quantity of leather, 136.

CHAPTER XV.
TAN OR POWDERED OAK-BARK.

Bagnall's machine for chopping bark and fleshing hides, 138.—Weldon's mill for grinding oak-bark, 143.—Farcot's bark-chopping machine, 146.—Bourgeois's bark mill, 150.—Lespinasse's bark mill, 153.—Birely's mill, 159.

CHAPTER XVI.
TANNING EXTRACTS.

J. Connel's concentrated extract, 161.—A. Steers's process, 162.—The Author's process, 163.

CONTENTS.

SECTION III.
SKIN.

CHAPTER XVII.
PROXIMATE PRINCIPLES OF LEATHER—STRUCTURE OF THE SKIN.

Proximate principles of leather, 165.—Structure of the skin, 166.—Behavior of the epidermis and cutis with reagents, 167.

CHAPTER XVIII.
CONSTITUTION OF THE SKIN.

Composition of the skin, 169.—Fibrin, 169.—Gelatine, 171.—Albumen, 172.

CHAPTER XIX.
THE PROPER TREATMENT OF HIDES AND SKINS—KINDS OF SKINS SUITABLE FOR TANNING—SALTING OF THE HIDES.

Ox-hides, 177.—Calves' skins and kips, 178.—Horse-hides, 178.—Sheep-skins, 179.—Goat-skins, 180.—Deer-skins, 181.—Hog or pig-skins, 181.—Seal-skins, 181.—Porpoise-skins, 181.—Hippopotamus hides, 181.—Mode of salting hides, 181.

PART II.
TANNING.

SECTION IV.
PRELIMINARY TREATMENT OF SKINS.

CHAPTER XX.
WASHING AND SOAKING.

Soaking of foreign hides, 186

CHAPTER XXI.
INFLUENCE OF THE WATER UPON THE QUALITY OF LEATHER.

Rain water, 192.—Snow water, 192.—Spring water, 192.—River water, 193. Lake water, 193.—Marsh water, 193.—Well water, 193.

CHAPTER XXII.
SWELLING OR RAISING OF THE HIDES.

Lime process, 195.

CONTENTS.

CHAPTER XXIII.
STACKING OF THE HIDES, 198.

CHAPTER XXIV.
INCONVENIENCE OF THE LIME PROCESS, 201.

CHAPTER XXV.
METHOD OF RAISING BY ACID, 202.

CHAPTER XXVI.
DEPILATION BY STEAM, 203.

CHAPTER XXVII.
DEPILATION BY CAUSTIC SODA, 204.

CHAPTER XXVIII.
DEPILATION BY SULPHURET OF CALCIUM AND SODA.

Preparation of the hydrosulphate of lime, 206.

CHAPTER XXIX.
COOL SWEATING PROCESS, 208.

CHAPTER XXX.
RAISING BY BARLEY DRESSING, 210.

CHAPTER XXXI.
WALLACHIA LEATHER.

Method of working the dressings, 223.—Bran dressing, 225.—Decomposition of the white dressings, 226.

CHAPTER XXXII.
RYE DRESSING, OR TRANSYLVANIA LEATHER, 227.

CHAPTER XXXIII.
RAISING BY SOUR TAN-LIQUOR.

Preparation of the tan-liquor, 233.

CHAPTER XXXIV.
RAISING BY YEAST, 236.

CHAPTER XXXV.
WORKING ON THE BRAM, 237.

CONTENTS.

SECTION V.
TANNING PROCESS.

CHAPTER XXXVI.
TAN VATS.

Wheat's patent vat, 244.

CHAPTER XXXVII.
HEALD'S APPARATUS FOR TANNING HIDES, 247.

CHAPTER XXXVIII.
TIME NECESSARY FOR TANNING, 251.

CHAPTER XXXIX.
PROPORTIONS OF THE BARK USED, 252.

CHAPTER XL.
DRYING OF THE LEATHER, 253.

CHAPTER XLI.
BEATING OF THE LEATHER, 257.

CHAPTER XLII.
BEATING AND ROLLING BY MACHINERY.

Debergue's machine, 260.—Flotard and Delbut's machine, 264.—Berendorf's machine for pressing hides, 270.—Cox's machine, 275.—Wiltse's rolling table, 277.—Seguin's machine to flesh and gloss leather, 279.

CHAPTER XLIII.
TISSUE AND QUALITY OF LEATHERS—THEIR DEFECTS AND THE WAY OF ASCERTAINING THEM.

Action of frost on leather, 282.

CHAPTER XLIV.
BELT LEATHER.

How to manufacture cow-leather into uppers of a superior quality, 288

CHAPTER XLV.
TANNING OF CALF-SKINS, 291.

CHAPTER XLVI.
TANNING OF CALF-SKINS FOR THE PREPARATION OF WAXED CALF-SKINS.
BY M. RENE.

Classification of untanned calf-skins, 295.—Washings, 295.—Liming, 296.—Salted skins, 298.—Dried calf-skins, 298.—Dry calf-skins from foreign countries, 299.—River work, 300.—Operation first, 302.—Treatment with strong liquors, 316.—Dressing, 321.

CONTENTS.

CHAPTER XLVII.
TANNING OF GOAT AND SHEEP-SKINS.

Bleaching of goat-skins, 326.—Coloring of whole sheep-skins, 327.

CHAPTER XLVIII.
MOROCCO LEATHER DRESSING—CORDOVAN LEATHER, 329.

CHAPTER XLIX.
TANNING OF HORSE-HIDES, 335.

CHAPTER L.
TANNING OF DIFFERENT SKINS, 337.

CHAPTER LI.
TANNING OF THE SKINS OF SHEEP'S LEGS FOR MAKING TUBES WITHOUT SUTURE, FOR COVERING THE CYLINDERS USED IN COTTON AND WOOL SPINNING.

Leather bottles, 338.

CHAPTER LII.
RED LEATHER, 339.

CHAPTER LIII.
DANISH PROCESS, 339.

CHAPTER LIV.
CHEMICAL THEORY OF TANNING.

Chemical researches on the art of tanning. By M. Knapp, 344.

SECTION VI.
IMPROVED PROCESSES.

CHAPTER LV.
SEGUIN'S PROCESS, 352.

CHAPTER LVI.
PROCESS OF PREPARING GLOSSED LEATHER BEFORE THE TANNING OPERATION.

Details of the work of the preparation of the leather, 353.—Hides, 353.—Smelting, 353.—Liming, 354.—Cleaning, 354.—Description of the apparatus, 354.—Tanning, 356.

CHAPTER LVII.
TANNING WITH MYRTLE, 356.

CHAPTER LVIII.
TANNING WITH GRAPE-SKINS, 357.

CONTENTS.

CHAPTER LIX.
TANNING WITH STATICE, 358.

CHAPTER LX.
LEPRIEUR'S TANNING PROCESS.

Sugar of lead bath, 360.—Tan liquor baths, 360.—First series of infusions 361.—Second series of infusions, 362.—Tanning in the vats, 363.—Quantities of tan employed for tanning 220 lbs. of leather, 365.

CHAPTER LXI.
D'ARCET'S PROCESS BY THE SULPHATE OF SESQUI-OXIDE OF IRON, 366.

CHAPTER LXII.
NEWTON'S PROCESS, 367.

CHAPTER LXIII.
PREPARING DRY FLINT HIDES, 368.

CHAPTER LXIV.
PROCESS OF TANNING OF H. C. JENNINGS, 370.

CHAPTER LXV.
BERENGER AND STERLINGUE'S PROCESS, 371.

CHAPTER LXVI.
CORNIGUET'S PROCESS OF SUBSTITUTING THE FRUIT OF THE PINE FOR THE BARK IN TANNING, 379.

CHAPTER LXVII.
VAUQUELIN'S PROCESS.

Description of the figures, 383.

CHAPTER LXVIII.
OGEREAU'S PROCESS, 390.

SECTION VII.
AMERICAN, ENGLISH, AND OTHER PROCESSES.

CHAPTER LXIX.
PROCESS OF TANNING WITH A DECOCTION OF OAK BARK, 391.

CHAPTER LXX.
DESMOND'S PROCESS, 393.

CONTENTS.

CHAPTER LXXI.
J. BURBRIDGE'S PROCESS WITH EXTRACT OF OAK BARK AND CATECHU, 393.

CHAPTER LXXII.
KLEMAN'S PROCESS, 394.

CHAPTER LXXIII.
SPILSBURY'S PROCESS BY PRESSURE, 396.

CHAPTER LXXIV.
M. W. DRAKE'S PROCESS, 398.

CHAPTER LXXV.
ROTCH'S QUICK PROCESS OF TANNING LEATHER, 399.

CHAPTER LXXVI.
J. F. KNOWLIS'S PROCESS, 402.

CHAPTER LXXVII.
TANNING APPARATUS OF D. ALDRICH, OF ST. LOUIS, MO., 403.

CHAPTER LXXVIII.
TANNING WHEEL OF V. E. RUSCO, 413.

CHAPTER LXXIX.
NEW MODE OF TANNING SKINS BY A LIQUOR OF TAR AND SOOT.

Preparation of the tan liquor, 417.—Preparation of the soot liquor, 418.—Preparation of the skins intended for leather, 418.—Preparation of leather for soles, 419.

CHAPTER LXXX.
INDIAN METHOD OF PREPARING ELK-HIDES, 419.

CHAPTER LXXXI.
HATCH'S PROCESS OF TANNING, CALLED ILLINOIS FRENCH TANNING, 420.

CHAPTER LXXXII.
IRISH PROCESS, 425.

CHAPTER LXXXIII.
PROCESS OF MANUFACTURING LEATHER CALLED CUIRS A MURON, 425.

CHAPTER LXXXIV.
KALMUCKS' PROCESS, 427.

CONTENTS.

CHAPTER LXXXV.
LEATHER MANUFACTURE IN TURKEY, 429.

CHAPTER LXXXVI.
J. HANNOYE'S PROCESS, 433.

CHAPTER LXXXVII.
M. NOSSITER'S PROCESS, 438.

CHAPTER LXXXVIII.
SQUIRE'S PROCESS, 442.

CHAPTER LXXXIX.
ENGLISH PROCESS FOR TANNING NETS, SAILS, AND ROPES, 443.

CHAPTER XC.
EXPERIMENTS IN THE TANNING OF CALF-SKINS WITH TAN, DIVI-DIVI, CATECHU, AND ELECAMPANE BARK.

Oak bark, 444.—Divi-divi, 445.—Catechu (terra japonica), 445.—Elecampane bark, 445.

CHAPTER XCI.
TANNING HIDES, BY J. W. JOHNSON, 447.

CHAPTER XCII.
TURNBULL'S PROCESS, 447.

CHAPTER XCIII.
S. SNYDER'S PROCESS, 452.

CHAPTER XCIV.
H. HIBBARD'S PROCESS.

Preparation of the skins, 455.—Composition for tanning, 455.

CHAPTER XCV.
HEMLOCK TANNING.

Process of tanning as performed at the Shaker Tannery, New Lebanon, N. Y., 458.

CHAPTER XCVI.
HALVORSON'S PROCESS FOR RENDERING HIDES HARD AND TRANSPARENT, 461.

CONTENTS.

CHAPTER XCVII.
TAWING.

Kid leather, 463.—Imitation kid, 466.

CHAPTER XCVIII.
THE BEST METHOD OF TANNING SMALL LAMB-SKINS CALLED CHAMOIS, AND ESPECIALLY WHITE PELTRY FOR FURRIERS, 467.

CHAPTER XCIX.
NEW METHOD OF COLORING WHITE TAWED LEATHER, 469.

CHAPTER C.
QUICK TANNING.

S. Dunseith's process, 473.—M. D. Kennedy's process, 474.—I. L. Wells' process, 475.—J. Cochran's process, 475.—W. R. Webster's process, 475.—Bunting's process, 476.—Thompson's process, 476.—L. Robinson's process, 476.—T. G. Eggleston's process, 476.—A. Dietz's process, 477.—P. Daniel's process, 478.—D. Needham's process, 479.—R. Harper's process, 479.—A. Hill's process, 480.—J. Nuessley's process, 480.—M. A. Bell's process, 480.—Blet's process, 481.—Baron's process, 481.—Quick process, 482.—Guiot's process, 483.

CHAPTER CI.
RESIDUES AND PRODUCTS OF TANNERIES, 484.

PART III.
CURRYING.

SECTION VIII.
GENERAL WORK OF THE CURRIER.

CHAPTER CII.
DIPPING, 488.

CHAPTER CIII.
SHAVING, 492.

CHAPTER CIV.
POMMELLING, 493.

CONTENTS.

CHAPTER CV.
STRETCHING, 494.

CHAPTER CVI.
WORKING WITH THE ROUND KNIFE, 496.

CHAPTER CVII.
PREPARATION OF STRETCHED LEATHER, 498.

CHAPTER CVIII.
PREPARATION OF SLEEKED LEATHER, 499.

CHAPTER CIX.
COMPARISON OF SLEEK LEATHER WITH ALUM-DRESSED LEATHER, 502.

CHAPTER CX.
TALLOWED OR GRAINED LEATHER.

Grain black; how to improve it, 506.

CHAPTER CXI.
WATER LEATHER, 510.

CHAPTER CXII.
OIL LEATHER.

Oiled leather, 515.

CHAPTER CXIII.
WAXED LEATHER, 518.

CHAPTER CXIV.
ENGLISH HIDES, 518.

CHAPTER CXV.
WHITE LEATHER AND COMMON RUSSET, 521.

CHAPTER CXVI.
CURRYING OF CALF-SKINS—OILED CALF-SKINS, 522.

CHAPTER CXVII.
TALLOWED CALF-SKINS, 524.

CHAPTER CXVIII.
ENGLISH CALF-SKINS, 525.

CONTENTS.

CHAPTER CXIX.
WAXED CALF-SKINS.

Fleshing and shaving, 526.—Bleaching or Whitening, 542.—Graining, 545.—Mode of making the blacking and its applications, 547.—Finishing, 550.

CHAPTER CXX.
GRAINED CALF-SKINS, 556.

CHAPTER CXXI.
CALF-SKIN LEATHER FOR BELTS, 557.

CHAPTER CXXII.
GREASING TANNED HIDES, 557.

CHAPTER CXXIII.
SATURATION OF LEATHER WITH GREASE, 563.

CHAPTER CXXIV.
CALF-SKINS CALLED ALUMED SKINS, 564.

CHAPTER CXXV.
F. JAHKEL'S PROCESS FOR MANUFACTURING LEATHER FOR HARNESS-MAKERS, 569.

CHAPTER CXXVI.
CURRYING OF GOAT-SKINS, 571.

SECTION IX.
RUSSIA LEATHER.

CHAPTER CXXVII.
PROCESS OF MANUFACTURING RUSSIA LEATHER, 575.

CHAPTER CXXVIII.
DISTILLATION OF THE EMPYREUMATIC OIL OF BIRCH-BARK FOR RUSSIA LEATHER.

Fischerstroern's process, 578.—Another process, 579.—Grouvelle and Duval-Duval's process, 579.—Payen's process, 580.

CHAPTER CXXIX.
NATURE OF THE ODORIFEROUS SUBSTANCE OF THE BIRCH-TREE BARK, 582.

CHAPTER CXXX.
PREPARATION OF RUSSIA LEATHER, 583.

CONTENTS.

CHAPTER CXXXI.
COLORING OF RED RUSSIA LEATHER, 584.

CHAPTER CXXXII.
EXTRACT FROM A MEMOIR ON THE PROCESS OF TANNING SKINS IN RUSSIA BY THE COUNT OF KARTSOFF, 586.

CHAPTER CXXXIII.
RED LEATHER, 590.

CHAPTER CXXXIV.
SHAGREEN AND PARCHMENT.

Shagreen, 592.

CHAPTER CXXXV.
PARCHMENT, 595.

SECTION X.
PATENT LEATHER.

CHAPTER CXXXVI.
FABRICATION OF THE PATENT LEATHER, 600.

CHAPTER CXXXVII.
DIDIER'S PROCESS.

White polished leather, 603.—Red polished leather, 603.—Blue polished leather, 604.—Yellow polished leather, 604.—Polished leather of leather color, 604.—Black lacquer for shoes and leather work, 604.—Process for varnishing leather for belts, &c., 605.

SECTION XI.
WATER-PROOF LEATHER.

CHAPTER CXXXVIII.
PROCESS OF J. SMITH AND J. THOMAS, 606.

CHAPTER CXXXIX.
NENORY'S PREPARATION TO RENDER LEATHER WATER-PROOF AND IMPERVIOUS.

Preparation of siccative oil, 607.—Preparation of the elastic gum, 607.—Preparation of the compound, 608.—Process of using the composition, 608.

CONTENTS.

CHAPTER CXL.
DEAN'S PROCESS FOR RENDERING LEATHER IMPERVIOUS.

First composition, 608.—Second composition, 609.—Third composition, 609.—Fourth composition, 609.—Application of the composition, 610.

CHAPTER CXLI.
DIFFERENT PROCESSES.

Cheap method of making leather water-proof, 611.—Jenning's process, 611.

PART IV.
HUNGARY LEATHER.

SECTION XII.

CHAPTER CXLII.
GREASE AND ANIMAL OILS.

Lard, 615.—Mutton suet, 616.—Beef tallow, 616.—Medullary beef tallow, 616.—Fish oils, 616.—Dolphin oil, 617.—Porpoise oil, 617.—Different fish oils, 617.—Process by which to give to a mixture of different oils and greases the properties of fish oils, 618.—Process for rendering vegetable oils fit to take the place of fish oils, 618.

CHAPTER CXLIII.
RIVER WORK, 618.

CHAPTER CXLIV.
ALUMING THE HIDES, 619.

CHAPTER CXLV.
SECOND ALUMING, 622.

CHAPTER CXLVI.
DRYING AND STRETCHING, 622.

CHAPTER CXLVII.
TREADING OUT THE HIDES, 623.

CHAPTER CXLVIII.
TALLOWING, 624.

CONTENTS.

CHAPTER CXLIX.
FLAMING, 628.

CHAPTER CL.
EXPOSURE TO THE AIR, 629.

CHAPTER CLI.
WEIGHING.—MARKING.—PILING, 630.

CHAPTER CLII.
HUNGARY LEATHER MADE OF COW AND CALF-SKINS, 631.

CHAPTER CLIII.
HUNGARY LEATHER MADE OF HORSE-HIDES, 631.

CHAPTER CLIV.
M. KRESSE'S PROCESS OF PREPARING BLACK HUNGARY LEATHER, 633.

CHAPTER CLV.
DEFECTS IN THE QUALITY OF HUNGARY LEATHER, 634.

CHAPTER CLVI.
USES OF HUNGARY LEATHER, 635.

CHAPTER CLVII.
IMPROVEMENT OF M. CURANDEAU, 636.

PART V.
GUT-DRESSING.

SECTION XIII.
PREPARATION OF THE INTESTINES OF CATTLE.

CHAPTER CLVIII.
OPERATIONS FOLLOWED IN THE PREPARATION OF INTESTINES OF CATTLE.

Description of the workshop, 638.—Scouring, 638.—Turning over, 639.—Putrid fermentation, 639.—Scraping, 640.—Washing, 640.—Insufflation, 640.—Desiccation, 641.—Disinsufflation, 641.—Measuring, 641.—Sulphuration, 641.—Folding, 642.

CONTENTS.

CHAPTER CLIX.
DISINFECTION OF THE WORK-SHOPS.—MODE OF SUPPRESSING PUTREFACTION, 642.

CHAPTER CLX.
GOLD-BEATER'S SKIN, 643.

CHAPTER CLXI.
LATHE-CORDS, 644.

CHAPTER CLXII.
MANUFACTURE OF CORDS FROM THE INTESTINES OF SHEEP, 645.

CHAPTER CLXIII.
DIFFERENT CORDS.

Cords for rackets, 647.—Whip cords, 647.—Hatter's cords for bowstrings, 648.—Clock-maker's cord, 648.

CHAPTER CLXIV.
CORDS FOR MUSICAL INSTRUMENT STRINGS, 649.

PART VI.

DIFFERENT KINDS OF APPARATUS USED BY LEATHER MANUFACTURERS.

CHAPTER CLXV.
IMPROVED MACHINE FOR ROLLING GREEN OR WET LEATHER.

Operation, 659.

CHAPTER CLXVI.
MACHINES FOR FINISHING LEATHER, 661.

CHAPTER CLXVII.
LEATHER POLISHING MACHINE, 673.

CHAPTER CLXVIII.
JACOB PERKINS'S MACHINE FOR POMMELLING AND GRAINING LEATHER, 675.

CHAPTER CLXIX.
NISBET'S GROUNDING AND PUMICING MACHINE, 678.

CONTENTS.

CHAPTER CLXX.
EMBOSSING OF LEATHER.
Bernheim and Labouriau's process, 682.—F. W. East's process, 686.

CHAPTER CLXXI.
DEGRAND'S MACHINE FOR SPLITTING AND SHAVING LEATHER, 687.

CHAPTER CLXXII.
GIRAUDON'S MACHINE FOR SPLITTING AND SHAVING LEATHER, 688.

CHAPTER CLXXIII.
MACHINES FOR SPLITTING AND SHAVING LEATHER.
Richardson's machine, 694.—Chapman's improved leather splitting machine, 697.—Introduction of splitting machine into German heavy and upper leather tanneries, 699.

THE

ARTS OF TANNING, CURRYING,

AND

LEATHER-DRESSING.

INTRODUCTION.

THE art of tanning is that by which animal skins are converted into *leather*, a product possessing certain characteristic properties, differing entirely from those of the same material, and eminently adapting it to the useful purposes for which it is employed. Those properties are of a physical nature, and vary with the kind of skin employed, and the modification of the process which it undergoes. Chemically considered, however, leather proper, whatever its kind, is a definite compound of tannin and gelatine, possessing the all-desirable requisites of durability, pliability, inalterability, insolubility in water, and great power of resisting the action of chemical reagents. When mineral or earthy substances are used as the leather-making agents, the result is a compound of gelatine with the base employed, and is more or less indestructible, according to the nature of the material and the circumstances under which the combination takes place.

It is much to be regretted that so little has been done by science for the improvement of the art of tanning, although many years have elapsed since the chemical union of tannin and gelatine was first demonstrated; discovery has not yet shown that abundant fruitfulness which it seemed to promise positively and almost immediately. It is true that a long step forward has been made, but has it not been effected by automatic rather than by natural movement? by mechanical force rather than by scientific combinations? In a word, is not the art of tanning in America almost as strictly empirical now as it ever was? If the production of our tanneries has been increased and the time of their work shortened, it is not owing so much to the introduction of new principles and to scientific theorizing as to the use of improved apparatus for facilitating old processes. Take away our bark and hide-mills, improved vats, and other constructions, and our steam power, turn us out of doors to work amongst the rude contrivances of a hundred years ago, and would the result of our labor show an extraordinary gain over those of our predecessors?

The modern appliances, of which American tanners boast, are certainly ingenious and praiseworthy, and we would not be understood to depreciate their importance, or to slight the intelligent enterprise of which they are the offspring. But we wish to record and to direct attention to the fact that in tanning, as in other occupations, the habits of the American mind lead to *invention* rather than to *discovery*. Now, in many other occupations, the fertile invention of our countrymen may insure perfect success; but in tanning it cannot; for here invention is only the servant of discovery, and must follow instead of preceding it. It is skill, not force, chemical combination, not steam power, which is principally to accelerate and cheapen the process of tanning; and the sooner the trade acts on this conviction, which every day's experience ought to strengthen, the better. If they can supersede our present machinery by the discovery of more effective and economical methods, it will furnish causes for congratulation and none for mourning. They must aim to be good chemists, as they are already good mechanics. With the analytical taste of the French and Germans superadded to their over-ingenuity and energy, what results might not be expected from their studies? The field to be explored is a broad one. Long as the art of tanning has been known to the world, not one step in its practice seems to be complete. There is still room for inquiry after tanning materials, and still a doubt whether tannin, or what is equivalent to tannin, may not be produced in quantity by artificial means. The hide itself should be examined and analyzed at every stage of its manufacture. Its structure cannot be too minutely scrutinized; its preliminary preparation is a problem; the nature of gelatine is a study; the manufacture of ooze, simple as it appears, is not uniform; the proper consistency and strength of the liquor is yet to be graduated and fixed. Most of all, the union of the tannin and the gelatine in the interior fibres is to be critically observed and facilitated by every possible means. The object is, of course, to produce leather in less time and at less cost than heretofore.

To these remarks the tanner will probably reply that he has neither taste, time, nor means to employ in chemical experiments. But if this is so, he can at least join with his brethren and endeavor with them to effect, by concerted action, that which it may be impossible for a single individual to accomplish. It is worth while to inquire whether our associations might not advantageously employ educated chemists to unlock for them the secrets of nature.

There is no denying that ignorance is the real bar to our progress; that our pathway to success winds up the hill of science. If we cannot travel it alone, we should secure guides, and accept whatever assistance is at hand.

Leather is employed for many useful and ornamental purposes, and numerous are its applications to various branches of industry. Besides its extensive use for covering for the head and feet, wearing apparel, saddles, harness, etc., it is largely employed for the embellishment of objects of taste and ornament.

Independently of the direct importance of the leather trade, it exerts a very decided incidental influence in developing the resources of a country, by giving value to certain materials used in, and resulting from the manufacture. Besides the immense quantity of bark which it consumes, it furnishes the raw material which gives employment to thousands of artisans. Even the waste material of slaughter-houses, tanneries, currier's shops have important applications; the horns serving for the manufacture of combs, buttons, and umbrella furniture; the hairs for plasterer's use, the spent lime for the farmer, the skin clippings for the glue boiler, etc. etc.

The following statements will suffice to give an idea of the vast extent and rapid increase of the trade in leather in the United States.

INTRODUCTION. 21

Imports of Hides at New York, for the past Sixteen Years.

Years.	January	February	March	April	May	June	July	August	September	October	November	December	Total
1848	109,324	54,400	112,732	113,976	91,160	26,967	109,761	97,435	53,962	58,710	40,219	101,018	972,654
1849	70,929	65,481	112,604	135,448	114,141	70,502	155,260	74,527	46,290	146,584	64,946	173,025	1,229,727
1850	113,329	141,900	58,200	118,400	144,500	146,400	113,000	117,965	169,900	83,100	120,700	156,000	1,483,305
1851	115,500	103,000	134,400	136,000	114,150	73,000	100,000	108,480	110,900	110,600	118,000	142,400	1,366,030
1852	50,000	101,000	76,000	75,500	139,000	98,800	93,300	140,600	103,000	70,000	195,000	235,000	1,437,200
1853	50,000	78,000	130,540	110,100	117,460	99,000	111,500	150,000	105,500	71,300	164,200	71,700	1,259,300
1854	176,519	121,758	130,247	108,900	198,956	125,650	176,700	142,635	142,500	135,800	125,000	98,360	1,679,995
1855	106,200	76,200	108,500	163,800	127,700	146,700	93,600	123,000	160,800	156,700	116,000	170,800	1,550,000
1856	212,103	188,259	101,898	203,500	203,364	139,212	91,316	129,817	121,648	143,981	150,977	130,837	1,715,900
1857	128,709	123,190	120,908	152,697	210,513	122,929	150,144	114,729	81,742	171,577	164,138	160,477	1,796,753
1858	96,030	60,530	111,351	158,181	134,412	220,020	137,348	113,138	172,939	315,195	180,719	249,612	1,950,044
1859	216,351	157,081	255,626	247,879	257,178	195,076	136,040	181,011	218,675	89,061	287,851	155,941	2,397,797
1860	212,612	137,036	159,941	137,724	141,275	144,082	103,190	177,393	136,089	100,845	150,744	147,826	1,716,257
1861	137,127	182,377	103,700	142,811	123,604	59,730	95,932	56,207	25,697	100,154	55,402	105,502	1,188,243
1862	102,554	107,580	125,069	109,155	194,316	147,005	181,333	158,368	182,513	176,810	121,196	156,275	1,762,174
1863	107,947	149,238	111,516	165,237	206,217	114,431	185,184	92,702	88,684	91,791	155,232	172,299	1,770,578

22 INTRODUCTION.

Imports of Hides at the Port of
Compiled from the Weekly Official Tables

FOREIGN.	Jan'y.	Feb'y.	March.	April.	May.	June.	July.
African	3,426	15,200	2,113	...	414	2,738	23,511
Bahia	...	20,301	4,476	7,033	7,323	...	3,294
Buenos Ayres	20,632	25,611	18,703	20,915	91,930	70,191	16,126
Carthagena	1,709	73	...	1,227	...	...	2,663
Chagres	...	...	...	...	...	...	...
Curacoa	56	227	276	1,738	329	...	1,628
East India	...	...	1,297	...	...	...	...
Honduras	697	343	10	49	...	159	...
Maracaibo	...	...	...	...	...	...	4,933
Maranham	...	...	...	...	...	...	...
Mexican	8,435	1,648	8,719	5,532	5,809	7,777	7,435
Monte Video	17,915	14,580	...	27,595	26,001	15,000	51,415
Orinoco	...	26,123	...	...	20,697	12,051	...
Para	20	11	...	173	...	1,075	3,453
Porto Cabello	...	5,585	100	1,910	2,412	...	4,533
Porto Platte	...	...	...	...	...	...	...
Rio Grande	6,545	5,203	11,393	25,903	44,870	12,895	18,633
Rio Hache	...	...	...	...	...	...	...
Savanilla	...	5,089	1,176	...	...	3,362	1,865
Sierra Leone	...	...	...	...	...	...	...
West India, &c	5,581	3,697	3,436	4,669	2,130	1,619	6,795
Sundry Central American	4,847	6,890	4,951	20,087	4,463	7,336	6,828
Sundry South American	...	...	4,252	3,480	990	123	...
From Antwerp	...	...	4,896	...	...	...	...
From Bremen	6,703	3,000	...	...	...	...	...
From Genoa	...	...	...	7,117	...	3,060	...
From Hamburg	...	...	...	...	...	...	...
From Havre	...	6,122	9,099	...	...	...	...
From Liverpool	1,750	..	1,194	1,746	...	...	...
From London	1,500	...	3,615	8,433	...	...	...
From Marseilles	...	...	...	...	...	...	...
Sundry Foreign	...	581	...	31	...	101	315
Total Foreign, 1863	79,816	140,284	79,706	137,638	207,368	137,487	153,427
" " 1862	77,992	61,297	106,275	62,791	158,173	108,948	110,804
" " 1861	81,581	133,014	58,114	87,763	58,656	52,367	44,116
" " 1860	188,875	87,211	91,443	51,212	58,285	73,322	84,845
" " 1859	184,263	120,570	175,563	200,973	216,413	158,242	97,718
DOMESTIC.							
California	...	...	21,762	...	36,059	...	21,353
New Orleans	2,564	2,081	693	509	...	2,500	24
Texas	...	...	...	...	...	...	...
Sundry Coastwise	10,627	264	4,688	15,650	913	11,999	8,854
Railroad	14,940	6,609	4,667	11,440	1,877	2,445	1,526
Total Domestic, 1863	28,131	8,954	31,810	27,599	38,849	16,944	31,757
" " 1862	24,562	46,283	18,794	46,364	36,143	38,057	70,529
" " 1861	55,546	49,353	45,586	55,048	64,948	7,363	51,816
" " 1860	83,237	49,825	68,498	86,512	82,990	70,600	18,345
" " 1859	82,091	36,511	80,063	46,988	40,730	36,834	38,322
Total For. & Dom'tic, 1863	107,947	149,238	111,516	165,237	206,217	114,431	185,184
" " " 1862	102,554	107,580	125,069	109,155	194,316	147,005	181,333
" " " 1861	137,127	182,377	103,700	142,811	123,604	59,730	95,932
" " " 1860	252,612	137,036	155,941	137,724	141,275	44,082	103,190
" " " 1859	216,354	157,081	255,626	247,879	257,178	95,076	136,040
Calcutta, &c., in bales	...	...	...	...	...	...	50

INTRODUCTION. 23

New York, for the Year 1863.
of "The Shoe and Leather Reporter."

August.	Septem'r.	October.	Novem'r.	Decem'r.	Total 1863.	Total 1862.	Total 1861.	Total 1860.	Total 1859.
...	...	7,593	...	4,920	59,915	24,028	35,803	26,542	26,690
2,851	...	12,716	...	221	58,215	36,616	4,000	130	47,508
24,581	13,748	21,862	17,162	54,537	395,998	303,552	146,606	263,364	470,393
...	873	856	182	2,266	9,849	15,684	6,582	3,379	27,821
...	...	...	...	...	...	...	...	77,582	97,663
...	496	...	964	89	5,803	3,248	8,088	5,680	8,043
...	402	...	400	...	2,159	...	18,208	15,718	11,783
111	...	...	365	...	1,734	3,925	2,846	20,781	...
483	1,221	2,833	500	1.836	11,756	12.498	25,079	42,870	46,324
...	...	...	...	...	...	15,288	2,208	8,087	22.219
10,382	603	6,947	6,011	3,266	72,564	51,538	34,238	24,684	66,241
15,661	5,525	...	30,588	55,510	259,790	82,688	54,243	82,264	184,996
...	15,804	...	37,363	15,957	127,995	160,780	139,879	121,176	282,877
3,632	...	6,350	...	1,051	15,765	28,575	5,512	4,667	16,800
6,147	...	...	9	...	20,696	33,625	34,390	24,352	25,860
...	...	...	...	...	...	5,146	7,320	16,936	18,606
9,504	7,993	...	13,144	14,362	170,445	173,248	46,082	138,888	178,641
...	...	...	...	...	...	1,872	857	2,544	12,808
442	...	...	1,598	...	13,532	18,181	5,994	49,218	28,547
...	...	...	...	...	...	18,421	24,300	9,120	36,523
1,783	849	1,059	4,319	4,114	40,051	25,516	9,319	12,655	34.117
8,800	4,114	5,388	4,097	4,630	82,431	74,447	33,263	16,427	31,138
...	...	903	...	...	9,748	18,564	42,421	10,312	10,932
...	...	...	...	...	4,896	2,190	5,092	1,985	6,552
...	...	...	...	...	9,703	23,504	...	...	...
...	...	...	...	...	10,177	28,958	...	...	...
...	...	...	...	...	...	425	2,986	...	49,030
...	...	...	971	...	16,192	26,859	6,083	...	24,369
...	...	...	...	...	4,690	4,249	7,408	7,068	42,077
...	...	1,030	2,500	...	17,078	6,841	1,020	...	11,860
...	...	...	...	...	...	...	...	...	19,368
...	...	...	...	1,806	2,834	20,484	4,169	5,913	62,840
84,327	51,688	57,537	120,173	164,565	1,424,016	1,219,950	713,962	992,622	1,852,856
132,802	118,110	118,441	60,216	104,101					
33,806	21,781	89,897	25,332	77,935					
43,640	99,667	57,217	53,433	96,416					
154,271	181,086	71,603	220,243	121,881					
...	11,458	...	22,109	27,584	140,325	297,907	186,956	169,150	160,542
266	...	...	...	...	8,637	9,184	50,704	92,769	69,498
...	...	...	...	...	...	...	74,258	212,769	101,147
6,407	24,382	31,115	11,938	20,150	146,937	142,884	118,788	158,844	122,427
1,702	1,206	8,139	1,112	...	50,663	92,249	43,764	90,103	90,321
8,375	36,996	34,254	35,159	47,734	346,562	542,224	474,265	723,635	541,935
25,566	64,403	58,369	60,980	52,174					
22,391	3,916	60,657	30,074	27,567					
33,747	32,422	138,628	97,311	51,860					
26,741	37,589	17,458	67,608	34,063					
92,702	88,684	91,791	155,332	172,299	1,770,578	1,762,174	1,188,243	1,716,257	2,397,791
158,368	182,513	176,810	121,190	156,275					
56,207	25,697	100,154	55,402	105,502					
77,393	136,089	100,845	150,744	147,820					
181,011	218,675	89,081	287,851	155,941					
...	158	100	558	...	866	646	1,721	2,094	823

INTRODUCTION.

Imports of Hides at the Port
Compiled from Official Sources for

FOREIGN.	Jan.	Feb.	March.	April.	May.	June.	July.
Bahia	...	...	...	...	...	...	2,000
Buenos Ayres	11,150	6,853	4,900	30,467	5,583	...	14,788
Cape of Good Hope	1,037	...	...	...	856	...	...
Chili	...	...	...	...	4,936	1,003	...
East India	...	...	...	...	...	...	...
Manila, Singapore and Penang Buffalo	...	...	...	...	...	...	...
Manila, Singapore and Penang Cow	...	...	...	...	...	...	...
Sandwich Islands	...	...	...	...	...	...	...
Sierra Leone	11,315	13,360	21,131	24,054	17,440	...	8,781
Other African	...	...	...	4,000	...	...	12,641
Truxillo	1,030	...	...	1,699	...	...	2,463
West Indies	...	...	...	...	25	1,628	200
From England	105	...	1,878	...	...	...	...
Other Foreign	365	281	...	...	100	...	...
Total Foreign, 1863	25,002	20,494	27,909	60,220	28,940	2,631	40,873
" " 1862	7,388	14,155	13,100	17,208	38,853	44,965	11,790
" " 1861	4,381	3,871	17,864	3,696	49,803	2,017	1,027
" " 1860	31,668	4,893	38,489	5,526	40,764	6,600	10,462
" " 1859	13,167	12,589	39,689	29,513	30,023	43,006	19,554
DOMESTIC.							
Baltimore	...	...	...	...	600	...	...
California	...	15,605	...	...	...	...	11,154
Charleston	...	...	...	...	...	...	...
Mobile	...	...	...	...	...	...	...
New Orleans	397	2,486	4,279	6,173	3,171	618	866
New York	...	2,576	...	...	1,000	...	...
Philadelphia	772	3,015	687	...	...	4,111	...
Portland	790	1,348	199	715	...	1,840	379
Savannah	...	...	...	...	...	...	...
Southern	...	...	...	...	...	...	...
Texas	...	...	...	...	...	...	...
By Rail	27,032	24,738	13,811	13,943	10,183	15,854	13,371
Total Domestic, 1863	28,991	49,768	18,916	20,831	14,954	22,423	25,770
" " 1862	9,642	12,415	12,183	7,680	12,792	12,227	5,649
" " 1861	9,355	13,288	14,110	13,698	6,532	1,000	217
" " 1860	27,303	17,477	24,377	40,804	26,400	23,697	7,843
" " 1859	62,933	28,208	28,926	39,960	51,193	24,630	21,503
Total For. & Dom'tic, 1863	53,993	70,262	46,825	81,051	43,894	25,054	66,643
" " " 1862	17,030	26,570	25,283	24,888	51,645	57,192	17,439
" " " 1861	13,736	17,159	31,974	17,394	56,335	3,017	1,274
" " " 1860	58,971	22,370	59,866	56,030	67,164	60,292	18,305
" " " 1859	76,260	40,792	68,615	69,473	11,426	67,736	41,057
CALCUTTA STOCK, &c.							
Buffalo (bales)	395	897	176	160	...	449	...
Cow	511	21	148	260	...	23	...
Goat	485	...	481	249	186	134	753
Sheep	110	642	258	...	...	95	896
Calcutta via England	...	...	...	...	...	...	...
Total Calcutta (bales)	1,501	1,554	1,063	669	186	701	1,649

INTRODUCTION. 25

of Boston, for the Year 1863.

"The Shoe and Leather Reporter."

August.	Sept.	Oct.	Nov.	Dec.	Total 1863.	Total 1862.	Total 1861.	Total 1860.	Total 1859.
4,200	...	...	4,000	...	10,200	...	...	...	...
12,042	...	2,000	...	...	87,783	80,517	19,814	62,629	95,730
...	...	...	...	...	1,913	2,462	250	8,568	12,189
...	...	...	548	6,430	12,717	7,299	4,108	23,327	17,055
...	...	...	...	...	...	4,142	12,386	...	...
...	...	...	...	...	...	...	5,209	12,159	4,584
...	...	...	...	...	...	12,500	7,255	15,287	12,263
4,900	...	1,155	...	...	6,055	...	...	...	...
...	...	17,700	5,424	...	119,205	79,601	38,046	81,732	24,000
...	295	6,600	6,376	2,000	31,912	...	...	...	...
...	...	...	...	...	5,192	6,411	5,546	6,713	2,323
...	...	207	...	...	432	2,104	811	388	3,685
...	...	...	...	2,595	6,206	8,785	3,212	10,908	59,256
...	...	...	...	...	746	13,550	1,660	31,325	60,000
20,332	295	27,662	16,148	11,025	281,531	204,996	98,298	202,972	291,729
6,964	22,414	26,751	4,080	19,410					
13,972	50	78	...	1,539					
12,543	23,620	9,585	7,916	4,256					
23,563	50,296	14,861	8,507	14,581					
...	...	...	598	...	1,198	5,684	4,249	33,281	24,805
...	9,891	4,943	11,373	6,976	44,337	11,375	...	856	2,370
...	...	...	...	...	...	...	4,363	10,596	13,587
...	1,100	6,297	1,434	3,049	29,810	18,008	27,621	77,957	95,052
...	1,390	...	423	601	5,990	15,450	9,829	...	29,605
100	870	...	...	...	9,555	12,685	862	490	1,686
103	784	954	102	...	7,162	1,646	12,399	12,141	14,468
...	...	...	...	...	...	...	3,098	6,067	12,269
...	...	310	...	...	310	...	2,879	13,218	21,595
...	...	...	...	...	...	...	4,813	20,031	7,709
10,979	16,349	21,374	19,507	25,305	212,446	120,815	120,888	45,082	112,159
11,182	30,334	33,878	33,437	35,931	326,415				
10,785	3,177	31,060	50,075	17,978		185,663	190,951	230,388	339,235
1,708	504	8,732	...	889					
12,608	12,329	4,221	18,478	17,241					
17,772	9,428	5,825	27,860	21,052					
31,514	30,629	61,540	49,585	46,956	607,946	390,658	289,249	43,336	638,984
17,749	25,591	57,811	54,155	17,978					
15,680	554	8,810	81	889					
25,151	35,940	13,806	23,391	21,491					
41,275	59,724	20,686	31,367	35,633					
...	120	...	573	...	2,764	704	2,087	2,080	3,583
...	165	60	165	...	1,353	2,128	1,333	1,772	3,664
68	379	12	1,036	354	4,137	803	1,336	1,867	2,996
...	101	3	141	57	2,303	...	36	2	135
...	...	58	...	...	58	612	...	...	...
68	765	133	1,915	411	10,615	4,247	4,792	5,721	10,378

Imports of Hides at Philadelphia.

The following table exhibits the foreign importations, also the arrivals coastwise, of hides at the port of Philadelphia for the past ten years.

Years.	Foreign.	Coastwise.	Total.
1854	174,597	10,451	185,048
1855	156,102	12,300	168,402
1856	109,755	9,399	119,154
1857	125,180	22,320	147,500
1858	101,258	33,200	134,458
1859	128,029	29,400	157,429
1860	100,250	8,730	108,980
1861	65,271	6,254	71,525
1862	98,133	11,913	110,046
1863	53,109	11,724	64,833

The foreign importations in 1863 amounted to 53,109 hides, and were divided as follows:—

Porto Cabello and Caraccas	29,645
Pernambuco	14,053
African	6,258
Rio Grande	1,680
West India	1,473
	53,109
Bundles of deer, goat, and sheep-skin	70
Dozens " " " "	649

Imports of Hides at Salem, Mass., for the year 1863.

Zanzibar	42,825
West Coast of Africa	25,789
Cayenne	2,518
New York	120,403
Total, 1863	191,535
" 1862	162,281
" 1861	184,701
" 1860	318,986
" 1859	430,774
" 1858	424,000

INTRODUCTION.

Below will be found an abstract from the Preliminary Report of the Eighth Census, showing the amount of leather produced for the years 1850 and 1860 respectively, also the quantities furnished by each State during the same period. The tanners of the United States produced in 1850, exclusive of morocco and patent leather, goods to the value of $37,702,333, and in 1860 the product reached $63,090,751, being $25,388,418 greater than during the corresponding period of 1850. The largest producers of leather are, in their order, New York, Pennsylvania, and Massachusetts. The former turning goods to the value of $20,758,017, the second, $12,491,631, and the last $10,354,056, being an increase in the three States of $10,955,347; $6,195,268 and $4,681,497 respectively on an aggregate increase of $21,832,112.

We can have no better evidence of the immense benefits of the leather trade to the commerce of the entire country than is manifested by the growth and increase of this single article of production, as set forth in the following table during the ten years ending June 1, 1860, and the exhibit of 1850.

States and Territories.	Value of product in 1850.	Value of product in 1860.	Per cent. increase.
Maine	$1,701,299	$2,011,034	18.2
New Hampshire	944,554	1,933,949	104.7
Vermont	640,665	1,000,153	56.1
Massachusetts	5,672,559	10,354,556	82 3
Rhode Island	133,050	80,897	Decrease
Connecticut	775,325	953,782	23.0
Total N. E. States.	9,867,452	16,333,871	66.6

INTRODUCTION.

States and Territories.	Value of product in 1850.	Value of product in 1860.	Per cent. increase.
New York	9,802,670	20,758,017	111.7
Pennsylvania	6,296,363	12,491,631	98.4
New Jersey	1,269,982	1,297,627	2.1
Delaware	213,742	37,240	Decrease
Maryland	1,426,734	1,723,033	17.2
Dist. of Columbia	56,000	37,000	Decrease
Total Mid. States.	19,065,491	36,344,548	90.7
Ohio	2,110,982	2,799,239	32.6
Indiana	750,801	800,387	6.6
Michigan	401,730	574,172	42.4
Illinois	337,384	150,000	Decrease
Wisconsin	181,010	498,268	175.2
Minnesota		11,400	
Iowa	24,550	81,760	23.3
Missouri	366,361	368,826	.6
Kentucky	1,108,533	701,555	Decrease
Kansas		850	
Total W. States.	5,281,351	5,986,457	13.3
Utah		93,255	
California		223,214	
Oregon		14,500	
Washington		17,500	
Total P. States		351,469	
Virginia	927,877	1,218,700	31.3
N. Carolina	363,647	313,020	Decrease
S. Carolina	282,399	150,985	Decrease
Georgia	403,439	393,164	Decrease
Alabama	344,445	340,400	Decrease
Louisiana	78,085	47,000	Decrease
Texas	52,600	123,050	132.0
Mississippi	241,632	223,862	Decrease
Arkansas	78,824	115,375	46.3
Tennessee	804,631	1,118,850	38.9
Total S. States	3,777,579	4,064,407	13.8
Aggregate in U. S.	37,791,878	63,090,751	66.9

The production of leather is a leading industry of much importance to the agriculturist and stock raiser, as well as to the commercial interests, inasmuch as it consumes all the material supplied by the former, and feeds an active branch of our foreign import trade. Including morocco and patent leather the aggregate value produced in the Union in 1860 exceeded sixty-seven millions of dollars.

If we add to the sum total of this manufacture the aggregate value of all the allied branches into which it enters as a raw material, or take an account of the capital, the number of hands, and the cost of labor and material employed in the creation and distribution of its ultimate products, it is doubtful if any other department of industry is entitled to precedence over that of leather.*

The principal steps in the manufacture of leather are—

1st. The *washing and soaking* for the purpose of cleansing and softening the skins and preparing them for—

2d. *The depilation or removal of the hair.* This is effected by the use of lime, or other substances, which destroy, dissolve, and soften the bulbous roots of the hair, and thus facilitate their removal by mere mechanical scraping with a blunt-edged knife. During this part of the process another important end is generally accomplished in the swelling of the tissues, and their preparation for the more complete and easy absorption of the tanning principle. The primitive mode of removing the hair was that of shaving it off with a knife, but the use of lime for this purpose was known even among the early Egyptians. When the rationale of the depilation is better understood by practical tanners, the slow and

* Preliminary Report on the Eighth Census, 1860, by Jos. C. G. Kennedy, superintendent.

inconvenient process of depilation by means of lime will probably give place to more effective, rapid, and economical methods, such as the use of the hydrosulphuret of calcium.

3d. *Tanning.* This step consists in promoting the combination of the gelatinous tissue with tannin by immersing the softened and unhaired skins in an infusion of oak bark, or other substances containing tannin. The tanning influence is, probably, not exerted solely by the tannin, but also partly by the extractive matter, more or less of which always exists in tanning material. During the soaking, the epidermis of the skin disappears, and the tissue of the latter is gelatinized, and thus predisposed to chemical union with the tannin. This gelatinization of the tissue is all essential, and is promoted doubtless by the gallic acid fermentation of the tanning material. This is the more probable, since the same effect may be produced by the use of very dilute acetic and sulphuric acids, and since gallic acid has no primary or direct influence on the tanning. Since exposure to moisture, to air, and a temperature of 77° to 86° are the requisites for this fermentation, which is developed by the action upon tannin of a ferment which is always present in tanning material, converting it into gallic acid. In consequence of this change, the prolonged exposure of the liquor diminishes its tanning power.

4th. Drying, rolling, and other operations intended to perfect the quality and appearance of the leather.

ORIGIN AND DEVELOPMENT OF THE ART OF TANNING.*

Upon the conviction that it will be agreeable to all in the trade to possess authentic data of an art, the practice of which is their vocation, and to follow its gradual development *ab initio*, we beg leave to present our readers with the following faithful sketch of the gradual rise and progress of the art of tanning, and we shall take pains to carefully collect all other notices on this subject of interest and value to the craft, and as a retrospect of its history.

The origin of the tanner's art is lost in antiquity; but it is supposed to have been an oriental invention; at least it was earlier brought to a state of perfection in the East than in Europe.

According to Chinese authors, it was their ruler, *Schinfang*, who taught them to prepare the skins of animals, and to remove the hairs with wooden rulers. Pliny ascribes the invention of tanning to *Tychius of Bœotia;* but this is also uncertain. At that time those who first introduced anything into a country generally received the credit of having invented it. The use of the skins of animals for clothing was known in the remotest ages, and but moderate attention, and inventive power, are requisite to conceive and follow out the idea of their employment in this manner.

The inconveniences of raw hides, and their roughness and hardness preventing their adaptation to the body, awoke reflection; men thought to discover the causes of these defects, as well as the means of remedying them,

---

* From the "Gerber Courier," Vienna, Austria.

and thus arose with a gradual progress towards perfection the art of converting the raw hide into leather and for clothing, which mode of preparation is now called *Tanning*.

The more nations increased in number, the greater became the demand for the necessity of civilization and luxury, and thus forced and attracted by necessity and gain, many experiments were made with a view to the improvement of tanning, until those excellent inventions were attained which have brought tanning to its present state of perfection. In these experiments the principal properties of tanned leather were not lost sight of. Attention was paid to the preparation of the hide so as to render it pliant and more impervious to moisture.

New inventions and discoveries are still making every day by workmen and scientific men; often accidentally, but often by study and reflection; and who knows but that in a few years tanning will be brought to a much higher point of perfection than it has hitherto attained. Chemistry, the fundamental science of tanning, has made astonishing progress in the last few years, and ought this not also to be the case in the tanning art, especially as it is based upon chemical principles?

The oldest method of tanning is red, or bark tanning, or that in which, in addition to the wooden and iron scraping and rubbing instrument used in the preparation or improvement of the hide or skin, lime-water, and astringent extracts from oak and other kinds of bark, or from other vegetable substances are employed. It is called red tanning because the tanning substances always contain more or less coloring matter, which dye the leather through and through of a more or less reddish color.

The ancient orientals understood the art of preparing

not only common leather, but even good, and often finely colored varieties, similar to our Morocco and Cordovan. Persian and Babylonian leather has been celebrated time out of mind. Many centuries back, such leather was brought from Asia into Europe, first into Turkey, Prussia, and Hungary, and thence later to Germany, Holland, England, France, Spain, etc., and these countries learned subsequently to manufacture leather themselves. In the first centuries of Christianity, the Turks, Russians, and Hungarians were the most celebrated tanners; subsequently England, the Netherlands, and Spain endeavored to equal them.

Among fine sorts of leather of foreign origin, *Cordovan, Morocco, Shagrin, and Russia* leather have at all times been especially famous. Cordovan, a soft, small-grained, colored leather, had already been prepared by the ancient orientals. Its name is derived from the Spanish city of Cordova, where it was probably first introduced into Europe, and where, for a long time afterwards, it was chiefly manufactured. It enjoyed a great reputation in the eleventh century, when the most distinguished persons wore shoes of Cordovan leather. The French name for shoemaker, "*Cordonnier*," appears also to be derived from this leather. The best qualities are now made in Constantinople, Smyrna, and Aleppo. The best known German Cordovan is the Bremen variety.

From the gradual improvement of Cordovan sprang Morocco, called also Turkish and Spanish leather, a still handsomer leather than Cordovan. This beautifully colored and brilliant leather has always been most excellently manufactured in Morocco, in the Levant, in Asiatic and European Turkey, in Krim Tartary, in Aleppo and Smyrna, and in the Island of Cyprus, and very well also in Russia, Poland, Hungary, and Spain, but especially in England, France, Holland, Switzerland, and Germany (in the latter country at Offenbach on the Main, and Calin in Wurtemburg).

Shagrin (in Turkish, *Sagri*, and Persian, *Sagre*) is chiefly celebrated for its hardness and strength, and for the peculiarity of the grain side, which appears as if covered with globular granules; it is also of eastern origin. The best Shagrin is now made in Persia, Constantinople, Algiers, and Tripoli. The production of the small globular granules on the grain side was for a long time kept secret. We were first informed years since by the celebrated traveller, Pallas, that they were produced by stamping the hard seeds of the *wild orach* (CHENOPODIUM ALBUM) into the hide, spread on the ground; the seeds were afterwards knocked out and the hide scraped on the indented side, and soaked in water for two days. There is another description of shagrin totally different, made from fish-skin, called *fish-skin shagrin*; it is used for covers, wood polishing, etc.

Russia leather is a strong and pliant leather, generally red or black, with a peculiarly penetrating odor, and was undoubtedly invented by the ancient Bulgarians. It is only lately that we have learned the mode of preparing this leather. Among other things, we first perceived that the peculiar odor arose from the birch oil which was rubbed into the leather. *Inuften*, the German name of this leather, is derived from the Bulgarian word "*Jufti*," a pair, as the Bulgarians, when they colored hides, always sewed them together by pairs in the form of a bag, with the grain side inwards; the coloring liquor was then poured in and the hides kept in motion. The best Russian leather is made in various Russian and Lithuanian provinces.

By tanning (*i. e.*, white tanning), which appears to

have been invented in Hungary before the twelfth century, a white pliant leather is obtained by tanning with alum instead of bark. This leather is used principally by glovers and harness makers. In Hungary, also, not long after the invention of tanning, chamois dressing was invented. In this method neither bark nor alum is employed;. the leather is simply dressed by rolling and other powerful operations, first with bran and subsequently with animal fat (train oil). In order that the fat may the better penetrate through and through, the grain side is cut away with sharp instruments. For this reason chamois leather is rough or velvety on both sides. Lately gloves and breeches are made from this kind of leather, the latter principally from white tanned buckskin. The Hungarians were, in ancient times, especially celebrated for their white tanned leather, which was imitated in France as long ago as three hundred years. In chamois leather, the most famous is the fine, white, shining French and Dane's leather (made from lamb and goat skins), from which, by means of a peculiar varnish, the so-called kid gloves are made.

A profession continues progressive, and cannot reach its highest point until its limits can be precisely defined. An excellent means by which to improve a profession, consists in pointing out the goal and end to be attained, and the bounds within which it must be confined. Without this precaution, we exhaust ourselves in single and unconnected researches, without reference to each other, and the knowledge which we acquire is dissipated and loses in force as it recedes from the common focus.

A small number of principles and a great mass of conclusions; this is the history of all arts, all sciences. The principles must rest upon reliable facts derived from experience and observation; but an author cannot render all conclusions and explanations. The principles are not numerous and are easy of comprehension, but the conclusions arising from them are innumerable, and lucidity is only to be arrived at by placing them in order under the general laws to which they respectively belong, and, therefore, a judicious classification is requisite.

Tanning, in general, is divided into various branches, although all may be practised together by the same tanner. We will first give nearer data upon the origin and development of our system of tanning, and subsequently consider minutely and singly every process and the different methods and systems in our tanneries at home and abroad, keeping constantly in view the statistics of the foreign leather trade and manufactures as compared with our own. We beg our readers to go back some centuries in history, and they will be convinced that the products of our trade were known in the time of Moses; for at that period, leather carpets were already used in tents; these we may still meet with at present among the Arabs. Colored leather seems, also, to have been common, for Ezekiel speaks of fine red leather which was probably our splendid red morocco. Leather was also used in the remotest ages by the Israelites as a material to write upon, for they used strips made of leather for this purpose. According to the testimony of Herodotus, the ancient Ionians wrote their annals upon sheepskin, and the ancient Persians, likewise, according to Diodorus of Sicily.

According to the accounts of Herodotus, the ancient Libyans wore leather clothing; the *Ichthyophagists* on the banks of the Araxes dressed themselves in sealskins, and in the time of Alexander, the wild inhabitants of Geodrosia used the hides of animals for clothing and covered their dwellings with leather.

Homer praises the splendid half boots of Agamemnon, and Hesiod recommends leather shoes lined with fur. For many years leather was used by the Greeks in the construction of ships; especially by the Phœnicians, who originally inhabited an arid sandy corner of the earth, between the Red Sea and the Mediterranean, where the soil was not favorable to the growth of timber, and they were obliged to supply its place by covering their boats, constructed of willows woven together, with leather or hides, which even thus early were subjected to a certain amount of dressing. The ancient Germans, also, who lived on the sea-coast, and the original Britons equally possessed this custom.

It is asserted that the art of dressing leather in general upon the so-called Hungarian method, was first brought from Senegal, in Africa, and made known to us in the middle of the sixteenth century, by one *Buscher*, the son of a tanner in Paris; at that time leather was common in Hungary, and that dressed there was very highly esteemed. In the year 1584, two German tanners named *Lasmagne* and *Aurand* came to Neuchatel in Lorraine, where they worked at their trade; from thence they went to St. Diziers, in Champagne, and finally to Paris, where they prepared very good leather.

The theory that the preparation or tanning of hides was discovered centuries ago, and that the leather produced was employed for the same purpose as at present, is further confirmed by the following old proverb, which is a proof that leather shoes were already worn at that time, viz: "*We must not steal leather to give away shoes in God's name.*" This refers to the legend of St. Crispin, who stole leather to make shoes out of it for the poor. In the old form of speech, "*To draw from the leather,*" signified to draw the sword. In low Saxon the same expression signifies to undress.

PARCHMENT DRESSING.—Parchment was known long before the invention of paper; for sheep and goatskins were used to write upon in the time of Herodotus, 484 A. C.; the name is derived from the City of Pergamus, in Asia Minor, where it was excellently manufactured. The best parchment is prepared from calfskin, and inferior qualities from sheep, goat, ass, and pig skins. The fine *virgin parchment* is made from the skins of new-born lambs.

Artificial parchment, which was discovered in England, consists of linen, cloth, or paper, which is tightly stretched, and then a paste composed of gypsum, white lead, powdered lime, water, and parchment glue, is laid on with a brush four times: it is then smoothed with pumice stone, and lastly steeped in a bright oil varnish.

The use of parchment is not very extensive; beyond the ordinary purposes it is sometimes used for printing, for organ bellows, and for sieves, and in England for sounding boards in stringed musical instruments. In Germany it is principally manufactured at Bentheim and Schuttorf in Hanover, and also in Augsburg, Nuremberg, Breslau, and Dantzic. Holland, England, and France manufacture excellent parchment.

Such is the historical origin of our leather trade. The gradual development and progress of technical tanning have been promoted and assisted by many, and among the most zealous are *MacBride, St. Real, Proust, Hermstadt, Vauquelin, Chaptal, Seguin, Desmond, Von Meidinger, Aikin,* and others. Attempts have been made to discover new methods by which hides and skins could be better tanned, and in a shorter space of time, than by the usual mode of treatment. In the year 1778

MacBride discovered the process of raising with diluted sulphuric acid (1 part acid to 400 parts water).

Later great attention was attracted to the system of quick tanning, discovered in 1795 by Seguin, by which hides and skins were tanned in much less time than formerly. This new process was tested by experts, and found to be partially good and partially deficient. In 1801, Banks discovered the tanning property of *Terra Japonica* (Catechu). Since that time tannin has been discovered in a great number of plants.

The English discovered, in the last century, the art of varnishing leather, which was soon after imitated in Germany with complete success.

Bellamy, Von Hildebrandt, Edward, and others introduced the art of preparing water-proof leather.

Whatever may be facts, it is to be presumed that the most ignorant races of antiquity, whose chief occupation was the chase, possessed the knowledge of giving a certain preparation to the raw animal hides to protect them from decay, and to render their necessary clothing convenient; they were certainly driven to invention by necessity, and thus the invention of the art of tanning was probably the work of accident, like the invention of most of the other arts. To them, consequently, must the invention of the art of tanning leather be ascribed, although it must be conceded that this art owes its proper cultivation and perfection to more recent ages.

PART I.

CHEMISTRY OF TANNING.

SECTION I.

TAN AND TANNIN.

THE second principal component of leather, such as that manufactured into boots, shoes, &c., is *Tannin*, or *tannic acid*, a substance of vegetable origin and very extensively disseminated in plants and trees. For a long time the agents which gave such virtues to oak bark, in converting prepared skins into leather, were little known, and, consequently, the peculiar relation of the proximate principle of this article could not be understood, notwithstanding that, in the absence of this knowledge, the leather manufactured was sometimes of prime quality. Dr. LEWIS was the first who drew the attention scientifically to the subject. He observed, during an investigation of the nutgalls, that they contained a substance which gave a black compound with a sesqui-salt of iron and precipitated isinglass. Deyeusæ, who also studied the subject, noticed this substance, but considered it a peculiar resinous matter. It was not, however, till Seguin published the results of his labors, that any definite account of it was given. This chemist showed that the unknown body differed from the acid of galls—*gallic acid;* that it combined with animal matters, more particularly albumen and gelatin, and formed with them unalterable bodies, the analogue of which constituted the main bulk of leather. Since then, manufacturers have given great attention to this principle in the tanning material, and the consequences are that a greater variety of substances producing tannin, or desirable for making leather, have been discovered, and that considerable expedition in the process has been attained. Although the beforementioned chemists, with DAVY, CHEVREUL, PELLETIER, LAGRANGE, GUILLOT, HATCHETT, TROMSDORFF, RICHTER and PROUST may be justly said to have given a scientific exposition of tannic acid and its behavior, and likewise pointed out its quantity in those plants that yield it most abundantly, still several more recent investigations have contributed to the stock of information on this subject. According to WAHNLENBERG, tannin exists only in perennial plants and almost solely in the permanent parts. For example:—

1. In the perennial roots of certain annual plants, as the *Septfoil* and *Bistort* or snakeweed.

2. In the bark of the trunks and roots of nearly all perennial trees, especially in the true cortical portion.

3. In the trunk and sap of many trees.

4. In the leaves of perennial plants.

5. In the leaves of different varieties of oak, of the *Rhus coriara* (SUMAC), of the *Arbutus uva ursi* (BEARBERRY), of the *Arbutus unedo* (STRAWBERRY), etc., in large proportion.

6. In the capsule of the unripe fruit of the *Quercus suber ægilops* (VALONIA OAK), *Juglans regia* (WALNUT); *Æsculus hippocastanus* (HORSE-CHESTNUT).

7. In the pulp of the fruit of the *Punica granatum* (POMEGRANATE); *Rosa pimpinelli folia; Garcinia mangostana* (MANGOSTEEN), and in different species of Anona.

The following table exhibits the names of the principal materials used by tanners.

Common Name.		Botanical Name.	Growth.
Oak	bark	Quercus pedunculata	Every country.
Larch	"	Pinus lariæ	Scotland.
Mimosa	"	Acacia sp.	New South Wales.
Baboul	"	Acacia arabica	Bengal.
Cork Tree	"	Quercus suber	Laruch, Rabat, etc.
Hemlock	"	Abies canadensis	United States.
Sumach	"	Rhus coriaria	Sicily.
Valonia		Quercus ægilops	Smyrna, Trieste, etc.
Divi-Divi		Cæsalpinia coriaria	Maracaibo, Rio de la Hacha, Savanilla.
Myrobalans		Terminalia sp.	Bengal.
Algarobilla		Prosopis pallida	Valparaiso.
Terra Japonica		Acacia catechu	East Indies.
Cutch		" "	Calcutta, Singapore.
Kassu		Areca catechu	Ceylon.

Besides the foregoing, which are partly well known in the trade, other astringent substances have been brought before the public to be employed *per se*, as tanning materials, or with oak bark as an adjunct. These are various extracts from species of the *acacia* tribe; Gambir, the extract of the *Nauclea gambir* from Singapore; Maiyrove bark (*Rhizopora mangle*), from Arracance; Turwar or Cassia bark; Avaraputtai (*Cassia auriculata*), from Vazigapatam; Saracondraputtai (*Cassia fistula*), from Madeira; Saul tree bark from the *Saul Forests;* Pomegranate rind; Darunka pucke (*Dahima jegota*), from Kemaon; Dalumka Khola from Calcutta; Jamoon bark (*Eugenia jambolana*); Pearl bark from Cuttah; Samah bark from Singapore; Vangay or Gum kino, (*pterocarpus dalbergoides*), from Malabar; Kino extract of the *Buchanania patifolia*, etc. etc.

We must note here—

1. That tannin is never found to any extent in the interior of the trunks of trees.

2. That it does not exist in poisonous plants, nor in those with a milky or viscid sap.

3. That its proportion is greater in old than in young plants.

4. That the tannin is converted into bitter principle, as the plant increases in age.

5. That it is most abundant in the cortical layers of the bark, and is usually absent altogether in the epidermis.

6. That the proportion of tannin in bark varies with the season, decreasing as the severity of the winter increases.

7. That the true extreme in quantities are allowed in winter and spring.

CHAPTER I.

PURE TANNIN.

CHEMICAL PROPERTIES OF PURE TANNIN—COMPOSITION—PREPARATION.

Chemical Properties.

By examining any of the numerous substances mentioned above, it will be found that they yield a product which is capable of precipitating a solution of gelatine, and also of giving a greenish or bluish-black one, with solutions of sesqui-salts of iron. To matter exhibiting this reaction, and having an astringent taste, the name of *Tannin* was given, irrespective of whatever difference might be exhibited upon further comparison. Now many of those bodies which, in common with the true type of tannin (that which is extracted from galls), precipitate gelatin, and so far show that they are eligible for tanning materials, are known to differ in that characteristic; for instance, some possess acid properties, whilst others are devoid of them; and although towards gelatin, their reactions are similar, their atomic constitution is widely different. Regarding their effect in converting skin into leather, this dissimilarity is not very material, as, when the components of each one are compared, a distinction is also made with respect to the physical appearance of the precipitate they afford with a sesqui-salt of iron, and by this all the known tanning materials are divided into two classes. In the first of these are placed gall-nuts, and the barks of the several oaks, and the second include the quinquina, the cachou, kino, pine barks, etc. The tannin afforded by the first throws down a bluish-black or purple combination, whilst the precipitate afforded by the second is greenish. Experiments have shown that such distinctions are not very marked, since the tannic acid from nutgalls or oak bark, in the presence of an alkali, will occasion a greenish precipitate when added to a sesqui-salt of iron, and a bluish or violet compound when acids are present.

HATCHETT first observed that many plants contain a carbonaceous principle, which, when acted upon by nitric or sulphuric acids, according to the method of CHEVREUL, yield a substance which, like the tannin of the foregoing barks and fruits, throws down gelatin, and renders it imputrescible. This variety has been designated artificial tannin; but in the present state of chemical science, it could not be compounded with the natural products. BERZELIUS, GEIGER, WALTL, and CAVALLIUS are of opinion that tannin, from whatever source it may be obtained, is identical, and that the difference of the reaction with the iron salt must be attributed to impurities which are accidentally present. STENHOUSE, in his more recent researches, has shown that such is not the case, but that all those forming precipitate with sesquioxide of iron, varying from the color of that which the tannin of nutgalls affords, must be regarded as a distinct substance, in which case there seems to be an almost endless variety. Even when the iron reactions of some tannins agree, and also appear analogous in other chemical relations, the same chemist states that the composition is frequently diverse.

In its purity tannic acid is colorless, inodorous, possesses a highly astringent taste, and is very soluble in water. It is, however, devoid of all bitterness, notwithstanding its astringency is so powerful. On testing the aqueous solution with litmus, the reaction evidences the acid nature of the tannin; and further, by treatment with an alkaline carbonate, carbonic acid is freely displaced, showing that a combination of the alkaline base and the tannin has taken place. With the oxides of the heavy metals it in a great measure combines, giving rise to precipitates which are the tannates of the respective bases, and generally possess a color more or less remarkable. Thus an infusion of nutgalls reacts in the following manner:—

With a *neutral* solution of salts of

	Precipitates given.	
	BRANDE.	DUMAS.
PROTOXIDE OF MANGANESE,	*Dirty yellow,*	—
" IRON,	*Purple tint,*	—
SESQUIOXIDE OF IRON,	*Black,*	*Blue black.*
OXIDE OF ZINC,	*Dirty yellow,*	—
" TIN,	*Straw* "	*Yellowish.*
BIOXIDE "	*Fawn* "	"
OXIDE OF CADMIUM,	—	—

	Precipitates given.	
	BRANDE.	DUMAS.
PROTOCHLORIDE OF COPPER,	*Yellow brown,*	*Gray.*
PROTONITRATE, "	*Green,*	"
OXIDE OF LEAD,	*Dingy yellow,*	*White.*
TEROXIDE OF ANTIMONY,	*Straw* "	"
" BISMUTH,	*Yellow,*	*Orange.*
OXIDE OF COBALT,	—	*Yellowish-white.*
SALTS OF CERIUM,	—	*Yellowish.*
" TITANIUM,	—	*Blood color.*
" TELLURIUM,	—	*Isabelle yellow.*
" CHROMIUM,	—	*Brown.*
" TANTALUM,	—	*Orange.*
" MOLYBDENUM,	—	*Brown.*
" URANIUM,	—	*Brownish-red.*
" SILVER,	—	*Pale yellow.*
" PLATINUM,	—	*Greenish shade.*
" GOLD,	—	*Brown.*
" OSMIUM,	—	*Bluish-purple.*

In making the foregoing experiments, it is necessary to employ neutral solutions of the salts, otherwise any excess of the acid may not only alter the shade of the precipitate but prevent it altogether. This is especially the case with salts of iron and titanium. When a solution of tannic acid is added to another of protosulphate of iron, according to Mr. Dumas, no precipitate occurs; but if one of the sesquisulphates be substituted there is an abundant deposit of a blue-black color.

By exposing a solution of tannic acid to the air, at a moderately elevated degree of heat, oxygen is freely absorbed, and an equal volume of carbonic acid is disengaged. Upon examination, the matter in solution will be found to be wholly transformed into two other substances, gallic and ellagic acid, the former of which is in excess, and is dissolved in the liquid, whilst the latter remains insoluble in the form of a yellowish powder.

This transformation takes place in the aqueous extract of gall-nuts, much more readily than in one of pure tannin; this is particularly the case if the marc or insoluble residue of the galls be left in contact with the liquid, as it induces a fermentative action, which brings about the transformation the more readily. When boiled with hydrochloric or sulphuric acids, gallic acid is also formed, together with grape sugar, which, as *Strecker* states, remains in the mother liquid after the newly-formed acid is removed by crystallization. The change here induced may be represented thus:—

$$\underbrace{C^{54}H^{39}O^{34}}_{\text{Gallo-tannic acid.}} + \underbrace{10HO}_{\text{Water.}} = \underbrace{{}^{2}(C^{14}H^{3}O^{7}3HO)}_{\text{Gallic acid.}} + \underbrace{C^{12}H^{10}O^{12}2Aq.}_{\text{Cellulose.}}$$

A concentrated solution of caustic potash at the boiling point, has also the effect of transforming tannic into gallic acid; and if air or oxygen be admitted, of converting the latter into an ulmin-like substance. Hydrochloric, nitric, phosphoric, and arsenic acids occasion in strong solution of tannic acid white precipitates which are, as stated by *Berzelius*, compounds of the tannin with those acids; all these precipitates are, however, readily decomposed, and their tannin changed into gallic acid, beseizing them with dilute sulphuric acid, or with an excess of alkali. If a cold aqueous solution of tannin be mixed with another of gelatin, isinglass, bone-size or glue in excess, an opaque white precipitate is obtained of tanno-gelatin, that is soluble in the supernatant fluid by the help of heat. When, however, the conditions are reversed, and an excess of tannin is taken, it happens that, instead of dissolving, the precipitate agglutinates, and forms a membranous matter of a grayish hue, that possesses considerable elasticity, and thus approaches caoutchouc. The solutions filtered from these bodies strongly tinges those of the sesqui-salts of iron. It appears that tannin solutions react in a similar way with protein compounds in general.

It was thought for a long time that the insolubility of the tanno-gelatin offered a means for insuring the purity of tannin, and of detecting the absence or presence of gallic acid in the sources affording tannin; but this insolubility, excepting in water alone, does not answer the purpose. *Pelouze* employed a piece of skin, cleaned in the ordinary way from hair and epidermis; this was immersed for some hours in the extract, and the whole agitated occasionally, and finally the liquid filtered. When pure tannin was operated upon, the whole combined with the integument, so that the fluid has no astringent taste, nor did it color a solution of a sesqui-salt of iron, but if gallic acid had been mixed with it, the bluish-black tint would present itself in the latter case.

Freshly precipitated alumina, agitated with a solution of tannin, absorbs the latter rapidly and forms with it an insoluble compound; gallic acid behaves in a similar manner. At the temperature of an oil bath, tannic acid is decomposed, water and carbonic acid being formed; but when the heat is increased, other products are generated, and nothing remains but charcoal, which, if heated on platinum wire, burns, leaving no residue. Strong ether dissolves tannin, and forms a syrupy liquid, which does not combine with fresh ether. Alcohol behaves with tannin in the same way, the solvent power of the spirit decreasing in reference to it as it approaches purity or dehydration.

Composition.

According to Berzelius, tannin such as it was prepared, *i. e.*, impure, was composed of

Carbon	52.69
Hydrogen	3.86
Oxygen	43.45
	100.00

Pure tannin, according to Pelouze, is thus formed:—

Carbon	51.40
Hydrogen	3.51
Oxygen	45.09
	100.00

These numbers nearly correspond with the formulæ $C^{18}H^8O^{12} = C^{18}H^5 O^9 3HO$. But STRECKER, in his later researches, gives the equation thus, $C^{54}H^{22}O^{34}$, showing that it contains less oxygen and hydrogen than is indicated above.

Preparation.

When tannin is to be obtained in its greatest state of purity, recourse must be had to the process known as that of PELOUZE, but which was first broached by LAMBERT. The latter chemist directed the formation of an extract of 60 grains of powdered nutgalls in 120 grains of ether, the digestion to be continued for twenty-four hours, after which the ethereal extract was to be filtered and evaporated. PELOUZE followed the foregoing method in principle by employing the apparatus of ROBIQUET and BOUTRON as used for the preparation of Amygdalin. Fig. 1 represents this digester. It is an elongated glass vessel *A*, having an orifice at the top, which is fitted with a ground glass stopper, and contracting towards the other extremity, which fits tightly into the neck of a bottle

PURE TANNIN. 51

or matrass *B* which receives the extract. Sometimes the lower bottle has a second tubular opening, *D*, for the purpose of receiving a cork furnished with a tube, to which a connector, *C*, of caoutchouc is appended, the other end being attached to a similar tube fitted in cork which closes the top orifice. Between *F G* is the powdered gall, and in *E* is a little batting cotton. This adaptation causes the filtration to take place more readily, whilst it prevents contact with any further quantity of air beyond what is contained in the apparatus. Common sulphuric ether is then poured upon the galls, and as it traverses the powder it takes up the tannin and gallic acid. The latter, however, gives a lighter and more fluid solution than tannin, and forms the upper stratum of the ethereal solution which has traversed the galls and dropped into the receiving bottle. The dense and dark-colored stratum below contains tannin. The galls are treated successively with new quantities of ether until they cease to yield soluble matter. The several ethereal solutions are then mixed together and poured into a separating funnel. When the two strata have formed, the lower one containing the tannin is drawn off into a retort, distilled to save ether, then repeatedly washed with pure sulphuric ether to remove traces of gallic acid, and evaporated over a warm sand-bath or under the receiver of an air pump; the tannin is obtained in the form of a spongy, iridescent,

Fig. 1.

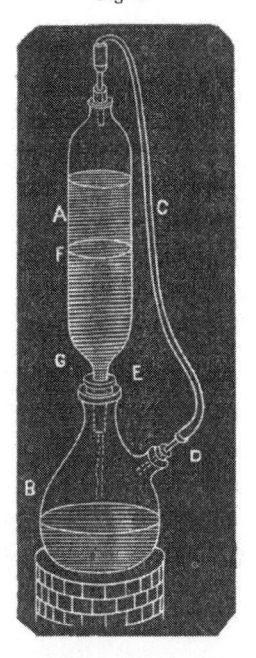

uncrystallizable mass having a light shade yellow color. So prepared, tannin is in its purest known state; but as sometimes it results almost colorless, doubtless it is not free from impregnation arising from decomposed tannin, apothema, or some other matters.

Another modification of the method just detailed was introduced by DOMINE, and offers the advantage of yielding a larger product, while it admits also of being applied on the large scale for the purpose of the manufacturer. He places the powdered galls in a damp cellar for several days, during which they absorb moisture; the powder is next transferred to a wide-mouthed jar, and made into a paste with ether of a specific gravity 0.75. After this the vessel is hermetically closed, and the contents allowed to digest for 24 hours. At the expiration of this time the pasty contents are transferred to a strong linen bag and subjected to gradual pressure, when the ethereal extract of tannin, having a dark syrupy consistence, flows off into the receiver. This liquid must be evaporated to dryness at a gentle heat, by which the tannic acid is left in the form of light-colored resin-like scales. The compressed residue is further treated with ether, to which six per cent. of water is added in the same manner as when preparing the first extract, and on expelling the fluid by a gentle heat, a residue of tannin is obtained. It is, indeed, more impure than the above, as it contains chlorophylle, volatile oil, and gallic acid; still the tannin thus prepared answers very well for many industrial purposes.

CHAPTER II.

IMPURE TANNIN.

CHEMICAL PROPERTIES OF IMPURE TANNIN—PREPARATION—VARIETIES IN THE IMPURE TANNIN.

IMPURE tannin is solid, brown, transparent, friable, uncrystallizable, odorless, has a very astringent taste; it is heavier than water, reddens the solution of litmus, softens in the fingers, melts at a low temperature; it is very soluble in water, principally while warm; by cooling it precipitates a light yellowish powder. The solution has a brown color, and is not decomposed when exposed to the air even at a middling temperature. Little soluble in absolute alcohol, it dissolves in it only by the addition of a little water in the proportion of 0.10. According to the experiments of Proust, Deyeux, and Davy, it combines with oxygen, but then it is decomposed or altered in its nature. According to Bouillon-Lagrange, it is transformed by this absorption into gallic acid. It precipitates albumen and gelatine from their dissolutions and forms insoluble combinations.

Hydrochloric and sulphuric acids precipitate the aqueous solution of impure tannin; the precipitate, which is very slightly soluble in cold water, but very soluble in hot water and alcohol, is a combination of tannin with the acid employed.

Acetic, arsenic, malic, oxalic, and tartaric acids precipitate the infusion of nutgalls; this precipitate, washed with cold water and dissolved in boiling water, has all the properties of the tannin. Nitric acid and chlorine destroy it easily; the first transforms it into a brown yellowish substance, soluble in alcohol and similar in its properties to an extract. According to Proust, it is the same for the stannic acid. Pure and carbonated alkalies form with this substance combinations nearly insoluble. Metals have not a sensible action on impure tannin, but the greatest number of oxides combine with it and render it insoluble in water.

Baryta and lime-waters decolorize the solution of impure tannin and produce a precipitate which is a combination of tannin with the oxide; this precipitate is nearly insoluble in water and without action on gelatine; it differs from the combination of this last substance with the tannin in which they cannot be separated, because they form a new compound. In the combination of the tannin with an alkali or earth it can be isolated by treating the combination by an acid which dissolves the oxide and sets free the tannin.

By agitating recently precipitated magnesia or alumina in a solution of tannin, it forms a tannate of magnesia and alumina, insoluble in water and decomposable by acids which render the tannin soluble in that liquid. If we treat the infusion of nutgalls by baryta, strontia, or lime-waters, the precipitate has an olive color, and is composed of tannate and gallate united with the extractive.

If we boil magnesia with an infusion of nutgalls, the precipitate has a dirty yellow color, insoluble, composed of tannin, extractive, and magnesia, while the gallate of magnesia stays dissolved in the liquor.

Alumina in small proportions gives the same results; in large quantities it separates all the substances which constitute the infusion. The alkaline carbonates separate from the gallic infusion the tannin and extractive; the formed gallate stays in solution; the solution of tannin does not decompose salts of the first section, but on the contrary it operates the decomposition of many belonging to the four last.

In *solution of copper* it produces an olive precipitate.

In *sulphate of manganese* it produces a fine light green precipitate.

In *nitrate of mercury* the precipitate is light yellow.

In *that of titanium* it is blood red.

In *binoxide of iron* it is bluish.

In *teroxide of iron* it is gray black.

Tannin unites and forms combinations nearly insoluble with some other principles, such as starch, gluten, ligneous fibre, albumen, casein, mucus, etc. Tannin submitted to the action of heat swells and is decomposed; by distillation it gives a black liquor which precipitates black the dissolutions of iron. This precipitation is due to a little pyrogallic acid. The residue in the retort is a very voluminous charcoal which amounts to the 0.0263 of the decomposed tannin.

Preparation of Tannin from Nutgalls.

In the art of tanning, the decoction used contains, besides tannin, gallic acid, extractive, and other soluble vegetable principles. Different processes have been proposed to isolate it; they do not produce it pure, but in a state sufficiently so for many purposes.

Proust's Process.

This chemist advises exhaustion of the nutgalls by water, and to pour into the liquor a dissolution of hydrochlorate of tin till it does not precipitate. Proust called this precipitate tannate of tin; it is yellowish-white. When washed and diluted in cold water he passes through it a current of hydrosulphuric acid gas, filters, and evaporates to dryness. According to this chemist it is pure tannin, but it has been ascertained that it contains a little gallic and hydrochloric acids and extractive matter.

Deyeux's Process.

He makes a strong infusion of nutgalls and precipitates it with a concentrated solution of carbonate of potash. He obtains an abundant precipitate, yellowish-white, which by drying forms a whitish powder. This product is far from being pure. Davy and Tromsdorff have ascertained it was a combination of tannin, gallic acid, carbonate of potash, and lime.

Dize's Process.

This chemist has ascertained that by pouring concentrated sulphuric or hydrochloric acid into a concentrated infusion of nutgalls, a white precipitate was obtained. Proust considers it like a combination of tannin with the acid employed. To purify it, it is sufficient to wash it with cold water, dissolve it in warm water, and saturate the acid by carbonate of potash. This tannin is not pure. Besides the extractive precipitated by sulphuric acid, it contains gallic acid.

Merat-Guillot's Process.

He precipitates the infusion of nutgalls by lime-water, and treats the precipitate by diluted nitric or hydrochloric acid. An effervescence is produced, and the liquor takes a dark color. The filtration separates a bright black substance that this chemist calls pure tannin, but as Davy has demonstrated it is united with extractive combined with the lime.

Bouillon-Lagrange's Process.

His method consists in precipitating the infusion of galls, by carbonate of ammonia, washing the precipitate with cold water, and digesting repeatedly in fresh portions of alcohol at 0.817. This process is as defective as the others.

Tromsdorff's Process.

He infuses, for three days, at a temperature of 65° a mixture of

Powdered nutgalls	3 lbs.
Water	5 gals.

Stir often, filter, add a new quantity of water, and repeat the operation until the liquor does not precipitate with sulphate of iron. Mix all the liquors, evaporate them at a gentle heat, and filter through a cloth to separate the extractive. Evaporate anew until it has the consistence of a jelly, and dry in the oven; treat several times with alcohol at 0.796 till it does not contain gallic acid. For this purpose he treats the tannin twice by alcohol at 0.10. It then contains a little mucous and extractive matter. To separate them he dissolves the tannin in water and exposes it to the air. It forms a moisture that he separates by filtration and evaporates to dryness. The residue is pure tannin, containing, however, a little sulphate of lime; to eliminate it he dissolves it in water and adds carbonate of potash until no more precipitate is formed. He filters, and to the dissolution he adds acetate of lead, which forms a precipitate or combination of tannin with oxide of lead. He washes the precipitate, and when dry makes a paste with it and water, and decomposed with sulphuretted hydrogen gas to separate the oxide of lead at the state of sulphuret. He evaporates the filtrate to dryness. The tannin is as pure as it was possible to obtain it at that time.

Serturner's Process.

This chemist precipitates the alcoholic infusion of nutgalls by warm carbonate of potash. He decants and washes the residue with alcohol, he dissolves in water, separates the carbonate of potash by sulphuric acid, evaporates and treats the residue with alcohol. The excess of sulphuric acid is precipitated by carbonate of lime. He filters and evaporates the filtrate to dryness. The residue is tannin containing very little gallic acid.

These different processes are for giving pure tannin; for the properties to be astringent, soluble in water, and precipitate the gelatine belong to some other substances of a different nature which are confounded in the generic name of tannin.

Varieties of Impure Tannin.

We have said that notwithstanding the numerous works of the old chemists, they never succeeded in obtaining pure tannin. It was impossible for them to separate it from foreign substances principally from the extractive with which it forms a very intimate combination, as it is to the extractive that were due the varieties observed in the different tannins. The less impure was that extracted from grape-seeds; as that of nutgalls it precipitates the gelatine in blue white.

That of *sumach* precipitates it YELLOW.
" " *quinquina* " " DARK ROSE.
" " *catechu* " " DARK-BROWN RED.

That of *Brazil wood* forms with gelatine a precipitate very soluble in water.

Proust affirms that there exist several varieties of

tannin, but it is very probable that these varieties are combinations of tannin with the above substances. In many cases, tannin has much analogy with gallic acid; it is nearly impossible to completely deprive it of the latter, at least they have the property in some circumstances of being transformed, the tannin into gallic acid, and the gallic acid into tannin.

The moulded infusion of nutgalls gives more gallic acid than a fresh infusion, by treating it with absolute alcohol. This example proves that the tannin can be transformed into gallic, and reciprocally.

Tannin of Catechu.

Davy has indicated the following process for extracting tannin from catechu. He treats it by alcohol, evaporates the extract, treats the residue by water, and evaporates to dryness. This tannin is astringent, sweetish, soluble in water and alcohol; the dissolution is of a dark-red brown. Potash, ammonia, magnesia, increase the color without precipitation. Sulphuric and hydrochloric acids precipitate it pale brown. The salts of protoxide of iron are not precipitated by this tannin. Those of peroxide of iron are precipitated olive-green; starch, gluten, ligneous fibre, gelatine, albumen, form with it an insoluble precipitate.

Tannin of Bark of Trees—Sumach—Kino.

Tannin from bark of trees is not different from that from nutgalls. The others have more or less analogy with those of catechu or nutgalls.

Tannin, according to the nature of the substance from which it is extracted, precipitates the dissolution of iron in blue or green, which is an indication of a variation in its constituents. The following table indicates the principal tannins which give these two precipitates.

1. TANNIN WHICH FORMS A BLUISH-BLACK PRECIPITATE IN SOLUTIONS OF A SESQUI-SALT OF IRON:—

Tannin from *nutgalls*,
" " the barks of *oak, beech, poplar, hazel, chestnut, maple, horse-chestnut, cherry, apricot, plum, elder, winter,* and other barks.
" " the bark of *sumach.*
" " *logwood.*
" " roots of *lithrum, salicaria, iris, pseudocorus, geum urbanum, polygonum bistortum, alchemilla vulgaris.*
" " the leaves of the *arbutus uva ursi, amothera biennis, geranium pratense,* etc.
" " the husks of the *cœsalpina coriaria.*
" " *lentils,* etc.

2. TANNIN WHICH FORMS A GREEN PRECIPITATE IN THE DISSOLUTION OF IRON.

Tannin from *catechu* (*juice of the* MIMOSA CATECHU).
" " *kino* (*juice of the* COCCOLOBA UVIFERA).
" " *cinchona barks.*
" " the roots of the *rumex aquaticus, tormentilla erecta, polypodium filix mas.*
" " *the tea and badiane.*

CHAPTER III.

ARTIFICIAL TANNIN.

PROPERTIES—COMPOSITION—FIRST VARIETY—SECOND VARIETY—THIRD VARIETY—PREPARATION OF AN ARTIFICIAL TANNIN FROM TURF.

Properties.

BESIDES the foregoing, chemists distinguish other varieties of tannin, which result from the chemical action of several powerful agents upon many substances; as, for instance, from the action of nitric acid upon charcoal and indigo, and likewise from the effects of sulphuric acid upon resin and camphor. The first notice of artificial tannin was published by HATCHETT in the Transactions of the Royal Society in 1801; he discovered it whilst making experiments upon the slow carbonization of plants. This tannin is different, however, from other varieties of this substance at present known.

Artificial tannin is a brown inodorous substance, having a vitreous fracture, and very soluble in water. THOMSON states that alcohol of sp. gr. 0.80 dissolves it, and so far it manifests a difference of behavior from natural tannin. The aqueous solution of this substance precipitates gelatine of a brown color, but the shade deepens as the liquids are more dense. This precipitate is a compound of tannin and gelatine, in the proportion of 36 parts of the former to 64 of the latter. It is insoluble both in hot and cold water. With the alkaline bases it combines, forming more highly colored solutions, which in the course of time get cloudy. The ammoniacal solution of artificial tannin on being evaporated to dryness and redissolved will not precipitate with gelatine till after the alkali which it retained is neutralized with an acid. The alkaline earths precipitate it, but the precipitates are slightly soluble in water; the heavy oxides precipitate it in combination as a puce-colored substance. On treating the precipitate with nitric acid the artificial tannin dissolves without change, whereas the natural product is altered by this agent. Heated alone in a retort it yields water and nitric acid, ammonia, carbonic acid, and another gaseous substance, probably nitrogen.

Composition.

According to M. Chevreul artificial tannin is formed of

$$\left.\begin{array}{l}\textit{Carbon}\\ \textit{Hydrogen}\\ \textit{Oxygen}\\ \textit{Nitrogen}\end{array}\right\} \textit{in undetermined proportions.}$$

First Variety.

Digest diluted nitric acid on powdered charcoal till entirely dissolved. The proportions are

Charcoal	1 part
Nitric acid at 1.40 . . .	5 parts.
Water	10 "

Mix the acid with the water and treat the charcoal in flasks that you heat in the air. A quick effervescence takes place due to the disengagement of nitrous acid. After a digestion of a few days add nitric acid and leave to digest until the carbon is dissolved. Evaporate to dryness and a brown mass is obtained, which is the artificial tannin. By this process you obtain 99 grains of artificial tannin from 88 grains of charcoal.

Second Variety.

This process consists in treating some substances rich in carbon, as indigo, resin, etc., with nitric acid. The dissolution of indigo in nitric acid gives a residue with an orange color, very bitter, soluble in water, forms with gelatine an insoluble precipitate, and has an action similar to tannin on metallic salts. This variety contains nitrous acid.

Third Variety

Is obtained by dissolving camphor and resins in sulphuric acid and leaving them together till the liquor becomes black, adding cold water, which precipitates a black powder, which is digested in alcohol. By evaporation a black substance soluble in water and alcohol is obtained. It forms an insoluble precipitate with gelatine, and has a weak action on salts of iron. According to M. Chevreul this tannin contains hyposulphuric acid.

Preparation of a Tannin from Turf.

Mr. H. C. Jennings has prepared a tannin from turf in the following manner: He takes black turf and moulds it into small bricks from 2 to 4 inches thick, and exposes them to the air until dry. He reduces them to fine powder, introduces into a vessel and moistens the surface with nitric acid from 10 to 20 per cent. of the weight of the turf, stirring well. The mixture becomes warm and swells.

When red nitrous vapors appear he hermetically shuts the vessel and leaves until all vapors have disappeared, then he adds 6 to 10 times the weight of water and stirs well.

When the mixture is thoroughly homogeneous he

treats it with boiling water. The tannin dissolves in the water.

Mr. Jennings has ascertained that leather can be tanned with this tannin, but after its use the skins must be dipped in a solution composed of 30 to 40 parts of carbonate of soda in 100 of water.

CHAPTER IV.

TANNIN FROM VARIOUS SOURCES.

It is demonstrated that several substances by combining with certain acids, produce natural and artificial tannin. The combination of an acid is indispensable for the existence of tannin, or rather tannin is not an immediate principle, but the compound of a peculiar substance and an acid united with more or less extractive matter.

1. Thus the tannin of nutgalls, of the barks of oak, sumach, etc., is united with gallic acid in greater or less proportion. It is very difficult to separate them, and we believe that it is to the gallic acid that is due the black precipitate formed by tannin in salts of sesqui-oxide of iron. This acid plays an active part in tanning. Its action has not been yet studied. The older the vegetable substances, the more gallic acid they contain, and consequently less tannin.

2. Artificial tannin is always combined with nitric or sulphuric acid, according to the acid used.

3. It is in acid fruits that tannin is found; in this case it is united with gallic acid and even with the acid from the fruit.

Chemists name four kinds of tannin.

1. *Natural tannin,* presenting several varieties, according to the proportions of extractive matter and gallic acid.

2. *Artificial tannin* resulting from the action of nitric acid on charcoal.

3. *Artificial tannin* resulting from the action of nitric acid on indigo, resins, etc.

4. *Artificial tannin* resulting from the action of sulphuric acid on rosin or camphor.

In the present state of things it is not rational to confound artificial with natural tannin, and the above statement is sufficient.

CHAPTER V.

GALLIC AND ELLAGIC ACIDS.

GALLIC ACID—PREPARATION—CHEMICAL PROPERTIES—COMPOSITION—ELLAGIC ACID.

GALLIC ACID.

THE tendency of Tannin to be transformed into gallic acid has been already mentioned; but it may be well to show more in detail the circumstances under which this change is effected, and to point out the properties of gallic acid generally, as also with regard to the operations of the tanner. Its name has been derived, as is evident, from galls, on account of those excrescences containing it ready formed. It likewise exists in the *cypress nut, arnica flowers, white hellebore, meadow saffron, colchicum autumnale,* and in a number of astringent barks together with tannic acid, but in small quantities. Its most prolific source is tannic acid, which by oxidation yields it abundantly. The conditions affecting the change, such as exposure of the solution of tannin to air and at an increased temperature, have been already mentioned, as likewise the decomposition of the same body by the mineral acids. All the methods recommended for the production of gallic acid from tannin are based upon these properties of the latter.

Preparation.

Scheele's Process.—He makes a concentrated aqueous solution of nutgalls, filters and leaves exposed to contact with the air. Tannin is decomposed little by little, and gives place to a moulding, which is taken after one or two months; he takes out the yellowish or grayish deposit from the bottom of the vasis and dissolves it in boiling water; he filters, and by a gentle evaporation, obtains gallic acid in the form of brownish crystals. He redissolves it several times in boiling water, and purifies it with a little animal black.

Fiedler's Process.—In one pint of water he boils one ounce of nutgalls, filters, and adds to the liquor a solution of two ounces of alum, the alumina of which has been precipitated by carbonate of soda. He stirs the mixture and leaves it in till the next day. The precipitate is treated with hot water until it does not blacken sulphate of iron. He reunites the liquors and evaporates so as to obtain crystals by cooling.

Braconnot's Process.—Take powdered nutgalls and pour on them water in sufficient quantity to cover them, and then leave at a temperature of 70° to 75°. After a while a quick action takes place, and when this subsides the paste is expressed and treated with boiling water, which dissolves the gallic acid and yields it upon evaporation in impure crystals. These by re-solution in water and filtration of the liquid through animal black afford a menstruum which gives the gallic acid in a state of purity when concentrated.

Ure's Process.—In a strong solution of nutgalls pour hydrochlorate of tin until no more precipitate is formed. Filter, dilute the matter in water and pass through it a current of hydrosulphuric acid gas, filter, evaporate; crystals of gallic acid deposit by evaporation.

It would appear from various researches that the change of tannin to gallic acid, on exposing the extract containing the former to air and moisture, is due to a fermentative process, which is considerably expedited if the vegetal matter in the bark or gall, or whatever else the source may be, is permitted to remain in contact with the liquid. Such is the case, especially with the extract of gall-nut; and it may be inferred that the tannin from all other sources, and which is capable of being transformed into gallic acid by oxidation in the above manner, is similarly affected. Mr. LAROCHE has shown by comparative experiments the effect of the marcs of gall-nuts after the extraction of the tannin with ether in the ordinary way in operating this change. By inclosing an aqueous solution of tannin and a portion of this residue in a bottle or flask, and allowing it to remain for some time, he found that the tannin was entirely converted into gallic acid, whilst a strong extract of tannin, freely exposed to the air at the same time, retained nearly the whole of its tannin unaltered. Hence, doubtless, the insoluble matter in galls in the presence of moisture, is capable of acting on tannin as a ferment, and that the change of tannin into its derivatives is the result of a fermentation. It is well known that fermentation by contact of yeast, blood, and albumen effects the same transformation of the astringent extract as the residue of the galls which have been digested in ether, and also that the latter will excite the various fermentations in solutions of grape sugar, and, therefore, these reactions may be taken as mutually corroborative. Further, the gallic fermentation may be intercepted by antiseptics like the vinous. Protochloride of mercury completely prevents the decomposition; and pyroligneous acid, or carbonic acid, on account of some aromatic matters which it contains, likewise considerably retards the fermentation.

It has been shown that sulphuric and hydrochloric acids at a boiling heat rapidly change tannin into gallic acid, and without the intervention of air; but if the mixture be kept at a common temperature, Mr. ANTOINE has shown by his researches that the decomposition of the tannin is retarded by a small quantity of these acids. On the contrary, malic, tartaric, and vegetable acids in general, expedite the decomposition of the tannin. The rapidity with which sumach ferments may be referred to the quantity of malic acid it contains.

Properties.

When pure, this acid crystallizes in long silky needles, which are unalterable in the air; its taste is acrid and styptic. BRACONNOT states that it dissolves in a hundred parts of cold and in about three parts of hot water, four or five parts of alcohol in the cold dissolve it, but one part of the hot spirit will take it up. It is soluble in ether, but in less quantity. The aqueous and spirituous solutions, but the former more readily, undergo decomposition, so that the surface of the liquid becomes mouldy, and a brownish matter is produced, which DAEBOEREINER considers ulmin. Added to a solution of gelatine no precipitation occurs, a behavior which at once distinguishes gallic from tannic acid, and which indicates that it is unavailable in converting skin into leather. This being so, and, as has been already pointed out, tannin being readily convertible into this body, it becomes of the utmost importance to the tanner to guard against this transformation, which, in the usual way of tanning, is so apt to take place. The researches of LAROCQUE have shown that, as regards the tannin from galls, the decomposition is completely and readily effected, provided the insoluble residuary matter be allowed to remain in contact with the liquor containing the tannic acid, and it is equally well known that the tannin from sumach is liable to decomposition, as well when it remains in contact with the insoluble portion of this body as when it is separated from it; but independently of the action of the residue, the malic acid here plays an important part. Though the evidence proving that the insoluble portion of the barks, etc., employed in tanning when allowed to remain in the tan liquor, does operate in the rapid conversion of tannin into gallic acid; thereby rendering the former valuable body useless is not definite. Still knowing that in the waste tan liquor a large quantity of gallic acid is found, it may be safely stated that its production is from the tannin, and also is owing more to the effects of the insoluble matter of the source of the tannin than to any oxidation which takes place during the tanning processes. Even those kinds of tannin which are incapable of producing gallic acid by decomposition, are subject to a metamorphosis which destroys the tanning agent, and this fermenting action is more readily produced where the insoluble matter is left in contact, than if the liquor were retained by itself. The only benefit that the tanner derives from gallic acid is that it aids in swelling the hides, and thus facilitates the absorption of the tannin; but when it is considered that a dilute solution of sulphuric or vegetal acids effects the same thing quite as well, it will be evident that he who relies on the swelling by gallic acid, and sacrifices a corresponding portion of tannin in its production, suffers a considerable loss, and is unable to compete with those who can obviate such a sacrifice.

At 410° to 420°, according to the observations of M. PELOUZE, gallic acid is entirely volatilized, producing a sublimate of beautiful white crystals and pure carbonic acid. If the heat be urged to 464° or 482°, instead of the foregoing change, another takes place, in which pure carbonic acid is likewise developed. But in addition to this a quantity of water is produced, and which runs along the sides of the retort, in the bottom of which remains a considerable mass of brilliant black insoluble matter, which at first sight might be taken for charcoal. Is is, however, a true acid, and is called by Pelouze *metagallic acid*.

The aqueous solution of gallic acid, upon treatment with potash, soda, or ammonia assumes a reddish-yellow color, which turns to deep brown by exposure to the air, probably by the absorption of oxygen. By the use of alcohol as a solvent and certain precautions, definite, crystallized, and soluble compounds of the acid with these bases may be formed. If the acid is associated with tannin, it decomposes nearly all metallic salts. With baryta, strontia, and lime, it forms slightly soluble compounds. Its affinity for magnesia is very strong, and the compound which it forms with that earth is insoluble in water, but soluble in an excess of acid. Gallic acid is also neutralized by alumina.

Gallic acid precipitates

Soluble salts of	MERCURY	in	*orange-yellow.*
"	" COPPER	"	*brown.*
"	" BISMUTH	"	*lemon.*
"	" LEAD	"	*white.*
"	" PROTOXIDE OF IRON	"	*blue.*
"	" SESQUI "	" "	*dark blackish-blue.*

Composition.

According to PELOUZE crystallized gallic acid is composed of

Carbon	.	.	.	.	50.10
Hydrogen	.	.	.	.	3.64
Oxygen	.	.	.	.	46.26
					100.00

Numbers which agree with the formula $C_7H_3O_5HO$. STRECKER, however, regards it as a tribasic acid; thus, $C_{14}H_6O_{10}2HO = 3HO, C_{14}H_3O_7 2Aq$, and capable of forming salts which correspond with the general formula $MO, 2HO, C_{14}H_3O_7$; $2MO, HO, C_{14}H_3O_7$, and $3MO, C_{14}H_3O_7$; MO being the representative of a metallic oxide.

As pyrogallic acid, $C_7H_3O_3$ or $C_{14}H_6O_6$, metagallic acid $C_7H_2O_2$ or $C_{14}H_4O_4$, ellagic acid $C_{14}H_2O_7HO$ and other derivatives of gallic acid, and, therefore, remotely from tannic acid, are of no importance in the making of leather, they will not be further dwelt upon.

ELLAGIC ACID.

Extract of gall, exposed for a long time to the air, contains in addition to gallic acid another acid, insoluble in water and to which the name of ellagic acid has been given. This latter acid is extracted from the deposit formed at the bottom of the vessels by treating it first with boiling water which dissolves the gallic acid, and then with a dissolution of potash, which dissolves the gallic acid in the state of ellagate of potash. The alkaline liquid, when evaporated, deposits the latter salt in the form of small crystalline spangles, insoluble in fresh water, but dissolving readily in alkaline liquid. Acids separate ellagic acid in the form of a slightly yellowish powder.

Ellagic acid is insoluble in water, alcohol, and ether, and its composition corresponds to the formula $C_{14}H_5O_{10}$. It loses two equivalents of water at 248°, when its formula becomes $C_{14}H_3O_8$. The formula of ellagic acid in combination with bases being $C_{12}H_2O_7$, that of the dried acid is, therefore, $C_{14}O_2H_7,HO$, and that of the hydrated acid $C_{14}H_2O_7,HO+2HO$.

Ellagic acid is said to be the chief agent that gives the *bloom* to the tanned hide. It will interest the reader to know the various derivatives of tannic acid. They play no part in tanning, but they are curious as a scientific fact.

Tannic acid	$C_{18}H_8O_{12}$.
Oxytannic acid	$C_{15}H_8O_{14}$, generated by the combined action of potash and the atmosphere.
Melanotannic acid	$C_{14}H_6O_9$, generated by the joint action of potash, air, and heat.
Melanogallic acid,	*metagallic* $C_{12}H_3O_3$, by the sudden action and continuance at a temperature of 480°.
Gallic acid	$C_7H_3O_5$, by the action of air and water or the action of heat, water, and sulphuric acid.
Ellagic acid	$C_7H_2O_4$, by the action of air and water.
Paraellagic acid	$C_7H_2O_4$, by the joint action of water, sulphuric acid, and a temperature of 285.°
Pyrogallic acid	$C_6H_3O_3$, by sublimation of galls and of gallic acid at 410°.

CHAPTER VI.

EXTRACTIVE.

THE term *extract* was employed by apothecaries to denote that portion of any vegetable substance which had been dissolved by digesting it in any menstruum whatever, and which had afterwards been reduced to a thick consistence by distilling off the menstruum, if valuable, or by evaporating it away if not worth preserving. So that originally the portions of plants dissolved by water, alcohol, wine, acetic acid, carbonate of potash, etc., and afterwards inspissated, were called *extracts*. This is the meaning which the word bears in the *Pharmacopée Royale Galenique et Chymique of Charras*, published in Paris in 1776. Thus the *extract of opium* of Charras was made by digesting opium, first in water, afterwards in alcohol, till everything soluble in these menstrua had been taken up. The two solutions were mixed, the alcohol distilled off, and the water evaporated at a gentle heat. What remained was called *extract of opium*. In process of time, these extracts were divided into two sets : namely, *watery* and *spirituous*, or *gummy* and *resinous,* according as the menstruum employed was water or alcohol. This distinction was attended to in the time of NEUMANN. Afterwards the term extract came to be restricted to what was obtained from vegetables, by macerating them in water and evaporating the watery liquid to dryness.

The extracts obtained in this way were generally considered as *soaps*, till FOURCROY and VAUQUELIN published some observations on the subject in 1790. According to them, *extract* is a substance at first soluble in water; but which, when the solution is exposed to the air, absorbs oxygen and becomes insoluble. Chlorine gas speedily converts it into a solid yellow substance insoluble in water but soluble in alcohol and alkalies. They inform us that they examined 12 different extracts and found the same characters in all.

In the year 1791, they published an elaborate analysis of the cinchona bark of St. Domingo, in which a great many experiments on extracts are stated; and soon after, Vauquelin made a set of experiments on the extractive principle of vegetables. FOURCROY, in his *General System of Chemical Knowledge*, published about the beginning of the present century, recapitulates the facts ascertained by Vauquelin and himself. The extracts from vegetables are very complex in their nature, but they all, in his opinion, contain a peculiar principle, to which he confined the term of extract. According to him it possesses the following properties.

It is at first soluble in water, but rapidly absorbs oxygen from the air, or other substances capable of yielding it. By this absorption it acquires a brown color and becomes insoluble in water. It has a strong affinity for alumina, and is taken away, and the liquid discolored, when alum mixed with an alkali is agitated in a solution containing the extract.

DE SAUSSURE afterwards showed that the substance called *extract* or EXTRACTIVE by Fourcroy and Vauquelin did not combine with the oxygen which was absorbed, but gave out hydrogen to it so as to convert it into water. The extractive, therefore, was not rendered insoluble by uniting with oxygen, but by being deprived of hydrogen. It contains a greater proportion of carbon than it did when soluble in water, and hence doubtless the reason why it assumes a brown color.

Berzelius has distinguished this brown extractive by the name of *apotheme;* it possesses the following properties:—

It is not completely insoluble in water, communicating a yellow reddish-brown or red color to that liquid, and is again deposited when the liquid is evaporated. But, it is dissolved with very great difficulty, and a minute portion of it communicates a great deal of color to that liquid. Boiling water dissolves more than cold, and the excess is deposited as the solution cools. It is much more soluble in alcohol than in water, and more soluble in hot than in cold alcohol.

Its best solvent is caustic potash, which dissolves a great quantity of it, and assumes a deep brown color. The alkaline carbonates dissolve it also. The acids precipitate it from these solutions.

The apotheme, thus set at liberty, combines with the excess of acid employed to precipitate it, and acquires the property of reddening litmus paper. It has a strong tendency to combine with acid bodies; this, doubtless, alters its character. But it is very probable that there are various species of apotheme, differing from each other according to the plants from which they have been obtained, though this subject has not hitherto attracted the attention of modern chemists. We need a set of experiments on this subject, with an ultimate analysis of apotheme, in as pure a state as possible, and extracted from different plants.

SECTION II.

TANNING MATERIALS.

SUBSTANCES which are available for the purpose of tanning, embrace a wide range of the juices, barks, leaves, roots, fruits, and excrescences of trees; vegetables which contain tannin, of one kind or another, may be taken into account. In looking over the researches and labors of chemists, many hundred substances which yield tannin have been discovered; but practice, or the trade, recognize only a few of these; probably owing to the quantity which can be annually produced, their yield in tannin, or because they offer some advantages, either in making a better leather, or in the time required to effect the operation. The tannin and other distinct principles in vegetable growth of every kind, are derived from the sap or soluble matters imbibed by the rootlets from the soil in which the plant exists, and the gases absorbed by the foliage. In many plants which elaborate tannin, it is met with in small proportions, owing, perhaps, to its being only a secondary and not a primary secretion. It is found in some vegetables equally in all parts, whilst in others, certain parts are richer in this substance, the remaining exhibiting only slight indications of its presence. The particular portions of plants that yield the greatest amount of tannin are, therefore, preferred in making leather.

The following is a list of the materials which contain tannin in the largest quantities, and which may be employed in the manufacture of leather.

Inspissated and Prepared Extracts.	Kino. Catechu or Cutch.
Vegetable Excrescences.	Galls.
Tree Leaves	of the different kinds of willow. of the common oak, Turkey oak, evergreen oak, and other varieties. of the common heath, and other varieties of the same plant. Garden artichoke. Sloe tree. Spotted hemlock. Bearberry. Several varieties of black and green tea. Sumach.
Seeds and Bulbs.	Grape. Hydro-sapathum and wild cornel. Hulls of the fruit of the cæsalpina coriaria, or divi-divi. Bulbs of the savilla maritima. Dried acorn hulls of the prickly copped oak.
Woods.	All woods of trees, the barks of which yield tannin, also afford more or less of this substance; they are scarcely employed.
Roots.	Leadwort. Malefern. Rhatany. Leopard's bane. Marsh rosemary.
Barks.	Birch, chestnut, horse-chestnut, sassafras, larch, hazel, beech, Lombardy poplar, blackthorn, pomegranate, ash, elm, cork tree, cinchona, willow, sycamore, tulip tree, wattle, oak, sumach, winter bark.

It will not be uninteresting to state briefly some of the properties of the substances mentioned in the foregoing table, with respect to their uses for tanning purposes.

CHAPTER VII.

TANNING SAPS—TANNING JUICES—KINO—CATECHU.

TANNING SAPS.

It is the general opinion of physiologists, that plants receive a considerable part of their nourishment by the root; that it enters into them in a liquid state and passes up in proper vessels towards the leaves. This liquid is distinguished by the name of *sap*. In the spring, when the buds begin to expand themselves into leaves, if we break off the extremity of a branch, or cut into the wood of a tree, this sap flows out, and may be obtained in considerable quantities. It was first examined by Dr. Hales; but chemical analysis had not made sufficient progress in his time to enable him to ascertain its constituents. Deyeux and Vauquelin have more recently analyzed the sap of different trees. To them we are indebted for most of the facts known respecting this liquid. A few additional ones have been ascertained by John.

The sap in all the vegetables hitherto examined is nearly as liquid as water. It always contains an acid, sometimes free, but more commonly combined with lime and potash. Various vegetable principles are also present; of these sugar is the most remarkable, and mucilage. Sometimes albumen and gluten, and sometimes tannin, can be detected. When left to itself, the sap soon effervesces and becomes sour, or even vinous when the proportion of sugar is considerable.

Hitherto, the sap of a few species of trees only has been examined. We are not in possession of any means of collecting the sap of the inferior orders of plants. The expressed juices of a considerable number of vegetables, indeed, have been prepared for medicinal purposes, but those are not sap, but a collection of all the liquid substances which the plant contains. At present, then, it is not possible to present a general view of the properties of sap. The following are the particular species in which tannin has been met most abundantly.

SAP OF THE BEECH TREE (*Fagus sylvaticus*).

Vauquelin collected two different specimens of this sap, the first in the end of March, the second about the end of April. It has a reddish-brown color, and a taste similar to the infusion of tan. It slightly reddens vegetable blues. Baryta, ammonia, carbonate of potash, and oxalate of ammonia, occasion precipitates in it; chlorine throws down yellow flakes, sulphuric acid blackens it, and disengages the odor of acetic acid. Sulphate of iron strikes a black, and glue throws down a copious whitish precipitate. When gently evaporated to dryness, it leaves a brown extract amounting to about $\frac{1}{138}$ of its weight, ductile while hot, but brittle when cold, and having the smell and somewhat of the taste of newly baked bread. It absorbs moisture from the atmosphere, and increases in weight about $\frac{1}{4}$. Lime disengages ammonia, and sulphuric acid, acetic acid from this extract. Alcohol dissolves only a small part of it. This sap contains the following ingredients:—

Water, *Acetic acid,*
Acetate of lime, *Gallic acid,*
Acetate of potash, *Tannin,*
Acetate of alumina, *Mucous and extractive matter.*

It contains, besides, a coloring matter, which may be fixed

on cotton and linen by means of alum, and dyes them of a fine solid reddish-brown color.

The sap of the oak contains tannin; the sap of the maple is composed as follows:—

Tannin,	Common salt,
Gallic acid,	Salts of lime, potash, and alumina.
Acetic acid,	

TANNING JUICES.

The sap passes from the root through peculiar vessels to the leaves, where it is altered by a process similar to that of digestion in animals, and formed into all the liquid substances requisite for the purposes of the plant. These liquids flow from the leaves towards the root in appropriate vessels, and have received the name of the *peculiar juices* of vegetables. They differ very considerably from each other in different plants. They have all a certain degree of consistency, and always contain much more vegetable matter than the sap. In the present state of organic chemistry, accurate details of their properties cannot be attempted; indeed, it is often difficult to procure them from any plant, unmixed with the sap. They sometimes exude spontaneously, and may always be procured in smaller or greater quantity, by incisions through the bark of the plant containing them. Many vegetable juices contain tannin, and we give below the three most generally employed.

KINO.

For a long time the origin of kino was unknown, but it has recently been ascertained to be the product of a lofty tree growing upon the mountains of the Malabar coast of Hindoostan, named *Pterocarpus Marsupium*, belonging to the natural order *Fabaceæ*.

Kino is the juice of the tree obtained by making longitudinal incisions in the bark; it flows abundantly, and is of a red color, and by drying it in the sun, it cracks into irregular angular masses, which are placed in wooden boxes for exportation. It sometimes comes to this country from the East Indies, but more generally from England. East Indian kino is usually in small, irregular, angular, shining fragments, in size between a pin's head and a pea, of a dark reddish-brown or blackish color, opaque, very brittle, easily pulverizable, and affording a reddish powder, much lighter colored than the drug in its aggregate state, and which becomes brownish on being kept for some time. It is inodorous and of an intensely pure astringent taste. Boiling water dissolves a large proportion of it, forming, when cold, a permanent intense blood-red solution; and which yields with sesquichloride of iron a dark green, coarsely flocculent precipitate, which is so abundant as to render the whole liquid pulpy. Acetate of lead affords a gray precipitate, and tartar emetic a gradually formed lake-red muddy jelly. Clear water forms with it a clear sherry red solution, leaving a crumbly, grayish-red residuum; alcohol dissolves about ⅜ of it, and forms a deep brownish-red tincture which is not disturbed by water. It contains 75 per cent. of tannin, and a peculiar extractive, 24 of red gum, and one of insoluble matter. Its aqueous solution precipitates gelatin, the soluble salts of iron, silver, lead, antimony, bichloride of mercury, and sulphuric, nitric, and muriatic acids.

AFRICAN KINO is rarely seen in commerce; it exudes from the *Pterocarpus erinaceus*. The DHA TREE KINO is the product of the *butea frondosa*, an East India tree; it contains from 70 to 90 per cent. of tannin. It is much used in India. The *Botany Bay kino* is the concrete juice of the *Eucalyptus resinifera,* or brown gum-tree of New Holland. It is easily powdered; the powder has an amber color; dissolves slowly in cold water, and rapidly in boiling water, forming a deep cherry red solution, which on cooling precipitates in a copious brick colored deposit, if the solution be made with 1 part of kino in 25 of water.

JAMAICA KINO. Product of the *coccoloba uvifera,* growing in the W. Indies. It contains 41 per cent. of tannin.

SOUTH AMERICAN, COLUMBIA OR CARACCAS KINO, is derived from the *coccoloba uvifera,* which grows upon the continent as well as in the islands. It is imported in heavy mass, and closely resembles the Jamaica kino in color, lustre, taste, and other properties. Cold water dissolves 89 per cent. and alcohol 94 per cent.

CATECHU.

Catechu is another of the same class as the preceding, and forms a most useful article for the tanner. There are several varieties, which are distinguished by various names, such as *cutch, terra-japonica,* and *gambir.* Formerly this extract, from its brownish-red color, was supposed to be a kind of earth, hence the title *terra* given to it. Catechu is extracted from the acacia catechu, a tree which grows to the height of 20 or 30 feet, and abounds in the forests from latitude 26° to 30°, known as the Bornese territory on the Malabar coast, and called Caucan. The heart and bark of the wood are boiled in water, and the solution evaporated, which leaves the astringent extract known as Caucan catechu. According to NEES VON ESENBECK most of the catechu exported from Bombay is prepared from the acacia catechu, whilst that brought from Bengal is derived from the *uncaria gambir,* a shrub cultivated in the countries lying on both sides of the shores of Malacca. It is obtained by boiling the wood, bark, and leaves of this shrub together with the inspissated juice in water, and evaporating, then adding a little sago to give it consistency; it is finally exsiccated in the sun, and then cut into square or circular cakes to suit the purchaser. Bombay catechu, which is the richest in tannin, is of a dark brownish-red hue, both externally and internally, and possesses a specific gravity of 1.38. DAVY examined the Caucan catechu, and found it to be 1.39; he also found in 200 parts of this as well as of the Bengal catechu, and known by the title *Pegu*, from the province of Bengal, where it is prepared, the following constituents:—

	CAUCAN OR BOMBAY.	PEGU OR BENGAL.
Tannin	54.50	48.50
Extractive	34.00	36.50
Mucilage	6.50	8.00
Earthy residue	5.00	7.00
	100.00	100.00

Cooper found in *cutch,* which is a commercial name for catechu—

Water	12.8
Tannin	47.7
Extractive matter	9.2
Gummy "	13.6
Resinous "	6.8
Insoluble residue	9.9
	100.0

The genuine catechu, of whatever variety, contains on an average about half its weight of tannin, and its efficacy in converting skin into leather has been estimated as being five times greater than the best oak bark; but this seems exaggerated. Besides the real tannin the extractive matter contained in it is another definite substance, which is called *catechin,* or *catechuic acid,* and which doubtless plays a part in the process of tanning. It possesses the property of coloring the leather deeply. This body differs from the tannin in being insoluble in cold water, although a solution of the tannin of catechu takes up a small quantity of it. The varieties of catechu of commerce are—

1. *Cake Catechu*, from its being in circular cakes. Their color varies from a light brown to a black, and their weight from several ounces to two pounds.

2. *Pegu Catechu*.—As already stated, this variety obtains its name from the province where it is prepared. It is generally imported in masses of a hundred pounds weight, but as seen in the shops it presents the appearance of angular, irregular fragments, in double layers with leaves between. It has a compact shining fracture and a deep brown color.

3. *Bengal Catechu* is manufactured into rectangular cakes, but in the course of transit they become reduced to fragments. Externally it has a rusty-brown color, and internally the shades vary from a brownish-gray to dark brown.

4. *Bombay Catechu*.—This variety occurs in globular lumps of the size of an orange flattened, and two pieces generally adhering together. In color it resembles that brought from Bengal.

5. *Gambir*.—It is stated by M'CULLOCH that no less than 4600 tons of catechu under the name of gambir are produced annually by the Chinese settlers in Rio. It takes the name from the shrub which is its source, the *uncaria* or *nauclea gambir*. It has a deep yellow or reddish-brown color on the outside, but within it is paler, and presents a dull earthy fracture. It comes to this country in solid masses of about a cubic inch in size. ESENBECK, who examined this variety, states that it

yields from 36 to 40 per cent. of tannin. Boiling water entirely dissolves it.

6. *Areca Catechu.*—The nut of an Indian palm known by this title affords this kind of astringent substances. These fruits are macerated with water, and the decoction is made, when a better sort of catechu results, known by the term *kassa*, and the semi-exhausted residue, upon further treating it with water, affords a solid extract, which is distinguished as *caury*. The former is of a black color and intermixed with husks, and the latter of a yellowish-brown with an earthy fracture. The *caury* is, of course, inferior to the extract known as *kassu*.

With regard to the application of catechu to the manufacture of leather, the natives of India have long practised it; but its introduction into the trade in this country for a similar purpose is of recent date. Its richness in the tanning agent causes its action to be very rapid in producing a gelatino-tannate of the substance of the skin, or, in other words, of making leather. The qualities of the article manufactured from it are not, however, so satisfactory as the rapidity of its effects, either to the tanner or the public; for the leather is very permeable to water, light and spongy, hard, and of a dark-reddish fawn color. The characteristic deposit from oak bark, and a few other tanning agents known as *bloom*, is not produced by catechu, and this want is a material objection to its use, as the existence of bloom upon leather is considered as a kind of guarantee of its goodness. One pound of catechu of good quality is capable of producing one pound of leather, and consequently, in tanning power is equivalent to five of oak bark, or thereabouts, as already stated.

CHAPTER VIII.

EXCRESCENCES CONTAINING TANNIN.

NUTGALLS.

There is no other natural product that affords so much tannin as those round, hard, woody excrescences known as galls. Formerly it was supposed that these were a kind of fruit, but naturalists and physiologists have ascertained that is not the case, but that they are excrescences or tumors, which form on the branches of different trees and vegetables, owing to the puncture of certain insects, for the purpose of depositing their eggs. The tree which affords those galls that are commonly known as *nutgalls*, is a stunted species of oak—*quercus infectoria*—which is generally found throughout Asia Minor. It grows to the height of four to six feet, has a crooked stem, and yields an acorn two or three times larger than its cup. The gall flies, which occasion the gall, belong to the genus *cynips*, and, from different accounts, there are several species; that which is concerned in producing the officinal galls, is the *cynips gallæ tinctoriæ*. The female insect of this variety, by means of an appropriate apparatus, perforates the cortical part of the plant, and in the wound deposits her eggs, together with an acrid liquor. In two or three days the part is, as it were, inflamed, and a swelling appears, and continues to increase till it results in a gall. The eggs which are inclosed in this excrescence are hatched, and in due time the young larvæ appear, and develop themselves, being supported by the juices of the plant till they become a perfect insect, when they perforate the galls and escape. When this happens, the excrescence loses much of its astringent principle, and becomes lighter; but if gathered or harvested before the entombed insect is completely devoloped, the nuts are not only heavier, but are richer in tannin and command a better price in the market. Galls gathered before the escape of the insect, have a black or bluish shade; but when the insect has left, their color is paler, and they generally attain to a larger size. To prevent this occurrence, great care is taken to harvest the galls before the insect attains its full growth, and eats its way through, leaving them, however, on the trees till they have acquired their greatest growth. In some parts, the governor, or *aga* of the district, levies a tax on the produce; and being thus interested in the success of the crop, he causes the cultivator to traverse frequently the hills and mountains, to report upon the advanced state of the galls, and whenever the proper growth has been attained, they are immediately collected. The selections thus made are known in the market as *green-galls*, and come to this country from Aleppo, Smyrna, and the interior of Asia Minor. Those which escape harvesting before the entombed insect has attained its full growth or emerged, are known as *white galls*, and are imported from the same place. Another kind of gall, produced upon the oaks growing in many departments in France, are nearly equal in size to the Asiatic green galls, but they are rounder, and possess a smooth and in some instances a polished surface. They have a brownish color, and rank, in their content of tannin, intermediate between the green and white Aleppo galls. A variety originating from the puncture of an insect allied to the *aphis* on the branches and shoots of the *dystylium racemosum*, comes from Japan. They are of an irregular shape, having in some instances both ends small, whilst the middle is much thicker, but more generally the stem end is the least and the more swollen part is nearer the other. Hence they are called apple-galls.

Annexed are the analyses of samples of Aleppo and Chinese galls by Guibourt and Davy.

	ALEPPO GALLS.		CHINESE GALLS
	GUIBOURT.	DAVY.	By BLEY.
Tannin	65.0	26.0	69.00
Gallic acid	2.0	6.2	4.00
Elagic acid	2.0	—	fat ⎫
Brown extractive	2.5	—	alb'en ⎬ 3.00
			resin ⎭
Starch	2.0	⎫	cellular ⎫ 16.00
Gum	2.5	⎬ 2.4	matter ⎭
Sugar	1.3	⎭	
Chlorophyl and vol. oil	0.7	—	—
Woody fibre	10.5	⎫ 65.4	—
Water	11.5	⎭	8.00
	100.0	100.0	100.00

CHAPTER IX.

LEAVES—TEA—FLOWERS AND FRUITS—SEEDS AND BULBS.

LEAVES.

OF the foliages of trees containing tannin, very few, if any, are now employed in the manufacture of leather. The leaves of the *heath* were once extensively used, but this material has long since been abandoned, preference being given to oak barks and other substances of native and foreign growth.

List of Tanning Leaves.

1. *Leaves of the different species of willow:* common white willow (*salix alba*), water willow (*salix caprea*), cracking willow (*salix fragilis*), red willow (*salix pentandria*), Downy-mount willow (*salix arenaria*), weeping willow (*salix babylonica*), Pyrenean willow (*salix aurigerana, S. grandifolia, S. pyrenaïca*), black willow (*S. nigricana*), sharp leaved willow (*S. cæsia, S. lanceolata*), yellow willow (*S. vitellina*), osier willow (*S. incana, S. viminalis*).

2. Leaves of the service tree (*sorbus domestica*), and mountain ash (*S. aucuparia*).

3. Of the pomegranate (*punica granatum*).

4. Of the beech-tree (*fagus sylvatica*), chestnut tree (*S. castanea*).

5. Olive tree (*olea Europæ*).

6. Of the common medlar (*mespilus germanica*).

7. Of the common dogwood (*cornus mas*).

8. Of the hazel-nut tree (*corylus arellana*).

9. Of the common birch (*betula alnus, B. alba*).

10. Of the red rose (*rosa gallica*), evergreen rose (*rosa sempervirens*).

11. Of the common ramble (*rubus fruticosus*), dewberry (*R. cæsius*), the cloud berry (*R. chamœmorus*) contains 7.3 of tannin.

12. Of the yellow-rooted water dock (*rumex aquaticus*).

13. Of the rosemary (*rosmarinus officinalis*).

14. Of the common European oak (*quercus robur*), Turkey oak (*Q. cerris*), sessile-flowered oak (*Q. sessiflora*), hoary oak (*Q. toza*), Apennine oak (*Q. apennina*), evergreen oak (*Q. ilex*).

15. Nearly all the *cistus* family.

16. Of the common heath (*erica vulgaris*), fine leaved heath (*erica anera*), cross-leaved heath (*E. tetralix*).

17. Of the French tamarisk (*tamarix gallica*), African and German tamarisk (*T. Africana and Germanica*).

18. Of the garden artichoke (*cynara scolynus*), of the twigs and leaves of the *cynara cardunculus*, cardom.

19. Of the sloe tree (*prunus spinosa*), common plum (*P. domestica*), briancon apricot (*P. brigantiaca*), common apricot (*P. armeniaca*), sweet almond (*amygdalus communis*), common peach (*A. persica*), common cherry (*P. cerasus*).

20. Of the spotted hemlock (*conium maculatum*).

21. Of the horse-chestnut (*æsculus hippocastanum*).

22. Of the crowfoot leaved cranesbill (*geranium pratense*).

23. Of the common œnothera, or evening primrose (*œnothera biennis*).

24. Of the lime-tree (*tilia europœa*).

25. Of the bearberry (*arbutus uva ursi*).

TEA.

The tea plant is a shrub or small tree, which in a state of nature may attain a height of twenty-five to thirty feet, but which, when cultivated, seldom exceeds six or seven. The tea plant is a native of China and Japan; it is an evergreen shrub from four to eight feet high. It is divided into black and green teas. The *green tea* is characterized by a dark green color, sometimes inclining more or less to blue or brown. It has a peculiar, refreshing, somewhat aromatic odor, and an astringent slightly pungent and agreeable bitterish taste. Its infusion is of a pale greenish yellow color, with the taste and odor of the leaves. *Black tea* is distinguished by a dark brown color, usually less firmly rolled, and lighter than the green. Its odor is fainter and of a somewhat different character, though still fragrant. Its taste is astringent and bitterish, less pungent and less agreeable than the green.

The composition of tea is shown by C. J. Mudler's analysis:—

	Green.	Black.
Volatile oil	0.79	0.60
Chlorophylle	2.22	1.84
Wax	0.28	—
Resin	2.22	3.60
Gum	8.56	7.28
Tannin	17.80	12.88
Thein	0.43	0.46
Extractive	22.80	19.88
Apotheme	traces	1.48
Muriatic extract	23.60	19.12
Albumen	3.00	2.80
Lignin	17.68	28.32
Salts	5.56	5.24
	104.94	103.50

Frank found the tea thus formed:—

	Green.	Black.
Tannin	34.6	40.6
Gum	5.9	6.3
Ligneous fibre	51.3	44.8
Gluten	5.7	6.3
Vol. matter & loss	2.5	2.0
	100.0	100.0

FLOWERS AND FRUITS.

Valonia.

Hitherto flowers and flower tops, though containing tannin, have not been used in the preparation of leather on the large scale. The same might be said of fruits with the exception of the acorn-cups of the *quercus ægilops*, prickly cupped oak, a tree which grows in abundance in the Morea and the adjacent countries. In commerce they pass under the name of valonia, and are imported from Turkey, Greece, Italy, and India. When the fruit is gathered it is conveyed to the nearest port to be shipped, then it is stored in a warehouse during several months, being laid out in beds of three to five feet in thickness. A slight heating or fermentation sets in during the above period, and as the moisture escapes the long spreading scales, which hitherto confined the acorn, become contracted and allow the latter to fall out from the cup. After being well dried the whole is picked, and the acorn, which contains no tannin, and the damaged cups are separated from those of the latter that are dry and good. The cup of this acorn, so long as kept dry, retains a bright drab color; but when exposed to moisture, it loses this appearance and turns black, losing by the change its tanning properties. Doubtless to the long exposure of the upper cups to the disengaged vapors from the bed, is owing their being invariably more or less damaged. Ordinary or common valonia, the cups of which average about 2 inches in diameter, differs from that kind known as carnata or *carnœtena valonia*, which are only about the size of a large cherry; the latter is said to be the fruit of a smaller species of *quercus* than that which affords the common valonia. It is in greater demand for silk dyeing than tanning.

Leather prepared by valonia is said to be harder and less permeable to water than that made with oak bark; and besides it presents the advantage of readily depositing a rich bloom upon the leather, a characteristic much sought by the traders in this article. Not less than 10,000 to 12,000 tons of this tanning agent are annually used in England, and it is stated that two pounds of good average quality are sufficient for making one pound of leather. Its price varies from $50 to $100 per ton. *Myrobalans*, the dried fruit of various species of *terminalia*, is extensively employed in tanning and dyeing factories. There are several kinds, all of which come, however, from the East Indies through Calcutta and other ports. This sort of fruit, when ripe, is pear-shaped, deeply wrinkled, of brownish-yellow hue, and weighing from 70 to 100 grains. The whole of the astringent matter which it yields is contained in the husk, which is easily separated from the unclosed nut by bruising the whole. Besides the tannin, a yellow coloring matter with mucilage and other principles is extracted. This tannin differs slightly from that found in nutgalls.

Divi-Divi is an article which has acquired, within a comparatively modern date, an interest with tanners and commercial men. It may be classed with the foregoing, since it consists of the dried pods of a leguminous shrub —*Cæsalpina coriaria*, which is indigenous to South America, and grows to the height of twenty and even thirty feet. The pods are about 3 inches long, of a dark brown color, and curled up as if they had been submitted to a high temperature during desiccation— the whole of the tannin is concentrated in the rind of the pod, immediately beneath the epidermis, and has consequently a very astringent taste, but the inner portion that includes the seed is very insipid. Besides tannin, it yields coloring matter, and a mucilaginous substance which interferes with its application in dyeing and printing. The leather prepared with divi-divi is very porous, and tinged brown or brownish red, according to the density of the ooze, time allowed, and state of exposure to the air. Its formation is attributed to a fermentative change induced by some of the extractive matter; this change occurs as well in cold as in warm weather, but more frequently in the latter. During the reaction a reddish matter deposits upon the leather in course of preparation, and on the side of the pit. By preventing exudation of some of the principles present, through the exclusion of atmospheric air, none of the fore-mentioned substances appear, and the leather retains the natural color. A solution or extract of divi-divi readily affords a deposit of bloom to leather. STENHOUSE has shown that the tanning matter of divi-divi, though similar to that contained in galls, inasmuch as it exerts a like reaction on solutions of sesquisalts of iron, is, nevertheless, different from the latter, since it produces no pyrogallic acid when submitted to dry distillation.

Of Tanning Flowers and Flower Tops.

Wild tansy (*potentilla anserina*).
Agrimony (*agrimonia eupatoria*).
Snakeweed (*polygonum bistorta*).
Malefern (*filix mas*).
Wood strawberry (*fragaria vesca*).
Dropwort (*spiræa filipendula*).
St. John's wort (*hypericum perforatum*).
Common cotton rose (*silago germanica*).
Greater and lesser periwinkle (*vinca, major and minor*).
Spotted persicaria (*polygonum persicaria*).
Plantain (*plantago major*).
Ladies' mantle (*alchemilla vulgaris*).
Everlasting (*graphalium dioïcum*).
Marsh horse-tail (*equisetum palustre*).
Common burnet (*poterium sanguisorba*).
Lungwort (*lichen pulmonarius*).
Cinquefoil (*potentilla reptans*).
Meadow sweet (*sporæa ulmaria*).
Wood cranesbill (*geranium grandiflorum*).

Red rose (*rosa gallica*).

Hop (*humulus lupulus*) contains more than 0.4 of tannin and gallic acid.

Clove tree (*Eugeniæ caryophyllata*) contains .13 of a peculiar tannin.

Common avens (*geum urbanum*) is an European plant. Its root is very rich in tannin, and contains, according to TROMSDORFF—

Volatile oil (heavier than water)	0.038
Resin	3.998
Tannin (soluble in alcohol and ether)	40.984
Adraganthine	9.196
Gummy matter	15.793
Woody fibre	29.991
	100.000

The water avens (*geum rivale*) which grows on this continent from Canada to Pennsylvania, likewise possesses tanning properties.

Seeds and Bulbs Suitable for Tanning.

Those of the grape contain much tannin, and give very good results. Those of the wild cornel (*hydrosapathum*). The bulb of the *scilla maritima*, a perennial plant indigenous to Barbary, Sicily, and Spain. There are two varieties of squills, the red and white bulb, but they do not differ in property. Before being sent to market they are thinly sliced and dried.

According to Vogel's analysis 100 parts of dry squill contain—

Gum	6
Bitter principle	35
Tannin	24
Saccharine matter	6
Woody fibre	29
	100

CHAPTER X.

WOODS—ROOTS—BARKS.

Woods.

This material has not been converted to any useful end so far as it immediately concerns tanning, notwithstanding, that tannin, as before stated, exists to some extent in many species.

Roots.

The *dentelaria*, or leadwort (*Plumbago Europæa*), a perennial herbaceous plant growing wild in the South of France, contains a considerable quantity of tannin. The MALEFERN (*aspidium filix mas*), grows in all parts of Europe, and in shady pine forests from New York to Virginia. The best root is about 6 inches long and an inch broad; externally it is of a brown color, internally yellowish or reddish white, with a peculiar but not very strong odor, and a sweetish bitter nauseous and astringent taste. It is collected in May and September.

MORIN has analyzed the root and PESCHIER the buds. Morin found—

Volatile oil,	Tannin,
Fatty matter comp. of elaine and stearin,	Uncrystallizable sugar, Starch,
Gallic acid,	Ligneous,
Acetic acid,	Gelatiniform matter.

Peschier found—

Aromatic vol. oil,	Reddish brown col. matter,
Aromatic fatty oil,	Extractive,
Adipocerous principle,	Acetic acid,
Brown resin,	Chloride of potassium.
Green coloring matter,	

RHATANY (*krameria triandria*) is a native of Peru, growing in dry, argillaceous, sandy places. It was discovered in 1780 by Ruitz. It consists of short root-stock from half to two inches in diameter. Its bark is dark brownish red, wrinkled and warty on the root-stock, brittle, inodorous, and of a strongly astringent and slightly bitterish taste. The woody interior is yellowish red, dense, tough, and of the same taste, but much weaker.

According to a recent analysis I made of this root, I found it thus formed :—[1]

Organic matters	93.60
Inorganic "	6.40
	100.00
Gum and albumen	1.257
Sugar	0.285
Extractive	0.628
Starch	1.064
Tannin	3.928
Coloring matter (resin)	20.578
Soluble salts	0.878
Insoluble "	5.428
Ligneous matter	65.954
	100.000

Gmelin found 38.3 of tannin, and Peschier 42.6; but in those analyses they calculate the coloring matter as tannin.

MARSH ROSEMARY (*Statica Carolinianæ*) is found along the sea-coast in marshy situations from Maine to Florida, flowering from August to October. The root is large, fusiform or branched, heavy, fleshy, and of a reddish or purplish brown color. It is inodorous, but has

[1] Journal of Materia Medica, vol. i., new series, page 141. Analysis of Rhatany, by Prof. H. Dussauce.

a saltish extremely bitter and astringent taste. According to Prof. Parrish it contains 12 per cent. of tannin, some gum, extractive, albumen, resin, volatile oil, caoutchouc, lignin, coloring matter, and various salts.

Barks.

The bark is the outermost part of vegetables. It covers the whole plant from the extremity of the roots to the extremity of the branches. It is usually of a green color; if a branch of a tree be cut across, the bark is easily distinguished from the rest of the branch by its color. If we inspect such a horizontal section with attention, we shall perceive that the bark itself is composed of three distinct bodies, which, with a little care, may be separated from each other. The outermost of these bodies is called the *epidermis*, the middle one is called the *parenchyma*, and the inner one, or that next the wood, is called the *cortical layers*.

The *epidermis* is a thin, transparent membrane, which covers all the outside of the bark. It is pretty tough. When inspected with a microscope, it appears to be composed of a number of slender fibres crossing each other and forming a kind of network. It seems even to consist of different thin, retiform membranes, adhering closely together. This at least is the case with the epidermis of the birch, which M. Duhamel separated into six layers. The epidermis, when rubbed off, is reproduced. In old trees, it cracks and decays, and new epidermides are successively formed. This is the reason that the trunks of many old trees have a rough surface.

Davy was induced by some observations of Mr. Coats, of Clifton, to examine the epidermis of the bamboo, the sugar-cane, and the *equisetum hyemale*. He found in them a great quantity of silica. When examined under the microscope, the epidermis of these gramineous plants constitutes a brilliant retiform tissue, which gives it the harsh feel by which it is distinguished. The epidermis of the bamboo was found to contain 17.4 per cent. of silica, and it has the appearance, when pulverized, of pounded glass. He found also silica in the epidermis of the sugar-cane, the common bog reed (*arundo phragmites*), wheat, barley, and oats. He found a still greater proportion of silica in some other of the gramineous plants.

The *parenchyma* lies immediately below the epidermis; it is of a deep green color, very tender and succulent. When viewed with a microscope, it seems to be composed of fibres which cross each other in every direction, like the fibres which compose a hat. Both in it and the epidermis there are numberless interstices, which have been compared to so many small bladders.

The *cortical layers* form the innermost part of the bark, or that which is next to the wood. They consist of several thin membranes, lying one above the other; and their number appears to increase with the age of the plant. Each of these layers is composed of longitudinal fibres which separate and approach each other alternately, so as to form a kind of network. The meshes of this network correspond in each of the layers, and they become smaller in every layer as it approaches the wood. These meshes are filled with a green-colored cellular substance, which has been compared by anatomists to a number of bladders adhering together, and communicating with each other.

Fourcroy supposes that the epidermis is the same in its nature in all trees, and that it possesses constantly the properties of cork; but this opinion is likely not to be verified. The cortical layers seem, at least, in many cases, to have a similar fibrous basis; a basis possessing essentially the properties of flax, which is itself merely the cortical layers of *linum usitatissimum*. Common cork, which constitutes the epidermis of the *quercus suber*, is composed of a cellular tissue, whose cavities contain a variety of foreign substances, which may be separated by rasping down the cork and treating it by various reagents, as is done with wood, in order to free the *lignin* from foreign matters. Ten parts of common cork, when treated in this way, are reduced to seven. This residue was considered by Chevreul as a peculiar substance, which he distinguishes by the name of *suberin*.

The properties of suberin have not been yet accurately determined, owing to the difficulty of obtaining it in a state of purity. Sulphuric acid readily chars it. Nitric acid gives it a yellow color, corrodes, dissolves, and decomposes it; converting it partly into suberic acid, partly into a substance resembling wax, partly into artificial tannin, and partly into a kind of starchy matter.

Suberin is very inflammable, burning with a lively flame, while at the same time it swells considerably, but does not melt. When distilled it yields water and a colorless oil, then a yellow colored oil. These liquids are all acids. If the distillation be continued, a brown oil comes over with a little ammonia, and a fatty crystallizable substance, which does not dissolve in caustic potash. During the process, combustible gases are disengaged, and there remains a porous charcoal, weighing ¼ part of the suberin employed.

Chevreul heated given weights of common cork, washed cork, and suberin with nitric acid, and obtained the following products:—

	Common Cork.	Washed Cork.	Suberin.
Fibrous, white, insoluble matter	0.18	0.9	1.0
Resin	14.72	17.5	10.0
Oxalic acid	16.00	10.6	7.6
Suberic "	14.40	19.6	22.4
	45.30	48.6	41.0

What is wanting to constitute the 100 parts is a yellow bitter substance held in solution by the mother water, together with carbonic acid and water formed at the expense of the constituents of cork.

Chevreul obtained from the epidermis of the birch, cherry tree, and plum a quantity of suberic acid, which was always the greater the purer the epidermis employed. Hence it would appear that these epidermides have a constitution analogous to that of cork. According to John, the young epidermis of the birch differs essentially from cork in this respect. It is soluble by boiling in caustic potash lye, and when the brown-colored solution is treated with an acid, yellow flocks fall, which become brown on drying. This precipitate is slightly soluble in boiling alcohol, but most of it falls again when the solution cools. The matter of the parenchyma, and the juice which exists in bark, vary extremely, and probably occasion most of the differences between them. Some, as oak barks, are characterized by their astringency, and contain tannin; others, as cinnamon, are aromatic, and contain an essential oil; others are bitter, some are chiefly mucilaginous, others resinous, etc. But in the present state of the subject, an enumeration of the different kinds of bark is not to be expected; I shall, therefore, satisfy myself with detailing the properties of those barks that have been subjected to examination in the art of tanning.

CINNAMON.—*Laurus cinnamomum* is a tree growing from 20 to 30 feet high, with a trunk from a foot to a foot and a half in diameter and covered with a thick scabrous bark. This tree is a native of Ceylon, the Malabar coast, Sumatra, Borneo. The bark of the root has the odor of cinnamon with the pungency of camphor. The leaves have a hot taste. The flowers have a disagreeable odor, similar to that exhaled from freshly-sawn bones. The bark furnishes the cinnamon of commerce. It is usually collected from trees about nine years old. The peeling commences in May and lasts until the latter part of September. The bark is dried in the shade first, and finished in the sun. The best bark comes from Ceylon. It has a light yellowish-brown color. It possesses a rich, pure, peculiar odor, and a sweetish, aromatic, slightly astringent, pungent, and peculiar taste. It yields its virtues to water and alcohol. Its tannin is of the same nature as the catechu tannin; it gives a dark green precipitate with the salts of iron. There are several other species of cinnamon, as the *C. aromaticum, C. nitidum, C. tamala, C. Loureirii, C. culilawan.*

Vauquelin has analyzed two kinds, and found them thus formed:—

CINNAMON OF CAYENNE.	CINNAMON OF CEYLON.
Volatile oil with a smart taste.	*Volatile oil more agreeable.*
Tannin.	*Tannin.*
Gum.	*Coloring matter.*
Salts of potash and lime.	*Gum.*
	Resin.

SASSAFRAS.—*Laurus sassafras* is a well-known tree growing through the United States and extending into Mexico, and flowering in the latter part of April or early in May. The flowers have a weak agreeable odor. The bark of the root is in small irregular pieces of a grayish-brown color outside, rusty-brown within. Hot water and alcohol take up its active properties.

According to Reinsch it is thus formed—

Water	9.0	*Sassafride* ⎫	
Essential oil	0.8	*Tannin* ⎬ ext. by w'k alcohol	6.8
Fatty matter	0.8	*Gum* ⎭	
Balsamic resin and wax	5.0	*Gum, col. matter, and salts*	3.0
Sassafride ⎫ extracted by	9.2	*Fecula, tannin (by water)*	5.4
Tannin ⎭ strong alcohol	5.8	*Fecula, tannin (by caustic lye)*	28.9
Soluble albumen	0.6	*Lignin*	24.7

100.0

BIRCH BARK.—*Betula alnus*, tree which abounds in the dry, barren portion of the Middle States, and grows to a great height. The epidermis consists of thin white layers. The inner bark is astringent, and is used for tanning *Russia* leather. According to Davy it contains 6.75 per cent. of tannin. Russia leather owes its odor and durability to a fragrant brown oil it contains.

CHESTNUT BARK. *Castanea vesca.*—We have already mentioned the chestnut-tree. The American species grows in gravelly or sandy soils, and yields a bark which contains upwards of four per cent. of tannin. Leather tanned with it possesses greater solidity and flexibility than that made with oak bark.

HORSE-CHESTNUT.—*Æsculus hippocastanum* is indigenous to this country, but is cultivated in Europe. According to Davy it contains 1.875 per cent. of tannin. The American variety is known as *Ohio Buckeye*.

BEECH BARK. *Fagus sylvatica.*—Indigenous to the North of Europe and North of America. Is very abundant in New York, Pennsylvania, Kentucky, and Tennessee. It is classified into two varieties, the white, *fagus sylvestris*—and the red, *fagus ferruginea*. Beech bark is of a silvery color, and contains nearly three per cent. of tannin. In places where oak is scarce the white beech is used for tanning purposes, and makes a white but inferior leather.

LOMBARDY POPLAR BARK.—*Populus fastigiata* contains 3.12 of tannin, and makes a lighter-colored leather than oak bark, imparting at the same time a fragrant odor similar to that of Russia leather.

BLACK THORN BARK.—*Prunus spinosa*, from the sloe tree or wild plum tree, contains 3.32 of tannin. The black thorn of the United States is the *yellow cratægus*.

POMEGRANATE BARK.—*Punica granatum* is a shrubby

tree of African origin. It is cultivated in the southern States. There are two varieties, distinguished by their fruit; one is sour and the other sweet. The rind of the fruit, the flowers, bark of the root abound in tannin.

ASH BARK.—*Fraxinus excelsior* is abundant in our forests and grows to a great height. The leaves and bark have a very astringent taste. According to Davy the bark contains 3.33 per cent. of tannin.

ELM BARK.—*Ulmus campestris* is cultivated in the United States, and contains 2.706 of tannin.

CINCHONA BARK grows in South America, and the number of species, as described by Guibourt, amounts to 25, but as many more have been described since.

As this bark is very costly and used only in medicine, we do not think it necessary to describe it here. All the cinchona barks are very rich in tannin.

POISON OAK.—*Rhus toxicodendron* is a creeping shrub from one to three feet high. The leaves are inodorous, have a mawkish acrid taste, and yield their virtues to alcohol and water. It grows wild through the United States. This plant contains tannin and gallic acid.

SUMACH. *Rhus glabrum.*—In its purity it consists of the powdered leaves of a shrub that grows extensively in the South of Europe, in the United States and in Asia, to which it is indigenous. It seems that there are several species, such as the WILD OLIVE, *Rhus cotinus*, rhus glabrum or coriaria, which is the best and most esteemed for the preparation of the finer kinds of leather. Italy, Sicily, Portugal, Spain, and France produce considerable quantities of sumach, varying in quality, and distinguished from one another by the habits of the tree, the color and other properties. The sumach obtained from the *rhus cotinus* is for the most part employed in dyeing, and the product of the *rhus coriaria* is that which is converted to the uses of the tanner, especially in the preparation of morocco and similar leather. The latter shrub, which grows wild in Portugal, Spain, and other countries named above, rises to the height of four to eight and in some cases to 12 feet; its stem is crooked and covered with a reddish-gray bark; the leaves present a green on the upper, and a whitish color on the under surface during spring and summer, but they assume a reddish hue in autumn. It flowers in July, the blossom being greenish-red, and yields a cluster of small crimson berries on ripening. Regarding the effects of sumach as a tanning agent, it is stated that it deprives the skin of much of its softness and elasticity, but it offers a great advantage of not coloring it during the process, and is on this account preferred in France and other places, notwithstanding its cost being much greater than other tanning agents, by the fabricators of morocco and glazed leather. It is utilized in the ordinary way of tanning mixed with bark or other matters, and affords good results.

Of the species of sumach in the market, the Sicilian is accounted the best. There are two kinds, one of which, the alcamo, is the most esteemed. It is a very fine light green powder, containing very little woody matter, having an agreeable odor analogous to that of the violet and a strong astringent taste. It contains very little coloring matter, though it gives a yellowish-green solution when macerated with water. The second variety inclines to a reddish-yellow, has a feebler odor, with a less astringent taste than the foregoing variety. Sicilian sumach is generally packed in bales weighing about one hundred and a half.

Spanish sumach is various in quality, being less carefully prepared, and, consequently more or less mixed with woody matters. The best sort comes from Priego, and is grown in the neighborhood of Malaga. It is, like the Sicilian, finely ground, and affords a color of equal or greater brightness; its odor reminds one of the tea plant. With water it gives a dark and more reddish solution than the foregoing. It is usually packed in bales of one hundred weight; the other sort, the Molina and Valladolic sumach, are next in quality to the foregoing; they are very similar.

Portuguese or Porto sumach is almost similar to the Priego, but is generally dirtier, and contains more mineral salts.

Italian sumach has a dark green color, is free from woody matter, but feels granular in the hand, and has an odor like that of the bark, which possesses similar qualities to the leaves.

French sumach is similar to the preceding. Three sorts are collected: the fauvis is almost equal to the Sicilian when well purified, and comes from Brignolles, near Marseilles. If less care be taken in its manufacture, it approaches more to the quality of Malacca sumach— it frequently goes under both these names. A second sort, Donzere, and a third Pudis, are commonly used in the tanneries. A fourth variety, called *redou* or *redoul*, obtained from the *coriaria myrtifolia*, cultivated in Languedoc, is of a grayish green color.

Willow Bark. Salix alba.—This bark is remarkable for its astringent taste. This tree grows in the northern and temperate parts of North America. The dry bark has an ash-gray color on the upper and a reddish yellow on the under surface. The white willow contains 2.3 per cent. of tannin and the Leicester willow 6.86 per cent. The black willow is the most common American willow, and grows in the Western and Middle

States. In the North of Europe the *S. alba* is used for tanning.

The leather which is made from kid and lamb-skins owes its agreeable odor to the willow bark with which it is tanned.

TAMARISK—*Tamarix gallica*—is a shrub plant indigenous to Spain, Italy, and the South of France. The bark is deep reddish brown on the upper and yellowish on the under side; both the wood and bark have an astringent slightly bitter taste.

HEMLOCK BARK. *Abies canadensis.*—This tree sometimes attains the height of 30 feet, with a trunk two or three feet in diameter. Its foliage is delicate bright green above and silvery white underneath. Hemlock is abundant in Canada, Nova Scotia, and the elevated and mountainous regions of New England and the Middle States. Its timber is very coarse grained, and its bark contains an astringent principle. The bark is largely used in this country as a substitute for that of the oaks in tanning. It imparts its red color to leather made with it, which is said to be inferior to that made with oak bark; but the two kinds united are supposed to produce better leather than either of them alone.

CHAPTER XI.

OAK BARKS.

THE oak, by its strength and greatness, is the patriarch of the forest. It lives three or four hundred years, and some authors have ascertained that it has lived six hundred years, according to the fertility and exposure of the ground. It is, and will always be, the most useful of trees. It seems that such a tree ought to be well known in its botanical, physical, and industrial character; but such is not the case, and unhappily all the varieties of oak are not yet known. The different species of oak belong to the *nonœcia polyandria*; all the parts and principally the bark contain tannin. We shall divide them into two classes :—

1. *European oaks.* 2. *American oaks.*

1. *European Oaks.*

Quercus robur.—This bark, so long and universally employed for tanning leather, has been but imperfectly examined. Davy found that 100 parts contain 12.7 parts of extractive and 6.3 of tannin. It contains also a considerable quantity of pectin. When oak bark, after having been exhausted by tanning, is put into water a kind of fermentation takes place, and an acid liquid is formed, which is employed in one of the preliminary processes of tanning. The acid thus formed is the lactic, and the liquid, called *jusée* by the French, contains acetate of lime, tannin, apotheme, a gummy matter, free acetic acid, and a great quantity of lactate of lime together with lactate of magnesia, potash, ammonia, and probably of manganese and iron.

Quercus nigra.

Quercus glomerata.

Quercus lamiginosa.

Quercus laciniata.

Quercus viminalis.

Quercus pedunculata contains about as much tannin as the quercus robur.

Quercus cerris.

Quercus haliphœos.

Quercus tauza.

Quercus esculus grows in Italy and Dalmatia.
Quercus apennina grows in Italy and the East.
Quercus lastigiata grows South of France.
Quercus lusitanica.
Quercus infectoria.

Quercus Ilex grows in Spain, Italy, and the South of France. Is much used to tan leather.

Quercus suber grows in South of Europe, principally in Spain. It requires dry and warm lands and fears the damp cool. Its height is from 24 to 30 feet. Its bark is very thick and soft and is known by the name of cork. It falls naturally every seven or eight years. It is used for tanning and burning, and after the tree has attained the age of thirty, the bark is collected regularly every seven or eight years to manufacture the cork. M. Chevreul has analyzed it and found it thus formed:—

Wax.	*Gallic acid.*
Cerine.	*Suberin.*
Soft resin.	*Acetic acid.*
Red coloring matter.	*Brown nitrogenized matter.*
Tannin.	*A salt of lime.*

Quercus coccifera is known by the name of *dwarf oak* and *garouille*. Its height is from 3 to 4 feet. The bark of the root is very rich in tannin and much used in Europe for tanning. It is on this oak that grows the vegetable *kermes* called *vermilion, Coccus Ilicis.* According to M. Bosc, the leaves and trunks can be used in tanning. It is much used in the South of France.

When this bark is used, the ox-hides are placed about 40 in a vat with plenty of water. In the vat is first put a small quantity of bark. Increase progressively the quantity of bark until about ⅓ of the bark destined to tan the hides is used. During the time, which lasts three months for heavy leather, draw and drop the hides, and put them back in the liquid. Leave them again three weeks, when draw them to put them into the pits.

The barking of this tree is done in every season; however, it is richer in tannin in the spring. In June it contains 8.9 per cent. of tannin, and in September only 8.3 per cent.

2. *American Oaks.*

White Oak. Quercus alba.—This tree varies in size according to the climate and soil, attaining the height of from 60 to 90 feet with a diameter of from 3 to 6 feet. It grows throughout the Union, but is more abundant in the Middle States. Its wood is strong and durable, and is extensively employed in ship building, etc. The bark is employed for tanning, but the red and Spanish oaks are preferred. The bark contains much tannin; it has a light yellowish brown color, a feeble odor, and a strongly astringent bitterish taste.

The *black oak* is a forest tree common to the United States, the bark of which is much used in tanning. It is preferable to the above. Its coloring principle is known by the name of *quercitrin*.

The *red oak* is more common in the Northern States and Canada; its wood is reddish and coarse-grained, and used principally for fuel. It contains considerable tannin.

Quercus Phœllos grows in North America, its height is about 100 feet.

Quercus primus is found in North and South Carolina. Its height is about 99 feet.

Quercus aquatica grows in North and South Carolina.

Quercus coccinea, or *scarlet oak*, is more abundant in the Middle States, and on the mountains of Carolina and Georgia, but is found as far north as latitude 43. Its height is about 80 feet and its diameter 3 or 4. Its leaves are of a beautiful green, and the first frost turns them a bright scarlet color. This tree produces galls, which are applied to the same purposes as the European galls.

Quercus virens, or *live oak*, is confined to the vicinity of the Atlantic coast, south of latitude 37° and of the Gulf of Mexico as far as the river Sabine. Its height is from 40 to 50 feet, and its diameter from 1 to 2 feet. The leaves have a dark green color above, and whitish beneath.

The bark is hard and thick, and of a blackish color. It is very good for tanning leather, but is not much employed.

Quercus falcata, or *Spanish oak*, inhabits all those parts of the Union which are south of the 41st parallel of latitude, but is most abundant in the Atlantic States.

This oak is remarkable for the great dissimilitude which exists in its leaves and general appearance in different climates. In the Southern States it grows to the height of 30 feet with a trunk 4 or 5 feet in diameter, while in New Jersey it is never above 30 feet high, with a trunk 4 or 5 inches thick. The bark is thick, black, and deeply furrowed, and the wood is reddish and cross-grained, with open pores. The leaves on the tree in the South are falcate, and as well as the young shoots to which they are attached are covered with a thick down upon the under sides. In New Jersey the leaves are three lobed, except a few upon the summit, which are slightly falcated. This tree fructifies once in two years. Its flowers put forth in May, and are succeeded by small round brown acorns, contained in scaly, shallow cups, supported by peduncles

$\frac{1}{6}$ of an inch in length. The Spanish oak is chiefly valuable on account of its bark, which is preferred to any other for tanning coarse leather, which it is supposed to render whiter and more supple. The quality of the leather prepared with it is said to be improved by the addition of a small quantity of hemlock.

Quercus ambigua, or *gray oak*, is abundant in Maine, New Hampshire, and in Vermont. Its height is 50 to 60 feet, and its diameter 15 or 18 inches. The leaves are large and smooth. It flowers in May. The wood and bark are similar to those of the red oak, and the latter may be employed in tanning.

CHAPTER XII.

BARKING OF THE TREES.

PART OF THE BARK CONTAINING THE MOST TANNIN—AGE OF THE TREES RELATIVELY TO THE RICHNESS IN TANNIN FROM THEIR BARKS—BARKING OF THE TREES—INFLUENCE OF THE SEASON AND LOCALITIES, IN THE TIME OF THE BARKING.

Parts of the Bark containing the most Tannin.

WE have already stated that bark is composed of 4 parts; all are not equally rich in tannin, or rather some contain none. Such is the case with the epidermis, the liber contains very little. It is in the inner layer of the cortex that it is principally found. Davy has found in oak bark of middling size and cut in the spring 0.604, while the inside white layers have given him 0.15. The experiments of tanners have demonstrated the fact. We see then theory and practice agree together. This remark is of much interest for the tanner who ought to reject the bark, with a thick epidermis, as poor in tannin.

It is the same case with medicinal astringent barks. Indeed quinquina barks are as poor in tanning principles, quinia and cinchona, as they are more fibrous or ligneous, while if the break is less fibrous, smoother, with a resinous aspect, they are richer in those principles.

Age of the Trees Relatively to the Richness of their Barks in Tannin.

It is a great mistake, which unhappily is believed by a great many, that the older the bark the poorer in tannin, however, while we have no doubt our opinion will be regarded as erroneous, we do not hesitate to say that the *older the bark the richer it is in tannin*. In this country this fact has been well understood as tanners use only barks of old trees. In Europe they employ only young trees from 18 to 30 years old. There is great variance of opinion regarding the age of oak to give a good bark. In some places they bark after 10 or 12 years, in some others they require a bark 20 years old. In this country we use barks, no matter how great their age, with the conviction that the tanning part never loses its properties. If the bark is covered with moss, it is taken out with the black and rough parts.

In some countries they bark the trees while standing, in others they bark only after being cut. This last method is the best, for in barking the tree while standing they cause a considerable damage to the woods. However, according to Buffon, if the tree must be cut a short time after, it is no harm to bark while standing.

Barking and the Most Convenient Time for it.

Experiment has demonstrated that it is in the spring, when the sap is in full activity, that the bark should be taken. We have said that all the regenerating and vivifying power resided in the bark. The suckers, the slips, the buds present us a proof of this first fact. Willow, olive trees, mulberries, and a multitude of others, the trunks of which are entirely rotted and the bark alone forms the partition. These trees, full of strength, are covered with leaves and flowers. This is due to the great quantity of nutritious juices conveyed by the bark. These abundant juices are sometimes different from those of the wood. Often, also, while of the same nature they are in so great a proportion that they break the bark to exude, or it is sufficient to make some incisions to have them run out. Almond trees, acacias, apricot trees, etc., are an example. It results from these facts, that while the sap is abundant in the bark in the spring, principally towards May, it is the proper time for barking. Tannin, as we have demonstrated, exists in the sap of several vegetables, and independently of numerous experiments of tanners, which demonstrate the superiority for tanning of the bark cut in the spring, chemical analysis throws light on this important fact. Indeed, Davy has demonstrated that

Oak bark cut in the spring contains of tannin · 6.04
" " " *fall* " " " . 4.385

Which gives nearly ⅓ more in the spring. Here again theory agrees with practice, both command to choose the spring as the time when the bark is richer in sap and tannin. Then we must cut every kind of oak at the time when the sap is up, and the barking must be done immediately by cutting circularly the bark from the trunk at both ends, and splitting it longitudinally. The bark is dried slowly in the shade.

Influence of Seasons and Place at the Time of Barking on the Richness in Tannin.

We have said above that the spring is the best time to bark, but this time may be more or less advanced according to the temperature. Thus, if the winter has been severe and the spring cold, it will be only in the middle or the end of May that vegetation will begin, and the barks will not be so rich in tannin. On the contrary, if the winter has been mild and the spring warm, April is the most convenient time. In temperate climates it is by the end of April, or the beginning of May, that this operation takes place. The barks are as much richer in tannin as they come from trees of warm countries, *i. e.*, the tannin is developed in greater proportions the further south it is. In the same locality oaks well exposed to the south and in dry and elevated places give barks richer in tannin. On the contrary, if they are in the shade in a low and damp locality they contain less. It is the same for rainy seasons which have great influence on the production of tannin. The barks are aqueous and sur-saturated with vegetable matter. These facts, while apparently trifling, are of great interest to tanners.

Decrease in Weight of Smooth Bark when Exposed to the Air.

Every tanner knows that his bark is somewhat heavier when it first comes from the store, than after it has been exposed for some time to the sun and air, and that it is therefore more advantageous to sell it before it leaves the store, instead of after it has lost some of its weight under the above circumstances. It will also be to his interest to learn how great a loss in weight the stored bark is liable to, when placed in the open air.

In order to ascertain this, Professor Nordlinger* allowed a bundle of smooth bark, weighing about 29 lbs., brought from the Hohenheim bark forests, which had reached its 15th year of growth, and whose strongest limbs were slightly split at the foot, to remain laid flat in a plastered room, having little draught through it, during May and June. On the 26th of June he took the bark out at about eleven o'clock in the morning, and exposed it, loosely spread out on trestles, to a tolerably strong wind, and a bright but not very warm sun heat—temperature 75° in the sun, and 72½° in the shade—and found, after weighing it again, that he had sustained a loss in weight, that is to say, a loss in moisture of 0.187, upon the store weight, and 0.191 after being dried by the wind, being about 2 per cent. of the weight of the bark.

In order to determine the degree of loss that a more thorough drying would cause, the small bundle of bark was again taken out of the store-room on a warm cloudless day, the 14th of July, and laid upon the ground in the open air as before, where it was allowed to remain from 9 o'clock in the morning until half-past two in the afternoon. The sun was quite strong, 93° in the shade, and 97½° in the sun, with little motion in the air. The loss in weight this time amounted to 0.383 upon the original weight, and 0.398 upon the first drying, making an average of four per cent. upon the bark's weight. After this, the bark was laid in a balcony entirely exposed to the sun, and covered with black shingles, making it close and warm, and after being allowed to dry there for another hour, there appeared a loss of 0.459 upon the original weight in the cool store,

* Gerber Zeitung. Berlin, Prussia.

and 0.481, when compared with the sun-dried weight, being on the average a loss of 5 per cent.

The above figures will correspond to most cases. If the smooth bark is taken out of a cool store and allowed to remain in the sun during a few hours, or if it is left in the forest over night, and not upon the earth where the dew may moisten it, but upon trestles elevated about a foot from the ground, it will lose about 2 per cent. of its weight in the first event, and becomes heavier in the latter. The difference will be greater, perhaps 4 or 5 per cent., if the bark is exposed to a stronger or longer-continued sun heat, or if it is allowed to remain on the low ground, or upon staves, as happens when bark is peeled in fine summer weather, and the binding together of the bundles deferred until evening.

We consider it obvious, that if the sun-dried bark is allowed to lie carelessly upon the ground where the dew has fallen, greater fluctuations, impossible to calculate in advance, may be the result.

CHAPTER XIII.

PLANTS CONTAINING TANNIN USED AS SUBSTITUTES FOR OAK BARK.*

OWING to the great lack of tanning materials which was felt several years back, and which gave rise to a multitude of experiments with native and foreign substances containing tannin as a substitute for oak bark, the general committee of the Bavarian Agricultural Society of Munich instituted a careful testing of those plants which seemed most adapted to supply this deficiency. The *Gemeinnutzige Wochenschrift* (No. 42),

* Gemeinnutzige Wochenschrift.

published at Wartzburg, contains the principal agricultural and chemical experiments there made, and we extract from it all which have reference to oak bark and its substitutes.

Plants which are intended to yield a substitute for oak bark must be susceptible of cultivation in large quantities, and the cost of cultivation and product should stand in such a proportion to the price offered by tanners that its culture may remunerate the farmer. To this end three species of plants, the common snakeroot, or *adder's wart*, the tormentil and the turmeric (but at first only the two first) were tested as to their cultivation and tanning properties.

The snakeroot cannot be well propagated from seeds, as many of these remain unripe or do not bud, and the ripe ones need from two to three years before they germinate, which is a great drawback. Therefore, it is necessary to take old roots and sprouts, cut them up with the seed capsules and lay them in furrows as potatoes are planted. This plant always requires a moist soil and can only be cultivated in ground suited to it; in clay or sandy soil it does not thrive at all. At Munich a lot of moist ground produced the following in one day's gathering, 16 cwt. of roots, 16 cwt. of leaves, and 8 cwt. of refuse, which together contained 4 cwt. 80 lbs. of tanning material, or 12 per cent. of the gross product, while the bark of oak saplings yields 15 per cent. Fraas reckons the net product per day's work, after deducting the cost of culture at about $4, which does not seem very tempting when we contrast it with potatoes, and consider the risk of sale.

The tanning experiments made with snakeroot, by Mr. Streicher, a tanner of Munich, give the following results as compared with tanning made with oak and hemlock barks. A slower tanning, a pale color, a lesser weight, and less firmness in the leather. One great disadvantage of this root in tanning, is the great quantity of starch flour that it contains, which forms a pasty sort of slime upon the hides which prevents the tannin from penetrating thoroughly. These experiments were made with roots of the crop of 1859. In 1860 the product of the crop was handed over to Mr. Kester, superintendent of factories at Munich, who made experiments similar in result to those of Mr. Streicher.

The *tormentil* grows everywhere, in meadows, heaths, and in light wooded grounds. Its roots form a hard tubercle varying in bulk from the size of a hazel-nut to that of a chestnut, having leaves similar to those of the strawberry plant, and the same sort of blossom, only of a yellow color. It contains about 16 per cent. of tanning material. The seeds are generally barren, and even when they germinate they require at the least two years' time to form a bulb of the size of a hazel-nut; moreover, they need a moist soil, and one enriched by decayed vegetable matter, a requirement which cannot be filled except by breaking up meadows or moor lands. They can be raised like potatoes from root eyes; but these eyes require three years before they come to a serviceable bulb, and moreover they are very difficult to cut off even with a sharp knife.

This will be sufficient to make it understood that this plant cannot be compared with the easily cultivated barks of the oak and fir. Reckoning the percentage according to the table, it takes only 123½ parts of young oak bark to effect the same results, for which tormentil root requires 845½ parts, or seven times as much of the latter to reach a like degree in the fermentation of the leather. Fraas, on his side, reckons that dry tormentil roots could be sold at about $1.25 per cwt.; but he doubts whether the grainer could produce it for that price. In addition to this Mr. Kester remarks that the leather tanned with tormentil is inferior in quality to that tanned with oak bark.

These interesting experiments, although they turned out negatively, are followed by still more instructive experiments upon the produce and tanning contents of the oak bark forests, in the palatinate and in central Franconia, facilities for the same having been accorded to the superintendent, Dr. Fraas, by the royal minister of woods and forests. This bark came from the forest districts of Ammer, Pirmaseus, Twerbrucken, Lauterecken, and Spier. Dr. Fraas tested the quality of tanning material therein contained, according to Muller's method; and in connection with their soil, age, time of stripping, etc. The following deductions are drawn:—

1st. The bark of oak grown in a sandy soil indicates everywhere a small content of tanning material (6 to 8 per cent.), especially in the forest districts of Twerbrücken and Ammer. The adjoining districts not only offer a poor sandy bottom of mottled sandstone, but they are situated at the highest point of land above the level of the sea in the palatinate.

2d. Trees grown on moorland are very rich in tanning material, containing about 21 per cent. at the age of twenty-two.

3d. Bark twenty years old is quite as rich, and still more tannin is obtained from that grown in a clay soil. The rich bark grown in the district of Schafferstadt is aided by the mild climate, and owing to the vicinity of the Rhine, by an underground dampness together with a deposit of best old Rhine soil.

4th. Roll barks from trees twelve to twenty-three

years old is richer in tanning material than the bark of twigs and branches.

5th. The middle part of good sized trunks contains more tannin stuff than the top or the lower part in trees from eighteen to twenty-two years old; but in trees ten years of age the top is the richest part.

6th. A mixture of the two seems advantageous to improve the tanning material.

7th. Barks, stripped from trees ten to sixteen years old, contained from 11 to 11½ per cent. of tanning material; from twenty to twenty-five years, 12 per cent.; and from thirty to forty years, 11½ per cent. Exception to this occurs from causes relating to climate and the condition of the soil.

8th. The amount of tanning material contained in bark, stripped off in the spring, is much greater than when it is peeled in summer and in autumn.

9th. The quantity of tannin held in young firs, grown in Central Franconia, is considerable, and the quality very good.

10th. The tanning material of young oak bark is so excellent in its effects that it cannot be equalled by any other sort of tanning material, and in nowise by snake-root or tormentil root.

To this we shall add that bark oak is sold at a higher price per cord than that peeled, because the heat given by it is quite equal to that of beech wood, and the charcoal produced by it is even preferred, in the foundries there, to the charcoal made from beech wood.

Barked oak burns in a dry state without crackling like birch wood; so that what it lost in the volume of the cord by peeling off the bark, is made up by the high price obtained. Therefore in places where they grow cultivated oak bark forests are most profitable. But tan bark containing 8 per cent. of tanning material, by comparison with tan bark containing 12 per cent., is not one third less in value, but one-half, because the cost of production and the tanning manipulations render this product disproportionally dearer, and still the heavier loses less in weight. The tanner's test of tan bark is the weight of his hides and the time taken to tan them, for time lost is money lost.

M. Brügl, of Ipsheim (Central Franconia), has compiled a most admirable work, giving fully the cost of procuring and a calculation of the return upon bark peeled in the oak and pine forests of his district. We are not able at present to give a comprehensive extract from this admirable book, which is well worthy of perusal.

1st. One hundred well-grown, fine-conditioned oak trunks, 16 feet long and 1½ thick were stripped, and the difference in the net proceeds amounted to 28 cents higher than for one hundred unpeeled.

2d. One hundred trunks 12 feet long and one thick were peeled and yielded 9 cents more.

3d. A cord of oak wood was stripped and lost ¼ of the cord measurement, despite which, counting the value of the tan bark, $1.58 more per cord was obtained.

4th. One hundred fagots after being peeled showed a loss in the cord size of 28 per cent., and yielded, counting the value of the tan bark, an increase of $1.53.

5th. Even 4 to 5 inches thick saplings yielded, when barked, an advance of $1.08 when compared with unbarked.

6th. Sixteen hemlock trunks, 14 to 36 feet in length, and 3 to 6 feet in thickness, between 50 and 60 years of age, were peeled; they yielded, counting the value of the tan bark, an advance of 27 cents. The day's work will yield, according to this calculation, of greater profit, about $3.25.

CHAPTER XIV.

METHODS OF ESTIMATING THE TANNING POWER OF ASTRINGENT SUBSTANCES.

EXAMINATION OF BARKS—CHEMICAL EXAMINATION—R. WARRINGTON'S PROCESS—DAVY'S PROCESS—BELL STEPHENS'S PROCESS—MULLER'S PROCESS—TANNIN CONTAINED IN THE PRINCIPAL ASTRINGENT MATTERS—RESPECTIVE QUANTITIES OF TANNING SUBSTANCES NECESSARY TO TAN AN EQUAL QUANTITY OF LEATHER—MODE OF ASCERTAINING THE RICHNESS IN TANNIN OR VALUE OF BARKS.

THE means of ascertaining the value of barks are of two kinds: 1st. By inspection of the bark. 2d. By chemical analysis. This last method is the best and surest.

EXAMINATION OF BARKS.

A good bark is known by its color. The most highly esteemed is that which is white outside and reddish inside, rough and dry on the side of the wood, breaks easily and gives less ligneous matter; the taste is the most astringent with a strong smell principally when ground. A sign of bad quality is when the epidermis and cortex are very thick and have a blackish color; then the bark is too old and has experienced a beginning of decomposition. It is the same with that which has been left exposed a long time to the rain. The bark which is red inside has lost its odor, and that which is dirty has lost a part of its property.

CHEMICAL EXAMINATION.

We have said that barks contained tannin, gallic acid, extractive, etc., and that they were more valuable for tanning in proportion as they contain more tannin. It is evident then that by chemically isolating this principle, and determining the proportions we could ascertain the value of a bark. One of the characteristics of the tannin is to form with gelatine an insoluble compound. It is then sufficient to ascertain the value of a bark to take the amount in weight of the precipitate obtained of equal weights of these substances put in infusion into water, and precipitate by gelatine. These precipitates filtered and dried give by their weights the proportion of tannin. We give below the different processes :—

R. WARRINGTON'S PROCESS.

This chemist speaks thus :* " Having often occasion to examine the value of astringent substances used by tanners, I think it will be interesting for the trade to know my method of operating.

" I have chosen gelatine as the basis of the determination of the value of astringent substances, and after many trials with several kinds of gelatine, I have found that isinglass of the best quality was the most proper for those assays. It is with isinglass that I prepared the proof liquor of a quantity such that each division of a graduated tube is equivalent to 0 gramme 001 of pure tannin. A given weight of the substance was treated by water, and the clear liquor was precipitated by the proof liquor till no more precipitation was formed.

" It is necessary during the operation to try from time to time a portion of the solution to be sure of the progress of the analysis. This operation, on account of the nature of the precipitate, has presented some difficulties. It was impossible to filter; then I adopted the following plan :—

---

* Memoirs of the London Chemical Society.

"I took a glass tube about 1 foot long and ½ an inch in diameter and introduced into it a little piece of a damp sponge that I fixed loosely at the inside end. When I desire to extract a portion of the liquor submitted to the proof for a particular essay, I immerse a few seconds this tube in the precipitated solution. The clear liquor filters by ascension through the sponge in the tube, and is decanted into another glass; if by adding a drop of the solution of gelatine a precipitate is produced, I pour back the liquor; and continue the operation till the saturation is complete. The numbers of degrees of the graduate glass indicate the quantity of tannin contained in the liquor."

DAVY'S PROCESS.

Take one ounce of the bark to dry, and reduce it to a fine powder, digest it in a pint of boiling water, stirring frequently; after 24 hours filter through a cloth. Also dissolve one drachm of isinglass in one pint of warm water, mix equal quantities of these two liquors, and filter; the precipitate is dried and weighed. The difference of weights indicates the degree of tannin; the precipitate formed of tannin and gelatine generally contains 40 per cent. of tannin.

BELL STEPHENS' PROCESS.

Stephens, while studying Davy's process, has given another less imperfect. Mr. Bostwick has ascertained that the precipitate obtained by the gelatine stays in great part in suspension in the liquor, and is not separated by the filter; in the second place, the proportion of gelatine is not constant. This chemist has ascertained that the first portions of gelatine give a precipitate which contains 50 per cent. of tannin, while at the end it contains very little. Stephens proposes the following method: Dip for a few hours, in a weak solution of tanning matter made with water at 90°, thin skins which in 7 or 8 hours extract all the tannin. The increase in weight of the skin indicates the quantity of tannin. As dry skin badly absorbs tannin, it is better before using it to soak it for ten minutes in water at 90° so to render it soft in all its parts. The skin ought to be weighed when dried before and after the treatment.

The process of Davy, while subject to the inconveniences named by Bostwick, is generally followed. That of Stephens is good in practice, as it indicates not only the strength in tannin, but also the appearance of the skin after being tanned.

MULLER'S PROCESS.

Dr. Muller has established a method for the determination of the tannin contained in tanning materials which justly deserves the name of technical experiment; very satisfactory results are gained by it in a short time.

The experiment is based upon the property possessed by tannic acid of forming with animal gluten a combination which is almost entirely insoluble in water and which is called *tanat* (leather). It is therefore necessary above all to ascertain how much of a solution of gluten, which is always prepared alike, is necessary to convert a fixed quantity of tannic acid into *tanat*. After ascertaining this proportion we have to find, further, how much gluten is necessary to completely precipitate the tannic acid in a given tanning material, and from these two proportions we have a ratio of which x represents the quantity of tanning material to be found. By means of a second proportion we can very easily learn the percentage of tannin in tanning materials—

Working out of this experiment according to Müller.—
4.38 grains of gluten* are to be dissolved in 140.1 grammes of water, and 1.09 gr. of burnt alum added to the solution; this addition of alum effects the separation of the tannin from the gluten in a much shorter space of time than in any other way. With the solution of gluten thus prepared, the proportions above named are to be fixed: a, the weighed part of the pure tannic acid is changed into tanat by b, the weighed part of the solution of gluten. Now let c be the weighed part of the tanning material, on which boiling water is poured and allowed to boil for a time, when the water will turn to a very deep brown color. Then let it be carefully poured off from the tanning material into a glass vessel. Upon the boiled tanning material water should be poured a second time and allowed to boil, and the extract then poured into the liquor produced by the first boiling; and this boiling and adding should be continued as long as the tanning material gives any solution; that is, as long as tannic acid is produced, which can be ascertained by the brown color of the boiling water. When the water remains colorless after long boiling, then the dyestuff of the tannic material may be known to be exhausted, and the residuum, the boiled-out substance, together with the water still covering it, is to be poured into the solution of tannic acid already obtained and added to the gluten after it is quite cold.

Suppose, for instance, b' to be the weighed part of gluten necessary to decompose all the tannic acid, then we have $b : b' = a : x$ or $b' : b = x : a$ according as b is larger or smaller than b'; but in both cases $x = \dfrac{a\,b'}{b} =$

---

* This substance is without doubt gelatine.

to the quantity of tannic acid contained in c weighed part of the tanning material; and, therefore by $c : 100 = \dfrac{a\, b'}{b}$, $x'-x' = \dfrac{100\, a\, b'}{5\, c}$, which is the percentage of tannic acid contained in two weighed parts of tanning material. The quantity of the consumed gluten will be fixed by weight. Fill a glass goblet with the solution of gluten and equipoise it on a scale, and add to the solution so weighed, the solution of tannic acid, as long as tannic acid remains, then put the glass which still contains some solution of gluten, upon the scale again, and it will be lighter than before the fixing; the additional weight beyond the equilibrium will give the amount of gluten consumed.

In order to fix this point completely, pour some solution of gluten and pure tannic acid, dissolved in water, into watch-glasses standing upon glazed paper. With two different splints dip a drop of the clear fluid above the separated tannic acid, either into the solution of gluten or the solution of tannin in the watch-glass; the smallest quantity of $\frac{1}{5000}$ of unprecipitated tannic acid or surplus gluten will appear in the glass in the form of a white speck, tanat, which comes up at the spot where dipped.

This experiment may be made more accurately and conveniently by estimating the quantity of gluten, not according to weight but by its volume as I have tried it. Weighing is liable to error, and it is not so accurate a plan as measurement. A vial of the capacity of 70 cubic centimetres (centimetre is $\frac{39}{100}$ of an inch) answers perfectly as a measure; with it we can calculate up to 0.5 centimetre, and regulate the addition of the gluten, even by drops—but it soon became evident that this solution of gluten was much too thick for this vial, as the narrow mouth of the vial soon became stopped up, and owing to this hindrance in the work, a thick solution of gluten does not precipitate tannic acid nearly as rapidly as a thinner and more freely flowing solution. I therefore prepared a solution in the following manner: I dissolved 2½ grains of gluten in 125 centimetres of water in which 0.75 gr. of alum had been previously dissolved. When the alum is put in the rough into the solution of gluten it dissolves very slowly.

Disposition of a quart of gluten: 0.71221 grain of chemically pure tannic acid was dried for such a length of time until its weight remained permanently at 0.6335; then this quantity was dissolved in 100 c. c. of distilled water; of this solution 4 analyses always of 5 c. c. in goblet glasses, and precipitated with solution of gluten prepared in the manner above laid down, required as follows: 5 c. c. tannic acid; 3.8 c. c. of gluten; 5 c. c. ditto; 4.1 c. c. do.; 5 c. c. do.; 4.1 do.; 5 c. c.; 3.5 c. c. do.; 3 minutes were required to clarify the liquid. If we take the mean of these results, it will appear that 5 c. c.=0.031675 grain of tannic acid, require 3.9 c. c. of gluten in order to become converted into tanat. 1 c. c. of gluten corresponds therefore to 0.031675; 3.9= 0.00812 grain of tannic acid.

By means of these data I have calculated the following tables, which will be found very serviceable in working out, as they render all calculations unnecessary. 1 c. c. of gluten corresponds to 0.00812 grain tannic acid, therefore 2 c. c.=0.01624, and so on; the quantity of tannic acid required for any quantity of gluten may be rapidly ascertained by multiplying 0.00812 by the number of c. c. Example: 4 grains of tanning material would require 75 c. c. of solution of gluten, therefore 4 grains of tanning material contain 0.609 of tannin, for 75 c. c.

corresponds to 0.609 of tannin. In order to reach the percentage, the following proportion must be made:—

$4 : 100 = 0.609 : x$

$x = \frac{60.9}{4} = 15.225$ per cent.

If, in each experiment, 4 grains of tanning material are employed, the per cent. contents may be easily ascertained by the following calculation. Gluten contained in 1 c. c. amounts to 0.203 per cent., in 2 c. c. to 0.406 and so on, multiplying the amount consumed in 1 c. c. by the number representing the accumulation of centimetres. With careful execution, this method gives results which are accurate even to 0.3, 0.5 per cent. as my experiments have established.

Special determination of Aleppo gall-nuts of 1839.

1st determination: 3.6386 gr. of matter required 75 c. c. of gluten, being equal to 0.6090 of tannin, therefore it contains 16.73 per cent. of tannin.

2d determination: 4.026 of the same substance required 84.4 c. c. of gluten, being equal to 0.685328 of tannin, therefore it contains 17.04 per cent.; the difference amounts to 0.31.

Marmorina gall-nuts (old).—*1st determination:* 3.25675 gr. required 75 c. c. of gluten, being equal to 0.609 of tannin = 18.89 per cent.

2d determination: 3.9186 of substance required 95 c. c. of gluten, being equal to 0.77148 of tannin, or 19.60 per cent.

Chinese gall-nuts.—*1st determination:* 2.1875 gr. of substance required 62 c. c. of gluten = 0.486388 of tannin = 22.23 per cent.

2d determination: 1.6555 of substance required 46 c. c. of gluten = 0.37352 = 22.55 per cent.

From the above examples the accuracy of my assertions regarding the correctness of the results may be seen. 0.5, 0.3 per cent. is the error.

METHOD OF DR. D. W. GERLAND.

We extract from the *London Chemical News* the following process, which we think very reliable. The importance of a sure and an easy method for the estimation of tannic acid as a means of determining the value of tanning materials, has been duly noticed, and a great number of processes described for that purpose.* An examination of these methods, induced by numerous samples sent to me for analysis, has convinced me that those recommended fail in answering the desired end, as some yield too high a percentage of tannic acid by the accompanying gallic acid being estimated as tannic acid, some giving altogether incorrect results, while others are too complicated to be of service to any but the skilled chemist.

After a long experience I have found that the estimation of tannic acid is accomplished with great accuracy and speed, as tannate of antimony precipitated by a standard solution of tartar of antimony, if the operation is conducted in the following manner:—

The solution of tartar emetic I prefer of such strength that 1 c. c. will precipitate 0.005 gramme tannic acid. One equivalent of tartar emetic dried at 212°,

$$= KO, SbO_3, C_8H_4O_{10} = 332.2$$

requires three equivalents of tannic acid,

$$3(C_{18}H_6O_{12}) = 636$$

to form one equivalent of tannate of antimony—

$$SbO_3, 3(C_{18}H_6O_{12}) = 789.$$

Accordingly, 0.002611 gramme of tartar emetic will precipitate 0.005 of tannic acid of galls, and, therefore,

2.611 grammes tartar emetic dried at 212° are dissolved in 1000 c. c. of water, each c. c. of which solution is then equal to 0.005 gramme of tannic acid. This liquor added to a dilute solution of tannic acid produces no change, but if a solution of chloride of ammonium is mixed with the latter, the tannate of antimony appears as a thick, curdy precipitate, which, after stirring, settles readily, leaving the supernatant solution perfectly clear, so that it is easy to perceive whether another drop of the antimonial liquor will again cause a precipitate. Its voluminous and opaque character makes it very perceptible to the last, so that I found less difficulty in observing the end of this reaction, than with the usual estimation of sulphuric acid by a standard solution of chloride of barium. If as much and no more of the tartar solution has been added as will cause a precipitate in the sample, the filtrate of the same will be found free from both antimony and tannic acid, and the precipitate, after filtering, washing, and drying at 212°, consists of pure tannate of antimony represented by—

$$SbO_3, 3(C_{18}H_6O_{12}),$$

and contains all the tannic acid of the original liquor. Any gallic acid that might have been present in the tannic acid is not precipitated under these circumstances, and consequently does not interfere with the estimation of tannic acid; for the ammonia salt, whilst it renders the tannate of antimony insoluble, keeps the gallic acid in solution. Nor do the coloring matter and other impurities, extracted by water from the tanning materials, affect this process. It is, however, to be observed that the reaction of the liquor is neutral or slightly acid. The number of c. c. of the standard solution used will, therefore, when multiplied by 0.005, give the exact amount of tannic acid in the sample, or the percentage, if 0.5 gramme were employed.

To illustrate the exactness of the method I add a few of my experiments. No. 1. 0.5 gramme of commercial tannic acid of galls was dissolved in 100 c. c. of water, of which 30 c. c. were mixed with a solution of chloride of ammonium and diluted with water to about 200 c. c. After having added 29.1 c. c. of the standard solution, the filtered liquor was free from tannic acid, showed a slight reaction of antimony, and contained gallic acid. The precipitate thrown on a weighed filter, and after washing with water and dried, weighed 0.1791, and was found to contain 18.01 per cent. of oxide of antimony; the formula—

$$SbO_3, 3(C_{18}H_8O_{12})$$

requires 18.13 per cent. The sample, therefore, contained, according to the quantity of standard solution used, 97 per cent. of tannic acid; calculated from the amount of precipitated tannate of antimony, 96.24 per cent. of tannic acid.

No. 2. 10 grammes of oak bark are exhausted with hot water, the filtered solution diluted to 300 c. c., of which 50 c. c. were treated as above. The amount of standard solution used was 12.51 c. c.; the weight of the dried precipitate was 0.1563 gramme, containing, according to calculation, 0.1257 gramme of tannic acid. The oxide of antimony in the precipitate was equal to 18.07 per cent.

No. 3. Dried valonia extract was treated in the same manner. 0.5 gramme required 38.8 c. c. of antimonial solution; the percentage of tannic acid was 38 92

It would be an interesting experiment to try the tanning strength of barks of different kinds and varieties of every country during the four seasons of the year at different ages; and it would be more interesting to analyze at the same time the roots, trunks, branches, leaves, etc.

We give below a table of the quantities of tannin contained in the principal tanning substances.

Substances.	Percentage of Tannin.	Authority.
Catechu, Bombay	55.00	Davy.
" Bengal	44.00	"
" Bombay, light color	26.32	Mulligan.
" Pegu, dark brown color	46.88	"
Rhatany root	42.60	Peschier.
"	38.30	C. G. Gmelin.
Kino	75.00	Vauquelin.
Butea gum	73.20	E. Solly.
Nutgalls, Aleppo	65.00	Guibourt.
" Chinese	69.00	Bley.
" Istrian	24.00	Roder.
Oak, old white, inner bark	21.00	Cadet de Gassincourt.
" " " " "	14.20	Davy.
" young " " "	15.20	"
" " colored or middle bark	4.00	"
" " entire bark	6.00	Davy & Geiger.
" " spring-cut bark	22.00	Davy.
" Kermes, bark of the root	8.90	"
" 100 years old	8.45	G. Muller.
" young	13.87	"
" British, 50 years old	8.90	Mulligan & Downing.
" " about 50 years	9.76	" "
" " " 70	6.12	" "
" Southampton, about 50	8.80	" "
" Coppice	12.55	" "
" Irish, 45 years old	9.50	" "
" Belgian, popering	8.33	" "
" " heavy	10.74	" "
" " light	8.52	" "
" Eschurgh	19.35	G. Muller.
Divi divi	29.80	Mulligan & Downing.
"	49.25	G. Muller.
Valonia, Smyrna	34.78	Mulligan & Downing.

Myrobalans	20.91	Mulligan & Downing.
Mimosa bark	17.87	" "
"	31.16	G. Muller.
Terra Japonica . . .	44.00	Esenbeik.
Avens root	41.00	Tromsdorff.
Squill, bulb	24.00	Vogel.
Statice	12.40	Parrish.
Birch bark	1.60	Davy.
"	1.40	Biggers.
Beech bark	2.00	Davy.
Larch "	1.60	"
" "	35.10	Mulligan & Downing.
Caratree bark . . .	12.16	" "
Hemlock " . . .	13.92	" "
Hazel " . . .	3.00	Davy.
Chestnut, American rose .	8.00	Cadet de Gassincourt.
" Carolina . . .	6.00	"
" French . . .	4.00	J. de Fontenelle.
" Spanish, white inner bark . . .	1.30	Davy.
" Spanish, colored bark	0.30	"
" " entire "	0.50	"
" horse . . .	2.00	J. de Fontenelle.
Poplar, Lombardy . . .	3.50	"
Black thorn	3.30	Davy.
Ash bark	3.30	"
Sassafras	58.00	Reinsch.
Elm	2.90	Davy.
Sumach, Sicily . . .	16.20	"
" Malaga . .	16.40	"
" " . .	10.40	Franck.
" Carolina . . .	5.00	Cadet de Gassincourt.
" Virginia . . .	10.00	"
" . . .	19.35	G. Muller.
" Palermo . . .	24.37	Mulligan & Downing.
Willow, Leicester, white inner bark . . .	16.00	Davy.
" colored, middle bark .	3.10	"
" entire bark .	6.80	"
" " .	3.95	Mulligan & Downing.
" bark of the trunk .	1.40	Biggers.

Willow, weeping	16.00	Cadet de Gassincourt.
Sycamore bark	16.00	"
"	1.40	Biggers.
Eder	2.30	Davy.
Plum tree	1.60	Biggers.
Cherry tree	24.00	Cadet de Gassincourt.
" Cornish	19.00	"
Tormentil root	46.00	"
Cornus sanguinea of Canada	44.00	"
Alder bark	36.00	"
Apricot bark	32.00	"
Pomegranate bark	32.00	"
Bohemian olive	14.00	"
Tan shrub with myrtle leaves	13.00	"
Service tree bark	18.00	"
Cloves	15.00	Davy.
Winter bark	9.00	Henry.

Comparative Quantities of Different Tanning Substances Necessary to tan an Equal Quantity of Leather.

Davy, who made a series of experiments of the highest interest, ascertained that Catechu is the most energetic substance for tanning. According to this chemist one pound of Catechu is equivalent to

Nutgalls	$2\frac{1}{4}$ lbs.
Sumach	3 "
Willow bark	$7\frac{1}{2}$ "
Oak	8 "
Horse-chestnut	11 "
Elm	18 "
Ordinary willow	21 "

In treating of extracts, we shall indicate the properties of a new preparation of oak bark which unites all the properties both of oak and catechu.

CHAPTER XV.

TAN, OR POWDERED OAK-BARK.

The more finely divided a substance, the sooner and more readily does it yield to the action of the liquid which dissolves its constituents. Water, accordingly, dissolves the tannin from bark in powder much more readily than from bark in coarse pieces. The grinding of the bark for tanning purposes is, therefore, indispensable. It must not, however, be reduced to impalpable fineness, else the solvent will act upon it too rapidly. Very fine powders also form a compact mass when wet, and thus obstruct or retard the infiltration of the solvent liquid.

Bark is ground in mills varying in construction in different countries, and driven or propelled by horse, water, or steam power. In England, it is crushed between chasers, or stones. There is a mill of ingenious construction used in Salleron's tannery in France, but as its rapid motion so modifies the bark as to cause it to impart color to the hides, we omit a description of it.

In the South of France they use a vertical mill of hard stone, similar to that employed for crushing oil seeds. It consists of two vertical stones (Fig. 2), of about 7½ feet in diameter, and 18 inches in thickness. The axle of these stones is fixed in a frame which incloses an upright shaft turning upon a pivot, and fixed in the centre of a strong stone bed. Rotary motion being communicated, imparts to each stone a double movement; that upon the other, and that which it undergoes in describing a circle upon the stone bed upon which it rolls.

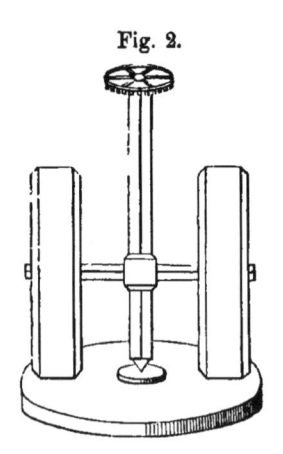

Fig. 2.

The axle of each stone should be so adjusted as to allow it to be raised or lowered according to circumstances. One of the stones is placed nearer to the vertical shaft than the other, so as to give a greater extent of crushing surface beneath. Two followers press the bark forward under the stones, and a cloth is attached to the outer one, for the purpose of rubbing off any pieces of bark that may adhere to the edges of the stones.

Bagnall's Machine for Chopping Bark and Fleshing Hides.—Fig. 3. General plan of the mill.

Fig. 4. Longitudinal section, showing the elevation of a part of the machinery.

Fig. 5. Section across part of the mill.

A (Fig. 3). Part of an undershot wheel moving the machinery. B. Shaft of the wheel, giving motion to the bevelled cog-wheel C. Another wheel F, placed upon a vertical shaft, is made to revolve by the motion of the wheel C, and the cogs upon its periphery move the hammer for beating the bark, and also the choppers, in the second story of the building.

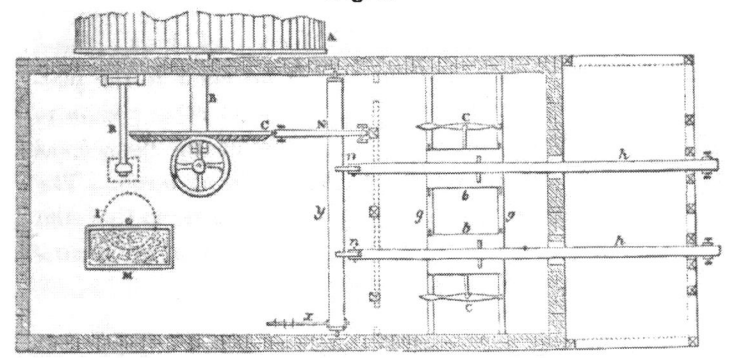

Fig. 3.

d (Fig. 4). A horizontal wheel bevelled upon its inclined surface, and toothed in an epicycloidal manner upon its

Fig. 4.

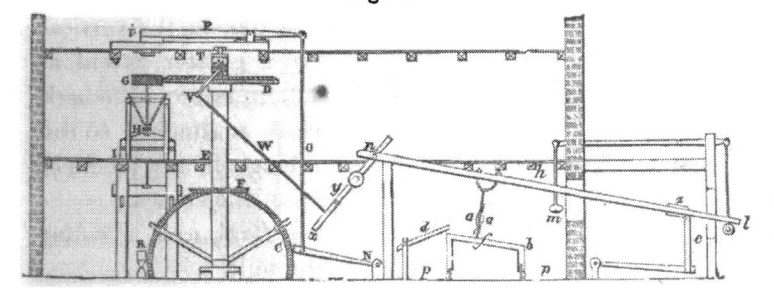

periphery. This wheel turns upon the upper part of the large horizontal shaft e, which passes through the first floor of the building. f. Cog-wheel, before referred to, gearing with the large bevelled wheel c.

g. Pinion upon the axle of the millstone i (Fig. 5).

p. The beam or handle of the cutting-blades, moving upon a pivot, and made to rise or fall, by the motion communicated to the lever N, by the cogs upon the wheel C. When one of the cogs becomes disengaged from the end of the lever, the beam falls by its own weight, and the steel blades upon its extremity come in contact with and divide the pieces of bark placed between them and similar knives fastened to the platform at *i*. The platform *i* is made of strong timbers firmly secured by bolts to the rafters of the floor, so as to enable it to resist the shock of the falling beam. The intervals between the knife-blades are open, so that the divided pieces of bark may fall through them into a con-

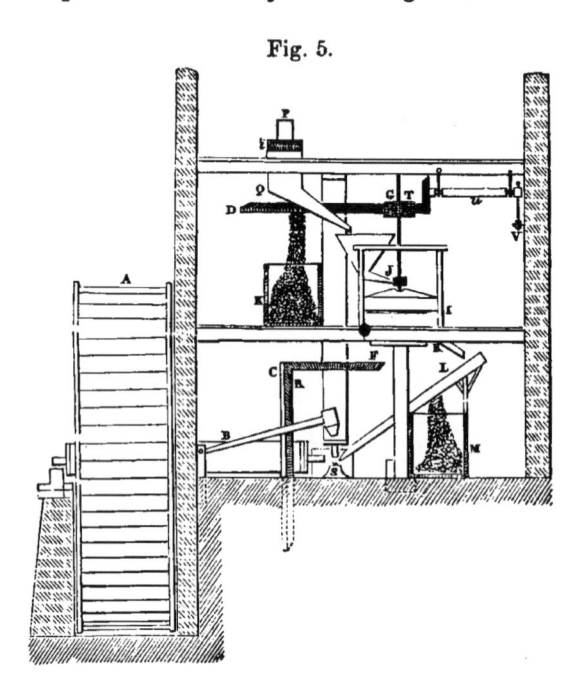

Fig. 5.

duit Q, from which they enter the hopper of the mill H, to be conducted to the latter by a guide J (Fig. 5). The lower part of the conduit Q is provided with a wire-cloth, which allows the powder to fall into a box K. The tan, ground in the mill, passes through the conduit O, and falls upon the sieve or bolter L, its finer particles passing through into the trough M; those which have not been sufficiently exposed to trituration being received upon the concave mortar or support S, and there reduced to a state of fine division, by the action of the round-headed hammer R, which is worked by the cogs upon the wheel C. The support is hollowed out in such a way that, at each blow of the hammer, the particles of tan acted upon are thrown out upon the side opposite to that at which they entered it.

T. Bevelled pinion, in gear with the upper surface of the wheel D, and having the end of its shaft connected with the crank V, by means of which the motion is communicated to the machinery for fleshing the skins. The crank is connected by means of the rod W with the lever X, the end of which is perforated with a number of holes, by which the bar is so adjusted that the length of the stroke may be increased or diminished.

y (Fig. 3). Shaft moving upon two axles, the sockets of which are imbedded in the opposite walls of the room; the lever y (Fig. 4) is connected with it near one end; and at about two-thirds of its length the cranks n, n, are attached, which give a reciprocating movement to the branches h, h, which support the fleshing-knives; so that, at each revolution of the crank V, to admit the movement of which there is an opening in the ceiling above it, the branches h, h, for fleshing the skins, are made to move in a transverse direction. In Fig. 4, the knife for fleshing is represented at f, fixed between two springs a, a, which render it sufficiently movable to prevent it from injuring the skins when passing across them. It is fastened by its forked extremity to the branch *h* by a screw and nut, so that it can be unscrewed and sharpened when necessary.

z. Stop on the branch *h*, which is connected with the forked lever *e*, by means of which the knife is made to return to the end of the skin without touching its surface. The extremity of the branch *h* rolls upon the roller *l*. By lowering the handle *m*, the knife is elevated, while the skin is being placed upon or removed from the table.

b. Table or bench upon which the skins are deposited. Each table is provided with four wheels *p, p*, running in the grooves *g, g*, which maintain it in position, and enable it to be moved at will by the levers *c, c*, so that each portion of skin may be in turn subjected to the action of the knife.

d. A spring, pressing upon the skin near the edge of the table, so as to prevent it from changing its position under the fleshing-knife. The iron support, or handle of the knife, is forked or divided, so as to receive the blade between its two extremities. The knife is 12 or 13 inches in length, and from 3 to 5 inches in breadth, and is adjusted in the open part of the handle, being prevented from swerving by the two springs *a, a*.

The roller *l*, with its forked lever, should be so arranged that the knife can be elevated to the proper distance from the table, by pulling the handle *m*, and hooking it upon a nail, so that the skin may be removed or placed upon the table without the necessity of ungearing the pinion T; the work being again commenced when the handle is allowed to rise.

Two benches or tables are used in this apparatus, in order that the knife may be in operation above one of them, while the workman is occupied in adjusting a fresh skin upon the other. These benches should be as wide as the largest skins, and should be made sloping at a

TAN, OR POWDERED OAK BARKS. 143

slight angle. The skins are kept in close contact with the surface of the support, by clamps pressing their borders down upon its edges. The pressure of the knives upon the skin is regulated by weights placed upon the beams or branches which support them. The inventor does not confine the application of this portion of the machinery to the preparation of skins for the tanning process; but also adapts it to the purposes of *tawing* and to those of the currier, by substituting hard brushes or other implements for the knives. Motion may be communicated to the machinery by the water-wheel already described, by a steam-engine, or by horse power; the labor of two horses being sufficient for the purpose.

Weldon's Mill for Grinding Oak-Bark.—Fig. 6, A. Wooden beam or cross-piece, imbedded in the walls of

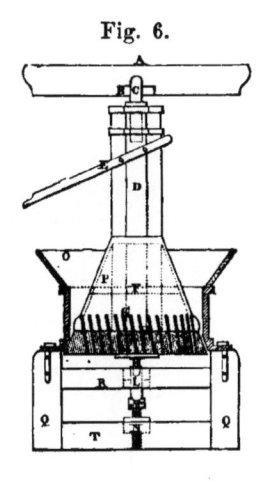

Fig. 6.

the building, and perforated for the reception of the upper axle of the main shaft.

B. Iron plate or socket for the axle.

C. Axle of the shaft, the dotted lines showing its connection with the latter.

D. The shaft, which may be square, octagonal, or of other suitable form.

E. Lever giving motion to the shaft by the power of horses harnessed to the end. When water or other power is employed, the lever is replaced by a wheel with the proper gearing.

F. Cylinder forming the lower part of the mill. It should be made of iron or brass, and may be either compact or hollow, as shown by the dotted lines in the figure.

G. Teeth, or projections for breaking and grinding the bark.

H. Lower teeth for the same purpose.

I. External iron or brass cylinder, provided with similar projections upon its inner surface, and firmly clamped and bolted to the solid framework Q, which forms the base of the machine.

K. Lower pivot or axle, firmly united with the main shaft, and turning in a socket like the upper one.

L. Iron or copper socket, fixed in the cross-beam R.

M. Regulating screw passing through the nut N, and the lower cross-beam T. By turning it, the teeth within the mill may be made to approach or recede from each other, so as to effect, at will, a coarser or finer division of the bark.

O. Hopper, made of strong wood for receiving the materials which are to be ground.

P. Conical lining of the interior of the mill, also made of strong wood. The whole apparatus is supported upon four uprights, Q, Q, firmly imbedded in the ground, and held together by the cross-beams R and T, there being two at R, meeting each other at right angles. Sieves of wire are placed between the cylinder F and the floor, which permit the passage through their interstices of the fine tan, and retain that which is too coarse.

Since its first introduction, Mr. Weldon has improved the construction of his mill, by making the teeth movable, and by other changes which we proceed to describe.

Fig. 7. Section of the improved mill.

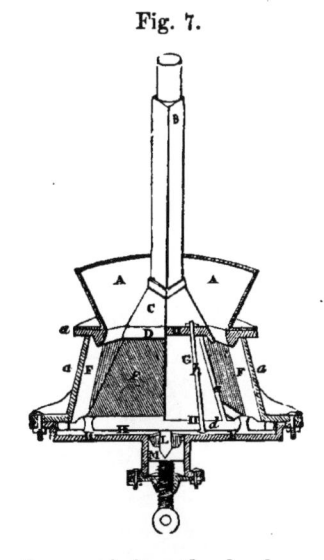

Fig. 7.

A, A. Hopper for receiving the bark.

B. Shaft of the mill.

C. Conical casing of the cutting surfaces, for feeding the mill.

D, D. Collar for staying the teeth, with four bolts, h.

E. Elevation of the conical part of the mill in which the teeth are placed.

G. Section of the opposite side, showing the manner in which the teeth are adjusted.

d, d. One of the teeth entering the lower neck.

H, H. Lower collar in which the teeth are imbedded.

a, a, a. Outer cylinder, or cone, cast in one piece, and showing the manner in which the movable teeth F, F, are adjusted.

i, i. Rim or collar for the attachment of the movable teeth; a part of it is seen detached in Fig. 8.

k, k. Support of the interior of the mill, fastened to the outer cone or cylinder by two bolts, *c, c*.

Fig. 8. Fig. 9.

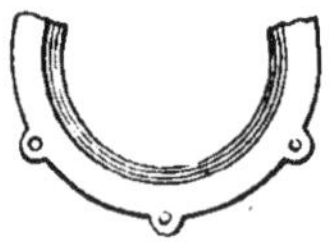

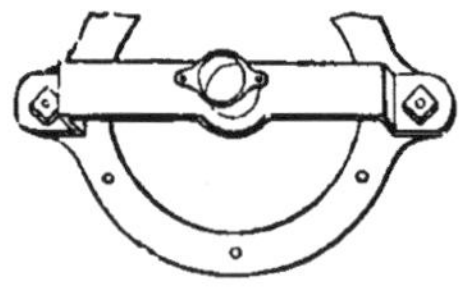

l. Lower part of the shaft, turning in a copper socket m, which rests upon the top of a screw by which the height of the inner part of the mill is regulated. Fig. 9 exhibits this part, with the collar of the rim, in which the socket and adjusting screw are placed.

Fig. 10. One of the movable teeth, detached from the exterior of the mill.

Fig. 10.   Fig. 11.

Fig. 11 is one of the teeth from the interior of the mill.

These teeth are blades of iron or composition-metal, ground to an edge, and so placed in the mill that the cutting surfaces are opposed to each other, and inclined in a direction opposite to that of the revolution of the shaft.

Farcot's Bark-Chopping Machine.—This machine consists of two feeding cylinders A, A. (Fig. 12), which convey the bark, previously spread out upon an inclined table *a*, to the edges of four large steel blades B B, which are fixed in a spiral direction upon the periphery of two parallel circles, revolving with the shaft c. The cylinders A, A, are grooved, and are moved by cog-wheels with long teeth. The power, from whatever source, is transmitted at the same time to these wheels, and to the bladed circles; b is a steel tie-piece, which supports the pieces of bark when exposed to the action of the knives,

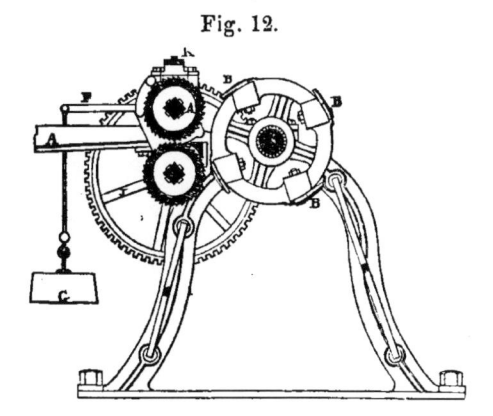

Fig. 12.

each of the latter passing over it, like one blade of a pair of shears over the other.

The levers F suspend the weight G, the object of which is to bear upon the shaft of the cylinder A, which is constantly elevated by the passage of the bark beneath it. Guides are so placed as to direct these levers in their vertical movements, and the bark is prevented, by guards or side pieces, from falling out of the grooves, over the sides of the cylinders. The feeding cylinders are 2 feet 2 inches in circumference, and the relation of the pinion of the wheel C to the wheel J which moves it, is that of 1 to 5. About 56 feet of bark will pass between the cylinders in one minute; in the same time the wheel makes 130 revolutions, and as it is armed with 4 blades, the bark is cut into 520 pieces, each one nearly $1\frac{3}{10}$th inches in length. More than 1600 pounds of bark can be chopped in an hour with this machine, when in good order and properly worked. Some are made, with which one man can work up daily more than 3000 pounds.

148   CHEMISTRY OF TANNING.

Fig. 13 is the plan in elevation.

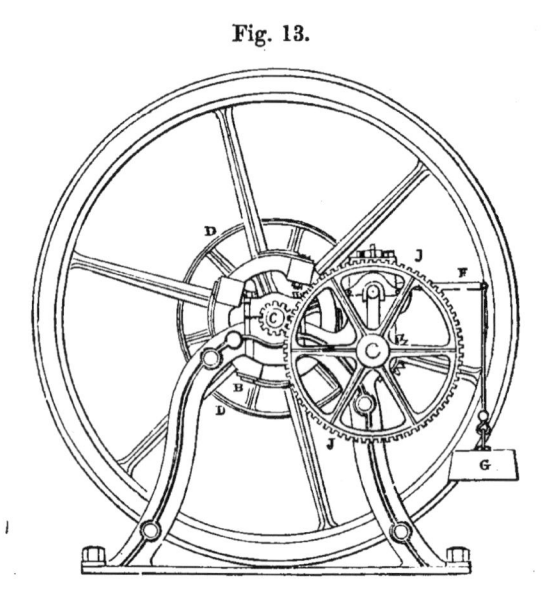

Fig. 13.

Fig. 14 is the ground plan.

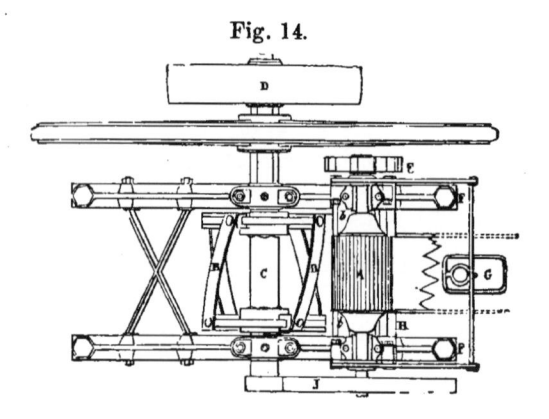

Fig. 14.

Fig. 15 shows the axle-pin of the bladed cylinder; and Fig. 16 is an end view of the latter.

TAN, OR POWDERED BARKS.

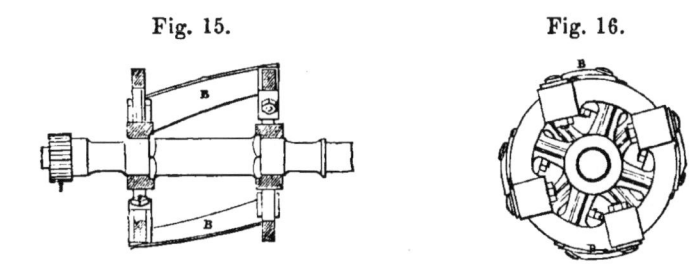

Fig. 15.

Fig. 16.

Fig. 17 represents the cast-iron frame which supports the channelled cylinders and bladed cylinder.

Fig. 17.

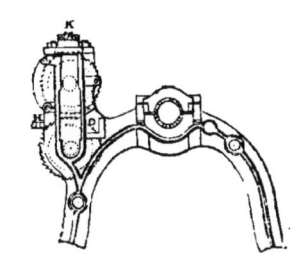

The bark, after being chopped as described above, is submitted to the action of the mill, which consists chiefly of two parts, the receiving and the revolving cylinder. The former is a thin, hollow cylinder, terminated below by a truncated cone, the interior of which is provided with spiral blades or teeth, some of which extend as far as the lower part of the cylinder. The base of the cone is attached by legs to the cast framework which supports the whole apparatus. Above the cylinder is a hopper, which is fed from time to time with chopped bark, the powdered tan falling down between the outer cylinder and the inner one. The outer surface of the movable cylinder is provided with spiral teeth, similar to those of the inner one, and made of a wedge-shape, so as to present a cutting edge to the fragments of bark, which are first cut and divided by the teeth which extend towards its upper part, and are then pulverized by those upon the two conical surfaces. The cylinder is made to revolve by a shaft set in a socket which is stayed by a tie-piece. This latter is traversed by a screw, by means of which the nut may be raised or lowered, so as to increase or diminish the space between it and the receiving cylinder, and to alter at will the quality of the powder as to fineness of division. A bar passes horizontally across the interior of the inner cylinder, and is firmly attached to the shaft passing through it. The horse moving the machinery is harnessed to an arm attached to a cast-iron plate on top of the shaft. This mill is calculated to make 25 revolutions in a minute, and is capable of grinding 8600 pounds of bark in 24 hours.

Bourgeois's Bark Mill.—This machine, which was invented in 1841, and is described in volume liv. page 193, of the French reports of expired patents, is used to grind bark by means of two cylinders, one of which (Figs. 18 and 19), serving as a case for the handle, is of a cylindrical shape externally, while the other and internal one is conical; the mill revolving in a vertical instead of a horizontal direction. The outer cylinder 12 is fixed by an iron framework, 10, to the wooden supports of the mill, while the inner cylinder, 11, is movable. This cylinder and the inner surface of the outer one, are both fluted with longitudinal grooves, describing curves along their length. Each of these grooves is divided into two, at the larger end of the cylinder, and into four at the smaller end, the separation commencing at the middle. The inner cylinder can be completely encased in the outer one, by the turning of the screws,

TAN, OR POWDERED BARKS.

14, and the arrangement of grooves is intended to effect a more or less complete division of the particles of tan.

When the cylinders are closely in contact, the bark is first exposed to the action of the larger grooves, which are deeper than the others, and then becomes engaged in the second and third divisions, by means of which it is reduced to a fine powder. If it be desired to produce a less complete trituration, the screws, 14, are loosened, and the spring, 13, then presses the inner cylinder from its place, in such a manner that the bark is only acted upon by the larger grooves.

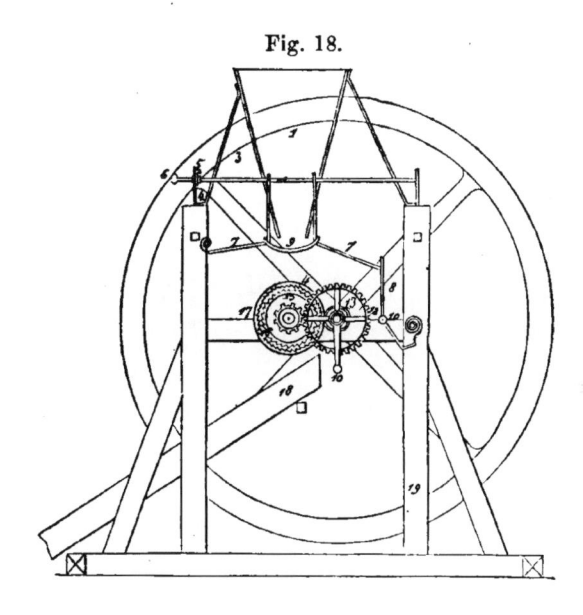

Fig. 18.

Fig. 18. 1. Hopper of the mill.
2. Spout of the hopper.
3. Regulator of the spout.
4, 5. Escapement wheel.
6. Handle of the regulator.

7. *bis*, strap attached to the spout.
8, 9, 10. The spout and its motive appliances—spring and strap.
11. Handle for turning the machine.
12. Arm of the lever turning the spout.
13. Trundle.
14. Large cog-wheel.
15. Small cog-wheel.
16. Internal conical cylinder.
17. External conical cylinder.
18. Trough for receiving the tan.
19. Wooden framework.

Fig. 19.

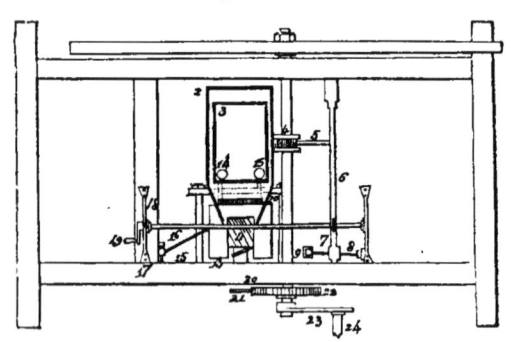

Fig. 19. 1. Fly-wheel.
2. Spout under the hopper.
3. Hopper.
4. Trundle.
5. Lever arm for turning the spout.
6. Axle of the lever.
7, 8, 9. The motor and regulating appliances of the spout.
10. Framework supporting the cylinders.

11. Internal cylinder, with grooves cut as before described.
12. External cylinder channelled like the inner one.
13. Spring, regulating the inner cylinder.
14, 15. Compressing screws acting upon this cylinder.
16. Spring acting upon the spout.
17. Escapement wheel.
18. Regulator of the spout.
19. Handle of the regulator.
20. Axis of the cylinders.
21. Small canting-wheel.
22. Large canting-wheel.
23. Axle of the trundle and fly-wheel.
24. Crank.
25. Wooden framework.

Lespinasse's Bark Mill.—This apparatus was invented in 1843, and is described in vol. lix. at page 428, of the French expired patent reports. Fig. 20, d, iron shaft turned by the pinion, moved by the power, and supporting and moving the stops of the rammers or stampers, c, shown at k in the figure. This shaft acts upon the conical pinion e, and through it upon the similar vertical pinion f, which communicates the motion to a small horizontal shaft, l, upon which there is another similar pinion, g, by means of which the horizontal pinion, h, is made to revolve. This latter transmits the motion to a vertical shaft, o, and gives a reciprocating movement by means of the pinions, e, f, g, h, to the curb, m, placed horizontally between the sides of the rammer, n. This curb, by its constant movement to and fro, forces the portions of bark divided by the knives of

154   CHEMISTRY OF TANNING.

Fig. 20.

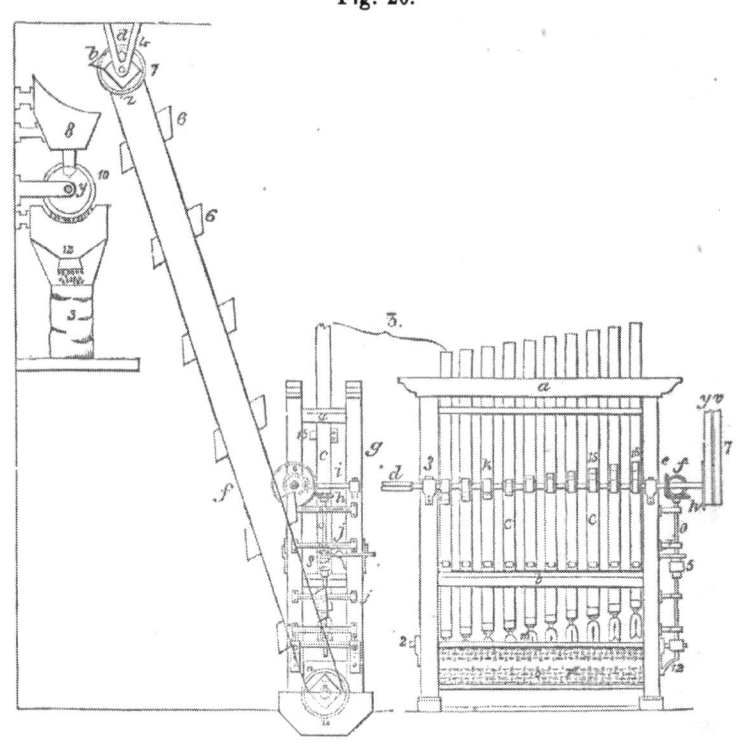

the rammer, *n*, through the holes, *x*, made of different dimensions in the sides of the apparatus, into the conduit, *t*, and the trough, *u*. Above this latter is a drum, *z*, connected by a strap, 5, to which the buckets, 6, are adapted, with a similar drum, *z'*. These two drums are made to revolve by a strap *v*, moving at one end over a drum, 7, placed at the extremity of the shaft, *d*, and at the other, upon another drum, 7', above the preceding, and which is connected with that supporting the strap, 5, with the buckets, so that these latter, in their revolution, become filled with the tan in the trough, *u*, and empty it into the wooden hopper, 8.

In the bottom of this hopper is an opening connected with a wooden conduit, leading to a sieve, which is divided lengthwise into three parts, each of which is perforated with holes of different sizes. This sieve is moved by an arrangement below it, which is connected with the strap, *y*.

12. Troughs to recieve the residue from the sieve, 10.

13. Bags in which the residue of tan is placed.

14. Cords keeping the bags in place under the mouth of the trough.

15. Lever of the rammers.

i. Arched framework for keeping the shaft, *o*, in a vertical position. This shaft is divided into two parts, connected by means of a coupling, *s*, which may be separated at will, by means of an iron tool, *j*, attached to the framework of the machine.

1. Small stops for regulating the movement of the rammers.

2. Cushions through which the arms of the curb pass.

3. Framework supporting the horizontal shaft, *l*.

4. Supports of the drums, over which the buckets revolve.

a. Wooden framework of the machine.

b. Beam supporting the pegs for keeping the rammers at rest.

c. Rammers with knives at their lower ends.

16. Cross-bàrs made to revolve by the shaft, *o*, so as to strike against the wooden box, *t*, and hasten the descent of the tan into the trough.

Wiltse's Mill.—This machine, known as the "Catskill Mill," and extensively used in the tanneries of the United States, is made by A. and B. Wiltse, intelligent and enterprising machinists of Catskill, Greene Co., New York. It is constructed upon the principle of the shears, the teeth being arranged with their edges at an angle, and thrown forward, so that the bark may be driven in and ground rapidly, and passed through without interruption. Fig. 21 represents the machine, which may be driven by

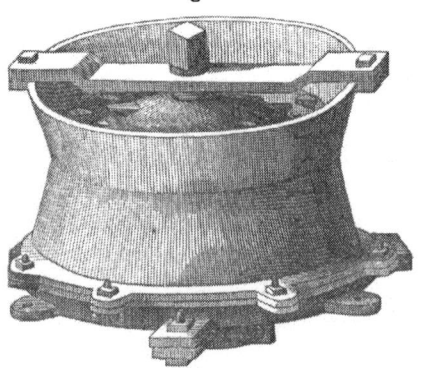

Fig. 21.

water or steam power, and so arranged as to receive the bark from the breaker and to deliver it ground in the leach-vats. To give a better idea of the manner in which it works, we give, on page 157, a plan showing the relative positions of the breaker, bark-mill, and leach-vat. Fig. 22 is drawn upon a scale of a quarter of an inch to one foot.

A is the water-wheel, and C its shaft; B is the bevel-wheel which drives the bevel pinion D on the foot of the main upright I, which also carries a spur-wheel E, and drives a spur-pinion F on the shaft G. The top of the mill sets ten inches below the second floor, in order to admit the bark running from the cracker J, K, above. This latter consists of a cast-iron curb or hoop J, of 18 inches diameter, and ten inches depth, with three jagged teeth, as shown in end and interior views at j. The top of the cracker K is made of two blocks of wood, firmly secured to two uprights, represented by the dotted lines,

Fig. 22.

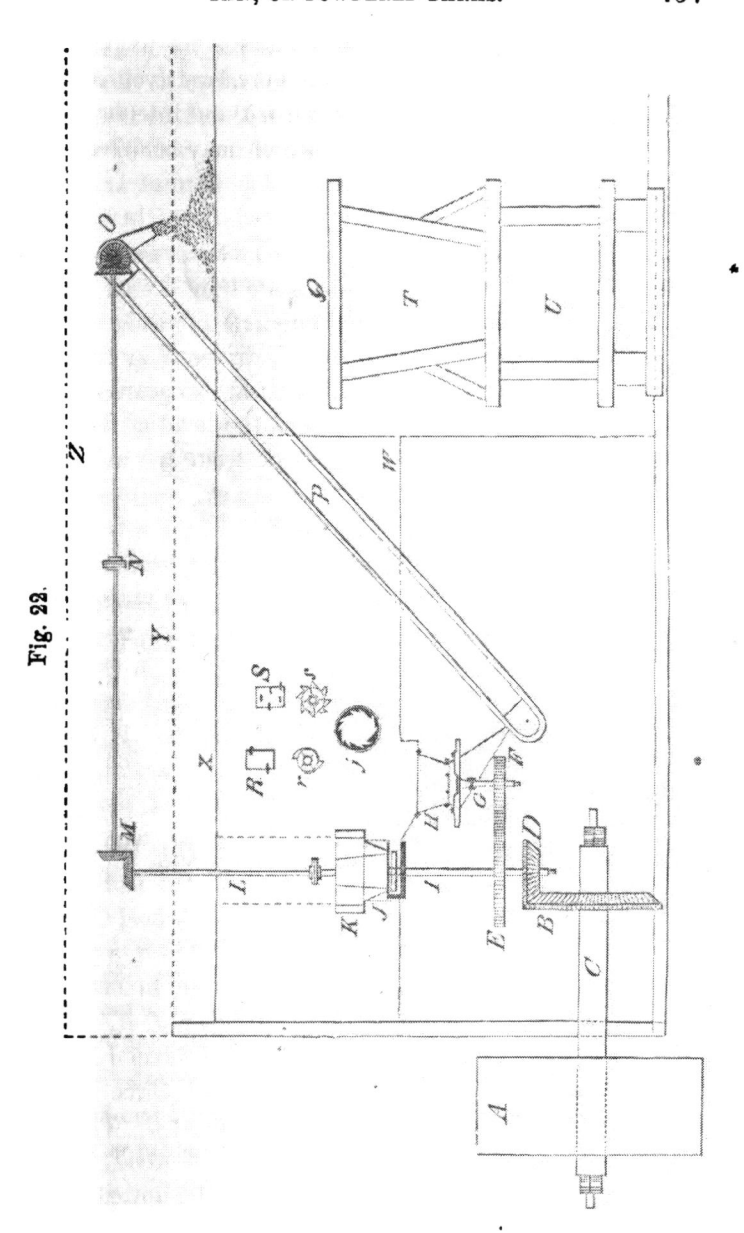

by means of bolts passing through the portion which laps them. The two blocks of K have openings in their centres, of 18 inches diameter at the base, and 24 inches at the top, to correspond with the size of the curb on which they rest. About 7½ inches from the bottom are four strong wrought-iron teeth, so inserted as to be in the centre between the teeth on R, r. The latter are secured to the shaft I, inside of K, as indicated by dotted lines; and S, s, is also similarly placed on shaft L, inside of J, j. A second length of the iron shaft L, drives N by the aid of the bevel-wheels M and N, which are so geared as to drive, in turn, the pulley-shaft O at the head of the elevators. The elevators take the bark from the mill and deliver it into a bark-room or loft above the leach-tubs Q, whence it may be drawn, as wanted, through a trap.

The drawing shows two leach-tubs, but the number may be increased according to the demands of the tannery.

The above mill possesses superior advantages, as it does its work effectually and with despatch. It cuts the fibre of the bark short, without flouring it, and passes it, even when wet, without becoming clogged. It is designed, also, for purposes of economy and durability, as well as of convenience; the arrangements of the parts being such, that when any of them, by wear, require renewal, they may be easily removed and replaced by others.

When worked to its utmost capacity, it will grind from one to two cords of bark per hour, and must be driven at the rate of 150 revolutions per minute by a ten-horse engine. At 100 revolutions it is less efficient. With one horse power, it may be driven at the rate of five revolutions per minute, and will then grind one cord in from one to three hours. The cracker should move at the rate of 30 to 40 revolutions per minute.

TAN, OR POWDERED BARKS.

If steam is used as the propelling force, the waste steam may be economized and applied to heating the leach-vats. A convenient arrangement for this purpose is constructed by the Messrs. Wiltse.

Birely's Mill.—Another ingenious grinding apparatus is that invented by Mr. Valentine Birely, of Frederick County, Maryland. It reduces the bark to shreds and strings, forms favorable to the entire extraction of its soluble matter by the liquor of the vats. Fig. 23 pre-

Fig. 23.

sents a perspective view, and Fig. 24 a vertical cross-section of the machine.

The framework is of cast-iron, with apertures at the sides for the journals of three cylinders, and flanges and ribs for securing a wooden hopper. These cylinders are of different diameters, and are propelled by means of a drum and cogs at the ends. Being denticulated on their surfaces, and revolving in concaves similarly studded with teeth, and arranged in alternate order to correspond with the reversed movements of the cylinders, the bark is reduced with great readiness, and the mill runs without obstruction. The coarse teeth of the first cylinder break it down preparatory to its passage through the next, and finally the last cylinder, which delivers it ground to the required degree of fineness.

These mills are made of three sizes, and the largest, driven by a ten-horse power engine at the rate of 80 revolutions per minute, will turn out twenty-five cords of bark every twelve hours.

The lengths of the cylinders in the three different sizes are, respectively, 21, 24, and 33 inches; and the smaller ones grind in proportion to the power applied.

CHAPTER XVI.

TANNING EXTRACTS.

For some years past, tanners have endeavored to accelerate the tanning process; and this end can be attained only by the use of materials very rich in tannin, and in small bulk. That is the reason why *Catechu* or *terra japonica* is so extensively used now. But many tanners, and we think they are right, object to the use of this substance, and prefer barks. We have been struck for a long time with the fact that no one has yet conceived the idea of manufacturing from bark an article having all the properties of oak or hemlock, and containing as much tannin as catechu. Several improvements have been made lately in the manufacture of extracts proper for accelerating the tanning process, but those improvements are not yet complete, for in these extracts a large portion of the tannin is destroyed and transformed into extractive. Before giving the process for manufacturing an extract containing all the tannin in an unaltered state, we shall give descriptions of the processes lately introduced.

J. Connel's Concentrated Extract.—This extract is thus prepared: He makes an inspissated extract of the bark, that is, he exhausts it completely by water, then evaporates it over fire in syrupy consistency, and dries it in connection with bark dust.

This extract has two inconveniences: 1st. A part of the tannin, by the action of air and heat, is transformed into extractive matter and a brown coloring matter is developed. 2d. This extract will not dissolve entirely in water.

Its only advantage is in being a little richer in tannin than the bark employed.

A. Steers's Process.—We are unacquainted with the mode of preparation of this extract; but from what we have seen we believe that the process is the same as the above.

According to Mr. Steers the process for reducing the tanning properties of the bark to an extract only $\frac{1}{12}$ of the original bulk of the crude bark offers the following advantages:—

The means of controlling the purchases of hides and sales of leather by enabling tanners to choose suitable city locations for their tanning operations, as the inducements of supply and demand may determine.

The means of securing a certain and permanent supply of tanning material at a uniform and unvarying figure to conduct their operations, and that figure less than the amount now paid by the most remote bush tanners.

To bush tanners the means of obtaining 25 per cent. more tanning material out of the same quantity of bark without increasing the cost of extraction.

To both city and country tanners the facilities of making liquors of any and every desirable amount of strength, to the want of which is generally attributed the tanner's greatest difficulty in attempting to compete with the European tanners in sole-leather.

To curers of bark and manufacturers of bark extracts for tanners' purposes, besides the basis of the proposed trade being of the most stable character, and giving to those who engage in it an unusual control over the subduing and settlement of wild lands, it secures to their operation in extract an immense direct profit, clearly exhibited and fairly calculated by assuming the difference of price between the place bark is procured at, and the place it is consumed as profits.

By this process of tanning butts and middlings, the hides being prepared in the usual manner and tanned with ordinary liquors, the most perfect tanning of the heaviest sole-leather is effected within four days, and an unusually great gain of weight is obtained, with a consequent rendering of the leather almost impervious to water, together with a susceptibility of a very improved finish. There is also a vast saving of tannic acid, as the unavoidable loss by volatility in the common exposure of present tanneries is equal to 50 per cent. of the bark used therein, as shown by the experiments of chemists and the statistics of large American tanneries.

As we have said above, the author of this book has had occasion to examine this extract, and it contains a large quantity of extractive matter, a sure sign of destruction of tannin. He tried it on a calf-skin, and it required two weeks to be completely transformed into leather.

It is true that the above advantages are exaggerated, but, nevertheless, the introduction of this extract is an improvement. We shall now describe a process we have tried, and which has succeeded with us very well.

We use the following apparatus:—

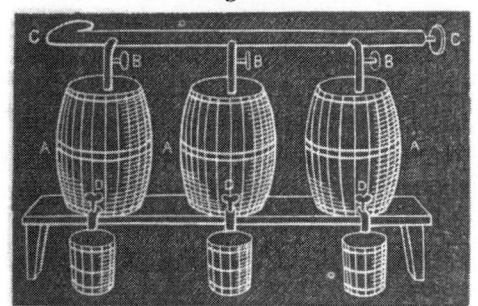

Fig. 25.

AAA, ordinary wooden barrels of a capacity of 40 gallons. The bottom of each barrel is covered with straw. Each is filled with the bark we mean to treat, which is covered with 20 gallons of water. Leave 24 hours, and then introduce the steam by the main pipe *CC*. Leave it to disengage until the barrel is full, then shut the cocks *BBB* and leave 12 hours. Draw the liquor by the pipes *DDD*. All the liquid is introduced into a vacuum pan and distilled at a temperature which does not exceed 120°. Continue to exhaust the bark as above described, till the water is nearly colorless, and evaporate all the liquors in the vacuum pan.

When the evaporation is completed the extract is drawn off in a jar and left to cool.

It is easy to ascertain when the evaporation is achieved; for that purpose take out a little of the extract and let it cool; on cooling it will become hard enough to be broken with the fingers.

Such extract has all the properties of the bark reduced to a small volume, and the evaporation being made at a low temperature without the contact of the air, the tannin is unaltered.

1 lb. Extract of *White-oak bark* represents	.	6 lbs. of bark.
1 " " " *Avens root* " "	.	4 " "
1 " " " *Sumach* " "	.	6 " "
1 " " " *Divi divi* " "	.	4 " "
1 " " " *Valonia* " "	.	4 " "
1 " " " *Hemlock* " "	.	4 " "

The above table shows that these extracts are richer in tannin than catechu, and have at the same time all the properties of the bark employed. We hope to see them used in preference to any other. The editor of this work has made many experiments on this subject, but unhappily they are not achieved and are uncompleted, but, when terminated, he will publish them, as they will be of great interest to practical tanners.

SECTION III.

SKIN.

CHAPTER XVII.

PROXIMATE PRINCIPLES OF LEATHER—STRUCTURE OF THE SKIN.

Proximate Principles of Leather.

As may be inferred from its nature, leather is formed by the combination of the substance of the skin with any other compound which has the property of rendering it imputrescible and elastic. Many substances possessing these properties in relation to skins of animals, are known to exist both in the organic and inorganic classes; but the one most generally employed as well as the most efficient is tannin. That a firm chemical union of the two bodies, such as that above referred to, exists, is evidenced by the modified form of the material, and the physical appearance and chemical behavior of leather, when subjected to microscopical and chemical examinations. The principle in the skin esteemed by the tanner is a gelatino-fibrous compound, which constitutes the basis of leather; and the combining agent —tannin—partakes of an acid nature, so that by uniting with the gelatino-fibrous material the former is, as it were, thereby salified, so that it is no longer subject to the ready putrefactive change which the skin undergoes under the influence of air and moisture. As the gelatino-fibrous principle forms only one of several others in the hide of the animal, so the tannin constitutes only one among many other substances in the sources whence it is extracted.

Structure of the Skin.

Strictly speaking, the skin of animals is composed of two parts, the CORIUM or *cutis*, and the CUTICLE or *epidermis;* the former is the portion which enters into the composition of leather, and forms the true skin; and the latter constitutes the exterior covering in which the fur, wool, or hair of the animal is rooted. Some physiologists, however, distinguish three distinct parts in the skin, namely the *corium, rete mucosum,* and the *cuticle.* These several parts are illustrated in the two following figures.

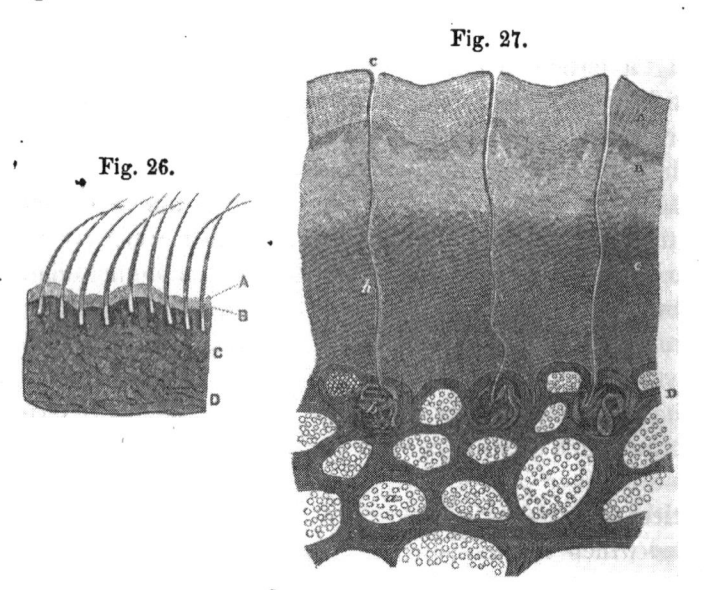

Fig. 26.

Fig. 27.

The former, Fig. 26, shows the position of the hair, and the latter, Fig. 27, the magnified layers of which the skin is composed. In both A represents the epidermis; B the rete mucosum in which the roots of the hair are imbedded; C, the fibrous tissue of the true skin; and D, the cellular tissue beneath the latter, showing the fat cells, *a*, in the latter figure, and sweat glands, *b*, with the follicles, *h*, through which this secretion passes out to the surface of the skin.

Behavior of the Epidermis and Cutis with Reagents.

When the fresh skin is immersed and macerated repeatedly in water, the matter of the cuticle is separated from the fibrous substance of the cutis, not by the solution of the former, but, as it would appear, by dissolving an extractive matter amounting, according to *Weinholt's* analysis, to about 8½ per cent., and which is probably, to some extent, intermediate between the horny matter of the cuticle and the cutis. Weak acids also abstract it, but solutions of the alkalies and of many of their salts are more effectual for bringing about the separation, since these agents dissolve it. The epidermis, which is analogous to horn, does not combine with tannin or any other substance, by the agency of which leather is produced. Hence it becomes useless to the tanner, and therefore the first process to which hides and skins are subjected by him, is that for removing the hair and epidermis, both being useless.

The corium, deprived of the epidermis, is a substance formed of a number of fibres ramifying and intersecting one another in every position, leaving, however, interstices contracting in size as they reach the other portion, and which are more or less charged with fluid matter, that serves to renew the cuticle, and keep the skin pliant and moist. On treating the skin with water these matters are removed, and ultimately there remains but the fibrous portion saturated with water. In this state it appears semi-transparent, and if the water be expelled by a gentle heat, it assumes the physical appearance of horn, constituting only about 32½ to 33 per cent. of the raw hide.

From Weinholt's researches, it appears that the skin deprived of the epidermis and its subjacent fluid, as also of the mucous membrane and fat on the interior, affords 43 per cent. of solid matter, yielding:—

Fibrous matter	74.42
Uncoagulated albumen	3.49
Extractive matter insoluble in alcohol	17.44
" " soluble "	2.32
Fatty matter and loss	2.33
	100.00

Digestion in water removes the albumen and extractive matter taken up by this menstruum; in alcohol the further portion of extract dissolves, and ether separates the fat with which the residue is impregnated. If the corium, deprived of the epidermis is treated with boiling water, it dissolves with the exception of a little fat and some nervous filaments; and when the liquid is evaporated slowly, a gelatinous residue is left, which when the entire skin is operated upon forms the glue of commerce.

This effect of the water does not arise, however, from the solution of the gelatine which, as might be supposed, the skin contains; but it modifies the components of the fibrous tissue, so as to bring them into this compound. The same property is possessed by acid and by alkalies in a more powerful degree, since the change is effected by these agents at the ordinary temperature.

CHAPTER XVIII.

CONSTITUTION OF THE SKIN.

FIBRIN—GELATINE—ALBUMEN.

Composition of the Skin.

HAVING treated of the structure of the skin we proceed naturally to consider its composition. The skin of animals consists of fibrin, gelatine, and small portions of albumen and fatty matter. The first two form, as it were, the basis or network of the whole tissue, a portion of which, if boiled with water, yields its gelatine while the fibrin remains. The epidermis of the skin does not combine with tannin. The properties of these substances which play such an important part in tanning are as follows:—

Fibrin

Exists in the animal structure as the basis of the muscular tissue. It occurs in solution in lymph, chyle, and blood, from which it separates by coagulation, as soon as these fluids cease to form a part of the living organisms. It is prepared by carefully whipping blood; it separates in elastic, stringy masses, which must be washed repeatedly with water to remove coloring matter, and digested frequently with alcohol and ether to free it from fatty substances. Dry fibrin is an opaque, yellowish mass; if transparent, it indicates the presence of some fat. Insoluble in alcohol and ether. Digested for a long time in water at 390° it is dissolved with a slight decomposition; it is thrown down from its solution by acids. Its solubility in saline solutions has been tested; when saturated it forms clear viscid liquids generally coagulable by boiling. When burned it gives the same smell as albumen and yields ashes composed of phosphate of lime and magnesia.

In sulphuric and mono or bibasic phosphoric acid it becomes gelatinous, and forms a neutral compound soluble in water. Nitric acid converts it into *xantho-proteic* acid. When dry it forms a blue solution in strong hydrochloric acid.

Muscular and venous fibrin both dissolve at a gentle heat, in acetate of soda, hydrochlorate of ammonia and nitrate of potash, forming solutions coagulable by heat, and exhibiting the properties of dissolved albumen; but neither arterial fibrin nor that of the buffy coat can undergo this change. By putrefaction it is transformed into a volatile fatty body having the characteristics of butyric acid. The same result is produced by heating it with potash lime at 320° to 356°.

Its ultimate percentage composition, according to Messrs. Dumas and Cahours, is:—

Carbon   52.78
Hydrogen 6.96
Oxygen   23.48 (with some sulphur and phosphorus)
Nitrogen 16.78
───────
100.00

Its formula is $C_{40}H_{31}O_{12}N_5SPh$, or $10PR+SPh$.

Pure fibrin, when added to water acidulated with hydrochloric acid and containing yeast, forms a clear solution similar to that of protein, and from which acid and alum precipitate a flocculent body. Without yeast a temperature of 212° will produce the same effect. By evaporation in vacuo it leaves a light yellow residue analogous to dry white of egg, soluble in warm water, but not coagulable by heat. After separating the dissolved part from the acid it has a composition closely approximating to *chondrin*, but without its chemical properties.

Gelatine

Is a solid, transparent, colorless, corneus substance, which forms with boiling water a solution that, on cooling, takes the consistency of a jelly. In its natural state and as existing in the cellular tissue, bones, tendons, etc., to which in their woof it serves to give form, it has the name of *histose*. This latter being treated with boiling water and dried, becomes gelatine; but, previous to this action, bears the same relation to the latter, in appearance and properties, as can exist between a completely organized body and its constituent elements in a state of complete desiccation.

Chondrin is the gelatine of cartilages, and is precipitated by acids, alum, and salts of lead. *Glue* is the technical term for the gelatine of bones, hoofs, and hides, *isinglass* for that from certain fishes, and *size* for the aqueous extract of parchment scraps and several animal membranes. At 212° gelatine softens and melts, but at a higher temperature it decomposes into animal products and a slight residue of earthy matters. In cold water it swells up and loses its solidity, but when impregnated with water, if heated at 140°, it becomes so minutely suspended as to give to the liquid the appearance of a solution insoluble in alcohol and ether. With tannin it forms a very intimate combination, and Müller considers this compound as definitely proportioned. Gelatine is transformed by nitric acid into oxalic acid; sulphuric acid transforms it into *sugar of gelatine*, or glycocol, *leucin*, and sulphate of ammonia.

Potash converts it into a mixture of sugar of gelatine and leucin, and though not of the protein series, it may, nevertheless, contribute to the nutrition of the gelatinous tissues. Bichloride of mercury coagulates and renders it insoluble, but an excess of gelatine dissolves the mercurial compound.

By long digestion at 212° gelatine loses its gelatinizing power, and forms, on evaporation, a gummy mass, readily soluble in cold water.

The ultimate composition of gelatine is:—

	Löwig.	Mulder.
Carbon	50.00	50.04
Hydrogen	6.41	6.47
Oxygen	25.64	25.13
Nitrogen	17.95	18.36
	100.00	100.00

Its formula is $C_{13}H_{10}O_5N_2$.

Albumen.

Albumen is a component of nearly all the animal solids; and when free from foreign matters is soluble in water. This solution coagulates at 160°, but the coagulum may be redissolved, by heating it with water in a digester at 400°.

As precipitated from the aqueous solution of white of eggs, or of the serum of blood, it is pure and soluble in acetic acid, very weak alkalies, and in soluble alkaline salts.

Albuminous solutions are precipitated by sulphuric acid; hydrochloric acid produces a coagulum soluble in water, and in strong hydrochloric acid by heat. Nitric acid throws down a flocculent precipitate, soluble in alkalies even from very dilute solutions. Acetic acid gives no precipitate even by heat, unless both acid and solution are concentrated. In that case, a gelatinous compound, soluble in both acid and in water, is formed; albumen is soluble in alkalies; water of lime, baryta and strontia have no reaction upon the aqueous solution of albumen, but with the alkaline earths themselves, it forms insoluble compounds. Earthy and metallic salts throw down double compounds, one with acid and another with metallic oxide, the latter of which is wholly insoluble, while the former is not entirely so.

Tannin precipitates albuminous solutions, but the resulting compound is not softened by heat like the tanno-gelatine.

Pure albumen is thus formed:—

Carbon	54.84
Hydrogen	7.09
Nitrogen	15.83
Oxygen	31.23
Phosphorus	0.33
Sulphur	0.68

CHAPTER XIX.

THE PROPER TREATMENT OF HIDES AND SKINS—KINDS OF SKINS SUITABLE FOR TANNING—SALTING OF THE HIDES.

Proper Treatment of Hides and Skins.

MR. H. F. LANGE, Cordovan leather tanner, in the late session of the Oschatz Trade Association, expressed his regrets that in the process of fabrication, that is to say, in the preparation of the hide for trade purposes, raw hides and skins labored under great disadvantages owing to the farmers' and butchers' handling, inasmuch as this was not carefully enough done with a view to the future operations to be undergone by the raw material. This subject of complaint was also concurred in by the bark and white tanners present at the meeting, who gave expression to the united wish that through the making known of the manipulations which experience has proved to be the most simple, and, at the same time, the most efficacious, hides or skins may be delivered in a condition perfectly suitable to the process of manufacture, and the evils more closely particularized below might gradually be done away with as much as possible.

It happens only too often that the hides and skins of slaughtered animals, or of those that have died from natural causes, are not at once taken off, but left for days together on the carcass. This is in the highest degree detrimental to the hides, as they acquire thin and defective spots, through the process of decomposition going on in the carcass, or the worms which are forming in the interior of the animal work destructively upon the hides. Great damage is also caused, although of not so great a nature, if, in flaying, the work is not done with all due care. The bits of flesh and fat, which are only too often allowed to remain adhering to hides and skins, become at once decayed and communicate decay to the skin; which is injured or eaten away in spots, becoming, consequently and subsequently, very thin or even worn into holes. Such damage is noticeable in a more especial manner after manufacture, when the leather is found bad in appearance, or inoculated with dark spots, as is the case with colored leather.

And leaving these defects out of the question, the suppleness and durability of the leather itself will be injuriously affected if the skins are not suitably and carefully treated in drying and hanging up, by the premature shrinking and imperfect drying of the material.

As an evidence that the evils just mentioned, arising from improper treatment, are of more importance than is generally thought, we give the statement of Mr. Lange to the effect that the sheepskins received in the summer season often yield barely one-third of a material perfectly adapted to the fabrication of imitation morocco leather.

In view of these evils, and in order to promote the interests of the leather trade, the following points are to be urgently recommended to the producers of the raw material in flaying hides and skins:—

1st. Immediately after the death of the animal the hide or skin should be carefully taken off.

2d. The fleshy or fatty portions still adhering to the skin should be detached down to the smallest pieces.

3d. The hide should, without the least delay, be hung up in a very airy place, one not exposed to dampness, with the hair side inward, so that a draught of air may play upon the entire length of the inward side of the hide.

4th. In order to prevent the hide from shrinking, the head and tail ends should be stretched out, and nailed to the pole.

5th. The hoofs and legs should be spread with skewers on both sides.

6th. The flaying of the hide should not be intrusted to inexperienced persons; for, unless a certain dexterity is brought into this operation, the value of the skin will be considerably lessened.

Only by observing these directions can skins and hides be properly dried, and delivered free from defects, suitable for valuable use.

The benefits that will accrue to the whole leather trade, by following such a course, cannot be rated too highly; for not only will it secure a serviceable material to manufacturers, but also a large quantity of hides and skins will be saved from destruction, and the market will be better and more fully supplied. A further consequence will also be that a better manufactured article will be produced, and lower prices be established.

Kinds of Skins suitable for Tanning.

The principal object of attention in the preparation of leather is the hides or skins of the animals. Three classes are specified in commerce: the term *hide* is applied to the skin of the larger and full-grown beasts; *kip* to the skin of the younger animals of the same class; and *skin* indicates the hides of the sheep, goat, kid, and the like. The term *kip* is qualified by the size of the skins. Generally speaking, the skins which are converted into leather are those of oxen, cows, and calves, of the sheep, the goat, and their young, of the horse, the pig, the dog, and a few others; but by far the most extensively worked, as well as the more important, are ox, cow, and horse-hides, kips, calf and seal-skins. Considerable difference is observed in the thickness and quality of the skins of various animals, even of those of the same class, owing to circumstances connected with the food, age, variety of breed, the state of health, and even the period of the year when they are slaughtered. Thus, large oxen are well known to afford hides which are tanned into thicker and heavier leather than bulls or cows, especially if the latter be old and have had several calves. Bull-hides are coarser-grained, and thinner in the back than those of oxen and heifers, or young cows, but much denser in the neck and parts of the belly. It would also appear that when cows have repeatedly calved, the skin becomes distended and thinner, and does not, therefore, afford as heavy a sole-leather as that of younger animals. Again, hides of animals, dying in a state of disease, are found to be much inferior to those of healthy ones of the same class, although the apparent difference is not very marked before tanning.

No very definite *criteria* are known to guide the purchaser in distinguishing the quality of hides and skins. If the hide be thin, flabby, soft, and will not bear handling, then such a one will not make good leather; but should it present the opposite quality, it may confidently be expected to be a good article. It has been remarked of sheep, that the finer wool variety have inferior skins; also that the skin gains in thickness and quality considerably in the course of a few days after shearing.

Ox-hides.—Under this head may be enumerated the skins of *oxen, cows, buffaloes,* and *calves.* In Great Britain and Ireland, the market draws generally upon the home produce, but the largest quantity used comes from South America, the East and West Indies, etc. The animals which roam along the Pampas and Llanos, or great plains, in herds of vast numbers, are, in addition to those owned by the extensive cattle owners or *hateros,* the stock whence the vast quantity of hides used is annually derived. They are imported in the dry state, and salted, and produce a very good sole-leather. It should be remarked, however, that the hides from animals inhabiting the tropical latitudes are not so well suited for tanning as those from the temperate and northern parts of the globe. The *green* or fresh hides of the home market always rate higher than other sorts, owing, perhaps, to the fact that they do not require so much labor as the imported dry kinds; still, in consequence of the amount of water they contain they prove to be much dearer than the others; for, allowing that for the production of 100 pounds of leather, 75 pounds of dry hide are requisite, the equivalent of this of salted hides would average 150 pounds, and 185 of green or market hides. Heavy hides are converted into sole, belt, and harness leather, also for carriage coverings, and the smaller and lighter kinds are made into leather much used for *skirtings*, and for enamelling. That which is used for ladies' shoes and for bridle leather, undergoes a bleaching process termed *fair finished*. Hides from the west coast of Africa make good upper leather, but are much employed in their raw state for trunk covering.

Calves' skins and *kips* of home produce are of very superior quality, and produce a leather, when made with good oak bark, very extensively worked into uppers of shoes and boot fronts. In France, where the calf-skin leather has been reputed for its excellence, they are taken off the animal when five or six months old. Kips are imported from the East Indies, Buenos Ayres, and Montevideo; those from the former places are dried and salted or merely exsiccated; and from the latter places they come simply salted. The lesser and inferior kinds of kids and calf-skins are tanned for bookbinders' use, for gloves, and the manufacture of ladies' boots and shoes.

Buffaloes' hides are tanned like ox-hides, but they make an inferior quality of sole-leather. When tanned in a particular way with oil, they constitute what is termed *buff-belt leather*, which is superior to the similar article made of cow-hides.

Horse-hides.—The skins of these animals are much inferior to those of oxen in thickness, texture, and strength, and, consequently, they are never prepared with the view of making *sole-leather*, though the better quality is used when tanned for uppers. The chief consumption is, however, as cordovan or enamelled leather, the hides being split by machinery to reduce them to the adapted thinness. Horse-hides are likewise made into tawed, white, or alum leather, and are in this state used as aprons for certain classes of mechanics, and as thongs for the manufacture of common kinds of whips, and for sewing common harness.

A considerable number of horse-hides is annually imported from South America. The imported hides are much superior to those which find their way to the home market, on account of the latter belonging generally to old and worn-out animals, while the former have been flayed from the captured wild horses of the pampas, lying between the chains of the Andes. Ass and mule's hides, tanned and so prepared, serve for the manufacture of scabbards; the leather is called *shagreen* or *shagri*.

Sheep-skins.—The home supply is very extensive, and although they are capable of making only a spongy, weak leather, the uses to which they are devoted are various, and their manufacture gives employment to numerous hands. Tanned with bark they constitute bazils, and are used for making slippers and as bellows leather; but when prepared with alum and salt, or with oil, white leather, much employed for aprons and by druggists, chamois leather result. A good many are split, the upper or grain side being tanned with sumach and dyed, then worked up as *skiver*, *roan* and *morocco* into pocket-books, hat-linings, and the under portion being made into white leather, and used very much by the chemist; but it is much the more general practice to reserve lamb-skins for the latter purpose; sheep-skins are sometimes tanned with the wool adhering to them and made into mats. In Asia Minor a considerable trade rises from the preparation of lamb-skins for ladies' glove-leather, for lining of morning-gowns, for slippers, and for winter gloves. On the hides from Asia Minor the wool is kept for the purpose of retaining the warmth. Considerable difference may be observed in the quality of lamb-skins; those from the animals killed shortly after being born are possessed of a very fine grain, and take a very uniform dye. The same qualities are in a great measure retained by the skins till a month old, but from this period they begin to deteriorate. In the Southern part of France and in Italy great numbers of lambs are killed averaging four weeks old, and the leather prepared and employed as a substitute for kid leather.

Goat-skins.—In this country a number of native skins are used, but the market is supplied almost entirely by imported goods, more especially from Switzerland, Mogadore, the Cape, and the East Indies. The Swiss skins are more esteemed because they possess a close, fine, and equal grain, which enables the dyer to give them a brilliant and permanent hue; the leather is also stronger, and weaves better than any other manufactured from goat-skins. Mogadore skins are made into a kind of black morocco leather, which still goes by the title of Spanish leather, or cordovan, in consequence of the first supplies of this article being obtained from Spain and Cordova, where the Moors originally brought the manufacture to great perfection. The sound skins which arrive from the Cape of Good Hope are much larger and superior in strength and thickness to any other variety. East India skins are small and light, and are generally converted into leather chiefly used for ladies' shoes and upholstery. Those from Mexico known as *Tampico* skins bear a very high character. Compared with sheep-skins, those of goats are much superior in texture, strength, and durability. Goat-skins are occasionally prepared so as to imitate chamois leather, and applied to most purposes to which the latter is adapted, and likewise with the hair on and used for matting. Kid-skins, manufactured into leather, are most extensively consumed by the glover, also for shoes, binding leather and the like.

Deer-skins.—A considerable number of these skins are manufactured into chamois leather, and also into glove leather.

Hog or Pig-skins.—Tanned pig-skin constitutes a very porous, light, but, nevertheless, very tough and valuable leather. It is largely used by harness-makers for saddle seats. The practice of skinning pigs is followed in Europe, where the hide is dressed with the hair on and used to cover portmanteaus, knapsacks, etc.

Seal-skins.—Of these a great quantity is imported yearly into France, and manufactured into upper and varnished leather. They are obtained from the animals captured along the shores of North America for their oil. The skin of the seal is light, but of a close texture, and when properly tanned, yields a leather which has greater strength, in proportion to its weight, than any other variety. Seal-skin is usually made into black enamelled leather for ladies' shoes.

Porpoise-skins.—The skins of the white porpoise have been tanned in Canada, and the leather is said to be soft, strong, and possessed of a beautiful finish.

Hippopotamus Hides.—About one hundred of these skins are annually imported from the South of Africa, and are tanned with oak. The hide, originally of great thickness, assumes the appearance of boards after being tanned. The only use which appears to be made of them are implements used for beetling in washing, and bleaching cotton and linen goods.

Mode of Salting Hides.

Delalande's method, which is that generally employed, consists in laying the hides open upon the ground, and sprinkling the flesh side with salt, more liberally at the edges and on the spinal portions than on other parts. They are then folded, or doubled lengthways, down the centre. The remaining folds are made over each other, commencing with the shanks, then the peak of the belly upon the back, afterwards the head upon the tail part, and tail part upon the head, and, lastly, by doubling the whole with a final fold, and forming a square of one or two feet. This being done they are then piled three and three together, and left until the salt has dissolved, and penetrated their tissue, which generally requires three or four days. Thus prepared they are sent to market.

Skins may be dried, even after having been salted, by stretching them upon poles with the flesh side uppermost, and exposing them to dry air in a shady place.

Ten pounds of salt in summer, and somewhat less in winter are requisite for each skin of ordinary size.

PART II.

TANNING.

SECTION IV.

PRELIMINARY TREATMENT OF SKINS.

HIDES, destined to be tanned and transformed into leather, are submitted to several preliminary operations before being tanned. We enumerate them successively. They are as follows:—

Washing and soaking.
Swelling.
Depilating.
Working on the beam.
Rinsing.
Tanning.

CHAPTER XX.

WASHING AND SOAKING.

THE first operation that the skins undergo is the washing and soaking. It is, therefore, convenient to have the tannery located near by a stream of water. The skins are taken in a *green, dry,* or *salted* state. The *green hides* are those from recently slaughtered animals. They are soaked in water for half a day, or longer if necessary, so as to remove all the blood and adhering dirt. They are to be well rinsed when taken out from the soaking. If they are to be soaked for a long time, it is necessary to handle them from time to time.

If the current of water is rapid, trouble will be saved by planting a kind of rake across the stream, and fastening the hides so that the friction of the water may loosen the dirt and carry it off. The skins must be carefully suspended, so as not to have them damaged by rubbing on the stones at the bottom of the stream.

When the hides are dry the soaking should be continued longer, and that operation is facilitated by handling them often, and stretching them each time, beating them under foot, and working them upon the wooden horse, as shown in Figure 28, with the fleshing knife Figure 29, and then leaving them to drain. The fleshing is repeated once or twice.

Fig. 28.

Fig. 29.

The working and scraping are continued until all animal matters which are prone to putrefaction are removed. The length of time cannot be prescribed. The hides are to remain in water until they have become supple, and it is for the intelligence of the workman to determine when this point is attained. If the soaking is too long, the skins have a tendency to putrefy. *Dried* and *salted* hides require a much longer soaking than those which have been only dried.

The working and softening of the hides upon the horse or beam are considered indispensable operations by every experienced tanner.

When the skins have all been soaked and washed, and are sufficiently supple, they are returned and left in the water for six hours. In running water they may remain eight hours. Reference is here made exclusively to large hides, for cow-skins may be left without danger for 24 hours, and calf-skins 48 hours, being careful to observe the nature of the water and the temperature of the air. Too long soaking in the same water exposes the skins to the danger of putrefaction, and the rapidity of the decomposition is proportional to the amount of filthy matters contained in the water.

Well-salted skins, but not dried, may be cleansed in 48 hours, but they can be left to soak three or four days without danger. They must be withdrawn once a day, left to drain two hours, worked with the back of the fleshing knife and well rinsed in water. The object of those manipulations is to remove salt and dirt, and render them soft and supple. When taken out from the water for the last time give a vigorous and thorough rinsing.

At St. Saens they commonly use dry hides from South America, which are placed directly in vats filled with lime-water and left for six or ten days, care being taken to work them in the usual manner at frequent intervals during the soaking. These vats are 8 feet long and 5 feet wide.

The skins are softened by the action of lime and rendered more easy to be handled. At this stage the defective parts may be detected, and sometimes they are so damaged as to be suitable only to manufacture glue.

At Liege, where they mostly use the dry hides from Brazil and Caraccas, there is no allotted time for soaking. After four or five days they examine each vat, and withdraw such hides as have become soft and leave the rest. This process is repeated daily until all the hides have been withdrawn.

As soon as the hides are taken from the vats, they are worked upon the horse and then returned to the water. On the following day they are thoroughly rinsed and placed in the drying room. The working is solely for the purpose of removing the wrinkles and stiffness of the dry skins. These manipulations are unnecessary for green hides.

According to some tanners the quality of the leather is improved in proportion to the duration of the soaking of the hides; but it is undeniable that when it exceeds a certain time the skin acquires a tendency to decomposition and the quality of the leather is impaired.

Soaking of Foreign Hides.

Before we speak of this soaking we must say a word or two regarding the employment of sulphuret of arsenic. This substance is produced by passing a current of hydrosulphuric acid through a solution of arsenic. The sulphuret is precipitated in the form of a bright-yellow, flaky substance.

By mixing the orpiment with a solution of lime in the proportion of 4 parts of the former to 96 parts of the latter a compact mass may be obtained which is easily used for depilating purposes.

Small hides or kips after being well washed and cleaned are soaked by laying them in foul bloody water. This method, which is of universal use amongst white tanners, requires much attention, like every other process by means of which the hide is almost restored to its original condition. It imparts a perfect softness to the hide, leads rapidly to the result, and is not costly; but it requires the greatest precautions. The method to which we give the preference is the one that we now propose to mention as offering certain guarantees, as we have lately had proven to us by actual experiment. This method is the softening of the hide by sweating, that is to say, heating it without fire and without steam.

The sweating pit is a pit about 12 feet long by $7\frac{1}{2}$ feet broad and 6 feet deep, flat on the top. In order to secure the desired result it should be constructed of good masonry, and, when practicable, built under ground. Moreover attention should be given to have the access of the air removed as much as possible from the entrance to the pit. The door, which should be 5 feet high by 20 feet broad, must be made of strong pine wood and furnished with three bars strongly fixed, so that it may be made air-tight when closed, and not warp from the effect of the dampness which fermentation produces. The sweating vat should contain poles planted in the ground at intervals of about $1\frac{3}{4}$ feet, according to the breadth of the vat, and rise to the height of $5\frac{1}{4}$ feet. It is important to observe these instances as nearly as can be, for if the sweating vat is too large, the same effect will not be produced. For sole-leather it is more desirable to use two smaller sweating vats than one very large one.

Small hides or kips should be thoroughly washed in very clean water, spread out after four days' soaking, well rinsed and drained, then laid together in packs in such a manner that the hair is outward, and the pairs of skins back to back. Hang them over the poles of the sweating vat, with the tail end upon one side, and the head on the other. Then close the door and stop it up well so that the air may be excluded as much as possible, and leave matters thus until the odor of the sweating process becomes quite strong, which is an indication that the process of depilation is about to begin.

The working of the sweating process is shown by a sharp lye which forms under the hair, and which drops off the instant fermentation sets in. After taking the skins out, the thick portions should be worked with an iron instrument, then lay the hides in water and let them soak for a day or two, after which the flesh side should be worked with the stretching iron, in order to bring out the grain again before consigning them to the lime pit.

Strange as this treatment of the hair side may appear, we do particularly recommend it, for in order to restore a cow-hide to its primitive condition, it is not sufficient to attend to the flesh side alone; we require to provide against the remaining of wrinkled places on the grain, as often happens, especially in Java and Calcutta hides. When we come to dress the leather, these cannot be removed by the grainer or stretching iron, because we have neglected to give sufficient care to the grain.

We cannot too often repeat that light hides should not be placed in too strong lime; this sort of hides should rather be operated upon by degrees and always with weak lime, and for this reason, it appears to us, that the surest method that can be followed in order to secure a successful result, is to use lime that has already been weakened by contact with fresh hides. For a dry hide, when acted upon by lime, may be compared to a flower, which is taken out of a warm forcing-house, and exposed to a cold temperature. It will be seen that its development will be arrested, it will shrink and draw together, and never will expand any further. The comparison may be incomplete, but yet it is apt.

With regard to the large hides of wild animals, such as those imported from La Plata and elsewhere, whether dried fresh or dry salted, we urgently recommend that they should be subjected to the sweating process, for, we repeat it, the sweating system has not only the effect of facilitating the process of depilation, but of giving to dry wild hides that development of which they stand in need.

The sweating process, as we understand it, regulates and hastens the expansion of the hide, opens the pores, and places the hide in a state similar to that in which it was at the time the animal was slaughtered. To prepare it for the leather dressing process, it will be found enough to work the hide lightly on the flesh side with the iron, when it is taken out of the sweating vat, so as to stretch out the wrinkles that may appear before the hide is placed in the lime pit, which, as has been said, should always first contain a weakened lime bath.

It is now for us to say something as to heavy hides, and it is necessary to state, that we restrict ourselves to the consideration exclusively of foreign hides, i e., the hides of wild animals.

We will begin with dry hides, those coming from Buenos Ayres, for instance, as being the best known. What is considered the most estimable property of Buenos Ayres hides? That they are a species of hide which softens easily and in a regular manner. It is admitted that hides which are allowed to remain continuously in water, soften less readily than those which are alternately soaked and piled. And now let us consider how piling compares with sweating. Piling is nothing more or less than a slow inward sweating, and while it is slow you run the risk of having the edges damaged, by giving the time necessary to effect a good result. So in order to save the back and extremities, you are obliged to dispense with a complete softening of the hide, and moreover lose time. This is always the result of irregular soaking. Now what, in fact, do we seek to attain in soaking the hide? Simply the raising up of the fibres, in order to save those parts of the hide which were wet, and became dried during its transportation; and we believe the best mode of doing this consists in accelerating the operation, so as to obtain a thorough soaking by the sacrifice of from seven to eight days.

Moreover, stagnant and hard water does not give the dry hide time to become completely softened again, at least it injures the grain, which becomes lost before the water has had time to penetrate the fibres of the hide.

Under these circumstances sweating is alone of use, and if necessary, a softening during 24 hours in open water will be sufficient to secure a satisfactory result, as experiment has proven.

Soak the hides in water for 24 hours, mark the flesh side well, and rinse the hair side thoroughly, so as to rid it of all foreign substances, so that no faulty spots may ensue; let them drain in a heap during four to five hours, and bring them to the sweating process as above described. Sprinkle them with fresh water through a gardener's watering-pot, provided with a sieve-like spout, and after the hides have been again allowed to drain off, put them back in the sweating vat.

Three sprinklings with the watering-pot will be found ample, in combination with the sweating process, to soften the driest and oldest hides to such a degree, that, even if they are of the heaviest, they can at once be divested of the hair. Then separate them after rinsing them, lay them again in running water, clean and scrape them, and do not interrupt the gradual course which the hide has to undergo.

What we have last mentioned should only be resorted to when suitable water is wanting for proper soaking, for we recommend above all things that the hide be carefully soaked in water, as this raises it well, but in all cases, whichever mode of soaking be followed, the hides should never, as a general rule, be allowed to stay in the water longer than four days, or from five to six days in severely cold weather. Of course the sprinkling with a watering-pot is then superfluous, and there will then only remain the piling up of the hides in the sweating vat, to be attended to. They should be left in it from four to six days, according to the season of the year.

With regard to salted wild hides, a proper softening in water will do, and this water should be changed every now and then, so that the hide does not remain long in briny water, and care should be taken to rinse them thoroughly before placing them in the fresh water; for the rest the same course is to be pursued as with dry hides.

CHAPTER XXI.

INFLUENCE OF THE WATER UPON THE QUALITY OF THE LEATHER.

It is a mooted point, whether the nature of the water used for soaking has any influence upon the quality of the leather. No positive experiments have been made yet, but in this case we think that it is better to take the affirmative side of the question. Calf-skin leather, which should be soft and supple, requires soft fresh water, and it will be difficult to manufacture them with hard water.

Modern chemists call water protoxide of hydrogen. When pure it is inodorous, colorless, transparent, elastic, a good conductor of heat and electricity. It boils at 212°, and freezes at 32°. The waters called *soft* dissolve soap, while those which do not possess this property are called *hard*. The former is nearly free from soluble matters, while the latter contains calcareous and other salts. The composition of chemically pure water is in weight—

	equiv.	
Oxygen	1 = 8	= 88.88
Hydrogen	1 — 1	= 11.12
	9	100.00

The agreeable taste of pure water is due to the air it contains; when expelled by ebullition it is insipid.

Rain Water.

The purest rain water is that which falls in the country where there are no noxious emanations.

The soluble impurities of rain water are those which it has dissolved from the atmosphere, and consist of minute traces of chloride of sodium, carbonic acid, and carbonate of ammonia. After a thunder-storm, rain water contains small traces of nitric acid formed by the atmospheric electricity.

Snow Water.

This water is the same as rain water, only it is crystallized, and by this crystallization it loses the gases held in solution.

Spring Water.

Water, in its transit through the soil, becomes charged with such constituents thereof as are soluble in it; and, consequently, the purity of the water is proportional to the insolubility of the earth through which it has flowed.

The purest spring waters contain air, carbonic acid, and minute quantities of hydrochlorate and carbonate of soda.

River Water.

There is not much difference between river and spring water. Sometimes, however, it is purer from having deposited its suspended matter, and also a part of that held in solution, which generally happens when it traverses a long and silicious bed. If it pass over or through limestone, or other strata containing soluble ingredients, it becomes less pure.

Lake Water.

Lake water contains more soluble principles of the soil upon which they rest than river water; this condition is promoted by their state of quiescence.

Marsh Water.

This kind is in a more permanent state of stagnation than lake water. This water, on account of the organic matters it contains, easily enters into a state of putrefaction.

Well Water

Contains more soluble constituents of the soil than lake water. Well water is generally *hard*, because among earthy salts it contains particularly sulphate, bicarbonate, and chloride of lime, which render soap insoluble in it.

Well water, in the vicinity of the sea, has a brackish taste, and contains the same constituents as sea water.

When well water is very hard the addition of a little carbonate of soda will decompose the lime salt and render it potable.

By what has been said it is evident that rain water is the purest, but all drinkable waters are applicable for tanning purposes. To soften hard waters the French tanners add a solution of pigeon or chicken dung to the vat, and stir it thoroughly by means of a shovel. The hides are then put into it to soak. Some tanners, instead of washing in the river, soak them in troughs. Water containing iron renders the leather brittle and blackens the hide.

In Paris, the water is purified by filtering it through spent tan. There is a series of three vats, charged similarly with spent tan; and as the water which is poured into the first vat is drawn through a cork at the bottom it is transferred to the second, and afterwards to the third. As, thus rectified, it contains a little tannin derived from the spent tan, which renders it particularly adapted for the early part of the tanning operation.

Some waters are preferable to others for tanning, but on what particular quality of the water this superiority depends has not yet been determined. The safest way is to prefer those which contain the less soluble matters, particularly earthy salts, for they certainly reduce the tanning power of the ooze by combining with some of its constituents.

The suspended matters, consisting of mud, as well as the soluble organic matters, which impart to water a bad taste, may be removed by filtering the water through clean gravel and fresh charcoal.

If the lime exists in the state of bi-carbonate, it can be separated by adding to the water some lime-water. Boiling produces the same result.

CHAPTER XXII.

SWELLING OR RAISING OF THE HIDES.

THE second process to which hides are to be subjected is termed *raising*, and is that by which the pores are distended, the fibres swollen, and the hair loosened. These results are effected by means of alkaline or acid solutions, and by fermentation. Milk of lime is the alkaline liquor generally employed. Lime-water has been proposed as a substitute, but it is less permanent in its action, and requires frequent renewal in order to insure the perfect cleansing of the hides.

Lime Process.

This process, which is the oldest, is the most defective, but in a complete work on tanning it is necessary to speak of it. It is an ascertained fact that the object of the vat work is to effect the swelling of the hide, to open its pores, and dispose them to the depilatory operation and absorption of the tannin. The tanner must be perfectly aware that he could never make a good leather with a hide which has not been well prepared in the vats.

The vats are prepared in two ways: they are of wooden work sunk in the ground or masonry. The vats destined to swell the hides to facilitate the depilation and raising are more or less large; they are square or round, about $4\frac{1}{2}$ feet square and of the same depth. The number of hides determines ordinarily the quantity of lime necessary for each vat; one peck is usually sufficient for a large hide, while under some circumstances it is necessary

196   TANNING.

to increase the quantity. In several manufactures to economize lime they add ashes, pigeon or dog dung, but we advise tanners to reject such processes.

To make a new vat throw in it quick-lime, cover it with water, and stir well with a stirrer, as represented below, till slacked and reduced into milk.

Fig. 30.

This operation done, leave a few days and it is then ready to receive the hides.

The vats are distinguished as *dead, weak,* and *live vats*. The dead vat is that which has been nearly exhausted of its strength; the weak is that which has only been used long enough to deprive it of a portion of its force, and the live vat is that which has not yet been worked.

It is easy to understand that the live vat becomes successively the weak and the dead vat. When a tanner uses more than three vats he establishes between the dead and live vats as many middling terms vats as convenient. The whole of the vat is called *raising series*.

Fig. 31.

The raising should be commenced in the dead vat, and continued in consecutive order through the series to the live vat. In some factories the series consist of as many as twelve vats; and in this case there should be a graduation in the strength of the liquors. The duration of this operation varies in different localities. Some tanners leave the hides for three months, while others soak them for eighteen months.

There is great variation in the composition of the vats. In Auvergne and Limousin they mix with the lime, ashes or lye of ashes, and in some other places the lime forms only ¼ in the composition of the vats. The old manufacturers gave the hide a soaking of ten, twelve, and even fifteen months; and then when they have become sufficiently softened, transferred them to a dead vat for eight days; at the end of which time they were withdrawn, hung up for eight days, and again placed in the same vat for eight more days, etc.

These consecutive operations are thus continued for two months or until the hair can be readily detached.

The graduation of the vat varies in different localities. In Angoumois it consists of twelve vats; the first two are *dead*, the four following *weak*, and the last six *fresh* or *live*.

In Poitou it consists of six vats; the first two are *dead* vats and the last three *live vats*.

In Britanny many tanners who believe that the hides are raised better with the hair on than in *pelt*, give six live vats and do not remove until the fourth and even the fifth vat.

In Auvergne they give three raisings of a month each with a mixture of lime and alkaline lye.

So many vats are useless; generally speaking, three or four vats skilfully managed suffice for any kind of skins. Some have asserted that ten to twelve months are requisite for a thorough soaking; but the experience of good tanners proves that two months are sufficient.

According to Curaudau only ten or twelve days are required for the transit of the hides through the three lime vats. He thinks a longer time will be useless, and that the shorter the soaking the greater is the weight acquired by the hides in tanning.

Malepeyre says it is now established—1st. That it is sufficient to leave the hides in the pits for twenty-four hours, and an equal length of time in stack. 2d. That this operation should not continue for more than six or eight weeks. 3d. That three or, at most, four good vats are sufficient. 4th. That after this interval the hides are easily cleansed, and, on the other hand, where the treatment is prolonged the hides become parched. 5th. That after three or four pits, the hides will have swollen to the fullest extent, and finally there is a great waste of time, lime, and materials in the old method of steeping from ten to fifteen months.

CHAPTER XXIII.

STACKING OF THE HIDES.

STACKING is to pile the hides one upon the other on the side of the vat as they are drawn from it, and leave them remaining a shorter or longer time before returning them to the bath for another wetting.

Piling enables the working of 60 hides in a vat of a capacity for thirty, by having one bath taking the place of the other in alternate operations. While one set of thirty is in retreat the other should be in the vats, and *vice versa.*

The vats should be covered; and as the skins in retreat are susceptible of becoming hard by exposure to the sun and air, they should not be kept in that state longer than is necessary. At every handling the water and lime at the bottom should be thoroughly stirred, and a workman at each end of the vat, by the aid of tongs, arranges the hides in it so that they may be smooth and firm. The suspended lime soon subsides upon the

Fig. 32.

hides, and the supernatant liquor which should cover the hides to a depth of some inches will be clear and transparent. As the greater portion of the lime is in contact with the skin at the bottom of the vat, its action is more powerful on them than on those above; and consequently in recharging the vat after stacking, the order should be reversed.

Should the vat become too weak to produce the desired effect, it must be strengthened by the addition of the quantity of lime necessary to restore its force. The advantage is thus obtained of giving the hide the benefits of two vats in one. The lime should be added while the skins are out of the vat.

To remove the hairs, the scraping knife alone is used. It is a dull-edged instrument which is not liable to damage the skin by cutting it, while it is all efficient in scraping off the hair. It is a bad practice to use the slate or rubber, which, being rough, may scratch and damage the hide upon its grain side.

Fig. 33.

The use of sand, ashes, etc., for removing the hair is very improper; it is also a bad practice to wait until the completion of the soaking before scraping off the hair, because the lime will in time act on the hair itself.

When the hair is removed, rinse the skins and replace them in the dead vat, and so on. It suffices to leave the hides for fifteen days in each of these vats, but care must be taken to stack and replace them every twenty-four hours.

M. Tournal says: "The force of habit and perhaps the use of the Kermes oak causes many tanners to continue the use of lime. But if, in rinsing, great care is not taken to remove every trace of lime, the minute traces remaining will, by abstracting carbonic acid from the air, become insoluble and render the skin dry, brittle, and perhaps useless. These faults are not entirely due to the carbonic acid of the air, but also to the formation of tannate of lime and of stearate and oleate of the same basis which are generated by the presence of fatty matters existing in the hides.

"Tanners who use the Kermes pretend that its *warm* nature imparts stiffness to the leather, and that the only available mode of raising is by lime. They own that the sour tan juice and barley processes distend the pores of the hides much more than lime, and that the tanning principle of the Kermes having a tendency to combine rapidly with the hide imparts an unnatural stiffness to the leather."

To the above statement we will add that the bark of Kermes oak is richer in tannin than the ordinary oak, and admirable leather may be prepared by tanning with it skins which have been raised by sour tan liquor.

CHAPTER XXIV.

INCONVENIENCE OF THE LIME PROCESS.

The inconveniences of the lime process are the following:—

1st. The contact of caustic lime alters more or less the texture of the hide, and permitting it to penetrate the pores, it remains in them in the state of caustic lime, carbonate, or lime soap.

2d. The rinsings in water and the workings remove it only partially, which is an impediment to perfect tanning.

3d. It hinders the ready penetration of the tan liquor, and the perfect combination of tannin with the skin, and so obstinately resists removal during all manipulations that a portion is always found in the best leather.

The experiments of Dr. J. Davy[*] show that the action of lime upon animal textures is rather antiseptic than destructive. Its corroding influence is limited to the cuticle, hair, nails, and all gelatinous tissues. These latter become soft and gelatinous owing to a combination which they form with lime, for on analyzing the ash of the cuticle thus treated a large increase of its normal contents of that earth was obtained.

The matters were steeped in milk of lime, kept caustic in close vessels, by the entire exclusion of air. After treatment they cease to be putrescent.

These disadvantages have led to the substitution of other agents, which we will proceed to treat of in the following chapters.

[*] Chemist, 1850.

CHAPTER XXV.

METHOD OF RAISING BY ACIDS.

An acid liquor has been used by some tanners instead of milk of lime. The Kalmucks use sour milk for this purpose. Pfeiffer has proposed the acidulated water obtained by the distillation of lime and peat. Sometimes a little sulphuric acid is added. This acid in a dilute state, as also all vegetable acids, produces the same effect. Acids have the double advantage of loosening the hair and swelling the hide.

Some tanners soften the skins by sprinkling one half with salt, and folding the other half over it; then they are piled and covered with straw. The fermentation follows; they must be turned several times daily, until they have attained that state in which they can be easily depilated. The use of salt is not necessary. They are to be piled on a bed of straw and covered in like manner. Twenty-four hours after they are turned and examined twice daily so as not to exceed the proper point. In some places the hides are imbedded in horse manure, in others they are covered with tan. The same effect could be produced by suspending the hides, which have been left lying in a heap for several days, in a close room kept above the ordinary temperature by a smouldering tan fire.

All methods of fermentation are termed *sweating processes*. But whatever is the process followed, the skins are to be spread upon a wooden horse, and scraped with a dull edged knife, as soon as the hair begins to yield readily. In this manner the hair and outer skin are fleshed or scraped off. The outer skin being of a different nature from that of the hide, and not uniting with tannin, must be removed in order to allow the free passage of the tan liquor through the skin, and to facilitate the tanning process.

CHAPTER XXVI.

DEPILATION BY STEAM.

In many places, instead of a milk of lime, they use another method, which consists in submitting the hides, in the heap, to a slight putrefactive fermentation in heated chambers. In summer it is difficult to control this fermentation, and sometimes it is necessary to salt the hides. After some days the epidermis becomes loose and detached, and may be readily scraped off from the hair.

Mr. Robinson, of Delaware, uses steam as the heating medium, in an arched chamber eighteen feet long, ten feet high, and ten feet in breadth, and lined interiorly with cement. The steam is introduced beneath a false bottom of wood, perforated with numerous holes. The condensed steam escapes through an opening at the basis of the chamber.

The temperature of the *heap* should be maintained between 70° and 80°, and care should be taken to keep it uniform, for the joint action of heat and moisture may dissolve the gelatine and cause the hides to be scarred with pits. The process is completed in twenty-four hours, and the hair is scraped off in the usual manner. Ox-hides weighing from eighty to one hundred pounds experience a loss of twenty-four to twenty-eight pounds.

CHAPTER XXVII.

DEPILATION BY CAUSTIC SODA.

M. F. BOUDET, for a substitute to lime for raising and depilating hides, proposes caustic soda. For this purpose the liquid is prepared by decarbonating a very dilute solution of soda ash with a sufficient quantity of lime, allowing repose, and decanting the clear supernatant liquor of caustic lye. Hides immersed in this liquor swell out rapidly and considerably, and are ready to scrape in two or three days. Moreover the alkali forming soluble salts with the fatty portions, facilitates the cleansing, and produces a smoother grained side than is common. Hides thus prepared imbibe the tan liquor more rapidly than those which have been treated with lime. They undergo the entire process of tanning in one-third of the time, and suffer less loss than those prepared by the usual method. Forty-four pounds of salsoda, dissolved in one hundred and thirty-two gallons of water, and mixed with thirty-three pounds of slaked lime, suffice for steeping two thousand two hundred pounds of fresh hides.

CHAPTER XXVIII.

DEPILATION BY SULPHURET OF CALCIUM AND SODA.

BOUDET, in trying the old method of depilating by means of a paste of orpiment and caustic lime, observed that the arsenic had no decided influence upon the hair, and that the depilatory action was due to sulphuret of calcium in the nascent state, formed by the reaction of lime upon the orpiment (sulphuret of arsenic). He replaced the orpiment by sulphuret of calcium, which, when made into a paste with lime, acted so promptly that, after twenty-four or thirty-six hours' contact, the skins were completely depilated. The lime alone has no depilating effect, and the sulphuret of sodium only a partial action.

This mode of preparing the hide is said to render it highly susceptible of being quickly tanned. Experience has to decide its influence upon leather. Tanners are opposed to this method, which, it is said, surcharges the leather with an amount of water that escapes by evaporation during storing, to the great loss of the dealer, but we do not think that this objection is tenable.

Messrs. Abram & Coste use the following process:—

Macerate the hides for three days, put them in the vat, raise three times, and then for each skin put

Potash	2¼ drms.
Lime	5 oz.
Orpiment	½ oz.

This same quantity is sufficient for three little goat or sheep-skins. For twenty-five hides take

Potash	1 lb.
Lime	2 lbs.
Orpiment	2 oz.

The whole is dissolved in fifty gallons of water.

This vat is much less commended than the preceding, and is liable to numerous objections, and the principal is the danger to health accompanying its manipulation.

Boëttger has proposed to depilate all kinds of hides with the hydrosulphate of lime, in paste, which is prepared as we shall see hereafter. To use it, the skin is put, with the hair up, on a table, when the hair is slightly impregnated with the paste, so as to penetrate as far as the roots. In the same way is treated a second hide, and it is placed on the other. These two hides are covered with a board loaded with stones. Two hours after the hair is transformed into a kind of soap, which is easily removed.

Preparation of the Hydrosulphate of Lime.

The hydrosulphuret of calcium, or hydrosulphate of lime, is prepared by saturating a very thick milk of lime with sulphuretted hydrogen gas. The necessary apparatus is shown below:—

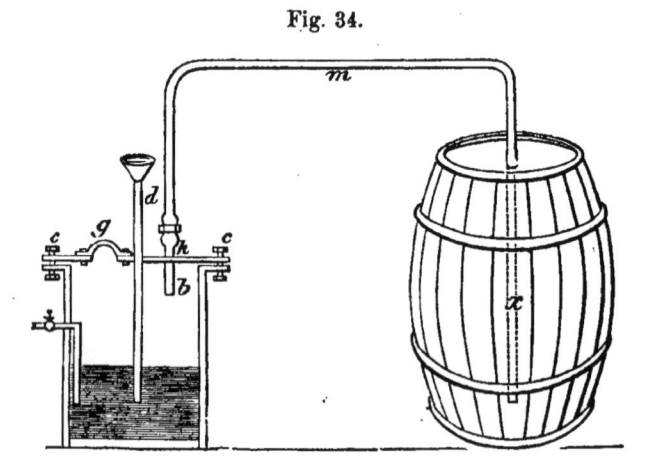

Fig. 34.

It represents a leaden generator, of cylindrical form, thirty-six inches high by twenty-four inches in diameter, supported by a wooden jacket. This vessel has a movable cover of cast iron, with a projecting ledge, through which pass the bolts *c, c,* for fastening it down. In this cover there are three openings, as shown in Fig. 35. The larger one, *g,* is the man-hole for the admission of the

DEPILATION BY SULPHURET OF CALCIUM AND SODA. 207

sulphuret of iron and for cleaning out. Of the two smaller, the centre one, d, receives the stationary funnel

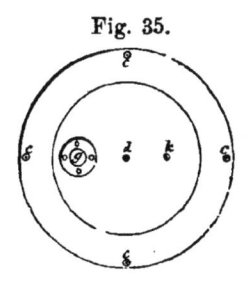

Fig. 35.

tube, d, through which the dilute sulphuric acid is to be introduced. The side hole, k, contains a short tube, b, with a screw at its upper end for coupling the flexible exit tube, m (made of vulcanized rubber), which is to convey the generated gas into the lime paste contained in the closely covered receiver, x. A pipe running down the side of the generator, interiorly, is for the coupling of the steam pipe when the admission of steam is necessary.

The protosulphuret of iron rests upon the bottom of the generator. When the sulphuric acid and water (one vol. of the former to three or four of the latter) are poured in through the funnel tube, d, to the height indicated in the figure, chemical action immediately ensues. The water, which is composed of oxygen and hydrogen, is decomposed, and the former gas goes at once to the iron, which is deserted simultaneously by its sulphur, and thus becoming an oxybase indulges its affinity for the sulphuric acid and unites with it to form sulphate of iron. The hydrogen unites with the sulphur to form sulphuretted hydrogen, which escapes through the tube, m, leading into the milk lime with which it combines as hydrosulphuret of calcium. The current of gas is continued until the lime is saturated. When the current of gas slackens, hasten it by the addition of a little acid and water. The occasional admission of steam facilitates the reaction. When the paste is saturated, stop the connection of the tubes m and k, and the generator is emptied by the main hole, g, so as to be ready for another operation.

The receiving vat should be of wood, strongly bound with iron hoops, and fitted with a cover and appliances for keeping it close enough to confine the gas, but not so tight as to cause an explosion.

The paste should be made in quantities as required, for it must be used immediately, as the action of the air soon converts it into sulphate of lime.

CHAPTER XXIX.

COOL SWEATING PROCESS.

THIS process, much used in New York, New Hampshire and the northern part of Pennsylvania, has all the advantages of the older processes. It gives a gain in the leather of 70 to 80 per cent., while the warm sweating process yields much less, and the liming only 30 to 40 per cent.

.The process is described as follows:* "A vault or pit is prepared for the reception of the hides; it should be 12 feet long, 12 feet deep, and 10 feet wide. The wall may be built of stone or of a planked frame. There should be one alley for entrance six feet long, having a door at each end; the outer one made double, and filled

* Journal Frank. Inst. 1843.

in with spent tan, to prevent the communication of warm air from without. A ventiduct, made of planks ten or twelve inches square should extend from the centre of the bottom of the vaults three or four rods therefrom, and placed not less than four feet below the surface of the ground. This serves both as a drain for discharging the water of the vault and to admit damp cool air, to supply the place of that which has become rarefied, and thus keep up a current through the ventilator at the top. The ridge of the roof may be level with the ground; and on the ridge, extending its whole length, set up two planks edgewise, two inches apart. The space between these is to be left open, but the remainder of the roof must be covered with earth, to the depth of at least a yard. The earth covering upon the vault and drain is to preserve a low temperature for the hides so that they may unhair without tainting.

"Spring water should be conducted either in pipes or logs, around the angles formed by the ceiling with the walls of the vault, from which water should be allowed to flow in small quantities, either forming a spray, or falling so as to raise a mist or vapor, and saturate the atmosphere of the vault. The temperature of spring water is generally about 50°. Water evaporating at all temperatures, it is plain that if a constant supply be afforded, this evaporation, by requiring a large portion of heat, would keep the temperature of the vault nearly uniform. To suspend the hides in the pit, place three bars lengthwise, at equal distances, near the ceiling with iron hooks, two or three inches apart, inserted therein. Soak the hides as usual for breaking, then hang them singly upon the hooks by the butt, so that they may be spread fully open. In the course of a few days, when the hair begins to loosen upon the upper parts, take them down, raise the middle bar, and hang them by the other end until they easily unhair. The hides should not be broken until they are taken from the vault and ready to unhair. In a good vault where the thermometer ranges from 40 to 56°, which it should never exceed, and where there is a free circulation of damp air, hides require from 6 to 12 days for unhairing. When the temperature falls below 44° the ventilator should be partially closed, and when it rises above 56° cold damp air must be forced in, or an increased quantity of cold spring water may be thrown from a hose."

Hides thus treated are free from all extraneous matters, and contain all their gelatine, albumen and fibrin, in an unimpaired state. "The action," says the author, "is confined to the *surface or grain* of the skin, expanding the outer portion, softening the roots of the hair, and thus rendering its removal easy. The effect is due to the *softening* action of the vapour, and it is a simple case of absorption and swelling of the tissues of the skin and roots of the hair."

This process has been proved by experience to obviate all the evils arising from *hot sweating* or from unhairing the hides by the lime process.

CHAPTER XXX.

RAISING BY BARLEY DRESSING.

THE swelling and depilation of hides by this process are more effective and rapid than when lime is used. Hides treated by this process require less working in the water.

This process requires a series of vats varying in

strength. The hides are soaked at first in the vat containing the weakest liquor, then pressed and washed.

Mr. Bouillerat, of Paris, operates as follows: The hides, after being soaked and fleshed, are put through the dressings, that is, are subjected to the action of barley water. They remain three days in the first or dead dressing, as much longer in the second, when they are freed from the hair, and placed in a third vat in which they dilate, swell out, and acquire consistence. They are taken out only once daily, from the dead dressing and twice from the others. At each time they are laid in heaps and there left during an interval of three hours. After these three dressings, the hides are submitted to a fourth, which is termed the new dressing, made with 145 lbs. of well-ground barley meal. From this quantity 10 lbs. are taken out and made into a leaven by being kneaded with warm water, and left to ferment from 12 to 14 hours, in which time it sours and becomes sufficiently ripe for the operation. In summer this leaven is thinned out with tepid water in sufficient quantity to form the dressing; in winter boiling and in spring hot water is used.

From the new dressing, the hides are passed into another similar one and allowed to remain four days in each. Eight or nine hides are generally worked at a time.

The series is composed of four or five vats. The first dressing is intended to wash the hides, the second for depilation, the third to swell them and impart body, and the two others, which are new, complete the action of the third. These preparations are termed *white dressings*, and require five weeks in summer and six in winter.

After having gone through the white dressings, the hides are carefully washed and placed in the red preparation, composed of 225 lbs. of tan well mixed with $2\frac{1}{2}$

hogsheads of water, and are left in the mixture for 15 days in summer time, and one month in winter. During the first five days it is necessary to take the hides out, once daily; to be sure that the supply of bark is sufficient when the skin comes from the preparation, they are to be washed and placed in the vats. Eight or nine skins may be handled at one working.

At Abbeville (France) tanners have adopted the following method. For 16 hides, they put 48 lbs. of barley meal into an open-mouthed tub, and mix with it some sour paste made of flour thinned out with hot water. They add to this mixture $\frac{1}{2}$ a lb. of yeast; fermentation soon follows, and in 15 to 16 hours the leaven is formed.

This leaven, being mixed with 150 lbs. of meal in a tub of water, forms the new dressing or preparation.

The same gradation as with lime is observed as to these dressings. Before the hides are worked, they should be cut into halves, and always placed with the flesh side upwards.

The time for the hides remaining in the dressing is as follows: two or three days in the old dressing, five or six in the weak, and twelve or fifteen in the third and fourth, which are the strong or new dressings. Sometimes the hides are sufficiently raised at the fourth dressing, and then they are taken out, while the unfinished ones are put into a fifth dressing and left until they have acquired sufficient swelling.

During summer the hides are drawn out twice, and in winter once, and left to drain for an hour, each time, upon a trough conveniently situated near the vat. This operation requires about six weeks in summer and much longer in winter, for cold retards the action.

In Sedan they use nine or ten small vats, each of about six hogsheads capacity. There is a regular graduation in the strength; for example, after the first operation the second becomes the first, the third second, etc. Five hides are placed in the first vat, where they remain from 24 to 48 hours; they are transferred to the second, which is a little more sour, and so on successively through all the vats. It often happens that the hides attain the necessary degree of dressing at the fourth, third, etc.; then it is useless to treat them further. These sour liquors, after having served for ten operations, still remain acid, and can be used again according to their degree of strength.

After the skins have been treated, they are washed in clear water for the removal of the dirt, and when they come to the last dressing they are rinsed and scraped over with the fleshing knife; at last they are again put in water and brushed over on the hair side.

Some, after this manipulation, lay the hides in the vats, but the greater number subject them at first to a red dressing. This dressing is given by spreading the hides in a vat, one above the other, and placing between each pair two or three handfuls of ground bark. They add water until the hides are submerged. This process requires two days, and the hides require only one withdrawal to allow them to drain.

Fig. 36.

In giving the finishing wetting, care must be observed to supply bark where it is wanted.

This method of cleaning and unhairing presents as many objections as the lime process, and besides has other disadvantages. The efficiency of the bath is destroyed when exposed to a low temperature, and it is not restored when the bath thaws. The leather is exposed to be injured by the putrid fermentation of the materials.

In England, for coarse hides, they have used for a long time the barley dressing, and they complete the operation in six days. The hides pass through four or five dressings, and from the weak progressively to the strong. The hides remain 24 hours in the last vat, which is new, and has been soured for 15 days. It is made by mixing 60 lbs. of barley meal in hot water. As a long time is allowed for the development of acid and consequently the dressing is more active than ordinary ones, it becomes necessary to watch carefully when the required point is reached, otherwise the hides will be injured.

Barrois operates differently. He works five series of four tubs each, at a time. These vats are $3\frac{1}{4}$ feet high and 5 feet in diameter, and of a capacity for 8 hides; each series comprising 32 hides. It is necessary to take out all the hides twice daily during the dressing. Every four days a new preparation is made up in one of the vats, which is deposited in that, the dressing of which was the weakest after running it off and washing out the vat. The third vat then becomes the last, and that which was the first and strongest becomes the second.

The hides remain eight days in the fourth or weakest vat, four days in the third, which then becomes the weakest; then the same length of time successively in the second and the first, after remaining six days in which they are stripped and deposited in a fresh series. In this they remain four days in a dressing which has only been used once, four days more in another similar one, and four days each in two fresh vats.

Each fresh preparation for eight hides is composed of 145 lbs. of ground barley, and the leaven is made with 30 lbs. of the above barley mixed with yeast and hot water.

This interval of thirty two days is sufficient for the requisite preparation of the hides, either in summer or winter; but in the latter season, hot water is generally used in the proportion of five to six buckets to each preparation in order to hasten the fermentation.

A hide dressed by this process weighing 100 lbs. takes about 200 lbs. of bark as follows: 25 lbs. in the red dressing, 30 in the first powder, 25 in the second, and 20 in the third. The preparation is maintained fresh by the addition of a few pints of vinegar.

When the hides have been sufficiently raised in the white dressing, they are put in the red, which is composed of clear water and two or three handfuls of bark placed between the hides. The hides remain thus three or four days, when they are again treated by the same quantity of bark as at first, and left three days longer; after that time they are ready to be laid in the vats in the same manner as in the lime process.

This process, a little modified, is one of the best that can be followed. A fresh vat can be used every two days, and thus there will be a gain of half of the time. Instead of clear water, it is better to use the liquor of the tan pits, and to place between each hide a layer of coarsely ground bark for the red dressing.

Two hundred pounds of bark are not sufficient for 100 hides averaging 200 pounds each. In some places they

216   TANNING.

use 300 lbs., but the quantity depends much upon the quality of the bark and the fineness of the powder.

The following is a very good method: For a dressing for eight hides averaging 50 lbs. each, from 100 to 140 lbs. of barley meal must be employed. Some tanners use all the meal at once, but others again make a leaven with 24 lbs. of the meal, which they do not mix with the rest until twelve hours have elapsed. Many tanners keep up the acidity of the dressing by throwing into each one three or four bottles of vinegar, at different times.

Other tanners put the whole of the meal in the tub and drench it with enough tepid water to form a fermentable paste, and leave it twenty-four hours. The dressing is made by adding to the fermented flour warm water in winter, and water at the ordinary temperature in summer. The quantity of water varies according to the number of hides. These are divided into two sides before subjecting them to the dressings, in which they remain three weeks in summer and four in winter. The hides are taken out daily, and placed on planks across the vats as shown in the figure, and there left for two or three

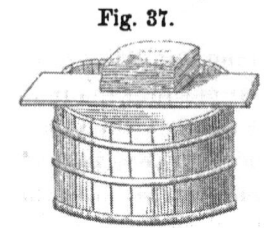

Fig. 37.

hours. The vats are 4¼ feet in height and as great in diameter. In some places, tanners use nine or ten vats, but three are sufficient; the first for the *dead*, the second for the *feeble*, and the third for the new preparation. The depilation is performed as soon as the hair can be pulled off without resistance.

Scrape the hides with the usual precaution, with the round knife, and throw them into the water, where they remain about two hours. Rinse, draw out, and place them in the second preparation. Experience alone determines the length of time necessary for the weak bath. While they are attaining the requisite body, they must be taken out daily, and replaced in the vats.

If the hides have not been fleshed before the dressings, it is necessary to subject them to this operation, after drawing them from the weak vat; but it is better to do it previously. After the fleshing, soak them for two hours in water, rinse carefully, and place them in the new dressing, which is prepared with barley meal, in the proportion of twelve pounds for each hide. A leaven is made with one-fourth of this quantity of meal, and when it begins to ferment, the residue is added, and the whole thoroughly diffused in an amount of water proportional to the number of hides to be worked.

The time in the third dressing varies according to the nature of the hide, the season, &c.

The hides during this, as in other dressings, should be daily removed from, and replaced in the vats.

The hides are then put into the red dressing, made of liquors from the tan vats, to which must be added about 6¼ lbs. of coarse bark for every hide.

You must be careful, in this operation, to avoid delay, and not give the bark time to settle to the bottom of the vat, for the skins will be unequally tanned.

It is better to commence work with the red dressing very early in the morning, so that the operation may be completed before night, and the leaving of the skins too long without stirring should be avoided. This way the hides may be taken out and replaced twice daily, once in the forenoon and once in the afternoon. The first time they are allowed to drain ten minutes, and then replaced. The second time they are drained for fifteen minutes, and in the interval the same amount of bark is added, and the vat thoroughly stirred. The next two days the hides are taken out and put back three times daily, and left to drip half an hour each time. Twenty-five pounds of fresh bark are added in the morning, and upon every removal of the hides the dressing is carefully stirred. No bark is added on the fourth day, and the hides are taken out only twice, and are allowed to drain three-fourths of an hour each time.

The last step, upon the fifth day, requires a new manipulation. After the hides have been taken out in the morning, and drained three-fourths of an hour, two workmen stir up the contents of the vat, while two others put back the hides, flesh side down, care being taken to spread some handfuls of bark upon each. When the vat is full, the last skin is put in with the hair side down, and some bark is sprinkled over it. After ten days take the hides out, rinse them in water used for dressing, and lay them in the vats.

The red dressing is a very important step in the process of tanning. It gives firmness to the hide, by an incipient tanning, which serves as preliminary to that which is to follow. A skin which has not received a red dressing is tanned so rapidly that it shrinks, becomes hard, wrinkled, and insusceptible of perfect combination with the tannin. The feeding of the vat, according to Dessables, can never be too strong, for the hide neither hardens nor shrinks in the powder. However, we believe that a strong feeding of a vat is injurious. Experience has proved that with a hide directly in contact with a concentrated liquor of bark, the tanning is very active, but the combination of the tannin with the gelatine is so rapid upon the exterior surfaces that the interior is unacted upon, as is the case in hasty tanning.

There are some tanners who contend that barley-dressed hides require about twenty per cent. more bark than those which have been limed. In many places they take for a barley-dressed hide averaging 100 lbs. in weight 225 lbs. of bark, as follows: 84 for the first, 75 for the second, and 66 for the third. The same results can be obtained with rye flour.

We do not recommend these processes to manufacturers; their use is now abandoned in consequence of the uncertainty of their action. We shall speak now of Wallachia leather, which is similar to this process.

CHAPTER XXXI.

WALLACHIA LEATHER.

This kind of leather is manufactured in Wallachia, and is made by barley-dressing, in a single vat. The hides are softened in water, and trampled under foot, then worked on the flesh side with the scraping knife to render them supple; at last they are rinsed in water and hung up to drain. They examine then if the hair can be easily detached, for, in warm climates, in summer, this is effected without any other preparation. If fresh skins are used, they are left to ferment so as to remove the hair, and, after removing the tail, horns, and ears, the skins are salted without being soaked.

The salting consists in sprinkling over each large hide from four to six pounds of salt, alum, and saltpetre, doubling it on the centre, so that one half is folded over the other, stacking it, and covering the pile with straw. The hides soon become heated, and it is then necessary to turn them once or twice daily, and change the folds, and the sides, so as to insure a uniform fermentation. When the hair can be detached readily, the depilation is immediately commenced, for any delays are injurious to the grain of the leather. If they cannot be depilated immediately, soak them in water for one or two days, but no longer, for fear of their undergoing an incipient fermentation.

Salt is not necessary, as we have said above; as a general rule the hair should give with a noise, when it is plucked out with the fingers, and the more difficult the depilation the better the skin, as it is a proof that it has suffered no alteration. The parts denuded during or previous to the operation should be moistened with a solution of salt, so that they may not be overheated before the other portions are ready for the depilation.

The depilation can also be effected with the help of stable manure. The three methods by fermentation are the most objectionable, as the skins nearly always suffer more or less from incipient putrefaction. In the following method it is better to employ the exhausted vats. As soon as the depilation is finished, the raising is effected in the following manner:—

For seven hides, each averaging eighty pounds, take twenty pounds of wheat flour that you make into a leaven, diffuse in water to a pasty consistence, and, to accelerate the fermentation, add a gill and a half of vinegar. This leaven requires twenty-four hours to be made, after which it must be kept covered in a warm place for three or four days.

The tub for six or seven hides should be five and a quarter feet in diameter, and three and a quarter feet in height, and well cleansed. Fill it with water and withdraw from it six or seven bucketsful, boil, and use a part for making a uniform paste out of ground barley, which afterwards thin out with cold water till of a syrupy consistence. This paste is boiled till it froths, constantly stirring with a wooden paddle, and when it has bubbled or foamed three times, it is to be poured into the tub destined for the dressing, and cooled by stirring with the paddle kept moving constantly in the same direction. The temperature should be such that the hand can be kept in it. Then stir in six pounds of salt, cover the tub, and leave it two weeks to sour. However, the mixture is stirred twice daily, and, in order to confine the heat, the cover should not be kept off longer than is necessary.

Take the skins from the rinse-water, strung in threes upon a rope thrown into the tub, and leave for four or five days. Each day withdraw them twice, rinse, leave to drain a minute, and put back in the tub. When the skins are well broken, and the hair side has become sufficiently soft to retain the impression of the fingernail, they are taken out and fleshed. If some portions

Fig. 38.

of the hair should still adhere, spread the hides upon the beam, and scrape them with the knife represented in fig. 38. When shaved, rinse in clean water, suspend and leave to drain twenty-four hours. In the mean time make and ferment in the same way a second leaven with sixteen pounds of meal.

The sour liquor is then transferred from the vat of the first dressing, and the clear supernatant portion poured into the second tub wherein is to be given the complement, which is nothing more than a repetition of the preceding operation. Six or seven bucketsful of the clear sour water of the tub are taken from each vat, are boiled, and a portion stirred up with about fifty pounds of ground barley, or about eight pounds for each hide. Add gradually the residue of the hot water, boil gently, and distribute in the new dressings, stir, take out a bucket or two, and heat it nearly to ebullition. The second leaven, made with eight pounds of meal, is distributed in the tubs; add to each four or six pounds of salt and and stir well. Take out several bucketsful and hold them in reserve, so as to have them ready for supplying any deficiency in the quantity of the liquid, which should not be greater than eight inches in height. If this method is too tedious, it may be simplified by making one step of the two, and using at once thirty pounds of leaven, one hundred and twenty of barley, and ten of salt, for each dressing of six hides.

By the ordinary process, tanners use at one time in their first new dressing, just twice the quantity of barley that would be employed here, and when their first new dressing is not sufficient, they make a second, which renders the process more tedious and costly than that of Wallachia. It is also necessary to say that, on the addition of salt, the dressing must always be well stirred, and two or three bucketsful of the liquor drawn out from each, and kept warm, to be poured into the vat in order to maintain the temperature. Several other bucketsful are poured into a reserved tub, so that no more liquor may remain in each dressing than is sufficient to cover the skins subjected to its action. Some tanners think it better to make the whole of the composition at once, for it may so happen that the complement made with the new quantity of barley may retard the progress of fermentation, and that the liquor must then be heated to a température which would be injurious to the skins.

The single composition is made in different ways: 1. From barley or rye meal without leaven, prepared over night with boiling water. 2. From equal parts of barley, meal and leaven, thinned out with water and heated nearly to ebullition just previous to putting in the skins. 3. From wheat bran in the proportion of a half bushel per hide, thinned out with hot water, and after a day's fermentation mixed with one pound of salt for each hide. 4. From leaven of barley or rye as substitute for that from wheat in the proportion of 6 to 8 lbs. of flour per hide. When the leaven rises, thin it out with water at 86°, and add the salt just before the skins are put in.

METHOD OF WORKING THE DRESSINGS.

When the fermentation is well established the *dressings* are ready to receive the skins; then take them from the hangers, and pass them in and out of the liquor several times to gradually equalize the temperature. Leave them a few minutes, on the cover of the tub, to drain. Stir the liquor and put back the skins, cover the vats, and maintain the heat of the dressings with the liquor kept warm and in reserve. Fifteen minutes after take out the hides, let them drain fifteen minutes, and put them back. Half an hour after remove them, let them drain a quarter of an hour, return them to the vat, and take them out again to drain twenty minutes. At last they are taken out after two hours, and the same round is repeated a seventh and eighth time after a similar interval. The liquor must be stirred every time, so as to cause the meal to rise from the bottom. Be careful to cover the vats immediately after putting in the hides. The heat of the vats should be maintained at from 105° to 120° F. by additions of reserved liquor kept warm.

Two workmen place the hides in the vats; they take them by the opposite ends, spread them out upon the flesh sides, and then push them down with a pole.

The action of the white dressing is completed in thirty-six hours; the acetic fermentation so expands the hides that they become as thick as leather into which they are about to be converted. Care must be taken not to leave them in the liquor after this point has been attained, for it injures the leather. The same result occurs if the liquor is too strong.

When the skins have been removed from the liquor, the clear portion is reserved for a new dressing, for which purpose it must be treated with a complement stronger than the first. This acid liquor facilitates the fermentation of the new composition, which sours rapidly. In this manner the white dressings are in train, and may be kept at one-half the expense of flour, time, and money.

After the hides are taken out of the dressings, they are left to drain on the cover; and, when cooled, they are soaked in water a few moments; in order to effect the removal of a viscous coating derived from the barley, they are drained anew.

Now they are submitted to the red dressing, which prepares them for the tanning. To prepare this dressing, charge the tub with about forty pounds of crushed bark, which is mixed in water, then place the hides in this mixture. Take them out at noon, allow them to drain seven or eight minutes, and again in the evening for a quarter of an hour. Before putting them back the last time, treat the liquor with forty pounds of crushed bark, thoroughly stirred. The mornings of the second and third days, add twenty-four pounds of bark, take out the hides daily, and every time drain for half an hour. The fourth day take them out only twice, morning and evening; add no bark, and allow forty-five minutes to drain. The fifth day take out the hides in the morning, drain, and stir the liquor thoroughly; return the hides to the tub, hair side uppermost. Throw some handfuls of bark between each skin, and on the top of the last one, which should have its flesh side uppermost. Leave the hides eight or ten days, remove, rinse, and put them into the vats.

Bran Dressing.

According to some tanners, the red dressings may be omitted, if the white dressings are made with bran, but the opinion of the majority of tanners is in favor of red dressing. However, we shall say a few words about the method employed.

The bran dressings are made either cold or hot. For the first, a leaven is prepared with yeast, or made with one and a half pounds of wheat or rye flour for each hide, and kept at a moderate temperature. The skins are freed from all adhering dirt which soils them; they are then fleshed and dipped. Boil a quantity of water, sufficient for a bath for all the skins, with bran, seven or eight pounds for each skin. Cover the boiler, and when the liquor has sufficiently fermented, pour it into a vat in which the skins, previously rinsed, have been deposited.

While the skins are getting warm, heat another quantity of water till it simmers, and mix it with the ferment made at the beginning of the operation. Take the skins out of the bath, pour the fresh mixture into the vat, mix with it salt in the proportion of a little more than a pound for each skin, stir, and deposit the hides in it. Six hours after withdrawing the skins replace them, after a portion of the liquid has been previously taken out, heated, and well mixed with the contents of the vat. Repeat this operation every six hours during the two succeeding days. As soon as the hair is ready to come off, remove it from the surface; then the skins are passed over lightly upon the flesh, soak them in cold water for a quarter of an hour, replace them in the vat, and leave them until sufficiently raised, being careful to keep the vat perfectly covered so as to retain the heat. The raising is generally completed at the end of three days, if a portion of the liquor in the vat has been reheated from time to time.

Rinse the skins, and let them soak for some hours in fresh water. Remove the hair where it is ready to be detached, rinse the skins, pass lightly over the flesh side, soak some hours in water, and deposit them again in the vat in order to *raise* them.

This method is very convenient for tanners who manufacture on a small scale, as it is inexpensive.

Decomposition of the White Dressings.

These dressings are sour pastes of barley, rye, or wheat, which, under certain circumstances, undergo a decomposition, and it is believed that lightning produces this effect. Some tanners place in the vat scraps of old iron enveloped in linen rags upon the approach of a thunder storm; while others dissolve from one-half to one pound of sal ammoniac in the vats, under the belief that these substances prevent the injurious consequences of the *turning* of the liquors. When the dressings experience this kind of decomposition, they are unfit for any further use, and render the skin so soft and spongy that the quality of the leather would be impaired.

The long continuance of the heat of the summer causes this decomposition, and the quality of the dressings is more likely to be injured in the three summer months than in all the rest of the year.

Cold has no influence upon them, it only diminishes their efficacy; and the skins may be allowed to remain in them even when the surface is frozen, if afterwards they are replaced in fresh dressings.

CHAPTER XXXII.

RYE DRESSING, OR TRANSYLVANIA LEATHER.

The Transylvanians work their hides about the same way as Wallachians. Their method differs only in this, the latter use 20 lbs. of barley while the former use only 15 lbs. of rye, which they divide into two portions. It enters 10 lbs. in the first composition, and eight in the second. As the grounds of rye keep their strength and quality longer than those of barley, on account of the gluten they contain, they are not thrown away, but are used even after decantation of the sour liquor, which renders this process less costly than the other.

We have given the above processes to satisfy manufacturers, rather than to induce them to use them;

for the dressings with barley, and generally with grains, are not followed now, on account of the influence of the temperature on them. The process described in the following Chapter is the most used now.

CHAPTER XXXIII.

RAISING BY SOUR TAN LIQUOR.

THIS method was first practised in Germany, but has since been adopted in many parts of France.

This process is the most difficult, but is very advantageous, as it is the beginning of the main tanning operations, and serves to abridge the time occupied by them, and the leather prepared by it is of much superior quality to that treated by lime, barley, or rye. We shall describe this process minutely and fully, commencing with the account of those originally employed.

The first is by Champion. When this method was first employed in France the depilation was effected by the action of heat; and to prevent the putrefaction, from one pound to one pound and a half of salt was sprinkled over one-half of the surface of each skin—the other half being turned over upon it, and the edges brought together so as to prevent the escape of the salt. From fifteen to twenty hides were salted in this manner, and placed one above the other, being left thus four or five hours in spring and autumn, and seven or eight in winter. At the end of this time the skins were folded again in the opposite direction, the bellies being placed upon the backs, and the heads under the tails, the whole being piled upon one another so as to be exposed equally to heat. The skins were first dried with the hair on, and were then soaked for eight days in running water, beaten with the feet or the mace, and again soaked during four to five days. They were beaten a second time, rinsed and drained upon the horse, after which they were salted as before described. After being freed from acid by the influence of heat, to which they were exposed in a tight vaulted apartment, they were soaked in running water. Then the skins were subjected to the steeping in sour tan liquor, which softens and enlarges the fibres, opens the pores, and raises them to receive the first tanning.

Another method was to deprive the skins of hair by stacking them on heaps, as represented below, and pro-

Fig. 39.

moting warmth by covering them with straw or manure, until the hair is ready to be removed. If it comes off with difficulty upon the horse, its separation is facilitated by the use of sand spread upon the hair side. This method is disadvantageous, and injurious to the skins.

To prepare the tan liquor for the bath, the bark which has been used for the second or third set of vats, in the tan-yard, is deposited in a vat thus arranged that the liquor percolating through it may be received in a draining-well or vessel placed under it; from which it can be returned into the main receptacle again and again, so as to secure an increase of strength by repeated filtrations and solutions. This liquor has a clear red color, an acid taste like that of good vinegar, and from this solution a number of baths can be made of different strengths. A series of eight baths may be made, the first one containing one part of the liquor and seven of water, and so until the full strength is attained. When the skins are freed from hair, washed and fleshed, they are soaked two days in clear water, in summer, and four or five in winter, being careful to change the water every day, and to let the skins drain for three hours. When the skins are ready for *raising*, upon being steeped, they are deposited in vats containing the infusion of spent tan, being first placed into the weakest. While remaining in these, they are taken out every morning and evening, and allowed to drain over the vats during three hours. Towards the end of the proceeding, when in stronger infusions, a removal of the vats once a day is sufficient.

The English tanners use baths with less acid than those employed in France; they are infusions of fresh bark in water. They use a large number of baths, increasing gradually in strength, and with vats of sufficient capacity for fifteen or twenty skins.

From all the methods primitively used in France, the best is that followed at St. Germain, and thus described by Delalande: They generally employ twelve infusions, the two last being new, and the ten first consisting of old infusions of tan. Each bath is prepared for twelve skins.

The skins having been scraped and washed, are deposited in the first infusions, the weakest of all. It is necessary to have the bath a little acid. Twenty-four hours after, raise the twelve skins, let them drain half an hour, and introduce them into a stronger infusion;

throw away the water of the above, which, having been used ten times, has no more strength.

The second infusion, while a little stronger, has no sensible acid action on the tongue; the third has a little more strength, and so forth. Every morning raise the twelve skins from one infusion to put them into another, until they have been treated in the ten vats. When taken out from the tenth infusion the skins are put into the first new infusion. This first infusion is composed of a sour water in which 20 lbs. of coarse tan are added for every skin. The skins stay ten days in this first infusion. At last the skins pass from this first infusion into another of the same nature, to which you add 20 lbs. of coarse tan for every skin. The skins stay ten days in this infusion, and then are ready to be tanned. An elevated temperature is injurious in the weakest infusions, and when the operation is conducted in summer, be careful to not let the temperature raise too high.

The sour liquor was prepared in the following manner; five ordinary vats being made use of:—

The *first*, or No. 1, being destined for the weakest, and the last, or No. 5, for the strongest infusions.

The spent tan from the pit in which skins had been imbedded for the third time was deposited in No. 5 and warm water poured upon it through a pipe or spout. The water filtering through the tan passed into a draining well, and was pumped out after four or five days constituting an amount of tan-liquor sufficient for four of the ordinary weak vats.

The pit was again filled with water, which after becoming tan-liquor was transferred into the vats Nos. 1 and 2, and the contents of Nos. 3 and 4 were composed of the liquors of Nos. 1 and 2; again it is passed through No. 5, and the infusion originally drawn from No. 5 was replaced in it. The 11th and 12th vats, originally referred to, were made up from the contents of No. 5, and the other ten from the contents of Nos. 3 and 4 diluted in the proper manner with those of Nos. 1 and 2.

The best tanners in France use now the following process:—

The skins are carefully fleshed and deprived of all superfluous parts, and soaked for 24 hours in fresh water. When perfectly clean and well rinsed, they are deposited in the liquors by which they are to be depilated and raised. These liquors are contained in a series of eight or ten vats made of oak, hooped with iron; they are 3 ft. 8 inches in depth, and 5 ft. 5 inches in diameter. In each vat deposit seven or eight skins, and cover them completely with the liquor.

Let them soak 24 hours in the first vat, which contains the weakest liquor, and during that time take them out twice to drain one hour, being placed on boards which are inclined so that the fluid dripping from them runs back into the vat. After two days, take them out, let them drain one hour, and place them in the second vat, which contains a stronger infusion. The same operations are repeated daily until the skins have passed through all the vats. If at the end of this time the hair appears ready to fall off, it is removed from the skins by working them in the ordinary manner upon the horse with the round knife. In cold weather it is sometimes the case that the process has not been sufficiently completed at the end of the time mentioned, and that the skins require exposure to the strong liquors for five or ten days longer, in order that the hair may be removed with facility.

The skins thus prepared have not yet been raised sufficiently to be tanned, and for this purpose must be exposed to the influence of four more vats of tan-liquor gradually increasing in strength. The mode of operating is the same as described above. After having passed through these four vats, they are deposited in a vat of the size before mentioned, nearly full of strong fresh tan juice, which has been previously thoroughly mixed by repeatedly stirring with 4 lbs. 6 oz. of sulphuric acid of 66°. During the first day of their soaking, the skins are taken out twice, and left to drain two hours; on the second day they are removed twice, being allowed to drain the same length of time, and on the morning of the third day they are changed to the last vat, which contains the strongest tan-liquor that can be procured, previously mixed as before with 4 lbs. 6 oz. of sulphuric acid. On the evening take out, drain for an hour, and replace in the vat. The next day and the day after, take out again, drain the same length of time, and deposite again in the liquor. Three hours after the last draining, they are finally removed and are ready for tanning. In cold weather the skins should be kept in the vats two days instead of one. The flesh side should always be placed upwards in the vats.

Preparation of the Tan-Liquor.

The tan-liquor used in the processes above described is obtained by the filtration of water through the partially exhausted bark of the second and third series of vats in the tan-yard, and derive from it their astringent and acid properties. This tan, after remaining for a time in contact with the skins in the vat, loses and gives up to them the greatest portion of its tanning ingredients, and then is readily disposed to ferment or acidify, still retaining some of its tanning properties, but becoming more and more acid as these are removed from it by absorption into the tissues of the skins. These qualities are calculated to injure the leather and make its removal from the vats necessary before it has been too long exposed to the action of the exhausted and acidified tan.

For the purpose of preparing the sour liquor, the tan is deposited in an empty vat in which a draining well composed of oak planks has been erected, as shown in the following figure. This well is so arranged that the

Fig. 40.

fluid can only enter it from below, and a pump adapted to it serves to withdraw its contents, or they may be removed in a bucket. The vat is then filled with water, and the solution formed by its filtration through the tan, is raised after a few days from the well, and is again poured over the surface. This proceeding is repeated over and over again until the tan is entirely exhausted of its soluble material. The top of the vat is kept close to avoid evaporation of the fluid. In place of this method the tan can be exhausted in the same manner as we have described in treating of tanning extracts.

From fifteen to thirty days are usually required to give to the liquors the proper degree of strength and acidity.

This operation can be done only in large establishments; however, with few vats only it is easy to make tanning juice; the following is the best method: Put the old bark into two vats that you fill with water after three or four weeks of maceration, make in the middle of the vat a hole large enough to introduce a pail, draw the juice and pour it back on the same vat, where it stays five days more, repeat the same operation until the juice has the required strength. Pass it through a sieve to have it clear.

This juice being withdrawn, pour some new water, leave eight days, and draw. The juice is weaker. For the depilation and swelling three vats and five solutions are sufficient. The first solution is very weak, and its strength increases progressively. Proceed as follows: Make a new solution, composed of pure water, or better, very weak juice, in which you put four baskets of tan. Introduce the skins, beat them, raise them three times a day, morning, noon, and night, and every time leave them to drain one-quarter of an hour; draw off the liquor.

The second day, put the skins in a weak solution composed of three-quarters water and one-quarter juice, with six baskets of tan, raise three times during the day, leave to drain one-quarter of an hour each time, and throw away the liquor. Introduce the skins in another solution composed of one-half juice, one-half water, and six baskets of tan, as shown in Figure 41. Leave two

Fig. 41.

days, raising three times a day, being careful to let drain half an hour.

The fourth solution, formed of the clear juice of the

above, lasts twenty-six days. The first day introduce the skins in the morning, and for six skins add thirty-six pounds of bark. The second and third, add in the morning twenty pounds of the same bark. During these three days, raise three times a day, leave to drain half an hour every time. The fourth day add twenty pounds of bark, and raise twice. The fifth, raise, leave to drain half an hour, stir, add forty pounds of bark, and leave eight or nine days without moving. After nine days pass in the last solution or pure juice, raise twice a day for three days, add twenty-one pounds of bark in the morning. The fourth day raise, leave to drain three-quarters of an hour, and put the skins back, being careful to throw between each four, eight pounds of bark. Leave eight days, and then the skins are ready to be tanned.

This process can be used by small tanners, and to terminate the swelling you can put sulphuric acid in the two last solutions, but instead of eight or nine days leave the skins only three days.

CHAPTER XXXIV.

RAISING BY YEAST.

YEAST has the property of raising skins, and has been used for this purpose. It is mixed in a vat with warm water, the vat is covered, and fermentation takes place. When this is fully established, a quantity of salt is thrown in, and the skins are deposited in the vat, the contents of which are then treated precisely as in the case of barley dressing. The operation can be conducted in the cold, but is much more rapid and successful if the temperature of the liquor be kept elevated.

CHAPTER XXXV.

WORKING ON THE BEAM.

AFTER the skins have been prepared for the separation of the hair upon them by any one of the numerous processes which have been described, the next proceeding is to remove it entirely by working them upon the beam. For this purpose the workman makes a kind of pad of two or three folded skins, which he places upon the horse, and over which the skin to be operated upon is laid with the hair side up, and he then scrapes the surface strongly from above downwards with the *scraper*. After the hair is completely removed the skin is washed and soaked in a trough, or vat full of water, and is subjected to the following operations:—

1. The flesh and other parts not properly belonging to the skin are removed with a sharp knife called the *flesher*, and the skin is again washed and soaked in fresh water.

2. The projecting filaments or shreds, and those parts of the borders of the skin which are thicker than the rest, are cut off with a sharp knife, and the skin is again immersed in cold water. The portions thus removed may be set aside to manufacture glue.

3. The hair side is then well rubbed and smoothed down with a stone, similar to that used for sharpening the knife-blades, but which is set in a wooden handle. This done, the skin is dipped for the third time in fresh water.

4. Both sides are well scraped and smoothed with a knife having a curved blade, so as to equalize the surfaces and remove all foreign substances.

A dozen skins can be worked in this way by one man in the course of a day.

SECTION V.

TANNING PROCESS.

HAVING completed the consideration of the various operations to which skins are subjected before they are prepared for tanning, we proceed to give an account of the latter process, beginning with a description of the vats in which it is conducted.

CHAPTER XXXVI.

TAN VATS.

THAT name is given to large square holes excavated in the ground, or to large vats in oak with a circular form. The first are still in use in several countries; they are seven and a half feet square by six feet deep. They are in masonry, and covered inside with a kind of mortar made with lime, sand, and cement. In Paris they use oak vats of a round form and sunk into the ground. The latter are preferred to the first, and are not subject to the same inconveniences.

1. Whatever care is taken, those in masonry always lose some of the infusion.

2. The lime of the cement combines with the tannin, and forms an insoluble tannate of lime.

3. The vats in oak wood, carefully made, do not lose any liquid.

4. Oak wood, instead of neutralizing a part of the tannin, furnishes to the liquor a new quantity of tannin.

These facts should induce all manufacturers to use them.

All tanners do not operate in the same manner. We shall be careful to indicate all the little changes they have made in the common process.

After the skins have undergone all the preliminary operations, they are cut in two, and stratified along with tan in the following manner:—

In the bottom of the vat put a bed of spent bark, about half an inch thick, cover it with about a quarter of an inch of new bark, well moistened, and place a skin on the top. In square vats, put two hides in one way and two in another, and set across them a fifth one; but in circular vats lay the hides all round, then be careful to turn exactly at the right, and fix them so that the tail of the last rests on the right leg of the preceding. By following this process a vat containing fifteen or sixteen skins can be filled in twelve hours.

On the first layer of skin spread another bed of powder, and continue thus by laying alternately a bed of powder and one of skin. Be careful to have powder between every part of the *skin, for if it has none the skin will not be equally tanned, and consequently will not be equally strong and solid. Some thicker places require more bark, but the shoulders and legs, being thinner, require less.

In Paris all tanners moisten the bark before using it. For this purpose they throw water upon it and mix it thoroughly with a shovel, then it can be divided more easily; however, some manufacturers use it just as it comes from the mill. The Parisian method is the best, as it is not injurious to the health of the men, who by using dry powdered bark are exposed to its inhalation.

In speaking of the tan, we have said that the English cracked the bark; several tanners have adopted this process, but it is not followed everywhere. It is generally admitted that the first ought to be fine, the second a little coarser, and the third very coarsely ground.

When all the skins are laid in the vat, it may happen that the vat is not entirely full, and, whilst the skins have been uniformly put up, some empty spaces are found, they are filled with powder; or rather when you have put in a sufficient quantity of new powder, distribute it so that the surface is equal all over.

In small tanneries, the pits are not always filled on the same day, and frequently only a small number of hides are placed in them at a time. As it is essential in these cases that they should be kept fully moistened, more water should be added each time that the new skins are deposited in them; and in order that the relative position of the contents may not be disturbed, the surface should be covered with a coarse cloth, and the water carefully poured over from a watering pot, and allowed to infiltrate gradually.

The water being equally distributed through, and in sufficient quantity, the vatting of the pit is completed. In establishments where they do not commence vatting until a number of hides sufficient to fill the vats has been prepared, the watering should be completed in one operation. When this is the case, it may happen that the tan rapidly absorbs all the water poured in, and in a day or two appears perfectly dry. More water should then be added, until it is certain that the vat contains enough to moisten all the hides thoroughly. The quantity required for each hide is about 12 gallons.

When, as often happens, particularly in small establishments, the tanner is compelled to place together in the same vat, hides in different states of progress, that is, those of the first, second, and third treatment, the following mode of arranging them must be resorted to. Those of the third treatment are to be deposited at the bottom, those of the second above them in the middle, and those of the first on top; so that, when those which have gone through the three treatments are taken out to dry, those of the second may occupy their place at the bottom, those which were before at the surface being in the middle, and the fresh hides which are to be subjected to the first treatment being placed at the top. This convenient method promotes an equalization of the tanning, and should always be adopted; because the continued exposure of the same set of hides to those parts of the vats which possess the greatest tanning power, and of others to the upper strata of bark which contains the least, is thus avoided. The substances at the bottom of the vat, undoubtedly, are those which possess the strongest tanning power, because the descending infusion, passing through the layers of tan above, becomes more fully impregnated with tannin and extractive matter than that portion which remains in contact with the upper strata of the solid materials. Moreover, the complete penetration and combination of these matters with the fibrine and gelatine of the skins is promoted by the pressure of the superincumbent hides, the tan, and the column of fluid.

When the ordinary arrangement is adopted, it is customary, in filling the second vat, to place at its bottom those hides which have been at the top of the first, and so on through the ranges of vats. This is done for the purpose of promoting a uniform impregnation of all the hides; since, if always kept in the same position in their progress through the yard, those occupying the lowest one would be the most thoroughly charged with tannin.

As oak bark is variable in quality, it is scarcely possible to give, with certainty, any proportion which it should bear to the skins. Skins weighing 110 lbs. usually require, however, about double that amount of bark. From 33 to 44 lbs. usually suffice for each of the skins from Brescia, which do not commonly weigh more than 26 lbs. Weak, thin and poor, or dry hides, being of inferior quality, require very little bark, and scarcely acquire any increase of substance. Common hides scarcely ever need exposure to more than three treatments, the first being given upon the grain, and the others upon the flesh sides. The finest powder is used for the first process, which should occupy three months. Coarser stuff is employed for the second, which should take four months, while the coarse bark alone is sufficient for the third exposure, occupying five months. This length of time may be considered sufficient for tanning, though the best tanners extend it, giving to their hides four, or for the best qualities, even five exposures in the pit.

Fresh hides exhaust the tanning ingredients to which they are exposed in the first process, much more rapidly than they do in the subsequent ones; and hence the necessity of a longer treatment in the second and third vats than in the first. After they have been thoroughly fed in the first, further contact with the spent materials would be useless, as these are almost entirely deprived of activity; and it may be very injurious to them by promoting putrefaction. In passing through the last vats, however, they run no such risks, for being in contact with strong solutions of bark, they are still constantly—though from the resistance of their already tanned surface gradually—absorbing tannin and acquiring density.

Small portions of alum are added to the tan by some manufacturers, with the intention of diminishing the impermeability of these tanned surfaces, and hastening the process in its latter stage. The practice is, however, neither a common nor a desirable one.

In changing hides from one pit to another, be careful to remove from their surfaces all the spent tan which covers them, so that there may be no mixture of effete matter with the fresh bark. Some tanners even take the trouble of beating and shaking the hides each time they are changed.

There is another form of vat, recently invented, and patented by J. S. Wheat, of Wheeling, Va., who makes the following statement:—

"I have my tanning process in full operation in this city, tanning leather in $\frac{1}{10}$ of the time required by the old process, and I warrant the leather to be of the finest quality for wear. This process combines the handling or moving of the hides in the liquor, the circulation of the liquor through the vats, the pressure upon the hides, and the circulation of the liquor through the tan bark in the leaches, all at the same operation, and the operation may be suspended upon one or more of the vats while it is continued in the others. Therefore amongst its advantages, in addition to the short time consumed in tanning leather, is the great saving of labor."

Fig. 42 is a perspective view of the apparatus, and Fig. 43 is a horizontal section through the middle of the vats combined with a horizontal section through the several reservoirs.

The leather is placed in the air-tight cylindrical vats X, X'', X''', X'''', and the tanning liquor which is prepared by mixing water with bark in the rectangular reservoirs E'', E''', E'''', E''''', below, is made to circulate through the

Fig. 42.

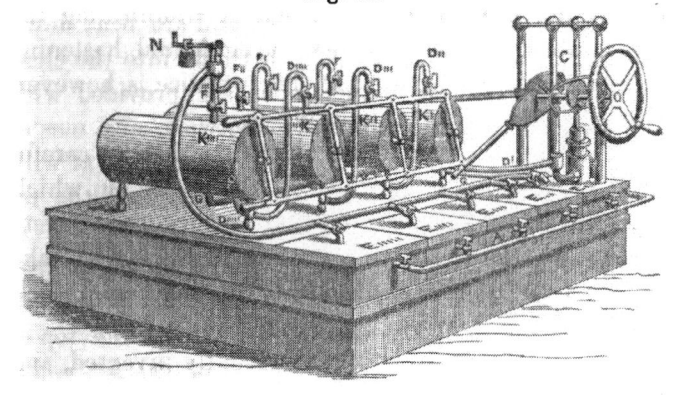

Fig. 43.

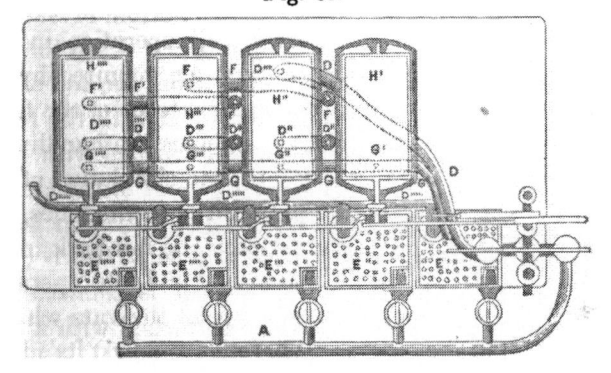

vats by means of a force pump C. The liquor in the vat is subjected to pressure regulated by a weighed valve, and the hides are forced through the liquor by being placed on vibrating frames H (Fig. 43) within the vats.

The water is mixed with the bark in the reservoirs E'', E''', E'''', E''''', and these reservoirs have perforated false bottoms through which the clear liquor is strained into the lower parts of the reservoirs.

From these places it is drawn out by means of the

pump, through branches from the pipe A, which pass through the ends of the reservoirs, and are bent down so as to extend through the false bottoms into the clear liquor below. These branch-pipes are provided with stopcocks, so that the connection between any one of them and the pump may be opened or cut off at will, and thus the liquor may be drawn from such of the reservoirs as the operator may desire.

From the pump the liquor is forced into the vats through the pipe D, which has two branches leading into the bottoms of the vats X, X''. From the top of vat X a pipe D'' leads to the bottom of vat X'', and a pipe F leads to the bottom of vat X'''. The pipe D''' leads from the top of vat X'' to the bottom of vat X''', and the pipe F'' leads from the top of vat X'' to the bottom of vat X'''. A pipe D'''' leads from the top of vat X''' to the pipe F''', which is connected with the top of vat X''''. All of these pipes are furnished with stopcocks, so that any vat may be thrown out of the circulation by simply opening and closing the proper cocks.

From the upper end of pipe F''' a pipe D'''' leads down to the reservoirs, with all of which it is connected by branch-pipes; each branch being furnished with a stopcock.

It will thus be seen that the tanning liquid is kept in constant circulation through the vats containing the hides, and through the reservoirs containing the bark; extracting in its course the tannin from the bark and carrying it to the hides. The liquor in its ascent may be passed through such of the vats and reservoirs as the operator may desire by simply turning stopcocks.

In the upper end of the pipe F''', but below the exit of pipe D'''', is a valve which is pressed down by a weight upon the lever N. By setting this weight at the proper point upon the lever, the pressure of the liquor within the vats may be adjusted to any desired degree. An emptying pipe G, connected with the bottoms of all the vats by branch-pipes, leads into the reservoirs E.

The frames H, in the vats, are hung upon shafts, which pass through stuffing-boxes in the ends of the vats, and they receive a vibratory motion from eccentrics on the pump-shaft, with which they are connected by levers in such a manner that by simply lifting the levers out of connection the action of the frame in any vat may be suspended. The hides are introduced into the vats through manholes provided for the purpose.

CHAPTER XXXVII.

HEALD'S APPARATUS FOR TANNING HIDES.

WM. H. HEALD, of Baltimore, invented and patented, in 1860, an apparatus for tanning hides. We give below a description of its construction and operation. The Fig. 44 represents a perspective view of said apparatus.

Figure 45 represents a longitudinal vertical section through the same.

The work of repeatedly raising the hides from the vat, for the purpose of exposing them to the air, constitutes one of the most laborious tasks in the operation of tanning. This invention relates to the construction of an apparatus to which the hides are united in such a manner that they will hang loosely and vertically in the vat, and may be raised from the vat with facility, and, when raised, lie in a pile, and the drippings therefrom all run back into the vat.

To enable others skilled in the art to make and use this invention, we shall proceed to describe its construction and operation.

Fig. 44.

A represents the vat which contains the tan-liquor. *B* represents a triangular frame, which is suspended within said vat by means of ropes or chains, *C,* and which can be raised or lowered by turning the crank *D,* and the drums *E,* around which the ropes or chains, *C,* are wound. The frame *B* has grooves, *a,* cut on its inner

HEALD'S APPARATUS FOR TANNING HIDES. 249

sides, into which the ends of the bars *b* are inserted. The hides, *c*, to be tanned are hung over these bars, as represented in Fig. 45, and one or more such grooves

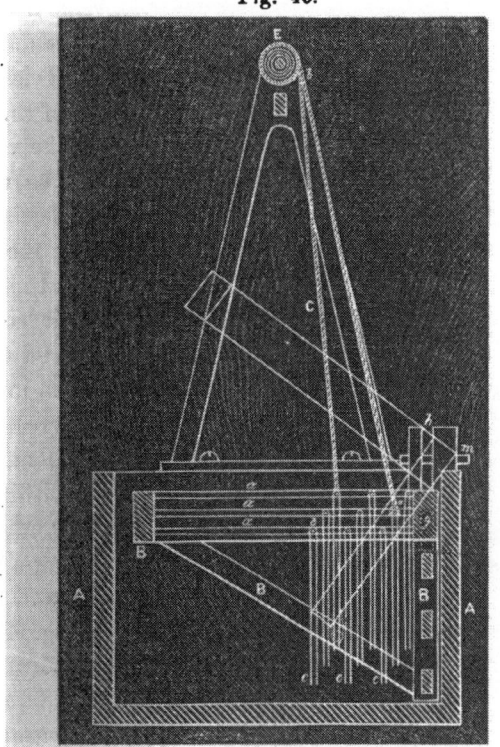

Fig. 45.

may be used for securing the bars therein. When three such grooves are used, the hides may be suspended, as represented in Fig. 45, where the bar of each consecutive hide is inserted in a different groove, by which arrangement they can be inserted and removed with greater facility than when they are all inserted in one groove, and when they are packed closely together. The frame, *B*, has pivots, *g*, at its side, which slide in corresponding grooves, h, in the sides of the vat, and which cause the frame to move perpendicularly on being raised or lowered. When the frame is to be raised for the purpose of exposing the hides to the air, or for removing them, the crank D is turned and the frame B rises, and as the side near the pivots, g, is somewhat heavier than its opposite side, the frame will lean towards that side, and when arrived at the top of the vat, it will be raised on the edge of the side of the vat, as represented in a, b, Fig. 45, and may then be raised to any degree of inclination, or almost to a horizontal position, leaving just sufficient inclination for the drippings to run back into the vat. The frame in this position may be secured by braces, stops, or their equivalents. To prevent the frame from being raised out of the groove, h, by inadvertence, the stop pins, m, may be used, by which the motion of the frame is arrested as soon as the pivots, g, come in contact with them. By this apparatus the hides, when once hung within the frame B, do not require any further handling, and can be raised and lowered with facility, thus saving a great amount of labor in the operation of tanning; and when frame B arrives at the position shown in Fig. 44 the hides lie on top of each other in a pile, and may be conveniently removed. In this position, too, the frame is more readily filled with hides, as it is comparatively clear of the vat, though ready to turn into it when desired. In the mere handling of the hides these machines save much labor, as they can be immersed in the vat or raised out again into a pile, whence they can be removed and others put in their place.

From the time the hides are placed in the frames until they are ready to be laid away in bark, is six weeks, thus saving four or five weeks over the old style of reels.

CHAPTER XXXVIII.

TIME NECESSARY FOR TANNING.

The importance of discovering some process which should shorten the time usually occupied in tanning, without injuring the beauty and durability of the leather, and which should also diminish the expense of the manufacture, by substituting some less costly materials for oak bark, has long been appreciated by chemists and practical men.

Among others, who have devoted much attention to this subject, is Seguin, who, acting upon his opinion that the combination of tannin with the gelatine and fibrine of skins might be much accelerated by presenting it to them in a liquid and concentrated form, succeeded in greatly shortening the time required for tanning. But experience has shown that, though the leather prepared by such means is, to all appearances, well tanned, it does not possess the requisite quantities. It is not thoroughly and uniformly impregnated; for, while the outer layers of the two surfaces combine rapidly with tannin, a deposit of gallic acid and extractive matter forms a compact coating, which prevents their complete penetration, and renders their interior inaccessible to the liquid. This leather is dry, and by no means durable, its interior consisting of untanned hides. We shall speak of it in treating of Seguin's process.

Experience has shown that, to insure the perfection of leather, all the gelatine and fibrine of the original skins must be made to combine with tannin, and that this combination must be effected in the most gradual way, the accomplishment of which is only to be procured by exposures to solutions, which at first are weak, and afterwards are increased in strength, until at last complete saturation is arrived at. After this entire conversion of substance has been attained, further exposure only serves to injure the texture of the hide by introducing into it a dry, hard, and horny matter, which renders them brittle and easily penetrable by moisture, and to consume uselessly the time and money of the manufacturer.

If, on the contrary, they have been exposed too short a time, they will be imperfect and wanting in the requisite weight and solidity. It is therefore an established fact that 12 or 18 months are required for the complete tanning of the best qualities of hides, they being found to increase in strength and weight up to the end of that time, which is the usual duration of the process in England as well as in this country. Still there, as well as here, skins are often sent into the market after an exposure of six or ten months, and even less.

CHAPTER XXXIX.

PROPORTIONS OF THE BARK USED.

The proportions of bark required vary considerably, according to the species, the quality and destination of the hides. For the skins of the butchers in Paris, weighing 112 lbs., at times from 336 to 393 lbs. of tan are used. Sometimes 292 lbs. divided into 4 parts are sufficient, 90 for the first, and 67 for the others.

In the provinces of France they vary much in weight. At Bordeaux the liquors are strong, while in Brittany they are weak. In some places they do not use less than 675 lbs. of bark for 225 lbs. of fresh skin, the weight of which after tanning has increased to 337 pounds.

CHAPTER XL.

DRYING OF THE LEATHER.

The drying of the leather, however simple a process it may appear, requires the utmost skill and attention on the part of the workmen, and the nicest determination of the point to which it should be carried. Skins dried too slowly, and in moist situations, are liable to mould, which is greatly to their injury, while those which are dried too rapidly, or during exposure to the direct rays of the sun, become hard and brittle.

In order to prevent either of these extremes, every factory should have attached to it a drying-room proportioned to its wants, in which numerous openings or windows admit a free current of air, while the leather is protected from the direct influence of solar heat.

The skins, when sufficiently tanned, are to be taken from the pits without being shaken or beaten, and are to be stretched on pegs or hung up by their heads from large nails, each one being kept expanded by two or three sticks passed through from side to side, so that all parts may be uniformly exposed to the air. When they have begun to whiten and have become slightly stiff, but before they are perfectly dry, they are stretched out upon a clean place and scoured with the spent tan with which they are still covered. When well cleaned in this way, they are then to be trod out and beaten with the soles of the feet in every direction, upon both sides; and after the inequalities and protuberances of surface have been made to disappear by this flattening process, they are assorted in sizes and piled up in heaps.

While the skins are stretched in the drying-room, they should be beaten twice daily, at morning and evening, upon the flesh side with a round-face wooden mallet. If the skins should be dry, the operation may be facilitated by moistening their surface with a wet brush. This process imparts firmness.

The *Shoe and Leather Reporter* has lately published a very good article on the drying of tanned leather, an extract of which we think will interest the reader.

"To overcome difficulties, we must first appreciate them. The difficulties and delays in drying leather as above described are very great. The amount of leather which tanners require to have in the loft exposed to the risk of fire is always very large, and at particular seasons of the year so large that some find it difficult to obtain the requisite amount of insurance, even at a very high rate of premium.

"We think it quite within our experience to state that a tannery turning out 150 sides per day must have exposed about 5,000 sides; which at 2½ per cent. would amount to $500 a year for the item of insurance. The loss of interest and inconvenience of delay must also be added, to appreciate fully the difficulties experienced under our present system.

"We hope to be able to show that no tanner need have over 1000 sides exposed at any one time, to enable him to roll and furnish 150 or even 200 per day. This estimate, it will be perceived, would cover a first class tannery.

"To make this improvement of practical value, it must

be adapted to our present buildings. But if we describe a perfect drying loft, the features which are new will be appreciated, and may be applied to each tanner as his circumstances may permit.

"The building should be as high as possible, not certainly less than twenty, and if fifty feet from the base floor to the peak, all the better.

"The lower floor should be closed against the dampness of the yard, or if placed on the ground, from the moisture which would arise. No opening or window should be allowed except from the lower part immediately over the base floor, and this opening should be by a *board trap* opening, say of one foot wide, so hung on hinges as to be easily regulated, and should extend all around the building. The other opening should be in the extreme peak of the building, and should also be so constructed as to be easily opened and closed. A drying loft thus constructed will always, by its own action, have a draft passing through it, even when the outside weather would indicate that there was *no air stirring*.

"In ordinary drying weather such a loft will dry wet leather from the vats in five or six days. But this will not of itself accomplish what we want. We must have some artificial means of drying when the weather is not favorable.

"This artificial heat can in no way, in our judgment, so satisfactorily be applied as by steam pipes. These are the best distributors of heat of any that have yet been applied.

"Heat or dry air can be forced by blowers into a loft, but to do this effectually considerable power is required. Steam pipes, when properly laid, are self-acting, and distribute heat more gently and uniformly than stoves, however placed.

"Some of the conditions to be observed are the following: The boiler which generates the steam must be lower than the base floor. The opening from which the escape steam pipe should enter should be from the top of the boiler, and the return pipe should enter at the bottom; when thus placed, there will be none of that bursting of pipe of which we hear so much.

"The pipe should be as nearly as possible on a level or incline towards the boiler, so that the condensed steam or water will run freely in that direction, but where eight or ten pounds of steam pressure is kept on the boiler, little difficulty need be apprehended. It is only when there is no pressure of steam that the water freezes in the pipe and gives trouble.

"But we omit practical details, since no tanner will attempt to adopt this improvement without consulting a practical pipe fitter, and they are now to be found in most every town.

"Experience has indicated that about five thousand feet of pipes properly laid will do all the drying that any ordinary tanner will require at eight pounds pressure. This pipe should be laid on the floor as near the centre as possible, and not around the sides of the building, as some have placed it. The pipe to be covered with lattice wood work to prevent disturbance.

"Experience may show that the side may be the proper place to fasten the pipe if placed opposite and inside the opening of which we have spoken; for the current of air from the outside may be sufficiently strong to force the heated or dry air to the centre, and thus form a current up to the top opening. But we are sure without such opening the air forms a current up the side of the building, and does not penetrate the centre.

"The effect of side openings, other than the kind here

recommended, is to create counter currents and destroy the whole effect.

"This whole subject is both new and interesting. We do not think there is any novelty in the use of steam pipes in drying lofts. But we think that most of the effect has been lost heretofore by reason of the improper construction of the loft.

"We think that a tanner may run partitions inclosing three or four bents of his tannery, from base floor to the peak, and dry more leather in these few bents than he does now in his whole loft.

"With a proper heating apparatus in connection with a properly constructed drying loft, sole-leather wet from the vats can be dried in forty-eight hours, ready for the roller."

CHAPTER XLI.

BEATING OF THE LEATHER.

AFTER the skins have remained in pile for a day, they are exposed to the air, as before, for four days. When nearly dry, they are taken down and pressed under planks heavily loaded with large stones. The next day they are spread out upon an oak or marble table and beaten with an iron mallet, so as to compress their tissue and render them smooth and compact. The operation is performed as shown in the figure.

This proceeding should never be omitted, whatever may have been the original preparation of the skins for the vat. Lime hides should, however, be treated before they are dried, as otherwise the hair side surface would be exposed to the danger of being broken and rendered uneven.

Fig. 46.

The process of beating leather is essential to give it firmness and durability, and to make it impervious to moisture. It is only the first step of the manipulation which the shoemaker finds it so necessary to continue upon the lapstone.

The leather, after being thus hammered, is now thoroughly dried for the last time, and piled up in a dry and well-ventilated loft. Before it is ready for market, the leather should be repeatedly shuffled, as it were; that is, the position of each hide must be changed, and the piles spread out in the manner of an open fan, and pressed as before, under planks and superincumbent weights.

Having undergone these different processes for nearly a month, it is again piled preparatory to being sent into the market. Not satisfied with this management of it, some tanners even take the unnecessary trouble of storing it away in cellars for some time before they consider it thoroughly seasoned.

CHAPTER XLII.

BEATING AND ROLLING BY MACHINERY.

THE process described above was a tedious and laborious mode of operating, which is rarely resorted to now, and has been superseded by machinery. The principal object of these machines was to accelerate the process and diminish the labor, and afterwards it was found that they also accomplished the desiderata of imparting smoothness, compactness, and uniform thickness to the leather.

In the earlier stages of this invention the imperfection of the machinery rendered it necessary to finish the beating by hand, but improvement grew with experience and has resulted in some perfect apparatus.

Sterlingue & Co. were the pioneers in this branch of ingenuity, and proposed the use of a hammer like those employed for forging iron, but grooved, and an anvil faced with brass. The other portions of their machine are a table for receiving the hides and cylinders for the cords or straps which kept the leather extended, their axes being connected with an endless chain in such a manner that the straps which are rolled upon them on one side are unrolled on the other.

The hides are allowed to be at rest during the descent of the hammer, and are moved from under it during its elevation. The blows may be increased in frequency and force at the will of the operator, and if it is thought proper to direct a number of blows upon one part of the hides, the movement can be suspended by a catch until the required number has been applied.

260   TANNING.

Having found that the horizontal position of the hammer interfered somewhat with the motion of the hides, they substituted a vertical hammer, like a pile-driver. By this improvement they obtained the alternate and successive action of a number of hammers upon the leather, and established a system by which rows of hammers of moderate weight are so arranged that those of the second row descend upon the prolongation of a line oblique to that of the first one, and fall upon the hides with a constantly increasing force.

Debergue's Machine.—This machine, invented in 1840, is described in vol. lvi. p. 40, plate 4, of French Reports of Expired Patents.

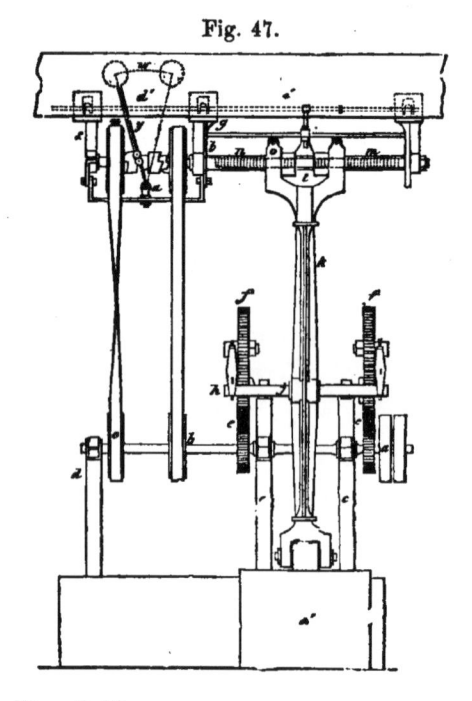

Fig. 47.

Figs. 47 and 48.
a, a. Pulleys, for communicating movement.

b. Longitudinal iron shaft.

c, c. Cast framework, supporting the shafts *b* and *g*.

d. Cast support, for the end of the shaft *b*.

e, e. Pinions, gearing with the wheels *f, f.*

g. Iron shaft, carrying the wheels *f, f*, outside of the framework.

h, h. Crank-rods, the iron pivots of which, *i, i*, are fixed by means of nuts in grooves cut in the wheels *f, f*, so that their position can be changed at pleasure.

j. Iron shaft, receiving an oscillating motion from the cranks *h* and *h*.

k. Cast-iron lever, carrying at its lower extremity a stamper or small cylinder in a fork, and having passing across it the shaft *j*, the movements of which it follows.

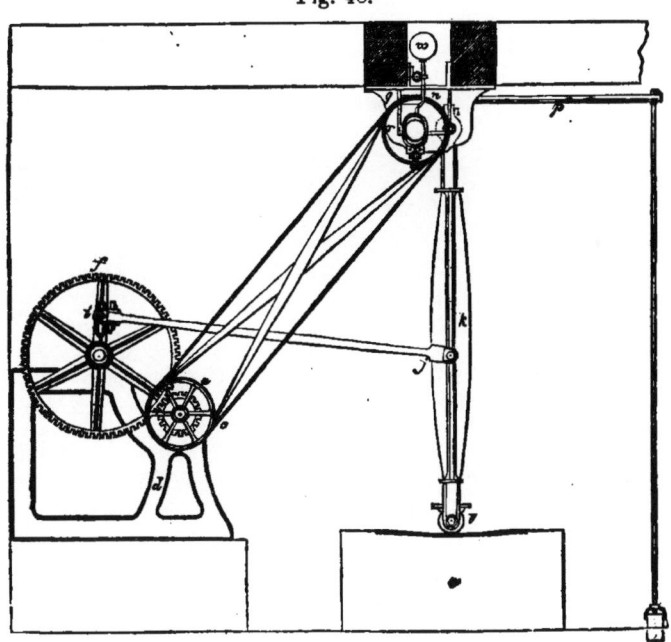

Fig. 48.

The upper part of this lever is equally divided into two branches, in each of which is a groove traversed by the iron shaft m, fixed at its extremities to double cast supports n, n. Above these grooves there are two rests, o, o, for the cast-iron lever p, which pivots upon the trunnions q, q, and to the extremity of which is attached an iron rod which supports a cast box or iron plate, or else a wooden box which can be weighted if necessary. Upon the line marked by the rests, the lever can be moved over the whole space between the two supports, and this part should be accurately adjusted, so that, whatever may be its position, the lever will weigh uniformly upon the rests. r. Iron shaft, adjusted between the two supports n, n, and resting at the other end upon a simple support s. The screw passes through the cast piece t, forming its nut, and having two projections pierced to receive the shaft m, upon which it moves when the screw is turned. As the projections of the nut t entirely fill the interval between the branches of the lever k, this lever must follow the movements of the nut exactly as if directly commanded by the screw. u, u are two pulleys, across which passes the uncut part of the screw z. These pulleys are commanded by the other pulleys v, v, the one by a straight strap, the other by a crossed one, and are turned in an opposite direction to each other.

x. Toothed shaft partaking of the rotatory motion of the main shaft, which, being traversed by a pin, but being movable to the right or left at pleasure, and fitting in the claws of the pulleys n, n, renders their movement uniform with that of the shaft. At the middle of this shaft there is a large groove, which receives two small iron stays, fixed to the interior of the oval which the lever y forms at its junction with the shaft. This lever is surmounted by a ball w, and is mounted upon an iron pivot, which is fixed upon the cross-piece a', fastened at its extremities to the supports n, n.

b'. Round iron rod having a square part at the end which slides in one of its supports, and is, by this means, prevented from being turned. This rod passes across a tail-piece, attached to the nut t, and carries two rings, c' c', fastened at a convenient part by a compressing screw. The rod also has upon it two little projections, $d'\, d'$, which engage the lever y, and give it an alternate motion to the right or left, when the tail of the nut encounters alternately the rings $c'\, c'$.

e'. Cast, marble, or wooden table, surmounted by a copper plate. The table, as the plan shows, may be either plane or concave, without any injury to the success of the process following.*

This machine is intended to produce the most complete contraction of the pores of leather that can be attained, by means of two different movements combined in one, and by a pressure of from 18 to 20 thousand weight upon a surface of some fractions of an inch, this pressure being transmitted through the whole thickness of the skins without injuring or abrading their surfaces, and compressing those of different thickness with entire uniformity.

The hides are placed upon the table e; the stamper l, to which a round, oval, curved, or straight form can be

---

* It will be observed that an occasional discrepancy between the lettering of the cuts and the references to them in the description occurs in this and a few other instances throughout the work. The errors are to be met with in the original French treatise much more frequently than in the present edition; and those which have not been altered from the originals by the engraver, will be detected at once by any machinist.

given at pleasure, directed by the whole weight of the lever k; and the additional one of the lever p, passes over the leather and receives the oscillating motion given to the lever k, by the cranks h, h. It also receives another motion which makes it pass progressively across the breadth of the table, first in one direction and afterwards in the other, and which is caused by the screw which receives an alternate rotatory motion to the right and to the left, by means of the toothed shaft which catches in the pulleys to the right and to the left, being governed by the lever with the ball on top, which is drawn away from its centre of gravity by the projections d', d', of the rod b, and falls back upon the opposite side.

The table being higher on one side than on the other, and the course of the lever passing the curved part where it is least elevated, the stamper leaves the surface of the leather at short intervals, which are determined by each revolution of the wheels f, f, and the pressure being thus taken off, the leather can be moved by the workman and replaced in another position, so that the force can be directed successively upon the whole surface.

The results of this operation are an immense economy of time, labor, and trouble, the greatest possible amount of compression and contraction of the substance of the leather, the securing of a perfectly uniform and smooth surface, and the accomplishment by one workman of what can only in common be effected by ten or twelve.

Flotard and Delbut's Machine.—The following is a description of a machine invented in 1842, by Flotard and Delbut, taken from the Reports of Expired French Patents, vol. lvii. p. 86; its object being to replace hand-beating by more active means, which will be free from the in-

BEATING AND ROLLING BY MACHINERY. 265

conveniences attaching to other machines. To attain this end, the inventors have endeavored chiefly:—

1st. To bring to perfection the construction of the mechanism moving the hammer, and

2d. To make the anvil elastic, so that injury to the leather by the hardness and roughness of the blows may be prevented.

3d. To use a table with a rolling surface, and with rollers attached to the feet.

Figs. 49, 50, and 51. *a.* Cam, intended to lower the arm of the lever *c*, so as to elevate the hammer *e*.

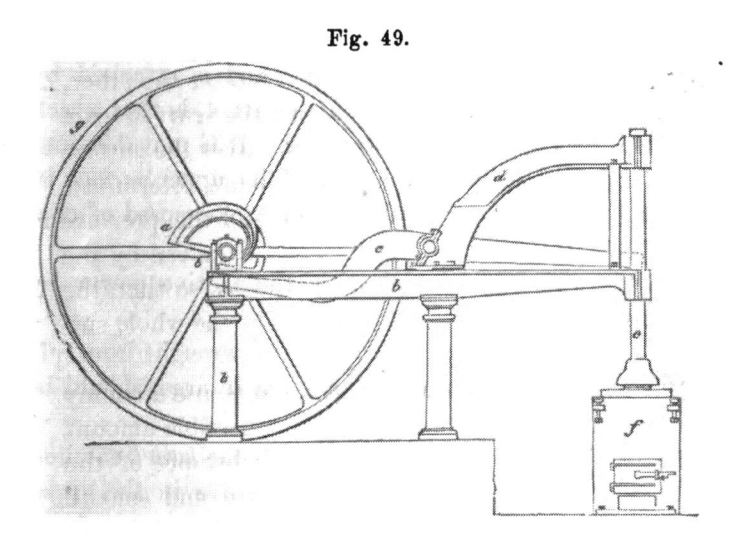

Fig. 49.

b. Framework, or cast beam, supported on three columns and sustaining the whole apparatus.

c. Lever, having one extremity furnished with a wooden cushion, and the other rounded off to enable it to move freely in the mortice of the hammer.

d. Cast arm, the end of which holds the helve of the hammer and maintains it in the vertical position.

e. Hammer, having its lower surface covered with copper.

f. Support, or anvil, composed of two principal parts: the one fastened to the ground, 1, is furnished with a

Fig. 50.   Fig. 51.

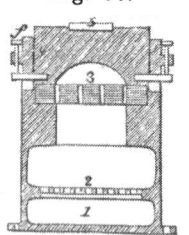

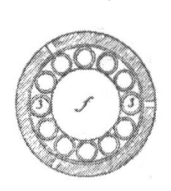

grating, 2, which receives the fuel, and is attached by screws to masonry-work; the other part, 4, is that which receives the impulse of the hammer. It is movable, and mounted on twelve springs, 3; and its upper surface is, like the opposing one on the hammer, composed of copper.

g. Fly-wheel, connected with the motive power by means of a band.

Figs. 52 to 55. Hammer, of cast or wrought iron. If sufficiently small, it may be solid, but if large, should be hollow.

a, a'. Wooden teeth, against which the cam *b* catches. These teeth are adapted to two mortises in the upper part of the hammer, and are retained in place by a wooden wedge. By means of the two teeth, the hammer can be elevated more or less, either by taking off the lower one *a'*, or by enlarging or diminishing their size.

b. Cam, acting upon the teeth *a*, to elevate the hammer.

d. Cylinder, directing the hammer and keeping it vertical. This is furnished with two projections 3, which support cushions for the shaft of the cam *b*. It rests upon a shoulder *d'*, upon the plate *b'*. The lips *i, i,*

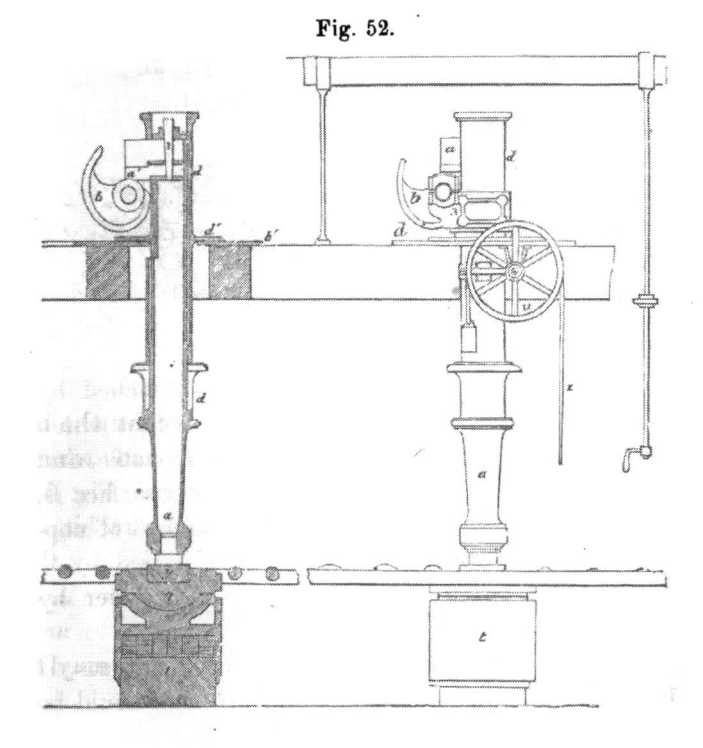

Fig. 52.

against which the wooden teeth slide, prevent the hammer from turning.

Two lateral openings, *o, o,* Fig. 53 (also seen in Fig. 52), allow the cushions *r, r* (Fig. 54) to pass, which press the levers *l, l,* worked by a screw, to the right at one end, and to the left at the other. Fig. 52 exhibits this arrangement.

The shaft *m*, Fig. 54, serves as a prolongation of the screw *n*, Fig. 53, and carries a pulley *v*, Fig. 52, upon which passes a cord having a weight at one end, and a stirrup for the foot at the other. The cushions *r, r*, produce a friction which slackens the fall of the hammer, and diminishes the force of the blow.

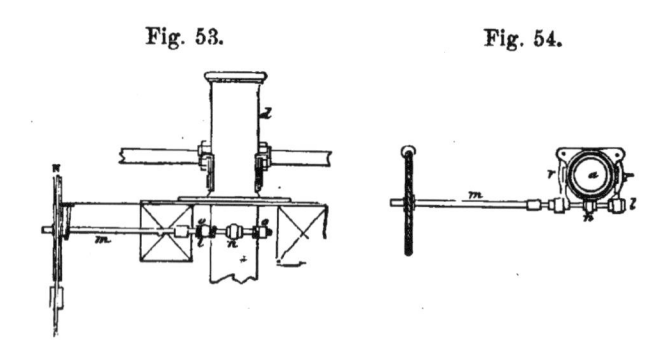

Fig. 53.   Fig. 54.

d. Circular plate, or cup, intended to receive the oil or grease dripping from the machinery, and which might otherwise fall upon and soil the leather. Fig. 51. Two vertical pieces, supporting horizontally a rabbit, or wooden spring, which is elevated or depressed by the screw attached to one end of it, so that the hammer *a*, in rising, touches it with more or less force, so as to augment the power of the blow. A metal spring may be used in the place of a wooden one.

f. Figs. 55 and 56. Table with rollers, *p*; its feet rest on iron rails.

r. Wheels, adapted to the feet of the table and running upon the rails. The skins to be beaten are placed on this table, and upon its middle the anvil, upon which the hammer descends, is supported.

The anvil is chambered for the passage of a current of steam, for the purpose of warming the copper face, *y*; and it rests upon springs, which are intended to render the shock of the hammer less severe, and to diminish the jarring.

Fig. 55.

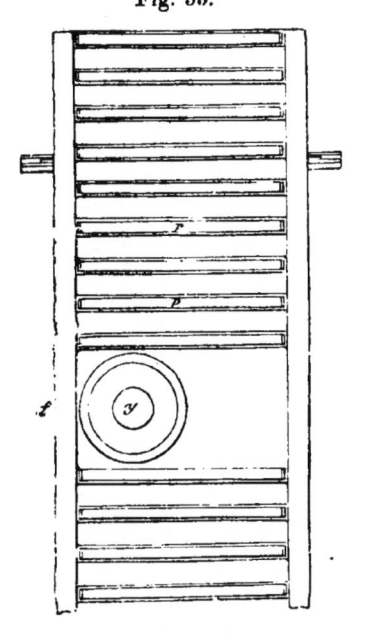

Fig. 56.

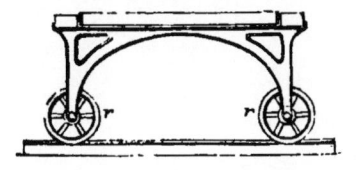

As the system of vertical hammers has long been in common use, the invention of Flotard and Delbut consists, really, only in the use of

1. The spring, for increasing the force of the blow.
2. The check, for diminishing it.
3. The cups, for receiving the oil drippings.
4. The movable table, with rollers.
5. The arrangement of springs, under the face of the anvil, and

6. In the passage of vapor.

M. Berendorf's Machine for Pressing Hides.—The following report upon and description of this machine is from the Bulletin of the Society for Encouragement of Arts, &c., of the year 1845, p. 68:—

"The necessity of hammering by hand skins intended for sole-leather, formerly a very essential though fatiguing means of compressing them, has now been almost entirely prevented by methods which much more effectually answer the same purposes. Among these means that of M. Berendorf, which substitutes for hammering a rapidly applied compression, somewhat analogous to it in operation, has been very successful.

"The peculiarity of the mode employed by him in the use of the machine invented in 1844, consists not so much in this substitution of rapid compression for hammering, as in the peculiar arrangement of the support for the leather, which, by its elasticity, makes it possible to confine the amount of pressure to any desired limits. The support is an anvil, resting upon a spring composed of hard wood, the amount of resistance of which can be modified at pleasure by the workman, who, holding the hide by one hand, turns with the other a screw which exactly regulates the pressure to which any particular part of the leather may be exposed.

"The machine of Berendorf is powerful, and simple in all its parts. A beam acts upon a lever, the fixed point of which is attached to a cast-iron support, which forms the top of a frame large enough to receive a great number of hides, and having in its middle an opening through which the piston which produces the compression by means of a lever about to be described, slides.

"The compressing surfaces in contact with the hides, are made of brass, are smooth, convex, circular, and

BEATING AND ROLLING BY MACHINERY. 271

have a diameter of from $3\frac{1}{10}$th to $3\frac{2}{10}$th inches. The skins exposed to their action are beautifully smoothed and perfectly compressed by it.

"The advantages of this process in improving the quality and appearance of leather, and its superior cheapness, have induced the council to bestow upon M. Berendorf a silver medal, and to insert in their Bulletin this report, accompanied by a description and plate."

This machine is composed, 1st, of a movable vertical hammer, which exerts pressure upon the hides. 2d. Of a fixed anvil upon which they are placed. 3d. Of a lever which gives the impulse to the hammer.

Fig. 57 exhibits a front view of this machine.

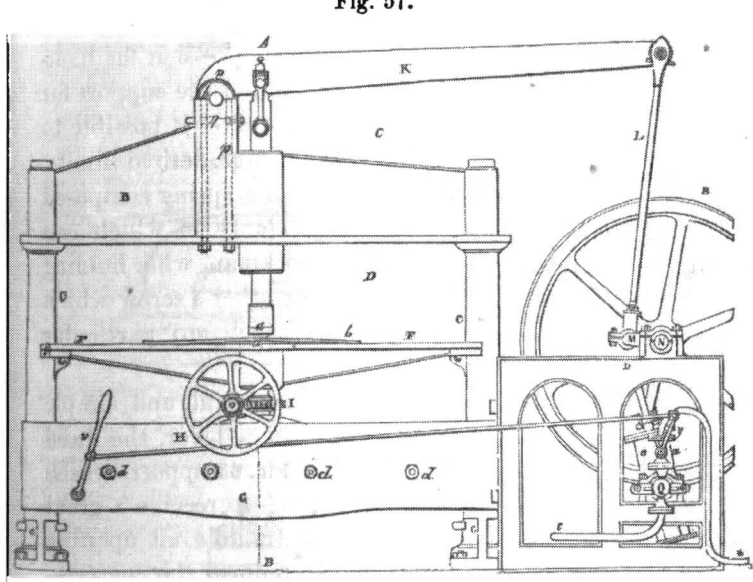

Fig. 57.

Fig. 58. A plan.
Fig. 59. Vertical and cross section, made upon the line A, B, in the first figure.

272   TANNING.

Fig. 58.

Fig. 59.   Fig. 60.

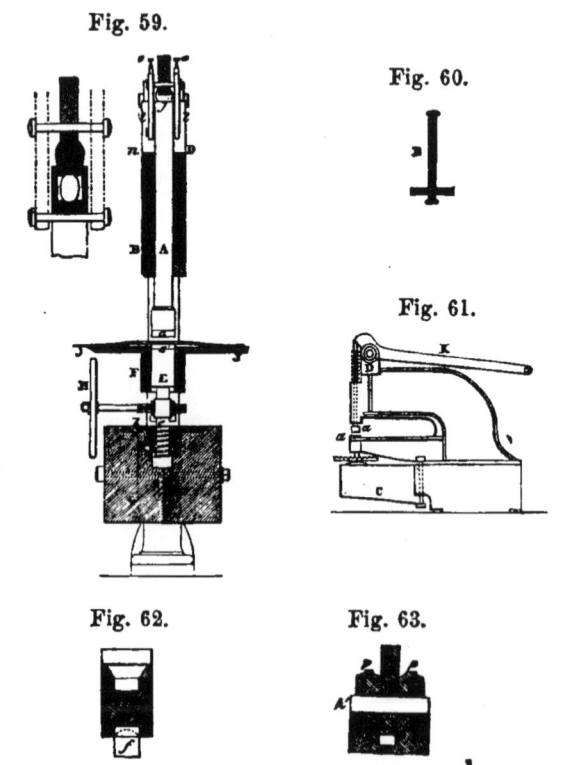

Fig. 61.

Fig. 62.   Fig. 63.

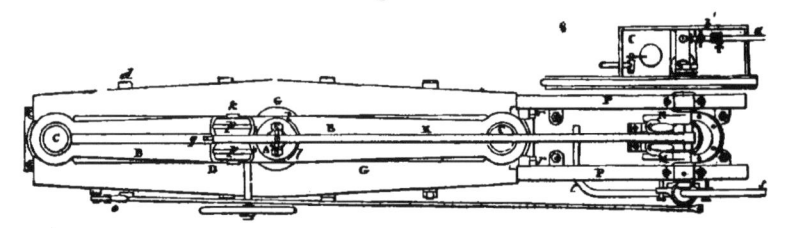

The same letters apply to all the figures.
1. The wrought-iron hammer, A, is furnished, at its inferior extremity with a face of bronze, and its cylindrical shank or helve passes through a vertical socket in

the large and strong cast-iron beam *B*. This latter, which is represented in cross section by Fig. 60 (upon the line *C D*, Fig. 57), is strengthened by mouldings, and rests, by its extremities, upon two cast upright columns *C C*, with which it is firmly connected. The space between those uprights, amounting to but 78 inches, only admits half hides, although M. Berendorf has also adopted another arrangement represented in Fig. 61, which admits of acting upon whole ones. About the middle of the upper part of the beam *B*, and near the socket, is a projection *D*, which supports the end of the lever that transmits its action to the hammer.

2. The anvil which receives the leather to be compressed, is composed of an iron cylinder *E*, having a brass face *a'*, like that of the hammer, and between these two the leather is pressed when the latter descends.

The cylinder passes freely through the socket of the large cross-piece *F*, and rests upon an elastic support, which allows it to descend a little under heavy pressure, and to rise again rapidly. This support consists of a thick wooden plank *G*, 20 inches square, fixed at its ends to the lateral projections *c*, which descend to the foot of the columns with which they are connected. This piece of wood-work is so large that it often has to be made of two pieces bound together by screws with nuts *d*. The cylinder does not rest directly upon this wood, but upon a steeled gudgeon, or pin, Fig. 62, *f*. The gudgeon or pin is threaded for part of its length, and traverses a copper nut *g*, sunk in a cast-iron rim *h*, which is let into the centre of the wooden support. By turning this pin to the right or left, the cylinder and the anvil face *a'* are made to rise or fall along with it. To effect this movement, the workman grasps a little fly *H*, the axle of which has an endless screw which works a toothed-wheel

I, mounted upon the gudgeon. The fly is turned more or less, as the thicker or thinner parts of the leather are being exposed to pressure.

The leather placed between the anvil and hammer is thus pressed to any desired extent, and, the wood below being elastic, bends or gives to some extent, and again rebounds to its original position.

The cast cross-piece *F* which guides the anvil, rests at its two ends upon the projections *i i* of the columns *C C*, and upon each side of it is placed a table *J*, upon which the workman moves the hide in every direction, so that it may be touched at all points successively.

3. The lever which acts on the hammer. The head of the hammer *A* incloses a steel block, upon which a prop *j* pivots, which is of ovoid form and well-tempered steel (Fig. 59); and upon this prop the large lever *K*, moving upon the axis *k*, Fig. 63, is supported. When it descends, it rests upon the prop *j*, which oscillates a little upon its centre, and forces down the hammer in a vertical direction, and, in order that it may rise again with it, they are connected together by two iron bars, terminated by arms, which are attached on one side by the bolt *m,* which passes through the lever, and on the other by a similar bolt *n*, which goes through the head of the hammer (Fig. 59). The play given to these arms is regulated by small compressing screws above them.

The steel axis *k*, upon which the lever moves, rests upon the upper part of the projection *D*. A steel ring, traversed by the axis *k*, is adjusted upon the centre of the lever-head, and can be easily replaced when worn out. In order to retain this axle in place, it is covered on each side of the lever by two strong stays, the branches of which extend to the top of the beam, as well as to the projection D, and are kept in place by strong nuts.

M. Berendorf moves his machinery by a small oscillating cylinder engine, the power being transmitted to the lever K by the two beams $L\ L$, joined together by the double crank M. The vapor enters the conical box Q, from the boiler through the pipe s, raises the piston, and escapes by the pipe t. The fly R turns the small crank z, and works the feeding pump S, which is plunged in the reservoir T. The water is returned into the boiler by the tube a'', when the cock b' is open, and a ball-cock keeps up the communication between a reservoir above and the one below.

This machine works ordinarily at the rate of 140 revolutions in the minute, during which time more than a square yard of surface is compressed by it. In M. Berendorf's establishment, where a number of machines are constantly working, from 70 to 80 half-skins are pressed by each apparatus in twelve hours.

Berenger and Co. have three mill-hammers at work, at the rate of 100 blows a minute, each one turning out from 35 to 40 whole skins in a day.

M. Berendorf has taken out a patent of fifteen years' duration, dating the 7th of October, 1842, and, still later, two additional ones of improvements upon this interesting machine, which is now completely established in favor.

Cox's Machine.—A more modern method of rendering leather smooth and compact, is by passing it between rollers. This mechanical arrangement, being free from tremulous motions, and easily adjusted to any desired rapidity of action, produces a uniform and powerful compression throughout the side of leather, without any liability of damaging it, as is the case in machine *beating*.

276   TANNING.

Cox has invented a rolling mill in which the roller is fixed at the end of a lever, which, being suspended, oscillates like the balance of a pendulum.

This roller, made of copper or brass, 5 inches in diameter and 9 inches in length, is suspended by its axes in the chaped end of an iron lever 6 inches in diameter and 11 feet 10 inches long. The upper end of this lever, also terminating in a chape, is movable upon pivots attached to a beam or block 15 feet long and 2 feet wide. This beam is free at its anterior extremity, and is so jointed at the other as to enable it to move upwards and downwards, and it rests on each side upon two supports placed below it. The weight is in a box resting upon the body of the lever, which is moved by the aid of a crank attached to it at a distance of rather less than two feet above the roller. The lever should move through a space of 3 feet 8 inches, but this can be

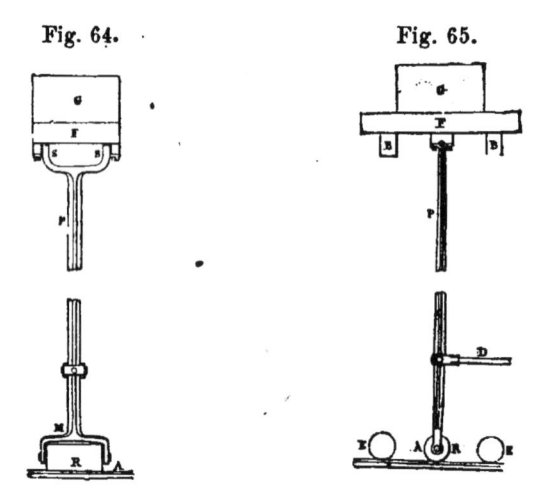

Fig. 64.   Fig. 65.

increased or diminished. The copper or brass support is hollowed out, so that the roller can pass along its whole extent, and reach all parts of the leather. As soon as the hide is placed upon this support, the block or beam is made to rise, and the whole weight bears directly upon the leather. At the end of its course, where the support is flat, the roller is raised up by the beam, the weight is borne down again upon the leather when it reaches the middle, and is again elevated by the supports placed under the beam.

Fig. 64 is a front view, and Fig. 65 a side view, of this machine. *F*, beam, movable at its hind end by a hinge *C* fixed in the wall (Fig. 66), and maintained in a horizontal position at the other end by the supports *B B*. *P*, lever joined to the beam *F* by the pivots *S S*, and terminated by a fork *M* which holds the roller *R*, running over the curve *A*. This curve has, at either end, a plane surface *E*, where the roller leaves it and is raised up by the pivots *S*. *D* is the horizontal shaft connected with a crank which moves the lever *P*, and *G* is a box containing a weight heavy enough to cause the necessary pressure at the moment when the roller reaches the plane end of the support.

Fig. 66.

Wiltse's Rolling Table.—This machine, somewhat similar in construction to the preceding, is shown by the accompanying drawing, Fig. 67, made to a scale of the eighth of an inch to a foot. The machine consists of a spring pole, a lever *b*, to which the head of the vibrator *d* is attached, and which is rendered compound by a connection with a second lever *c*. This combination acts through the vibrator *d* upon the roller *g*, and is propelled by the foot working the treadle *e e*. The bed *h* is of lignum-vitæ wood, and the table *i*, upon which the leather is spread while being gradually drawn under the roller, is 8 feet wide and 16 long. The bed is the part upon which the leather is rolled, and is firmly sup-

278   TANNING.

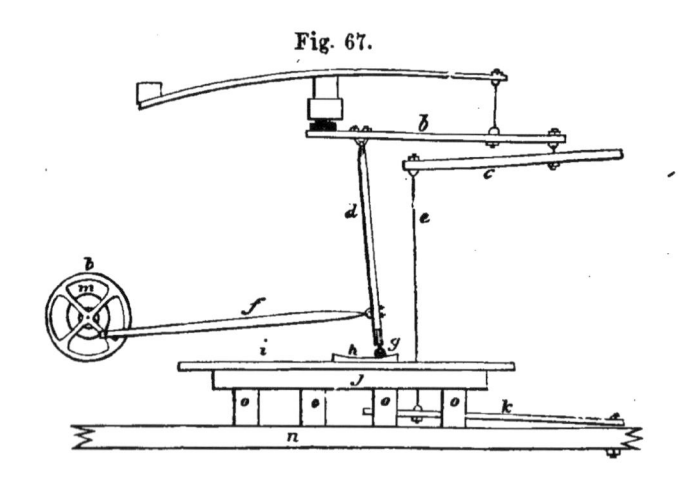

Fig. 67.

ported by a heavy log *J*, which, in its turn, rests securely upon the supports *o o o o* and the sill *n* of the building.

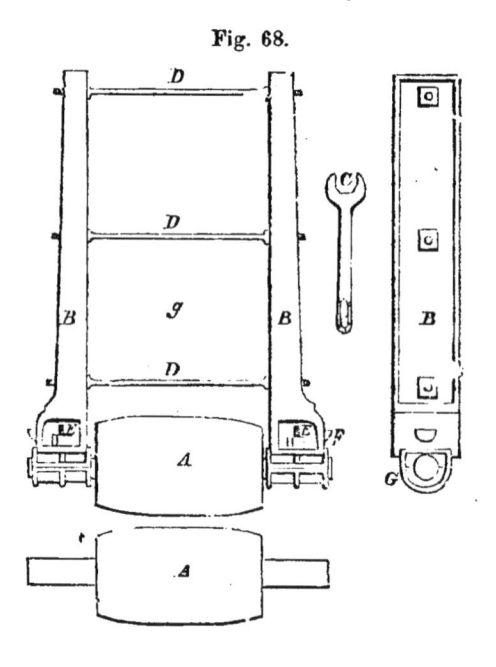

Fig. 68.

The connection f with the balance-wheel b forms a crank by which a vibrating motion is communicated to d. The pulley m on the same shaft is the driving medium, and the roller should move at the rate of 130 revolutions a minute.

Fig. 68 is a view of the rollers $A\,A$, one of which is represented as it is retained in working position by the straps $B\,B$, and the other detached. A side view of the strap is also given in a separate figure B. The wrench C is used for turning the nuts E. The lips $F\,F$ are oil-holes for lubricating the journals of the roller.

The roller is made of a composition of copper and tin, with a steel shaft penetrating through it.

These mills and appliances are made in a creditable style of art by Wiltse and Co., Catskill, New York.

Seguin's Machine to Flesh and Gloss Leather.

This machine is composed of two metallic rollers six feet long; one carries a sharp blade spiral in form, and is destined to flesh the skin enveloped on another roller $2\frac{1}{4}$ feet in diameter, while the first is but six inches. On the circumference of the lower roller and parallel to its axis a groove is made in which the end of the leather maintained by hooks, is engaged; the sharp blade is thus disposed to form from the centre of the roller a spiral which makes a full turn to the two ends. The pivots of the rollers turn those of the lower roller in fixed steps, and those of the upper roller in true levels by which they raise or lower this last roller to make it stand on the large roller. The movement of these rollers turning in opposite directions is combined so, that when the upper roller makes a full revolution, the lower one advances only $\frac{1}{12}$ of its circumference. The pressure of the upper roller on the leather can be regulated by loading the levels with weights, more or less heavy, the leather, being engaged by the end in the groove of the lower roller, rolls around this roller as soon as it turns.

At that moment they put the sharp blade of the lower roller in operation, so that the skin is fleshed from the centre to the ends on all its length.

CHAPTER XLIII.

TISSUE AND QUALITY OF LEATHERS—THEIR DEFECTS AND THE WAY OF ASCERTAINING THEM.

We have made known the composition and structure of the skin; it is then evident that well-tanned leather ought to form a homogeneous body from which it is impossible to extract fibrin and gelatine. These principles are in a state of perfect combination, and while the fibrous tissue is not destroyed, it is, however, reduced to such a state that it is not fibrin. According to what we have indicated before, it is evident that if barks of good quality have been used, if the operation has been well conducted, the leather must be of good quality; but if one or several of these operations have not been well executed, and if the barks are poor in tanning principles, the leather presents imperfections which diminish its quality. It is ordinarily by cutting, that the quality of leather is ascertained; that well manufactured presenting a bright cut and a hard body. It is everywhere, except on the hair side, of an equal color, and the inside has the appearance of an open nutmeg. The tail, the back, and the throat being the thickest and most essential parts, are those which are cut in order to ascertain the quality of the leather.

You can judge a leather is badly manufactured or impaired when its edge is yellowish or blackish, when you perceive in the centre a black or whitish line, and at last when its tissue is loose and spongy.

Too long a stay in the vats, the vat being badly composed or managed, a want of dampness in a vat which loses water, and other different circumstances, may deteriorate the leather. Then you perceive that it is spongy, too open, wants weight, has not the proper color nor the requisite hardness to be good in use; but the evil is without remedy, and the quality cannot be restored. Generally the outside color of leather depends on the manner in which it has been swelled and tanned. The leather swelled with lime is nearly black on the hair side, and red on the flesh side, the inside is light red; the color of leather raised with barley is slatish on the hair side, and whitish on the flesh side and the edge. That with garouille bark is of a blackish-brown, and has a strong and disagreeable odor that it always keeps, while leather tanned with birch has an agreeable odor.

It is impossible to tan perfectly the thin, hollow, and dry skins, those which are difficult to swell, or those which do not swell in a satisfactory manner.

It is also difficult to prepare well, skins which are full of cuts, and those from Ireland, and Brazil. Skins put into muddy waters are often pricked; there are some others so difficult to depilate, that there remain on the side foreign substances, thus explaining the reason why in working on the beam they are cut, because those parts which are hard resist the knife.

When the skins have remained too long in the lime, sometimes they are burned in such a way, that by taking them with the nippers they are torn, and it is nearly impossible to flesh them. It is a fact beyond question that a fresh, clear, and pure water is the only one proper for the preparation of leather.

Leather is called *horny* when some parts of it are dried and hard as horn, because not having been softened the tan has not penetrated them. To obviate this defect you must be careful not to leave them in the open air.

Some leathers contain a multitude of small holes; these holes deteriorate the leather to such an extent that it lets in water. A good plan to test the quality of a leather is to put into water a piece previously weighed, and leave it in for a few days. If, when withdrawn, this leather has acquired a considerable weight in proportion to its volume, it is a sure sign that it is spongy and consequently badly tanned. If, on the contrary, its weight is nearly the same as before, the leather is of good quality; consequently the more dampness a leather absorbs, the more spongy it is.

Leather kept more than two years does not improve in quality. It dries and diminishes in weight, which is a loss to the manufacturer, who should keep it in a damp store.

Action of Frost on Leather.—Many inquiries have been made for the purpose of ascertaining whether the freezing of leather will add to its weight. We answer no, quite the contrary. The particles of water freeze within the pores of the leather and become expanded, and to that extent that the sides appear *bloated*. But when the icy particles melt away, the side is left in a spongy, softened state, which very much injures the fibre of the leather, and to some extent takes from the weight of the side. We are not unaware that some tanners infer, because they get a larger gain in weight in winter than in summer, that this gain is in some way the result of frost, but this fact is attributable to other agencies, which we will not consider at this time.

The influence of frost upon color is very marked, and is attributed to a chemical change, and it is a fact that leather *frozen dry* will be many shades lighter in color than if dried by any artificial heat. It is also true that leather thus dried is much softer, but then this is clearly attributable to the *heaving of the fibre* by the frost. It is a sad mistake to suppose that frost adds either to the weight or quality of leather. The only good it can accomplish is on short, tanned or crusty hard leather, it directly tends to overcome those difficulties; but upper leather and calf frozen dry will always cut a flesh more open and coarse than when dried by the natural air without freezing. We do not allude to this subject just now so much to correct errors on this point, as to suggest that the whole subject of drying leather should receive more attention. Suppose it can be demonstrated that sole-leather can be dried in forty-eight hours without injury either to the weight or color; how valuable would such an improvement be. Under such circumstances no tanner would require more than 1000 to 1500 sides exposed at any one time, besides saving the interest for at least one month on his whole stock.

It is believed that steam when properly applied can accomplish this result, and it has been done as we shall see hereafter.

CHAPTER XLIV.

BELT LEATHER.

The name of *belt*, or *crop leather*, is applied to leather made from the skins of cows or small oxen, provided they possess sufficient thickness, as their tissue is more compact than that of ox-hides, at least, if the cows have not already calved. The skins of young oxen are deficient in thickness and firmness, and are only used for conversion into belt leather.

This kind requires a much more thorough currying than thick hides, which are almost fit for use when taken from the tanning. It is employed principally by shoemakers for second soles and uppers for women's shoes and men's light shoes and pumps. Young ox-hides are regarded by shoemakers as inferior to cow-hides; and they use the latter for upper and thin soles. The tanning of these hides is conducted in a somewhat different way from that of thick hides.

At first, they are placed in the lime pits; and, when ready for depilation, which is generally in eight days during summer, and ten or twelve in winter, are repeatedly fleshed and scraped, care being taken to rinse them each time in clean and running water, if possible, so as to remove all the lime. Those intended for uppers require at least four or five rinsings, while two will suffice for those which are to be used as soles. They are then deposited in wooden vats, 4½ feet in height and 6½ feet wide, which are nearly two-thirds filled with weak infusion of oak bark, and are handled daily.

If the hides are worked in the same vat, the strength

of the infusion must be restored as rapidly as exhausted by fresh additions of bark.

When transferred to other vats the liquor must be made successively and successively stronger. Usually, tanners prefer this method; but, sometimes skins are treated in hot infusions, prepared in vats similar to those just described, by adding hot water to bark in the proportion of five baskets for every twenty-four cow-skins. After being placed in the vats, the skins are repeatedly handled or moved about by the workmen. This working is frequently repeated, the skins being taken out daily to drain; and a little fresh bark being added to the vats in the interval. This manipulation is continued from four to six weeks. The following figure represents the operation.

Fig. 69.

Whichever of these methods is adopted, the hides are next subjected to a mixture of ground bark and strong liquor in other vats. For this purpose the bottom of the vat is covered with a layer of fresh tan, carefully moistened, upon which a skin is spread out to its full extent; this is covered with another layer of tan, and the hides and bark are alternately packed in till the vat is full. The top hide must have a "hat" of bark, and the contents of the vat be then drenched with the solution.

The workman should be careful to place the skins in every direction around the pit, the end of the contiguous ones forming slight angles with each other, and to deposit tan in all the creases and doubling made by the bending of the edges. This process usually requires six weeks. Five baskets of tan are used for a dozen ordinary cow-skins, and about six for six dozen young ox-hides. The skins, having undergone this preparation, are then further exposed to two treatments in the vats in precisely the same manner. After remaining in the first pit for three months, they are taken out, and, before being transferred to the second one, are beaten or trod out for the purpose of rendering them more supple. This process having been completed, they are placed in the second and last pit. Some tanners are satisfied with five weeks' exposure in this last pit; some others extend the time to three months. This latter period is not too long for leather of good quality. After withdrawing, the leather is dried in the usual manner, being careful not to expose it to the sun, a strong wind, or a cool or damp atmosphere, in which it might mould; then it is transferred to the currier, who prepares it according to the kind and quality of the leather required.

Cow-skins differ much in quality, those of the younger animals being much superior to those of cows which have frequently calved; the latter having become weak and thin by the distension to which they have been subjected. Young ox-skins also, long regarded as inferior to the latter kind of cow-skins, are equally serviceable; and the shoemakers now use them indifferently.

The above process is employed in the best establishments of Paris; but, in the provinces, some tanners vary it more or less.

In Brittany this leather is made by the process of

tanning in sacks. After having been exposed in the lime pits for two months, and placed for eight days in hot ooze and water, they are then filled with the decoction, and left for a week or more, being careful to change their position five or six times a day. Then they are unripped, placed between layers of bark, and allowed to remain untouched during eight days before being finally taken out and dried.

In Limousin they are limed for four days, then placed in the tan pits, in which they are allowed to remain for three months.

In Dauphine they are limed for fifteen days, then exposed for four weeks to two different treatments with barks, and transferred to the vats, where they remain for $1\frac{1}{2}$ month.

At Metz and Verdun, after having lain for eight days in old lime pits, and as much longer in fresh ones, they are exposed to the action of ooze for one month, and afterwards to two stratifications with tan for five months longer.

At Bourges and in different places in Berry they are allowed to remain three months in the lime pits and six months in the tan vats.

At St. Germain, cow and calf-skins are passed through three old lime pits and one fresh one, and then undergo five cleanings and rinsings. They are then beamed and relieved with the knife of all superfluities, and worked upon the hair side with a whetstone, and when thus well softened and clean, are again thrown into the water. After being worked for the third time upon the horse with the round knife on both sides, so as to expel the last portion of lime, they are again rinsed; and a fourth and fifth time treated in the same way. The final rinse water should come from them perfectly clear, and leave them in a proper state for the ooze bath.

How to Manufacture Cow-leather into Uppers of a superior quality.—In order to be good, upper leather should have the following properties:—

1st, the pores should be very close, constituting its solidity. 2d, the leather should remain pliant and not break easily in use. 3d, the leather should be waterproof, so that the feet may be kept dry in the dampest weather.

The following instructions should be observed in manufacturing cow leather uppers possessing the above named properties. In choosing the hides such skins only should be selected as are of light weight, and whose exterior promises leather of a superior quality. In the selection, attention should be given above all things to the hair; if it is fine and glossy, it is an evidence that the animal was well fed. The next point is the horns; if they are short and sharp pointed, then the animal was young. With regard to the flesh side, it should be as even as glass and devoid of the bites of cattle worms. If otherwise the skins are free and thin, they may be considered in a suitable condition to be transformed into fine upper leather.

In places where this sort of cow-skins accumulate, it is advisable to work them while they are still fresh. It is true that it is necessary to pare them before putting them in water, still the drying operation is gained by this, and the leather made from them is as good and even more heavy than that produced from milled hides.

But as the tanner does not receive many fresh hides, he is obliged either to buy dry hides or to have them dried himself. In the drying operation great care must be taken, especially in summer and autumn, that the hides while suspended on poles do not rot and lose their hair, which unfortunately happens very often.

In order to avoid rotten spots, Mr. V. Mathesias proceeds as follows: When the hide is laid on the table, first remove all the fat, then stretch it well out, and sprinkle it with about one pound of salt, and as soon as it has been rubbed in hang the hide up. It is not then necessary to stretch it so carefully. Thus, this advantage is gained, that the hides being dry they are seldom attacked by moths or worms. Another advantage is, that they are much easier to refreshen than hides which are not salted. In my opinion, there is no need to give heed to the fresh, especially when one is able to use block salt.

It is not advisable to put more than from twenty to twenty-four hides into the water at a time, even where upper leather tanning is carried on on a large scale; still, in the spring the number may be doubled, for the reason that the vats can be filled at several stages.

The first day, the skins to be refreshened should be hung in running water; and in places where this is not practicable stretch them out, and pour water upon them time and time again.

After the hides have become softened by this operation, they should be placed in the vat, and, if possible, add spring water until the hides are entirely submerged. The next day raise them, and put them back. This is necessary to make the tanning uniform. The fourth day raise them again. This should be done often if the weather be warm, and also if the water in which the hides are soaked be hard; then they may be stretched on the apparatus for that purpose; but, before doing this, it should be ascertained that they are soft to the touch. Then they are to be cleaned, in order that they may be stretched lengthways on the table which has been previously covered with one hide.

When hides have been salted before drying, or when they have not been salted at all, provided that they have not been dried too much, the stretching operation is easy; but there are cases, especially if the skins have been dried in the sun, when this operation requires much force, especially when the skins known as *kips* are concerned. After having properly stretched the skins, they should be put back into the same water from which they have been taken. The next day raise them, and examine whether they have become well-soaked. If you find any that do not appear to give satisfaction in this respect, put them back; but if there are any that are still very hard, these should be stretched again. It is absolutely necessary that the hides should be completely refreshened before being placed in the lime pit. If they are placed in it in a hard state they will remain hard, even after they have become converted into leather. Therefore, we may look upon the refreshening as the first basis of the tanning of pliant leather.

East India kips, which for many years past have been tanned into upper leather, require a special mode of treatment for the refreshening. In India, they are first stretched, and dried by the heat of the burning sun; then, in order to protect them against worms, while they remain in store and during their long voyage, they are sprinkled with lime or nitre dissolved in water, or with arsenic. They are, therefore, often very difficult to soak; some of them cannot even possibly be well refreshened, as they are half burned. This species of hard hide is tanned for the purpose of making inner soles. At least, this is the best use to which they can be put.

CHAPTER XLV.

TANNING OF CALF-SKINS.

The tanning of calf-skins is conducted much in the same way as small cow-hides. After being pressed to expel oleaginous matters, they are passed three times through old, and once through fresh lime vats; but, being too weak to bear the full strength of the lime, this should be done after the passage of cow-skins through the vats has somewhat diminished its activity. If they are dried when brought up into the tannery, they must be first trodden out and soaked. Then they are scraped, carefully fleshed and rinsed, after which they are ready for a part of the process differing from that used for cow-skins.

Place from fifteen to eighteen skins in a tub, beat them for eight or ten minutes. This operation softens the fibre, and is repeated after each rinsing, but it is omitted in establishments where the skins are rinsed as often as six times. The beaters are wedge-shaped, from $8\frac{1}{2}$ to 10 inches in diameter.

The skins, being entirely free from hair and lime, are placed in the hot ooze and water, and treated like cow-skins, excepting that they require more frequent and careful handling. Be careful to put fresh tan each time into the vats. Submit them to the action of stronger ooze, and tan in the same way as other skins for a month, when they are afterwards transferred to the pits. In these they are folded lengthwise and unequally, and thus spread over with tan, being careful to cover the heads and tails with rather more tan than the other parts. The tan used should be of the first quality. They are exposed in the first pit for three months. They are then taken out, freed from all particles of tan which adhere to them, and placed in the second pit with tan which is reduced to the finest state of division. They are folded double, and unevenly as before, but in such a manner that the part before covered shall now be exposed. Fill up the pits as usual; moisten the whole with warm water, and leave three months, then the skins are ready to be curried.

Some tanners, instead of using cold water to moisten their pits with, employ a warm infusion of bark, which is an improvement upon the old process.

As it is important to have the skins soft and ready to absorb the tanning liquor, some tanners remove all traces of opposing substances, such as grease, lime, etc., with the help of an alkaline lye, which consists of water impregnated with pigeon's or hen's dung, and is technically called a *bate*. Ten or twelve gallons are sufficient for one hundred skins; and during the time they remain in the last liquor—from eight to ten days—they are frequently handled and scraped. After the action of the bate, the skins assume the form of *pelts*, in which state they are placed in the ooze vats. The bate acts by means of its hydrochlorate of ammonia. The lime in the skins decomposes it, takes its acid, and becomes hydrochlorate of lime, which is soluble, and carried away by the washing waters, while the ammonia disengages in a gaseous state. If the *dung* is fresh, the organic matter it contains is liable to putrefy, which involves a partial decomposition of the gelatinous tissue and a loss, and at the same time imparts a very disagreeable odor to the leather.

CHAPTER XLVI.

TANNING OF CALF-SKINS FOR THE PREPARATION OF WAXED CALF-SKINS. BY MR. RENE.[1]

I.

BEFORE entering into the details of the manufacture of waxed calf-skins, which within the last thirty years has attained to so great an importance, we wish to say a few words on the origin of this speciality, and of the time when this kind of work began to be seriously developed in France.

About fifty years since, the fabrication of waxed calf-skins was scarcely known in France; only black-grained, stamped, and white calf-skins were produced. The first two articles were already well made; they alone with cow-hides in oil being used for men's and women's shoes. The white skins were exported to Spain, Portugal, Italy, Constantinople, Smyrna, Alexandria, Malta, and Sicily.

Let us describe in a few words how those white calf-skins were prepared. We shall not, at present, speak of the method of tanning. We wish only to make known the processes to which they were subjected after tanning, in order to prepare them to be delivered for exportation.

On being taken from the pit they were piled lightly for drying, then scraped, either over a horse with a tanner's knife, or on a table with a stretching iron, but this was done very lightly; then they were placed in oil of a rather thin consistence mixed with fish oil. On the

[1] From "La Halle aux Cuirs." Paris.

fleshy side they generally used fine degras, such as is used by chamois dressers; they were then hung up to dry. The calf-skins being dried after laying some days in a pile, were folded muff-like, and pressed on the bickern, beaten well on the bench with a cork-club, then turned again and scraped against the grain with the same, and finally grained with a cork board from the four false quarters, and then they were ready for exportation. These calf-skins presented a clumsy resemblance to the rough Milan skins.

About 1808 four Irish curriers established themselves in France. They were expert workmen, and they brought with them a new branch for us in the leather business, and the speciality at length placed French currying in the first rank, for it may now be said to be without a rival in this particular kind of manufacture. These Irish workmen formed apprentices; and, after Paris, Pont-Audemer had the first instructed workmen. It was also through those Irishmen that we learned to curry horse-hides.

At that time France was in the middle of a long war with England, the ports were blockaded, and the demand was only for home consumption. Consequently few waxed calf-skins were manufactured, except for large cities where they were used for elegant shoes. Waxed calf-skin was then employed much as varnished calf-skin has been within the last ten years, during which the fashion of wearing patent leather shoes has been common in the cities, while in smaller towns, cow-hide in oil and grained calf-skins formed the principal staple of consumption. Horse-hide, when known, became a rage; every currier produced smooth horse-leather, until it came to be the *patent leather* of the time. In 1814, the style of boot introduced by Russians, of white calf-skin, diminished the call for horse-hide. We may say at once that the English were then far from having reached the perfection attained in our day in the preparation of upper leather. The waxed calf-skin alone was finished of about the same quality as now, and even better.

The fabrication of boot legs, then, from 1814, rapidly improved in France; but waxed calf-skins, properly so-called, were still in the back-ground, if not as a manufacture, at least as an important article of sale.

II.

Classification of Untanned Calf-skins.

Untanned calf-skins, the manufacture of which we are about to describe, may be divided into four classes, viz:—

1st. Calf-skins fresh from the butcher's.
2d. Salted calf-skins.
3d. Dry French and European calf-skins.
4th. Dry calf-skins from the East and West Indies.

Washings.—On receiving the skins fresh from the butcher, they are placed in water for washing; not in running water, because it is too cold in winter and too warm in summer. In the absence of spring water, we use that from the pits. In the centre of the work-house or in the corner is a large reservoir rising at least 6 feet above the ground; there the water is collected and distributed about the establishment. Soft water is preferred as less charged with calcareous matter than hard water, which often holds in solution earthy salts.

I use a pit built of wood. As soon as the skins come from the butcher I plunge them into this pit, unfolding them one by one, and being careful to scatter them about the vessel with a stick.

One hundred calf-skins weighing from 1000 to 1200 lbs. are enough for any allowance of water; fewer may be taken, but if more are put in they will not be well cleaned. In summer I let the skins soak six hours, and twelve hours in winter, according as the temperature rises or falls, after which I take them out of the water. Then I empty the pits and refill them with clear water, and replace the skins as at first. In about six hours in summer and twelve in winter, I examine them, the flesh is white, the little veins have lost their blood. I draw them and give them, while on the horse, light blows with the iron on the flesh side.

LIMING.—The calf-skins being now sufficiently cleansed and drained, I set about placing them in lime-pits. The lime-pits are three in number, each 52 cubic feet. In one is the dead liquor or the oldest, in another the gray or the second in strength, and in the third, the fresh strong lime, which is the most active. By means of a large hoe, I agitate the contents of the dead vat as much as possible, and when sufficiently stirred I cast in my calf-skins, one by one, unfolding them well and sinking them in the liquid as fast as I plunge them in. This done, they are left undisturbed for twenty-four hours; at the end of which they are drawn off with iron tongs. When they are out I stir up the lime-water anew, and immerse the skins in it for another twenty-four hours.

This is done with fresh skins from the butcher; but if they are slightly tainted, I pass them in the gray solution, and even into the strongest one, in order to help their preservation. If they begin to decompose when received from the butcher, I rinse them carefully, beat them on the flesh side, and cast them immediately into the strongest lime-pit. I take up the skins which have been immersed in the dead solution for the second twenty-four hours; I pass them into the second solution, where they are worked as in the first, and left forty-eight hours, being careful to raise and beat them after each twenty-four hours.

At the end of these four days of liming, it frequently happens in summer that a third, a half, sometimes even all the skins are stripped of hair. In such a case they are immediately taken out; otherwise, I pass them in the quick vat, where I leave them until the process is completed. But, generally, in twenty-four or forty-eight hours the end is attained. I allow the skins to drain, and put them into a tub with just water enough to cover without floating them; there they are submitted to the first disgorging process. They can, if necessary, remain in this water ten or twelve days.

I prefer this method to piling, for in the water calf-skin parts with the lime, and the action of the latter is weakened. While in the pile it continues to work, and if my men in piling do not exercise care, they catch what curriers call the *plis de pelain*, a disease almost impossible to banish from currying establishments. But the sum of all this is, as soon as the skins are unhaired, they are to be taken out and rinsed in a vat or washed immediately in the river; in this first process, then, it is advisable to be as quick as possible, for I repeat that liming calf-skins is not tanning them. We have heretofore omitted to indicate the manner in which the three pits, called the strong, gray, and slake pits, are prepared.

Into my pit, the capacity of which is about fifty-two cubic feet, I turn about one hundred and ninety-eight gallons of water, and add thirty-nine gallons of fat lime; this is for the strong pit. In the gray pit I mingle the same quantity of water and twenty-five gallons of lime;

in the dead put for the same quantity of water from twelve to fifteen gallons of lime.

I keep alive my pits while they are in use with slacked lime, in such a way as to preserve the relative strength. I renew my live pit; for about every six weeks, or at most two months, it degenerates to the strength of the gray pit, and the gray to that of the slack. In order to re-make the live pit, I first empty and cleanse the dead pit, for I believe this step to be necessary to the health of the workmen and salubrity of the establishment.

Salted Skins.—These hides are cleansed from the salt and blood in twenty-four hours; then they are taken from the water and struck with the iron upon the fresh side, then replaced in clean water for twelve hours, after which they are removed and allowed to drain off; finally, they are put into the slake pit, following the same course as with fresh skins.

Dried Calf-skins.—For calf-skins, dried in hair from France and other parts of Europe, I pursue the following method:—

The skins are soaked forty-eight hours; at the expiration of that time, I raise and lower them in the same water, and let them remain another forty-eight hours. I then raise them again and straighten them very carefully with the stretching iron, especially on the parts not affected by the soaking.

The edges and the necks should be worked with minute attention; every fold should be opened, and the stiff parts of the neck should be unrolled with the hand. This work finished, and I replace them in water for twelve hours, then withdraw them, let them drain, and send them to the dead pit, which I have taken care to weaken, because, for calf-skins dried in the air, the pits ought not to be so strong as for salted and fresh calf-skins.

I use this method of softening dry skins during about eight or nine months in the year, but when the temperature falls, my remedy is found in my wells of water. It is very rare that in a tannery one has not one pit unoccupied; availing myself of this pit, I pile in it as many dry calf-skins as it can hold, and having covered them with heavy stones, set my pump in motion, and, instead of sending the water into the reservoir, direct it all warm into the pit where the skins are. I fill this pit with water, place three or four poles over it, and carefully cover the whole with empty bags in such a manner as to exclude the air as far as possible. This done, I wait 48 hours for the light skins and 62 for the heavy. The water in the pit undergoes a partial fermentation, and at the end of this time the calf-skins, perfectly restored, may receive the action of the stretching-iron.

Dry Calf-skins from Foreign Countries.—This class of skins is of Eastern production; they come from Madras, Calcutta, Java, etc. etc. In France few of these skins are tanned, but in England and Germany considerable quantities are manufactured.

To soften them I put them to soak in my vat for three or four days, and then withdraw and pile them up. When well drained, I give them heavy blows with the iron; the water worker by the strength of his arm must tear away the fatty tissues, the thin skin which envelops the hide; he thus frees it, breaks down its contractility, and expands it one-third. When this work is done intelligently and boldly, it may be taken for granted that the skins will be well softened. I replace them in clean water and leave them there 24 or 48 hours, according to the season of the year; they are then worked on the hair side, and in the direction that the hair runs. This done, they are piled one above another, the best on the top, and the following solution is applied: For about 100 skins, weighing from 6 to 8 lbs. each, I take a cask holding about 50 galls., fill it two-thirds full of water, and throw in some good lime so as to make it boil for a time. While still warm, add 4 lbs. of orpiment, mix the whole, and let it cool. I proceed as follows: To the end of an old broom I tie a stout piece of linen canvas, and soak this mop in the liquid, and make an application of it to the hair of the skin. When well smeared, I bend it double, as one would a hide in salting it, and deposit it in a vault constructed for the purpose. The same course is pursued with all the skins, taking care to pile them in the vat, in the best possible manner, and when the last is reached, I pour the remainder of the solution over all the skins, so as to cover them. They are thus left for three days; on the fourth they are withdrawn from the vat, and I rinse them in running water; I leave them to drain and place them for 24 hours on a solid platform in order to have them swell a little. At the end of this time I prepare for the *river work*.

RIVER WORK.—The river work must be arranged so that the men lose the least possible time in taking out and replacing in the tubs the skins that they are making.

Three tubs are necessary to five or six men working with a bench; these tubs should be of a capacity of from 375 to 400 gls. each, and the water should be introduced and drained off rapidly.

The working benches are four and a half feet long, and they are all covered with a heavy plating of zinc, giving an even surface, in order to facilitate operations, and to avoid breaks on the hair side, and knife cuts.

The sheet of zinc is three feet long by two feet broad, and the bench is arched about seven inches.

The zinc is fastened down by round-headed nails well driven in; it should not reach the head of the table, but about one inch lower, for the following reason: It oftens happens in working, that one is obliged to lay from 20 to 25 calf-skins on a table to drain off, and to leave them there during several hours. And I have noticed that the undermost skin having the hair side next the border of the head of the table becomes strongly marked with a curve in the neck, and that this impress cannot be effaced either in the tanning or currying. The hair side at this spot became like parchment, and would not absorb the tannin. I looked and attributed this to the ridges of my tables. I brought my sheet of zinc one inch lower, and from that time I found no more wrinkles on the hair side of my skins.

The table for rounding off skins, and for thinning the necks is broader, and less arched than the other; it is lens shaped. This facilitates the work of the knife, for by having a broader surface, the edge is less liable to make flaws, and the work progresses more rapidly, as the operator is not forced to change the position of his calf-skins so often, and when he reduces a throat or a head, he does so in a more uniform manner.

The tools we use are:—

1st. A knife having a blade one and a half foot long, and provided at either end with convenient handles.

2d. A tanner's knife with a strong handle; the blade should be 13 inches long, and the curve nearly one inch.

3d. A smoothing stone, having the stone part 11 inches long, fixed in a holder or perforated iron, and held in its place by iron rivets. Its curvature should be about one inch, and the handles should be strong and solid.

It is necessary that each workman should have a double set of tools, namely, two No. 1 knives, one lighter than the other, and that most used necessarily becomes the lighter of the two; then two knives No. 2, one to depilate and work on the hair side, another to flesh and work the skins; one good smoothing is sufficient.

OPERATION FIRST.—The first operation is the depilation. In order to depilate freshly slaughtered calf-skins, I place on the table two skins as substratum; for medium skins three, and four for middle skins.

To avoid scratches and to make the action of the knife easier, the workman must give great care to the edge, and leave no trace of hair upon them; then I place them in water, and rinse them.

Next a skilful workman removes the necks; he cuts the navels and nipples, trims the rump and the tail, going entirely around the skin, and reaches the throat.

After this operation the skins are folded crossways, starting from the lump on the shoulder. In working fresh slaughtered hides I lay them on a bare table, but for small medium sized or thin skins I lay two skins underneath, to avoid breaking the hair side.

To execute this operation well, short quick strokes should be given with the knife, allowing the edge to cut as little as possible. The work should be sharply and briskly done upon the cripper, where the nerve of the skin should be entirely crushed, but the hinder flanks and towards the breasts should be passed over lightly, without even attempting to take off the tissue covering these parts. The neck should be treated carefully, and the throats and heads, when the skins have them, should be briskly worked. By pursuing this course the nerves of the calf-skins are crushed on the nervous parts, and the weak or hollow spots are spared. After the skins have all undergone this process I soak them six hours in a tub of clean water.

I next give them a counter-fleshing, placing two skins as a layer on the table. I return them to the water for an hour, I then take them out to work them; for this purpose I lay on the table, when the skins are fresh, two for foundations, and more if they are small skins. I use the stone lightly at first, and then smartly, to rid the skins of lime. After using the stone I clean the hair side with a knife not too sharply whetted, so as to avoid scratches. Then I put the calf-skins again to soak in clean water during three or four hours; at the end of this time I take them out in order to work them once more on both sides. I then rinse them for the last time, and stack them up until I am ready to put them in the vats.

In order that my manner of conducting my dressing, and that the whole of my work may be well understood, I am obliged to enter into indispensable details. In the first place I have to fix a basis of fabrication, and determine as clearly as possible how many skins I can produce in the course of a year by my method of management, the number of operations I must employ, the quantity of tan which I require to provide myself with; in a word, I have to estimate approximately the price of calf-skins when tanned and in the pits.

I will adopt as a basis the manufacture of 12,000 calf-skins per annum, such as they come from the general slaughter-house. We reckon these skins, large and medium together, as weighing, one with the other, $14\frac{1}{2}$ lbs.

each. We have, therefore, 174,000 lbs. of fresh hides to tan, and I use three pounds of tan to tan one pound of fresh hide. I shall have to provide myself with 522,000 lbs. of tan. Reckoning extra heavy skins, which will require three layers and a large piece of bark which I use in my liquor vats, I may estimate the amount at 555,000 lbs. of tan to be used during the year.

Six men at the lime pits and river work will suffice, and two men for dressing and to tend the pits, can do the work, with the help from time to time of one of the men employed in the river work.

The foreman intrusted with the management of the lime pits and with the river work, will work with the men and turn the skins. These men will turn 250 calf-skins weekly. The foreman dresser will attend to the pit, make his liquors and return the skins to the pit. A good workman will be assigned to aid him, and as it is necessary they understand well each other, it is better to leave the choice of the assistant to the foreman. The same is done in regard to the foreman of the river work.

The staff of workmen being well organized, my pits well arranged, and my river work complete, we next come to the dressing operation.

In order to work 1000 calf-skins monthly we need 26 vats of oak wood, three feet in depth by five feet and one half in diameter. They should be of oak, for the edges of a pine vat cannot long stand the daily work to which they are subjected.

Twenty-six vats with 50 calf-skins in each will work 1300 skins monthly, but as we have vats of large skins, only 32 of which can be held, the number becomes reduced to 1000; for before preparing the river work for a vatful, we equalize the weight of the skins intended for that vat as much as possible. 50 medium skins weighing 13 lbs. each, make 600 lbs. of fresh hides for our vat, and if having calf-skins, only put in 35, weighing on an average 17 lbs. each, making 612 lbs. in all. It is very important that the contents of the vats should be equalized, so that the quantity of tan used in each may secure the same result, and in order to reach accuracy in this, we weigh all the calf-skins as they come from the butcher. The weight is marked on each, and before putting a lot to soak, the foreman reckons up the aggregate weight, so as not to exceed the limit of 612 lbs. of fresh hides.

We give the calf-skins six days in the liquor, and as we can put 100 skins in each vat, we therefore require six vats for this operation.

In the handling we put 200 skins together, and leave them during one month, consequently we require six large vats for this process. They may be built of pine, and should be $5\frac{1}{2}$ feet in depth and $6\frac{1}{2}$ feet broad. They are raised $1\frac{1}{2}$ foot above the level of the ground to prevent their being stepped on. The oak vats first mentioned should also rise $1\frac{1}{2}$ foot above the ground in order to assist the workman who stirs the hides by offering a support to his knees on the edges. The risk of his pitching in is thus avoided; still, despite this precaution, it happens that a man will plunge head foremost into a vat now and then. This seldom occurs, but it has happened, and we have witnessed it.

We need also 12 racks of solid oak capable of supporting 100 calf-skins if necessary. We lay the skins to drain on the frames when we take them out of the vat, to turn over the contents, and to add the quantity of tan necessary, when they are returned to the vat.

The vat is entirely covered with bitumen so as to prevent it from rotting at the level of the ground, and it is also more clean. If the row of vats is against the wall, fill in the intermediate vats and apply bitumen to the intervals between them, so that when the skins are stirred, the ooze falls back into the vat and is not lost.

Twenty-six vats in operation for the dressing liquor, six vats for the liquors, six large ones for handling, total 38, to which number two more are added to provide against accidents or unforeseen stoppages, making in all 40 vats; and as we require at least four vats to each pit, although the calf-skins remain longer in the pits than in the vat, we have ten pits. They are 6½ feet in depth and 7 feet in breadth at the mouth. They will hold about 300 calf-skins, and we do not have them larger, so as to use one a week. This is the result of the general arrangement of our work, which should progress steadily without any stoppage.

We require also three ooze pits, which are also 6½ feet in depth and 7 feet in breadth. We lay in them a double flooring of pine pierced with holes for the ooze to filter through. Then we have a square upper work of plank to hold the pump, which reaches down to the double floor.

In the new pit, which we will designate under the name of ooze pit No. 1, we lay from 18 to 24 inches deep of coarse bark to support the ooze. In it we place the spent tan of the first and second pulverization, and it serves to prepare the third vats as well as to aid the strength of a feeding vat. At the end of a week this becomes pit No. 2; its liquor serves to fill my pits. At the end of a week this becomes pit No. 3, whose strength is almost negative, but which serves to keep pit No. 2 from giving out too soon; it receives the spent tan of the last set of pits, and the liquor of the second; in a word it filters the last essence of the spent tan, and it serves also sometimes to modify the strength of pit No. 1, when we prepare a third vat. At the end of a week it becomes totally exhausted; then we have it emptied among the spent tan, and use it again as a new pit, and thus continually. These ooze pits are of the greatest utility, and nothing can be done well without their employment.

Having given a sufficiently full account of the material arrangement of the factory, we come now to the operation of placing the calf-skins in the vats.

The third vat, which is the last given, is always a new one; the liquor pit No. 1 serves to prepare it. Its strength should be about 3° by the tanninometer, less rather than more. It becomes the second vat, and the second vat becomes the first, and the first becomes the discharging vat. We only use the tanninometer for the third vat, for this instrument gives only the strength of the liquor when this liquor is free from all gelatine. It would not be successfully used to estimate the second vat, whose liquor is already charged with gelatine. The same applies with regard to the first and also to the discharging vat. The latter is prepared in the following manner: Begin by extracting one-half of the spent tan and taste it; its liquor should be barely able to affect the palate, and as it is almost always too strong, add to it liquor from the pit No. 3, and fill it about ⅔ full, so that when the calf-skins are placed in it, the whole contents will reach to about six inches from the top. Have the calf-skins brought up from the river-work. The workman takes them one by one and lays them flat in the vats. Another man, armed with a long oak wood pole, of the length of about five feet, plunges them down the one after the other all around the vat. After this operation, the same man takes a longer pole, also of oak wood, 8 feet long, and strong enough not to bend too much under the weight of the load. He plunges it along the sides and uses it as a lever. From 12 to 15 calf-skins are at the end of his pole, which he lowers on the edge of the vat, and swings them right and left for about ten minutes.

In this manner he sets the entire contents of the vat in motion, and then raising his pole two-thirds, he makes it describe half a circle to the left, then raises up his pole and lets the skins go, plunges in again, seizing about the same number of skins, and continues in this manner until he has gone completely around the vat; then he takes a tanner's iron hook, disentangles the skins, equalizing his vat, and recommences his work with the pole and so on during two hours. At the end of this time, the calf-skins being well cleaned and well washed, will have lost all the lime remaining in them after the river work. This operation is complete when the flesh of the skin begins to turn black; then they are promptly taken out by the two men, one fishes for them with the hook, and the other takes them one by one, and places them on the rack, and this operation being speedily ended, they are carried in a wheelbarrow to the first vat, which is prepared in advance in the following manner.

All the spent tan is extracted and tasted, and as its juice is always too strong, add to it some barrels from the liquor pit No. 3. Fill it two-thirds full, and throw the skins into it, in the same manner as in the discharging vat, the workman continuing to swing them in the same manner.

The flesh of the skins begins to bleach at the end of an hour; throw in 11 lbs. of fine tan of the best quality, and continue to stir them. A quarter of an hour later, add a like quantity of tan, and the stirring continues;

at the end of another quarter of an hour, examine the skins, and you find that a slight grain begins to appear on the hair side. Stir them then during ¼ of an hour longer, putting in 11 lbs. more of fine tan, and when you are certain that the grain is well worked, wishing to obtain more (so as not to affect the hair side by trying to get a premature grain), remove them promptly to the rack placed above the grain. Then stir the vat with a stirring pole; the second workman takes a wooden shovel and works the liquor, while the other workman stirs. Then plunge back the skins again into the vat, one by one briskly, taking care to watch that the workman performing this does not drive them to the bottom with the first stroke of his pole, after he has plunged a skin about half way down, he should change the place of his pole, in order to avoid making folds in the skin, or as they are called in tanners' language, *umbrellas*. By beginning the stirring operation at six in the morning, it is finished by ten o'clock, but leave the skins quiet till noon, then take them out and lay on the rack, folded in half from the rump to the head, with the hair side inwards. Stir the vat again, and plunge the skins in once more, adding the while 3 lbs. of tan, of the best quality, ground to nut size. At 3 o'clock repeat the operation, except that you add no tan, stir the vat briskly, so that the froth rises to the top, put the skins in and at six o'clock take them out. Stir the vat as usual, and, replacing the skins, add 20 lbs. more of the same kind of tan. Above the vat is a board painted black, upon which you write the day that the skins are first placed in the vat, the number of skins contained therein, and score two bars to indicate that 88 lbs. of tan have been put in the vat.

Next day, as soon as the workmen arrive, look at the vat, examine the hair side of the skin, the grain begins already to be better defined, stir the contents vigorously, and while the skins are being again plunged into the vat, add 22 lbs. of tan, nut size, and then leave the skins alone the whole day. At six o'clock in the evening raise the vat, and proceed in the same manner as before, but in replacing the skins in the vat, add 22 lbs. of tan. Next day raise the skins again, and add 20 lbs. then, and 20 lbs. more when the skins are replaced in the vat, stirring the while. Next day the operation is repeated, after which they are allowed to remain undisturbed during four entire days. The first vat has taken about 220 lbs. but gradually, so that the grain of the skins cannot be affected. Throw out the contents of the discharging vat, and take care not to have it put into the liquor pits, for this liquor contains too much lime and gelatinous matter; this liquid would injure the purity of the liquor pits.

In many tanneries the stirring is done with a shovel, and in large establishments where there is mechanical motive power, the stirring is effected by the agency of floating mills in order to economize manual labor; this is an improvement, but the floaters should not be abused, for if used without caution, they often scrape the skin.

Upon the ninth day after the skins have been placed in the vat, have them taken out and drained on the frame one hour. Then prepare the second vat. Have all the spent tan which it holds taken out in order to assure the strength of its liquor. Taste it and add almost always two pailfuls of liquor of the pit No. 1, and one pailful of the pit No. 3 or No. 2, according as it is more or less to the required degree. In order to aid the estimate, take care to taste the liquor of the first vat, and raise the strength of the second about one degree above the first. Have 22 lbs. of tan, nut size, thrown into it, and stir it strongly for five minutes; then have the skins brought to the frame above No. 2; agitate its contents again, and do not wait before putting in the skins for the liquor to become still, on the contrary put them in quickly, and after about two-thirds of them are in the vat, throw on about 11 lbs. of tan and keep on. When the last skin is reached, two men pack the skins well down on the bottom of the vat, so as to exclude the air, and then throw upon them the 11 lbs. of tan remaining. This operation is repeated each morning for four days, adding each time 44 lbs. of coarse tan of the best quality; and take care each day to have the skins drained for one hour on the frame, between the time of taking out and of replacing them. The day that the operation is begun, mark on the board the number of skins placed in the vat, and the quantity of tan put in, and after the fourth day, leave them quiet for four days in summer and six in winter. The skins therefore remain in the second vat during eight days in summer and ten days in winter. Each day examine the progress made by the skins. If they rise too much, diminish the quantity of tan; if, on the contrary, the skins seem to be sinking down, put in 20 lbs. of fine tan, and often even a bucketful of liquor from the vat No. 1. This is a matter of practice, and too much care cannot be given to the skins while in the vats. The tanner should devote each forenoon to this important matter.

In the second vat use about 175 lbs. of coarse tan, nut size, and of the best quality, which will be sufficient if the tan is good. The ninth or the tenth day prepare the third vat with the liquor of the pit No. 1. Fill it only half full, and its strength should be about three degrees by the tanninometer. If it is stronger than that, reduce it, and if inferior, throw in 20 lbs. of fine tan, then let the contents be stirred about ten minutes. Next empty the second vat and let the skins drain off for two hours, when they are placed on the frame of the third vat, which is stirred again, and 22 lbs. of coarse tan are added. Then put in the skins briskly, in the same manner followed for the previous vat. During four days, operate in the same way, putting 44 lbs. of tan into the vat each day, and the fourth day leave them quiet. This vat takes also about 175 lbs. Thus the preparation of from 610 to 620 lbs. of fresh slaughtered skins, has taken, with the aid of the liquor pits, about one lb. of tan to every pound of fresh hides. The work goes on gradually, the hair side of the skins remains soft, the grain comes out more and more each day, the texture of the skin is slowly and progressively penetrated with the tannin. The hair side becomes as white as milk, the skins have acquired a certain firmness, the necks and flanks are full, and nothing more is requisite. Being satisfied now as to the result, leave them quiet for six days, taking care that the liquor does not rise above the vat, for the fermentation that takes place therein is often so active that it requires to be looked to daily.

In order to prepare a vatful of dry calf-skins with the hair on, equal to the vatfuls of fresh calf-skins, put in from 440 to 450 lbs. of skins; for 50 lbs. of fresh skins do not give more than 20 lbs. of skins thoroughly dried. Treat them in very nearly the same manner as the fresh calf-skins, but have them stirred an hour longer, as the grain of a dried calf-skin comes out much less readily than that of a green skin, and take great precautions that the grain may not be affected, which, having been dried, already contracts more readily under the action of the tannin. Pursue the same plan for Calcutta and Java kips. Put in 55 lbs. of skins to each vatful, for kips before they are dried receive a preliminary preparation, which makes them much more difficult to moisten than ordinary skins.

The action of the orpiment used to depilate them speedily has softened the flesh side a little, and this grain being more tender requires most careful treatment in the vat process. In this manner kips have been dressed, having a grain as soft as that of green calf-skins, but the work is slower and requires constant watching.

The calf-skins having been long enough in the vat, take measures next for the treatment with ooze. For this purpose clean the vat into which you intend to place them and turn into it the liquor of the vat No. 2. Put about six inches of this liquor at the bottom, and have the two No. 3 vatfuls raised, those which you propose to use about three hours in advance, so that the liquor may thoroughly drain off. Moisten about four hundred and seventy-five pounds of fine tan of the best quality. This tan you throw in, a handful at a time, upon the skins as they are placed in layers in their liquor. It is necessary that this tan should be lightly sprinkled with water in order that none of it may be wasted, and so that one may be able to see clearly the bottom of the vat. If it were not moistened, the dust, the flour of the bark would be lost, and the men would be incommoded by it in their work.

All these precautions having been taken, have the skins brought close to the vat on a wheelbarrow, where you take them up one by one. The first workman takes them up by the hind legs, and casts them with the hair side upwards upon the liquor which covers the bottom of the vat. The second workman, who is provided with a pole, stretches out the feet or neck which may have doubled under in throwing them in; then the two together, each with a pole, push the skins squarely down into the liquor. They then throw in three or four handfuls of bark, seize another skin, and the same operation is gone through with each skin. When the liquor becomes all absorbed have more poured in, so that the skins are always floating and yet as compact as possible. Care should be taken not to pour in too great a quantity of liquor; this is very important, for with the commencement of this operation the skins having floated sufficiently in the three vats, should begin to draw together, otherwise the fibrin of the skin will become too soft and weak. For this stage of the process use about four hundred and seventy-five pounds of fine tan of the best quality, this quantity being sufficient for the fifteen days that the skins are to remain in the vat. When this work is complete have about five or six inches of spent tan laid upon the pile so as to keep the skins squarely in the vat; for without this precaution, the work of fermentation going on, the skins would rise up and get out of the liquor, and often in half a day they would have spots on the portion of the grain exposed to the air, and such stains can never be effaced.

We have said that the skins are left in for fifteen days. At the end of this period have two vatfuls taken out and rinsed in good liquor, and prepare them for the next process, after allowing them to drain for three or four hours. This is how to proceed in that operation which is done with the object of giving a body to the skins before placing them in the pits, and in order to thoroughly tan the grain side of the calf-skins. In order to secure a white and soft grain, that will not change color in currying, this grain should be tanned entirely through, before replacing the skins in the pits; and this is the reason why the skins are placed in a half floating pit with the grain upward, taking care to use only very fine bark, so as not to dimple the grain, which is yet tender and which has to undergo a certain amount of pressure in the next operation.

After having had the large vat, in which it is intended to place the calf skins of the two liquor vats carefully cleansed, put in the bottom of this vat about two inches of fine spent tan, then take a skin, and throw it quite flat with the grain side upwards, upon this layer of bark; the men spread out this skin with their poles, making it lay quite flat, so as to make the least creases possible, and then they throw handfuls of tan over it, especially upon the centre of the body and the neck, so that the grain on the flanks may be but slightly covered, but the body of the skins well covered. Each skin has the same done to it, and in order that the layers may have an equal depth, have the tail parts turned towards the walls of the pits, which equalizes and regulates its strength. This operation being ended, when you come to the last skin, have it laid with the grain underneath. Select a large skin for the last, and take care to cover the flesh side well with bark. The skins should not entirely fill up the vat; there should remain a space of at least from ten to twelve inches from the surface of the upper-most skin to the rim of the vat, and for this reason give to the contents of the pit no other pressure than that of their own weight, and the weight of about six inches of spent tan placed at the top it. In supplying this vat with juice from pit No. 1, lay canvas upon the spent tan, so that the liquor when poured in may not disturb the bark. Filter gently and gradually; the liquor penetrates the interior, and its weight makes the contents rise slightly, and the skins bear themselves up. At the end of a day or two, after fermentation has begun, it often happens that the whole mass rises from ten to twelve inches, therefore if the vat is too full the liquor will run over and be lost. For this reason take the precaution not to fill the vat clear up to the rim, and do not place any weight in it, because it is necessary to have the skins float a little. By employing a heavy pressure, as is done with skins relaid in the pits, the tan would imprint itself upon the grain of the skins which would create difficulties subsequently in the currying process. Use no more tan for this operation than in that preceding it, but the liquor used to darken the skins is much superior. Then, again, use a lesser quantity of bark, which, however, contains necessarily more tannin principle in this operation than that which is used for the liquor vats. The work goes on progressively and the skins grow more and more compact. During this process the saturation of the grain is completed, without its becoming hard, for one of the most important points is to tan the grain thoroughly without rendering it dry, and above all things, if it is hoped to curry well, the grain should be soft.

Leave the skins in this for one month. This time is enough; they would gain nothing by being left longer. It must be well understood that each time that you take a lot of skins out of the vats, the liquor and the spent tan contained in these vats are removed to the liquor vat No. 3. Nothing should be lost in the work.

Treatment with Strong Liquors.

Upon this stage of the operation of tanning we will amplify a little.

After a month in the pit, the calf-skins are again taken up; the grain side is tanned, it is white and well saturated with the tanning material, and since the operations of working, of coloring, and of saturating with the liquors succeeded each other without interruption, the grain side of the skin almost vanishes under the pressure of the nail. It is important to guard against hardening the skins by the employment of too strong ooze, and in order to avoid this, wash and rinse them in pit No. 3. Then lay them together in pairs, always with the grain side within and let them drip upon the beam for twenty-four hours. Now prepare the tanning pit and cover the bottom with a layer of spent tan two inches deep. For the middle layers for tanning the skins employ as much bark as possible of the first quality. Six hundred and fifty or eight hundred and seventy-five pounds of this are moistened with good tanning liquor and are carefully mixed. The moistened mass is put in as small a compass as possible in order to obtain for it a greater fermentation in the pit. In every one of the pits there is a box made of boards, which serves in watering the pits to prevent the bark with which the skins are covered from being washed about, and at the same time, its outlet is serviceable in ascertaining whether there is sufficient ooze in the pit. For eight days be careful to see that the pits are sufficiently watered and that they have not lost any tanning liquor. This is necessary, and by observing it, you never have pits in which the upper skins become dry, and heat, and become greasy on this account.

When all these preparations are made, the workman who arranges the skins descends into the vat. A man is detailed to assist him, who hands him the skins over the edge of the vat, so that he can take them one after another without any further assistance. The carrier also brings him the tan in baskets, and the work begins. He takes a skin, folds it up, the grain side in, lays it flat down, the tail part of the skin directed to the outside of the pit, so the hind shanks of the skin, when they bend up together, lie at the extreme edges. In this fold he puts a large handful of tan; he covers the ends of the skin of the legs afterwards with another handful of tan. The tail part of the skin and the part by the navel are also covered with tan. He then turns the fore-shanks upon the back of the neck, and puts a handful of tan amongst these folds. After this he puts a light covering upon the neck and breast, and here he puts a handful of tan upon the grain side; finally he covers the back of the neck, and the butcher's cut in the throat with a thick layer, for those parts which are the strongest have need of a double portion of tan. When one skin is prepared in this way, the one who lays them in takes another, and lays it in such a way that the succeeding layers shall go around the vat in a circle, so that they will rise regularly. Thus the thinner part of one layer of skins must be upon the thicker part of the layer beneath, by which depressions are avoided, which a bad workman, in order to make the layers even, often fills up with good tan, to the great detriment of the proprietor, who often cannot control this.

A good arranger of the pits is a valuable workman in a tannery, for he makes use of a very dear material. When the skin is left in the vat the workman tries it with his fingers, and thus knows how to estimate how much tan should be applied to it.

In the first pit, one should not spare the tan, and it must be wet with good tan liquor. The liquor of vat No. 2 serves for this purpose; as soon as the workman has come to within eight or ten inches from the brim he stops laying in, and throws upon the last layer of skins a layer of tan about two inches thick, and fills the rest of the eight or ten inches with good spent tan, covers this with boards loaded with stones, so as to have a certain pressure; for as soon as this vat is wet, the force of the liquor pressing in often raises up the whole. Let the calf-skins remain two months in this pit; at the end of this time the tan is spent, and the process of tanning will not go on if they remain longer in this pit. Now take them out, and beat them with switches, in order to get off the spent tan which commonly clings to the flesh side. After this the skins will be put to tan again in the same way, but on the other side. This time, however, less is used than the first time; the workman presses the skins together as hard as he can, and takes especial care that the tail part of the skin, and throat, and back of the neck, which parts most resist the influence of the tanning material are well covered with tan. This pit is weighted and wet the same as the first, and if one wish, he can finish them up in forty-five days, but it is better to let them stand two months.

If we make a *résumé* of the time of the various operations, we have the following:—

Depilation, including river work	15 days.
Three vats for coloring	30 "
Soaking	15 "
Treatment with liquor	30 "
First pit	60 "
Second pit	60 "
The whole	210 "

At the end of this time the skins, in case they are not treated with too strong ooze in the first and second vats, though they must have been sufficiently long in the third coloring vat, and likewise in the soaking pit, and in the ooze pit, as also in the mixed pit, are completely tanned, and ready for currying, unless they have been neglected between these successive operations, and they are very tender, soft, and clean from grain.

A calf-skin for dressing should be tanned with great care. Should you leave the calf-skins three or four months in every pit, and neglect to lay them down flat, or to put them carefully in pairs, the grain side within, they would become hard. The grain side of this skin would be too brittle for dressing; the nerve of the skin would be brought up too sharp, and it would be impossible for the dresser to make a soft skin of it; blood vein would hinder the table worker, and make it too hard for finishing upon the table. In order to soften it sufficiently a great quantity of oil, tallow, and degras must be employed; the grain side will assume a brownish color like oiled cowhide; and when this grain side is compressed it will tear and spring upon the pressure; in stretching the pushing iron will stick fast in the texture of the substance which has acquired a too strong power of resistance, and the workman will not get on well.

To get a fine and good dressing, therefore, the calf-skin must be well filled with tanning material, but only with the right quantity. If it is too little tanned, it does not take up the particles of fatty matters which are supplied for it in dressing, does not gain in weight, for it grows then too much in finishing, and because the texture of the latter is not sufficiently saturated with the tanning matter it becomes fibrous in skinning. Consequently we get skins that are flat and full of cavities upon the neck pieces and upon the grain side; even more, we obtain a grain side which, in eight to fifteen days after it is curried, changes its color. The same thing happens if they are too strongly saturated with the tanning material; they remain hard, and show an enormous weight.

Seven months' tanning, well carried on, is sufficient for middling calf-skins of from twelve to fourteen pounds without head; from eight to ten months for large calf-skins that we put in the pit a third time. If the tanning is extended beyond this space of time, provided, always, that the operations are carried on in proper succession, little cow-hides are produced and consequently a bad material for dressing because it is too hard.

A good currier recognizes all these wants when he has to dress a calf-skin tanned in a defective manner. By the employment of great carefulness he may indeed restore it so as to make it passable; but he can never make from it a skin of the first quality. Therefore if one tans for his own dressing he must follow the simple method which we lay down as far as possible, and he can then be sure of obtaining magnificent results.

Dressing.

Have the calf-skins taken from the pits in which they have been treated the second or third time with tan, and have them beaten with switches to clear off the tan which clings to the flesh side. Then have them brought up upon dry ground in order to dry them in the air. In great manufactories in which the arrangements are complete, from one hundred to one hundred and fifty skins are brought under a hydraulic press and are dried uniformly in a moment. By this much hard labor is saved, and the operation answers nearly the same purpose as drying in the air; it is to be preferred, even, because the calf-skins which are laid out to dry in the air need a careful watching that the neck-piece and the extremities may have the same degree of dryness as the rest; negligent workmen often let the extremities become dry and then moisten them up again. This carelessness injures the quality of the parts of the skin dried first. In the treatment with oil it happens if the workman does not take great care that the oil will too freely penetrate those parts from which the tanning liquor has not been evaporated by the action of the air; great attention must be paid to this so that the calf-skin may dry uniformly in all its parts. When the calf-skins have dried in the air, they are spread out and then stacked up in a pile. An apprentice takes a hard brush and goes over both sides of every skin and then it goes into the hands of the currier.

CHAPTER XLVII.

TANNING OF GOAT AND SHEEP-SKINS.

Goat and sheep-skins are used by tanners to manufacture *morocco*. Owing to the scarcity of goats, the tanners use very few fresh skins, the supply being drawn from Switzerland, Germany, Africa, the East Indies, and Asia Minor. As imported they are dried and covered with hair; they require breaking and softening, which is done by soaking them several days in water, treading them under feet, rinsing, and scraping them on the flesh side to produce evenness. They are then passed through three old lime pits, the same precautions being observed as in the treatment of calf-skins. The process is continued until the hair can be easily detached, which generally requires about one month, then scrape them on the beam, re-immerse in lime milk for two days, and flesh with the scraping knife. Goat-skins require more rinsing than others, and the operation must be repeated several times in running water. Bait the unhaired skins with pigeon's, hen's, or dog's dung, to remove the excess of lime. Sometimes bran-water is used as bate.

The skins, after being scraped, are sewed into bag form with the grain side outward, and partly filled with a strong solution of sumach; inflate them by the breath, close them tightly and throw them into a vat containing a shallow depth of weak liquor of sumach, and make them float by means of a constant agitation so as to assure the uniform action of the tanning material through the surface of the skin, as represented below. Leave a few

Fig. 70.

hours, take out the bags and pile them upon each other so as to insure the uniform action of the tan liquor through the pores of the skin.

Repeat the process with new liquor, then unstitch the bags, rinse and scrape them on the beam, and suspend them in the drying loft. These *crust* skins are moistened, rubbed out smooth with a copper tool upon a sloping board, and hung up to dry previous to coloring. By this method a goat-skin can be dyed in one day.

Another method is to steep the skins for several days in a fermenting mixture of bran water, scrape them on the beam, soak and rinse in clear water. Lime in the usual manner; work or rub them over with a tool of hard schist to press out the lime; smooth and soften the grain; full them by agitation in a revolving cask, lined inside with pegs, and containing water.

Tan as above, two lbs. of sumac being required for each hide. The French process is the same as the above.

This method constitutes the preparation of the *true morocco*. The *imitation morocco* is prepared from *sheep-skins* in the same manner as the above, except that after being stripped of wool, they must be subjected to powerful hydrostatic pressure for the expulsion of oleaginous matters, which being contained in a large amount would otherwise seriously interfere with the tanning.

Lime them in pits containing thirty-three pounds of lime for every dozen skins, and allow them to remain from three weeks to a month. Then deprive them of hair; resteep them in the pits for five or six days; rinse; beat in tubs, and when perfectly clean deposit them in ooze for one month.

When sheep-skins are tanned for common leather, use oak bark instead of sumach.

The color is imparted in the same manner as cloth is dyed by means of a mordant.

Some dye the skins when they reach the state preparatory to going into the tan liquor, by sewing them together with the grain outwards; then mordanting, and afterwards giving them two immersions of a half-hour each in the dye bath.

The most common method is to take the tanned skins as they come from the drying loft; place two together, and rub them exteriorly with a brush containing the mordant solution, and applying the color afterwards in the same manner. When the dyeing is finished, rinse, drain, spread out; sponge with oil to preserve the flexibility, and send to the currier.

The *black* is imparted by the application of a solution of red acetate of iron; *crimson*, by a mordant of alum, or tin salt, and decoction of cochineal; *puce*, by mordant of alum and decoction of logwood; *blue*, by a solution of sulphate of indigo; *olive*, by a weak solution of copperas as a mordant, and decoction of barberry, containing a little of the blue bath as coloring liquor; *violet*, by the consecutive application of a decoction of cochineal and weak indigo bath.

The *skiver* is a kind of leather made from sheep-skins, split while in the state of pelt by machinery. It is tanned by sumach in vats, being spread out instead of sewn into bag form, as from its lesser thickness it is more readily impregnated with the tan material.

Fig. 71.

The extreme thinness of sheep-skins renders necessary a peculiar apparatus, and nice manipulations for its bisection. The above figure represents a splitting machine, with the skin undergoing the process of being split.

This manipulation presents a double advantage; one skin being made into two portions which are then respectively adapted to uses, for which the original skin, on account of its thickness, was not suited. The vibrating knife and rollers are so arranged as to give an equal thickness to both sections of the skin, or a greater thickness to one side than to the other, as may be desired. The knife acts slowly, but completes the section in about two minutes. This kind of leather is used for hat linings, pocket-books, box covers, &c.

The *roan* is sheep-skin morocco, tanned with sumach, but wanting the grained appearance of true morocco, which is imparted by the grooved roller in the finishing.

Bleaching of Goat-skins.

Bleaching goat-skins in winter, by natural means, is a difficult and tedious operation, which can be materially shortened by the employment of chemical bleaching means. Sulphurous acid is usually used for this purpose, but a better result can be obtained by the careful use of chloride of lime, which being sufficiently diluted and completely neutralized, will bleach skins perfectly in two days. The solution is thus prepared. Treat two pounds of chloride of lime by twenty pounds of water; let stand some time, stirring frequently; when the liquid has become quite clear mix with it $2\frac{1}{2}$ pounds of glauber salt dissolved in water. Leave to settle; decant the clear liquor, and lay the skins in until entirely bleached, which takes about two days. Rinse the skins well in water. They could be softened and rendered pliable by placing them in a lukewarm soap bath, both prepared from white soft soap.

Coloring of Whole Sheep-skins.

At the first industrial exhibition held in London in 1851, there were exhibited whole sheep-skins sent from various places and beautifully and durably colored in the principal colors that can be brought out on wool, and a path has been opened to their use as rugs, carriage mats, and many other purposes, where such soft and long-haired sheep-skins, dyed to present a handsome appearance, can be used. The handsomest specimens, as far as cleanness and beauty of color are concerned, were undoubtedly sent for exhibition, first of all from the London establishments, and then from Paris and Brussels houses.

The mode of dying the skins above named must have been a special coloring method, for the wool showed a uniform color even to the hide, and was at the same time perfectly firm. The method of stretching the skin and then brushing it over with hot dye-stuffs, a mode that furriers now and then follow, could not have been employed in this case, as such can be easily recognized; although there is very little difficulty in dyeing wool, there is a great deal of dyeing entire skins, where the hide, the leather upon which the single wool fibres grow firmly, cannot stand the high temperature of the bath necessary to the dyeing process, and must not therefore be placed in it.

As the matter was one of general interest, efforts were made at the time in London to discover the mode of operation, which was kept secret in some degrees, and after many useless attempts the whole simple method became known.

We communicate this method, although twelve years have since elapsed, partly because these whole dyed sheep-skins created a great sensation in the trade, and yet the method of coloring them is almost unknown, and again because the question is brought up in a German paper, which copied it from an old number of the *Muster Zeitung*.

Long-haired sheep-skins, having the hair two, three, or four inches long, are usually dressed by white tanners and furriers by the ordinary process, then cleansed and brought wet to be dyed. For this purpose they are stretched upon a suitable board and tacked to it with small nails, the flesh side downwards; and in order to make them adhere well, both the skin and the board are previously wet, thereby securing a very firm and uniform level. The board is provided on the under side with transverse pieces which prevent it from warping under the dampness, it being vitally requisite to have a perfectly level board. Besides this the four corners are furnished with rings to which are attached four slender chains of equal length, the ends of which come together in another ring at the centre (as in a weighing scale, only the chains are shorter in proportion), and to this central ring is attached another chain which is wound around a roller or pulley, so that the board remains in a horizontal position, and can be raised or lowered at will. After the skin is thus stretched the wool hangs down on the under side. This is the preparation for dyeing.

The coloring itself is done in flat boxes which should be larger than the board and 12 inches in depth. They are made of copper, and can be tinned if requisite, and they have a double bottom that they may be heated by steam. The boxes are to be filled with water mixed with wool refuse, and the dye-stuff according to the nature of the color to be produced. The dye-stuff should be quite concentrated in order that the hair may not remain over long in the bath; then the vessel should be heated by steam until it seethes, that is, as high as to avoid the bubblings of the contents.

The pulley above referred to should be immediately over the vessel, so that the board can be raised or lowered by the single chain. The board should be lowered at the surface of the liquid for a moment, to give a lustre to the leather, then let into it and then draw out in order to color only the wool, which is soon accomplished. The liquor should be kept hot, not in a state of ebullition, but simmering only; and the water turned into steam should be made good in exact proportion. After the color develops itself rinse and dry the skins.

Every wool dyer can employ this mode of coloring with an ordinary kettle, if he takes care to observe the main points. They are a uniform stretching of the skin, a horizontal and level immersion in the liquor, a gently simmering, not bubbling color bath, made rather strong, and a restitution of the water changed to steam. The leading colors are deep scarlet, yellow, green, bronze, Saxony, blue, orange, brown, black, etc.

CHAPTER XLVIII.

MOROCCO LEATHER DRESSING—CORDOVAN LEATHER.

Morocco Leather Dressing.

ALTHOUGH enamel oil cloth, having its surface finished to imitate morocco leather, has come into very extensive use during the past ten years, still it does not seem to have injured the manufacture of the genuine article. Morocco dressing establishments are still increasing in number and extent. Real morocco leather is made of tanned goat-skin, but the term is now applied also to tanned sheep-skin, which is colored, and dressed with a polished and corded surface in imitation of morocco. The manufacture of sheep-skin into colored leather is carried on extensively in Albany, N. Y., by the old firm of A. Williamson and sons. In this establishment, colored sheep-skin is principally used for shoe bindings, and the majority of the pelts are obtained green from sheep and lambs slaughtered in the vicinity. About 100,000 skins are dressed annually, and from this about half a million pounds of wool are obtained and sold.

The first process through which they are made to pass is that of soaking and softening by water, to fit them to receive the unhairing preparation. Formerly, hydrated lime was sprinkled in the inside of each pelt; it was then folded over with the wool side out, and laid down on the floor, sometimes called the *pit*. In this manner a whole pile or heap was made, and a heating action was engendered, by which the roots of the wool were loosened, so that the fleece could be easily pulled or scraped off on a table afterwards. This method of loosening the roots of the wool was tedious, occupying several days to complete, and the skins required constant watching, as they were liable to overheat and injury, both to the wool and the gelatinous tissue. This was especially the case in warm weather; but a remedy for this trouble and these ills was lately introduced by Mr. Williamson, and is one of the most important improvements made for many years in this art. This is effected by a calcined orpiment compound which they import. It is made up into a thick creamy consistency; then applied to the inside of the skins, which are folded over, wool side out, and laid in a heap. In twenty-four hours the skins can be deprived of their wool, and if they have to lie longer no injury will result. In all cases the depilatory action is certain without injury to wool or skin tissue.*

The next operation is that of washing the skins prior to unrolling them. This latter operation is executed by placing them upon an inclined bench, and rubbing off the wool with a blunt tool. The flesh side of the skin is also scraped to remove slime and loose flesh; after which they are ready for the liming operation. They are now placed in vats containing milk of lime, in which they are treated for about two weeks.

The next operation consists in passing the skins through a bath of hen or pigeon manure mixed with water, which softens them. After this they are washed, and passed through a bath of dilute sulphuric acid, which neutralizes all the lime that may remain in the pores of the skin. After this they are dipped into a solution of common salt; sewed up at the edges with the grain side out, to form bags, partly filled with tanning liquor, inflated and tied. They are now placed in a tub containing an extract of Sicily sumach, in which they float, and are kept in constant motion for several hours, and when they have absorbed a sufficient amount of tannic acid they are taken out, drained, and rinsed; and, if not to be colored, they are ripped out, and dried in the atmosphere in sheds constructed for this purpose.

They are stretched on boards, rubbed out to render them smooth, and tacked down, so as to dry without wrinkling. These skins are generally filled three times with fresh liquor to tan them fully.

The next operation is that of coloring. If the color

* By referring to Chapter XXVIII., the reader will see that this so-called improvement was a process known for a long time, and orpiment and lime have been the first agents fixed for the depilation.

is to be applied topically, by putting it on the surface with a sponge, the skins are first dried. If they are to be dyed in liquors they are sewed, so as to have the grain side out; then mordanted, and afterwards handled in a tub containing the coloring agents. Prussian blue color is imparted by handling the skins, first in a dilute solution of nitrate of iron for about one hour; then in a warm bath containing yellow prussiate of potash, and a little sulphuric acid. A beautiful blue is thus obtained. A scarlet is prepared with a mordant of chloride of tin and cream tartar; the red color is afterwards obtained by handling them in an extract liquor of cochineal; purple is dyed by applying a cochineal color on the top of a Prussian blue; bronze is obtained from a strong extract of logwood and alum. After being dyed the skins are rinsed, stretched on boards; rubbed smoothly down; tacked around their edges, and dried.

Topical colors are given to the grain surfaces in many instances; they simply consist of a strong extract applied with a sponge on a piece of cotton cloth; almost any color can thus be put on. A scarlet color is made by a topical application of an extract of turmeric upon a dyed cochineal red. To enable some of the coloring agents to go on evenly, milk and the white of eggs are frequently mixed with them. These applications also serve to impart a metallic lustre to the surface. Prior to rolling, the dyed skins are slightly shaved on the wrong side and trimmed at the edges.

The subsequent finishing operations consist in rolling the skins on a table under a small weighted roller having a grooved face, and which is attached to a suspended arm which the operator moves back and forth until the roller has traversed the entire surface. This operation imparts a glossy Cordovan surface to the leather. A second rolling with the grooves running in an angular direction, gives the surface a diamond corded finish, the true morocco style. Formerly these skins were all finished by hand labor. The operatives stretched them on inclined boards, and rubbed over their surface with grooved balls of ebony held in the hand. Sometimes an extra finish is still imparted in this manner to skins.

This establishment is to our knowledge the first who applied (in this country) aniline dyes on leather. The colors thus produced are magnificent. However, we do not recommend them, as they have no stability.

Cordovan Leather.

Cordovan leather, which takes its name from the city of Cordova, in Spain, and of which the original preparation is attributed to the Moors, is plain, but handsome, with a fine grain, and similar to the morocco which is ordinarily tanned with oak bark, nutgalls or sumach. The best kinds, especially the yellow Cordovans, are brought from the Levant. Those of Spain, France, and Hungary are also highly esteemed, and in Germany the cities of Dantzic, Lubec, and Leipsic enjoy a reputation for like productions. The material used in the manufacture comprises goat-skins, dog-skins, and even hog-skins; they are produced of every color and quality, but those made from the goat-skins are the best.

The skins, after having been cleaned and stretched in water, are placed in lime pits; they are then replaced in water for a space of from eight to fifteen days, care being taken to renew it from time to time, and to work the skins by treading upon them with the feet. After a lapse of a fortnight a bath is applied composed of water and dog's dung, the temperature not being higher than that of new-drawn milk; then a second bath, equally composed of water and of wheat-bran. Immediately on being taken from the bath the skins are stretched, pressed between two boards, and rubbed with kitchen salt. They are then immersed in a third bath prepared of figs and water. Only skins which it is intended to color black are dyed after having been tanned. Black leather is tanned in liquor of the extract of oak bark; that of lighter color must be placed in an ooze made up of water and the extracts of sumach and nutgalls.

When the operation of tanning is completed, the leather should be withdrawn, taking with it as little moisture as possible, and spread in the shade, where care should be taken to rub on the bloom with Sesam oil before the sides can become perfectly dry. After the oil is laid on, the process of drying in the shade may be completed, and the skin may be folded on the flesh side. When it is desired to give to the Cordovan a rough aspect, the surface may be rubbed off with a dull knife immediately after spreading.

In many parts of Southern Russia, particularly at Karaszubazar, a city of the Crimea, of which the Cordovan manufacturers enjoy a high reputation, wormwood (*artemisia absinthium*) is employed to make fast the color in the leather. If, for example, it is proposed to dye the leather black, a decoction of wormwood is mixed with pulverized cochineal, and then alum is added.

In the island of Cyprus, Cordovans are dyed red in the following manner: The skins, generally about fifty at a time, are placed in a fig bath; they are then passed into a strong solution of alum heated to a temperature equivalent to that of fresh milk; they are afterwards strung up on poles to drip, and at length stretched, in order to expel as much of the dampness as possible; finally, the skins are extended on a table, and after being uniformly stretched the red color is applied with a cotton rag. The coloring matter is prepared by taking ground cochineal, and boiling it in soft water in a well-tinned kettle, and during the ebullition five ounces of powdered alum are added for every five ounces of cochineal, and the liquor boils until it has been reduced ⅓ or ¼ by evaporation, when it is poured through a filter. The skins are coated four or five times with this preparation, and after being placed in the tanning liquor, are submitted to the operation of dressing.

In Hungary and in Transylvania, where the manufacturers of Cordovan produce goods which are highly esteemed for their quality, the red color is laid on in a different manner. When the skins have been properly prepared for the process, they are fastened together by couples in the form of bags, care being always taken to place the sides to be colored within and facing each other, and to leave but one opening. Into this opening the warm coloring matter is poured; the mouth of the bag is then tied, and if the color does not readily penetrate all parts of the skins and readily unite with them, they are agitated or rolled around.

CHAPTER XLIX.

TANNING OF HORSE-HIDES.

About sixty years ago the tanning of horse-hides was considered a problem, but now they are largely converted into leather, and they make excellent material for uppers and the legs of boots.

They are lined in the same way as calf-skins, but being much thicker they require a longer exposure in the tan pits, eight months being necessary.

Horse-hides can be easily tanned, and transformed into excellent leather in fifty days, by the following process:[*] "Soak the skins for one night, and pass them successively through three lime pits; let them remain one day in each, the fresh pit containing one bushel of lime for seven skins. Take out, and wash in running water; work them in the usual way on the beam, and pass them through the vats, remaining six, eight, and in winter, ten days in the first one. During this part of the operation take them out, and replace them from time to time, as often as eight or ten times daily for the first five days. The liquid of the first vat should mark $0.7°$ by Baumé's areometer; that of the second should be $0.9°$, and while in this the skins should be taken out only once daily. After nine or ten days, remove them to the third liquid, which has a density of 1.2; allow them to remain in for the same length of time; and finally keep them for ten or twelve days in the last vat, which marks $2°$. During this last period, two baskets of fresh tan, weighing 55 lbs., should be daily thrown into each vat.

"After removal from the last vat the skins are thoroughly tanned. They are then rubbed upon a marble table, first on the flesh, then on the hair sides; half dried upon hooks attached to the ceiling of the drying room, and sent slightly moist to the currier.

"A horse-hide weighing 22 lbs. loses 6½ lbs. by cleaning, but gains 8½ lbs. in the tanning." This process is very simple, but requires all the attention and care of the workmen, and differs from that for other hides, in their not being placed at all in pits, and in being subjected to the action of tannin while floating in liquid.

[*] Dumas, "Traité de Chimie Appliquée aux Arts."

CHAPTER L.

TANNING OF DIFFERENT SKINS.

THE skins of bucks, wolves, elks, dogs, and other animals can be tanned as those of goats and sheep. Those of lambs, kids, cats, rabbits, and hares, do not require exposure to as strong infusion, nor for so great a length of time as sheep-skins, while those of hogs, wild boars, and bears, are prepared like them. When these skins are fresh, and when it is intended to prepare them with the hair, the time is considerably lengthened. Human skins can be tanned like others. They have more body than cow-skins, and are thickest upon the abdomen. They require a greater number of limings and of exposures to the infusions of bark, and they swell up a great deal under these operations.

CHAPTER LI.

TANNING OF THE SKINS OF SHEEPS' LEGS FOR MAKING TUBES WITHOUT SUTURE, FOR COVERING THE CYLINDERS USED IN COTTON AND WOOL SPINNING.

A PARISIAN tanner, M. Delvau, introduced this process, which consists in cutting the skin of the sheep's foot above the spur, and stripping it off in a manner similar to that after which rabbits are uncased. This tube is then limed, until the wool falls off, is *daubed* with oil, and curried so as to make it of an equal thickness through.

To apply these tubes to the cylinders without suture, two burnishing tools are used for spreading them out. Each tube, which is made of such a size as to exceed the cylinder a little in diameter, is drawn over it, and stretched upon it by means of pincers, and the parts which pass beyond the ends of the cylinder are folded down, smoothed out, and glued over them. These extremities are then rubbed with the burnishers, in order to make the glue enter the substance of the leather, and they are left to dry five or six hours. The shreds of leather are then removed, and those parts which project from the middle and ends are cut away on a turning lathe. To finish the surface and give it lustre, it is well rubbed with a hard linen cloth.

Leather Bottles.

These bottles are used in France to carry oil and wine. Cow-skins are used for this purpose. They are dried upon pegs by the butchers, and are then softened in lime which has been previously used, and in which they remain for eight days. Then they are thrown into a fresh lime pit until the hair readily comes off; they are cleaned, rinsed, and fleshed after having been cut into pieces of the proper shape. Then expose them to dry upon a smooth, clean and dry spot of ground, great care being observed that this drying takes place uniformly and gradually. When thus deprived of moisture, and at the same time preserving all their suppleness, they are hung up for a month, and exposed to the direct rays of the sun, being taken down and stored at night, so that no moisture shall have access to them.

Before being sewed they are placed in water to allow the stretches to be made. These bottles last a long time, but liquids kept in them always acquire an unpleasant taste.

CHAPTER LII.

RED LEATHER.

THE butts used to manufacture this kind of leather are imported from Buenos Ayres. Soak them from four to five days, deposit them in an old lime vat, extend them evenly so they may not wrinkle; the largest hides being cut in half along the line from head to tail. Handle repeatedly in this pit for five days, and deposit them in a fresh vat where they remain for two or three months; handle them twice a week, and add a little fresh lime during each of the last five handlings. When they are ready to be fleshed, take them out, rinse them four times only partially, so that the lime may not be entirely washed out.

Place the hides in the pit, and stratify them with the bark of the root of the evergreen or scarlet oak, which has been soaked in water.

Leave three months in the first pit, place in a second one, and expose them to the action of the bark for the same length of time, take them out, dry and carry them to the currier. Each hide requires about 120 lbs. of bark.

CHAPTER LIII.

DANISH PROCESS.

BY this process *dressing leather* may be made in two months.

Soak the hides, flesh and free them from hair, and rinse them in the ordinary manner; color them like barleyed skins. Sew them into form of bags, leaving an aperture about ten inches long, by which you fill them with tan and water. Sew those openings, and beat the closed sacks in every part, for the purpose of distributing their contents equally through; then deposit them in pits containing sufficient ooze to completely cover them. These pits are 4¼ feet in depth; the same in breadth, and from 8½ to 10½ feet long. Place upon the skins planks heavily loaded with weights, and press them towards the bottom to increase the penetrating power of the infusion. To have them equally tanned, remove the boards three or four times a week, beat the sacks and change their position.

These skins are supple and pliable, have a finer color than strong leather; they are thinner than those made by the ordinary process, owing to their not swelling up by the slow process of feeding, and to the pressure to which they have been submitted. It is doubtful if the durability and other qualities of the product are equal to those of leather prepared by more tedious processes.

CHAPTER LIV.

CHEMICAL THEORY OF TANNING.

THE operation by which skins are converted into leather has been known and practised since the most remote antiquity; but the nature of the tanning principle was unknown before the experiments of Lewis and Deyeux, and the experience of Seguin. This latter chemist has given the following theory of the art of tanning:—

1st. The skin stripped of its flesh, is a substance which

can be easily converted by a convenient process into an animal jelly which, concentrated and dried in the air furnishes glue.

2d. A solution of this latter substance being mixed with an infusion of tan, an insoluble precipitate is formed, and this precipitate is not susceptible of putrefaction.

3d. The solution of tan is composed of two distinct substances, one precipitates the glue, and is the true tanning matter, the other precipitates the proto-sulphate of iron without precipitating the solution of glue, and produces only the disoxygenation of the skin and of the substance which unites the hair to the skin.*

4th. The operation of tanning is not a simple combination of the skin with the principle which precipitates the glue, but a combination with the skin disoxygenized by the substance, which, in dissolution in the tan has the property of precipitating the sulphate of iron. Thus all substances to be used to tan ought to have the properties of precipitating glue and sulphate of iron.

5th. The operation of tanning consists, first, in the swelling of the skins by an acid principle. Second, a disoxygenation by gallic acid. Third, in disoxygenating the skin with the same principle, and by this disoxygenation it is in a middle state between glue and skin. Fourth, in combining it by this disoxygenation.

Whatever are the merits of Seguin, and the services he has rendered, we cannot but expose all the errors of the above theory.

We persist in looking at the swelling of the skin as an effect less chemical than mechanical, which is principally due to the interposition of the water, or to the effect

* Seguin does not speak of the extractive, which, according to Sir H. Davy, is necessary to form a flexible and firm leather.

of the caloric produced by the fermentation. Acids and alkalies, as we have said, act only as a means of preserving the skin from putrefaction; afterwards they exercise a chemical action. Thus the lime with which the interior of the skin is saturated, notwithstanding all the washings, forms with the tannin a tannate of lime, which takes away the suppleness of the leather; and for this reason it is that the lime method is injurious. It is not the same with acids. Besides preserving the skin from putrefaction, the produced acetic acid reacts on the fibrin, softens it and transforms it partly into a transparent jelly, soluble in boiling water and combining with the tannin. Besides this acid, by which the skin is more or less saturated, it precipitates the solution of tannin and fixes a larger quantity in the leather. This softening renders the swelling very easy. However, it can be operated without these means, which are in antagonism with Seguin's theory.

We do not agree with Seguin that gallic acid is the principal and indispensable agent in tanning. No experiment has demonstrated the durable disoxygenation which he asserts, and which is impossible if we compare the respective constituents of gelatine and fibrin. Thus

Fibrin contains . 19.615 *per cent. of Oxygen.*
Gelatine " . 72.207 " " "

From this we see it is impossible that gallic acid disoxygenizes the fibrin and transforms it into glue, whilst pure gelatine contains nearly one-third more of oxygen. If such were the case, gallic acid must oxidize instead of disoxygenizing it. We therefore see that this theory is inadmissible. Let us now record the experiment :—

Catechu contains from 48 to 54 *per cent. of Tannin.*
Tea " " 34 " 40 " " "
Herb Bennett " 42 " " "
Scille " 24 " " "

These substances, so rich in tannin, are applied with success in tanning, while, however, they do not contain a particle of gallic acid. Seguin does not mention the extractive, however; this substance has some action in the tanning, and according to the experiments of Sir H. Davy its presence is necessary to form a flexible and firm leather, and in some way it may take the place of tannin. In England, where tanning material is very scarce, they have used the decoction of cicuta; and Schwerger has shown by analysis that 100 parts of fresh leaves contain 2.73 of extractive without tannin or gallic acid.

To resume, we regard tanning as a combination of five principles, *fibrin, gelatine, tannin, extractive,* and *acid.*

1st. Gelatine and fibrin are transformed into a jelly, by acetic acid with tannin, extractive and gallic acid.

2d. In tanning, the epidermis disappears, and no portions of the skin have been disoxygenized.

3d. The action of gallic acid is similar to that of acetic acid, and its presence is not necessary in the operation.

4th. Extractive, like tannin, unites with the altered gelatine and fibrin, and renders leather flexible and firm. It is also the principle of their coloration; thus leather tanned with gall is pale, that with oak bark is brownish, with catechu is reddish, etc. It is the extractive which gives to the leather a brownish color, without rendering it insoluble in boiling water.

5th. Lime forms with tannin a tannate of lime, which destroys the suppleness of leather, and renders it dry and brittle.

6th. Dried skins well tanned increase in weight about 33 per cent. This increase is due to the fixation of the tannin, extractives, gallic acid and a little water.

7th. In saturated infusions there is less extractive than tannin, while in weak infusions the extractive predominates. That is the reason why it is necessary to place the skins at first in very weak infusions, and, lastly, to saturate them, little by little, with tannic acid and extractive, so as to have a complete tanning and a more supple leather.

8th. By presenting to the skins strong infusions, the leather contains but very little extractive, and is tanned only on two surfaces, the centre containing little, so that the leather obtained is hard and brittle.

9th. At last, gallic acid exercises so slight an influence on tanning, that Sir H. Davy thinks it is doubtful if oak bark contains any.

Chemical Researches on the Art of Tanning.*
By M. Knapp.

Every one knows that it is not the skin which is worked by tanners, but the prepared skin, or the *corium*, or the skin separated, as much as possible, from the useless parts by mechanical and chemical treatment.

The prepared skin, when damp, has the appearance of a tissue of a milky color; seen by the microscope it appears to be composed of parallel fibres without color, and transparent.

The transparency and the milky appearance are the effects of the dispersion of light. The skin, by drying, contracts, assumes a homogeneous appearance, and becomes *horned*. But by working it it becomes again white and pliable, as before the desiccation.

This change of nature is due to this, when the skin dries, the fibres which compose it agglutinate, one on

* Répertoire de Chimie.

the other, exactly as the surfaces of the intestinal skin, which composes violin strings; thus the spaces which separate them disappear, and it no longer transmits light.

The object of *tanning* is at first to destroy, as much as possible, the tendency of the skin to putrefy principally, and it is its characteristic function to cause the skin, when dry, to remain a fibrous tissue without transparency, and to remain pliable. Three operations are necessary to transform the skin into leather, the *anterior preparation*, the *tanning*, and *currying*.

The PREPARATION consists in taking out the *flower* of the epidermis, and the hair which covers it, and the flesh of the adhering membranes. The maceration and the working are sufficient to prepare the flesh; the treatment of the flower requires chemical substances, such as lime, sulphurets, etc.

The *modus operandi* of these two substances is different. Lime acts by rendering the tissue of the epidermis softer, which admits of its easy depilation, whilst on the contrary, sulphurets act on the basis of the hair, render it milky, so that if a piece of skin is macerated in this reagent, the hair can be taken out only by rubbing it with a piece of wood.

TANNING is generally considered as a chemical operation.

Every one agrees that there is found in the skin an immediate principle, which combines with the tannin or with tanning substances, and then it is compared to *gelatine*, some even consider the leather as a *tannate of gelatine*.

The known facts are sufficient to demonstrate how far this theory is from the truth.

At first, acidulated bones, which give gelatine as the skin, are not capable of giving a product similar to leather, *whatever is the quantity of tannin and the time of contact*. Then the salts of iron and alumina, which tan leather, do not precipitate the gelatine. At last, grease, which tans perfectly well, has no similarity to tannin.

It may also be said that, generally, when a chemical combination takes place, the form disappears; and it is sure that, in tanning, not only the texture of the skin does not disappear, but is rather developed; however, as in gun-cotton, it will be admitted that the substance of the skin can combine, without apparent change, with the tannin, as the cotton with the nitric acid.

A more serious objection is in this known fact, that tanning substances, such as alum, can be *taken from the skin by a sufficiently long washing*, then the skin reappears with its primitive character.

Tannin itself can be taken from the skin. If we take a skin which has been immersed in *pure* tannin and is transformed into *leather*, we can by a weak alkaline solution, separate all the tannin, and the skin can be tanned again. However, skin which has been tanned with *tan*, and treated by carbonate of soda, loses the greater part of the tannin it contains, but it *does not cease to be leather*, as is the case with skin tanned with pure tannin. It retains a *tanning* substance *peculiar to the tan* and differing from pure tannin, which the carbonate of soda cannot dissolve. Evidently these facts do not agree with the theory which sees in tannin a chemical action. Mr. Knapp thinks that analytical experiments alone can resolve this question. For this purpose he takes a prepared and purified skin, dries it in vacuo, and operates on a determined weight that he submits to the action of tanning dissolutions, and weighs anew after a thorough washing and drying in vacuum. These experiments have given the following results.

Skin immersed in a solution of alum contained, after the operation, 8.5 per cent. of additional matter. The increase in weight was due only to the incorporation of the *alum in nature;* there is no chemical decomposition in this operation. With sulphate of alumina the result was the same; the skin fixed 27.9 per cent. of anhydrous sulphate of alumina. The chloride of aluminum acted in the same manner; it united without decomposition, and the skin contained 29.3 per cent. Acetate of alumina gave the same results, and the skin contained 23 per cent. of this salt.

It results from these facts, that not only is it no decomposition of the tanning salt, as in acid and basic salt as Berzelius thought; but that the quantities absorbed are without relation to their equivalents. The author adds that these numbers are not absolute; that they vary with circumstances, principally with the concentration of the liquids, and that the fixed salt can be taken out by washing with pure water. Thus the proportion of chloride of alumina after a washing of three days, has been reduced from 29.3 per cent. to 3 per cent.

The corresponding compounds of chrome and iron behave in the same manner as the salts of alumina, only they are absorbed in less quantity, and they color the skin, while the salts of alumina do not.

Fatty bodies, as sesquioxide salts, will tan. This fact alone is in opposition to the idea of a chemical combination of the tanning matter with the skin. Nevertheless, the author has tried to prove by experiment, if there was in the quantity of the bodies absorbed to convert the skin into leather, any evidence in favor of the theory which he was disputing. He dipped skins into alcoholic solutions of stearic and oleic acid; or ethereal solutions of fish oils, and he ascertained that the *tanning was perfect*, and that the fatty body was not modified, and the absorbed quantity was from 1 to 1½ per cent. Resins have acted like greases. This small quantity of tanning substance represents only the proportion kept in solution by the reagent in which the skin is macerated.

All the above experiments demonstrate that tanning is not a chemical action, and Mr. Knapp has substituted for the old theory a more solid one. To this chemist, tanning substances have the function of enveloping the fibres of the skin, so that their adherence becomes impossible, and that the skin keeps its pliable qualities after the desiccation, or at least recovers it by a mechanical action; *this is to him the true character of tanning*. To demonstrate his proposition, he established a series of experiments, the object of which was *to tan the skin without the use of tanning substances*. Considering that the fibres agglutinate together only when they are penetrated by water, he conceived the idea of putting the skin in contact with a liquid (alcohol or ether) which, expelling the water by endosmose, takes away from the fibres that property of agglutinating together. According to his views, he has obtained by *the action of alcohol alone*, a tanned skin very white, and of such a constitution *that practical men have recognized it as a tanned skin. Then this is a true leather without tanning matter*, which in water becomes again skin, and by the coction is changed into glue.

This last experiment shows that tanning is not a chemical action. When Mr. Knapp speaks of tanning, he understands only *the conversion of the skins, which in drying will become horned, into a matter which remains flexible even by desiccation*. For the other qualities that leather requires in tanning, such as imputrescibility, etc., they are not absolutely inherent in the nature of the leather; they are only relative, and they are obtained at variable degrees according to the products obtained, and the operations to which the skin is submitted.

The conclusions of Mr. Knapp's experiments are the following: Tanning is not a chemical operation, leather is no more tannate of gelatine than tanned skin is a combination of gelatine with a sub-sulphate of alumina.

The proof of it is in the following facts: Some substances, which, like skins, can be converted into glue, do not give leather.

Tanning substances are not absorbed by the skin in definite proportions. The different tanning salts do not unite with the skin in equivalent proportions.

Tanning salts, and tannin itself, can, by washing, be separated from the leather which becomes skin again.

Fatty bodies which have no similarity to astringent compounds, will tan leather.

Skins may acquire the properties which are given by tanning without the use of tanning compounds.

At last some substances unite with the skin and render it imputrescible, and incapable of forming gelatine; without giving it the qualities of leather.

According to Mr. Knapp, leather differs from the dry skin in this, that in the last the fibres adhere one to the other, while in the first they are isolated; the part of the tanning substance is to maintain this isolation.

The tanning substances surround each fibre instead of uniting with it as chemical substances.

To realize an industrial tanning, you want reagents which can be fixed on the fibres of the skin, prevent the adhering of these fibres, operate with rapidity, and give to the skin the required suppleness and the property of resisting putrefaction. These conditions are partly fulfilled by the use of salts of sesquioxide.

The tanning action of iron salts has been known for a long time, but it has not been much utilized yet.

Leather tanned with iron salts is often flat, hard, and brittle, even when the solutions are the most nearly neutral possible. The acid reaction of the salt is sufficient to destroy the quality of the leather. It is a known fact that an alkaline reaction is favorable to the swelling of skins.

The above experiments have conducted Mr. Knapp to the following process:—

Prepare two baths, one with soap-water, the other with a solution of iron, alumina, or chrome.

The solution of soap must not contain more than $\frac{1}{20}$ or $\frac{1}{30}$ of soap. If hard soap is used (soft soap is better), the bath is kept at 100°.

Prepare also the solution of tanning-salt, which should be one-tenth, with the chloride of iron, which colors the skin brown red, or with the chloride of chrome, which gives a gray-blue color, or with the chloride of alumina, which is colorless.

Dip the skins in the metallic solutions, stir them, draw them, dip them again, and so forth, till they are well-penetrated. Forty-eight hours are sufficient to obtain this result.

The skins, being well drained, are thrown into the solution of soap. When the reaction is complete, wash and dry them.

This operation is very rapid, and it may be rendered more so by substituting alcoholic for aqueous solutions.

We see that this process, while very different from

tanning, conducts to the same results; is quicker and cheaper, and gives a simpler, brighter, and softer skin.

Tanning can also be obtained by dipping the skin in a very weak acidulated water, then in soap water, and repeating this operation two or three times till all the skin is tanned. Wash and dry.

In the course of this paper we have spoken of an experiment consisting in impregnating the skin with an alcoholic solution of stearic acid. The author insists on that experiment as giving a new and quick process of preparation. Leather thus obtained is very flexible, and as white as white kid leather; the grain is fresher and brighter.

SECTION VI.

IMPROVED PROCESSES.

In order not to interrupt the series of the operations of tanning we think it better to devote a special section to the improved processes. We shall make no comment, and we leave it to intelligent manufacturers to consider as our judgment of the different processes we describe, that which agrees with what we have before expressed.

CHAPTER LV.

SEGUIN'S PROCESS.

The preliminary processes are the same as those of others, excepting that after soaking and fleshing, he rinses the skins in running water, so as to expose all parts to it. He depilates them with lime and deposits them in tan juice mixed with $\frac{1}{500}$ or sometimes $\frac{1}{1000}$ part of sulphuric acid.

For raising, he uses a vat lined with a cement containing lime and filled with water containing $\frac{1}{1500}$ part of sulphuric acid, but he finds that the acid instead of mixing with water combines with the lime. For these vats he substitutes wooden tubs and fills them with water containing $\frac{1}{1500}$ part of sulphuric acid, which increases to $\frac{1}{1000}$, and by this arrangement he was enabled to raise skins in forty-eight hours. According to this chemist this raising is not necessary, as he could make excellent leather from skins not submitted to this treatment.

He placed the skins in vats filled with *ooze*. To obtain this solution he filled a number of tubs placed in a row, with ground tan. In each tub he put a certain quantity of water, which filtered through the tan, dissolved its soluble particles, and was received in vessels beneath. He passed the liquid of the first vat on the second, and so on till the liquid was completely saturated. As the two still contained a certain amount of soluble material, he treated the tubs until the tan was completely exhausted.

The skins being taken from the acid bath, he placed them in a very weak infusion of tan and allowed them to remain only one or two hours to color the hair sides. He then immersed them in a stronger solution, and continued thus, increasing each time the strength of the solution until the tanning was completed.

CHAPTER LVI.

PROCESS OF PREPARING GLOSSED LEATHER BEFORE THE TANNING OPERATION.

THIS new process of preparation of hides, invented by Messrs. Monier and Ray, consists in trampling them in a fulling machine, disposed so as to contain any liquid put in, and having below holes for the water to run off.

Details of the Work of Preparation of the Leather.

Hides.—Soak them for 48 hours in cold water.

Smelting.—Introduce the hides into the fulling machine, which according to the size of the hide will con-

354   TANNING.

tain 8 or 10 or even 16 of them. Trample them for half an hour, which is sufficient to render them sufficiently supple.

Liming.—After beating them a few minutes to free them from water, put them into the lime vat, the lime being of the consistency of thick milk, and in sufficient quantity. The hides being thus exposed, beat them for four hours, withdraw them, pile them one upon another, leave them for five days, the time necessary to warm them, and then put them back into the fulling machine to clean them.

Cleaning.—Work them in the fulling machine for 1½ hour, take them out and scrape them well. The first cleaning not being sufficient to take off all the lime, leave them one hour in a water containing $\frac{1}{100}$ of sulphuric acid, handling often. Wash them well in running water.

Description of the Apparatus.

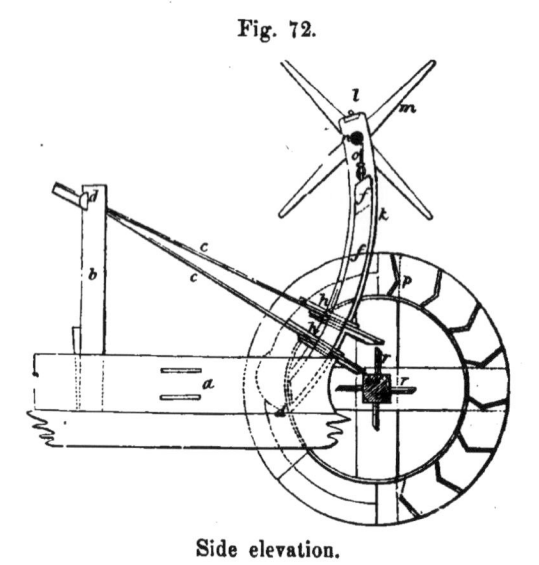

Fig. 72.

Side elevation.

PROCESS OF PREPARING GLOSSED LEATHER.

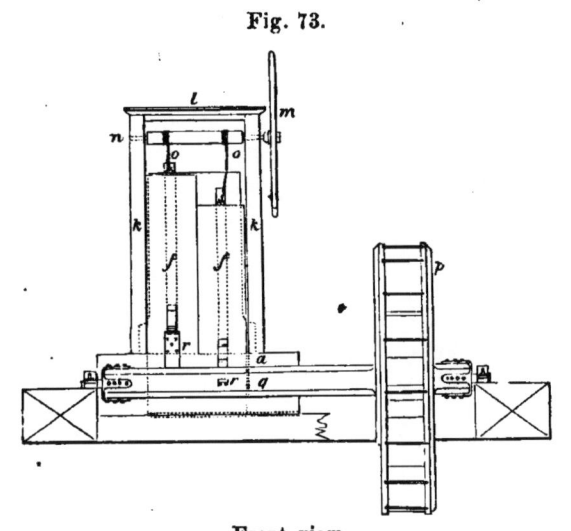

Fig. 73.

Front view.

Fig. 74.

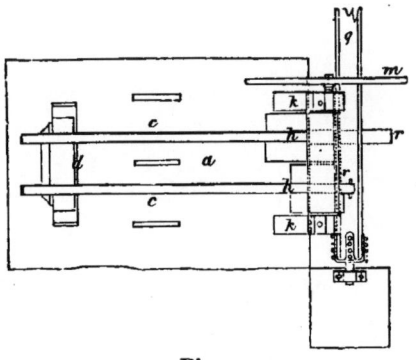

Plan.

(*a*). Trough in which the skins are placed.

(*b*). Post raised above the trough, and supporting the levers (*c*) near their upper end, where these levers are attached to a piece of wood (*d*).

(*e*). Key to press the post (*b*) and to give it the necessary inclination.

(*f*). Mallets fixed to the lower end of the levers (*c*), and working on the skins, in the hollow part of the trough (*a*) formed by the curved line seen in (*g*).

(*h*). Keys disposed so as to keep the mallets conveniently inclined to the form of the curve *g* of the trough.

(*i*). Other keys having the same uses as the above.

(*k*). Two curved posts, raising above the trough and preventing the mallets from swaying.

(*l*). Piece of wood joining the posts *k* at their upper extremity.

(*m*). Vertical turnstile with four branches, the axis (*n*) of which is received and turns in the posts *k*, and is used as a shaft to the ropes (*o*) which keep the mallets suspended.

(*p*). Wheel put in motion by water, its axis (*q*) carries cams (*r*), which by turning let the mallets (*f*) rise and fall alternately.

Tanning.—After the cleaning of the hides, and before putting them in the tan vats, they are submitted to the action of an ordinary press, then they are placed in vats filled with tan water, in which they are left for six days.

After six days the leather is pressed again, and is put back in the vats containing tan water stronger than the above. It is left in for ten days. Press again and carry to the pits, where the leather is left two or three months.

CHAPTER LVII.

TANNING WITH MYRTLE (*Vaccinium Myrtilus*).

THIS process was discovered by a tanner of Bern-Cassel, Mr. Rapenius, who found that a superior leather could be made by tanning with the myrtle plant. This plant is collected in the spring of the year, is dried and ground. One hundred pounds of leather require three hundred and fifty parts of this substance, while it requires six hundred parts of oak bark, and its use saves four months of the time generally employed. Leather made with it is of a superior quality. Shoes made with it last two months longer than those made from common leather. The skin of the neck becomes as strong and elastic as other parts when thus prepared. The myrtle should be cut off, and not pulled up by the roots. After it is cut it is not injured by water as oak bark, which loses by exposure to moisture.

CHAPTER LVIII.

TANNING WITH GRAPE-SKINS.

In 1829, a chemist of Narbonne proposed to substitute grape-stalks for oak bark in tanning. His process is thus spoken of by Nachette, in the *Journal of Pharmacy*.

"A substitute for oak bark has long been sought for, but no one yet has before thought of employing for this purpose the stalks and skins of the grape. This chemist prepared skins for tanning by the ordinary process; he placed them in vats filled with stalks and skins of grapes (previously distilled to save the alcohol); he allowed them to remain from thirty-five to forty-five days, which time he found sufficient. The advantages of this process are the following: 1st. Less time is required. 2d. A refuse material of some localities is substituted for the expensive oak bark. 3d. The leather produced has a slightly agreeable odor. 4th. The leather obtained by this process lasts twice as long as that obtained by the ordinary process."

CHAPTER LIX.

TANNING WITH STATICE (*Marsh Rosemary*).

This process was discovered by Mr. Tournal, and we give below the full details, extracted from a paper written by him on the subject.

'Mr. Gayraud and himself commenced an experiment with an ox-hide, while another tanner, M. Mallaret, undertook to prepare some goat-skins. Mr. Gayraud prepared the hide in the same manner as with the bark of the root of the kermes-oak, except that he divided it into two equal portions; one he tanned with the statice and the other with the root of the kermes-oak, in order to determine what difference in weight would be produced by the two materials.

Six months had passed when the heat of the weather produced, in the statice liquid, so active a fermentation that it burst the vessel containing it, so the experiment could be carried no further. The tannin had penetrated nearly to the centre, and probably two months more of exposure would have completed the process. The leather, examined by good judges, was declared of the very best quality. Mr. Mallaret declared that goat-skins tanned by this process were superior to that with oak bark.

M. Tournal, in one year, tanned perfectly a piece of thick Buenos Ayres hide, which in the ordinary way would have required eighteen months.

M. Gayraud then commenced the tanning of more than 100 horse-hides and 50 imported cow-hides, while M. Mallaret tried 150 goat-skins, and M. J. Calas, 80 horse-hides, the cow-skins being intended for soles, the horse-hides and goat-skins for upper leather.

M. Gayraud placed the cow-skins in the lime pit, to depilate and rise them. The lime revealed many defects and injuries, so that out of the fifty hides, one-third were more or less damaged, and some had to be trimmed to one-half their size in consequence of being injured. This prevented ascertaining the difference in weights in the process, but it was found that the hides were tanned in a third less than the usual time. They were remarkable for weight, beauty, color, and strength. The same operator weighed exactly a certain number of perfect skins; he tanned them by the statice, and obtained the most satisfactory results.

In the preparation of horse-hides, the superiority of statice as tan was evident in the finer structure of the product, shortness of the process, economy of material, beauty of color, increased weight, power of absorbing fatty bodies, etc. The same advantages were perceived in goat leather.

All the skins thus prepared have been sold, and workmen who used them preferred them to those tanned by the usual process. They equal skins tanned with kermes-oak bark for wear in damp weather, while in dry weather they are much superior. As to flexibility, they hold thread better, and are more easily worked. The leather for uppers is remarkable for suppleness and firmness, and for the brilliancy, intensity, and durability of the black color which can be given to it.

CHAPTER LX.

LEPRIEUR'S TANNING PROCESS.

Four operations, about similar to those followed by tanners, constitute Leprieur's process.

1. *The rinsing*, comprising the softening of dry hides, washing, swelling, etc.
2. *The sugar of lead bath.*
3. *The tan liquor bath.*
4. *Tanning.*

A. SUGAR OF LEAD BATH.

This operation comprises the following manipulation: 1st, the hides being well washed and drained are put into the bath ten to twelve hours in summer, and 24 to 30 in winter. This bath is thus prepared:—

Acetate of lead (sugar of lead)	1 lb.
Water	125 gals.

Such a bath is sufficient for 6 to 8 hides.

It is to the precipitate formed by this salt and the albumen that the author attributes the solidity of the leather, which is neither hollow nor brittle. When out of this bath put it in another prepared in the same proportions, being careful in the two immersions to stir the hides every three or four hours. After remaining 12 to 24 hours in this bath, wash carefully in running water.

B. TAN LIQUOR BATHS.

The author contends that the raising is not an essential condition for tanning, and if necessary it can be obtained by adding acid in the first infusions; he gives the proportion of 1 part of tan for 10 parts of dry hides, with enough sulphuric acid to impart a decided acid taste, as being all-sufficient for the purpose.

First Series of Infusions.

First Bath.—This bath for every 110 lbs. of hides is composed of 22 lbs. of tan; infuse the hides for 24 hours in enough water to cover, but not completely sink them. To this mixture add from 9½ to 9¾ ounces of sulphuric acid at 66° B. If after a maceration of 24 hours the liquid is not sensibly acid, add some more, if it is desired to raise by it.

In summer keep the hides in this bath 30 or 40 hours, for after that time it will putrefy. In winter they may remain one day longer.

Second Bath.—For 110 lbs. of hides use 33 lbs. of tan and acidify this bath as the above. Keep the skins in for 36 hours, take them out to drain, immerse them 30 hours more, and drain again. This bath is no longer serviceable except as a putrid ferment for new infusions.

Third Bath.—For 110 lbs. of skins use 44 lbs. of tan, and add 9½ ounces of sulphuric acid, if the previous raising has been considered sufficient. Take out the skins by intervals, wash in water, drain and replace. If after a stay in the bath of four or five days it shows 3° or 4° by the acid hydrometer, allow the skins to remain 24 hours longer, or better, the liquid may be used in the same manner as the first bath for thin skins.

Fourth Bath.—Operate as above, using 55 lbs. of tan, and leaving the skins in it for six or eight days. The skins before being placed in the vat are drained for eight or twelve hours, and are taken out at least three times to ascertain that the liquor has not become too weak.

If the degree shown by the acid hydrometer is four or five tenths, prepare a fresh liquid and reserve the old one for skins which are undergoing the second series of baths. According to Leprieur, it is better to deposit fresh skins in old baths which they quickly exhaust, than in those more advanced.

Second Series of Infusions.

First Bath.—According to Leprieur a new set of skins begins with the fourth bath of the first series of infusions, and require 330 lbs. of bark to tan them as completely as the others.

Second Bath.—Since the fifth bath of the first series would not be disposed of in time to answer for the second bath of the second series, and would moreover be too strong, a new one should be prepared like that of No. 2. After the fourth bath stratify the leather and tan, alternately interposing willow twigs so that the surfaces be equally soaked.

FIRST SERIES.—*Fifth Bath.*—For 110 lbs. of hides use 66 lbs. of tan. Keep the hides in the vats 6 to 8 days, take out, draw, and replace three or four times during this period. If strips of wood are placed between them, it will be sufficient to cover the last layer of tan with the infusion to the height of ½ an inch.

SECOND SERIES.—*Third Bath.*—The fifth bath forms the third of the second series.

Sixth Bath.—To 110 lbs. of hides use 66 lbs. of tan, leave 10 days, take out and drain at intervals of two or three days. When the infusion marks more than 5 or 6 of the acid hydrometer, take the skins out, and the bath is reserved for others which are less advanced in preparation.

Fourth Bath.—The fifth bath like the sixth, not being

unoccupied soon enough to answer for the fourth of the second series, it is necessary to prepare it with fresh materials, like No. 4. It is then the sixth of the first series under the denomination five.

Fifth Bath.—The hides can remain in this bath until the fifth bath of the first series is fully prepared; there is then no more danger of the putrefaction of the hides.

Seventh Bath.—For 110 lbs. of hide use 88 lbs. of bark. Leave the hides to remain twelve or fifteen days, or until the liquid marks no more than from six to seven by the hydrometer. After that time it will serve for the second set of skins. When the hides are taken from this bath and cut, the section shows a well-tanned surface, while the inside is unchanged. The operation has taken nearly fifty days, and every 110 lbs. of hides have consumed 385 lbs. of bark. Supposing that 1100 lbs. of tan are used to tan that weight of leather by the ordinary method, there still remain 717 lbs. to be used in the pits to make the expenditure the same.

Sixth Bath.—The seventh bath of the first series is the sixth of the second; but it is a matter of indifference whether the hides are at once deposited in the vats, or again exposed to a bath of 110 lbs. of tan to an equal weight of leather.

C. TANNING IN THE VATS.

Leprieur uses tan well mixed with water, to which he adds sulphuric acid in the same proportions as above indicated. Upon the bottom of the vat he deposits a layer of this mixture; he spreads a hide upon it, and he continues the stratification until the vat is filled. The last hide is covered with a stratum of one inch of the mixture; he throws in a quantity of water sufficient to rise above the surface, and covers the whole with weighted boards to prevent the skins from floating. The liquid of the vat is tested every three or four days with the hydrometer, to ascertain if any diminution of strength has taken place. In this case the skins are taken out, and deposited in another vat. Taking into consideration that 110 lbs. of good tan give 1320 lbs. of infusion marking 1° of strength by the hydrometer, and 10° or 12° of the acid hydrometer after forty-eight hours, it will be easy to ascertain, day by day, from the diminution of density, how much of the tanning principle has been absorbed. When the infusion has lost one-half of its strength it will still serve for other processes, and another supply of tan is given.

First Tanning in Vats.

For the first vat use one hundred parts of tan for one hundred parts of hides, the water being mixed as before with a little more than nine ounces of sulphuric acid. Leave the skins in this first vat, twelve to fifteen days, and besides testing the liquor by the hydrometer, the skins should be cut from time to time, to ascertain the progress of the tanning. If considerably advanced, and if the liquid is reduced to five or six-tenths, the vat should be changed.

Second Series.—The contents of the first vat are not exhausted, but furnish a strong infusion for a sixth bath for the second set of skins.

Second Tanning in the Vat.

Expose 100 parts of skins with 120 parts of tan, for fifteen days.

First Tanning.—The preceding or second tanning of the first series forms the first tanning of the second series. The skins taken from the first tanning are then exposed to the second.

Third Tanning.—Expose 100 parts of hides with 130 parts of bark, from fifteen to twenty days; the preparation is the same as before. Examine carefully the hides, as probably the thinnest ones are tanned.

Fourth Tanning.—This is the second of the second series. Use 140 parts of tan for 100 of hides; expose from fifteen to twenty days.

Third Tanning.—The preceding, or the fourth of the first series, serves as the third of the second series.

Fifth Tanning.—Use 160 parts of tan for 100 parts of hides; expose from twenty to thirty days. This quantity of 176 lbs. completing the 1100 lbs., used for the first series.

Fourth Tanning.—This is the fifth of the first series.

If after twenty days the tanning is not completed, from fifteen to twenty days more may be allowed to elapse before the leather is taken out; this being the last tanning.

If it should be necessary to add 220 lbs. more of tan to the amount already used, 220 lbs. of leather would be completely tanned by means of 1650 lbs. of bark.

Quantities of Tan Employed for Tanning 220 lbs. of Leather.

First Series.

Tan for baths	385 } 1101
" " pits	716

Second Series.

Tan for baths	88 } 264
" " pits	176
	1365

According to the author:—

Strong and supple hides are tanned in from 100 *to* 130 *days.*

Middling ones in about 150 *days.*

Refractory ones in about 180 *days.*

Sometimes a sixth tanning is required, which does not much increase the duration or expense of the preparation.

CHAPTER LXI.

D'ARCET'S PROCESS BY THE SULPHATE OF SESQUI-OXIDE OF IRON.

ACCORDING to this author, this process is simple and economical, the time of working it short, the price of the material very low, and it seems at first that this process is to be preferred to any other.

A solution of sulphate of peroxide of iron poured in a solution of gelatine or albumen produced an abundant precipitate similar to that obtained with tannin; thus a skin dipped in a solution of sulphate of sesqui-oxide of iron can be perfectly tanned. It had some inconveniences: it is that some free sulphuric acid was left free in the leather, and the other was that salts of iron disorganize the leather. Boucherie has seen that by introducing linseed oil, this last inconvenience was removed. The destructive action of sulphuric acid can be avoided, as we have seen, by dipping the leather in a weak solution of soap. This process is very short; four days are sufficient for thin skins and eight days for thick ones. We have no doubt this is an advantageous process, and before rejecting it we must wait for the results of the experiment on a large scale.

CHAPTER LXII.

NEWTON'S PROCESS.

THIS method is an accelerating process combining the use of mineral and vegetable substances. It consists in the employment of certain earthy alkaline or metallic salts for the preliminary treatment and of an astringent for the tanning. This joint action promotes the combination of the albuminous matter of the skin with the bases. When other material than catechu is used, the latter of good quality and containing 50 per cent. of tannin is taken as standard for regulating the proportion of the former. The skins must be unhaired and free from lime.

FOR 100 CALF-SKINS.

Take:

Alum	20 lbs.
Salt	10 "
Catechu	100 "
Sulphate of alumina	4 "

This latter can be used either alone or mixed with 2 lbs. of common salt. The three mixtures are dissolved in water and kept apart in separate vessels.

In a vat place $\frac{1}{5}$ of the first solution, $\frac{1}{10}$ of the second, and $\frac{1}{4}$ of the third; immerse the skins in this liquor, handle and stir them repeatedly for a short time, then take them out. Then refresh the vat by the addition of $\frac{1}{5}$ of the first solution, $\frac{1}{10}$ of the second, and $\frac{1}{4}$ of the third. Replace the skins in this mixture, treat as before, but a longer time. Remove the skins a second time, refresh the vat with $\frac{1}{5}$ of the first solution, $\frac{1}{10}$ of the second, reimmerse as above. Let them remain some time, handle occasionally, remove again, and mix in the vat the residues of the first and third solutions and $\frac{1}{5}$ of the second. Put back the skins, a few days after, take them out to add to the vat the remaining $\frac{2}{5}$ of the second mixture; four or five weeks are sufficient to complete the tanning.

This process may be modified by laying the skins in a vat and stratifying them with 3 lbs. of moistened tan. Other skins can be thus tanned, but the proportions vary as we could see below.

One hundred goat-skins require—

Alum	10 to 12 lbs.
Catechu	50 to 60 "
Salt	6 "

One hundred cow-hides require—

Sulphate of alumina	2 to 300 lbs.
Salt	100 "
Catechu	500 "

One hundred and ninety ox-hides require—

Sulphate of alumina	14 to 16 lbs.
Salt	8 "
Catechu	60 to 70 "

CHAPTER LXIII.

PREPARING DRY FLINT HIDES.

As a green hide becomes dry by evaporation of its liquid, the flesh side absorbs oxygen from the atmosphere which, combining with the fresh fibro-gelatinous surface, forms a hard, flinty scale. To free the hide from the scale and facilitate its softening, tanners submit it to hard beam breaking, or to the action of a hide-mill, both of which have the detrimental effect to some extent of disturbing the uniform relations of the interposed gelatine and loosening the small bundles of fibres composing the structure of the hide, thereby weakening the hide in its textile strength, nor have any of the modern soaks proved less detrimental, depending as they do upon a putrefactive condition. The first effect of such soak is to decompose the parts of the hides easiest affected, generally the fibro-gelatinous structure, immediately beneath the scale; hence the frequent water peltings and running of hides in the soak, particularly in warm weather. M. Aldrich, of St. Louis, Mo., to obviate those objections and at the same time render the hide soft and pliant, as when first taken from the animal, has invented a chemical process for preparing dry flint hides, and accomplishes it in the following manner:—

First. The hides are soaked in clear water until limber, then placed in the following acid bath—

Acetic acid	1
Water	16

which will in from 24 to 36 hours dissolve the scale by combining with its oxygen or swell the fibres of the hide; when they are placed in the following bath—

Water	70
Carbonate of ammonia	1

which having a strong affinity for the acid absorbed in the first bath, saturates in from 48 to 72 hours all the acid remaining in the hide, leaving a hide in a naturally pliant and soft condition, so perfectly transformed from a dry to a green condition, that no tanner can detect the slightest difference between stock tanned from dry hides so prepared or from green hides.

The first cost of the acid solutions is two cents a gallon, or $20 for a large poolful, after which it can be used continually, attended with no expense except pumping up and passing it through the apparatus to renew its strength after it has been used.

The second solution is prepared from all bate water attended by no expense but pumping.

This process obviates all danger of damage from taint or running, for its action is so perfectly antiseptic that hides so softened may be kept for weeks in water before being placed in the lime, also by keeping fibrous and flanky hides in the first bath, double the ordinary time, they will plump up and be materially improved and all without any breaking whatever. Hereafter we will treat of the full process of tanning of the same inventor.

CHAPTER LXIV.

PROCESS OF TANNING OF H. C. JENNINGS.

A SHORT process of treating hides, with the use of very little tan bark, to make leather has been patented by H. C. Jennings, London. In the preparation of thick ox-hides by this process, the hair is first removed in the usual manner, either by steeping them in a lime bath, as in the old mode, or by sweating, according to the new methods. If lime is used, the hides are steeped in dilute muriatic acid after they are unhaired and washed. This opens their pores and fits them for the succeeding operations; they are now piled in batches of a dozen hides in each, with a hurdle or wicker between each pair; and they are then alternately lowered into tanks filled with the following solution :—

Tank No. 1 is charged with a strong solution of alum, to which ten per cent. each of sulphuric and muriatic acids are added.

Tank No. 2 is charged with a concentrated solution of soda ash, to which is added five per cent. of tungstate of soda.

The skins or hides are immersed six hours at a time in these tanks, then withdrawn and drained, and transferred alternately from the first to the second, and *vice versa*, until the hide is sufficiently hardened. This condition of the hide is known by cutting a small piece off with a knife. At this stage they are immersed for six hours in a strong solution of tungstate of soda alone, then lifted, drained, and placed in a liquor of soap made by dissolving twenty pounds of soap in every ten gallons of water, and the hides agitated in this until the strength of the soap is exhausted by being absorbed in the hides. Wash them well in soft water, and finally steep them for 24 hours in a common liquor of oak bark, after which they are dried and finished in the usual manner. This process is too costly.

CHAPTER LXV.

BERENGER AND STERLINGUE'S PROCESS.

In 1842 Messrs. Berenger and Sterlingue patented the process described below. Their method reduces the time occupied in tanning, within the reasonable limits of from four to five months; thus avoiding the extreme of allowing too short a duration for a process which, to be successful, must be more or less gradual or prolonged.

When skins are deposited in vats with water and layers of tan the infusion marks generally 25° of the hydrometer. As the combination progresses the strength diminishes, and after four months it generally marks 4°. At this time the skins are transposed in fresh vats, and this change is repeated a third, and often a fourth time, at every interval of four months; each time the hydrometer sinks from 25° to about 15°, 12°, 10°. The introduction of tannin into the skin becomes more and more slow, owing to the obstacles to the penetration into the tanned surfaces. The object of these manufacturers was to find means of tanning which keep the skins in contact with infusions gradually increasing instead of diminishing. For this purpose they placed in the vat a wooden cylinder through which the infusion could be removed by pumps, and replaced by fresh and stronger liquor when necessary. Thus, they succeeded in tanning in a comparatively short time and avoiding the renewal of the contents.

To moisten a freshly filled pit requires eighty tubs of water; the tan absorbs the largest portion, leaving about only ten tubs of infusion, which can be pumped without injuring the hides and altering their relative positions. Messrs. Berenger and Sterlingue avoided this difficulty by removing the old infusion from the pits at the same time that it was exactly replaced by the introduction of fresh and stronger liquids; but their mode was irregular, and it was necessary to devise better means to attain their objects.

They provided a row of vats with wooden cylinders which were connected above at a depth of six inches below the surface of the pits by means of a pipe passing from one to another, which communicated below by means of a perforated tube with an open space under a false bottom in the pit. By this arrangement it was only necessary to open a stop-cock and admitting fresh liquor into the weakest pit to enable the fluid, which had no other means of escape, when this was filled, to traverse the entire range of pits, filling each one from the weakest to the strongest in succession before it was possible for any of it to enter the next one.

Let us suppose a series of eight pits thus arranged, each provided with its cylinder opening by a perforated tube into the false bottom, and connecting with the cylinder of the next pit at a depth of six inches below the surface. Stratify the hides with the tan, in the end of the pit, pour water into it in the ordinary way. Leave from fifteen to twenty-one days, then fill a second pit with dry tan and skins, and since eighty tubs of water were required for the saturation of the first one, the same quantity properly graduated is poured into the first pit; this liquid, on descending, takes the place of that originally contained into it, then it has no other means of escape than to pass out in the second pit in quantities exactly proportioned to those which enter the first one. Fifteen or twenty days after repeat that operation, a stronger infusion being introduced into the first pit for the purpose of filling the third one with the contents of the second, and the second with those of the first. Continue the same way and at the same intervals until the eighth or last pit is filled. Close the communicating pipe, pump the infusion from the first pit, take out the leather to dry; deposit in the pit fresh hides and tan; this pit now becomes the eighth pit of the series. The second becomes the first, and is supplied with eighty tubs of strong infusion.

We see that one application of tan is alone required; the pits are not changed until the leather is removed, securing thus a great economy of time and labor. It generally lasts from four to six months.

An exposure of six months in eight pits is sufficient, if the strong infusion is added every fifteen days; if the operation seems to progress too rapidly, lengthen the interval to three or four weeks; in this case the process requires from six to eight months. The number of pits could be increased or diminished.

The infusion for watering the pits is prepared in the following manner:—

As the leather is taken out to dry, the infusion is transferred to a set of vats which are provided for the purpose, and which are like those used to furnish the liquor for a tan bath. Lixiviate these infusions as we have described, and mix with them some fresh tan to give the requisite strength. If the liquid is only at 30° and is required to be at 60°, place it in a large reservoir which connects with a trough. This trough, by means of a pipe, communicates with a second, a third, and a fourth below each other. All have pipes running longitudinally along their bottoms.

Pass steam along these tubes so as to heat the infusion which passes successively from one trough to another, and to concentrate it to any desired point, so as to increase its strength and deprive it of the fatty matter and gallic acid which it may have absorbed during its passage through the pits. Let it off by a stop-cock into a reservoir below where it cools, then pour it into the pits.

This system is applied to a bath of tan liquor. However, the skins are not daily transferred from the vat containing the weaker liquor to that of the stronger, as in the ordinary method, but are placed upon horizontal shelves adapted to each vat and are not taken out until ready for the tan-yard, the liquor being passed from vat to vat as in the pits. It may replace the old system of tanning the skins by floating them in tan and water. In that process, the skins, tan, and infusion are all thrown into the vats; after a certain time, the skins are taken out, the infusion is drained off and replaced in the vat with the same skins and fresh barks, the change being frequently repeated until the tanning is complete. By this new method, these removals are unnecessary; it is sufficient to introduce fresh liquor into the oldest vat and keep it constantly full; so that the others will be filled in succession. The tanning by this process is more complete, regular, rapid, and economical; it saves much labor necessary in the other process.

The following is a description of the different apparatus:—

Fig. 75.

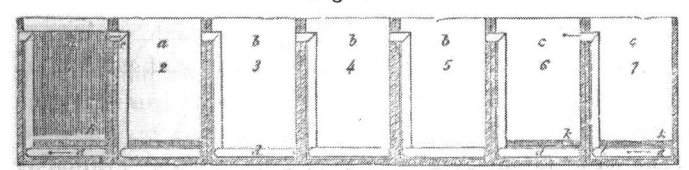

Figs. 75 and 76. Apparatus, for giving the baths to hides; 1, 2, 3, 4, 5, 6, 7, square vats, forming a series.

Fig. 76.

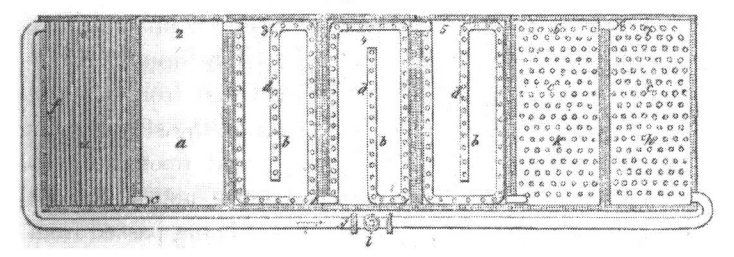

376　TANNING.

a. Skins *h*, placed from head to tail, across horizontal crosspieces *f*, and resting upon them without touching each other.

b. Exhibits the bottom of the pit, with the false bottom taken out; and *c* shows the latter in place.

d. Tubes in the bottoms of the pits, pierced with holes to receive the infusion. Their vertical parts, *e*, are not pierced, but conduct the fluid upwards from the bottom of one vat to the top of the next one. Their upper extremities turn horizontally into the adjoining pits, so that they cannot communicate excepting through these tubes.

g. Horizontal tube, connecting vat No. 7 with No. 1. As all the vats communicate, fluid poured into one readily passes through all.

i. Cock, to prevent connection between Nos. 1 and 7, when it is not desired.

k. False bottom.

l. Arrows, indicating the direction of the motion of infusion from 7 to 6, etc.

Figs. 77 and 78. Series of pits. 1, 2, 3, 4, 5, 6, pits, forming a series.

Fig. 77.

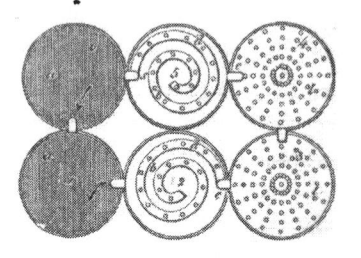

a. Skins deposited in pits, alternating with beds of tan.

BERENGER AND STERLINGUE'S PROCESS. 377

b. View, or plan of pits, with the false bottoms removed, and showing *d*, tubes curved and pierced with

Fig. 78.

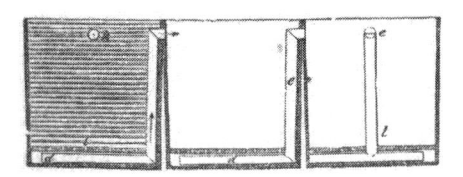

holes in this part alone: the vertical portion of the tube passing up and turning over under the surface, into the next pit.

c. Plan of pits with the false bottoms in place, above the tubes.

i. Arrow, showing the movement of fluid from one pit to another.

k. Bungs, or stoppers, used when necessary, to prevent the passage of fluid.

l. False bottoms, cullendered.

Fig. 79.

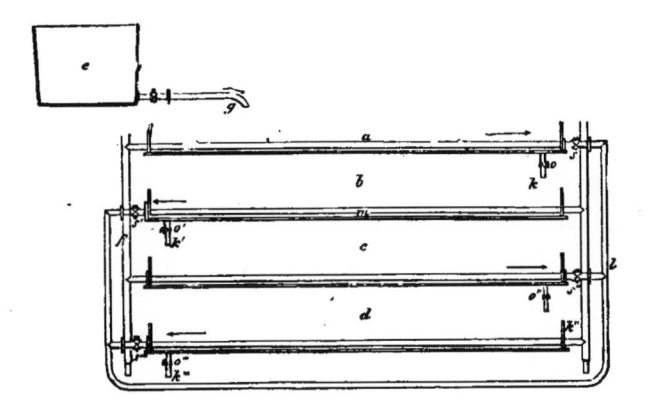

Figs. 79 and 80. Apparatus for regenerating old tan-liquor, and concentrating it to the desired strength.

Fig. 80.

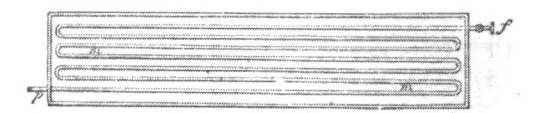

a, b, c, d. Troughs placed one above the other, so that the infusion in a runs down into b, into c, and into d, through the tubes k, k', k'', k''', with the stopcocks o, o', o'', o'''.

At the bottom of each trough is a serpentine tube m, extending over the whole surface, as seen in the plan. The vapor enters each tube upon opening the stopcocks s, s', s'', s''', in the tube l.

e. Reservoir, in which the liquor to be purified is first placed. It escapes from this through the tube g, into the first trough. When this is full, the fluid still running from the reservoir, the cock o is opened, and the warm and already partly concentrated fluid runs into reservoir b, and so on successively, until the concentrated liquor passes through the cock o'''' into a trough in which it is allowed to cool.

f. Escape-pipe, conducting the condensed water and waste vapor into the open air.

p. Pipe, for the entrance of steam.

The drawings represent only six and seven elements of the series of pits and vats, while reference has been had in the text to eight.

CHAPTER LXVI.

CORNIGUET'S PROCESS OF SUBSTITUTING THE FRUIT OF THE PINE FOR THE BARK IN TANNING.

Put the skins in the lime, draw them once every day, and keep them till they depilate easily.

Wash them carefully. Put them into the vats. For 100 calf-skins, weighing from 400 to 500 lbs., are required 200 lbs. of powdered fruit, which is introduced into the vat in five hours at the rate of 40 lbs. every hour. Stir them for six hours, raise every day, change them every eight days in summer, and fifteen in winter, let them drain two hours above the vat.

Put them back in half of the water used in the preceding operation, and then withdraw the first powder, spread them one by one, covering them with fresh powder so as to use 300 lbs. Leave them six weeks in summer and three months in winter, raise, wash, and drain them 24 hours.

Lay them in dry vats, putting alternately a layer of powder, and a layer of skin, putting more powder on the thickest parts; leave three months and they are ready.

The fruit of the ordinary pine tree, and the larch tree reduced into powder, can be thus substituted for oak-bark, but that of the larch tree is better as containing more tannin.

CHAPTER LXVII.

VAUQUELIN'S PROCESS.

The means employed by Vauquelin to perfect the process of tanning rest on different principles, and we have combined them so as to make the four following effects clear:—

1st. Not to alter the skins by a chemical reaction.

2d. Prepare the hides, by mechanical means, so as to render them more apt to receive the tanning matter.

3d. Shorten the work.

4th. Handling in tallow, and dressing the hides by mechanical means.

The first operation consists in preparing the hides for tanning by soaking them while fresh for a few hours, then submitting them to the action of the machine described hereafter. When the hides are dried they are treated in the following manner: Soak them some time, about forty-eight hours. Place them in a fulling machine, in which they are submitted to the action of wooden pestles for about one hour. The blows soften the hides and render them fit to be cleaned.

In that state they are placed in another apparatus, in which they are treated for some time by introducing steam into the apparatus, so as to raise the temperature to 104 or 122.° From there the hides are carried in another vessel or oven, in which they are submitted to the action of tepid water which penetrates and humects them for twenty-four hours. The temperature must be uniform, for if the operation is conducted better on one place than on another, you run the chance of producing a hollow skin, and diminish its quality.

When you operate on small quantities at a time, this operation is sufficient to depilate, but on large quantities it is important to act quicker. In this last case weak lime-water is used instead of a milk of lime, and the temperature is regulated according to the number of skins operated upon.

When these operations are complete the hair is taken off easily. These skins are then submitted to the fleshing with the help of machinery. The machine, put in motion by a man, acts on the hides, takes off all the fleshy parts which adhere to it, and prepares them for the subsequent operations. The advantages of this preparation are, to submit to the tanning process only the parts really useful, while in the old method all the skin was tanned, and afterwards cut, thus causing a great loss. The parts of skins thus separated are used to manufacture glue.

The hides thus treated are put into the fulling machine, and worked with tepid water for a certain time according to the nature of the hide. Then they are brought into the vat, where they are impregnated with a weak solution of tanning liquor for a few hours, raised and piled up, and two hours after placed in a stronger liquor. The three first days raise them three times a day, and afterwards only once. Submit them to the action of the fulling machine every forty-eight hours, and put them back for half an hour in the same tanning liquor, where they are left until completely saturated.. The action of the pestles of the machine opens the skins, and renders them more apt to receive the tanning substance, and by using the apparatus hereafter described, all the parts of the skin are put in contact with the liquor, which acts on it rapidly and uniformly. At last, by this process the operation is executed much quicker than by the old process.

The following is another method of operating:—

The hides being placed in the vat, pass through it a current of steam, so as to raise the temperature to about 104° or 116°. The skins by the rotative movement given to this vat are projected on its partitions, then fall back on the bottom from whence they are successively retaken. This operation is continued for some time, till the hides are entirely deprived of hair. In that state they are placed in another apparatus to which a rotative movement is communicated. It is a drum to cleanse, which has in its inside a series of immovable pins, and which turn in a reservoir of water which raise to about half the height of these pins. The hides in projecting on the pins are deprived of their hair by the rotative movement of the drum, and this hair falls to the bottom, and is carried away by the water, while a metallic grate prevents the hides going out from the drum. In that state the skins can be cut, and submitted to the operation above described.

The following gives an idea of the manner of passing the skins through the tallow, and preparing them.

After the skins are tanned by the above or any other process, cover all their surface with a fatty matter, composed of oil and tallow. These skins, thus greased, are placed in a cylinder, presenting on its inside surface a series of pins as we have explained above. Turn this cylinder, and the skins are projected on the pins during the rotation. This operation is continued for half an hour, after which time it will be found that the greasy matter has uniformly penetrated the skins, and that their surfaces present a dry aspect. Take them out, spread, dry, and prepare them as usual.

This cylinder is not absolutely necessary, because this system of tanning prepares much better the skins destined to receive the greasy matters, but in many cases it is advantageous to use them. We now give a description of the different apparatus which will cause this system to be better understood.

Description of the Figures.—Fig 81. This represents

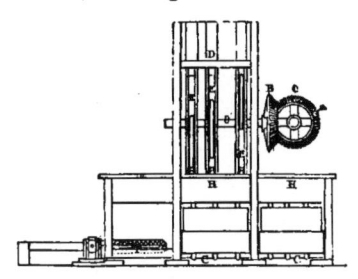

Fig. 81.

the beating or fulling machine. A, B. Cog-wheels, giving motion to the shaft o, and to cams upon it, which alternately raise and lower the hammers E, E, E, to which the bar D serves as a guide. A movable trough for the skins is seen below. c, c. Cocks, which allow the liquid matters contained in this trough to escape. H, H. Openings, through which the skins are introduced into the trough. I. Rack and pinion, by means of which the trough is moved to and fro, so as to bring all parts of the skins successively under the hammer.

Fig. 82. Churning vat. This may consist of an open vessel, but a closed one will enable the operator to maintain a more uniform temperature. A. Vat, closed by its lid. B. Shaft, carrying the cams or arms C, C. D, D. Tubes, through which cold and hot water, the tanning liquor, and steam are introduced. E. Ladder, by which the workman descends and regulates the cocks. F, F.

384 TANNING.

Ground level. G, G. Water level in the vat. H. Door, which closes the opening in the vat. *a.* Toothed wheel,

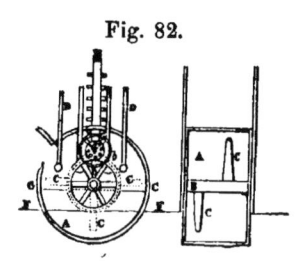

Fig. 82.

communicating its movement to the wheel *b*, and the shaft. The arms of the shaft are straight, but may be made of various shapes.

Figs. 83 and 84. These figures represent the machine

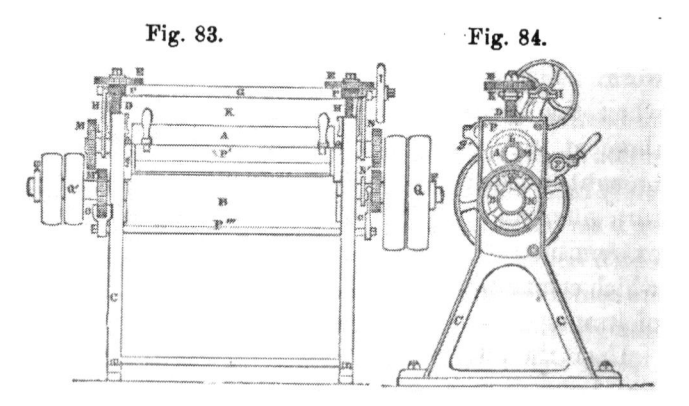

Fig. 83. Fig. 84.

for fleshing and paring the hides after they have been properly soaked and softened.

It is composed of two cylinders, A and B, of copper, or other suitable metal, mounted upon a framework C, C, and forming a kind of cylindrical press. The upper one can be elevated or depressed by means of screws D, D, in the upper crosspiece of the frame, which act both upon the fixed supports H, H, and upon the sides of the frame. Upon this crosspiece, a shaft with a small fly-wheel I, works the endless screws F, F, which turn the cog-wheels E, E, by means of which the screws D, D, are turned in either direction. These screws carry, just below the wheel F, two shoulders or collars, upon which the bar K is supported, and at the extremities of this bar, two descending cushions L are attached, which support the shaft of the cylinder A, and which are elevated or lowered by the bar, in accordance with the movement of the screw D. At the two extremities of the cylinders are cog-wheels of different diameters, M, N, M', N'. Those on the shaft of the lower cylinder B, are so attached to it, that it shares in their movement, while they are movable upon it, and can be slid to the right or left by two forks Q, Q, fastened to the bar P''', which passes across the framework. The wheels M, M', are geared with each other when the cylinders are a certain distance apart, and those at N, N', engage in turn, when the cylinders are brought in contact with each other, so that the cylinders turn simultaneously in either of these positions. At the extremities of the cylinders, there is a system of pulleys which communicate the motion to the machine by means of straps.

Upon the interior and posterior faces of the machine, two knives, P, P', are fixed, which turn upon cushions supported by the pieces q, q', seen on the frame. The knife P has a cutting-blade, which is retained in place and adjusted by means of screws, but the knife P' is dull.

The skin, placed upon the upper cylinder, is drawn in, compressed, and stretched out in the direction of its length, between the two rollers. The wheels M, M', are then put in gear, and the knife P' is made to pass over the skin by pressing it against the upper roller by means

386 TANNING.

of a movable piece with two handles. The skin being now pressed between the rollers and gradually advancing through them, the cutting-blade, which is parallel to the surface of the cylinder, is put in action, and, like the ordinary fleshing-knife, it removes all the projections from the flesh side, and equalizes the thickness of the skin.

Figs. 85, 86, and 87. These figures represent the re-

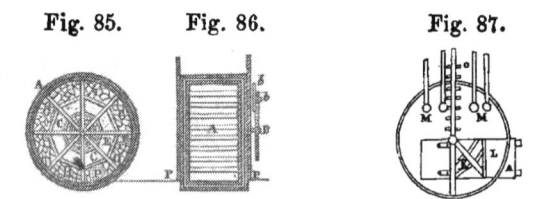

Fig. 85. Fig. 86. Fig. 87.

volving cylinder or drum for depriving the skins of hair, which has already been partly described.

A. Exterior of the drum; B, B, shaft of cylinder; C, cylinder; D, crossbars, forming the framework; E, F, separate pieces of the set of crossbars; G, G, internal surface of the cylinder; H, wooden projections, fixed upon this surface; I, metallic plate, closing the surface of the cylinder; L, door, closing the aperture; M, M, tubes, through which water, tanning liquor, and steam are introduced into the cylinder; O, ladder, for the workman who attends to the stopcocks, to descend; P, level of liquid in the cylinder; b, b, cog-wheels, communicating motion to the cylinder.

Figs. 88, 89, and 90. These figures exhibit different

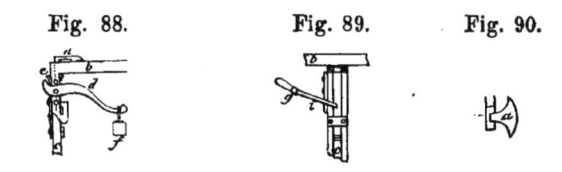

Fig. 88. Fig. 89. Fig. 90.

means of keeping the skins pressed upon the table when they are subjected to processes of paring by hand.

a, a. Clamp or press for maintaining the skin in place; *b, b,* the table; *c, c,* a vertical bar sliding in a groove; *d,* the lever which acts upon the press; *l,* a catch which stops the lever *d; f,* weight at the end of the lever; *g,* another lever by means of which the press is raised, as has been before explained.

Fig. 91 represents the press commonly used in this mode of preparing leather.

Fig. 91.

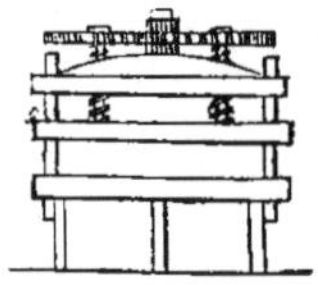

The committee on chemical arts of the *Société d'Encouragement*, reported, in the Bulletin of the Society, most favorably upon the processes of Vauquelin. They believe that the expense of the various methods used by him does not exceed that of those ordinarily employed, while a great gain is secured by the rapidity of the process, and the smaller quantity of tan required by it.

This process being described, we shall give the results of experiments made by the *Société d'Encouragement,* and reported in its Bulletins of 1841 and 1844.

"African cow-hides, so dried by the sun that tanners thought them impossible to be tanned, have been chosen by Mr. Vauquelin to demonstrate the advantage of his process; they have been marked and treated by the above process. To obtain all desired certainty in the quality of the leather, the committee invited the best leather dealers and manufacturers to assist in his researches.

"After the skins had been tanned they were examined, and they were unanimously declared of good quality, all but one, that one of the judges declared incapable of being well curried.

"That skin was marked and all were curried, and all of them without exception were found perfect.

"The leather could be smoothed and greased. By the first process the benefit would have been greater; the second was more difficult, and Mr. Vauquelin chose it to prove that skins tanned by his process present a peculiar character for currying—that of gaining in weight instead of losing.

"One of the skins was converted into black leather which was of good quality, and it is a great advantage of this process to obtain skins apt to be used in different ways.

"The following are the details of the operation:—

23 skins weighing with hair 77 K. (154 lbs.) weigh when curried 99 K (198 lbs.)

1 Curried marked anew	3.500	(7 lbs.)	" "	6 K (12 lbs.)
1 Dry in crust	3.500	(7 lbs.)	" "	4.500 (9 lbs.)
3 For legs.	10.	(20 lbs.)	" "	"
1 For black leather.	5.500	(11 lbs.)	" "	9.500 (19 lbs.)
3 To smooth.	14.	(28 lbs.)	" "	21 (42 lbs.)
1 For strong leather.	5.500	(11 lbs.)	" "	" "
1 Bad and six fresh.	21.500	(43 lbs.)	" "	" "

140.500 281

"The work lasted two months, the currying had been put back on account of damp weather, and the difficulty of drying.

"The quantity of tan used has been 1800 lbs., an inconsiderable proportion, but easily accounted for, if we remember that it is a quick process, and the transformation of the tannin into gallic acid is less considerable than in the ordinary process."

Later, in 1844, a new report gives the results of some new experiments.

"100 calf-skins weighing 360 lbs., three cow-hides weighing 14 lbs., and two horse-hides were put in experiment the 9th of January.

"The eighteenth of March the calf-skins were tanned, the 4th of April the cow-hides were completed, and the horse-hides on the 12th of April.

"One calf-skin was reserved for another experiment, the 99 others weighed 340 lbs., the three cow-hides 18 lbs.

"We see that calf-skins have been tanned in 68 days, cow in 85, and horse 87, while by the usual methods, it requires from 12 to 15 months. Col. Chompre, of the French Army, gives the following notes on the use of M. Vauquelin's leather.

"1st. A piece of calf-skin forming a patch on a pair of trowsers, which were ridden in by a dragoon every day for eight months, was found at the end of that time in a perfect state, and as pliable as at first.

"2d. A number of pairs of calf-skin boot-legs wore exceedingly well, preserving their firmness and pliability without any unusual care being used for their preservation.

"A pair of boots with ordinary tops, and with soles made of the tail part of the horse-hides, was worn by a non-commissioned officer, who generally wears out a number of shoes. These are in good order, and have lasted, by his account, as long as two pairs of shoes.

"Five other pairs of soles of shoes given to lancers, who wear out a great many in service, are in an excellent state of preservation.

"3d. The blackened leather used for belts, girths, etc., has also worn well."

The conclusions of the report of the administrative council of the regiment are—that the leather submitted to, and tried by them, was superior to any which had before come under their notice.

CHAPTER LXVIII.

OGEREAU'S PROCESS.

An eminent Parisian tanner, Mr. Ogereau, proposes to lessen the duration of the tanning process by a methodical arrangement of materials. The skins are properly prepared by the ordinary method of separating the hair and raising; then he places alternate layers of tan and skins in a vat with a perforated false bottom. This vat being full to the ¾, is drenched with water for the first operation, and with weak tan liquor for the succeeding ones. The liquid penetrates slowly into the mass, and having moistened the contents, runs through the false bottom into a reservoir, from which it is carried back upon the surface of the materials.

His arrangement consists of six vats,* each one contains 100 domestic or 120 imported hides. The liquid passing through into the reservoir is daily distributed over the surface by pumping. This operation is continued for one month, at the end of which time the vat is emptied and the spent bark replaced by fresh, and the same process is recommenced. A third exposure to fresh tan and repeated filtrations is necessary to obtain a proper tanning. This full process occupies four months, and the leather it furnishes is equal in quality to that obtained by the old method, one hundred parts of dry Buenos Ayres hides gives 150 parts of leather.

* Dumas' Chimie Appliquée.

SECTION VII.

AMERICAN, ENGLISH, AND OTHER PROCESSES.

CHAPTER LXIX.

PROCESS OF TANNING WITH A DECOCTION OF OAK BARK.

THE principle of this process is the same as that established by Seguin. Oak bark is boiled for four hours in a large copper kettle, and when the tan is exhausted the liquor is conducted by pipes into vats, where it is left to cool. Soak therein the hides, press them often, draw out and soak again. Place them from time to time in a fresh liquor, if the first is too weak before the operation is terminated; by this method a larger quantity of tannin is concentrated in a given space, and the labor is less. If the leather is desired whiter, mix with the liquor a certain quantity of powdered bark. By this process the hides are tanned better, and ten or twelve days produce the same effect as nine or ten months by the usual method. This is true, but the leather thus produced is not completely tanned. The great quantity of tannin which is present rapidly tans the two surfaces, then they refuse passage to the solution, and the inside remains in the state of skin. There were the same objections to Seguin's process.

Besides oak bark, the inventor uses again oak shavings and sawdust, and the ordinary heath. It has been ascertained that the bark of nearly all trees with a heavy wood, contains tannin. They recommend, also, the use of buds, roots, and branches of oak. They obtain thus a decoction of tannin stronger than that of the bark of the trunk which contains a thick matter difficult to separate.

It had been shown, as early as 1819, that the trunk, roots, middle parts, branches and leaves of the oak, contained tannin in sufficient quantity to be used successfully in tanning. These are reduced into shavings, or coarse powder, boiled and used in the following manner:—

To tan calf-skins or other light skins, take 200 lbs. of the middle part of the tree, or shavings of oak branches, boil them in a copper kettle, containing 50 galls. of water, until it is reduced to 37 galls. Draw the liquor, pour on the residue 37 galls. of fresh water which by ebullition you reduce to 20 galls. Keep this liquor apart. It is used to immerse calf-skins, when they have been worked on the beam. Pass afterwards in the first solution.

For ordinary hides, take 200 lbs. of the middling part of the tree or branches, 150 lbs. of coarse powder of oak, and 25 lbs. of root, that you boil in 63 galls. of water until reduced to 42 galls., draw the liquor, and on the residue pour 50 galls. of fresh water and boil until reduced to 25 galls. This liquor is used for the first operation of the tanning. Pass them afterwards in the first decoction. When the hides have been submitted to these two operations, add to each solution some oak bark, as much as necessary to complete the tanning. This quantity varies according to the strength of the decoctions.

This method seems to us very incomplete, and the authors do not even indicate the number of hides the above proportion will tan, nor the time they must remain in the solution.

CHAPTER LXX.

DESMOND'S PROCESS.

This process, like the preceding one, is a modification of Seguin's process. He recommends saturating the water with tanning principles by infusion of successive portions of oak bark, or any other tanning vegetable; and when the bark is exhausted, he extracts what is left of gallic acid by fresh water. To this last liquor he adds $\frac{1}{1000}$ in measure of sulphuric acid, and leaves the hide in till the hair is easily removed. When the swelling is necessary, he leaves the hide ten or twelve hours in water, acidulated with 0.05 part in measure of sulphuric acid, he washes anew and fleshes with the round knife. He then leaves the skins for a few hours in a weak solution of tannin, afterwards several days in a stronger solution, which must be renewed as the strength becomes exhausted, till the skin is completely tanned.

CHAPTER LXXI.

J. BURBIDGE'S PROCESS WITH EXTRACT OF OAK BARK AND CATECHU.

Mr. Burbidge prepares leather with the extract of oak bark. He says that in ten days he obtains this extract without any loss of tannin, which requires two or three months in the ordinary tanning process. He regulates the use of this extract with an hydrometer called barkometer; in three or four months the tanning of sole-leather is complete. The only precaution necessary to be taken, is to begin with a weak extract at 3°, and to increase successively the strength by changing the liquor three times a week, so as to carry it to 20°, being careful to use the strongest extract when the leather is nearly tanned. His process increases the weight of the leather. Tanners take one year to tan a hide weighing 80 lbs. when green, and it weighs only 40 lbs. when tanned. In three months Mr. Burbidge tans a similar hide which shows a weight of 48 lbs., which demonstrates that the excess of time employed is injurious to the leather. He does not use more oak bark than they do, that is to say, about four to five lbs. for every pound of leather.

England using yearly 117,000 tons of oak bark, of which 100,000 are imported from Holland, Mr. Burbidge wishing to liberate his country from this kind of tribute, proposes to substitute for oak bark the terra japonica, which, according to Mr. J. Dauks, has ten times greater tanning properties than oak bark. According to the experiments of Sir H. Davy, the specific gravity of catechu and oak bark are : : $8\frac{1}{2}$: 1. Then catechu worth in England £33 the ton, then as it is equivalent to $8\frac{1}{2}$ tons oak bark, which at £10 the ton makes £85. It is clear that there is a large saving. The previsions of Mr. Burbidge have been realized, for catechu is now extensively used.

CHAPTER LXXII.

KLEMAN'S PROCESS.

OAK bark, such as is used in tanning skins, is usually taken off while the tree is in sap. It is dried in order to preserve it, and it is introduced into the tanning pit at the same time as the skins, together with the requisite quantity of water. But it will be understood that the tanning property as well as the chemical composition of the bark must vary, according as the drying is quick or slow, and the greater or lesser period of time during which the bark is allowed to be exposed to dampness before the tanning begins. In most cases the bark undergoes a commencement of acetous fermentation, which is completed in the tanning vats.

Mr. Kleman recommends the following mode of operation, in order to utilize to the best advantage the tanning principle existing, whether in gall-nuts or in oak bark.

The bark, while still fresh, should be reduced to small pieces and placed in a cask. Add sufficient water to cover the stuff, and close the cask hermetically, so as to prevent the action of the oxygen of the atmosphere. Leave the mixture undisturbed during a few weeks, in order that the principles soluble in water may become thoroughly dissolved, and dissolve the liquid to separate it from the bark. If this liquid is subjected to a gentle heat of 113 to 115°, it will enter into vinous fermentation, and will then contain enough alcohol to mark 1 to 2°. If a skin is placed in this solution, it will become very rapidly tanned, but it will be hard and horny, because the liquor is too much concentrated. If on the contrary it be diluted with water, one part liquor and four parts water, excellent results will be obtained, skins thus tanned are more supple and the grain is closer than when they are tanned by the ordinary method. Moreover, by this new method, the same quantity of bark will produce more tanning matter. It is not advisable to boil bark in water, because boiling coagulates the albuminous matter which induces fermentation. The author has assured himself by experiments of his own, that bark which has only undergone vinous fermentation gives much better results than that which has been subjected to acetous fermentation.

CHAPTER LXXIII.

SPILSBURY'S PROCESS BY PRESSURE.

THE hides are very carefully depilated and prepared. They have all the holes sewed up, so as to render them water-tight; they are then stretched by means of clamps upon rectangular wooden frames. The frame is exactly overlaid by another similar frame, which is screwed down to confine the edges and make them water-tight.

Another hide is stretched as before over the upper ledges of this second frame, and a third frame screwed upon it as above. The whole three are bolted together by means of clamps, so as to form a water-tight vat. The frames are then set upright, and the ooze allowed to flow into the space intervening between the two others through a pipe leading into it from a reservoir above. A hydrostatic pressure is thus maintained, and the liquid column forces the ooze through the hide by slow infiltration, and brings thus all parts in contact with the tannin.

In the bottom of the vat is a stop-cock to allow the escape of the air as the ooze enters, and the exit of the spent liquor when the operation is done; but it must be closed carefully when the vats are full of liquor and in operation. There is also a stop-cock in the pipe leading from the reservoir to the vat, to shut off communication when the operation is completed.

Let off the exhausted liquor by the stop-cock, replace it by fresh, and when the skins are completely tanned take the frames apart, pare off the edges, and dress the leather as usual.

This process is rapid, but the time varies according to the pressure, the strength of the solution, and the quantity of the skins. There is more or less loss on account of the clippings and sewing of the skins. This method has not been as successful as it was originally anticipated.

Messrs. Drake and Chaplin have modified this process. Mr. Drake gives to the hides prepared as usual an incipient tanning by immersion in weak ooze. After the necessary handling, he takes them out and sews them together at the edges, grain side within, in pairs, so as to form water-tight bags, with small holes at the end for the admission of the tan liquor. By means of loops, he suspends the bags between two upright wooden racks, to prevent bulging when full. The cold ooze is introduced by a funnel, and by keeping the bag distended, creates a pressure, which causes the liquid to infiltrate through the skin.

The fluid passing through is received in a vessel beneath, and returned to the sack. When the skin becomes firm and hard towards the close of the operation, the temperature of the room is raised from 68 to 149°, and is maintained till the skins begin to darken in places, and the liquid ceases to lose strength. Take them down, empty them of their contents, and prepare as usual.

The elevation of temperature promotes the infiltration of the ooze. To prevent indentations, the position of the bags should be occasionally shifted.

By this process a skin can be tanned in ten days; the appearance is very favorable; but we can say nothing about the quality and durability.

Mr. Chaplin lays the bags in an inclined position, and turns them frequently so as to equalize the tanning.

One great objection to this process is, that the hides are not equally permeable—some portions imbibing the liquor more readily than others. The leather is weakened by the prolonged distension of the hides.

CHAPTER LXXIV.

M. W. DRAKE'S PROCESS.

M. W. Drake has modified Spilsbury's process. After the hides have received the usual preliminary operations in a weak liquor of tan, they receive a first tanning before being submitted to the cold infiltration. Then he places skins, as much as possible of the same size, and same form, and sews them with waxed thread so as to form a bag, solid enough to retain the solution of tan. Then he suspends these bags with the help of ropes, sewed to their sides with tapes. At the upper end of the bag is an aperture large enough to introduce a funnel, by the means of which the cold liquor is introduced until the bag is full. After a certain time, variable according to the quality of the skins, their exterior surface becomes moist, and drops begin to form below the bag. This liquid is received in a convenient vessel, and when a sufficient quantity is collected, it is poured anew into the bag. When the hides become hard and firm, while all the parts are equally moist, raise the temperature from 68 to 149°; maintain this temperature until all the skins have become hard and firm at all the points. When the skins begin to blacken in some parts and the liquor does not diminish in strength, the skins are tanned. Then empty the bag by cutting the sewing, and terminate the operation in the usual manner. By this process a skin can be tanned in ten days, while by the ordinary method it requires ten months.

CHAPTER LXXV.

ROTCH'S QUICK PROCESS OF TANNING LEATHER.

This process consists in causing tannin to penetrate the skins by moistening them with tan liquor upon one side, while the water which passes through the pores is made to evaporate upon the other by artificial heat. Thus the greater part of the tannin remains in the leather, and the strength of the liquid increases instead of diminishing. By this method leather can be tanned in ten days.

The skins are limed in the usual manner, soaked, and handled in a weak tan liquor for raising and coloring them. They are prepared and cleaned, carefully examined, and if any holes are found they are pieced and sewed.

They work two skins at a time, and they stitch together at the edges those of equal size with tarred thread; they suspend them by cords (Fig. 92) to the pegs s, s, s, s, which project from the bar (a). This bar is the top of a wooden rack a, b, c, and there is a similar rack on the other side of the bag of skins, so that the latter can be compressed in such a manner as to make it retain its shape when full of fluid; between the two ranges of uprights, which are made to approach one another by screws e, e, an opening about an inch in length is left on the upper part of the bag for the reception of the funnel, through which the tan liquor is

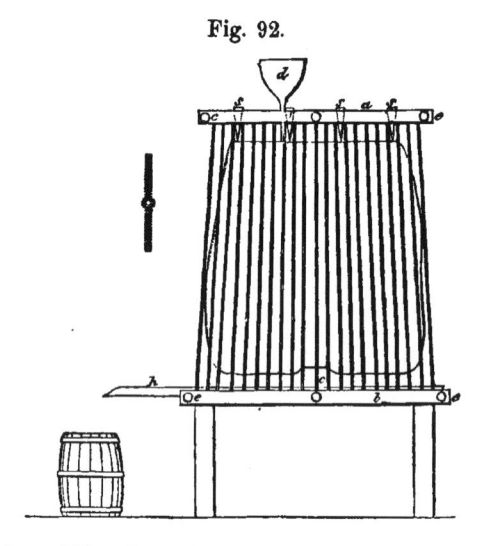

Fig. 92.

poured in. The funnel may be conveniently placed in the neck or collar, seen in the figure alongside of the rack.

The figure 93 represents a section of the side view of the rack, and *s, s*, the pegs upon the head of the rack, from which the bag of skins is suspended. The inner sides of the central bars comprising the rack are hollowed out in the form of arcs of a large circle, as seen below. The skins being thus suspended, pour the cold tan liquor into the bag until full. After a certain time, varying according to the thickness of the hide, the outside becomes moist, and the water which filters through drops into the gutter *h*, and flows into a receptacle placed below its spout. This liquid, as soon as cold, is poured back into the bag to keep it full, and the supply of the fluid is kept constantly in proportion as it loses by evaporation.

ROTCH'S QUICK PROCESS.

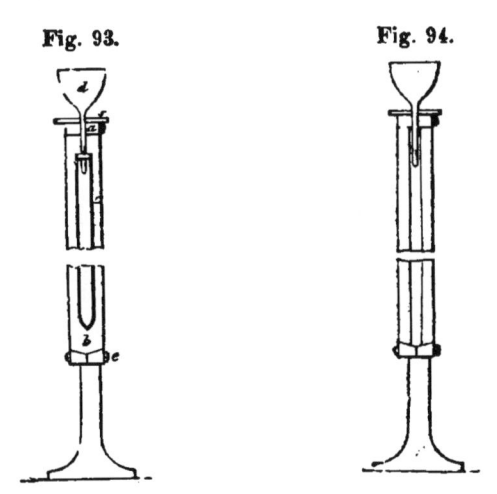

Fig. 93.   Fig. 94.

When the surface of the skin becomes firm to the touch, and equally moist, the air of the room is gradually heated from 70 to 150°, and kept thus until the skins become firm and hard in every part, and assume a brown color, and until the strength of the liquid in the bags remains the same. The skins are then thoroughly tanned.

Take them from the frame, empty them, dry and prepare them as usual.

The position of the skins, during the process, must be changed often, so that the bars of the frame may not press for too long a time upon the same parts.

Fig. 95.

The time of tanning varies according to the thickness of the skin, their change of position, the strength of the liquor, the regulation of heat, etc.

The annexed figure shows a section of the rack; *b, b,* lower part of the rack; *c, c,* bars of the two racks placed so as not to be opposite to each other.

CHAPTER LXXVI.

J. F. KNOWLIS'S PROCESS.

Knowlis's process is an improvement of the above. He suspends the hides in an air-tight vessel, of a capacity larger than their dimensions. He hangs the hides at regular intervals, and keeps them distended by means of weights attached to their lower ends. In the upper portion of the vat is an opening, with a movable cover for the entrance of the workman. In the side, and near the top, is a tube with a stopcock, and coupling screw for connecting with an air-pump, and in a corresponding position on the opposite side, is a similar tube for the admission of air to create external pressure as may be required. As soon as a vacuum is obtained, the contents of the vat are left in repose for 24 hours, after which the tanning liquor is drawn off, and the apparatus allowed to remain empty for two or three hours to permit the entrance of the air. Repeat this operation several times till the hides are perfectly tanned.

The ooze is renewed after each exhaustion of the vessel, and the first liquid should be weak, and as the operation proceeds, the strength is increased.

This process really accelerates the absorption of tannin by the hides, and saves time and labor. But these processes we prefer the one described in the following chapter.

CHAPTER LXXVII.

TANNING APPARATUS OF D. ALDRICH, OF ST. LOUIS, MO.

Mr. Dennis Aldrich, of St. Louis, Mo., patented, in 1860, the following apparatus, of which we shall give a full description, as we look upon it as a decided improvement.

Fig. 96 is the plan of a tan-yard, with its apparatus

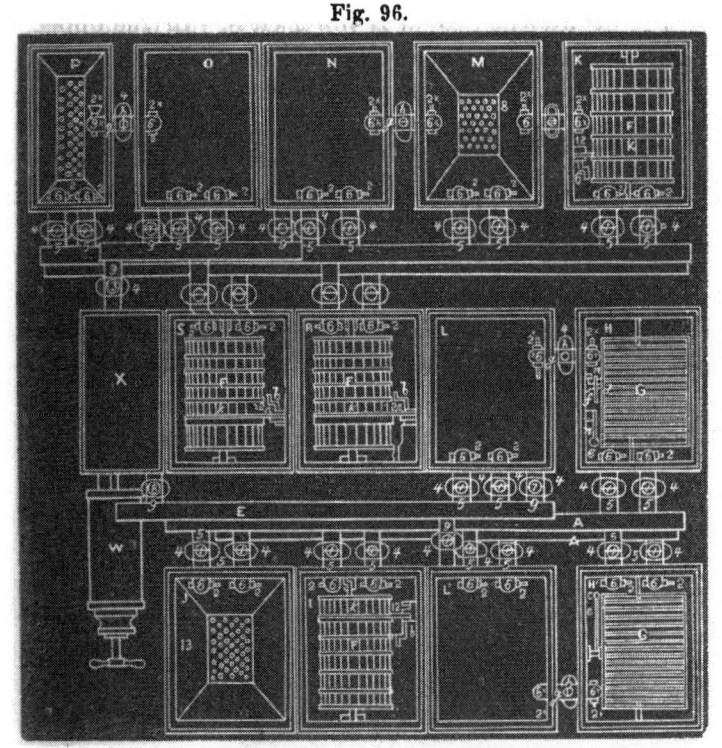

Fig. 96.

constructed and arranged according to his invention, the vats and tanks having their covers removed to show the apparatus inside of them.

404 TANNING.

Fig. 97 is a vertical section of the apparatus in the plane indicated in Fig. 96.

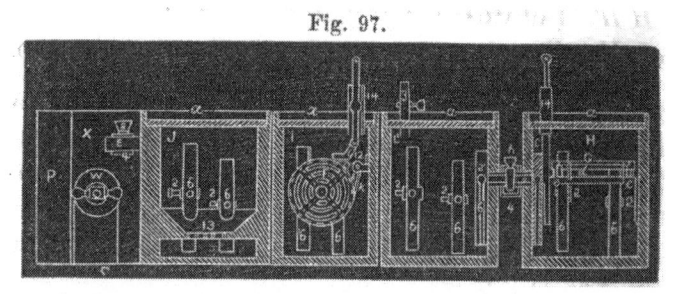

Fig. 97.

Fig. 98, vertical section of the same in the plane indicated in Fig. 96.

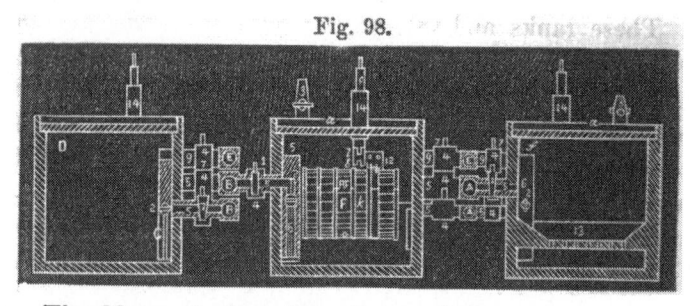

Fig. 98.

Fig. 99, vertical section of one of the tan vats in the plane indicated in Fig. 96.

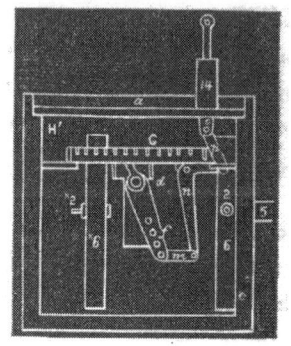

Fig. 99.

Similar letters of reference indicate corresponding parts in the several figures.

H H'. Tan vats.
I. Handler.
J. Tan leech.
K. Bat vat.
L L'. Tan liquor vats.
M. Bate leech.
N. Bate tank.
O. Lime tank.
P. Lime leech.
R. Pool.
S. Lime vat.

These tanks and vats are arranged in three rows, as shown in Fig. 96, for the convenience of making the several pipe connections. The said tanks and vats are all made of wood, calked and pitched inside to make them tight, of the usual or of any convenient horizontal area, and of about 6 feet deep, and every one is provided with a movable lid, *a*, fitted into a deep rebate formed recess provided round the top of the tank, such recess being deep enough to allow the lid to be covered with water, and to enable its edges to be covered with suitable paste or cement, to prevent the entrance of air, when a partial vacuum is produced in the tank or vat as hereafter described; *A A* are two pipes, which he calls liquor pipes, arranged one above the other between the middle and one of the outer rows of tanks and vats, and each one connecting with tan vats, *H H'*, and with tan liquor tanks, *L L'*, with the handler, *I*, and tan leech, *J*, by means of a number of small branch pipes, 5, 5, each fitted with a stop-cock, 1, by which either of the said tanks or vats may be shut off from the liquor pipes.

The said branch-pipes, 5, 5, do not terminate in the

walls of the tanks or vats, but enter upright pipes, 6, 6, which are arranged close to the interior of the said wall within the said tanks or vats, such pipes, 6, 6, being closed at their upper ends, but open at their lower ends, which are within about one inch of the bottom of the tanks or vats, and being furnished, just below where the branches 5, 5 connect with them, with three way-cocks 2, 2', by which the said pipes are made to communicate either with the bottom or the upper part of their respective vessels. $b\ b'$ are two pipes, which he calls conduct pipes, arranged one above the other between the middle and the other outer row of tanks and vats, and each one connecting the pool R, lime vat S, lime leech P, lime tank O, and bate vat K, bate leech M, and bate tank N, by means of short branch-pipes 5, 5, which, like the branch-pipes of the liquor pipes $A\ A$, are furnished with stop-cocks 1, 1, and like these pipes terminate in upright pipes 6, 6, which are arranged within the tanks and vats, and provided with three way-cocks 2, 2, in all respects like the pipes 6, 6, first described. These pipes and cocks are all best shown in Fig. 98.

$E\ E'$ are two air-pipes arranged one between the middle, and each of the other rows of tanks and vats, above the liquor-pipe, and conduct pipes with branches 9 9 connecting the two tan liquor tanks $L\ L'$, the bate tank N, and lime tank O with the air-tank X. These branches 9 9 communicate with the tanks and vats near the tops thereof, and each of those connecting the air-pipe with the air-tank, is furnished with a stopcock 8, and each of the others with a stopcock 7.

The air-tank X, which must be a perfectly air-tight vessel, has connected with it an air-pump W, by which to extract it, said pump being worked by hand or by steam.

Each of the tan vats HH' is connected with the adjacent tan liquor tank L or L' by means of a short pipe 9 filled with a stopcock h. These pipes do not open directly into the vat or tank, but connect with the vertical pipe 6 having closed the upper ends, but opened the bottoms, arranged close against the sides of the vat, and tank, like the pipes 6, with which the branches 5 of the liquor pipe and conduct pipe connect.

These pipes 6 are fitted with three way cocks 2 like those 2 connected with the branches 5. The bate leech M is connected with the bate vat K and bate tank N by similar pipes 9 and 6, and said pipes are furnished with similar stopcocks h and three way cocks 2, the said pipe 6 running through the false bottom of the lime leech. The tan liquor tanks are each furnished with an air cock 3 in its cover for the admission of air, when necessary. The stopcocks 1 1 and $h\ h$ are each surrounded by a boxing 4, which serves to collect any leakage, and by keeping these boxes filled with water, the cocks are rendered air-tight.

The leeches J, M, and P, are each constructed with a false bottom 13, which is about two inches above the main bottom. The central portion of these false bottoms is perforated; but towards the sides of the leeches the said bottoms have an upward inclination, and the inclined portions are not perforated.

The pool R, lime vat S, vats K, and handler I, each contain a cylindrical reel F, whose ends are composed of narrow, radial slats, and rings of wood, and whose sides are composed of narrow longitudinal slats and hoops of the same material. These cylinders have central shafts fitted to work in bearings in the ends of the vessels in which they are placed, and each is divided into four compartments by slatted partitions, as exhibited in Fig. 97, in the handle I; and each of these compartments is furnished with a hinged door, of the whole length of the cylinder, for the introduction of the hides.

To provide for the rotary motion of the cylinder F, each of the vessels containing the said cylinders, contains also a pulley 12, which is secured to a short shaft working in bearings in brackets secured to one side of the vessel; a band K is applied to run round the outside of the reel. The shaft of the pulley 12 is provided at one end with a crank 6, which is connected by a short vibrating connecting rod b, with a vertical piston rod c, whose piston works air-tight in an upright cylinder 14, attached to the lid of the vessel, said rod passing through the top of said cylinder, for the purpose of enabling it to be worked up and down by hand, or by suitable motive power applied outside of the vessel to promote a rotary motion of the pulley 12, and reel.

Each of the tan vats H, H', contains a horizontal frame G, of wood, having slats extended from side to side, to hang the hides upon. Each of these frames is balanced upon the ends of the rockers e, e, attached to a rack shaft d, which extends across the vat, and works in bearings in the sides thereof. The said shaft is furnished with an arm f, which is connected by a link m, bell crank lever n, and vibrating connecting rod p, as shown best in Fig. 99, with a vertical piston rod C, which works through a cylinder 14, attached to the lid a, of the vat, in the same manner as the piston rods by which the reels are operated. By working this rod c, c, up and down, a reciprocating motion in a nearly horizontal direction is imparted to the frame G.

The process of tanning with this apparatus is conducted in the following manner: A number of hides are placed in each of the compartments of the reel F, in the pool R, in which there must be sufficient clear water to keep the reel submerged; and the same reel is then set in motion by power applied to its piston rod C, and kept rotating for about six hours, or until the hides are perfectly cleansed of dirt, blood, oil, or saline matter that may have been in them—the water being changed as often as it becomes dirty, during this part of the process, by allowing it to run off and introducing fresh water by pipes and cocks not necessary to be described here.

From the reel F, of the pool, the hides are removed to the reel F in the lime vat S, which then has its lid put on and secured closely, the lime leech having been charged with slacklime water, is introduced above the charge by suitable means not necessary to be described, and the lime vat S is placed in communication with the lime leech P, and with the lime tank O, by means of the conduit pipes B, B, and its branches 5, by opening the stop-cocks 1, 1, and the lime tank O is placed in communication with the air tank X, by opening the proper stop-cocks 7 and 8, in the branches of the air pipe E. Vent is then given to the lime leech P by removing its lid, leaving it loose; and the air tank X, lime tank O, and lime vat S are exhausted by setting the air pump W in operation; and the lime vat S is filled with lime water forced from beneath the bottom of the lime leech P, by atmospheric pressure; said water passing up the pipe 6, of the lime leech, through the branches 5, and pipes B, into the lime vat S. When it is desired to strengthen the lime water in the vat S, the lime leech is put in connection, as before described, with the vat S, and put in direct communication with the lime tank O, by opening the stop-cocks h, between them, after which, by giving vent to lime vat S, by opening its lid, the lid of the leech P being in the same time closed, and placing the lime tank into communication with the air tank and starting the air-pump, the water is forced back into the lime leech *P*. For this operation the three way-cocks 2, of the pipes 6, in the lime leech should be turned to admit the water above the lime-that it may percolate through it. The lime being thus strengthened may be forced back in the lime vat *S*, as before described. By the use of two lime tanks, *O*, a constant circulation of liquor can be kept up through the lime leech *P*, and lime vat *S*; while the hides are in the lime vat *S*, the cylinder may be kept in motion constantly or set in motion from time to time.

When the hides have been sufficiently limed they are removed from the lime vat *S*, and prepared for the bate, and put in the reel *F*, of the bate vat *K*, whose connection with the bate leech *M*, and bate tank *M*, and air tank is similar to the connection of the lime vat with its respective leech and tank, and with the air tank, and the operation of the bate vat is conducted in the same manner as that of the lime vat, the bate leech having been previously charged with bating material. Having been thus prepared for coloring the hides are placed in the reel *F*, of the handler *I*, which by opening and closing the proper cocks in the liquor pipes, *A A'*, and air pipe *E*, can be put in communication with the tan liquor tanks *L L'*, and tan leech *J*, and the hides be operated upon in the same manner as in the lime vat and bate vat, except that tan liquor is used in place of the lime or leech liquors.

After having been sufficiently colored the hides are suspended from the slats of the frames *G G*, in the tan vats *H H'*, and after the covers of said vats have been put on and secured, the tan vat *H* is connected with the tan leech *J* by one of the pipes *A A*, and its branches 5 5, by opening the proper cocks 1, 1, and is connected with its adjacent liquor tank L by opening the cock h of their respective direct connection pipe 9, and the said two liquor tanks L are, by means of the air pipe E, and its branches 9, brought into communication with the air tank X, and the other tank liquor L' is, by means of the other of the pipes A' A', and its branches 5 5, brought into communication with the tan leech J. The pipe 6, of the tan leech, which is in connection with the tank L', having its cock turned to such position as to open the upper aperture of the said pipe, and the other pipe, 6, of the said leech having its cock reversed. Then by opening the cock 3, of the tank L', and setting the air pump in operation to exhaust the air tank X, the liquor is forced by atmospheric pressure from the said tank L to the tank leech, where it falls upon and percolates through the tanning material and passes through the false bottom 13, from below, which is caused to pass by the opposite pipe 6 of the leech to that from which it enters, and the liquor pipe A or A', to the tan vat H. By opening and closing the cocks to place the tan vat H' in the same relation to its respective tank, and L, as just described, of H and L, and reversing the above described relation of the tanks, L, L', with the tan leech and air tank, opening the air cock of L and setting the air pump in operation, the vat H may be filled from the tank L, by completely reversing the communication between the tan liquor tank, air tank, and tan leech from either of the above described conditions, the liquor may be returned through the tan leech; and by a proper manipulation of the cocks, while the air pump is in operation, a constant current of tan liquor through the tan leech, where it receives the tannic principle, and the tan vats where it is absorbed, may be kept up. The reciprocating motion of the frames, *G G*, of the tan vats already described is kept up during the tanning process.

The practical advantages derived from the use of an apparatus composed of a series of air-tight vessels with air pump and system of connection, such as above described, are as follows: It is well known to tanners that when a hide is limed in open vessels, and frequently exposed to the air, it becomes so hard and crusty that in order to soften it such a decomposing beating process is necessary, that the hide is brought so nearly to a putrefactive condition that its substance is materially changed, and it is not unfrequently seriously damaged, and it is also well known that in using tan liquors in open vats, the liquor readily absorbs the oxygen of the air and the tannic acid is so changed to gallic acid, which latter not possessing any tanning property, but having a dissolving effect on the fibre of the hide, thereby damaging its textile strength, and being of the same color as tannic acid, is a dangerous obstacle in the way of successful tanning; on the contrary, by using air-tight vats for liming, the change and loss in quality of the lime liquor is avoided, and by using such vats for tanning every species of chemical change in the liquor is avoided; and in bating the use of air-tight vessels is of no less advantage, as it permits the retention of all of the free ammoniacal gases, which gases perform so important a part in facilitating the neutralizing of any remaining lime in the hide, and cleansing the cuticle of all extraneous matter.

By the use of the reel in the lime tanks the positions of the hide are constantly changing, and they are presented to the action of the lime liquor to the best advantage, the hair and epidermis being loosened, and the hide being left in a naturally soft condition in a short space of time. Corresponding advantages result from the use of the reel in the bate vat, and in the handler by the use of the reciprocating frames G, in the tan vats, the hides being suspended at a distance, a point just sufficient to permit the circulation of the tan liquor between them, are caused to be brought very uniformly and rapidly into contact with the tan liquor, the absorption of which is thereby accelerated.

By the use of the perforated false bottom, with inclined sides in the leeches, the different substances are leeched by percolation, by which means from 15 to 25 per cent. more strength can be obtained from tanning material than by either of the old modes of maceration or filtration.

CHAPTER LXXVIII.

TANNING WHEEL.

THIS new apparatus, invented by V. E. Rusco, of Chicago, was patented in November, 1863, and has been used by many tanners, who consider it a great improvement.

Fig. 100.

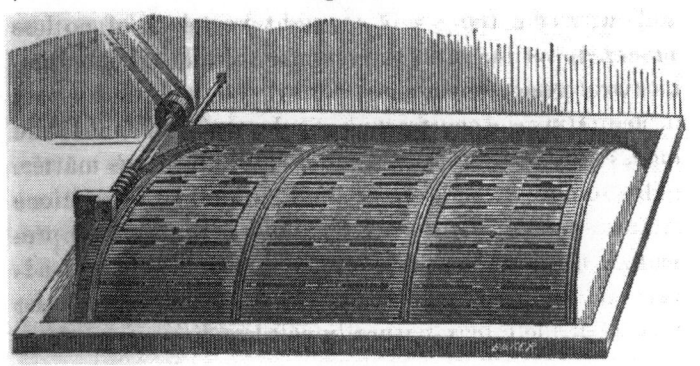

414   TANNING.

Fig. 100 is a view of a single wheel. Fig. 101 is an end view of the same, showing the internal arrangement

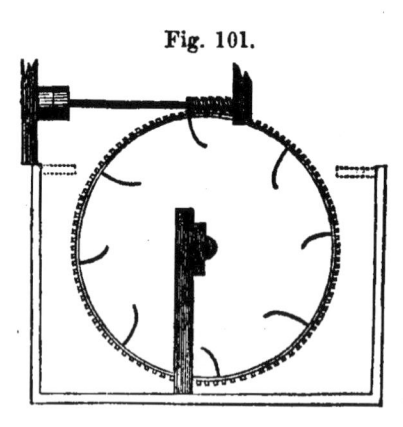

Fig. 101.

of the wheel and the hooks by which the leather is kept in motion.

Fig. 102 shows how a number of wheels may be operated by one shaft and pulley. Any number of wheels can be driven in this manner, and each one can be thrown in or out of gear by means of a clutch and shipper.

Fig. 103 shows how the wheel can be driven by a rope without the expense of a worm shaft and segments. This way of driving will answer when gear cannot be procured, but is not to be recommended either for durability or economy.

Fig. 100 is a perforated wooden cylinder, made of staves and hooped with iron bands; the ends of the cylinder are closed. In the inside of the cylinder are wooden hooks, in the form of a seekle, which keep the leather in motion as the wheel revolves. This wheel is best driven by a screw pinion working in a segment placed on the circumference, and when but one wheel is

Fig. 102.

used in a tannery it should make from 1½ to 2 revolutions per minute. When a number of wheels are used a slower motion is desirable. The small amount of power required to drive this wheel is greatly in its favor. No more power is required to operate ten of these wheels than it takes to operate one England wheel. The wheel is submerged nearly to its surface, and turning with a slow and regular motion, produces plump, firm, and yet very soft and pliable leather. Many first-class tanners give it as their opinion that the highest speed of other

Fig. 103.

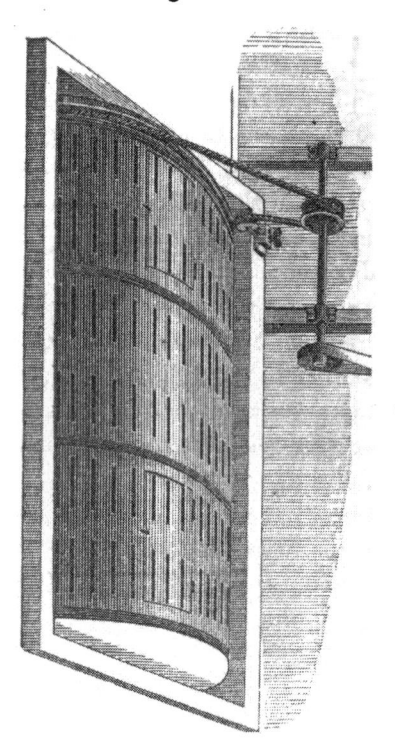

wheels makes thinner shoulders and flanks than is made in the ordinary way of tanning; while in the submerged wheel there is no strain to draw out the thin parts of the leather.

When the hides are ready for the liquor they are placed in the wheel through trap-doors, which are closed and fastened. About 300 calf-skins, 125 sides of upper, or 100 sides of harness is the capacity of a wheel, such as can be worked in a vat 9 by 10, 5 feet deep. Particular attention should be paid to running the liquor for the first two days in a green pack to draw a fine grain. The third run of a leech is quite strong enough. The vat should not be drawn down more than ten inches at a time two or three times a day for the first two days. Draw the leather once a day for the first two days. After increase the strength and quantity of fresh liquor.

After running a few days in the wheel the leather may be laid away in the ordinary manner. When laid a proper time it may be returned again to the wheel with great advantage.

Care and judgment are necessary in proportioning the continual increasing strength of the liquor to the requirement of the leather in the different stages of this process. The liquor should be kept cool, never to exceed 80°, too high a temperature with a strong liquor being highly injurious to the life of the leather. It is well known to practical tanners that a certain time is necessary to produce a certain quality of leather. It is claimed for this wheel that it will save much of the labor, and greatly lessen the time in the ordinary way of tanning. If this wheel has no other merit than coloring, it should recommend it to all tanners. It also works equally well for bating and liming. Tanners will understand that it requires a larger wheel for liming, as the hides full up more.

CHAPTER LXXIX.

NEW MODE OF TANNING SKINS BY A LIQUOR OF TAR AND SOOT.

Preparation of the Tan Liquor.

TAKE 100 gallons of boiling water and throw into it from 18 to 20 pounds of good tar, add enough lime to form a thick paste. Pour cold water on to this composition, to precipitate the lime in the form of a powder; then add a pailful of tar and an equal quantity of powdered lime; stir until you obtain a thick paste.

Distribute this composition in several vats. The hot water is then drawn off from the kettle and poured in the vats—being careful to stir the composition three or four times with a shovel while you pour in the hot water. When the water is thus distributed cover the vats, and twenty-four hours after the liquor can be used.

Preparation of the Soot Liquor.

In a kettle for every 100 pounds of soot pour 55 gallons of water and 4 pounds of powdered lime; stir three or four times during the filling of the kettle; cover this kettle, and in twenty-four hours filter the liquor.

Preparation of the Skins intended for Leather.

The skins destined to be converted into polished leather are depilated and cleansed by the ordinary processes. They are then put in cold vats of oak-bark paste, and left in four or five days, and even a week. Handle them three or four times a day, and withdraw them. Dip them afterwards into the warm tar liquor of half strength, and increase gradually the strength until it has reached the primitive degree. Leave them fifteen days in this liquor; put them anew in the oak bark as the first time, then in the weak liquor of tar. Handle them three or four times a day for the first two weeks; place them in the strong liquor; handle them twice a day, and leave them till they are well penetrated. This operation done, the skins are put, for a week or more, according to their thickness, in a warm solution of sumach. Withdraw and dry them.

Preparation of Leather for Soles.

The hides are deprived of hair and flesh by the usual process. Put them for a few days in a cold vat of oak bark. Take them out and dip them as for polished leather; introduce them into a vat containing a weak and warm liquor of soot—the degree of strength is about one-third or one-half of the primitive liquor.

The skins are handled three or four times a day; put them in a vat containing the warm liquor with all its strength; handle them three or four times a day till well impregnated; dry them; dip them again, for half an hour, into a vat containing hot water. Brush and wash them well.

The skins thus prepared are dipped in a strong solution of oak bark. Handle them three or four times a day until the operation is achieved. Dry the skins every time they have been dipped in the last liquor.

CHAPTER LXXX.

INDIAN METHOD OF PREPARING ELK-HIDES.

IMMEDIATELY after the skin is taken spread it to dry; take out the brains of the animal: which dry in the sun on the grass. When the hunting season is over the women prepare the hides by soaking them first in water, and afterwards taking off the hair with an old knife, and putting the hides in a large earthen vessel, adding to them the brains; then heat these hides to about 95°, which operation cleans them very well. They take the skins and wring them, without taking out the water entirely; they spread them on a kind of rack composed of two perpendicular posts and two sticks placed horizontally. With ropes they spread them well, and during the drying they rub them all the time with a stone or with a round piece of wood to expel the water and grease, till they are perfectly dried. The operation is then completed.

In one day a woman can prepare from eight to ten skins.

CHAPTER LXXXI.

HATCH'S PROCESS OF TANNING, CALLED ILLINOIS FRENCH TANNING.

WE mentioned that Mr. Hatch, of Princetown, Illinois, has taken out two patents for his process. The first was patented in 1856, and consists in preparing hides and transforming them into leather by using smoke of wood or its equivalent combustible, in the following manner:—

The nature of his invention consists in smoking hides after being unhaired, and heated previous to putting them in tan, which changes the nature of the gelatine into an admirable condition for the rapid absorption of the tannin, and, at the same time, preserving the full texture and strength of the fibre, thus enabling him to tan calf-skins in from two to twelve days, upper and collar leather in from eight to twenty days, and other leather in a proportionate time according to the thickness. By smoking the hides and then handling them in sumach, bran, and water, for half a day, and then putting them in alum, tan, and sumach, the tan struck through heavy uppers in three days.

Hides prepared in this way preserve the gelatine in such a condition as to keep longer even poor weak liquor devoid of tan. He uses smoke from various kinds of combustibles, all producing the same effect.

Some of the great beneficial results in this kind of tanning are these: With a small capital he can compete with any tanner using bark; the leather is better and more durable. By using smoke in connection with tanning, it enables him to use terra japonica with or without acids in the tanning, with pretty good results. In the West, where no bark is to be obtained, he can successfully tan in much less time than in tan bark districts.

That this principle of smoke, the great desideratum, is applicable in bark tanning, the world over in terra japonica, or other tannin. By it he has been able to bring 8 lbs. of prepared hide through in 36 hours, cowhide, upper-leather, and collar leather in eight days, making good leather, yet he prefers from four to twelve days' time for tanning the same.

The leather tanned by this process has been well tested, and given good satisfaction. The method of operating is as follows: The hides are bated in the usual way, either in hen bate, or wheat bran, as it leaves the hides more plump, until the lime is thoroughly worked out; after working it off the last time, they are rinsed in clean water to plump up, and open the hide fully wet, in order, while smoking, the grain may not become too dry, as well as to rinse off all uncleanliness; then hang up in a tight smoke-room sufficiently large to hang up by but and neck, grain side out, then make a smoke in such a manner that the hides may not become heated from the fire. Smoke upper and collar leather hides six hours, other hides, time according to thickness, then take them out and soak them an hour in clean water, to assure the hides a fully wet condition, before coming in contact with tan; then put them in tan ooze of moderate strength. Stir, and handle often, until the grain is colored even and struck through, then increase the strength of the ooze, by tannin from day to day, until the hides are tanned.

To get a light color in the terra japonica or hemlock ooze, add a little sumach in the first, handled in such proportion as half a pound per side for upper leather.

For heavy leather, such as harness and sole-leather, after being prepared in the usual way, should be smoked six hours, then soaked in clean water one hour, then smoked again six hours, soaked again, and passed in tan as above stated.

As regards the above process on *smoking, or preparing hides for tanning*, the author says: "I am well aware that *smoke* has been used in dressing glove leather, out of deer-skins in the old Indian manner, but not used in the manner, and for the purpose, as I use it under the patent, namely, in *preparing hides for tanning*, to tan with any vegetable tanning astringent."

The novel application of smoke, as done under this patent, has the following great and desirable effect on hides: It toughens the epidermis, retains and coagulates the albumen, permeates, toughens and preserves the gelatine and fibrin, and disposes them to readily unite with tannin, producing leather rapidly and of great firmness. It also plumps up the flanks and shoulders of leather, causing them to readily fill up with tannin; therefore much better weight to the profit of the tanner and also to the worker of leather; as they are enabled to cut out more solid, serviceable leather than is generally obtained from old fashioned tanning. The leather also generally retains its pliability and smoothness longer in wear through all kinds of weather. The tan liquors also become impregnated with the potent principle and are thereby rendered in preserved condition so that they do not sour, thereby a great saving of tannin. As in the old way of tanning fresh tan liquors are often drawn off into vats of sour liquor, or the latter is drawn off into leeches of pure fresh tan, thereby the sour liquor precipitates a portion of the tannin in flakes to the bottom of the vat, in this manner much tannin is utterly lost to the tanner and the country, the saving of which alone, by this simple and almost costless improvement, is no small item. Hides but slightly tanned have been known to keep a long time in a perfectly sound condition in such impregnated liquors devoid of tannin, this improvement thus preventing damage by decomposition of hides in process of tanning, when the tanner may happen to be deficient in supply of tanning material.

The best results from this improvement are seen in oak bark or japonica tanning. This system, now called *Illinois French tanning*, lately reorganized on the previous and following process, reconstructed and systematized since 1858. The system, *as now* organized, having other very important filings in ingredients and a method not here, nor ever yet made public, or communicated to any but the purchasers of the process.

The melilotus, or trefoil plant, mentioned in the following process, is a very useful and cheap plant in tanning; it is a substitute for the imported Sicily sumach; besides possessing equal and similar coloring matter it also possesses certain saccharine properties that sumach does not contain. It gives valuable conditions to leather, a beautiful oak color, softness, toughness, and a cheesy condition; it rectifies terra japonica in leather, so as to modify its caustic nature and entirely do away with the japonica smell, giving leather a pleasant aromatic odor. The proportion of the plant in the system is small; it is a hardy, rapid growing plant on low damp soil, yields heavily, producing from four to six tons per acre, and two yearly crops from one seeding.

All other cloves or grasses have a weakening effect on leather, causing it to be thin and flanky, and to suffer a great loss in weight. The melilotus in effect is to the reverse of all that, and favors all the desirable conditions in leather.

This new process was patented in 1861, and consists in the use of the sweet-scented clover (*Melilotus*), in connection with terra japonica, cutch, tan bark, or other material used in the tanning of or manufacture of leather. Mr. Hatch operates as follows: He extracts the virtue from the melilotus by steeping in water, or tan liquor, and mixes the same with the terra japonica, cutch, or other tan in the proportion of 4 pounds of the green, or 2 pounds of the dry plant to each side of upper leather, or according to heavier or lighter stock—measuring the amount of melilotus to the proportion of tan used, as greater softness or toughness of leather is desired; or decreasing the proportion of melilotus as greater firmness of leather is desired. Put the raw hide into the liquor of said melilotus, and tan combined, or into each separately—changing from one to the other until tanned; and also drench tan leather in the liquor of said melilotus to soften it, and likewise to improve the color to that of oak-tanned leather.

The plant should be gathered when in flower, or when about going into flower.

It is a well-known fact that terra japonica, and cutch, are powerful astringents, and that, used alone, tend to make leather harsh and brittle, and thus liable soon to crack and break to pieces in wear; but, using the melilotus plant in connection with them, has an admirable effect in neutralizing their harsh nature, and thus to improve their condition in tanning leather.

CHAPTER LXXXII.

IRISH PROCESS.

IN 1766 Mr. Rankin announced that the heath, which is very common in Ireland, contained a tanning principle susceptible of taking the place of oak bark. Several experiments having succeeded, he published the following process: He puts the heath in a large kettle full of water, and leaves it to boil three hours, which time is sufficient to exhaust it. He decants this water in large vats which must be fixed in such a way that the water can be exhausted a second time. Be careful to put the skin in this last water when the temperature has fallen at 95°. This method tans the skins more easily than in the ordinary process. The solution of heath must be changed often; and, when used, the temperature must not be higher than 95°. This process gives a good tanning.

CHAPTER LXXXIII.

PROCESS OF MANUFACTURING LEATHER CALLED CUIRS A MURON.

WHEN the hides are fresh, soak them for eight days in particular wells, or in the river; draw them out every day to soften them. When they have been sufficiently soaked, take them out and put them in a solution composed of two parts of ashes and one of quicklime; dissolve the ashes and lime by boiling water, stirring all the time. Afterwards pour this mixture in a vat, dilute it with the necessary water, and soak the hides in it. Not to have them in contact with the residuum, which always settles to the bottom, cover it with a grate. Leave the hides in it until the hair can be pulled easily, which is generally the case after eight days. Take them out and depilate them with the round knife. Then tie the skins two by two, suspend them to poles, and place them in a current of water to cleanse them entirely from ashes and lime. Let them drain, flesh them, and trample upon them with the feet.

The small hides are put in a mixture called *kakscha*, composed of warm water and dog dung. Leave them to soak for twenty-four hours; take them out, clean, and wash them; macerate them in a liquor composed of oat flour and malt; leave them twenty-four hours. Put them in tan water, where they stay three days; afterwards they are worked in the following manner: Fill the vat half with pure and half with tan water; lay the hides on the grate, after having covered each one with powdered oak bark: the little hides may remain eight days; leave the strong and thick ones a longer time. When you draw the hides empty that vat, wash, trample the hides with the feet, wash, and flesh them; repeat the same operation four times, being careful to cover each time the skins with oak bark; the fourth time leave the skins in the vat for three weeks. When they are sufficiently tanned, they are spread two by two, and as soon as they are dry they are sent to the currier.

For red leather they generally take buckskins and calf-skins of every age. The red leather is dyed with red sandal-wood, and the black with logwood. A large skin requires 1 lb. of sandal; ½ lb. is sufficient for a small hide. To dye 100 hides black, dissolve with the logwood 3 lbs. of green vitriol; and for 100 red skins 3 lbs. of alum. Before dyeing the skins, give them the form of bags, leaving only a small aperture to introduce the dye; shut this opening, and shake the skin in in every way. This done, leave the skin to dry, and give it a second and even a third dye. When the skin is colored enough, coat it on the flesh side with birch tan or whale oil.

CHAPTER LXXXIV.

KALMUCKS' PROCESS.

WITH the Kalmucks, the women have the charge of tanning the hides. To prepare the skins of young lambs, they wash them in tepid water, spread them in the open air, and keep them till nearly dried, then they flesh them, and expose them anew to the air on the grass. During three days, they coat them three times a day with sour milk, in which a little salt is dissolved; the fourth day the skins are dried, and are worked all over with the hands, until entirely supple.

To have the hides resist the dampness and rain, they are smoked; for this purpose, a fire is lighted in a little vat, on which rotted wood, dry manure, etc., are thrown. They also use sheep dung, and the *stipa capillata*.

All round the pit they plant sticks disposed in form of pyramids, which are covered completely with the skins destined to be smoked. From time to time the position of the skins is changed from top to bottom. They continue thus, for one hour, then they work them to render them supple; they are rubbed on the flesh side with chalk, or gypsum; they are polished with knives, bleached anew with chalk, and well beaten.

Buck, and sheep-skins, destined to make riding pants,

or travelling summer dresses, are prepared in the following manner. The fresh hides are rolled, and left in a corner, until the wool, or hair, can be pulled; they are coated with sour milk, and worked in the same manner as lamb-skins; then they are spread on the ground, and the flesh side is coated with a strong decoction of *statice*, to which alum, and a certain quantity of mutton suet are added, then they are dried. Begin again the operation until the color of the root has exactly penetrated the skins. The hides thus prepared resist the dampness well.

The Kalmucks who live on fish, skin the large sea carp, dry the skin, remove the scales, and tan it afterwards. For this purpose they use sour milk, or a decoction of statice. These hides are almost transparent, and are used to make hoods as a protection against the rain.

Nearly all the house utensils of the Kalmucks are made from leather. For this purpose they use ox, and horse-hides. The back part is considered the best. To prepare them, they heat them in boiling water until the hair can be pulled off, others depilate them with ashes, afterwards they flesh, and wash them in running water. When withdrawn from the water, they are spread in the sun. Before being dried, they are cut into pieces, to which the intended form is given, and those pieces are sewed; the form is then given, and they are dried before a fire.

Those vessels have a very disagreeable odor, which communicates to everything which is put in. They soften by the introduction of a liquid too cold or too warm. These defects are obviated by exposing them to a heavy smoke for several days; by this means they take the appearance of horn, and have a solidity so that they can be kept many years without injury.

CHAPTER LXXXV.

LEATHER MANUFACTURE IN TURKEY.

The chief manufacture of leather in Turkey is in Trebizond, Mosul, Amaziah, Constantinople, and Ternova. The colored goat and sheep-skins, generally used to make slippers, come from Diarbeker, Aleppo, Damascus, Mecca, Smyrna, Sarohan, Kutahiah, Seras, Uskuff, Salonica, Philippopoli, Tirhala, Scyros, Randos, Eukare, Rustchuck, Widdin, Constantinople, and Erzeroum. There are great varieties of these skins. The red and the yellow are brilliant and solid; they are used chiefly for slippers, especially the latter color, which is usually reserved for Turkish ladies. The red and the black are much sought after for the making of saddlery of the oriental fashion.

All these skins, and more particularly the sleeked cow, are usually a little too dry; they have not sufficient flexibility, nor are they thick enough. These defects arise chiefly from the imperfect tanning processes employed in the provinces. The sheep and goat-skins are well curried.

It is known that the European process of tanning lasts a long period. None of the attempts made in Europe during the last 30 years to discover means whereby to expedite the operation of tanning have completely succeeded. The hide must remain, on an average, at least one year in the pit before it becomes properly tanned, and the preparatory operations to which the hides must be subjected before the process of tanning is entered upon are also quite long and complicated. They are divided into cleansing, swelling, depilation, and table work. Then comes the operation in the vats and pits.

A tannery is built quite close to a river, or to a spring of water able to furnish all the water necessary in these various operations.

The hides are first of all carried to a river and plunged in the water during half a day in order to wash away the blood and dirt with which they are soiled. Care is taken to turn and stir them from time to time, and they are rinsed before being taken out of the water. Dry hides, of course, need to remain longer in the water than fresh skins. These are briskly washed several times each day, and they are stretched with the stretching iron, trampled under the feet, cleansed, and the water then allowed to drain off. They are also worked once or twice at least with a round knife, having no edge, in order to stretch them perfectly, and to clean and soften them, the fleshing having been previously done; cellular tissue, the viscous matter, the muscular fibres, and in general all those parts which are apt to putrefy readily, are removed.

After the skins have been sufficiently softened they are replaced in the water and allowed to remain there from five to six hours. Care is taken not to let them remain too long, especially if the water is not fresh and running, for too long a stay in the water brings about a putrid decomposition of the hide, which affects it more or less deeply. However, all species of water are equally suitable for this operation, provided that the hide is only left therein long enough to wash it thoroughly, the sole object being to cleanse it and remove all hardness and stiffness. It has been ascertained by experience that hard water is more suitable when heavy leather is to be produced, and soft water for soft leather.

The second operation to which hides are subjected is the swelling or raising. The method used in the Ottoman provinces is a preparation of barley in a warm vat. According to this method as soon as the hides have been softened in the water they are trampled under the feet, and the round knife, above mentioned, is passed over the flesh side to make them supple. Then they are cleaned and placed on poles to drain. They are next examined to ascertain whether the hair comes off readily from the skin, which may appear in summer without further preparation. When fresh hides are treated they salt them without soaking them by sprinkling them with about 5½ lbs. of a mixture made up of sea salt, alum, and saltpetre. Then they pile them up and lay a mat over them.

Hides thus arranged speedily become heated, and they are turned over several times each day so that the fermentation may take place uniformly in all parts, and when it is perceived that the hair will come off easily it is at once removed as a too prolonged fermentation will damage the flesh side of the hide.

As soon as the depilation is completed the swelling is begun. For this purpose they make a leaven of wheat which is securely covered and kept in a warm place. It takes 24 hours to prepare this leaven. In swelling the hides a vat is used, which is partly filled with water. Then a few pailfuls are drawn from it and boiled, and in this boiling water are mixed 68¾ lbs. of barley, coarsely ground, made into a paste of the consistence of a thick glue by the admixture of cold water; then they put the paste back into the boiler and let it boil thoroughly, stirring it incessantly with a stick. After it has risen three times they pour it into the vat and stir the contents with a wooden shovel, turning always to the one side.

The vat is then very carefully covered after having taken out two pailfuls of the liquid that it contains, which is placed on the fire, and as soon as this composition begins to bubble they mix in the wheat leaven first made and pour the whole into the vat. This constitutes the first operation, which is intended to do for 6 or 7 hides. Such a temperature should be maintained that the workman cannot bear his arm in it without pain. They then add 5½ lbs. of sea salt; mix the whole well together and let it sour during 15 days, taking care to stir it several times each day, and to cover up the vat again immediately thereafter so that it may lose none of its heat.

At the end of that time the hides are thrown into a spring together by threes on a rope, and they are left there from four to five days. Each day they are taken out twice, rinsed, drained a little, and then put back; and this operation is kept up until the flesh side of the hide becomes soft enough to retain the imprint of a finger nail, when the finger is pressed against it. They are then taken out to be fleshed, and if any hair remains it is shaved off, after which they are rinsed in clean water and laid to drain upon poles during twenty-four hours.

A second leaven of wheat is then made, a little weaker than the first. The sour liquor, which was used in the first operation, is next poured out, keeping only the clear portion of the liquid, which is poured into a second vat in order to receive its complement; that is to say, the addition, as in the first operation, first of a quantity of ground barley, a little less than the first, then of the second leaven already prepared, and finally of a little sea salt. Thus two vats are prepared for the operation. Care is taken to withdraw a few pailfuls, which are kept in reserve on the fire; and when the fermentation is well established, which is ascertained by the sourness of the water, the hides are removed from the framework of poles to plunge them in, for a minute or two, that they may gradually acquire the temperature of the vat. They are then laid on the cover of the vat so that they may drain off a few minutes without becoming cold; then they are pressed down into the vat, and after it is covered again the heat is kept up by the aid of the hot water held in reserve. At the end of a quarter of an hour, the hides are taken out for the second time, and are allowed to drain in the same manner as before during a quarter of an hour, after which time they are again plunged into the vat and left there half an hour.

CHAPTER LXXXVI.

J. HANNOYE'S PROCESS.

ANOTHER method, analogous in principle to the preceding, consists in producing an equable and active filtration of tan-liquors through the skins, while they are exposed to pressure, the kind, temperature, strength, and mode of employment of which can be varied at will. For this purpose, the filter-press of Real, with some modifications, is made use of, not merely with the intention for which it has before this been employed, of extracting the active principles of bark, but as a direct agent in the tanning process itself; the skins being stratified in it with layers of bark, and the extraction of the tannin, and the absorption of it by the skins, being both effected under pressure, and without contact of air. The apparatus, which has been prepared upon the principle of the filter-press, is provided, like it, with a tube having air-tight joints, by means of which a forced and uniform filtration is effected by the pressure of a column of fluid, and the tube is of such a height that the pressure can be increased or diminished at pleasure by altering the height of the column, while the character of the operation can be varied at will by the employment of different fluids. The pressure of the column of fluid can be directed alternately upon either the upper or lower surfaces of the skins, by means of tubes provided with stopcocks, and entering the vessel at the top and bottom.

The inventor claims this new application of the principle of the filter-press, as being entirely original, and

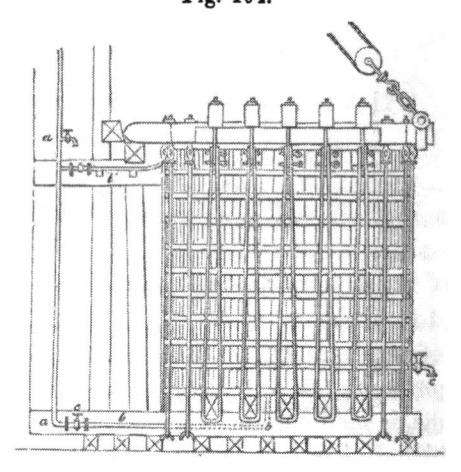

Fig. 104.

asserts that, by the employment of it, he has been able to arrive at a perfection, rapidity, and exactitude of the method of tanning, which have not been attained by any other process.

Figs. 104, 105, 106. Vessels of a cylindrical or square form, of a suitable capacity to hold the number of skins

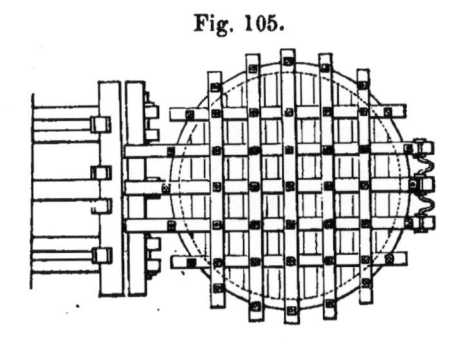

Fig. 105.

intended to be operated upon, and which are capable of resisting a considerable pressure. A tube a, a, Fig. 104,

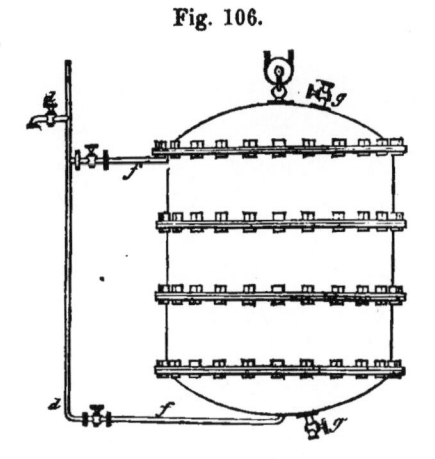

Fig. 106.

is attached to each, and is proportioned in height to the mode of making pressure which is to be adopted, whether it be that of a column of watery fluid, of mercury, or of the hydraulic piston. Branch-pipes b, b', connect this tube with the upper and the lower part of the reservoir, and the opening of one or the other of the stop-cocks upon them causes the pressure and consequent infiltration of tan-liquor through the skins to take place either from above downwards, or in the opposite direction. A pipe with a stop-cock e, allows the liquid within the vat to escape.

"The reservoir may be composed of different materials. It may be constructed of solid masonry, covered in its interior with lime cement, over which a coating of tar or of some resinous substance is placed, so as to defend the leather from the action of the lime. It may be made of wood, lined with sheet-lead; zinc or copper, well soldered in all parts; or may be composed of cast-iron, lined throughout with lead or zinc, so as to prevent the injurious effect of oxide of iron upon the leather. In either case, the rim of the neck of the vessel consists of a solid plate or disk of metal, firmly attached to it, and a disk of thick leather is interposed between it and the top or lid, which is tightly fastened down by means of screws and nuts upon the plate. This top may consist of thick wood or of metal plate, also lined on its lower surface with sheet-lead or zinc. The copper or leaden tube d, d, for the column of fluid, is from one to three inches in diameter, and is connected with the vessel by two tubes f, f', one entering it below the lid, the other at its base. By opening the stop-cock upon the upper tube, the pressure of the fluid is made upon the upper surface of the skins, and in the opposite direction by opening that upon the lower tube. Two other cocks, g, g', the one proceeding from the lid, the other from the lower part of the reservoir, conduct the liquid which has traversed the skins into a suitable receptacle, the upper one being left open when the pressure is from below, and the lower one when it proceeds from above. The skins are stratified in the vat between beds of tan; water alone is usually employed for the pressure upon its contents, and for the extraction of the tannin, and the cocks for the egress of fluid are only left so much open as to allow it to escape drop by drop.

"Calf-skins may be tanned in twenty days by this method, and ox-hides in sixty days, but the tanning may be much expedited by the following arrangement: Instead of simply stratifying the skins with layers of bark, a framework of wood, with an open space in its interior, rather smaller than the skins, is placed upon each one. The interior of this frame is filled with tan, another skin is extended above the frame thus filled, and is in turn surmounted by other frames and skins arranged in the same manner. To prevent the fluid from being forced through the spaces between the outsides of the frames and the walls of the vessel, these are filled up with mastic, or some impervious cement like the *fatty lute* of chemists, or a mixture of tallow and rosin. A similar application of lute is made around the edges of the skins, and the weight of the tan and frames soon makes the cemented parts perfectly tight.

"After each tanning is completed, the mastic or luting can be taken off and used for a similar purpose again. Skins tanned by this last method are as perfectly prepared in a few days, as those which have been exposed in the pits for sixteen months."

CHAPTER LXXXVII.

M. NOSSITER'S PROCESS.

This new method was patented in England in 1844, and consists in depositing the skins in pits so that they shall not be subjected to the pressure of those placed above them, and in pressing out the exhausted infusion contained in them, before immersing them again in fresh ooze.

1. The skins being superposed, in the old method of tanning in vats, those which are below are so compressed that the tan-liquor penetrates their structure with difficulty. To avoid this objection, the inventor proposes to deposit the skins in square vats, and to separate them by the interposition of rectangular frames with ledges. By this means the skins are perfectly free from contact with each other while in the tan-liquor.

Fig. 107 represents a horizontal section of the vat, and a frame with a skin stretched over it.

Fig. 107.

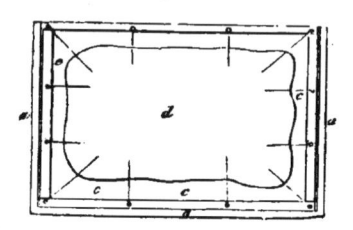

Fig. 108 is a vertical section, showing the frames in stack, and the skins between them.

NOSSITER'S PROCESS.

Fig. 108.

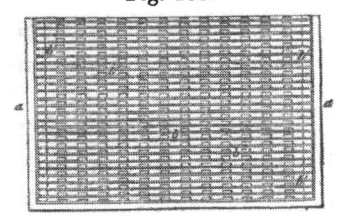

Fig. 109 shows the plan of the bottom of the vat.

Fig. 109.

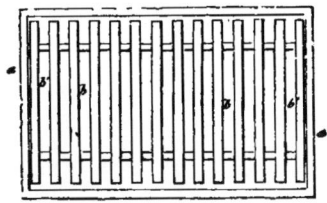

Fig. 110, plan of the frame.

Fig. 110.

a, a. Vat, of the ordinary form; *b, b*, wooden frame, with crosspieces; *b'*, ledges for maintaining the pieces in position.

This method of tanning is much more expeditious than the old way; for although fewer skins can be tanned by it at one time, it admits the working of a greater number in a given time, and in the same vat.

The vat is first filled with the skins and frames, and the tan-liquor is then introduced. When this latter is exhausted or weakened, it is pumped out and replaced by fresh ooze.

The skins are deprived of exhausted liquor, in many establishments, by pressure between rollers; but as this method does not fully effect the object, Nossiter subjects them to the action of a screw-press, which is seen in vertical section in Fig. 111, and in the plan, Fig. 112.

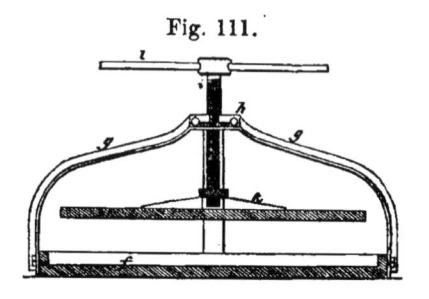

Fig. 111.

This press consists of a strong rectangular support f, from the four corners of which arches spring, which

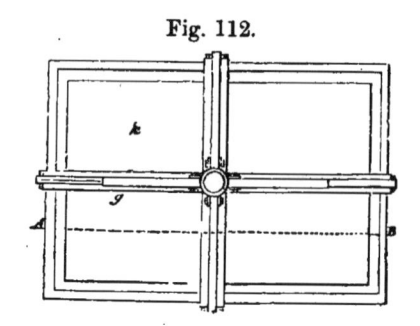

Fig. 112.

meet in the centre in a square nut h, in which the strong screw i turns. The skins are placed above each other on the table of the frame, and are pressed by the plate

k, at the lower end of the screw, which is turned by the lever l. The skins are subjected to this pressure until all their fluid contents are expelled.

Fig. 113.

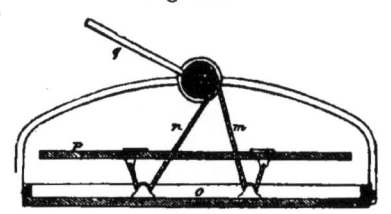

In place of the screw-press, one with an axle, seen in Fig. 113 in vertical section, and in Fig. 114 in plan, may

Fig. 114.

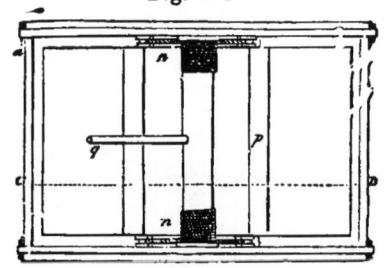

be used. Around the axle m, the cords n, n, are rolled, which pass through pulleys in the supports. The cords are passed at their ends through screw-rings on the sides of the under surface of the plate p. By turning the axle with the lever q, the upper plate is made to compress the skins which are placed below it.

CHAPTER LXXXVIII.

SQUIRE'S PROCESS.

This process, patented in 1844, consists in depositing the skins in a horizontal wooden cylinder, which is made to revolve slowly, under the surface of hot tan-liquor, so as to insure constant agitation of the hides and skins, and perfect exclusion of air.

Fig. 115 represents a transverse vertical section of the

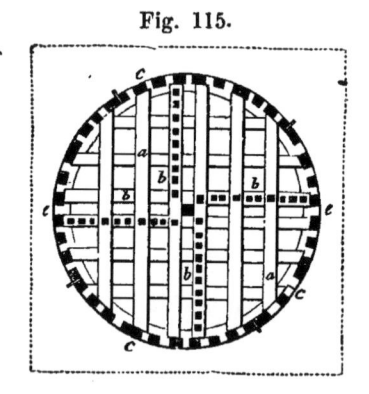

Fig. 115.

apparatus, as placed in the vat: *a*, wooden drum 12 feet long and 7 feet in diameter, lined with ridges, and divided into four compartments by the partitions *b, b*, which are composed of wooden staves, or bars with open spaces between them. Hot ooze, and some of the tanning material are then introduced with the prepared hides through a water-tight door *c*. The vat should be deep enough to admit the submersion of the whole cylinder, which is to be kept in uninterrupted motion, at the rate of six or seven revolutions per minute; and for this purpose its axle d, resting upon upright supports, is turned.

This is really an accelerating process, for the use of hot ooze, and the continuous contact of the skins with the tan-liquor, shorten the time for complete tanning to two weeks. Moreover, it permits the use of divi-divi, catechu, and other readily oxidizable tanning materials, which, when used in open vats, color the leather and render it unsalable. The access of air in this process being limited, this disadvantage is avoided.

The ooze spends its force very rapidly, and must be replaced by fresh hot liquor as fast as it becomes exhausted.

CHAPTER LXXXIX.

ENGLISH PROCESS FOR TANNING NETS, SAILS, AND ROPES.

The following method of preserving, and increasing the strength of nets, sails, and ropes, has been proposed by a ship builder of Bridgeport. He boils, in 89 gals. of water, 100 lbs. of oak branches, and the same quantity of tan, until it is reduced to 71 gals. He decants the clear liquid, and introduces into it the articles to be tanned, being careful to have them entirely covered, and not touching the bottom of the vessels. He boils them three hours, withdraws, and dries them.

This is not a regular tanning process; its object is only to combine the tannic and extractive matter with vegetable substances, which are very different from the gelatine of the skin. Linen, steeped two or three days in a solution of oak bark at the temperature of 150°, was kept in a damp cellar for ten years, without being rotted, while an untanned piece, placed in the same circumstances, was completely rotted.

CHAPTER XC.

EXPERIMENTS IN THE TANNING OF CALF-SKINS WITH TAN, DIVI-DIVI, CATECHU, AND ELECAMPANE BARK, BY M. KAMPFFMEYER.

THESE interesting experiments were published in the *Mémoires of the Société d'Encouragement of Berlin*, and the *Technologist*. We shall describe them with details.

To proceed to these experiments, twenty-five calf-skins were chosen; they were identical as nearly as possible. Of these twenty-five skins, seven were tanned with oak bark, six with the elecampane bark, six with catechu, and six with the divi-divi.

The twenty-five hides, during the operations, were submitted to the same manipulations. When those manipulations were finished, all the skins treated by the sulphuret of calcium and by the lime were cleansed as much as possible from the lime, and deposited in the vats.

Oak Bark.—Amongst the skins tanned with this bark the three pieces treated with sulphuret of calcium weighed, when raw, 12 lbs. 14 oz.; weighed anew, after the tanning, and passed to the tallow, they weighed 12 lbs. 5 oz., consequently they had lost 9 oz. There had been used 84 lbs. 2 oz. of bark; that is, 6 lbs. 8½ oz. of tan per pound.

The four skins treated by caustic lime weighed, when raw, 14 lbs. 11 oz.; after tanning they weighed 13 lbs. 14 ounces, consequently they had lost 13 oz. They required 107 lbs. 12½ oz. of tan; that is, 5 lbs. 8½ oz. per pound. They were similar to the commercial leather, and their grain was finer than in the other experiments.

The skins treated by sulphuret of calcium were firmer and soft.

Divi-Divi.—The three skins treated by the sulphuret of calcium weighed, raw, 12 lbs.; when tanned, they weighed 11 lbs. 3 oz.; they had lost 9 oz. They required 13 lbs. 2 oz. of divi-divi; that is, 1 lb. 11½ oz. per pound.

The three skins treated by caustic lime weighed, raw, 10 lbs. 8 oz.; and when tanned, 9 lbs. 15 oz.; they had lost 9 oz. They had required 11 lbs. 3 oz. of divi-divi, or 1 lb. 11¼ oz. per pound.

The edge and the color were very fine, and the tanning more satisfactory than in the other skins. The grain had not so fine an aspect as the skins tanned with oak, but it was satisfactory.

Catechu (Terra Japonica).—The three skins treated by sulphuret of calcium weighed 9 lbs. 10 oz.; and after tanning, 11 lbs. 13 oz.; they had thus gained 2 lbs. 3 oz. They required 13 lbs. 1½ oz. of catechu, or 1 lb. 2¾ oz. per pound.

The three other skins treated by lime weighed 12 lbs.; when tanned, they weighed 12 lbs. 4½ oz. They had gained 4½ oz. They required 13 lbs. 1½ oz. of catechu, or 1 lb. 4½ oz. per pound.

The tanning was perfect; the color slightly orange; the side was unequal and rough; the grain was thin and spongy in the skins treated by quicklime. They were inferior to the others.

Elecampane Bark.—The three skins treated by sulphuret of calcium weighed, raw, 11 lbs.; and when tanned, 11 lbs. 4½ oz.; they had gained 4½ oz. They required 155 lbs. 3 oz. of bark; that is, 14 lbs. 1½ oz. per pound.

The three skins treated by quicklime weighed, raw, 10 lbs. ½ oz.; and when tanned, 9 lbs. 10½ oz.; they had lost 6 oz. They had required 121 lbs. 5½ oz. of bark, or 6 lbs. 2 oz. per pound.

Notwithstanding the large quantity of bark, the skins were more or less imperfectly tanned—principally those treated by the sulphuret of calcium; they were so hard and dense that the grease could not penetrate them entirely; the grain was flat. The skins could be tanned easily even after the greasing; their color was brown.

We see by the above experiments that the tanning with oak bark and divi-divi were the best, and the latter can be compared with the oak.

The use of catechu, as a dry matter in the tanning of skins, is inadmissible. The porous and thin texture of the leather thus manufactured is a poor guarantee against dampness and permits of little duration.

The results obtained with the elecampane bark are less satisfactory.

For the expenses, there is little difference between oak bark and divi-divi. Divi-divi, it is true, is more costly; but as it possesses six times as much tannin as oak bark, the balance will be rather in favor of the latter.

Trials were also made with green Buenos-Ayres hides, and the results were about the same as above. The divi-divi is superior to catechu and elecampane, and can be compared to the oak in many respects; but it requires more care in its use on a large scale, while the operation is one-third shorter.

According to the author, the divi-divi is the best substitute for oak; and while it is difficult to grind it, reduced into the form of an extract it can be advantageously employed by its mixture with oak bark.

CHAPTER XCI.

TANNING HIDES, BY J. W. JOHNSON.

Mr. J. W. Johnson proposes to employ for the purpose of tanning hides a new vegetable decoction prepared from *Maruta Cotula*, to a gallon of which are added 4 ounces of catechu and 2 ounces each of common salt and alum. In this mixed tan liquor, the skins or hides, with or without hair upon them, are to be immersed, and there left for a period determined by the thickness of the hide, and by other circumstances which ordinary experience will dictate.

Sir Humphrey Davy was the first to show that catechu alone could be employed as a tanning material. We are unacquainted with any special property possessed by the vegetable decoction referred to, which would render advantageous its employment in conjunction with the foregoing.

CHAPTER XCII.

TURNBULL'S PROCESS.

The *Technologist** has given, on this process of tanning, details that we propose to reproduce here.

In the tanning of skins, as every one knows, it is very difficult to bring the tannin immediately in contact with the gelatinous matter of the skins, and that for the following causes:—

* Sixth year, page 442.

1. Hides macerated in lime absorb a certain quantity of this earth, which takes a portion of the gelatinous substance in form of soluble gelatine, that is, alters the fibre enough to render it incapable of combining efficaciously with tannin, and the pores of the skin are so impregnated with lime that the tanning principle cannot operate freely and penetrate to the heart of the skin.

2. When catechu is used, the leather produced is very permeable to water, light and spongy and of a dark red color. This state is produced by catechuic acid and some other extractive matters which are found in the catechu.

3. When we macerate tan or other similar substances, such as divi-divi and sumach, with water for tanning, those substances by the action of the oxygen of the air produce gallic acid, which is a solvent of gelatine, and consequently noxious in the tanning, at the same time that it causes an expansion in the pores of the hide, and as it does not help in the combination of the tannin with the gelatine, the leather remains spongy, porous, and of an inferior quality.

The principal object of M. Turnbull has been to remove these inconveniences and difficulties and to produce a rapid and efficacious combination of the gelatine of the skin with the tanning matter.

The first point consists in removing the lime contained in the skins, or to use other means of raising sugar and saccharated matters contained in vegetable substances, having the property to combine with lime and to dissolve it. It is the same with pyroligneous acid or wood vinegar, consequently to extract the lime contained in skins prepare a solution consisting of 14 pounds of sawdust, 4 pounds of raw sugar and 300 quarts of water. It can also be composed of sawdust alone in the proportion of

28 pounds for the same quantity of water. The solutions are made either cold or warm, but always used cold; macerate in the skins for two or three days, which is sufficient to dissolve all the lime.

To raise the skins without lime Mr. Turnbull dips them first in a solution of sugar or any saccharine matter; second, in a solution of common salt. By the first means sugar dilates the gelatine, and renders the raising easier. In the second the salt contracts the epidermis without acting on the gelatine, separates it from the true skin, so that the hair can be taken off without producing any alteration in the gelatinous matter of the skin. The solution of sugar is thus formed : 14 lbs. of raw sugar or molasses for 112 gals. of water kept at a temperature between 50° and 77°. The skins are left in from five to ten days. The solution of salt is formed with 14 lbs. of salt in 112 gals. of water kept at a temperature between 68° and 86°.

Turnbull's process to separate catechuic acid from the other principles contained in catechu, from tannic acid, and to avoid the formation of gallic and ellagic acid when gall, oak bark, divi-divi, etc., are used, is the following :—

Reduce the catechu to a fine powder, treat that powder by cold water until no more is dissolved. Pour the cold solution into a vat or cylinder provided with a metallic tissue or cotton cloth. The catechuic acid insoluble in cold water stays on the filter and the solution of tannin is freed from these matters.

To prevent the formation of gallic and ellagic acid he reduces the material into powder and prevents the contact of the air during the tanning, as we shall see hereafter.

The skins thus prepared are well washed and tanned by two different processes. First, by the application of a certain physical force different from capillary attraction and hydrostatic pressure. Second, in vats communicating one with the other, as we shall explain hereafter, so as to maintain a constant agitation and circulation in the tanning matter, until the skins are tanned.

The physical force that Mr. Turnbull proposed to apply to the tanning of the skins is that one which produces the *endosmose* and *exosmose*. For this purpose he takes the skins to form bags in which he introduces the tan in the proportion of 2 lbs. for every pound of damp leather. He shuts the bags in which he keeps a small aperture by which he pours in cold or warm water, then hermetically closes the hole. These bags are then introduced in closed wooden vats filled with a purified solution of catechu. In this manner during the operation the solution is not attacked by the air, and the formation of gallic acid is thus avoided. Thus, to increase the density of the vats, he adds 14 lbs. of sugar for every 112 gals. of liquor.

The two liquors thus prepared and used, the effects of *endosmose* and *exosmose* are produced, and tannic acid passes rapidly through the skins until they are perfectly tanned. Draw the bags from time to time, and when they are partly emptied by the filtration they are filled again with water.

During the tanning it is necessary to keep the density of the liquor of the vats by adding to it sugar from time to time. Instead of catechu you can use Valonia and even tan in the proportion of a half of the first. For the catechu it must be introduced in the bags only purified and in solution in the proportion of 2 lbs. of catechu equal to 8 lbs. of tan for 10 lbs. of skins.

You can dispose a series of vats, closed so as to maintain a constant movement and circulation. For this purpose fill these vats with a liquor composed as above, leaving in them a space sufficient to introduce the skins one on another, then close these vats so as to exclude the air, and finish by filling with the liquor, then establish a forcing pump, which by means of an aspiration pipe goes to the bottom of each vat. Draw the tanning liquor, raise it and pour it in another distribution pipe, which by means of little pipes forces it to the upper part of the vats.

When you operate on catechu to separate the tannic acid from the catechuic acid, and other useless matters, the deposit which forms in the vat is at least five per cent. in weight of the catechu put in dissolution. This deposit can be purified, and rendered proper for tanning. Deposit it in an oven, or in an evaporating vessel, and heat it at 161°, then expose to the air, and stir it until it takes the color of the powdered catechu. This matter, dissolved and filtered, contains as near as much tannin as the catechu dissolved in the first place.

The skins from which the lime has been separated, or those treated without lime, can be tanned in the usual way with catechu purified as above, or with other tanning substances. The leather produced by this process is heavier, and of better quality than by the old method.

Later, Mr. Turnbull gives the following details.[*]

"The economy obtained by my process is immense, and I will prove it in a few words.

"Thus, 100 lbs. of hide in the green state furnish only from 45 to 50 lbs. of tanned leather, requiring 300 lbs. of oak bark, and the operation lasts 18 months. By my method, 14 days are sufficient. For the same weight of skin, I use only 100 lbs. of oak bark, and after the operation I obtain 60 lbs. of leather; while

[*] Comptes Rendus. Acad. des Sciences, Janvier 12, 1846.

by the old method the tanner can prepare only one skin, I can prepare 39.

" The tanning of calf-skin requires by the usual method from five to six months; from two to four days are sufficient by my process.

"At last, if the tanner will use only the first part of my process, that is the saccharated solution, destined to prevent the action of the lime, he reduces the operation for calf-skins from six months to ten days."

CHAPTER XCIII.

S. SNYDER'S PROCESS.

EVERY one knows how important it is to saturate the hides with tannin as quickly as possible after they have been prepared to be put into the tanning vats, but till now this saturation has been done so slowly that it is often the cause of losses difficult to avoid. We will describe now a process which enables us to attain this object quickly, and which we have no doubt can be used in practice.

Mr. Snyder takes the hides after the working in the river, when they are very soft and flexible, and he *acupunctures* them on the entire surface, that is, he perforates them with an instrument presenting a surface armed with fine steel needles. A man can prepare from 30 to 40 hides daily, but the operation can be rendered more economical and rapid with the help of a machine. For some kinds of leather you must *acupuncture* on the grain side, while in some others on the flesh side.

Every one admits that a hide thus treated will be tanned much quicker than one which is not; but this idea to perforate thus an article, the object of which is to be water-proof, seems a paradox. But its author remarks that it is when the hide is in its greatest state of softness that the operation is performed, and he affirms by experiment that in this state the skin is not altered. As a proof he presented some skins, perforated and tanned, in which the puncture was not perceived above the grain. Indeed the soft skin contracts by the desiccation, and the tannin with which it is impregnated gives it back its thickness and its primitive firmness, in obliterating all the pores and perforations.

A better leather can be prepared by this method than by the other, for the following reasons :—

1. Because it accelerates the tanning so as to require a more frequent renewal of the liquor, which has no time to become acid; for it is a known fact that a tan liquor becomes acid in ten days, and in the ordinary process the leather is left sometimes 6 or 8 weeks in the same liquor, which consequently becomes sour. He surmounts this difficulty by exposing a more considerable surface of fibres to the immediate action of the tannin, which causes a quicker combination, requires a more frequent renewal of the liquor than by passing it through a bed of powder, and insures its being fresh and sweet.

2. Because by bringing the tannin into immediate contact with the interior fibres a chemical change is produced at the same time as that on the exterior surfaces, which need not be over-tanned. This exterior surface is rendered hard and brittle as usual, by continuing the action until the tannin has penetrated inside.

According to the author he can tan in half the time of the ordinary process, and consequently save much cost and labor. If you want to operate quicker, hydrostatic pressure can be applied, which does very well with the acupuncture, and it requires less pressure than that usually employed, which often weakens the fibres of the skin.

CHAPTER XCIV.

H. HIBBARD'S PROCESS.

This process unites in a high degree the advantages of economy, time, and labor. It is applicable to all kinds of skins, and produces a solid and durable leather. The process is described by his author as consisting:—

"*First*. In the use of a composition of lime, wood, ashes, and salt, the object of which is to remove hair and wool, also for *liming* instead of using lime alone. We have described the objections to the use of lime and ashes separately, but when combined in proper proportions the salt modifies the action of the alkalies and protects the skin from their caustic properties, so that the process of unhairing is rendered more expeditious and safe than by the old process. The texture of the skin is uninjured and the leather is much stronger.

"*Second*. In the use of a composition of salt, sulphuric acid, and sumach, oak, hemlock, or any other tanning material. The salt, sulphuric acid, and tannin being mixed together in water in certain proportions, a portion of the salt is decomposed by the acid to form sulphate of soda, and set at liberty hydrochloric acid, which is redissolved by water, acts on the skins, opens the pores, and prepares them for the tannin, which being present in the mixture, readily unites with the principles of the skin and forms leather more expeditiously than by the old method.

Preparation of the Skins.

"Prepare the following composition:—

Quicklime (freshly slacked)	½ bushel.
Wood ashes	½ "
Salt	3 pints.

"To remove the hair mix the above composition with water sufficient to make a thick paste, apply it to the flesh side of the hides, fold the skins and keep them at a temperature of summer heat. In a few hours they are ready to pull.

"For the liming process I use the same composition, mixed with a sufficiency of water in a vat to immerse the number of skins proposed to be limed. One bushel is equivalent to one bushel of lime alone. The liming is done at the temperature of 60°.

Composition for Tanning.

"For six dozen of full sized sheep, deer, goat, or similar skins, prepare the following composition:—

Salt	18 lbs.
Sulphuric acid	2 "
Sumach or quercitron bark	36 "
Hydrochloric acid	2 ounces.
Dried clover	18 lbs.
Water	125 gals.

"Exhaust the sumach by water, add the salt, enough to insure perfect solution. Add then the acids and incorporate by stirring."

CHAPTER XCV.

HEMLOCK TANNING.

The hemlock forests of New York and Northern Pennsylvania are very extensive, and the readiness and cheapness with which the bark may be obtained have brought it into general use, in those States, as tanning material. It may be employed alone, or in combination with oak bark.

In order to produce heavy weights the hides should not be reduced too low in the beam house, and should be tanned quickly with strong, good liquors, principally in the last stages of the operation. Nothing is more injurious to green hides than to leave them too long in weak ooze; they become too much reduced, grow soft, flat, and flabby; lose a portion of their gelatine, and refuse to plump up.

The soaking and sweating are made in the ordinary manner, and the following table shows the time employed for these operations at different temperatures:—

Soaking.	40°. Days.	50°. Days.	60°. Days.	70°. Days.
Buenos-Ayres hides	10 to 12	8 to 12	6 to 8	3 to 6
Carthagena "	8 to 12	7 to 9.	5 to 7	2 to 3
Sweating.				
Buenos-Ayres "	15 to 20	12 to 16.	8 to 12	2 to 3
Carthagena "	15 to 20	10 to 15	6 to 8	2 to 3

Soaked hides do not require more than two-thirds of the time to soak, but rather longer to sweat.

After these operations are done, pass to the *handling*, which is performed two or three times a day in a weak *ooze* until the grain is colored. New liquors, or mixtures of new and old are preferable for dry hides, old liquors for slaughtered. They are then, after a fortnight, laid away in bark, and changed once in two or four weeks until tanned. Much care and judgment are necessary in proportioning the continually increasing strength of the liquors to the requirements of the leather in the different stages of the process. The liquors should also be kept as cool as possible, within certain limits, but ought never to exceed a temperature of 80°. Too high a heat, with a liquor too strongly charged with the tanning principle, is injurious to the life and color of the leather. If too strong a solution is injurious, the use of a too weak one must be avoided. Hides treated with liquors below the proper strength become relaxed in their texture, and lose a portion of their gelatine. The leather loses in weight, and is much more porous. The greatest strength of liquor used for handling must mark 16° by the barkometer; and that employed in laying away must mark at its greatest strength from 30 to 45°.

After the leather has been thoroughly tanned and rinsed, or scrubbed by a brush machine or broom, it will tend very much to improve its color and pliability to stack it up in piles and allow it to sweat until it becomes a little slippery from a kind of mucus that collects upon its surface. A little oil added at this stage of the process has been found very useful.

The average time of tanning by hemlock amounts to five months twenty-seven days. The English tanners employ from eight to ten months.

We need not dwell much longer on this process, which is the same as with oak bark. The leather it produces is good, and easily recognized by its red color.

To tan sole-leather with hemlock takes from four to

six months, according to the strength of the liquor and number of sides in the vats; and the quicker tanned the better. The weight of the hides if heavy requires more time than if comparatively light. If the hides are fresh, they are capable of being properly softened; and if so, the process of tanning may be completed sooner than in the case of old and hard hides that cannot be softened so easily. If the hides have sufficient room in the vats they will tan much faster. As the tanning advances the liquor should be renewed seasonably, and its strength increased in a ratio proportionate to each stage of tanning.

Process of Tanning as Performed at the Shaker Tannery of New Lebanon, N. Y.

We are indebted to M. Fred. Sizer, the Shaker tanner, for the following account of the process of tanning as performed in that village. All those who are acquainted with the products of that society will know the value of this process, which we, without hesitation, recommend as purely practical. We give it in the words of its author:—

"I take a pack of calf-skins—say one hundred dry skins—and put them in a water vat to soak; after they have soaked two or three days, I take them out and mill them (a wheel is best for milling hides). I then beam them on the flesh side, removing all the lean meat and grease from the skin, stretching them out well with the beaming knife, and put them into a vat of clean water until they are soft enough to go in the lime. They must be as soft as they were when they came off the animal, or as near that as you can get them. If the hides are not soft before going in the lime, they never can be, and the leather will always be hard.

"Fresh hides that come directly from the butcher are

put in the water a day or two; change the water once; beam on the flesh side to get the meat and grease off, then they are ready for the lime.

"I make my lime in a vat 8 feet long, 4 wide, and 4 deep. One bushel of slaked lime and 2 gallons soft soap, put in the vat two-thirds full of water, will make a lime sufficient for 100 calf-skins, or 50 sides of upper leather. The hides should be hauled out every other day, while in the lime, to air and change their position; then stir the lime well before they are put back.

"The lime needs strengthening every time a new pack is put in, by adding say half bushel lime and two or three quarts soap. I lime my calf-skins and upper leather hides until the hair comes off easily (but sole leather should be limed as little as possible and get the hair off); then unhair them, wash them out in the mill, beam them on the flesh side, trim off the pates and shanks, and put them in the bate.

"I put 5 or 6 bushels hen dung into a vat of the same dimensions of that used for the lime, and fill two-thirds full of water, and let it stand two or three days to ferment. I let my skins remain in the bate two or three days in warm weather, and longer in cold; haul them two or three times while in the bate, and work them twice on the grain with a common worker on the tanners' beam; mill them before working the last time; then beam them, and they are ready for the tan vats.

"I make a liquor of moderate strength to handle them in, put them in this liquor, and stir them with pole a while; then I handle them up smooth on a box or rack three or four times in the course of the day; let them remain in this until the next morning, then change the liquor, giving them about the same strength they had the first time; handle them two or three times a day in this liquor, and when the liquor is exhausted change again and handle less as the skins get colored and the grain set. I make my liquors of hemlock bark, ground and put in leeches, and pump in exhausted liquor. The first strength of my leeches I draw off into my sole leather vats; I draw off my leeches two or three times before taking it for my upper leather and calf-skins, and these I keep in mild, sweet liquors through the whole tanning process.

"I handle my hides and calf-skins through until tanned, changing the liquors as they get exhausted. After they get well along, I handle three times a week. They will do to lay longer, but will tan faster to handle often.

"When my calf-skins have been in the tan two or three weeks, I shave down the necks; and after my upper leather has been in four or five weeks, I shave it down to a proper thickness.

"In my experience in tanning, which has extended through forty-two years, and I have used both hemlock and oak bark, I find that mild, sweet liquors are far the best for tanning all kinds of upper leather. The hide in the raw state is tougher than when tanned, and that toughness ought to be preserved as much as possible and make good pliable leather, and the slow process of tanning with mild liquors will do it. Strong liquors have a tendency to make the leather hard and liable to crack.

"The hides for upper leather should not be tanned any more than thoroughly through; if tanned longer than this, it has the same effect upon them as strong liquor. But the longer sole leather is tanned the better.

"When I think my leather is nearly struck through I try it by cutting into the thickest edge, and when tanned through take it up and scour it out in the wheel to cleanse it from the tan and soften the grain; then take them to the currying shop, and the calf-skins I skive and upper smooth down with the currying knife; then put them in a tub of water and scour them on the table with a brush, stone, and slicker; dry them a little to temper them, and then put them on the table and set them on the grain side to work the grain out smooth. After that apply some thin stuffing made of oil and tallow; then turn them over, the flesh side up, and set them out with an iron slicker; then apply the stuffing more plentifully, made thicker with more tallow; then hang them on sticks and dry them, and then pack them down in a pile and let them stay two weeks. I then take them and rub off what stuffing does not strike in, and whiten them with a currying knife or slicker.

"I commonly whiten my calf-skins and kips with a slicker, and finish in the French style.

"Since the French dégras has come into use I have used it for calf-skins and kips. I have also, for some time, used tansy in my liquors. There is an acid in tan that injures the leather which tansy neutralizes, and keeps the liquor sweet."

CHAPTER XCVI.

HALVORSON'S PROCESS FOR RENDERING HIDES HARD AND TRANSPARENT.

This method, patented by H. Halvorson, is thus described:—

"I take the raw hide and submit it to the sweating operation sufficiently to remove the hair, or I immerse the hide in a solution of lime or alkali proper to remove the hair. I then submit it to the action of a boiling bath of any powerful astringent and alkaline, or any other substance sufficient to remove the fatty matter and make it thicker.

"So far as my experience goes I find sulphuric acid, salts of tartar, and alum, dissolved in water, to answer a good purpose. I keep the hide in the boiling solution, stirring frequently, and handling the hides while under the influence of the bath, in order to cause the liquid to penetrate it.

"After having fulled it to the desired thickness I rinse it in warm and clear water and dry it. The hide is opaque, and is very easily affected by the atmospheric changes. In order to render it semi-transparent and capable of resisting the influence of atmospheric changes I immerse it in a vessel full of boiling drying oil, and keep it in until a white or yellowish scale begins to form on its surface, then I remove the hide from the fire. While hot it can be pressed or moulded into various shapes. When cold it is converted into a substance resembling horn or tortoise shell, and may be worked like them or ivory.

"If the hide be designed for embossed works, it is advisable to remove it from the oil as soon as it acquires the desired transparency and softness.

"After being thus prepared it can be moulded. During the last portions of the process the material may be stained by adding to it any material proper to produce any desired color.

"Where it may not be required to thicken a hide to its greatest extent of capacity the use of an astringent solution may be dispensed with, it being only necessary in such cases to employ the alkaline solution, and afterwards expose the skin to the action of boiling oil as above described."

CHAPTER XCVII.

TAWING.

THIS process is applicable to the manufacture of soft leather for gloves and furrier's uses, as skins may be subjected to its action even in their hair state. It is sometimes called *alumed leather*, because a salt of alumina is the basis of the process. The skins usually submitted to this treatment are sheep, lamb, kid, and other light skins.

Kid Leather.

The first operation is to soak the skins well in running water and to break them upon the beam by working on the flesh side with the back of the fleshing knife. Then they must be immediately dried to prevent putrefaction, which will render them spotted and tender. Dry skins require a soaking of one or two days.

Then rub the flesh side with a cold milk of lime, place them back to back in pairs with the back outwards, stack them in piles, and leave them several days until the hair *gives* readily. Rinse them in running water, to remove the lime, and fleece them; this operation consists in *plucking* out the hair with spring tweezers, and smoothing by rubbing with a whetstone or rolling pin. Cleanse, and soak again in the lime vat, whence, after being removed, they are transferred to an old or weaker vat, and there remain for a fortnight or more, being careful to take them out and drain them frequently. They are now ready for the *branning*. For this purpose they undergo a steeping for 10 or 15 days in a fermenting mixture, or drench of 40 galls. of bran and 20 galls. of water. As soon as the skins sink in water they are sufficiently *raised;* this operation requires two days in summer and four days in winter, and great care is necessary to observe when they reach that stage, which may be attained earlier by frequently turning the skins.

When taken from this liquor they are put in the *white bath*, composed, for 100 skins, of a boiling solution of 10 to 12 lbs. of alum in 12 galls. of water, to which you add, in summer, 2½ lbs. of common salt, and in winter 3 lbs. Divide the skins into four equal parcels, and pass each parcel separately and successively in this bath, and then immerse the whole together for ten minutes.

Make a paste by gradually adding, during a constant stirring, firstly, 15 lbs. of wheat flour to the alum bath gently heated, and subsequently the yelks of fifty eggs, and then incorporating the whole thoroughly. The skins, after being passed in this paste singly, are transferred to it in bulk and left for a day.

This paste has an emulsive action, softens and whitens the skins, counteracts the hardening influence of after exposure to the air, and tendency to brittleness.

After this operation stretch the skins upon poles in a drying loft and there leave for a week or more, as may be necessary. They are then ready to be worked upon the *softening iron* to stretch them, reduce unevenness, and develop whiteness. For this purpose they are soaked in water for 5 or 6 minutes, and then spread and softened by the process of *staking*.

Next they are stretched on hooks, dried, and worked on the stretching iron, but some tanners, after the skins come from the smoothing iron, spread them upon the beam, with a clean undressed skin beneath, and work them with the fleshing knife.

Sometimes the prepared skin is polished by being rubbed with pumice. The lustre and finishing stroke are given with a smooth flat-iron carefully heated.

In some places the process is slightly modified. For example, by the use of a large barrel churn, or *roundabout*, which receives both the skin and the alum bath. Rapid rotation of the apparatus promotes constant contact of the skins and tanning material, and accelerates the operation. The tanned skins, after coming from the paste, and being washed and dried, are subjected to the *staking*, which consists in the use of a semicircular iron plate, fixed perpendicularly, with its round edge uppermost, to the top of a wooden stake about thirty inches high. The workman, holding the skin distended by both hands, draws it forcibly, and in every direction,

Fig. 116.

over the blunt edge of this tool, and thus imparts softness and smoothness to it.

Tawed leather is raw skin combined with chloride of aluminum. The alum is decomposed. Its aluminum combines with the chlorine of the chloride of sodium (salt), and the sulphuric acid of the alum forms a double sulphate of potash and soda, as represented in the following reaction :—

$$\underbrace{KO,SO_3, Al_2O_3\, 3(SO_3)}_{\text{Alum.}} + \underbrace{3Cl\, Na}_{\substack{\text{Chloride of}\\\text{Sodium.}}} = \underbrace{KO\, SO_3}_{\substack{\text{Sulphate of}\\\text{Potash.}}} + \underbrace{3NaO\, SO_3}_{\substack{\text{Sulphate of}\\\text{Soda.}}} + \underbrace{Cl_3\, Al_2}_{\substack{\text{Chloride of}\\\text{Aluminum.}}}$$

Imitation Kid.

Imitation kid is made from lamb-skins. Lime is not used in order to remove the wool without injury. Steep the skins in water, and break them on the flesh side; suspend them in a subterranean vault twelve feet square, protected as much as possible from atmospheric changes, so that the temperature stays the same all the year round. An incipient putrefaction is promoted, the roots of the wool are loosened, and it is readily plucked from the pelt; and when this state is reached, which takes from five to seven days, the skins are removed, to avoid injury.

The skins are then *slimed;* that is, are scraped on the flesh side, stripped of wool, and steeped for a week in lime water, fleshed on the beam, drenched for some days in a fermenting bran-bath, and treated with alum and salt in the same manner as true kid. Dyeing, softening, and polishing complete the preparation of the leather.

CHAPTER XCVIII.

THE BEST METHOD OF TANNING SMALL LAMB-SKINS, CALLED CHAMOIS, AND ESPECIALLY WHITE PELTRY FOR FURRIERS.

M. A. BRUGGEMANN describes a process, the principal result of which is, that the skins retain their fur, and that they remain dazzlingly white; further, that they become strong and exceedingly soft, which is best attainable in the following manner:—

The skins should be allowed to soak about eighteen hours in water, but not longer, or the fur will become loosened and the skin be rendered useless as peltry. Then they should be taken out of the water, and rinsed in running water. After the water has been drained off, or pressed out, the skins should be laid separately, with the fur sides uppermost, on a table or suitable board, and then carded, one after another, with the coarsest description of wool comb, especial attention being paid to the dirtiest spots, and great care taken that the fur may not be injured. The dirtiest spots should be rubbed with soap, and, that it may thoroughly take effect, the soaked skins should be allowed to remain untouched one or two hours. When there are large lots to be dressed together, the work goes on without interruption on this account, the skins first soaped being the first ready for the next state of the process. After the soaping, and after it has been allowed the necessary time to work in, the skins require to be once more carded, especially upon the soaped places. Then will be seen which portion of the pelt stands in need of a more further soaping; this should be done at once, and the skins allowed to lie a short time longer, that the soap may take effect; then they should be carded and washed clean.

Those skins found to be quite clean should be washed or rinsed in running water, which ends this part of the process. The washing out of the pelts, like all the preceding operations, requires great care in order to make them of uniform cleanliness. The skin should be held by one of the hind legs, that the other leg and the entire hinder part of the skin may be turned in washing evenly right and left, so that the other portions of the skin may continue in level motion on the water. If this particular, however insignificant it may appear, be not attended to, clean pelts cannot be obtained without much loss of time. After the skins are cleaned on the fur side, and the water drained off or squeezed out of them as much as possible, the flesh or fibrous part of the skin is removed by drawing it over a stationary iron instrument contrived for the purpose. This *fleshing* operation is also intended to render the skin pliant, and is of importance to its ultimate softness. After fleshing, the skins should be laid singly on a board, with the fleshy side uppermost, and carefully examined, heads, legs, tails, etc. Then take barley groats, or, in the absence of this, a mixture made of 3 parts wheat bran and 2 parts rye flour, which will answer the same purpose, and strew a layer of barley groats or the other mixture over each skin, covering the surface uniformly. Then roll each skin together, with the wool or fur side, of course, outward, with the legs, head, and edges well tucked in, and pack them thus rolled one by one in a water-tight vat. When the vat is tolerably full, or the stock of skins exhausted, pour salt water, that will bear an egg, upon the skins, and sufficient to cover them entirely. They should be left to remain there about twenty-four hours. It must be noted that the vat containing the skins should stand in a cellar, or in some other cool place, where it can be protected against frost. After the specified time the skins should be carefully unrolled, so that the bestrewn parts be as little disarranged as possible; then lay them with the fur side inwards, by twos flat together, the head of one being upon the tail of the other, and pack them thus flatly in another vat. Care must be taken not to press out the moisture remaining in the skins, as their peculiar nourishment or fermentation would thus be removed. During fourteen days, or ten will be sufficient at a high temperature, the skins must be daily re-packed and changed to another vat, so that all their parts may absorb the liquor uniformly. If this is not carefully attended to daily, the skins will certainly be speckled, and possibly entirely ruined. After the time mentioned, the skins should be taken out of the vat, drained, and the moisture got rid of by pressing or squeezing; then they are dried, and the dressing process begins.

CHAPTER XCIX.

NEW METHOD OF COLORING WHITE TAWED LEATHER.

Pelts, to be well colored, should be made perfectly smooth on the flesh side before being cleaned, this is accomplished by reducing the thickness of the skin on that side by means of the flesher and then making it perfectly even. In order to facilitate this operation, and that the flesher may take better hold of the portion which it is desired to remove, the side of the pelt operated upon ought to be well rubbed in with thin chalk paste. After the skin has been properly smoothed it is cleaned, wrung out, dried, and stretched out. The next operation is to place it on a tin or zinc table, with the flesh side outward, to stretch it tightly, and then to apply to its surface the desired coloring matter by means of a soft brush with long hair. After this, and while the pelt is still damp, it should be well rubbed in with pumice stone, being for that purpose stretched out on a frame. The workman performing this part of the operation holds with his left hand the frame, on which the skin is extended, and rubs it downwards with the pumice stone which he presses as hard as he can. The skin should be thus pumiced from the tail to the head, then again from the head to the tail, and then from flank to flank, the latter if the condition of the skin requires it. After pumicing the pelts are dried on wooden platforms or scaffoldings, provided with hooks, in a room where they can be so hung as not to touch each other. The dried skins are again placed on the table as before, receive the second coating of color, and are again carried to the scaffolding to dry. This operation is repeated a third time, and if the color answer the expectation the labor is completed; if it should not prove sufficiently dark, a fourth coating will bring it to the desired shade, but this is seldom required, except for skins intended for the best description of gloves.

This method is called the *Parisian method;* it differs from the one called the *Grenoble method.* In the former the skins are colored three or four times, while in the latter the operation is performed but once. The disadvantage of the *Parisian method* is that the repeated removal of the skin from the table to the scaffolding and back again subjects them to the danger of being soiled;

this, however, can be avoided by careful handling, and the disadvantage is counterbalanced not only by the color being more uniform and true, but by the suppleness which the skin acquires by this operation.

CHAPTER C.

QUICK TANNING.

Tanners and leather dealers are often charged with being opposed to innovations, and slow in adopting or introducing improvements. This, to a certain extent, may be true, but we can hardly believe that tanners, as a class, are more indifferent than others to their own interests. It is undoubtedly true that the various steps in the process of tanning have been, and still are, to a large portion of American tanners, merely mechanical. They do not understand the principles, and know results only as a matter of experience. This want of knowledge has left a large field for fraud and imposition, which has not been unimproved. There is hardly a tanner in the country, who has not, some time or other, paid dearly for some alleged important information, new invention, patent process, etc., which have proved worthless, and smarting under the failure of some impostor's theory, is it any wonder that the tanners became jealous and backward in adopting new processes. We believe, if it be fully proved to the tanners that an invention is an actual improvement, that there is no class of men more willing to receive, use, and pay for, such inventions. They are a class more sinned against than sinning.

Many tanners maintain that there is no advantage whatever in keeping leather in process after the gelatine and tannin have united. There is much diversity of opinion upon the length of time necessary or advantageous, to keep leather in the tanning liquor, but it doubtless depends very much upon the preparation of the hide. Tanners generally do not pay proper attention to the early steps—those of unhairing and raising. Is there any necessity that time be given after the tannin and gelatine have united, for leather to consolidate and grow? Is there any gain in weight, if even made more durable by such delay? What length of time is it necessary to let hides tan which are limed or sweated in the common method? These are questions often asked, and on which the views of practical men are desired.

The fact is, that when the tannin and gelatine are completely united, the process of the formation of leather is exhausted. But in the ordinary manufacture it is never the case that the hide has received all the tannin of which it is capable, and therefore an extension of time is followed by an increase of weight. If all the gelatine of the hide could be exposed at the same moment to the action of the tannin, the process would be instantaneous, and this is what the patented processes profess to facilitate. There is no doubt that improvements in this direction are feasible, and that a considerable time is now actually gained over the old periods of manufacture without any injury to the leather. But no improvement has yet so facilitated the quick production of leather, that a material gain in weight may not be secured by a protracted stay in the vats, while attempts of this kind by the use of deleterious substances have often resulted in rotting the fibre of the hide.

Has there ever been any leather tanned in two, three, or six months, by any patented process, which has claimed to be equal to the English band leather; and what gives the great superiority to this class of leather if not the length of time it is in tan? It is well known that the oak tanners of Pennsylvania and Maryland are about twice as long in tanning leather as the hemlock tanners. May it not be this length of time in tanning which gives the general superiority to oak leather? It is a general complaint that leather tanned by quick processes is wanting in solidity and strength. It is porous, easily filled with water, and wanting in durable qualities. A few years since a tanner in Pennsylvania had several hundred sides of leather in vats tanned the usual time. A part of this leather had been dried out and sent to market, when an event occurred that entirely stopped the working of the yard for six months, and the residue of the leather remained undisturbed in the vats. This was finally sent to market, and on comparison with the stock sent six months earlier, was found to be a much superior article, besides having gained from 6 to 8 per cent. in weight. We do not mention this as an example for imitation, but simply to show that tanners, under the common system, frequently hurry out their leather before they realize the full gain.

We give below a few of the quick tanning processes. We could have given more, but in reality they are all much the same; they vary only in proportions.

S. Dunseith's Process.—The skin, with or without hair, is submitted to a tan liquor composed of one gallon of strong decoction of *Anthemis Cotula*. To this decoction he adds—

Catechu	$\frac{1}{4}$ lb.
Alum	$\frac{1}{8}$ "
Common salt	$\frac{1}{8}$ "

Stir well.

Then the hides are immersed in that solution for a

time more or less long, from three hours to twenty days, stirring and handling frequently. If desired, terra japonica may be used without the anthemis, in the following proportions:—

Terra japonica	12 lbs.
Water	15 gals.

To which are added—

Alum	1¾ lbs.
Salt	1½ "

But the first formula is better.

When the skins are tanned without removing the hair, they are soaked in water until perfectly soft and pliable, and then they are worked on the flesh side. When the skins are prepared in the lime vat instead of the bat vat (hen-dung), for neutralizing the lime the following composition is used, and the skins are soaked in—

Water	30 gals.
Sulphuric acid	1 lb.
Salt	6 lbs.
Wheat bran	1 bushel.

Stir and mix well.

Prepare the skins on the beam in the usual manner, and they will be ready for the tanning liquor.

M. D. Kennedy's Process.—In this process the author uses the divi-divi, catechu, oak. He combines the tannin with the sulphates of soda, magnesia, alumina, carbonate and borate of soda. The liquor of the vats is prepared with—

Tanning material	30 lbs.
Sulphate of soda	8 "
Sulphate of magnesia	4 "
Alum	1 "
Carbonate of soda	2 "
Borate of soda	1 "
Ammonia	1 "

I. L. Wells' Process.—The composition used by the author is the following:—

Soft water	128 gals.
Catechu	100 lbs.
American sumach	150 "

J. Cochran's Process.—The hair is removed from the hides by any of the known processes, after which they are handled from two to four days in the following compound or solution:—

Water	8 gallons.
Terra japonica	8 lbs.
Salt	16 "
Elder extract	8 ounces.
Saltpetre	2 lbs.
Alum	1 lb.
Aloes	1 "
Opium	1 ounce.

This composition is too costly to employ in the usual practice, and we doubt its efficacy.

W. R. Webster's Process.—The hair is removed by the usual process, and the hides are passed through the bate, and then are saturated by passing them in the following solution:—

Water	100 gals.
Hypochloride of lime	3 lbs.

After the perfect saturation, they are passed in a combined solution of tanning material and hypochloride of lime. This bath is thus formed:—

Water	100 gals.
Hypochloride of lime	3 lbs.
Catechu	30 "
Alum	6 "
Salt	3 "

The originality of this process consists in the use of bleaching powder (hypochloride of lime), in combination with the other substances, or with any material used in the process of tanning; but we believe that the use of the bleaching powder is more injurious to the hide than beneficial, and we will not advise tanners to employ such a powerful agent.

Bunting's Process.—The following are the proportions used in this composition:—

Boiling soft water	7 gals.
Dry elder leaves and bark	4 oz.
Terra japonica	15 lbs.
Powdered nutgalls	6 oz.

Stir thoroughly until completely macerated, add then 8 gals. of water, 1 lb. of potatoe starch, and 1 lb. of salt; the whole is stirred when it is ready to receive the skins, after having added 4 ounces of alum, and 14 ounces of whiting. In this process is not explained the utility of starch and whiting, and the materials used are too costly to permit their employment in the practice.

Thompson's Process.—The composition used by this tanner is the following:—

Polygonum bistorta	10 lbs.
Geranium maculatum	2 "
Sulphate of copper	¼ "
Catechu in weak solution	1 bbl.

Instead of catechu, tan bark or hot water can be used.

L. Robinson's Process.—This process consists in the employment in combination with catechu, which has been purified by sulphuric acid, of carbonate, sulphate, or calcined magnesia, and sulphate of potash, for the purpose of tanning hides of every description.

T. G. Eggleston's Process.—This process is similar to the above, and we do not think them worthy of consideration, as being impossible in large tanneries. The author uses terra japonica purified by sulphuric acid, in conjunction with carbonate and sulphate of magnesia, and sulphate of potash. He prepares the tanning liquid called No. 1, with—

  Water . . . . . 112 gals.
  Terra japonica . . . . 15 lbs.

He stirs until dissolved, and adds:—

  Sulphuric acid . . . . . 3 lbs.
  Stir well, leave to cool and decant.

For upper leather, to the above quantity of the liquor he adds ¼ of an ounce of carbonate of magnesia, and $\frac{1}{16}$ of an ounce of sulphate of potash, and as much water to reduce the liquor No. 1 to one-half its strength.

This liquor is good for ten good sized hides. The hides are put in and well stirred during the first two days. He keeps always the liquor No. 1 prepared, so as to increase the strength of the vat. Thirty-five gallons are added every second day, with 1 ounce of sulphate of magnesia. The hides are raised up to put in the fresh liquors. The operation is continued until the skins are tanned.

This method is good for every skin the hair of which has been removed. According to its author, this process is a little quicker than the ordinary one, and the leather is better.

A. Dietz's Process.—The features of this invention consist in swelling the tissues and fibres of the skin previous to and during the process of tanning, by the use of saline liquors, so as to fit the skin to receive most easily and effectually the tanning material, and in using in connection with such saline liquors, tanning liquors of different and increasing strength, whereby the centre and inner parts of the skins are tanned as quickly, or nearly so, as the outer surfaces.

The author makes a weak liquor, at 2° or 3° by the barkometer, from any tanning material; in such liquor he mixes salt or alum, two ounces to the gallon, stirs well the whole; immerses the skins in this liquor and handles them till they are well saturated and the fibre fully swollen. The saline substance may be dissolved in water alone without any tannic material, and the skins saturated with this liquor, and after being completely saturated they are passed in the tanning bath.

The strength of the bath in tannin has to be increased from 2 to 4 every day, and the skins are stirred and handled until they are tanned.

The time required to tan is the following:—

Sheep-skin	2 or 3 days.
Calf "	8 days.
Heavy leather	30 to 40 days.
Sole leather	40 to 50 days.

P. Daniel's Process.—The author prepares a bath of terra japonica at 10°.

The first day for 30 skins he makes a bath with 8 ounces of tartaric acid; he immerses the hides in and handles them four or five times. The second day he takes half a pail of the tannin solution, he dissolves ½ a pound of sal soda and adds to it a quarter of a pound of tartaric acid; stirs well and puts in the vat containing the tannin solution, and repeats the operation as often as requisite.

In the last week he adds ¼ of a pound of bi-chromate of potash, and the leather is finished in the usual manner.

Whatever are the merits of this process, the use of tartaric acid, on account of its high price, renders this method impossible in practice; and in addition we can never recommend the use of bichromate of potash on account of its oxidizing action on organic substances.

D. Needham's Process.—The following bath is prepared:—

Hempseed	1 peck.
Hops	1 ℔.
Sal soda	¼ "
Animal brain	¼ "

The whole is boiled in 8 gallons of water. When ready it *is* diluted with 40 gallons of water.

The hides are soaked in this solution from 6 to 36 hours. Then they are put in a tanning solution consisting of—

Catechu	12 lbs.
Divi-divi	4 "
Alum	4 "
Salt	2 "

The originality of this process consists in the application to the hides of the above solutions, preparatory to treating them with the tanning liquor.

R. Harper's Process.—The author takes—

Wormseed	50 lbs.
Thoroughwort	50 "
Boneset	50 "
Goldenwort	50 "

He makes a liquor by steaming them, and uses this liquor in connection with—

Terra japonica	15 lbs.
Alum	10 "
Saltpetre	1 "

These quantities are for 100 skins. According to its author, the use of the above-mentioned weeds, in combination with the aforesaid drugs, facilitates the process of tanning, and is cheaper than the usual process with bark.

Our opinion is different. This process is more costly,

and the leather must be of inferior quality to that made from bark, and this is easily accounted for, the above weeds containing very little tannin and much extractive matter.

A. Hill's Process.—He takes—

Soda	1 lb.
Gum tragacanth	1 "
Terra japonica	12 lbs.
Alum	4 "
Common salt	3 "
Saltpetre	$\frac{1}{2}$ lb.
Prussiate of potash	$\frac{1}{4}$ "

He dissolves in water, and leaves the hides in for ten days. We hardly believe such a mixture will work, and we do not see the necessity of using alum in connection with the prussiate of potash, which will render the process unhealthy on account of the prussic acid disengaged; and, besides this inconvenience, the materials used are too costly.

J. Nuessley's Process.—He takes—

Pyroligneous acid, from wood-tar, properly obtained by distillation	1 gal.
Water	3 gals.
Hydrochloric acid	4 ozs.
Catechu	$1\frac{3}{8}$ lb.
Alum	$\frac{7}{8}$ "

He mixes the acid with the water and adds the hydrochloric acid to the solution. Stir well.

For 100 gallons of the above, he adds—

Catechu	40 lbs.
Alum	10 "

And when cold put the hide in this bath. In three or four days the skin is tanned; heavy skins require three or four weeks.

M. A. Bell's Process.—The hair is removed and the

skins are prepared in the usual manner. They are immersed in the tanning liquor from two to four days. The tanning liquor is prepared as follows:—

Wood ashes	1 bushel.
Water	50 gals.
Let to settle and draw	40 "

He adds 40 lbs. of terra japonica, and boils until dissolved. He allows to cool, decants, and it is ready for use.

The author claims in this process that, by the combination of lye with tannin, he is enabled to prevent the tanning liquors becoming sour or decomposed, and he is enabled to strengthen them without accumulating more than is necessary, and will tan skins in a shorter time and with less labor than by any other known process.

Blet's Process.—He operates in vats of oak or pine wood, which are kept in a room, the temperature of which is always between 77° and 86°. The hides are put into a vat containing river water; for 1000 lbs. of leather the vat contains 63 gals. of water and 5 lbs. of urea. Raise the hides four times a day; after three days the hides are well peeled, then they are well worked with a stone bottle, and immediately after they are peeled they are thrown into water and put anew in the vat with 5 lbs. of urea; let run on them tan juice strong enough; raise four times a day, adding every day some new tan juice stronger and stronger. Fifteen days after put them into a vat with water, and the juice which has been used to raise them. Six weeks after the hides are tanned.

Baron's Process.—The river work and depilation by lime are the same as in the ordinary process, only that the author passes the hides during three hours in river water containing $\frac{1}{1000}$ of spirit of salt (hydrochloric acid), to destroy the small quantity of lime the skins may contain, and afterwards he washes in river water. This treatment with the acid terminates the perfect swelling of the hides, and they are ready to be tanned.

Before tanning the color of the leather must be fixed so as to be of the usual shade. For that purpose he prepares a juice of oak bark, at 1° of the barkometer; in this juice he dissolves $\frac{1}{100}$ of madder, and passes the hides in this bath for six hours, so as to have the color take evenly. He leaves to rest one hour, and turns them over every hour.

Twenty-four hours after the hides are ready to be tanned in the following manner: In river water dissolve catechu according to the number of hides to tan. The liquor is placed in a receiver, covered with a filter, and provided with a rubber pipe to transfer the juice to the vats.

The first vat contains juice at 1°, with a weak solution of alum; the hides are put in this mixture and are occasionally stirred during the first hours, afterwards they are raised every three hours. Next day they are placed in a vat containing juice at 2°. Raise four times a day, and let them drain two hours; increase the strength from day to day until the hides are well tanned. Complete in the usual manner.

Quick Process.—In this process the vessel has to be airtight, and, at the same time, no metal can be used but copper. When the hides are taken from the wash all the water is expelled by pressure, they are then packed in a barrel, fixed so as to have a rotary motion, and with them the necessary amount of tanning material is mixed, and enough water is added to keep moist the contents of the barrels. The main hole of the barrel is now closed, and the air pumped out as completely as possible; this being done the stop-cock is closed, and a piece of lead pipe is added to the conducting tube. This lead pipe communicates with a tank containing a solution of tanning material of the proper strength. If the stop-cock is now opened the tanning fluid rushes rapidly into the barrel, and when a sufficient quantity has been admitted the stop-cock is closed, and the barrel is now rotated for one hour, or half an hour, according to the quantity of hides contained in it. After two or three hours' rest the rotation is again continued, until the operation is completed. The advantages of this process are to open the pores of the skins, and the tannin is not converted so quickly into gallic acid.

The rotary motion facilitates the absorption of the tannic acid from the bark, and helps its absorption by the hides, which are then tanned in less time than without rotary motion, as shown in the following table:—

	Time required for tanning in vacuo without motion.	Time required for tanning in vacuo with motion.
Calf skins, from	6 to 11 days.	4 to 7 days.
Horse hides	35 to 40 "	14 to 18 "
Lighter hides	30 to 35 "	12 to 16 "
Cow hides (middling)	40 to 45 "	18 to 20 "
" (heavy)	50 to 60 "	22 to 30 "
Ox hides (light)	50 to 60 "	20 to 30 "
" (first quality)	70 to 90 "	35 to 40 "

In this process a large percentage of bark is saved.

Guiot's Process.—The hides are swelled and depilated as usual. A vat containing 50 hides has the following dimensions: 3 feet wide and 4½ feet high. The proportions of material to use are, for 50 hides weighing 500 lbs.:—

Catechu	150 lbs.
Water	50 gals.

Stir well until dissolved, and add 50 gals. of fresh water, and a solution containing 3 lbs. of lime. Mix the whole.

Put the hides in this bath and leave them in for eight weeks. During the first two weeks raise them once a day; the last 6 weeks raise them only once a week. Prepare another bath, and for this purpose take 25 gals. of the above which has been used, 25 gals. of fresh water, and 6 lbs. of white vitriol; mix, put the hides in and leave them 4 days, being careful to stir every day. Raise and put them in 125 gals. of fresh water, leave them in for three days and then they are perfect. Complete them in the usual manner.

CHAPTER CI.

RESIDUES AND PRODUCT OF TANNERIES.

TANNERS call waste or residue, 1. The cuts and other parts of skins which being of any use are employed to make glue. 2. The wadding, horns, hair, spent tan, and old lime.

The glue, or the cuts, is sold according to the quality; those of calf are always considered the best for the fabrication of glue.

Mr. De La Laude has advanced that cuts from skins prepared with tan juice were not fit to prepare glue. It is a mistake, for in Paris where heavy leathers are prepared in this manner, the cuts are sold for this purpose.

The hairs, when they are mixed, are sold in France from $2 40 to $3 00 the hundred weight. Those of calf without any mixture are sold for $3 60 the hundred.

The horns are sold by the hundred, according to their size and length. The old lime can be used for fence walls and even for foundations, or for manure.

The spent bark can be used by gardeners for hot-beds

and hot-houses. In France it is sold for this purpose by the wagonful at the rate of $1 00 to $1 20.

According to Mr. De La Laude, 50 leathers prepared with lime give yearly a product of 66 francs ($13 20), the same quantity of leather prepared with barley 211 francs ($42 20), and at last 50 leathers prepared with infusion of tan produce 254 francs ($50 80).

A hide weighing 100 lbs., after being separated from the horns, hair, blood, grease, etc., gave by tanning 55 lbs. of leather, sold at about 30 cts. per lb. Thus a hide of 100 lbs. cost $7 00, and is sold for $16 50.

The industry of tanning gives a great value to the woods for the use of the bark. The price of the bark extracted from one hectare (2½ acres) of wood is valued at $30 00.

PART III.

CURRYING.

SECTION VIII.

GENERAL WORK OF THE CURRIER.

The derivation of *Currier* is from the Latin *Corrigere*, which means straighten, weaken, etc., or better, from *Coriarus*, workman who works leather, called *Corium* by Latins. The ancients, as with us, understood by currying the art of working or continuing to work tanned skins or leathers to give them suppleness, polish, color, etc., according to the use for which they were destined. If the art of tanning has necessarily preceded the art of currying, it is easy to ascertain that currying has created the arts of the harness-maker, shoemaker, carriage-maker, etc.

Of old, the currier applied himself only to hides of small oxen, cows, calves, goats, and sheep. Horse and mule hides were the lot of the Hungarian tanners, who alumed them, and passed them to tallow to manufacture the *so-called German leather*. Now these hides are curried, and the leathers they produce take the place of goat and sheep-skins for upper leathers and boot legs.

We must observe that, of old, curriers gave the name of cow-hides to small ox-hides, which will not produce strong leather, while now they distinguish the hides by the name of ox, cow, etc. It is a known fact that cow-hides are to be preferred for currying to those of young oxen. Curried leathers have different names, according to their preparation and their use. The principal are *tallowed leather, oiled leather, waxed leather, oiled cow,* etc. The principal operations to which leathers are submitted are the following: *Soaking* or *dipping, treading* or *beating, stretching, oiling, tallowing, dyeing,* and *polishing*. But before working them, the tails, foreheads, teats, and parts of the extremities are cut off, and these remnants are used for uppers, soles, heels, etc.

According to some manufacturers, there are some places where they work heavy leathers with the *pommel*. This process, which can be used only when the leathers are damp, strengthens them and renders them finer. However, this work being very hard, we indicate it without advising its use. In some countries curriers pass strong leathers in tallow and render them water-proof. The only objection to this process is that it is too long and difficult.

CHAPTER CII.

DIPPING.

THE first operation of the currier is that of *dipping* or *softening* leather. For this purpose, after cutting off the tails, foreheads and teats, they are put in a tub in which they stay until they are sufficiently moist to be worked. Of old the curriers used to dip a broom in water and sprinkle the leather until it was completely moistened. When the skin is well moistened, it is placed on the ground in a clean place, or better on a hurdle, and it is beaten with the feet until the water has penetrated all

DIPPING. 489

its parts and it has become supple. That hurdle is represented below.

Fig. 117.

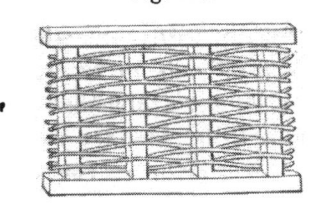

There are two kinds: one, manufactured by basket-makers, is composed of two strong posts about one yard long. In each post make seven or eight holes equally spaced, in which you introduce strong sticks to keep them spaced about a yard. Between these sticks interlace some ashed sticks. The other kind is made by a carpenter. It is formed with 15 strong posts; seven of them are placed below at equal distances, and eight above, notched to a wood and screwed to each other. These posts form eight ranks of parallel lines in one way, crossed at right angles by eight other ranks of parallel lines, leaving between each empty spaces of about 3 inches square. The workman to beat the leather wears large shoes made for this purpose, with three thicknesses of soles. For a quarter of an hour or longer, with the heels the workman tramples upon the leather in every direction.

Fig. 118.

The left foot maintains the leather firm, while the right heel pushes it with great force. For this purpose is also used a *mace* with a handle $11\frac{1}{2}$ feet long, with a mallet $4\frac{7}{10}$ inches long, $5\frac{1}{2}$ inches square, upon the two faces of which, parallel to the lines of the handle, are four egg-shaped pegs of wood, one and a half inches in length, which are finely polished, so as not to tear the moistened leather when beaten with it. Experiment has demonstrated that all the skins destined to be tallowed, not only ought to be beaten by the feet, but also rounded, and these two operations require more care where the skins are hard and difficult to work. Firm skins require to be more humected than others; it is the same for all the dry parts of these same skins. It is a bad process to moisten with a broom; they are much better done when dipped in a tub.

Fig. 119.

The leather, after having been properly softened by these means, is placed upon the *horse* and subjected to the action of the *cleaners*. The *horse* consists of a strong

Fig. 120.

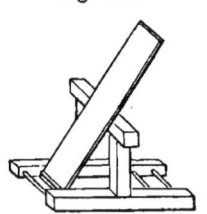

firm flat board, supported upon a frame by two uprights and a cross-piece, so that it can be made to slope at a greater or less angle. If not sufficiently heavy to be immovable, it may be loaded with weights placed upon the frame.

A more convenient beam is that patented by N. Sargent. The upright is filled with adjusting screws, by which it may be elevated or lowered to any desired height, as may suit the comfort and convenience of the workman.

DIPPING.

Fig. 121.

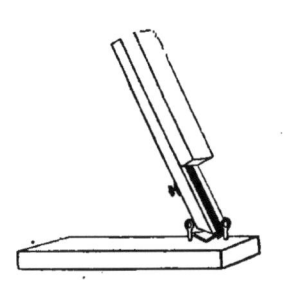

Formerly, and in some places now, three instruments have been and are used for cleaning and paring the leather: the sharp edge cleaner, the blunt cleaner, and the head knife. The latter alone is now used in Paris for this first working. This knife, called in French *couteau à revers*, on account of the form of its edge, which is very much turned over, is from 12 to 14 inches long, and from 4½ to 5½ inches broad, and has two handles, one in the direction of the blade, and the other perpendicular to it, for the purpose of guiding the edge more correctly over the surface of the skin.

Fig. 122.

The round knife (*lunette*) is a circular knife from ten to twelve inches in diameter, with a round 4 or 5 inch hole in the centre, for introducing the hands. It is concave, of the form of a spherical zone; the concave part being that which is applied to the skin, and having an edge a little turned over on the side opposite to the skin, so as to prevent it from entering too far into the leather. Besides these, the sharp-edged and blunt-edged *cleaners* are sometimes used. The latter is usually made of an old knife, and is provided with two handles; the former may be made of an old sword.

Fig. 123.

Curriers are recommended to dispense with these cleaners, to use the head and round knife for shaving and paring the skins upon the horse, and to confine themselves to the employment of the stretching-iron for smoothing and scraping the leather, for filling up its weak parts, removing the creases, and the filamentous particles which project from its surface.

CHAPTER CIII.

SHAVING.

THE second operation of the currier is to shave the skins with the head-knife, above described. When the leather has been smoothed, it is shaved to secure uniformity of thickness and regularity of surface, and that is the reason why every cow-skin which is destined to be tallowed or oiled must be shaved. When weak and thin parts are found in the leather, this operation is dispensed with; they are filled up with the stretching-iron.

The head-knife is the only one used for calf and sheepskins. Parisian curriers shave with the round-knife and head-knife. They use the *French horse* for paring off the borders of the skins, and the *English horse* for the other operations.

Fig. 124.

For the purpose of paring with the round-knife the French horse is used also. However, in nearly all the shops, the table has been substituted for the horse, and it is on the table that the leather is smoothed.

The above represents the workman smoothing the leather.

CHAPTER CIV.

POMMELING.

ALL kinds of leather should be submitted to the action of the *pommel*, so-called because it clothes the hand and performs its functions. This instrument has a rectangular shape, and is of different sizes, but is generally about 13 inches long and 5 broad, and is made of dogwood. The upper surface is flat, and provided with a wide leather strap nailed to the sides, which is intended for confining the hand of the workman. The lower surface is rounded and furrowed over with transverse straight ridges and grooves. These grooves are sharp-edged isosceles triangles in section, and vary in fineness according to the size of the pommel, the largest being from seven-hundredths to one-fifth of an inch deep, and two or three-tenths of an inch wide.

Figs. 125.   126.

A large kind of pommel, called the *marguerite*, is now employed for nearly all the operations in which the ordinary one was formerly used. It is from 15 to 19

494   CURRYING.

Fig. 127. inches long, 5 inches broad, and of a thickness in the middle of from 3½ to 4½ inches, and at the end of from one and nine-tenths to two and two-tenths inches. As it is much heavier and more difficult to manage than the pommel, a peg or handle is placed at one end for the workman to grasp, while his arm is placed under a large strap, and his elbow rests upon a cushion at the other end. The grooves are larger and farther apart than those of pommels, and differ in size with that of the *marguerite*, which may be made for particular purposes, larger or smaller than the one which has been described.

These instruments are those which are the best adapted to the purpose of giving flexibility and a granular appearance to the leather. The skin is first folded with its grain side in contact, then stretched out upon a table, and rubbed strongly with the *pommel*, or *marguerite*, each quarter successively being made to slide under the instrument, over the leather below it, first towards the centre, and then back to its original position. This mode of working leather makes it extremely flexible. To give the proper grain, the skin is then stretched out upon the flesh side, and pommelled from head to tail and crosswise.

CHAPTER CV.

STRETCHING.

THIS operation is performed with the *stretching-iron*, which is a flat piece of thin iron or copper, a fourth of an inch thick at the top, and thinning off at the bottom into a blunt edge, shaped like an arc of a very large circle. It is about 6 inches long and 4 inches high, and

STRETCHING. 495

is provided with a handle ten inches in length and five in height. An iron or steel instrument is generally em-

Fig. 128.   Fig. 129.

ployed, as being less likely to wear out than a copper one; but the latter is preferred by many, since the leather is sometimes blackened and spotted by the iron. One made of steel is less objectionable on this account. Stretchers of other forms and dimensions than the one described above are sometimes used, but they vary very little from each other in construction. Those formerly used were without handles, and had a copper rim to protect the hands of the workman.

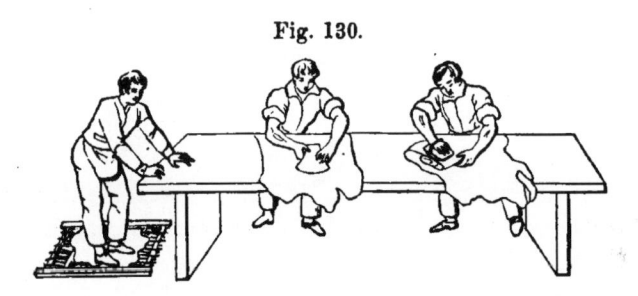

Fig. 130.

The skin being placed upon a table, the workman grasps the stretching iron in both hands (central figure), and holding it nearly perpendicular upon the leather, forcibly scrapes the thick places so as to render them of uniform thickness with the rest, to remove particles of flesh or projecting filaments, and to fill up the thin and weak spots. The leather is rendered smoother, softer, more compact, and equal throughout by this operation, to which all kinds of skins should be subjected; and when thus treated, there is no absolute need of the application to them of oil or tallow.

CHAPTER CVI.

WORKING WITH THE ROUND-KNIFE.

Fig. 131.

THE round-knife, as shown in the figure below, has already been described. The leather is submitted to its action after its edges have been sloped off with the head-knife, an operation which is performed upon the horse by shaving off a layer of two inches in breadth all around the borders of the skin. They are then worked with the round-knife upon the *dresser*, a cylindrical wooden bar fastened at a height of five feet three inches from the ground, by its two ends, to two buttresses projecting from the wall.

Along the upper surface of this bar a thick cord is stretched. Separate the end from the dresser, fold the breadth of the skin over it, the grain being within, turn over the skin and stretch it around the beam, its end being firmly held between the bar and the cord, which is still more tightly pressed down by the leather which envelops it. The figure below represents a skin stretched upon the dresser.

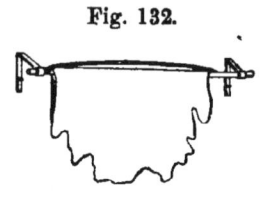

Fig. 132.

After the skin is stretched, the lower part of it is seized and confined in place by a pair of pincers attached to the girdle of the workman, and grasping the round

WORKING WITH THE ROUND KNIFE. 497

knife with both hands, he works the leather with it from above downwards, removing the fleshy, thick, or projecting parts. This paring requires the utmost care, and is generally done from tail to head, and sometimes across the grain.

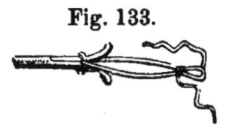

Fig. 133.

The round-knife is occasionally sharpened upon an oiled stone, and the edge is kept turned over by a steel, so as to prevent it from entering too far into the leather.

Fig. 134.

This operation is performed only or chiefly in France for goat-skins, all the other kinds being pared with the head-knife. An ordinary skin can be pared upon the dresser in one hour, and six or eight dozen goat-skins in a day. Before being curried, hides are frequently cut in half, and are still oftener made into an almost square form by cutting off the head and belly parts, leaving the tail still attached to them. These square hides contain all the best and strongest parts of the leather; the head and belly portions being the weakest, and only used by shoemakers for the finest or upper soles.

CHAPTER CVII.

PREPARATION OF STRETCHED LEATHER.

The skins of cows and of young oxen made into crop-leather are the only ones fit for *stretchers*, and when thus prepared do not require the application of oil or tallow.

All curriers do not follow the same method; some preparing the crop-leather, or that which has been tanned in bags, by the Danish plan. They dry the leather, moisten it, flesh on the horse, moisten a second time, scrape with the stretcher, and when thoroughly dry, slick it with the glass polisher so as to smooth the grain. Formerly to stretch a cow-skin the head was removed, as being too thick to be properly smoothed; but it is now usually left on, as it forms a considerable addition to the weight of the leather. The skins are first cut in half from head to tail, the whole skin being too large to be properly worked, and are then deposited in tubs full of water, in which they are allowed to remain for twelve hours.

When thoroughly wet, they are taken out and spread on the table and worked from head to tail with the stretching iron, or, if preferred, they are lightly pared on the horse. These operations being completed, the skins are well pommelled and worked with the *marguerite*, from head to tail and crosswise, and then dried.

When stretched and deprived of the greatest part of their moisture, they are slightly dampened with a wet cloth upon the hair side, and scraped again with the stretching iron. The hair side is well moistened with a wet cloth, then the skins are dried, placed under the press, and after an exposure of three or four hours, they are hung up to dry. When nearly dry, pile them up in a dry and clean place, cover them with loaded planks, and the operation is completed.

Leather prepared in this way does not require oil or tallow, and is not blackened. It is used by saddlers, harness-makers, and shoemakers for the soles of pumps, and the upper soles of heavy shoes.

CHAPTER CVIII.

PREPARATION OF SLEEKED LEATHER.

THIS kind is principally intended for saddlers' and harness makers' use, and is made of strong hides. Ox-hides and thick cow-skins are generally preferred.

After they have come from the tanyard, the hides are cut in two and are deprived of the head parts, soaked in a tub, and trod out, being careful not to allow them to become too thoroughly saturated with water. Then they lightly flesh them with the head knife, pommel and half dry them by exposure to the air. In this state they tread them out, hang them up to dry and tread out a third time; pommel on both sides, and at last hang them up until thoroughly dried. Each skin then has its weight marked with Roman characters.

Before tallowing, the flesh sides are rapidly *flamed*, by being drawn over a blaze of fire from lighted straw, the object of which is to make them more penetrable to grease. The fatty matter to be used is left to the choice of the operator, but mutton suet is the best, and gives a finer lustre to the leather than any other, but is more expensive. In Paris the curriers use suet obtained from kitchen drippings. A hide of an ordinary size requires 6½ lbs. of suet.

Melt and heat the grease to the proper point, stretch the skin upon the table, and spread the tallow over the surface with a tallowing cloth or mop made of the fleecy parts of blanket stuff. This kind of mop is 15 to 19 inches long; the handle is made by binding or tying up from 11 to 13 inches of its length, leaving a tuft long enough to answer the purpose.

Fig. 135.

Apply at first the grease on the flesh side, and then upon the grain, and more of it is rubbed over the groins, edges, and thin parts than over the rest, so as to increase their strength and body. A hide can be tallowed in five minutes. After being greased, fold the skins square, the hair side in, and soak in a tub during eight or ten hours; then tread them out in water, and beat with the mace until deprived of the watery contents. Moisten them again with a wet broom, or soak for a time; beat once

Fig. 136.

more in every direction. Pommel then with the *marguerite* upon the flesh side; the hair side is pommelled from head to tail and crosswise, until the grain is well smoothed, then the skin is placed upon the table with the hair side up, and the surface is smoothed by the use of the stretching-iron.

Blacken the leather now while still upon the table; if the leather has become too dry, moisten it before the

PREPARATION OF SLEEKED LEATHER.

blackening, because a certain degree of humidity is necessary to enable it to receive the color. For this purpose dip a brush of horse hair in the composition and rub thoroughly with it in every direction. After the

Fig. 137.

first blacking, dry the leather to three quarters, by exposing it to the air; pass again the stretching iron over the surface, being careful not to scratch it. You secure uniformity and smoothness of surface by moving the instrument constantly in one direction. To make the leather appear thicker and uniform, pare off the edges with a hooked knife.

For sleeked leather two applications of black are required, and if any part of the surface remains of a red color, a third may be requisite. The second coat is applied in the same manner as the first; the leather is then partially dried, and the surface sleeked, until all the marks of the stretching-iron have disappeared. When the leather is of a fine black color and perfectly dry, expose it to the press for two weeks, which increases its density and firmness, the excess of tallow being pressed out. If moist when placed in the press, it is usually found covered with mould when taken out.

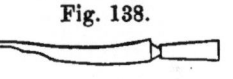

Fig. 138.

In order to give the last dressing, wipe the hair side well so as to remove any portions of remaining grease, or the mould formed on the surface. Polish it with sour beer or barberry juice, and sleek the surface with a very smooth stretching-iron.

If any spots of grease or defects remain on the surface, rub gently those parts with a cloth dipped in the polishing liquid, until perfectly bright. At last hang up the leather to dry in a shady place.

Parisian curriers use for blacking hatter's black, composed of logwood, nutgalls, gum, and sulphate of iron. The last dye is made as follows: Cover with sour beer, in a deep wooden vessel, scraps of old iron, and leave them in contact for three months. It forms a red liquor of acetate of iron, which blackens the leather better and quicker than the solution of sulphate of iron.

Another liquor, less expensive and more quickly made, is thus prepared: Mix sour beer with barley yeast, leave twenty-four hours, and then add it to a solution made by boiling sulphate of iron in vinegar, being careful to remove all the yeast from the surface.

CHAPTER CIX.

COMPARISON OF SLEEK LEATHER WITH ALUM-DRESSED LEATHER.

LATELY the Imperial Board of Military Horse Inspectors at Vienna put the questions to the Austrian Chambers of Commerce, whether, taking into consideration the quality and nature of sleek leather, and the greater cost of articles of horse gear made of this material, more durability was possessed by it than by alum-dressed leather proportionally, and inquiring as to what per cent. sleek leather excelled alum leather on this head. The questions propounded were answered as follows:—

"Although the various articles manufactured out of sleek leather, as a rule, come higher in price by at least 20 per cent. than similar articles made of alum-dressed leather, still the price of the former, in view of their respective qualities, can only be said to be apparently higher, for which reason the use of articles made of sleek leather is to be recommended. Alum-dressed leather is far from possessing the durability of sleek leather, and it is a well-known fact, that if alum-dressed leather is exposed to humidity it grows soft and therefore ductile, by which when the horses draw the traces are stretched out, and the power employed to set the load in motion is weakened.

"On this account, especially for the harness of teams used in transportation and in the artillery service, where a greater amount of strength is necessary, sleek leather must always be preferred to alum-dressed leather.

"And even if, independent of what we have already said, the articles of horse gear from alum-dressed leather do come cheaper, still this economy is only seeming and not real, for the articles made from sleek leather will generally stand almost double the wear of those made from alum-dressed leather, and therefore they are in fact worth more, by at least 20 or 30 per cent.

"It is unnecessary to remark on what account sleek leather possesses a greater durability than alum-dressed leather. The one is a bark-tanned leather, the other a so-called mineral-tanned leather, whose pores are simply filled out with the material in an insoluble form, and when worked upon by water and solvents they easily become cleaned out again. In fact, alum-dressed leather when exposed merely to a damp air, untans itself; that is to say, it returns to its original raw condition. When bark-tanned leather happens to untan, the untanning is a very slow process indeed, because the combination formed between the tanning material and the fibres of the hide is much closer and firmer than in the other case, where merely the pores of the hide are impregnated with the tanning stuff. With regard to the estimate of the difference in cost and the durability of both kinds of leather, we believe a practical calculation will show that no other estimate could be given truthfully."

CHAPTER CX.

TALLOWED OR GRAINED LEATHER.

GRAINED or tallowed cow-skins are those, the grain of which has been brought out, instead of being smoothed down and polished, as the sleeked leather. They are softer and more flexible than the latter, and more waterproof, and are consequently much used by trunk-makers, saddlers, and harness-makers. The largest ones are employed for carriage tops. The finest cow-skins, not cut in half, but entirely dressed, are selected for the preparation of this kind of leather. Tread out the skins with the feet until all irregularities of surface have disappeared, then pare them with the head-knife to secure perfect uniformity. The edge of the knife should be straight and even, so as not to streak or scratch the leather; then dry the skin partially and work it again with the foot while in this state, and tread it out so as to free it from all depressions of surface.

Dry the leather partially, beat it once more, roll it up first upon the flesh, and afterwards upon the hair side, the creases then disappear; if too hard, moisten it by sprinkling water over it. Pommel it with the cork from tail to head.

Dry the leather sufficiently to allow an insensible amount of moisture to remain in it, *flame* on both sides and tallow as already described. Some tanners are in the habit, before this process, of sprinkling water with a brush over both surfaces, so as to increase the pliability of the leather. This practice is improper, as the excess of water prevents the grease from thoroughly penetrating the substance. A cow-skin requires from three to four pounds of tallow, and a thick calf-skin about one pound.

After being tallowed, the skins are rolled and left folded with the hair side within for some days. They are folded square, and placed to soak in a tubful of water for eight or ten hours, and worked in the water until the excess of grease is worked off. The soaking has been sufficient when the surface assumes a uniformly white appearance.

To bring out the grain, the leather is well worked with the *marguerite*, and the hair side is pommelled, then both sides are cleaned with a horse-hair brush, and the creases are taken out from the parts which have been folded, by the use of a smooth stretching-iron, the operation being conducted on a clean table. Then the skins are sprinkled with water, cleaned again, doubled up and hung out to dry, retouched with the stretching-iron, and at last slightly moistened before the application of the black.

Fig. 139.

The blacking composition is prepared and applied as for sleeked leather. Then dry partially the skins, black them a second time, smooth them with the stretching-iron, wipe, fold up with the hair within, and pile them upon each other. Then take them down, blacken a third time, smooth and wipe as before, and then dry them perfectly. Then give them a coat of sour beer, and work the four quarters with the *marguerite*, pommel the hair side across, and rub with a piece of old blanket and apply a second coating of sour beer. When thus smoothed and cleaned, bring out the lustre by the use of the stretching-iron by mopping with the old flannel, and by rubbing the surface lightly with a smooth, compact piece of woollen stuff dipped in the barberry juice. Then pommel the surface at first obliquely, afterwards across the breadth of the skin, and at last from tail to head, so as to round off the grain as much as possible.

To give the last dressing to the leather, treat it again with sour beer, expose anew in the air until dry, and rub once more with a cloth dipped in barberry bush juice.

It takes a man from eleven to twelve days to prepare completely a dozen black skins.

Tallowed hides are used by trunk-makers, harness-makers, and saddlers, and serve for saddle flaps and carriage covers, the largest being used for carriage tops.

Different materials are used to give a lustre to skins of this kind, as sumach, hot ooze and water, sour wine, or weak brandy. Gum Arabic and sugar dissolved in sour beer furnish an admirable liquid. Many other means are employed for the purpose of giving a gloss to the surface, some consisting of sugar and molasses dissolved in beer, others of infusion of cassia in beer and vinegar, etc. All these substances are less expensive than barberry, and quite as efficacious.

Grain Black. How to Improve it.

If this subject was given to a chemist for solution, he would analyze the blacking, and hope by changing its component parts to cause the desired effect. The most that can be said for the best *patent liquid grain* which is now sold is, that it is a great improvement both as to quality and economy over the *home-made black*, made from pyrolignite of iron.

We do not ignore the fact that many curriers of grain leather profess to make a perfect black which will stand on hemlock; but we have never seen such black, and think we should have seen it if produced in this country.

Black, as applied to the coloring of leather, is a relative term. We have recently seen some *tanned grain leather, i. e.*, leather tanned in salt and alum, which came from Japan, which was so much blacker than any black we can make, that ours looks brown in contrast.

Now if the curriers of Japan can thus grain black tanned leather, we certainly should not despair of grain blacking all bark tannages.

While the chemist seeks a remedy in a new analysis of the blacking, a practical tanner must seek a remedy in the preparation of the leather.

Our curriers have little or no difficulty in grain blacking leather tanned in oak bark or sumach. Why is this? The practical answer is, that they hold more acid than hemlock, but whatever the cause, we know that the presence of either of these will unite with or take blacking and retain the color for a long period.

In furtherance of this view of the case, we think it will have been observed by curriers that hemlock leather that has been tanned in old sour liquors, will take grain black much more readily than leather tanned in fresh bark and liquor. Some leathers have an *old sour smell*. These leathers of hemlock when otherwise well prepared, will be found to retain the black much longer than the fresh leather tanned out mostly by handling and by frequent change of liquor. If this is true, then it goes to show that the acid in the hemlock is the same in kind, but not in quantity, as in the oak and sumach.

We must then remove as far as possible the hemlock tanning from the grain, and substitute sumach or oak. How can this be done?

The hemlock skins or sides should be milled either in a wheel or stock, until the liquor with which the leather was tanned is removed from the surface as far as possible, then the grain should be well scoured on a table; after which the leather should be handled for a few days in a warm oak or sumach liquor. If this process is thoroughly carried out, hemlock leather may be made to take a tolerably fair leather.

This is the process in use by most curriers in Newark and New York, who have the proper facilities, but unfortunately too few have such facilities, and hence the miserable attempt to black grain hemlock. We have not noticed the various methods employed to *kill the grease,* nor have we said anything about the various *secrets* for manufacturing the blacking, as we assume the cause to be want of acid, so we would supply this, and that of a quality and kind which is known not to injure the wearing qualities of the leather. This done, and hemlock leather may be blacked on the grain successfully.

But the harness leather manufacturer says, this milling and scouring process removes the weight. This is true. But the old grain must be scoured out, and the milling or wheeling process will greatly facilitate this. Besides the old grain to be removed, there is a large amount of tan liquor and bloom which must be removed; if not, the leather will *spew the oil,* and otherwise make a slovenly finish.

If we can successfully compete with the French in

grain blacking calf, colt, and horse leather, then there is no reason why the prevailing and very desirable fashion of shoes for ladies and children should not be maintained. But if hemlock leather is used as at present, so imperfectly blacked that a few days' wear will change the color to a *foxy brown*, then we may expect to see the fashion change as soon as the price of cloth or morocco shall again come within reasonable bounds.

Why is it that goat morocco does not thus change color? Simply because hemlock tanners have not ventured to lay their hands upon the manufacture. What would be thought of the sanity of a hemlock tanner who should insist upon tanning goat-skins in hemlock, because forsooth he might save a few cents on each skin, as between the cost of hemlock bark and sumach? While the hemlock tanners would not think to venture on grain goat, they do venture and insist upon tanning grain calf, and the result is what we all see.

Now the difference between the cost of oak bark and hemlock in the tanning of calf is so trifling as hardly to be worth mentioning, and yet a very large majority, perhaps eight-tenths, of all the calf-skins taken off in this country are tanned in hemlock bark.

The effect of our system of calf-skin tanning has been to throw the business into French hands of supplying our people with the finer descriptions of skins, both grain and wax. But this should not be, and must not longer continue.

CHAPTER CXI.

WATER LEATHER.

The name of water leather is applied to the larger and finer neat-skins sent directly from the tanner to the currier, who does nothing but pare and expose them to the air before sending them, still in the wet state, to the carriage-maker. The latter does not receive those skins until about to make use of them. He places them upon the carriage, fixes them in position, and without making other changes, blackens and varnishes them.

CHAPTER CXII.

OIL LEATHER.

Two kinds of oil leather are manufactured, one black, intended for harness-makers, the other uncolored, for shoemakers' uses. This leather is exceedingly durable, and the most entire and well-tanned skins are always selected for its preparation. Whether skins are intended to be blackened or not, in either case they are dipped, but after this operation has been gone through, they are kept separate, as the process is different for both kinds.

The kind intended to be blackened on the hair side should alone be beaten. The operation is then finished with the round-knife. At first they are treated like tallowed hides, that is, dipped and then beaten, if the intention be to trim them with the round-knife, and

OIL LEATHER.

they are fleshed if this is not the case. They are then worked with water in a cask with a long pestle. A

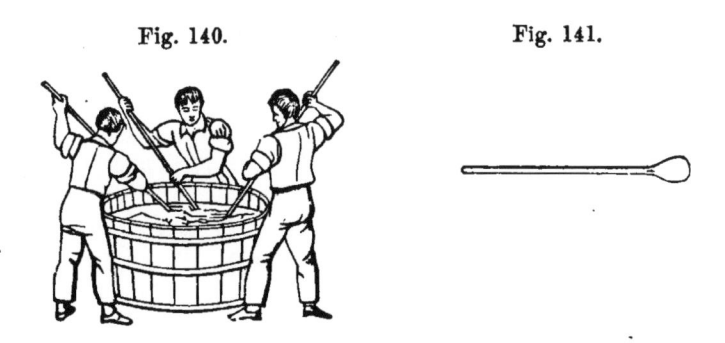

Fig. 140. Fig. 141.

number can be operated at a time, and as the object is to make them pliable and soft, they are often treated in this way seven or eight times, being each time redipped and worked in the same manner.

After the skins have been thus worked, the flesh side is stretched upon marble tables, and the hair side worked with the stone, and to extend them thoroughly the stretching-iron is well laid on, by which process all the water is pressed out. The stone used for the purpose is a piece of good grit stone, set in a handle in the same manner as the stretching-iron. The skins having in this way been freed from the greater portion of their watery contents, are then exposed for the purpose of drying either in the open air or within the building, one hour's exposure usually being sufficient in summer, while in winter many more are required. After being sufficiently dried, they may at once be held in readiness for the application of the oil.

Fish oil is sometimes used for this purpose, but it has been proved by experience that train scouring oil is the best for this purpose. Train scouring oil is a mixture of fish oil and potash which has already served to clean skins converted into chamois leather, and many advantages are obtained by using it. It has more density than fish oil, and is more completely absorbed by the leather. Its saponaceous quality contributes to give softness and tenacity, and less of it is required than of oil. Its qualities should be well ascertained before using it, for if it has not been well boiled, and if it contains water, it will not possess the proper penetrating power.

According to De La Lande, neat's foot oil adds to the qualities of the leather. To obtain it it is only necessary to boil the foot thoroughly in water, draw off the liquor and place it in a kettle with water to the boiling point. Boil this for twenty-four hours; the pure oil rises up to the top; draw it and place it in another kettle at about 125°. Let it remain at this temperature for twenty-four hours; cool off. Three different layers of oil rise to the surface; draw them off separately. The heaviest of these, according to De La Lande, is found to render leather perfectly water-proof.

It is impossible to employ the scouring alone, whatever is its quality; it must invariably be mixed with fish oil. The proportions of the mixture cannot be accurately given, as they depend upon circumstances, the temperature of the air, quality of the leather, dressing intended to be given to it, peculiar mode of operation, etc. etc. In summer a small quantity of oil is added to make the mixture, while in winter a larger quantity is required. Poor and thin hides, which have been left too long a time in the lime pits, require but little oil and a good deal of scouring, because they cannot retain much of the oleaginous matter, and will absorb too quickly that which has the greatest penetrating power. When the skins are exposed to the action of the mixture, they imbibe upon the first application much more than upon the second. The denser the scouring oil the more oil is required, but the quantity of the latter which is often made to amount to one-quarter of the mixture, should never exceed one-half of it.

Experience has shown that for a neat-skin weighing from 15 to 16 lbs., 4 lbs. of oil material are required, and that 10 lbs. are expended upon a dozen calf-skins weighing 28 lbs., thus giving the proportion of about one-quarter of their weight of oil for the former, and one-third for the latter.

Skins intended to be oiled should contain just enough water to enable them to yield a small quantity upon being wrung out. If they be dry or slightly moist, they will absorb the oil too rapidly, while it is essential that their substance be gradually penetrated by it. When they are too wet they take it up slowly in proportion as they lose their water. Therefore before oiling them the operator should carefully ascertain that they are just wet enough for this purpose, and should moisten again those parts which have become too dry. The other extreme should be as carefully guarded against, because when the hides are too wet, too much of the scouring oil is consumed in forming a soapy compound with the water.

After the skins have been oiled on both sides, and the workman has uniformly distributed the oil over the surfaces with the hand or the tallowing cloth, he hangs them up by the hind quarters and allows them to remain in the air long enough to absorb their contents of oil, taking care not to let them be exposed to the extreme heat of the sun, or to a great draught of air, as, if they be dried too rapidly, the oil will not penetrate them gradually. Ten or twelve hours of exposure are sufficient in summer, while in winter it requires two or three days. The bellies of neat hides require less oil than the other parts, while on the contrary those of calf-skin absorb more.

There is no uniform method for oiling skins. In some establishments the oil alone is applied to the hair side, while a mixture of oil and scouring is placed on the flesh side; in others the mixture is applied to both surfaces. Again some curriers make use of no oil whatever, but apply the scouring oil to both sides, taking care only to stuff the flesh side most plentifully with it. These different modes appear to succeed equally well, and we refrain from condemning any of them, but we must observe that care should be taken not to give the hair side too great an amount of scouring, or it will be very difficult to give a gloss to the surface. Skins intended for saddlers require by one-third less of oil stuffing than is needed for shoemaker's leather.

After the skins have become sufficiently dry, they are fulled and recharged with some fish oil and a lesser quantity of scouring oil, again fulled, and at last the hair side is to be thoroughly scoured by a brush dipped in a lye of potash. Immediately after this the skins are blackened, care being taken to keep the borders clean. The blacking has already been described, and is applied in the same manner. After the first blacking, pommel the skins crosswise, apply a second coating of black, and expose them to the air until completely dry. Then beat, pommel, and trim them, pass over with the head of the round-knife, rub with the cork, and terminate the process by lightly rubbing the hair side.

These last operations are differently performed by different curriers. Some, after the first coating of black, do not full the skins, but stretch them with the stretching-iron upon the table. They moisten the hair side, pass over it the solution of potash, and give a second coat of blacking. To smooth and to impart grain they pommel them from tail to head, and across the grain. This last method is preferable.

As harness-makers need for their purposes very strong skins, square oiled hides are prepared especially for them, or skins the head and belly pieces of which have been cut off, by which each skin is reduced to 4½ feet in length, and about three feet in breadth. The following figure represents a square oiled hide or croupon.

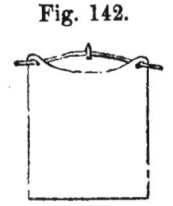

Fig. 142.

Oiled Leather.—We class under this head a kind of leather prepared without tannin or alumina, and having the grain surface of the skin removed. Fish oil is the principal substance employed, and has no chemical action on the tissue. The skins imbibe the oil by mechanical force, which expels the moisture and with it all putrescent matters soluble in cold water. This leather is commonly known by the name of *Chamois*, because it was originally made from the skin of the wild animal of that name. It is also called *Lash* leather. Its use is now almost exclusively limited to domestic purposes, being employed chiefly for washing and polishing furniture.

The preliminary operations are the same as for tanning, and the process can be applied to goat, sheep, lamb, deer, etc., skins, care being taken to choose the finest and most perfect.

The skins are brought to the state of *Pelt* by washing,

liming, fleecing, beaming, and branning, in the same manner as for kid leather; they are subjected to the *frizzing* operation, which is rubbing them with pumice stone, or working them under the round edge of a blunt knife. This operation removes the *grain surface*, equalizes the thickness of the skin, renders it pliable, and exposes a softer surface.

Wring out the skins and transfer them to the trough of a fulling mill, and subject them to the continuous

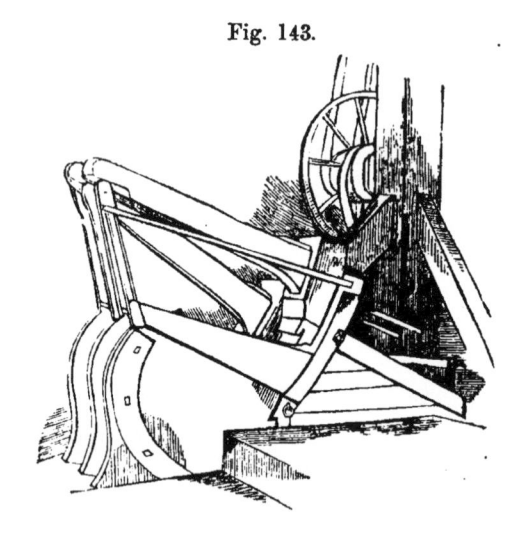

Fig. 143.

action of the wooden hammer until nearly dry, then remove them, spread them upon the table, and sprinkle them over the surface with fish oil. Fold them in bundles of four, and return them to the trough and beat them as before from two to four hours, as may be necessary to produce a perfect impregnation with the oil, after which take them out again, open, expose them to the air for a short time, and then besmear them with grease and full as before. Repeat these manipulations eight or ten times, until the skin becomes thoroughly impregnated with oil. One gross of skins requires from three to five gallons of oil.

After the oil has been well beaten into the pores, and there is no appearance of greasiness, take the skins out and suspend them by hooks, to wooden hangers running across a drying chamber, about six feet high and twelve feet square, heated by steam pipes. This treatment causes a slight fermentation, which dilates the pores, and promotes the intimate incorporation of the oil with the animal fibre.

Remove the excess of oil by immersing and handling the skins for one hour, in slightly heated potash lye at 2° Beaumé, which converts it into a soluble soap. Wring them at the peg, dry, finish at first on the stretcher, and smooth at last with rollers. To give them a buff color, dip them merely in an infusion of oak bark, which in this case is used as a dye.

The fulling mill consists of two stocks, the head covered with copper, being attached to a long beam or handle lying in an inclined position. Near the lower end of each a wheel revolves, by which each hammer is raised and dropped through a space of about a foot into the trough beneath. The upper or handle end of each stock is adjusted so as to work on a pivot or axis, and the stocks being set in action the two descend and rise alternately, and beat the skins uniformly until perfectly dry.

CHAPTER CXIII.

WAXED LEATHER.

WAXED skins are those which have been rubbed over with melted wax, and maintained at a heat sufficiently great to allow it to penetrate the leather. This mode being costly very few are now prepared, principally as saddlers and harness-makers no longer buy them. The name is now, however, applied almost entirely to tallow hides which have originally had great consistency, being very carefully prepared. Some curriers, to give great firmness to certain skins, add to the tallow from one-eighth to one-quarter of wax. Generally smooth, sleek skins, with this property of great firmness, are used and sold by carriage-makers as waxed skins, and are held in great esteem for their beauty and durability.

CHAPTER CXIV.

ENGLISH HIDES.

THESE skins are so called which are made pliable by means of tallow, and retain their reddish or yellowish color. They select for this purpose tanned skins of the best quality, white on the hair side, clean, and free from greenness. They are dipped in the same manner as sleeked leather, and are carefully handled, as the least spot renders them unfit for use. After having been dipped and exposed to the air, they are then worked and pared, and are well pommelled on both sides to efface the wrinkles; they are thoroughly dried before being tallowed.

When done, wet the hair side with a clean cloth dipped in pure water, so as to prevent tallow entering the weak parts. The tallow applied to the flesh side should not be as warm as that used for the tallow hides and sleeked leather, and as the principal object of the process is to make them retain their natural color, only a small quantity should be applied, so that it shall not fully penetrate to the hair side. The skins are soaked half an hour in clean water after they have been tallowed. The process is thus described: "After the skins have been soaked, they should be worked in water, and a light and uniform coating of fish oil, or what is better, linseed oil, is spread over the hair side with a piece of wool or cloth. Then they are dried, and the process is finished as for sleeked leather, except that a stretching tool of copper is used instead of iron, which might spoil the surface. Dry thoroughly the skin, and apply on the hair side a color made of French berries. One-half a drachm of berries dissolved in one quart of beer is sufficient to color six hides. The color is laid on carefully so as to secure an uniform coating, and as briskly as possible, otherwise the skin will be spotted or discolored.

"After the skins are colored, dry them in the open air in the shade, because, if exposed to the heat of the sun it will cause the oily matter to penetrate through to the hair side and discolor its surface. The barberry is not required, but it is sufficient to rub the skin until it becomes dry with a small cloth or piece of linen, by which the surface is rendered sufficiently smooth and polished. Some do not even color skins of this kind, but content themselves with smoothing them.

"Another different method is sometimes followed.

CURRYING.

When the skins meant to be yellowed have been prepared, pommel them to make the inequalities of the surface disappear, and full them in a cask containing

Fig. 144.

clean water. Place them then upon a marble table, with the flesh side uppermost; replace again upon the stone with the hair side up for staining, and drawn out with the stretching-iron. This should be pressed down very firmly, for the purpose of stretching the leather and of making it compact and firm. Then dry them a little, and again and again treat them with the stretcher of copper, care being taken to dry them well after each dressing with a clean woollen cloth. After this apply linseed oil to the hair side; and a composition of equal parts of fish oil, scouring oil, and fine white tallow, melted together and passed through a hair-cloth sieve, is used for the flesh side."

In order that the shoulders and legs should have a uniform color with the body, it is proper to apply a less amount of liquid to them. After this oiling, the skins are dried by hanging them upon a rod with its ends passed through the tail and one of the legs. When dry they are placed anew upon a marble table, the flesh side is stretched out with a warm stretching-iron, for the purpose of cleaning them and making them compact. The hair side is then placed upwards, moistened with a little clear water, treated with the copper stretcher, dried carefully with a clean rag, and passed over with the stretcher once more before the final drying. Sometimes they use a color made with a little Brazil wood, Yellow berries, and glue heated together. This color is passed rapidly and lightly upon the hair side, and the leather is then stretched and exposed to the air until perfectly dry, and is finally *sleeked* with a piece of glass attached to a handle like that of a stretching-iron. Skins thus prepared are higher priced than tallowed leather, and are chiefly used by harness-makers.

CHAPTER CXV.

WHITE LEATHER AND COMMON RUSSET.

White Leather is used principally by shoemakers for the uppers of large shoes, the hair side being placed within. The skins are not worked up whole, but are made into square hides by cutting up the heads and belly pieces, which, being too thin for the purpose for which the leather is employed, are used for the first or upper soles.

Dip the skins well at first and scrape them carefully with the head-knife without being shaved. Then treat both sides with oil and train oil scourings, dry, beat out with the feet, trim on the borders, press and pommel them to efface the creases. Complete the preparation by pommelling with the cork, so as to smooth the flesh and grain the hair side.

This leather is well stuffed, each skin absorbing usually 3¼ lbs. of oil and train scouring oil. Some curriers pommel only these skins on both sides, and dry them. They assert that they are finer than when beaten.

Common Russet is prepared as blackened leather, except it is allowed to absorb grease to saturation, so as to increase its strength and pliability. For this purpose, after the skins have been tallowed and partially dry, they are saturated with train oil scourings on both sides, about 1½ lb. being used for each skin. This leather preserves nearly its original color, and is used principally for pump-valves, mail bags, etc. etc.

CHAPTER CXVI.

CURRYING OF CALF-SKINS.—OILED CALF-SKINS.

CALF-SKINS are sometimes prepared in the same manner as neat's leather, the thickest and largest of them being used for the same purpose as square hides; but the latter being commonly employed in the manufacture of soles, the calf-skin leather being only used for uppers, and being consequently required to possess more pliability and softness, must be treated by processes differing from those to which thick leather is subjected.

Oiled Calf-Skins.—As soon as the skins are taken from the pit, dry them immediately, scrape and tread them out under the feet, and then oil on both sides. In winter you can use warm oil. As for cow-skins use a mixture of equal parts of oil and scouring train oil. If the train oil is very clear, it can be used alone. A dozen of calf-skins weighing from 30 to 36 lbs. generally require from 10 to 12 lbs., though experience alone can guide the workman to judge the amount the skins will absorb without injury. Avoid the use of an excess of fatty matter, as it tends to make the leather too soft and flabby. If the skins have been exposed too long in the lime they do not take up as much oil as those which have not been thus injured. After the oiling, dry the skins and dress and soften them by beating them with the feet, and bring the grain in the usual manner. If the skin is intended to be waxed, or converted into grained or stamped leather, they do not require to be worked with the feet.

In order to cleanse and soften the leather and prepare it to receive the black, dip a brush in a solution of potash, made by dissolving about one pound of potash in a bucketful of water, and pass it over the hair side. If the solution is stronger it injures the leather, but the above is sufficient to saturate the excess of oil and enable the black to adhere more readily to the surface. When this operation is completed, apply at once the liquid blacking as above, being careful to not lay on a large enough quantity to penetrate below the surface of the leather.

Pommel the skins then from head to tail with a medium sized pommel; use four parts of oil and one of scouring train oil to smooth down the long ridges which traverse the leather in different directions.

Apply then a second coat of black, and, if necessary, charge again the leather with the oily mixture, and dry thoroughly in the air. Then tread it out, pommel on both sides, pare down on the borders with the head-knife and scrape with the round-knife. To complete the preparation, pommel with the cork, and rub lightly over the grain with fish oil to deepen the color, which would have been injured by the previous operations.

Sometimes curriers follow another method. After the skins are dried and oiled, they soak them in a tub until sufficiently damp, while they are not thoroughly penetrated through. They are then pommelled lengthwise and blackened. Then they are pommelled crosswise, blackened a second time, charged with the oily mixture, thoroughly dried, worked with the pommel from head to tail, and oiled as before.

CHAPTER CXVII.

TALLOWED CALF-SKINS.

A LARGE proportion of the calf-skins used are oiled, but those which are tallowed are less liable to be penetrated by moisture. To prepare them, sprinkle the dry skins with water, scrape them with a dull knife or the stretching-iron, unless it is desirable to diminish their thickness by paring. Then pare down the head with the head-knife as far as the junction of the neck, flesh the body lightly, being careful to moisten the surface to prevent the knife entering too deeply. Dry the skins and pommel them upon the flesh side with a large pommel, and upon the grain with the cork instead of pumice stone. Tallow in the same manner as cowskins, dry, then work under water, pommel and blacken twice; after this operation pommel again, polish and rub upon the grain side with clear oil. A dozen of calf-skins weighing from 38 to 40 lbs. require from 12 to 15 lbs. of tallow.

Harness-makers and saddlers use these skins for covering horse-collars, and for other purposes. They are also used for manufacturing thick shoes, and to cover trunks, chairs, and tables.

CHAPTER CXVIII.

ENGLISH CALF-SKINS.

To prepare this kind of leather, choose the best kind of skins, and the process of manufacturing is similar to that employed for cow-skins intended for corresponding purposes.

Tallow the skins upon the flesh side, but use only a small quantity of grease, so as not to penetrate the leather. This and the succeeding operations must be very carefully conducted, to avoid injuring or soiling the surface.

The thinner skins are used for thin soles, while the thicker ones are curried white for the uppers of thick shoes. Formerly this white leather was used for heel-vangs. Moisten the skins slightly, pommel them in every direction, and after oiling and thoroughly cleaning, shave them down on the borders, pare from tail to head until soft, then pommel and scrape them with the round-knife, and pass over with the cork. During all these operations avoid scraping or scratching the surfaces, which are more liable to be injured than those of neat's leather. If the skins come from still-born calves, you avoid injuring them by passing them through tan liquor and exposing them for a time in the pits.

CHAPTER CXIX.

WAXED CALF-SKINS.*

Fleshing and Shaving.—In a preceding chapter we have given the best process for tanning calf-skins; we now give a description of the different processes to which the currier submits such tanned skins.

Good dressers of waxed calf-skins have become in our day very rare. For about twenty years past the manufacturers of patent leather have appropriated all the good workmen and have kept them busy, and since more is earned on patent leather than in dressing waxed calf-skins, the currier is almost the only workman left who carries his work mechanically and without principle.

The English taught us to dress the skins which we understood how to tan better than they. We have excelled them and now they are tributary to us, thanks to the improvements which we have made upon their lessons. The Germans do as well with their glazed leather and dressing hides as we do, but in the manufacture of sole leather, waxed calf-skins, boot legs, and saddle leather we are far beyond them.

For the first process use the plate knife, and to sharpen it proceed as follows: For this purpose use the finest sand-stone, which is long and round, and hold the knife turned to the back and inclined about two-thirds; to begin press upon it hard, taking care to turn the sand-stone every two or three minutes in order to keep it even, which is

---

* This process of manufacturing waxed calf-skins is extracted from "La Halle aux cuirs," Paris, 1864, and is the work of M. René, one of the best Parisian curriers.

essential in order to have the edge of the blade remain exactly regular. As soon as you reach an edge, assure yourself of it by holding it up to the light, when you notice a light feather which follows the whole length of the edge. Continue with the sandstone, but do not press hard, the mere weight of the hand and blade being sufficient. Then make two or three strokes upon the other side, and in five minutes the feather vanishes. When the edge upon the sandstone is gained, take the Scotch stone, which is the best of all the stones. It is an eight-cornered stone with a very sharp grain, and with it the edge can be burnished in ten minutes. The action upon this stone shows a new feather almost imperceptible to the eye, but you can feel it very plainly if you let your finger nail glide along the edge. This is removed in the same way as that which first appeared upon the sand-stone, taking care, however, to carry the knife lighter. When the feather has disappeared the edge feels smoother, and then you take the whetstone and proceed as before. In a very little while you obtain a smooth edge, and if, when you run your nail along upon it, you feel its sharpness, and the nail meets no resistance, the edge is ready and can now be turned.

In this operation proceed in the following manner: Cover the edge with tallow, take the plate of steel which must be carefully polished, and let yourself down upon your knees. Take the cross handle between your legs, incline the knife to the right and bring the steel to the edge; give the first stroke to the right, turn the knee slightly and give a second stroke, giving lighter strokes as you proceed, you come to the edge which turns under the pressure. You rest no longer upon the end than upon the middle to obtain a uniform edge, and if when you press the knees together you have raised the knife nearly perpendicular, you stop, for if you went on, you should fall and break out the edge, a fault of which many workmen are guilty.

In order to flesh and shave calf-skins, it is necessary that the edge should remain a little open, and especially that it is not set too strong, for it is better to take off two shavings than one. The workmen who work with their edges set too strong, shave almost all their skins too hard, and when they come to the sides they often press deep into the leather. We have often seen how unmercifully skins were handled in this way, and observed also that workmen of this kind work with too open a grade and penetrate the skin against their will. A middling edge, not too open, is the best.

Use the English beam, the surface of which is always very even lengthwise. Of this one must assure himself by using a very exact straight edge, for the least hollow, the smallest bunch, must be removed. Then look to breadth in the same way, and see whether it is exact. This you ascertain by laying the back of the knife upon it. Move it up and down and observe whether it meets with any obstacle. The currying board must be rounded quite lightly and even at the edges. The thinner a skin is the evener must be the surface of the beam. The upright frame of the beam must be inclined towards the side of the workman at least two inches.

After the instrument is well ground and set, and the board well prepared, proceed to flesh the calf-skin; and that the knife may not suffer by bits of tan, if such should remain sticking in the flesh side, have the skin well brushed upon the flesh and grain. Then take the skin and lay it crosswise upon the beam, a ravel in each hand, the tail piece toward you and the breast part hanging down. Begin upon the right side of the skin, give it a light blow with the sharpening steel to press it down, drive the knife into the flesh at the navel, and go down over it to the end of the breast points. Cleave only the flesh and preserve the membrane upon the skin everywhere. Bring the skin from left to right, and give the second stroke. Go down as far as the arm will reach, in such a way as to cleave the flesh only, without cutting into the skin. When you come to the back lines, and especially to the skin at the back of the neck, take good care to have the knife sharp, for since there is a stronger membrane in the lines of the back than in other parts, you might go in too deep and make a hole like an egg. We often see in the middle of a handsome calf-skin a defect like this, caused by an awkward workman. Go on with the work from left to right. Spread out the skin over the upper corners of the beam with great care, and hold it fast with the knees, so that it cannot move from its place in one direction or another, for the least displacement often damages the skin.

When you have done here, turn the skin from right to left, and begin the work again at the right fore-leg. Move this twice in order to get around the joints, and to sever the nerves of the shank, which, since it is stronger than that of the sides, may make you commit a like fault to that mentioned above. Proceed with all possible caution to flesh the neck lengthwise, taking care to press sharply against the knife, and draw, or rather mow, the flesh off, but rest upon the knife only lightly. When you come to the breast or to the head, press on more in the stroke, but take only the flesh, and take no particular care to leave the skin smooth; this matter is attended to in finishing.

When the calf-skin is well fleshed upon the neck and breast, turn it back to its former position, and treat the tail part in the same style. In this way you finish the skin in three operations. Avoid forcing the strokes on the tail part, and everywhere mow off the flesh, and never double the stroke. By means of a little piece of steel preserve the sharpness and set of the blade.

When the calf-skins are fleshed, hand them over to the grainer, who breaks the vein, stretches the skin out, works them, in a word, gives them the grain. This process is useful, and it can be made up for by nothing else: a calf-skin cannot be curried to perfection if it is not first grained with the grainer's wood.

When the calf-skin is grained, take it again to the beam, and even off the throats and the cheeks. Feel carefully through them first so as not to make useless strokes in the same direction, and these strokes must cross each other in order to even off the head part well. When the head and breast are well evened, the object is accomplished. Fold the skin once and go over quite lightly with the shaving knife. For this purpose the back must be up. The cut goes straight, and do not rest or press upon the beam with the knife. It must be carried down quite naturally, but with a sure hand, taking off the rest of the flesh and bringing with it the bunches of flesh. We do not, however, approve of a style of finishing which takes off a great shaving, for by this the skin loses in weight. On this account have the calf-skin shaved over crosswise, very lightly only, but should it be necessary to manufacture them to sell by the dozen, take off all the thick places, even off the fore-shanks and the joints uniformly, take off one or two membranes from the sides, and also from the tail; in a word, you must use shoulder power, as one must if he will really complete his work. But we repeat that selling by weight has debased the hand of the workman, and he is compelled to go over a calf-skin very lightly to preserve the weight. Hence you shave the skin on both sides, then repeat the stroke on a quarter of the back. Everywhere the veins are shaved through a second time; the shoulder piece retains its strength, the extremities are spared, not the least unevenness nor the smallest cut is perceptible, and the calf-skin is curried as the necessities of the trade require.

Before passing over to the process which is now followed, we shall make a few remarks in reference to currying. In the majority of manufactories calf-skins are now no longer shaved transversely, but only lengthwise, and indeed it is done to save a few cents. In our opinion it is better to spend on a skin a little more and have it completely finished.

We proceed now to the finishing, which is called by the trade the setting out, or the settling to the wind. This process is the most important of all table work, and it is likewise the most neglected, for routine has taken the place of the knowledge of our first teachers.

In finishing, bring the shaved calf-skins together in a tub with weak liquor, if you have any ready, or in clean, pure water. It is well, if there is time, to have them rinsed in this water at least 24 hours; then they are taken out and laid with sides turned in, rolled up or set to the wind in a cask in a circle around it and in the middle. It is better to full quite a quantity of skins together, for thereby we reach a better result than if taken singly. Pour into the cask two or three pails of water of weak liquor, then each workman takes a pounder and begins in time with the next, to pound the skins in the tub. The strokes should never be repeated in the same place. In this way the calf-skins are sufficiently fulled in seven or eight minutes, upon one side. Turn them about, and the work begins again and goes on till they fall down, or are fulled as soft as a rag.

In the great workshops where mechanical power is used, there must be a fulling cask. The calf-skins are brought to it, bent into a muff form, the proper quantity of water or tanning liquor is poured in, and the cask is made to revolve. Thus the skins full and cleanse themselves. By this much hand work is saved, and the work is better, for they are allowed to full the necessary length of time to become perfectly tender; while in fulling by hand, the workmen, to whom the business is not specially pleasant, perform it negligently, which is a great fault, since a bad calf-skin fulled before the setting out is almost like a dry skin which one should put into the pit before it is prepared for the tanning process. Before the table workman can become master of his skin, he must soften it thoroughly again, and it should be half cleansed, that the nerve may be broken. By this the work will be forwarded; but this process is often slighted, especially in piece work, and hence we would advise that it be performed by mechanical means whenever possible. When this work is done, rinse the skins in clear water or in weak ooze. Pure water is preferred.

The tools used in the table work are the scouring-stone, the smoothing-iron or sleeker, and the scouring-brush. These tools being well known, we do not think it necessary to describe their form and appearance. When the tools are put into shape, take a calf-skin from the cask where it has been soaking, and place it upon the marble, the flesh side up, the tail part turned to the right, and the whole hinder portion of the skin upon the marble, and the neck four inches from the edge.

Take the sleeker and go to work on the back strips, make the first stroke in the direction of the tail, beginning at the shoulders, and the second stroke proceeds from the same centre, and is directed straight along the neck between the ears. If by both these strokes the calf-skins are not smoothed down flat along the back, repeat them, and begin them upon the throat almost transversely. Leave the fore shanks and turn to the tail part of the calf-skin. The strokes from the shoulders begin along the back and go on one after another, taking in an inch to an inch and a half in width, and from twenty to twenty-four inches in length, at every stroke, till you come to the navel. The purpose of this operation is to free the neck and other parts from superfluous thickness. First of all, endeavor to even the skin well and to make the thickness as uniform as possible, and to gain this end begin with the fulling of your leather by the first working, which is the stretching of the flesh side.

When the neck part is well evened and the rear part well beaten, stretch the skin as much as you can, since the more you extend it the thinner will the skin become on each side. The fore shanks are stretched and evened by themselves. Then repeat the strokes upon the tail part, pressing hard upon the roots of the tail and upon the rear of the skin, and when you come to the hind shanks trim these by oblique cuts right and left. After this, gather up all the cuttings, take the brush, dip it in water, and wash off clean the flesh side of the skin. Now turn it about in order to use the iron upon the other side, proceeding as before. Then fold the skin square, and rinse it out in clean water.

Take the calf-skin again and spread it out upon the marble just as you did in working the flesh side; take the scouring-stone and stretch the skin, going down from the shoulders along the back to the tail. Then turn around and stretch it in the direction of the neck, always along the back—stretching it with all your force. If the calf-skin possesses too much nerve, do not hesitate to cover the marble with a thin coating of tallow, so that there may be no displacement of the skin at this point. After this is done, begin upon the neck, pressing the stone upon it hard without holding it too fast in the hands. The weight of the fore part of the body is enough, for if you hold the stone too firmly your hands become tired too soon, and as you go to and fro with the strokes let the stone slide along easily over the skin to clear off the grain. When you repeat the stroke, lean upon the tool, but do not press hard upon it, for strength would be wasted to no purpose.

When the neck is well stretched, turn back again in the direction of the rear of the skin, and beginning the strokes at the shoulders, work down, taking about 1¼ inch at every stroke towards the navel. You come to the breast part, which you work by straight strokes from you, taking off the superfluous leather which appears here. The fore shanks you stretch by cuts right and left. Then take the tail part, which you press as hard as you can, for this part, always full of nerve, must be worked down at any cost. Then stretch the belly and carefully work down the hind shanks. When this is done, take the brush and carefully wash the grain side with it, and take the scouring-stone again, letting it play at pleasure over the skin. The drier the operation becomes, the more the grain is compressed. All the veins must vanish, and the lines show themselves upon the epidermis. It is only when you perceive this that you can regard your skin as sufficiently dressed. Then take your brush, wash the grain again, and use the smoothing-iron, the blade of which must be in good order, in order to avoid a change in the grain. Use your sleeker in the way you did your scouring-stone, only seize it firmer in the hands, so that it will not hop, and do not touch it to the grain in the back stroke. We have seen workmen who neglected to press the skin with the stone, and sought to make the veins disappear by stretching the skin by strength of arm alone, and they did; but when their skin came upon the marble, the veins appeared again, and showed their work to be incomplete. The scouring-stone alone can take out the veins, the stretching comes after it, but cannot take its place.

When the calf-skin is well pressed and stretched, turn it around and begin the work on the other side in the same way. Take good care always to have the back strips well stretched, for the least displacement will cause the skin to be stretched crosswise and you should be obliged to full it over again.

After exposure to the wind, come the stiffening and drying. In summer, after calf-skins have been thoroughly exposed to the wind, they may be oiled without being dried, but in winter it is advisable to have them dried, especially the skins of males. In large establishments, there should be a hydraulic press for that purpose, and the operation can be done successfully by that means, but in ordinary establishments, where machinery is lacking, the skins should be exposed to the air until the moisture has completely evaporated. This greatly facilitates the workmen's tasks, the skins tend better, and the action of the stretching-iron is much stronger, and the veins do not rise; besides, the skin will be more compact. Male calf-skins especially require much care, chiefly in the necks, the flanks, and the edge of the rump; to these portions an intelligent workman should devote all his skill.

In stuffing the skins, use in summer a substance composed of white whale oil, tallow, melted by the fire, and, in order to combine these to the fatty bodies, add a third, by mixing with them a little degras of the best quality, in the proportion of one-fifth of degras to four-fifths of other matter.

In winter, in the place of whale oil, use cod-liver oil, and try as far as possible to procure the cod-liver oil entirely pure, free from any admixture of vegetable oil. In general, all animal grease may be used to oil skins. Such is not the case, however, with vegetable oils. Not only do they not impart any body to the material, but they also give it no softness, and they are always apt to escape from the tissue of the skin, either on the flesh side by rising to the surface, or on the grain side by raising to the epidermis, forcing often little blisters which burn the grain or brown it.

When the skin has been well dressed and stretched upon the marble table, after every vein has disappeared, coat the grain side slightly, then fold the skin and leave it two or three days in this position before oiling the flesh side. The grain returns to its original nature under the wholesome influence of this application, which penetrates and spreads slowly through the tissues of the skin, and in three days the entire coating of oil will have penetrated all the pores of the skin, the tallow alone remaining in a paste on the surface, and serving to keep it fresh, when the skin is ready to be exposed to the air or heat to dry it.

If you should have smeared the flesh side with oil immediately after the operation of stuffing the grain, the workman who applied the oil, in pressing the skin to make it stick, would drive out all the oil by the pressure of the stretching-iron, and there would not remain matter enough on the grain side to soften it, or to preserve it from the too strong action of the air or the heat of the drying stove, and thus the object would not be attained, for we aim above all things at securing a soft, pliant, and mellow grain. In order that this end may be entirely secured, the grain must have been thoroughly saturated with tannin during the tanning, and this desirable result could not possibly be attained in calf-skins, when the tanning of the grain has been neglected. After the calf-skins have remained two or three days oiled on the grain side, you make preparations to oil them on the flesh side, and to effect this operation, which is one of the most essential in the preparation of calf-skins, operate in the following manner.

In its composition, use as far as possible only degras of the best quality. Sheep or buffalo is to be preferred; it is more penetrating and it leaves less deposit upon the skin. Both in summer and also in winter, add to it a certain quantity of good tallow, and in mixing it do not melt all the degras. Out of 440 lbs. of degras you melt about 110 lbs. You have it melted in a pot until it almost boils, then pour it gently upon the rest. Next you melt a potful of tallow, which you pour out at the same degree of heat, and you mix it together briskly by means of a stick.

When the mixture is nearly complete, take a stirring-pole and keep on stirring the contents until it is nearly cold, so that the substance may be so intimately mixed that the part of the separate ingredients will not appear. In summer, when it is warm, double the quantity of tallow, but in winter graduate this according to the temperature. Sometimes by drying with a stove it happens that you use as much tallow as in summer, so that the stuffing be made compact and not run after it has been applied.

This being done, take the skin by the two hinder shanks and lay it on the marble table as far as the shoulders. Feel the rumps and the shanks to assure yourself of their strength. Press it slightly upon the marble, without using too great an effort, so as not to displace the leather and in order not to remove the matter applied to the grain side. Take a smearing cork covered with smooth lamb-skin, or rather a soft brush, and dip it into the degras, which stands on a corner of the table within reach. Take up a certain quantity and apply it to the left buttock of the skin, then the same on the right buttock, and spread it uniformly all over. Cross the sweeps so that the coating may be everywhere equal, taking care to go softly over the grain, then pass the brush from one flank to the other and from the edges of the rump to the shoulder. After doing this, apply a fresh coating to the nerves of the hinder shank, to the rump, the centre, and borders of the belly. The skins being thoroughly tanned and having neither lime nor moisture will stand an enormous quantity, and you lay on a coating almost equal in thickness to the leather itself. The males, after their rumps have been well smeared, should have a uniform coating, their buttocks being as thick as the borders, but with the females it is different, the borders of their rumps and their flanks are thinner, and treat them accordingly. The centre of these skins being thicker and more compact than in the male skins, make repeated applications to those parts until at least one-third more is added.

All the parts being now placed on the marble, take the skin on the right side of the fore and hind shanks, and turn it round briskly. Then seize the two breast points and spread the skin out smooth. Take the stretching-iron and press down the neck gently so as not to change its shape, for were you to press it violently, the action of the stretching-iron would displace the skin, and you would have much trouble in readjusting it and making it as straight as it was. And even then you would not succeed so far as to avoid leaving wrinkles about the neck, which is a common defect among workmen in applying oil to calf-skins. Many do not know how to adjust a skin correctly, and nothing is more ugly than a finished calf-skin that has wrinkles on the neck, commencing at the shoulder, when spread out on a table.

To resume, the calf-skin lies down flat without requiring effort to put it so, as it has been already stretched and made even. Apply the degras to the thick part of the neck, then spread it out and equalize it. Next, lay another coating on the neck according to its thickness, and use more in proportion on the nerve of the fore shank, the brisket and the shoulder; but give great care to the sides of the neck, for a calf-skin impregnated with oil about the neck is very ugly.

Nothing more unmistakably indicates an inexperienced oiler than a skin that spreads unevenly and shows oil through the neck and shanks. After this is finished, take a little stick, which pass through the holes that you have taken care to make in the hinder shanks, and leave the skin to dry. You use about 6 lbs. of degras to smear 50 lbs. of calf-skins, when taken out of the pit on the flesh side; and about 1½ lb. to smear the same quantity on the grain side.

The drying of oiled calf-skins requires the greatest care. In winter, when the temperature is low and the air moist, calf-skins cannot be dried in the open air, for the degras would remain on the skin, the flesh side would mould, making spots, and the color would be hideous. Recourse must be had, therefore, to the drying stove, but in this case the heat should be temperate. Too much fire is to be avoided, for with calf-skins freshly oiled, the greasy matter would decompose and run, and as calf-skins are suspended by the rumps, and as this portion receives twice as much degras as the neck which hangs down below, the result would be that in running from the rump downwards, the grease would penetrate the neck to the detriment of the body of the skin, which would not be supplied with enough grease. From 86 to 100° of heat will be sufficient. With such a temperature Paris-slaughtered calf-skins, oiled and fresh from the pits, can be dried in eight days. A drying room should have one or more apertures in order to carry off the moisture that escapes from the skins, and thus the drying is better and more promptly effected.

When the calf-skins are entirely dry stretch them out, and have them piled for twenty-four hours; then bring them again into the air, where you leave them three, four, or five days before piling them up again. The freshness of the atmosphere spreads itself upon the skins, and restores to them that suppleness which cannot be gained when dried in a heated room. Their weight increases; they are easier to bleach, and the flesh becomes easier to cut. At the end of three, four, or five days, pile them up again, folded together, having the flesh side inwards. Stretch out the edges and hams carefully, so that no folds may be made by pressure; then load them with weights as heavily as you can, and leave them thus for eight days at least.

In regard to drying in spring time it regulates itself, and no other precautions are necessary except to change the places of the skins every now and then, and to pile them up as they become dry.

In summer, when the heat is excessive, precautions

must be taken. We have seen some calf-skins dried in twelve hours, but the flesh side was streaked like marble, and the flanks burned by the heat. In bleaching those skins the dust flew up before the scraping-iron. Often the greatest trouble is experienced in restoring them to their proper degree of drying heat. The best method when that happens is to pile the skins up in a cellar or other damp place, and leave them there eight days without changing the pile. At the end of that time bring them up out of the cellar, and pile them in the warehouse, where you leave them as long as you can in oil. Thus, the flesh side becomes equalized, and the coating of tallow, remaining on the flesh, combines intimately with it. When they are handed to the bleacher they cut well, and the difficulty is thus removed, although not without a loss in weight.

The season most propitious for perfect success in oiling is during the months of September and October, the heat being then temperate during the day; the nights are cool; the process of drying goes forward slowly and surely; the material retains its suppleness and weight; it is easily finished, and the quality is perfect.

After the skins have laid the proper length of time, clear them of fat upon the flesh and grain sides. For this purpose use a small stretching iron, not pliant, which you whet upon the sandstone till it is tolerably sharp, but do not bend around its edges for reasons which we will indicate. Lay the calf-skin lengthwise upon the marble table, and press heavily upon the iron, which is half bent towards the body; the strokes are given in the same direction you took before you oiled the skins; smooth out carefully the folds which sometimes appear along the edges. Take good care not to open the flanks, and those parts of the skins which have been worked together, so as not to disfigure the skin. This would be an evil that could hardly be obviated, as all the disfigured parts lie in folds and wrinkles, and can never be made even again. How often have we seen calf-skins cleared of fat by incompetent workmen in such a way that the finisher could never restore them to a good condition. He lost time and lessened the weight of the goods in the effort, but gained nothing. Therefore, watch this process to avoid the above-mentioned bad result, and do not bend up the edge of the instrument used in the operation, so that you can give the stroke according to your liking, and avoid making useless notches in your skins. If you wish to shave the calf-skins, take the folds out of them lightly and gently with a blunt sleeker.

Bleaching or Whitening.

The bleaching of waxed calf-skins is one of the most essential processes in its manufacture. It is the beginning of the end, and the defects of the bleacher will be noticeable by all, even by inferior judges. A streaked calf-skin attracts attention, and an ill-finished flesh side cannot be kept out of sight. Any slight cut should be made to disappear; if not, it will remain as a defect, exposed to the view of the buyer. Therefore, to make a good bleacher, a man needs to be skilful and intelligent at the same time, otherwise, he will be unable to turn out a perfect article.

The manufacture of waxed calf-skins in France became so largely developed in the years subsequent to 1830, that workmen capable of performing the bleaching process with the knife could not be taught fast enough. Another motive, and one equally powerful, the sale of calf-skins by weight, forced the manufacturers to look to it.

The manufacturers of the Loire-Inferieure, the Nantes tanners were the first to meet with these difficulties. Some workmen who did not like over much to whet their tools, and who were required to clean their skins when green, thought fit to set the edges of their stretching-iron bluntly, and, not satisfied with removing the dirt from the skins, they also took off the small morsel of flesh remaining. The better instructed perceived this and sought to draw advantage from this nascent invention. They bought good blades made of steel, which were carefully ground, and the edge curved conversely. With a fine butcher's steel the edge was set, and the workmen began to scrape properly. By degrees the more expert among the workmen got their hands used to this, and the process of bleaching with the stretching-iron became improved. Necessity, the great mother of invention, did not fail the seekers in this respect. Bleachers with the knife gained auxiliaries, and orders were no longer delayed in the filling through the lack of competent workmen. When a stretching-iron is wielded by a skilful and intelligent operator, it may be made to take the place of the knife; better than this, calf-skins are less put out of shape and better prepared by being bleached with a stretching-iron. But how few workmen combine the requisite qualifications, and how many among those who possess them will not give themselves the trouble to do it well?

In order to bleach a calf-skin well with the stretching-iron, it must first be worked lengthwise and then gone over transversely with care, working without interruption, removing the veins and knots of flesh, and especially the cuts, at least those which can be made to disappear. By taking all these precautions, a skin is often turned out that ranks in the first quality, otherwise some have ranked only as second rate.

The cost of the operation of bleaching with the knife, for medium-sized Paris-slaughtered calf-skins, amounts to forty cents per dozen, and of bleaching the same skins with the stretching-iron to thirty-five cents per dozen. It is to be understood that for this price the workman should remove all such defects as can be made to disappear—in fact, he should *put his calf-skins in full dress.*

The skins that are finished up with the shaving-knife, although they are cleared of fat before the process, cannot be grained without being gone over a second time. The reason of this is that the corners of the beam in shaving often make impressions upon the skin which subsequent operations cannot remove, and these marks injure the looks of the skin. After this, we advise the following means: Take a light brass grainer, round off its corners well, and put it first upon the sandstone, then upon the English stone till it is polished almost as bright as a mirror, then take the skins crosswise as in the working in. In order to avoid making wrinkles, remove all irregularities from the board, stretch the necks and flanks straight, take off and even the folds which have appeared in drying. Remove, by a single strong pressure, the veins which withstood the stretching process, or which have appeared since that. This operation makes the grain remarkably pliable and uniform. Then take a pushing-iron, not too pliable, make its edges very smooth, so that it will not be apt to gnaw in or make furrows. Begin now at the neck to clear the skin and to compress it. Take special care to avoid scratches, which give to the grain a marbled look and injure the whole of the currying work. This important operation is too often put into unskilful hands, and is executed very badly. **Many** manufacturers attach little importance to it, but we think it is best to devote to it great attention. First, it imparts to the grain a greater softness, while it also strengthens the fibres of the hide. You prepare the way for giving a grain to the skin, and with a skin prepared in this way beforehand one is sure of a grain of fine appearance. It is very difficult to grain a fine calf-skin alike in all parts if this operation has not been first performed.

In the same way treat calf-skins that have been whitened with the knife for that purpose, and such as have been entirely cleared of fat before whitening. The tallow which remains upon the grain hardens and equalizes itself under this operation of dry finishing. The grain will again become pliable and free, and often calf-skins that have been too quickly dried or rather bathed in the drying-room, or in the air in summer heat, are restored and made very soft. It is this way of working by which one gets that pearly yet tender grain, which to the common eye is a sign of fine work.

Graining.—There are several ways of graining calf-skins. Almost every manufacturer has a peculiar method. Some make a cross grain by taking their skins from the four quarters; this is the English method. Others make a barley grain, and in our opinion this grain is the handsomest, for it breaks the skin less and spares the flanks more. Others start it from the four quarters and end it by running straight from head to tail, which produces a very fine grain, but it can only be done successfully with female skins that have been very compactly tanned, and would not do for male calf-skins.

In order to grain a skin well one requires to be practically acquainted with skins so as to be able to judge at the first glance of the quality of the skin to be grained, for if a calf-skin is firm and compact, it can be dressed with cork without danger, and without fear of bringing too coarse a grain to the surface. But this is not the case with calf-skins that are a little flabby; their grain is tender, and they should be treated carefully or the grain surface will rise so that it will seem to be detached from the fibres.

This is the way to proceed in this operation: Take a grainer not over 6½ inches in breadth, and covered uniformly with cork. The grain should not be too convex, and should form an elliptical arch, and its length may vary from 10 to 11 inches. In the centre have a band of leather at the back, broad and soft so as not to hurt or fatigue the hand. This instrument should be very light and easy of use, as it is almost always worked with one hand, and this hand would soon become fatigued if the instrument were not of this condition as to its lightness and adaptability to the hand. Take the skin by the left shank and roll this shank closely until you come to the navel, so as to fix the direction of the grain that you wish to produce, starting from the left brisket to the right hinder shank. If the skin is firm, pass the cork, holding it by the right hand, under the left, and bear down heavily with both hands, taking care to follow the corners of the cork, which is essential to curve the grain, for if you draw it straight the grain will remain flat. You follow up without interval, taking care to push from left to right only a distance equal to one-quarter of the breadth of the cork in order to produce a uniform grain. When you reach the right flank, do not crush it, but pass lightly over it, pressing only lightly on your cork until you reach the hinder shank, when you press heavily.

The grain being well brought out through the whole length, unroll the skin and continue, passing carefully over the left flank, and pressing heavily upon the rump, for the grain of this part does not develop itself as easily as elsewhere, and often a double amount of work is required there. Still bringing out your skin, you arrive in this manner at the end of the shank, then you turn the skin around to work on the neck. This part you also roll and begin your grain again in the middle where the other commenced; there you proceed in the same manner, going carefully over the weak parts and pressing heavily upon the neck in order to break it down. When you reach the extremity, take the skin straight before you and roll up all the throat and neck with the left hand, thus reaching to the middle of the skin, there hold it rolled up with the left hand, while with the right you curve the grain lengthwise in a uniform manner.

Mode of making the Blacking and its Applications.

The blacking is made in the following manner: Take good light lampblack and let it soak in linseed oil for several hours. If you wish to make a quantity of blacking, put in one-tenth lampblack, which gives a beautiful color and does not dirty the brush. After it is well saturated in a small quantity of oil, crush it to mash the lumps either with the hands or upon a marble slab with a roller prepared for the purpose. When it becomes of the consistency of paste, and after all the lumps have disappeared, pour oil upon it and mix slowly. In winter mix in linseed oil, but in summer put one-half cod-liver oil, as the linseed oil penetrates and spots the skin. To this mixture of lampblack and oil add an ox-gall and five quarts of beer black, or rust black, or bark prepared with logwood, verdigris, gall-nuts, and gum Arabic. This last black is very handsome, and gives a magnificent blue-black basis. After the whole has been well mixed, making a solid paste, next melt of the tallow twice the weight of the lampblack in winter. You only melt it, and do not let it become too much heated, for if boiled it would coagulate and make little lumps when poured out. It is sufficient to simply melt the tallow before pouring it off, and as soon as it is poured it should be vigorously mixed. By this method the blacking will always turn out well. In summer use three times as much tallow as blacking, and we have known manufacturers who added yellow wax with a very good result, especially in small calf-skins, as this often imparts a certain appearance of solidity to the flanks which increases the general effect to the eye.

Let the blacking become thoroughly cold before using it. Take a dozen skins, and place the largest undermost, arranging them on the table so as to black them rapidly and avoid any marks being made by the brush. Lay all the skins with the flesh side uppermost, as a matter of course, and the whole rump part as far as the forepaw, so that in turning the skin around you may only have a small part of the neck still to black. Having done this, take your blacking-brush, which is of the shape of a mushroom upside down. Take it in the right hand and dip it evenly in the blacking, taking care, however, to use only a small quantity. Place it on the rump and rub the flesh briskly, sweeping the brush angularly, so as to apply it thoroughly, and use the left hand at the same time as the right to increase the pressure. The strokes are made from the rump towards the neck, and when you reach that part the brush is almost dry. In order to avoid penetrating that part, which is always weaker than the rump, pass at once carefully to the borders, where you use very little blacking. Take care not to let the brush touch the under sides of the borders, so as not to leave any spots of blacking, for the reason that the skins may be kept clean for the subsequent process and that you may not have to clean them with the stretching-iron.

After the skin has become quite black, rub your brush dry to remove the dirt, and even leave the brush and rub with the hand so as to roll all the small lumps, and, after the blacking has dried thoroughly, take a horse-hair broom and sweep them off at the skin. When this operation is well done, the finger may be applied almost without being blackened by the contact. This is the way to see whether a skin is well blacked. Having finished the rump, turn the skin round, and lay upon the left hand edges of the skin remaining upon the table a piece of leather or pasteboard, so as to prevent the blacking, upon the edges of the other skins, from staining the grain of the skin which you turn, after which you black the neck in the same manner as the rump.

A fault of many blackers is, that they spread the blacking without brushing it in enough. This is more rapid but not as good, for often in sizing the skin for the first time, the brush raises the flesh and the skins turn out gray instead of black; and even when the skins are quite smooth, the flesh remains reddish in color, which becomes apparent when they are sized for the last time, but then it is too late to remedy the evil.

A good blacker is a valuable workman, for when a skin is too pale after having been oiled, he will darken its color; if it should be too much saturated, he will also skilfully avoid adding to this. This operation, therefore, requires an experienced man, one thoroughly acquainted with his task. For medium Paris-slaughtered calf-skins this process costs eighteen or twenty cents per dozen, for an active expert workman cannot get through more than from five to six dozen per day.

Finishing.

Prepare your wax in the following manner: Take some cuttings of glovers' skins (these parings should be kid, we prefer such to all others, for goat-skins will give a much finer glue, and consequently it will be easier to use), and let these parings soak in water during twelve hours, then rinse them well so that no foreign substance may remain with them.

If you wish to make three pounds of gelatine, take one pound of these cuttings and boil them in five quarts of water. Skim off the first boiling carefully, and then let it boil for about three hours over a slow fire. At the end of that time strain it through a cloth, and let the liquid cool down. By this means you obtain a tender gelatine, which breaks easily. It should not be too strong, for it would then break with difficulty, and as you mix it with tallow it would not mix readily, if it was too hard, and it will be difficult to employ. Moreover, if the gelatine were too strong, it would prevent the polishing process, and the calf-skins will be streaked.

The great fault of many finishers is in using a first glue of too strong a consistency.

Therefore take, according as you may need, say two lbs. and one-fifth of the gelatine, which you break up by means of a piece of wood kept for this purpose, and you crush it during ten minutes; then take 1¾ lb. of tallow melted by boiling. Crush this tallow thoroughly, and, in order to make it more pasty, mix with it about 3½ ounces of linseed oil in summer, and 7 ounces in winter; for when the temperature is low tallow hardens, and this quantity of oil is necessary to render it more easy of handling.

When the tallow is well crushed, mix it by degrees

with the gelatine forming one substance of the two; this mixture should be made with much care.

Use in preference to other sorts, good beef tallow, and have it always melted by boiling. It is preferable to mutton tallow, which is too dry, and always more difficult to crush than beef tallow. Never use decomposed size, for it always gives the worst results. The material being well mixed take a soft brush, so that it will not streak. Place a skin on the table, and brush it with a hand-brush lightly, to rid it of any dust or pellets of waxing that may adhere to it still; then with the size brush spread the skin over with the first sizing, using a small quantity for the females, and a larger quantity for the males. With the latter, take especial care to cover the flanks well, and especially the necks of those that are old. Equalize the whole by a last light brushing, and then turn the skin over, and go through a like operation on the other side.

Having done this, hang up the skin to a wooden bar with hooks, by a little hole made in the centre of the throat.

Let each skin hang in summer only during the time that it takes to size four skins, and in winter while you are doing six. Do not let the size dry longer than this, for it would be too difficult to polish. Therefore, unhook the skins as you go on, and pile them up on the trestles.

After the first coating of size has been given to all the skins, prepare to polish them; and, for this purpose turn the pile of skins upside down, so that those first polished may be those that are first sized.

For this operation a very smooth polishing surface is necessary, for that no straps may be made. Polishing may be done upon smooth marble, or upon a table of walnut wood, and many are polished upon a foundation of leather. When the skins are large, and too much charged with oil, it is better to polish them upon marble.

If the skins are medium sized and in the same condition, polish them upon a walnut table; but if you have small skins or skins that are too full, it is better to polish them upon a foundation of leather, and take care to spread a little talc upon this basis from time to time, so that the skin may slide over it easily, and not stick, thus avoiding any crisping in the polishing process.

Polish all the skins transversely and often; when you find skins which do not polish easily, work them lengthwise and crosswise. Always begin at the neck, and make the strokes consecutive, avoiding any crisping or marks that will remain and appear at the last sizing.

If the skins are not oily, you need not fear to darken them, and polish them vigorously; but if, on the contrary, they are brown already, you pass over them as lightly as possible, so as to avoid darkening their color still more.

These two operations require great care and cleanliness. Before turning the skin over to give it the first sizing; take care to wipe the table with a woollen rag to remove the marks of the brush which, after the skin is turned, would soil the flesh side, and oblige you to scrape it clean with the stretching-iron, which would leave ugly traces on the grain side of the skins.

Pursue the same plan in polishing; and in this manner the skins are always scrupulously clean on the flesh side; and in our opinion these are precautions that should not be neglected, for a skin spotted on the flesh side always denotes a careless workman.

After these two operations are finished, you prepare to give your skins their last sizing. This size is made up in the following manner: First melt your gelatine, then add a quart of water to reduce its strength, and let it cool off. Next crush it with the size-beater, and mix in a little black soap, and 3½ ounces of tallow to each pound of gelatine. Then add about a quart of size in paste with the addition of a little linseed oil to render it more easy to dry, and mix the whole mass together with great care. Thanks to this composition, you produce a fine lustreless size, which is the most agreeable to the eye and the most advantageous, for it conceals all small defects.

But if you wish to obtain a finer and cleaner size, you set about it in this manner: Dissolve in water some white or black soap (white soap is preferable), and let it boil thoroughly, so that the soap may be perfectly dissolved, then put in your pound of gelatine, which dissolves at once, and while the whole is boiling gently, stir about 7 ounces of size paste into a quart of water in a separate vessel. When this has mixed well pour it into the first vessel and let the whole boil together thoroughly. Skim it carefully, and at the end of ten minutes take the size off the fire, strain it through a cloth and leave it to cool, taking care to stir it from time to time until it acquires the desired consistency. After it is quite cool crush it, and, without adding anything further, you are ready to give the skins their last sizing. This size is very fine but rather light.

Lustreless size is properly appreciated both in France and this country. The English do not like calf-skins sized according to the French process, and they bring their calf-skins white and all ready to be waxed. In waxing and sizing them according to their method, they generally wax them with very light wax, and size them with a size much more solid than the above, but their size has this defect, that it turns gray with age. In putting on the last size make use of a very fine sponge; dip it in water, and then squeeze it strongly so that the least possible mixture may remain in it. Take the skin and spread it out on the table with the rump towards you, then seize the sponge and take a quantity of size in proportion to the dimension of the skin. Dip the sponge as deep as possible into the size and draw it briskly towards the rump, then work it right and left to spread the size, and smooth the whole, commencing at the edges of the rump and the hinder paws. Follow your sweeps quickly, advancing towards the neck, pulling the skin by the tail with the left hand; as the right hand advances, the left descends, and thus you reach the neck transversely, of course. By this method you rarely spill any of the size. The first dip fills the sponge, and this suffices for the whole skin. Then hook it up to the bar and leave it to dry for at least twelve hours. This operation should take place in a room where neither steam nor dampness can penetrate, for either of these influences would tarnish the size, and in certain cases where the skins are put together by dozens, they would stick the one to the other, and, the goods would at the same time lose in appearance and value.

These precautions are especially necessary when the skins are destined to be exported to a long distance; for a case of calf-skins that comes to hand glued together is greatly depreciated. For this reason, in goods manufactured for exportation, too much care cannot be taken to allow the size to dry thoroughly. Twenty-four hours are often necessary, especially in winter and in foggy weather, when the air is overcharged with moisture. At such times the rooms in which the skins are placed to dry should be heated from 60° to 70° and carefully ventilated, so that no steam may remain to condense and adhere to the size, which would scarcely be noticeable upon taking she skins down, but which after causes a reaction at the end of a few days, especially when the skins are piled or packed up, and then it is too late to remedy it. The calf-skins arrive, having lost their fine appearance, for the want of due care in the last operation.

It is better to let the calf-skins rest in the wax a while for the following reasons: Although the skin be well rubbed and dry under the brush, yet the fatty particles of which the wax is composed quickly penetrate it; but if it has been dressed too thin in finishing, the impression is momentary and gives the grain a marbled appearance. We must let it take its time in quiet, in summer eight days, and in winter from ten to twelve days are sufficient. After this pile them up in dozens, and take care to cover them up properly to protect them from the dust.

A workman who makes waxing his business, always prefers calf-skins whitened with the shaving-knife; the flesh side gone over more lightly, is brushed better, the penetration of the dressing is more perfect and speedy; it is easy to clean, which is not so with skins finished up with the instrument for the purpose. With this the flesh side is left open; the wax penetrates them with difficulty, and it often happens that the workman, in order to get along faster, makes his wax thinner, and runs the risk of not penetrating them sufficiently. Calf-skins which have been whitened with the shaving-knife gain more in weight in waxing than those whitened with the knife for the purpose; but it must not be forgotten, in comparing the two, that the former lose in shaving as much as they gain in waxing, so that after waxing the difference between the two has disappeared.

We give the preference to calf-skins whitened with

the shaving-knife, and the English, who are celebrated for the fineness and finish of the flesh side, never use anything else. The American curriers, who have derived their principles from the English, likewise give their preference to calf-skins whitened with the shaving knife.

CHAPTER CXX.

GRAINED CALF-SKINS.

The first operation consists in moistening the skins selected for this manufacture. This done, pare down the heads in order to equalize the thickness; place them on the table, and scrape them with the stretching-iron.

Next, beat them with the pestle in a tub of water, smooth them on both sides upon the marble, in order to reduce the natural grain of the leather; then dry partially. Apply the blacking on the hair sides; smooth the skins again, and oil them on both sides. Dry them, and deprive them of the excess of oil by means of a lye of potash. Smooth them upon the grain with the stretching-iron.

In order to furrow the surface with the grain, place the leather upon the table, with the hair side up, and pommel first crosswise, then from tail to head, being careful that the lines which correspond in direction shall be perfectly parallel. Use for this purpose a pommel with 45 to 50 teeth to the inch.

Apply another coating of black, and when absorbed brush over the surface oil and scouring train oil, in sufficient quantity for the requirement of the leather; then dry it. Pommel the hair side in the same manner as before. Pare the borders upon the horse with the round knife, and at last spread over it a light coating of pure and clear oil.

CHAPTER CXXI.

CALF-SKIN LEATHER FOR BELTS.

CUT off the heads and extremities of the skins, soak them in a tub until sufficiently wet, shave them upon the horse with the head-knife until equally thick. Beat them in a trough with the pestle, dry them, and grease them slightly upon the flesh side with a mixture of equal parts of tallow and oil, and on the hair side with linseed oil alone. Then dry them and work them upon the flesh side with the stretching knife, and sleek upon the grain with the glass. Sometimes a grain is given as above described.

CHAPTER CXXII.

GREASING TANNED HIDES.

MR. GEORGE HUTTELMAIER, of Alleghany, Pennsylvania, has invented a new and useful improvement in the process of greasing tanned hides, and patented it in September, 1863.

In the process of greasing tanned leather, it is required

that the tallow should penetrate it thoroughly, and, in order to effect this, he finds it very desirable to expose the leather to a moist heat, sufficient to open the pores of the skin and to keep the tallow melted during the whole process, and at the same time to apply friction to the leather so as to rub the grease well in. Where this operation is carried on by hand, as is usual, it is obviously impossible to secure all these conditions as the heat required is too great, and even if the tallow be melted and sufficiently heated when first applied, it soon becomes cool when exposed to the external air.

His invention, then, consists in applying the tallow to the tanned hides in a suitable closed vessel, which is previously heated by steam, and which will retain sufficient heat during the continuation of the process and simultaneously applying to the leather a constant friction to rub in the melted grease. To effect this, he uses the following apparatus:—

Fig. 145 is an end view or elevation of the apparatus.

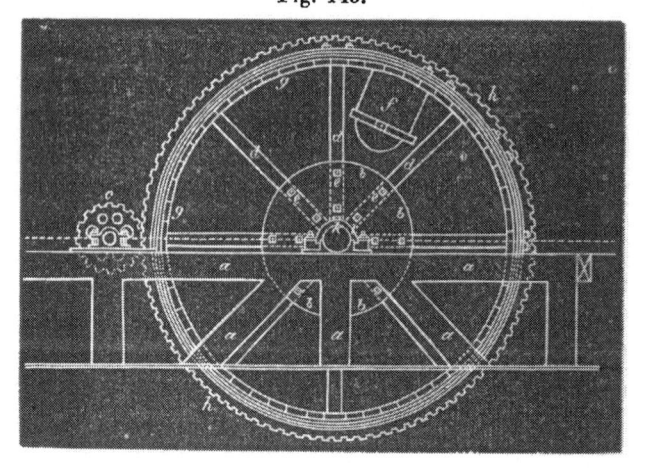

Fig. 145.

GREASING TANNED HIDES. 559

Fig. 146. is a side view.

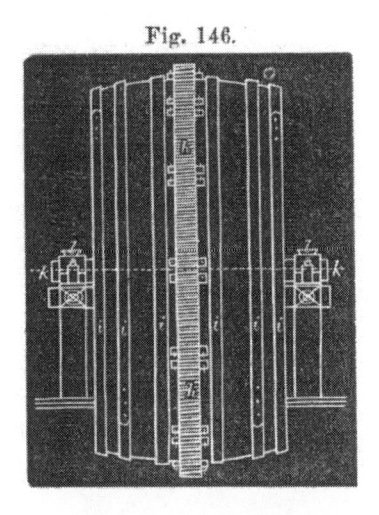

Fig. 146.

Fig. 147 is a section through the centre of the apparatus, in the plane of its axis, showing the construction of the interior.

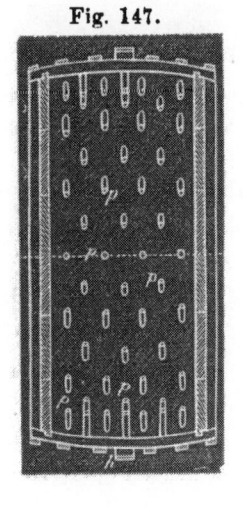

Fig. 147.

Fig. 148 is a transverse section of one-half of the apparatus at right angles to its axis.

Fig. 148.

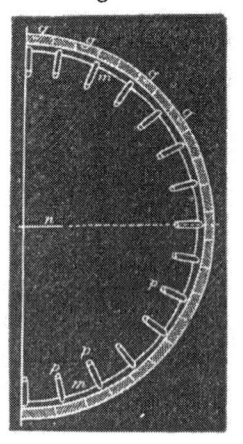

In the several figures, like letters of reference designate similar parts.

The apparatus consists of a large cylindrical wooden vessel, which should not be less than ten feet in diameter and of any convenient length, although its dimensions may be varied to suit any desired capacity. This vessel may be conveniently made like a barrel, the circumference being constructed of wooden staves, g, g, about 1¼ inch in thickness; these staves are bound together by strong iron bands or hoops i, i, surrounding the vessel at suitable distances apart; the hands or end pieces, u, of the vessel are also made of wood, and are supported by a circular iron plate b, b, in the centre of each end piece, to which are fastened arms d, d, which radiate from the centre of plate b, b; the arms are fastened to the central arm plates by screws e, e, and the end pieces are likewise bolted or otherwise fastened to the arms d, d; in one of the end pieces is a door f, through which the tallow and leather are inserted in the cylinder; from the centre of each of the circular iron plates b, projects a journal k, on which the cylinder revolves in suitable bearings l, which are supported by the framework a, a, sustaining the entire cylinder.

Around the outside of the cylinder at any convenient point is a band or hoop h, furnished with cog-teeth, which gear into a pinion g, to which motion is communicated from the steam engine or other primary motion.

Inside the cylinder, the staves comprising its periphery are studded with a number of pins p, p, projecting therefrom and pointing towards the centre of the cylinder. These pins should be about two inches in length, and may be fastened to circular ribs m, attached to the staves g, g.

The apparatus thus described may be varied in size, shape, or construction, so that the designed effect is produced.

Before inserting the tallow and the tanned hides into the cylinder, it is previously heated by injecting steam for a sufficient length of time, to make the staves and ends of the cylinder so hot as to be perceptibly felt from the outside, and so as to secure a temperature in the cylinder, after the steam is allowed to escape, of about 180°.

The injection of steam is then discontinued, and any condensed water allowed to escape at the door f, or other aperture for that purpose.

The tallow, previously melted by gentle heat, is then poured into the heated cylinder, and the tanned hides, in a half dry state, are inserted and the door securely closed.

The proper quantity of tallow will vary according to the quality and kind of leather to be greased, but one hundred pounds of calf-skins will require about 10 lbs. of tallow. The revolution of the cylinder is then commenced, and continued for two or three hours more or less, according to the quality and quantity of the leather inserted therein, care being taken not to fill the cylinder so full of hides as to interfere with a constant and violent motion of the leather, which, being carried round by the pins *p, p,* should be able to fall from the top of the cylinder on to the points of the pins at the bottom.

By the moist heat contained in the cylinder, the pores of the leather are kept open, and the tallow is kept so hot as to enter it readily, while the continued rubbing of the hides on the pins causes their complete saturation with grease.

Thus by means of the combined high heat and constant friction, a result is attained far superior to that which is accomplished by any degree of heat and rubbing which is attainable when the hides are greased by hand, or in vessels not so heated.

This process produces a very durable solid and yet pliable and elastic leather, superior in these respects to that made in the ordinary way. Care should be taken that the hides are of a uniform degree of moisture, commonly called half dry, before they are inserted into the cylinder; if too dry in spots, they should be wetted in those places before they are put in, otherwise the greasing will not be uniform. The leather greased by this process is finished in the usual manner.

CHAPTER CXXIII.

Saturation of Leather with Grease.

In the saturation of leather with grease, a very faulty system is in some cases followed, from its being believed that leather must be dry in order to absorb the grease, and become thereby more enduring and flexible. Precisely the contrary of this is the fact. However incomprehensible it may appear at first glance, moist leather combines easier with oil or grease than dry. This seeming paradox is, however, easily explained; dry leather is drawn closely together, its pores are closed; and, therefore, it absorbs fatty bodies only slowly; moist leather, on the contrary, is expanded and flexible, and its pores are open. If it is smeared over with oil or liquid grease, this penetrates the pores easily, entering even into the smallest as soon as the water disappears, and its evaporation is facilitated by the opening of the pores which have absorbed the oil. It is easy to convince one's self of this effect of oil upon moist leather.

Take a small piece of wet leather, or a wet boot, place it in a warm place where it can dry slowly, and it will become quite hard and brittle; but if you smear it with oil and grease, it will retain its pliability, and after being thoroughly dried, it will not have been in the least impaired. Moist leather smeared with grease may, therefore, be dried by heat without detriment. If dry leather be saturated with warm grease, the durability of the leather will be much impaired, because the heat contracts the fibres, and the oil easily acquires such a heat. The saturation of boot soles, as well as the rubbing in of sand or fine iron filings, is only practicable when the shoemaker turns the inner or flesh side of the leather outward. This possesses also another advantage. The flesh side has wider pores, and is less firm than the outer side. If the latter—the outer side—is made the outside of the sole, it will speedily give out, as soon as the hard external surface is worn away, for the soft inner side can offer no further resistance; and, moreover, it does not absorb the grease owing to the smallness and rigidity of the external pores. If, on the contrary, the soft side is turned outward, then the side takes in a considerable quantity of wax, grease, and oil, and it will be more pliable and enduring; and even after this originally soft, but now enduring portion has been worn out, there still remains the hard part, the outward hide side being a guard sole, which can be worn to almost the thinness of paper without giving out. The most enduring soles of this description are made from the neck of the hide, having the fleshy side outward, and properly impregnated with wax and grease. The only fault that they have is this, that in walking upon grass, on account of their smoothness, you are apt to slip; but soles saturated with grease are not only softer to the feet, but cooler, which is a great advantage in summer.

CHAPTER CXXIV.

CALF-SKINS CALLED ALUMED SKINS.

These skins are chiefly employed by bookbinders. The process of making them has been described at length by De La Lande, from whose work we extract the following:—

For the manufacture of this leather select dry skins of stillborn calves or others of low price; reject those injured by weevils or worms. When you open them, beat them strongly with a stick, and deposit them in a place not too warm or too damp. Work at a time thirteen dozen of dry skins. Deposit them in an oval pit, dug out in the ground; this pit is from eleven to thirteen feet long, by three and a half to four and one-third feet wide, and six and a half feet deep. Pass the water into this pit by an oval aperture, one and a half feet in height and narrow enough to prevent the skins escaping from it, and draw away by another similar opening.

Leave the skins in the pit for two or three days in summer and six or eight in winter. Take them out, stack them, and next day scrape them upon the horse with a blunt knife. Deposit them again in the vat, leave them two days, scrape them as before, and if they are not sufficiently soft, expose them a third time in the pit for one day and scrape them. Place them in the lime pit, which is a hole about five feet deep, with a proportionate breadth and length. Into this pit throw from forty to fifty buckets of water and a cask full of lime, which is left to slack for twelve or fifteen hours. Stir the contents of the pit with a long pole, deposit in it the skins singly, and dip them with a stick. Leave in the lime pit for a day, take out, spread, and stack them; pass them subsequently, in the same way, through new lime pits, gradually increasing the strength until the hair is ready to be removed. Wash them well in running water, depilate and deposit them again in a vat similar to the first described; let them soak one night, being kept in position by a long heavy pole placed longitudinally above them. This done, the skins are well fleshed upon the horse with a sharp knife until the flesh side can scarcely be distinguished from the grain. Thin down the necks until they become of equal thickness with the other parts of the skin. Cut off the ears, tails, and other extremities, and use them to make glue. Return the skins to the first pit, leave them over night in water, and work the hair side on the horse to expel the lime. After this, empty three or four bucketsful of dogs' or chickens' dung into a large vat and mix it thoroughly with a bucketful of water by stamping upon the mixture with the feet. Throw cold water in the vat until half full, and mix in some hot water. Throw the skins in, and stir for a few minutes with sticks, draw the liquor into a boiler and heat it, and the skins, after having been left for one hour are arranged in a corner of the vat, and kept in place by two sticks crossed over each other. Pour the hot liquor in the empty part of the vat, a bucketful at a time, stirring all the time; mix with the cold liquor so as to avoid injuring the skins by scalding. When the water is sufficiently hot, remove the sticks, and stir the skins around in the vat three or four times. Return the liquor to the boiler, and repeat the same operation, being careful not to add the hot water too rapidly to the contents of the vat and to try its temperature frequently with the hand. Leave the skins in for half an hour.

Collect the skins in a corner of the vat, and examine them; stretch them in every direction, and when perfectly pliable and soft they are ready to be taken out. At first, remove one or two dozen of those most advanced in preparation, deposit them in buckets; then empty the vat of water as before, and turn the skins three or four times. A quarter of an hour after fill the boiler again, collect the skins together; take out more of them, and so on until they are all removed.

This part of the operation must be done very carefully, for if the skins are allowed to remain in the hot mixture after reaching the proper point, they are rapidly softened and destroyed. A repetition of the process described, continued for six or seven hours, is sometimes necessary for imparting the requisite qualities to the stronger skins. Experience alone can guide to determine the proper time for removing them from the vat. When this is done take out the skins from the vat; stretch them and scrape them upon the beam, in order to soften, distend, and clean them; and if any are found too firm, they are replaced in the vat while the rest are washed. Then, allow the contents of the vat to escape through the bung-hole. Wash it well, and fill it half with clear river water while you throw in a basketful of fresh tan. Wash the skins and stir them in this water with sticks, and leave in the vat till next day. Take them out; drain upon planks, and transfer them to the care of the sempstress. She then examines every skin, and closes any holes which may exist in them. The skins, excepting the tail part, are then sewed with the flesh side outwards into the form of a bottle. For this purpose she uses a large needle, flat at the point, and with a double thick thread, stitches one part of the skin at a distance of one-fifth of an inch from the edge, and the other that of half an inch, turning over the latter upon the former in a hem, but not pressing it down tightly enough to prevent water from draining through, or to cause the production of dark spots and lines after tanning. A workman places in each bag a quantity of tan proportioned to its size; after which the sempstress sews up the tail part, closed by the hind legs, so as just to permit the introduction of a copper socket for a wooden funnel. The bags are then brought near to a vat in which the tanning has just been completed. The sacks in this vat are removed to a rack in order to be unripped. The vat is left half full of the old liquor, and there is poured into it a quantity of hot fresh liquor, sufficient to make the contents lukewarm.

This fresh liquor is prepared by pouring the contents of the already tanned sacks into a vat provided with an upright door or partition at one end, through which the liquor which has drained from the tan passes, and collecting in the empty space is transferred to a boiler. The workman then takes a bag of skins, and empties into it, through the funnel, a small bucketful of water, and closes the mouth by tying it up with a small strip or thong which had been previously cut from the skin for the purpose, and left hanging from the tail; the bags having each been filled with the same quantity of water and then placed in the vat, and left for an hour, while another portion of liquor, prepared by percolating through tan, is being heated in the boiler. The workman then places the bags upon a rack at one end of the vat into which the heated water has been poured, fills them again through the funnel from his little bucket, tying them as before, by which they are made to assume a pyramidal shape in the vats. Repeat this operation a third time at the expiration of one hour, increasing the heat of the liquor as before. The liquor should be less heated for those skins which have been a long time in the lime-pits than for those which have been a shorter time, but the skill exhibited in making this distinction can only be acquired by long experience. Next day perform a similar operation in a third vat, while the bags deposited the day before are left to soak in the vat. The third day take out the skins of the first vat, and leave to drain upon a rack placed over the vat. Throw them upon the rack in the vat, upon which they are unripped and emptied of their tan. Fold them with the flesh side within, and wash them in running water; place them upon a trestle to drain; open them at the hindquarters, and hang up in a shed, with the heads down, on nails placed some distance apart.

When dry, pile them up, and leave them until ready to be sent to market. Then moisten them, in summer, by exposure to the dew of night air; tread them out in order to render them supple and to efface the marks of the sewing; assort them, according to size, into packs of six each, which are tied together by the heads with pack thread.

Hog-skins used by bookbinders for Bibles and church books, are prepared in the same manner as calf-skins, but they differ from them in being exceedingly thick and strong.

Tanned sheep-skins, used by bookbinders, are not alumed as calf-skins, but are only limed and tanned. Some of these are sewed up and tanned similarly to the calf-skins, while others are tanned by stratifying them with bark.

CHAPTER CXXV.

F. JAHKEL'S PROCESS FOR MANUFACTURING LEATHER FOR HARNESS-MAKERS.

The fine brown leather made in England for saddlers' uses is very highly esteemed, and, notwithstanding its high price, is much sought after, being superior to any other in suppleness, density, and color.

Its excellence is not attributable to any novelty in the process employed in its manufacture, or to the use of complicated machinery, but solely to the care with which the materials are selected, and to the skilful and accurate manipulation of the workman. The finest skins used for this leather come from cattle raised in Wiltshire and Somersetshire, the climate of which counties seems to be the best adapted to secure the development of tissue in these animals, and particularly of the firm, elastic, and resisting integuments, which are so necessary for the production of grain leather.

Skins of cows or of young bulls are preferred. They are usually tanned in the neighborhood of Bristol, and sent to London, where the best are selected by the manufacturers.

The processes of tanning are similar to those elsewhere employed, and comprehend, besides liming and depilating, the use of *grainiers* of chickens' or pigeons' dung, dipping immersion in tan baths of different strengths, and two separate tannings in pits with fresh barks of the finest quality. The currying which this leather undergoes serves to remove its original dryness, stiffness, and depth of color, and to render it supple, elastic, and impervious to moisture, without diminishing the solidity and density of structure given to it by the tanning.

At first, cut the leather in half along the length of the skin, and repeatedly soak it; beat it, and wash it in cold water to dissolve and remove the gallic acid and extractive matter, which, if allowed to remain, might by oxidation deepen the color, and interfere with the proper absorption of the substances which are afterwards applied. After all foreign bodies have been removed by these means, the skins, although saturated with tannin, are yet in a condition which enables them to absorb sumach; and accordingly they are deposited in a bath containing one-quarter of their weight of powdered sumach.

Take the leather out, and dip it again in a new position two or three times every day while in this bath, stirring every time the powder which has settled to the bottom. At the end of the second day add a quantity of sumach equal to that already used. Take the skins at the end of three days; they are found to be not only improved in color, but more soft and pliable than before the treatment. To more completely develop the lustre-like yellow color of these skins, they are washed in water to remove the sumach, and then passed repeatedly through a very weak bath of sulphuric acid, being quickly taken out after each immersion, and immediately rinsed in pure water to take up the acid, which, if allowed to remain, will destroy the leather.

Dry the leather; then oil it upon the flesh side with pure cod-liver oil, and when thoroughly penetrated by this, oil it with a mixture of best whale oil with half its weight of tallow; in the meantime, scraping as usual upon the grain with the fleshing-knife. Then pare it, sleek and beat it out flat. All these operations are performed with the hand, without the help of any machinery. The excellence of the products depends entirely upon the skill and attention of the workman.

CHAPTER CXXVI.

CURRYING OF GOAT-SKINS.

The preparation of these skins, on account of their great thinness, requires as much care and labor as calf-skins. The currier receives them dried, after having been oiled. At first he softens them by soaking for 24 hours in a vat full of water; he treads them out under the feet three at a time, and scrapes them upon the flesh side with a blunt knife. When nearly dry, he oils them with a mixture of train and scouring oil. A dozen of skins weighing from 18 to 20 lbs. requires from 6 to 8 lbs. of oil. The oiling being completed, he again treads them out, scrapes clean and pommels with instruments smaller than those used for calf-skin. To free the surface of the excess of oil, and to soften and brighten them, he dissolves 4 ounces of potash in two bucketsful of water, and passes lightly the solution over the grain side, the saponaceous compound which it forms is wiped off. The above quantity of potash is sufficient for six dozen of skins.

After this operation, grain the leather with the pommel, and rub it with a bunch of straw to soften the grain. Wipe it well with a woollen rag, and black it with the following mixture: one ounce powdered nutgalls, one pound copperas, and a handful of Brazil wood; the whole is boiled some time in a little porter and then stirred in a bucketful of the same liquid. Black six skins at a time, and pile them upon each other on the table or floor. Then turn the pile, so that those which have been blackened first become uppermost, and wipe thoroughly each one with a woollen rag, and stretch them to dry. When the skins are partially dried, black them a second time with a hard brush, distribute the color over the surface rapidly and uniformly, then wipe them with a roller made of blanket stuff, and dry them in the air. Pommel them now across the grain, wipe, moisten with sour beer applied upon a piece of listing, and rub with a bunch of straw to reduce the grain.

This operation done, trim the borders upon the horse, pare the skins with the round knife, pommel and brighten with barberry juice. This last operation must be done carefully, and is performed by passing the listing, dipped in the polish, rapidly and lightly over the surface from head to tail and across, continuing to rub while the rag remains moist and until a polish is given. Then apply the roller equally and forcibly to the whole surface from head to tail, pommel the skin lengthwise and across, and dress upon the grain with pure linseed oil.

Formerly it was the fashion to form a diamond grain surface upon goat-skins, but now they are grained in straight parallel ridges, formed by pommeling from head to tail alone.

We will now describe another mode of preparing goat-skins indicated by M. Dessables:—

Sprinkle two skins at a time, upon the hair side, with water from a brush, and place them upon each other with their hair sides in contact, and fold them up into a cap-like form, beat them with the feet or the mace.

Pommel them from head to tail and crosswise, slightly moistening them at the same time with water. After you have prepared a dozen or more skins in this way, place them in a tub with a sufficient quantity of water to cover them, beat them with the rammer, stretch out and smooth them upon the marble with a stretching iron, and dry partially. Then wash the hair side over with a weak solution of potash, scrape the skins upon the flesh with the stretcher, rub over with a bunch of straw, stretch again and wipe with a piece of woollen cloth before blacking. The color is prepared as in the other process. Spread this blacking lightly with a brush over the hair sides, and dry.

Sometimes instead of pure water a solution of potash is used to moisten the skins.

When dry, apply to the skins a second coating of color with a hard brush made of hog's bristles, pass it rapidly over the surface, and press upon them with considerable force. Then wipe the hair side with a woollen cloth made into the form of a roller, and pommel lengthwise.

Pare the edges with the head-knife, scrape the leather, and wipe it again, and at last pommel so as to produce quadrilateral figures. Polish the blackened surfaces by rubbing them with a piece of cloth dipped in barberry juice, smooth with the roller, and oil upon the hair side with linseed oil; this completes the operation.

SECTION IX.

RUSSIA LEATHER.

The Russians have manufactured for a long time a variety of fancy red leather called by them *Juncten*. This leather has an agreeable and characteristic odor, does not mould even in damp places, and is not attacked by insects. This process was described by Pallas and by Fischertroem, and a factory was established in France at St. Germain more than 70 years ago, under the auspices of M. Feybert, but did not prove successful.

The process we are going to describe is taken from the prize work on the subject by Grouvelle and Duval-Duval, and of Mr. Payen,* but all these methods are defective, and the Russian process is not yet entirely known.

CHAPTER CXXVII.

PROCESS OF MANUFACTURING RUSSIA LEATHER.

Calf-skins and goat-skins dyed generally of a red color, cylindered and impregnated with a purified empyreumatic oil obtained from the birch tree, constitute Russia leather. For this object select the whitest and most perfect skins. Deprive them of hair by steeping them in a mixture of ash lye and quicklime made too weak

---

* Dictionnaire technologique.

to act on the fibres. Rinse; full them a longer or shorter time, according to their nature; wash in hot water, and ferment in a proper steep. Leave eight days; take out; full again; steep a second time if necessary to open their pores; clean with the flesh knife on both sides.

For 200 skins make a paste with 38 lbs. of rye flour fermented with leaven; work the dough with a sufficient quantity of water to form a bath for the skins; soak them forty-eight hours; transfer them to small pits; let them remain fifteen days; wash them well. This preliminary operation serves to prepare the skins for their uniform and complete combination with tannin and extractive matter.

Then make a decoction of willow bark, and when the temperature is sufficiently lowered to prevent it from injuring the fibres, immerse the skins in it; handle and work them for half an hour. Repeat this operation twice daily during a week, after which prepare a fresh decoction, and submit the skins to the same treatment for another week. Then dry them in the air, and they are ready to be dyed and dressed with the oil.

Dessables has given another method of preparing the skins for the chief operation.

Select the whitest and most perfect skins; soak them in water; scrape them upon the beam; full them; work with the pommel, and then oil them upon the flesh side with pure fish oil, and upon the hair side with train oil scouring. Dry them; pommel them again; wash over the hair side with a solution of alum, and then press under the cylinder. This cylinder, by which the diamond-shaped grain is given to Russia leather, is made of steel, 12½ inches long, and 3 inches in diameter, and is covered with a number of closed parallel threads or grooves like those of a screw, but cut perpendicular to its axis and not spirally. This cylinder is filled with stone weighing from 300 to 400 lbs. It is moved in two directions upon a wooden bench, by means of a cord passing round a wooden roller with a handle; this cord also passes over two cylinders attached to the floor and a fourth one upon the end of the bench. The cylinder having the handle upon its axle is divided into two different parts, over which the two extremities of the cord pass in different directions, so that two opposite movements can be given to the cylinder by one handle. The cylinder is sustained and directed by iron bars placed along the bench upon which it rolls. The skin which is to be grained is placed below it lengthwise upon the bench, and longitudinal grooves are impressed upon its surface by the track of the cylinder. The skin is then removed, and again placed upon the bench, either crosswise or at an angle, according as it is intended to give it a square or a diamond-shaped grain.

When the skins are properly grained, apply to them a second coat of alum water, and when nearly dry spread over the hair side the *Russian oil,* and give the black or red color. Then expose the skin repeatedly for a short time to the direct rays of a hot sun, until the color has sufficiently penetrated its substance; then full; pommel; sleek with the round knife upon the beam; and at last rub well upon the hair side with a hard brush.

The principal characteristic of the preparation of Russia leather is its impregnation with birch-bark oil, the fabrication of which is still in a measure kept secret. In order that the oil should penetrate the leather properly the latter must not be either too moist or too dry, but should contain just sufficient water to enable the oil to be spread equally over the surface, and to be absorbed in proportion as the moisture gradually evaporates. The leather thus prepared retains the characteristic odor for a long time. You must be careful not to apply too much of the oil, for fear of its passing through and staining the grain side. To fully impregnate a large cow-skin, from twelve to sixteen ounces are sufficient. In case the leather is not dyed, or of morocco to which you wish to impart the odor, only a very small portion should be applied to the flesh side.

The composition of the red color of Russian leather has not been accurately ascertained. It usually contains Brazil wood, alum, and some other substances. It is not very durable, and does not resist the action of boiling water or of potash, but remains unaltered in the air. Other dyes of better quality are sometimes used which enhance the price of the leather. Black Russia leather is prepared in the same way as the other, and is stained by the repeated action of acetate of iron.

CHAPTER CXXVIII.

DISTILLATION OF THE EMPYREUMATIC OIL OF BIRCH-TREE BARK FOR RUSSIA LEATHER.

Much attention has been bestowed upon the manufacture of the empyreumatic oil of birch bark, and quite a number of different modes of preparing it have been described, we shall give the most important.

Fischerstroern's Process.

Separate very carefully the whitish membranous epidermis of the birch from all woody matter. Introduce it into an iron boiler, which, when full, is covered with a vaulted iron lid, from the centre of which issues an iron pipe. Place over this boiler another one, into which this tube enters without touching its bottom. Bolt the edges together and lute tightly. Invert them so that the one containing the bark is uppermost. Sink in the earth the lower half of this apparatus, cover over the surface of the upper boiler with a lute composed of clay and sand, then surround it with a wood fire, and expose to a red heat until the completion of the distillation. As soon as the boilers are cooled, disconnect them. In the upper one you find a light charcoal powder, and in the under one, used as a receiver, is a brown oil, odoriferous, empyreumatic, mixed with tar and pyroligneous acid. Separate the oil from the other substances and keep it in a close vessel.

Another process.—Introduce the dark birch bark into a large earthen pot, having a hole in the bottom. When the pit is full, set the bark on fire; over that pot invert another similar pot with a hole for the escape of smoke, and this latter is placed upon a bucket, into which the tar and oily matters drop as they are formed.

If the preparation is made in the spring, some manufacturers mix the young branches of birch covered with buds with the bark. This arrangement facilitates the separation of the oil, which, when thus prepared, is of a lighter color, from the smaller quantity of soot it contains.

Grouvelle and Duval-Duval's Process.

They take the white epidermis of the birch bark, well separated from all ligneous matters, and introduce it into a copper still, similar to those used to distil wood to manufacture pyroligneous acid. They adapt to it a receiver immersed in water, in which the gaseous products are condensed. As in the fabrication of pyroligneous acids, the resulting products are pyroligneous acid, tar in larger quantity, and the empyreumatic oil more colored and less abundant. This oil is obtained nearly colorless by a rectification, but this rectification is not useful except in case the oil has to be used for skins very lightly colored.'

Payen's Process.

By repeating the distillation *per descensum* of the epidermis of the birch bark, Mr. Payen has ascertained that with a very simple apparatus, it is possible to obtain an oil less colored and in the proportion of one-fifth more, at a temperature less elevated.

His apparatus, represented below, is thus formed:—

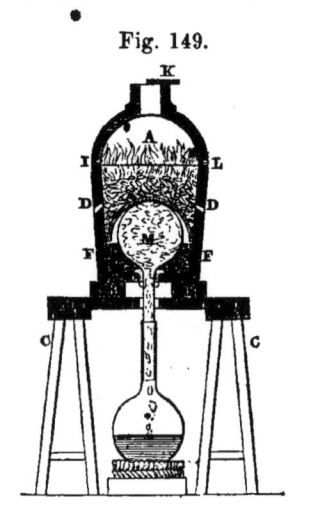

Fig. 149.

A hole is made in the bottom of an earthen furnace A, large enough to receive the neck of a matrass M. The furnace is supported by two bricks placed upon the plank, which is also perforated so as to admit of the passage of the neck of the matrass, and which rests upon the trestles

C, C. The matrass is filled to its utmost capacity with the epidermis of birch bark, it is inverted and passed through the furnace and the board. Then the neck is luted and placed in the position seen in the figure, being supported by sand thrown into the bottom of the furnace as high as F, F; and in order to expose the matrass to a uniform heat, it is protected by inverting over it an earthen hemispherical vessel or crucible. Around this, burning coals are placed, and the fire is kept up through two lateral openings D, D, the dome I, K, L, being placed upon the furnace top. Condensed water first trickles from the mouth of the matrass into a vessel placed beneath, and this is succeeded by drops, and then by a constant stream of an amber colored oil. After a time this ceases, and it is necessary to apply heat lower down to the neck of the matrass, so as to cause the discharge of the last portions of all and tarry matters which have condensed in it.

The products obtained by the distillation of 100 parts are as follows:—

A brown oily matter, light fluid empyreumatic, soluble in ether	70.00
Thick dark brown tar containing a little oil	5.00
Water acidulated with pyroligneous acid	10.00
Light spongy charcoal	12.50
Gases	2.50
	100.00

This oil may be readily obtained by distilling the bark in iron cylinders placed horizontally in a furnace similarly to gas retorts.

CHAPTER CXXIX.

NATURE OF THE ODORIFEROUS SUBSTANCE OF THE BIRCH-TREE BARK.

Messrs. Payen and Chevalier have examined the odoriferous substance of the epidermis of the birch-tree. This epidermis contains from 0.2 to 0.3 of an immediate peculiar principle, white, pulverulent, soluble in alcohol, volatile. Thrown on incandescent charcoal it exhales abundant vapors, whitish, with an aromatic odor, sweeter than that of Russia leather. It is to this principle, called *Betuline* by Mr. Chevreul, who discovered it first, that are due the characters proper to Russia leather. This principle can be assimilated to an insipid, odorless and colorless resin. By alteration it acquires a very fully developed odor. It is probable that by the distillation *per descensum* a greater portion of betuline is carried away without alteration and in the fluid part. It is possible that in this state, it contributes more efficaciously to the preservation of objects which are impregnated by it, a property which, as every one knows, is common, 1st, to resinous bodies not to be penetrated by dampness; 2d, to many volatile oils and odoriferous substances, to preserve vegetable and animal substances subject to spontaneous alteration.

CHAPTER CXXX.

PREPARATION OF RUSSIA LEATHER.

MACERATE calf-skins in a weak alkaline liquor, work them on the beam and wash them in water, dip them in a mixture of water and oat meal, and keep them in till a light fermentation is established. Birch-tree bark is preferable to oak bark. Stir all the time. The tanned skins are rendered supple by means of the oil; they are then rubbed several times with the tar of birch-tree bark; they owe their agreeable odor to this substance. Russia leather retains that odor for several years.

This leather is blackened by rubbing it after tanning with pyrolignite of iron. In Astracan they prepare a very fine leather with elk or goat-skins. The operation is similar to that operated on sheep-skins. The leather is left for three days in a bath of fermented bran. Spread each skin in a bucketful of water containing a certain proportion of honey; it is passed afterwards in a sour bath and then dried. This leather is dyed red by immersing it in a bath of cochineal containing an alkaline plant. It is then passed in a solution of alum and tanned. The red can be made brighter and more solid by using nutgalls instead of sumach. The yellow is obtained with the wild chamomile.

CHAPTER CXXXI.

COLORING OF RED RUSSIA LEATHER.

Mr. Jno. Wagmijster, a tanner of Paggstall, has successfully imitated Russia leather by employing the red dyed cow-leather. He operates as follows: As a basis, take 5 ounces of nitric acid and heat it in a glazed vessel in a chimney flue, but not over an open fire, until it begins to smoke, that is, until a red fetid vapor rises; which great care should be taken not to inhale. Then pour it over one pound of salt of tin and stir it with a long wooden stick. It is preferable to mix the salt of tin and the warm acid in the open air, or in a strong draught, so as not to be too much exposed to the danger of inhaling the vapor. The stirring with the skin should be carefully continued as long as the red vapor rises; but as soon as white vapors commence to ascend, one-quarter of a pound of hydrochloric acid should be poured into the mass, stirring it briskly all the while. After a few minutes pour the liquid into the bottle and keep it for use. In filling the bottles care should be taken not to have the liquid too hot, or a bottle may easily burst and hurt the operator.

The liquor until used should be kept in a place where the temperature is moderate, and in using it, from twelve to fifteen times its volume of clean water should be added to dilute it.

After being thoroughly tanned and well washed, hides may be *grained* with this, that is to say, this corrosive substance may be well rubbed in by means of a brush. For the dye take 1 lb. Brazil wood, and boil it an hour in six quarts of clean river water. Then the limpid coloring liquor must be strained off and three-quarters of an ounce of cream tartar dissolved in it. The coloring liquid with the tartar should be well boiled together for an hour. It is advisable to boil the coloring liquid separately several days before the tartar is added, as its strength will be increased thereby.

As in black dyeing the hides should be smeared only on the flesh side, then fulled and wiped off with woollen rags, so that the half-moist condition may leave the grain open. After the hide is thoroughly dry, it should be crimped and well rubbed two or three times with the above-mentioned corrosive liquid, and then spread over also two or three times with the warm dyeing liquor; if cold, warm it. In the preparatory operation as well as in the stirring, brushes should be used. The brush should not be dipped in the liquor, but the liquor poured upon the hide and the brush work begun at once in order to spread the stuff uniformly, and that the stained hide may show an even tone of color in all parts. The dye must be applied immediately after the first rubbing, because it is then moist and the color takes better and no small spots are left. Therefore it is better that two men should be used in this operation, each of whom dyes half a hide, both working together, thus the dyeing of one side and the staining of the other side will go on together. Should the color not take uniformly, the light spots must be gone over again with the dye.

This red dye is very lasting, and endures as long as the hide itself, so that hides treated with this preparation may be kept on hand in the storehouse for further dressing. Hides that have been coated and long kept on hand dye badly; such should be soaked in luke-warm water, and then treated like fresh-tanned hides.

As a last process, the stained leather should be moistened on the flesh side with tan liquor, sleeked, dried, and then grained and crimped; a handsome appearance may be given to that leather, by going over the colored side with lime water by means of a sponge; the color receives a fine gloss and a peculiar fiery tint; but the lime water should not be too strong.

CHAPTER CXXXII.

EXTRACT FROM A MEMOIR ON THE PROCESS OF TANNING SKINS IN RUSSIA BY THE COUNT OF KARTSOFF.*

The principal Russian manufactories are situated in the government of Misnie, Novogorod, Orlow, Moscow, Perm, Courks, and Wladimir. The city of Cazan possesses a very extensive establishment, but as it belongs to the government the products manufactured there are reserved for use of the navy. As for goat and sheep-skins proper for the fabrication of morocco, Cazan exclusively manufactures them.

The Tartars are the principal workmen in these shops. Their process of preparing goat-skins differs from the other in this: that they use sour mares' milk, into which they pass the skins after the raising. It is this preparation which gives to the morocco the suppleness which distinguishes it, and renders it proper for the different uses to which it is intended.

When the skins are dried, soak them in water to soften them; the degree of dryness and the temperature deter-

---

* Bulletin de la Société d'encouragement de l'industrie nationale, vol. xii. page 211.

mine the time of this operation. In summer they are left in water about five or six days, and in winter from ten to twelve days.

The skins are washed to free them from the blood and impurities adhering to the surface; for this purpose spread them and raise them as follows:—

Throw the skins in water, to which some hydrate of lime has been previously added, and let them stay in the vats a longer or shorter time according to the strength of the milk of lime. Begin at first to put 160 lbs. of lime in each vat, and when the liquor weakens introduce a new quantity of lime. The vats are built of pine wood; they are 8 feet in diameter, and 6½ feet in height. They are hooped with iron, and are sunk a few inches below the floor of the shop, so as to enable them to be covered with planks.

For heavy leathers another method is followed: They are carried in an oven, and are spread one on the other, covering them with earth to prevent fermentation. A sour bath prepared with rye bran is sometimes used, principally for thin skins.

The skins are inspected several times a day, to ascertain when the hair begins to loosen. Take it off then with the epidermis, by working the skins on the horse with a two-handled knife; then equalize the inside surface with a knife.

To destroy the lime which has penetrated the skins, wash them several times. For this purpose a man introduces them one after the other into a vat, and beats them with the feet in turning them; he soaks them with warm water till this water is clear; then he washes them, and lets them soak one or two days in running water.

To this operation follows the tanning; but to have

the tannin penetrate the skins, their pores are opened by swelling them; for this purpose they are dipped in an acid liquor prepared with flour. For a vat of the size described above, they use sometimes 1000 lbs. of rye flour and from 4 to 6 lbs. of salt dissolved in warm water; sometimes 2000 lbs. of oatmeal, 6 lbs. of salt, and a little yeast. In some places they use spent tan. When the acid fermentation is established, put the skins in, and leave them about forty-eight hours. Sixteen pounds of flour are used for a skin of an ordinary size.

The skins thus disposed are exposed to the action of a weak infusion of oak bark or willow. Then they are spread on a wooden grate above the bark. They are piled up, and covered with bark, coarsely ground; and, as you raise the pile, force the grate down the pit until it reaches the bottom, which is covered with a bed of the same bark. The pit being full, water the skins with spent liquor. They are covered with planks loaded with stones. Leave the whole from fifteen to eighteen days; raise the skins, and change the bark. Repeat this operation three and even six times according to the nature of the leather.

When tanned, the leather acquires a certain stiffness, which is corrected by dipping it from twenty-four to thirty-eight hours in a liquor composed of 120 lbs. of oatmeal and 8 lbs. of salt, both mixed with water, so as to form a thin paste. This quantity is sufficient for 150 skins of ordinary size; wash them, and leave them to drain, and they are ready to receive the oiling. Fish oil and tar from birch-tree bark are the substances used for this operation, which is practised in the following manner:—

The leather, being damp, is placed wrong side upon

a table. The operator, having dipped his hand into the mixture, passes it over the skin by spreading it as equally as possible.

The perfection of this operation depends upon the ability of the workmen. The proportions of oil and tar vary according to the size, nature, and quality of the leather. Generally one-third of tan and two-thirds of oil are used. Sometimes two-thirds of tan and a second coating are applied on the outside surface to render it less permeable to water. In some shops, where they desire to keep the skins as white as possible, they use pure oil, to which is added a little beef tallow, half a pound being sufficient for an ordinary skin.

This operation completed, the skins are spread on ropes under a well aerated shade, where they remain until perfectly dry. In winter they are exposed to the frost which renders them white.

The Baskirs and Kirguises used to prepare the skins with smoke, which takes the place of tannin.

They begin by strongly stretching the skins when green, and taking off the hair with a sickle. The skins dried by the sun are kept in till the following spring.

At that time a pit is dug, the size being according to the quantity of skins to contain; poles are suspended on the top, their ends reposing on the edges of the pit. Then at about five feet they make a round hole which communicates by a little trench with the bottom of the pit. In this hole the combustible is placed; this combustible is generally rotten wood, as the one giving the most smoke.

This done, the fire is lit by shutting the aperture: the smoke passing by the trench penetrates inside the pit and spreads over the skins. After fifteen or twenty-one days of smoking, the skins are impregnated with the volatile products of the combustion, and acquire some of the properties essential to the tanning. They are more water proofs than European leathers.*

The currying is done in Russia as anywhere else, only the leather is streaked with a long fluted copper plate about from 4 to 6 inches long and 3 inches wide, on which they bear the hand, which grains the surface.

The process of preparing the tar is as follows: Take large earthen pots, the bottoms of which are pierced with a hole, which are filled with birch-tree bark well packed. They are placed on pails used as receivers. After lighting the bark, they are covered with other similar vessels pierced with a hole by which the smoke escapes. The oil runs by degrees through the aperture of the lower vessel and falls into the pail which supports it.

This operation is done in the spring, and they mix with the bark some branches covered with buds. That mixture facilitates the running of the oil, which is less colored than by the other process, the reason being that they dissolve less soot. This is why fresh bark is preferred to that which is dry. As Russia prepares more oil than necessary for its consumption, a large quantity is exported.

CHAPTER CXXXIII.

RED LEATHER.

In former times this kind of leather was very largely manufactured, but is replaced now by Morocco sheep-leather; however, some is still manufactured, of a finer but of a less permanent color than Russia leather, and

* Bulletin de la Société d'encouragement, vol. xii. page 211.

without its odor. These skins, used by harness, coach, and trunk-makers, weigh on an average from 10 to 12 lbs.

To prepare red leather choose fine clean skins with a uniform smooth surface. They must not have been tallowed, but only softened with a little clear oil, which is passed lightly over the surface. Dip, pare, and wet them in water, give them a coating of clear oil on the hair side, and train-oil scouring on the flesh side. The proportions to use are half a pound of each. The skins are then dried. Press on the hair side with a brush, a solution of alum in water, which acts as a mordant to fix the color on the skin. The skins are then beaten to soften them, exposed to the air, and, when dried, they are rubbed with a cork. In that state they are dried. The color is prepared as follows:—

In a clean barrel put from 8 to 10 lbs. of quicklime, with as much water, and let it stand for two days. The third day decant the water without stirring the lime deposited in the bottom. Put this water into a copper kettle. To prepare two pailfuls of red, take 8 lbs. of Brazil wood, and boil strongly with the lime water; as the water evaporates, add some more so as to have two pailfuls at the end of the ebullition. Put this liquid back on to the fire, and boil it until reduced to one-half; keep that solution in a separate vessel. Fill the kettle with lime water, reduce to half. Mix the two liquors in the kettle, and add to this composition half an ounce of powdered cochineal, boil a few minutes and take off from the fire. While the liquid is yet boiling add a piece of lime the size of an egg, and let it cool. This dye is sufficient for eighteen to twenty skins. When the dye is ready, give to the skins a first coating, expose to the air, give a second coating, and leave it to dry completely. The skins are then pounded, and they receive a third coating to which a white of egg has been added. Expose to the air and sleek on the hair side. They are finally rubbed over in the usual way with barberry juice, dried, and strongly sleeked.

Dessables has given another process to dye the skins. He makes a solution of alum by dissolving in a kettle 1 lb. of alum in 1½ pint of water. When the solution is made he pours it into an earthen jar and adds to it 3 qts. of ordinary water. This solution is sufficient to mordant three dozen calf-skins. Afterwards take 3 lbs. of Brazil wood with a piece of lime the size of an egg. Boil the whole in 15 qts. of water for five or six hours.

The skin being in the same state as for the black, it is well rubbed with a piece of wool dipped into the alum solution, then well dried and rubbed with the Brazil. Dry again, and rub with a piece of wool, apply another coating of Brazil, dry, and repeat the operation a third time.

CHAPTER CXXXIV.

SHAGREEN AND PARCHMENT.

Shagreen.

The best quality of shagreen is manufactured almost entirely in Astracan and other parts of Asiatic Russia; gray and colored shagreens are imported from Constantinople and Tunis; an inferior article is also manufactured in Poland. True shagreen is not real leather, but a skin prepared by drying, and without the chemical action of any tanning material. The following process is that which is said to be followed in Astracan. The raw materials employed are the skins of horses, asses, camels, and only the small strip from the cropper along the chine to the neck can be employed. This is cut off just above the tail in a semicircular form, about 34 inches upon the cropper and 28 along the back. Soak these strips in water until the hair is ready to come off, then separate it by scraping. Afterwards dress the pieces with the fleshing knife until all extraneous matters are removed, and they have been reduced to the thinness of a hog's bladder. Stretch them tightly across frames, and occasionally dampen them to prevent them from shrinking unequally; after which, lay them on the floor with the flesh sides undermost, and the grain sides are then thickly strewed over with the smooth hard seeds of the alabuta or goose foot (*chenopodium album*). In some places, instead of this mustard seed is used. Then lay a felt over the whole, and force the seeds deeply into the soft moist skins by treading upon them or by the action of a press.

This operation gives to the hair side of the shagreen its characteristic granular appearance. Then dry slowly in the shade, the frames with the seeds sticking in the skins, until the skins are ready to drop off upon shaking. The skins are thus converted into hard horny membranes, with the surfaces deeply indented; they are laid upon a beam, padded with wool, are shaved down until the depressions caused by the seeds become very slight and uniform. First steep the skins in water, and afterwards in a warm alkaline lye; pile them upon each other while still warm and moist. By this means the parts indented by the pressure of the seeds regain their natural elasticity and not having lost substance by the shaving of the rest of the skins, they rise to or above the surrounding level, and form the peculiar grain of the shagreen; after this, cleanse the skins by salt brine and dye them.

Green color is given to shagreen by passing over the flesh side a concentrated solution of sal ammoniac, strewing it over with copper filings, rolling it up with the same side inward, and pressing each skin for 24 hours with a heavy weight. The sal ammoniac dissolves enough copper to give the skin a beautiful sea-green color.

Blue color is obtained with indigo dissolved in a solution of soda with lime and honey. Black with copperas and nutgalls; red with cochineal. Pure white is obtained by dressing the strips first in an alum solution, then in wheat dough, and washing away the latter with lime-water.

The preparation is completed by greasing, carefully working in hot water, currying with a blunt knife and drying.

Shagreen is rendered very hard by drying, but it softens in water, and in that state will take any shape given to it, and is used by sheath makers for the cases of spectacles, surgical and mathematical instruments.

An imitation of shagreen has been made so much like the genuine article, that it is impossible to distinguish the difference. For this purpose sheep or goat-skins are used. Deprive them of hair in the lime pits, steep them in water, flesh and soak again; rub them well down upon the horse with a hard polished piece of wood, after which they steep them a third time, beat out and trim them on both sides. Then steep them for two hours in a bath made of a bucket full of tan for fifty skins, mixed with enough water to cover the skins. An hour after a bucket half full of the same is thrown in, and another at the end of an hour and a half. After this, keep them in tan pits eight days, remove them, wring out, and reduce the thickness with the round knife applied upon the horse. Dry them partially, stretch in the direction of the length, cut in half, blacken in the usual manner and dry.

The grain is given to this shagreen by means of copper plates engraved in imitation of the roughened surface of the real article. These plates, previously warmed, are placed upon the skins and then subjected to the action of a press.

CHAPTER CXXXV.

PARCHMENT.

PARCHMENT is the invention of Eumenes, King of Pergamus, in Asiatic Turkey, about 200 years before Christ. It was known in early times, as *Pergamena*, and was used, on account of its great durability, for records and valuable manuscripts, and as a substitute for the *papyrus*, or writing paper of the ancient Egyptians. The finest quality, made from thin and perfect skins, and prepared by very careful manipulation, is called *vellum*.

Fine parchment, for writings, is made from the skins of calves, kids, stillborn lambs, sheep, and she-goats; but an inferior quality, for drum-heads and battledores, is prepared from the skins of he-goats, calves, wolves, and asses. Pig-skin is also sometimes converted into parchment for bookbinders' use. The operations are nearly the same, throughout, for all the varieties, but are more delicate for the finer quality.

The skins above mentioned are those generally employed for this branch of manufacture, but all other thin skins are applicable; and sometimes the thinner halves of thick hides, split by machinery, are dressed by this process.

"The skins, after having been soaked, limed, shaved, and well washed, must be set to dry in such a way as to prevent their puckering, and to render them easily worked. The small manufacturers make use of hoops for this purpose, but the greater employ a *horse*, or stout wooden frame. This is formed of two uprights and two crossbars, solidly joined together by tenons and mortises, so as to form a strong piece of carpentry, which is to be fixed against a wall. These four bars are perforated throughout with a series of holes, which are fitted with very smooth and slightly tapered box-wood pins. Each of these pins is transpierced with a hole like a violin screw, by means of which the strings used in stretching the skin may be tightened. Above the *horse*, there is a shelf for such tools as the workman may need at hand. In order to stretch the skin upon the frame, large or small skewers are employed, according to the size of the piece which is to be attached to it. Six holes are made in a straight line to receive the larger, and four to receive the smaller skewers, or pins. These small slits are made with a tool like a carpenter's chisel, and of the exact size to admit the skewers. The string round the skewer is affixed to one of the bolts in the frame, which is turned round by means of a key, like that by which harps and pianos are tuned. The skewer is threaded through the skin when in a state of tension.

"Everything being thus prepared, and the skin being well softened, the workman stretches it powerfully, by means of the skewers; he attaches the cords to the skewers, and fixes their ends to the iron pegs, or pins. He then stretches the skin, first with his hand applied to the pins, and afterwards with the key. Great care must be taken that no wrinkles are formed. The skin is usually stretched more in length than in breadth, from the custom of the trade; though extension in breadth would be preferable, in order to reduce the thickness of the part opposite the back bone.

"The workman now takes the fleshing-tool which is a semi-circular double-edged knife, made fast into a double wooden handle, seizes it in his two hands so as to place the edge perpendicularly to the skin, and pressing it carefully from above downwards, removes the fleshy excrescences, and lays them aside for making glue. He now turns round the *horse* upon the wall in order to get access to the outside of the skin, and to scrape it with the tool inverted, so as to run no risk of cutting the epidermis. He thus removes any adhering filth, and squeezes out some water. The skin must next be ground. For this purpose, it is sprinkled upon the fleshy side with sifted chalk or slaked lime, and then rubbed in all directions with a piece of pumice-stone, four or five inches in area, previously flattened upon a sandstone. The lime soon becomes moist from the water contained in the skin. The pumice-stone is then rubbed over the other side of the skin, but without chalk or lime. This operation is necessary only for the best parchment or vellum. The skin is now allowed to dry upon the frame, being carefully protected from sunshine and from frost. In the warm weather of summer, a moist cloth needs to be applied to it from time to time, to prevent it's drying too suddenly; immediately after which the skewers require to be tightened.

"When it is perfectly dry, the white color is to be removed by rubbing it with the woolly side of a lamb-skin. But great care must be taken not to fray the surface; a circumstance of which some manufacturers are so much afraid as not to use either chalk or lime in the polishing. Should any grease be detected upon it, it must be removed by immersion in a lime-pit for ten days, and by then stretching it anew upon the *horse*, after which it is transferred to the *scraper*.

"This workman employs here an edge tool of the same shape as the fleshing-knife, but larger and sharper. He mounts the skin upon a frame like the *horse* above described; but he extends it merely with cords, without skewers, or pins, and supports it generally upon a piece of raw calf-skin, strongly stretched. The tail of the skin being placed towards the bottom of the frame, the workman first pares off, with a sharp knife, any considerable roughnesses, and then scrapes the outside surface obliquely downwards with the proper tools, till it becomes perfectly smooth. The fleshy side needs no such operation, and, indeed, were both sides scraped, the skin would be apt to become too thin, the only object of the scraper being to equalize its thickness. Whatever irregularities remain, may be removed with a piece of the finest pumice-stone, well flattened previously, upon a piece of close-grained sandstone. This process is performed by laying the rough parchment upon an oblong plank of wood, in the form of a stool; the plank being covered with a piece of soft parchment stuffed with wool, to form an elastic cushion for the grinding operation. It is merely the outside surface that requires to be pumiced. The celebrated Strasburg vellum is prepared with remarkably fine pumice-stones.

"If any small holes happen to be made in the parchment, they must be neatly patched, by cutting their edges thin, and pasting on small pieces with gum-water.

"Parchment is colored only green. Boil eight parts of cream of tartar and thirty parts of crystallized verdigris in five hundred parts of rain-water; and, when this solution is cold, pour into it four parts of nitric acid. Moisten the parchment with a brush, and then apply the above liquid evenly over its surface. Lastly, the necessary lustre may be given with white of eggs, or mucilage of gum Arabic."

SECTION X.

PATENT LEATHER.

THE fabrication of varnished leather, or *patent leather*, has reached such a development in France within the last thirty years that this kind is exported to every country. This fabrication is not difficult, all that it requires is care and dexterity. There are several processes, but we think it only necessary to describe in detail the process now most usually followed.

CHAPTER CXXXVI.

FABRICATION OF THE PATENT LEATHER.

THE glazing of leather comprises two distinct operations:—

1st. The preparation of the surface. 2d. The varnishing.

The object of the preparation of the surface is to close the pores of the leather, and make a proper ground by repeatedly rubbing the surface with pulverulent substances and incorporating them with it.

The object of the varnishing is to obtain a soft, supple, and bright coat, unalterable by rubbing.

To prepare the surface, incorporate pulverulent matters

which have the property of forming a mastic in the pores of the skin, such as *chalk, ochre, lampblack*, etc.

In the varnish, on the contrary, no material used must destroy the transparency and brightness.

The basis of both preparations is siccative linseed oil, prepared as follows:—

For 25 galls. of oil, take—

20 lbs. of lead,

20 lbs. of litharge,

and boil them together until reduced to a syrupy consistence.

This composition is then intimately mixed with ochre or chalk, according to the fineness of the skin to be prepared, and is uniformly spread on either sides of the leather with appropriate tools.

Three successive coatings are given at such intervals of time as will permit each coating to dry, when the surface is rubbed with pumice-stone. A number of thin coatings are applied in the same manner, and rubbed down until perfectly uniform, and of sufficient thickness to prevent the varnish from penetrating the leather, by which its qualities would be injured and its structure rendered hard and brittle. The oily substance of the preparation and of the varnish should merely penetrate deeply enough into the leather to make the composition of which it is the basis adhere closely to it.

The foundation for the varnished surface being thus laid, a mixture of the above preparation without, however, the *addition of ochreous or other earthy matters*, and well rubbed up with fine ivory black and enough spirits of turpentine to make it flow smoothly and easily, is laid on by means of a fine brush, three or four successive coatings being applied. By this means a black and shining, pliable surface is obtained, over which, as soon as it is perfectly dry, the varnish may be applied.

After the application of each coating, the leather is dried, by hanging it up, or better, laying it out upon frames or racks in the drying room. Before varnishing, it is customary to give a polish to the surface by rubbing it over with a piece of woollen stuff and the finest kind of pumice-powder or tripoli.

The varnish is thus prepared: Take

    Oil prepared as above 20 lbs.
    Asphaltum,   1 lb.
    Thick copal varnish, 10 lbs.
    Spirits of turpentine, 20 "

The asphaltum and oil, being mixed together, are heated, then the varnish and spirits of turpentine are added, constantly stirring until the mixture is perfectly homogeneous. The asphaltum can be substituted by Prussian blue or ivory black. Leave the varnish to settle in a warm place for two or three weeks before using it.

During and after the varnishing, be careful to avoid dust falling on the prepared skins.

The temperature of the oven varies from 133° to 167° according to the nature of the leather and varnish.

The tint of color of varnished leather varies with the coloring material which has been added to the varnish. Asphaltum gives it a reddish hue, Prússian blue a greenish-blue metallic tint, and ivory black a pure brilliant black lustre.

Some manufacturers add to the litharge employed for boiling the oil, red lead, ceruse, powdered cuttlefish-bone, oxide of manganese, and various other metallic salts or oxides.

The success of the process depends very much upon

the care with which the skins prepared with it have been selected, tanned, and curried. It is very necessary that the dubbing should have been applied to them with great uniformity, and only in small quantities, for otherwise the surface will soon become tarnished and blotted.

CHAPTER CXXXVII.

DIDIER'S AND OTHER PROCESSES.

HEAT lampblack in a close vessel, and mix it with linseed oil varnish until the mass becomes sufficiently liquid to flow. Apply two coatings to the leather and let it dry. Mix then this varnish with an equal quantity of copal varnish and give another coating to the leather. As soon as this last coating is dried, polish the leather with a felt charged with finely powdered pumice stone; then pass on the leather a waxed sponge, wipe with a cloth, and then give the polish. For this purpose rub on a slab one part of copal varnish with lampblack, and give to the leather five or six coatings of this mixture with a brush. Dry, rub the leather with pumice stone, and give again two coatings of copal varnish.

White polished leather.—Rub ceruse with white oil varnish, and apply two coatings on the leather. Then rub Krem's white at first with water, let it dry and rub it with white copal varnish, give three or four coatings, and polish as above.

Red polished leather.—The first coating is given with shellac mixed with spirit of turpentine and the second with the same lac in copal varnish. This latter is prepared by dissolving one part of copal in two parts of turpentine and adding to this solution an equal quantity of linseed oil varnish.

Blue polished leather.—Give a first white coating with ceruse mixed with oil varnish, then a blue coating with Prussian blue mixed with copal varnish.

Yellow polished leather.—Yellow requires a white leather prepared by boiling it in a copper vessel containing a solution composed of fustic wood, lye, cochineal and alum; pass this liquid through a cloth, give a coating to the leather, and when dried, apply the copal varnish. If no white leather is at hand, give a first bottom with light yellow ochre and ceruse mixed with ordinary varnish. The second coating is given with the same color mixed with copal varnish. When dry, polish the surface, and apply three coatings of yellow cassel mixed with copal varnish.

Polished leather of leather color.—Apply a coating of a mixture of yellow ochre, white lead, and oil varnish; when dry, polish. Give a second coating with Turner's yellow mixed with copal varnish.

Black Lacquer for Shoes and Leather Work.

Mix four ounces of shellac and half an ounce of the finest lampblack in a stone bottle with 1¼ pint of strong alcohol, close the mouth of the bottle with a damp bladder. Add nothing more to the mixture for twenty-four hours, but shake it often in that time. Then pierce a hole in the bladder with a needle, and place the bottle in hot water, and let it stand half an hour, taking it out often to shake it. Unfasten the bladder, pour an ounce of Venetian turpentine in the bottle, close up the mouth again, and place it once more in hot water. The bottle should be kept always corked, and it requires to be shaken before using the contents.

Process for varnishing Leather for Bells, etc.

The varnish for leather is the same as for carriages, except that it contains less copal, and that the oil used in the varnish for certain coarse articles should be a little decomposed.

After having dressed and scraped the leather to be varnished, apply upon the flesh side a thin coat of glue water, to which has been added about one ounce of boiled linseed oil. The leather when dried is polished, and successive coatings applied until it becomes very smooth. Then mix one part of strong dying oil, and one part of copal varnish in an iron vessel, add well pulverized lampblack and spirits of turpentine, and set the whole over a fire. The leather which during this time has been kept in a closet artificially heated, is now stretched upon a table, a very thick coat of the mixture quickly laid on with a flat brush, immediately placed in a warm closet and allowed to dry slowly. When dried it is polished with pumice stone, or, which is better, with charcoal finely powdered and sifted. A second coat is applied in the same way, and the operation finished with a third coat which should be very lightly laid on and be very smooth. The leather is now dried without polishing.

SECTION XI.

WATER-PROOF LEATHER.

Many processes have been proposed to render leather water proof. Those processes which rest upon the increase of the density of the matter by the use of fat, resinous or gummy matters present no great interest; nevertheless for the satisfaction of the reader we shall give a few of them.

CHAPTER CXXXVIII.

PROCESS OF J. SMITH AND J. THOMAS.

Macerate the leather you want to render water proof in water for twenty-four hours; then press it between two iron cylinders, and let it dry in the air for five days. Then mix the following liquor:—

Linseed oil	4 pints
Olive oil	2 "
Spirit of turpentine	1 "
Castor oil	2 "
Beeswax	8 ounces
Pitch	4 "

Boil all these substances over a gentle fire in an earthen vessel, and during the ebullition dip in the leathers which leave more or less time, according to their nature.

Sole leather must stay about twenty minutes. Calf

and cow-skins about ten minutes. Those leathers thus prepared are drained and pressed between two iron cylinders covered with leather. Dry then in an oven heated at 77 to 86°, press them again and put them anew in the oven.

CHAPTER CXXXIX.

NENORY'S PREPARATION TO RENDER LEATHER WATER PROOF AND IMPERVIOUS.

The preparation of this compound is made as follows:—

Preparation of Siccative Oil.

Take 100 lbs. of linseed oil and 13 lbs. of litharge; boil them together at a moderate heat for several hours, until the oil is reduced to the two-thirds.

Preparation of the Elastic Gum.

Take—

Old linseed oil	7¼ lbs.
White wax	1 lb.
Glue	5½ lbs.
Verdigris	4 oz.
Water	2 qts.

Melt the whole at a gentle heat, in an iron vessel, until it forms a homogeneous mass.

Preparation of the Compound.

Take—

Siccative oil prepared as above	100 lbs.
Gum prepared as above	8 "
Beeswax	10 "
Spirit of turpentine	13 "
Balsam of Peru	2 "
Oil of thyme	2 "
White pitch	6 "

Melt the whole in an iron vessel at a gentle heat without boiling; then pour this composition in the bottles which must keep it.

Process of using the Composition.

Put the bottle near the fire, so to render it fluid without heating it. After having well dried and brushed the leather, pass the composition over it with a little sponge or a brush, and during the operation expose the leather to the sun or to a gentle heat. When the leather is dried, repeat the operation until saturated. If it stays on the leather, some composition which has coagulated, rub it with a rough cloth, then apply any kind of blacking.

CHAPTER CXL.

DEANE'S PROCESS FOR RENDERING LEATHER IMPERVIOUS.

First Composition.

1. Take: Linseed oil, rape-seed oil, and neats-foot oil, 251 gallons; boil until reduced to 21½ gallons.

2. Take: Mutton or tallow suet; melt it at a gentle heat; pass it through a sieve; boil it one hour in water,

filter and let it cool, and put the cakes on cotton cloth to absorb the dampness.

3. Take of the grease prepared above (2) 34½ lbs. and 34½ lbs. of fresh wax; melt them together, and keep them at a temperature of 158°, until the whole is well incorporated.

4. Take 2 lbs. and 2 drs. of India-rubber in shreds, that you dissolve in 8 quarts of rectified spirits of turpentine at a temperature of 248°, over a sand-bath.

5. Take 10 lbs. and 1 drachm of Burgundy pitch, that you melt with 2½ gallons of spirits of turpentine at 194°, over a water-bath; leave this mixture to cool until it reaches 158°, then add it to the above mixture, and stir the whole until well incorporated.

Second Composition.

1. Take oil, grease, and melted wax; mix as above at a temperature of 158°.

2. Take 4 gallons of turpentine, in which you dissolve 10 lbs. 1 drachm of yellow rosin over a sand-bath, at a temperature of 200°.

When the mixture thus prepared has cooled to 158°, add the resinous composition to that of oil, grease, and wax; stir the whole until cold.

Third Composition.

Take 21½ gallons of pure whale oil, and from 13 to 17 lbs. of India-rubber shreds; heat them together at 194° to 240°, which is sufficient to operate the dissolution of the India-rubber.

Fourth Composition.

Take rectified spirits of turpentine, sufficient to cover 13 or 17 lbs. of India-rubber shreds; boil gently over a sand-bath heated at 240°, until the entire dissolution of the India-rubber; add to this composition 21 gallons of pure whale oil at 194°, and keep thus until the mass is fluid and united; let the temperature fall to 158°; add 8½ lbs. of fresh wax; stir the whole until cold.

Application of the Composition.

The first and second compositions are used for skins, and the third and fourth for leathers.

The skins are saturated with the first or second composition, by spreading them in a vessel which communicates with a kettle in which is the composition. Introduce the composition heated from 144° to 212° in the vessel containing the skins until entirely covered; leave them thus two or three hours. The skins are then withdrawn, and submitted to a current of air gently heated, until dry. In this process hydrostatic pressure or vacuum can be used the same as we have seen for tanning.

The leathers, if thin, are impregnated with the third composition; if thick, with the fourth. They are placed on a metallic plate, heated at 104°, and they are covered with the composition by using a brush. The saturation is achieved by rarefying the air contained in a room purposely constructed.

You operate on leather by exposing it in a room at a temperature of 100 to 120°; then one or two hours after, when warm, coat them with one of the above compositions until well saturated; place them in a room at the ordinary temperature, and leave them in until dry.

CHAPTER CXLI.

DIFFERENT PROCESSES.

Cheap Method of making Leather Water-proof.

MELT together in an earthen pipkin

Tallow	2 lbs.
Lard	1 lb.
Turpentine	½ "
Beeswax	¼ "

Dry the leather well and warm it. Rub the composition into them with a piece of tow dipped into it, the articles being held near a hot fire until they have had rubbed on them as much as they can take up.

There is another mixture much used by fishermen, which consists in melting together

Beeswax	1 lb.
Rosin	½ "
Suet	¼ "

Jenning's Process.

Dissolve any metallic soap in an equal quantity of raw linseed oil, and immerse the leather in that solution heated at 225°. When the latter has become cold, take the leather out and dry it in the air. Forty-eight hours are sufficient for the whole process.

Canvas and similar fabrics can also be rendered waterproof by the following process:—

Dissolve

| Soft soap | 100 lbs. |
| In boiling water | 30 galls. |

Heat the solution to 212° with 66 lbs. of sulphate of zinc.

An insoluble salt of zinc is formed, while the sulphate of potash dissolves in water; the metallic soap rises on the surface of the liquor, and is boiled in fresh water to purify it.

Boil 5 lbs. of pearlash with 50 galls. of raw linseed oil, until the mixture assumes a soapy appearance, and to it while hot add, stirring all the time,

Sugar of lead	2½ lbs.
Litharge	2 "
Red lead	4 "
Black rosin	21 "

Boil one hour, constantly stirring, and at the end of that time add 30 lbs. of the metallic soap.

Add to the mixture two gallons of a liquor made by dissolving India-rubber, 24 ounces in one gallon spirit of turpentine. Allow the mixture to cool to 160°, and apply it with a brush. Two or three coatings are sufficient, but there must be an interval between each coating to insure a perfect drying.

PART IV.

HUNGARY LEATHER.

SECTION XII.

This method of preparing skins, analogous to tanning, was originally introduced into Hungary from Senegal. It was imported into France, in 1573, by a tanner of the name of Boucher. In the next century the great Colbert established a manufactory at St. Cloud, in which the process was adopted; and, in 1702, this establishment was removed to La Roquette, in Paris, in which it was in successful operation for a long time.

The process of manufacturing Hungary leather is a rapid one; it consists in impregnating strong hides with alum, common salt, and suet; and is almost the same as when first introduced from Hungary. The only improvement we know is the one introduced by Curaudeau, of which we shall speak hereafter. This kind of leather is manufactured all the year round, measures being adopted to counteract any injurious influences the temperature might exert upon it.

The workshop is divided into two parts:—

1st. A shed on the bank of a river in which are placed the beams, the fleshing and paring-knives, and the scraping-stones. In a corner is a furnace to prepare the solution of alum, and near it are two tubs to immerse the skins. Besides this a number of ordinary tubs is required.

2d. The other part of the factory consists of a room 6 feet high by 15 feet square, perfectly tight, so as to retain the heated air. In a corner of this room is a furnace, fed with fuel through a door opening externally, upon which is placed a copper kettle, capable of containing 160 lbs. of tallow. In the middle of this kind of oven is a square stove, upon which an iron grating, three feet square, is placed for the reception of coals. On either side of this oven, and occupying its whole length, are large tables upon which the skins are greased. The upper part below the ceiling is filled with poles, upon which the leather is hung in order to dry. The door of this room fits closely to its joints, so as to prevent the entrance of cold air.

The most suitable hides for Hungary leather are strong ox-hides, but bull and cow-skins can be prepared in the same manner. The process is rapid, and may be completed in two months or less time. These hides can scarcely be compared with those tanned and curried in the ordinary way, since they consist of the original tissue of the skins condensed and slightly altered in character by the process to which they are subjected, but not converted into true leather by combination with tannin. Moreover, they are employed for different purposes.

The chief operations to which hides are subjected are the following:—

1. *The river-work,*
2. *Aluming,*
3. *Second aluming,*
4. *Drying,*
5. *Stretching,*
6. *Treading out,*
7. *Tallowing,*
8. *Flaming,*
9. *Airing,*
10. *Marking and piling.*

Before describing these operations we shall say a few words on the different greases employed in this process.

CHAPTER CXLII.

GREASE AND ANIMAL OILS.

These substances of animal origin are white or yellowish, sometimes odorless, sometimes with a strong odor. The consistence is variable; the taste is sweet, lighter than water, without action on litmus, more or less fusible, alterable in the air, insoluble in water, soluble in alcohol which dissolves the oleine.

Greases are composed of two principles, one liquid, the oleine, the other solid stearine and margarine; and it is according to the proportions of the latter that depend the fusibility of the grease.

Lard

Is white, inodorous, soft; melts at 80°.6, is insoluble in water; 100 parts of boiling alcohol dissolve 2.80 which are oleine. Treated by caustic alkalines, it is converted into glycerine and oleate, margarate, and stearate, of these bases, which by their union constitute the soaps.

According to M. Chevreul, lard is composed of oleine and stearine, and its elementary constituents are represented as follows:—

	Chevreul.	Saussure.
Carbon	79.098	78.843
Hydrogen	11.146	12.182
Oxygen	9.756	8.502
Nitrogen		0.473
	100.000	100.000

This substance is employed in currying, Hungarying, etc.

Mutton Suet.

This grease is firmer than the above, odorless, insipid; brittle when pure; insoluble in water, and very moderately so in alcohol. 100 parts of alcohol dissolve only 2.26 of oleine.

According to Mr. Chevreul it is composed of oleine, stearine, and a small quantity of hircine. Its elementary principles are as follows:—

Carbon	78.996
Hydrogen	11.700
Oxygen	9.304
	100.000

Beef Tallow.

This tallow has a light yellowish color. It is firm, brittle, fusible at 104°, insoluble in water, soluble in boiling alcohol. Its properties and composition are the same as the above.

Medullary Beef Tallow.

This kind of grease is of a bluish-white color, fusible at 113°. It is composed of

Solid grease	76
Oil	24
	100

The oil has a very disagreeable odor, and is nearly colorless.

Fish Oils.

From fish a kind of greasy fluid is obtained which we call oil, giving to it the name of the fish it is extracted from. While spermaceti is not, properly speaking, an oil, however, as it has some of its characters, it may be included among them.

Dolphin Oil.

This oil is extracted from the dolphin, *Delphinus globiceps*. Its color is lemonish. Its odor similar to that of the fish. Its specific gravity 0.9178. 100 parts are dissolved in 100 parts of alcohol at 0.812, at a temperature of 158°. Its solution has no action on litmus. This oil exposed to a cold of 26°.6 separates into a crystalline substance and an oil which solidify at 28°.4. The crystalline matter is much similar to cetine. It is formed of oleine, phocenin, and a little phocenic acid.

Porpoise Oil

Is extracted as the above, from the *Delphinus phocæna*. It is yellowish. Its specific gravity 0.937; without action on litmus, soluble in alcohol, and saponifiable in alkalies. It is composed of oleine, phocenine, an orange-red principle, an odoriferous principle, and phocenic acid.

Different Fish-Oils.

This oil belongs to different fishes, particularly to the whale. The oil is separated by pressure from the solid grease. It is fluid, sometimes colorless, sometimes of a reddish-brown with a disagreeable odor. According to Mr. Chevreul, it is formed of oleine, stearine, two odoriferous and coloring principles. It possesses a great similarity to fixed oils. Its elementary principles, according to Berard, are—

Carbon	79.65
Hydrogen	14.35
Oxygen	6.00
	100.00

Process by which to give to a mixture of different Oils and Greases the properties of Fish Oils.

Take the inferior qualities of seed-oils and boil them several times in a kettle to separate the aqueous, earthy, and acid parts. Boil putrefied horse guts or bad fishes. Mix these two substances in the kettle. Add seed oils, horse-fat, residuum of seed oils purified by sulphuric acid, and at last whale or cod-liver oil. Stir this mixture for twenty-four hours in the kettle. Leave to settle; pass through a skimmer. You obtain thus an oil as good as cod-liver oil, which is the best.

Process for rendering Vegetable Oils fit to take the place of Fish Oils.

Melt in a kettle over a gentle fire 16 lbs. of lard, mixed with 100 lbs. of nut oil or linseed oil, or any other seed oils. Stir well, till the mass is homogeneous. Take off of the fire, and when partially cold, pour in it while stirring four ounces of sulphuric acid.

This oil has the same properties as fish oils.

CHAPTER CXLIII.

RIVER WORK.

THE first operations are similar to those of tanning and tawing. The hides are washed, cut in two, scraped upon the horse with a round knife, and are then carefully and slightly washed; the fat and flesh alone being removed.

Afterwards scrape off the hair from the hides, by placing them upon a bed of other skins folded double and so disposed upon the horse as to present a smooth and perfectly uniform surface. This operation must be carefully conducted to avoid injuring the surfaces, and it will take one day for a skilful workman to separate the hair from eight or ten hides. Then soak the skins in the river for

Fig. 150.

twenty-four hours, or in vats for three days, changing the water twice a day in summer and once in winter. If you soak in running water, drive a stake into the ground, and fasten the hides to it by a cord passing through the hide holes, or those left by the removal of the horns.

CHAPTER CXLIV.

ALUMING THE HIDES.

The aluming is the most important preparation to which Hungary leather is submitted. Not only does it prevent the putrefaction of the hides, but effects a chemical change in them, by which they are rendered stronger and more substantial. The exact nature of this chemical influence is not known yet, but the supposed reaction is as explained under kid-leather.

The hides are first treated with a mixture of alum and salt, by which a portion of the sulphate of alumina is transformed into chloride of aluminium. This salt softens the effects of the alum, attracts moisture of the atmosphere, and preserves the suppleness of the leather. Generally, the manufacturer works nine hides at a time. When the skins are ready to be alumed, dissolve alum and salt in a kettle disposed on a furnace. This kettle is round below, and of a size according to the quantity of skins to be treated. An ordinary kettle is 14 inches deep in the middle and about 22 inches diameter, and is large enough to alum nine skins at a time.

Fig. 151.

The proportions of alum and salt used are for each skin—

Alum	. . . . .	6 lbs.
Salt	. . . . .	3½ "
Water	. . . . .	7½ galls.

Heat the water at about 122°, throw in it the alum and salt, and stir until dissolved.

When the solution is ready, put the skins in two vats, 4 feet 10 inches long, 3 feet wide, and 27 inches deep.

When nine hides or eighteen strips are worked together, the whole is divided into three lots of three skins each. Three strips are placed in each vat, being prepared upon each other with the hair side up, and so arranged that the head of the second one is above the tail of the first, and so on. It may occur that the leathers are very strong and large, and require much care, then instead of three lots you make four.

ALUMING THE HIDES.

When the leathers are thus disposed you alum them. For this purpose take in the kettle two or three pailfuls

Fig. 152.

of the alum solution. This solution must be tepid, for if too warm it will burn the leather. Heat gradually, so that the last is warmer than the one before used. Pour this water on the hides. Then a man beats them with his feet. This operation is renewed three times. Each time the workman beats with the feet, twice the backs and once the bellies. Each three turns forms what is called one water. During this operation another man puts tepid water in the second vat, and disposes the strips as above indicated.

This first water done, the man passes in the second vat and begins the same operation. For each three skins you give four waters in the same manner, but each time the liquor must be warmer.

After the fourth water fold the hides double and deposit them in tubs 2 feet diameter and 2 feet deep. Fill this tub with alum water which has been used, and immerse the hides. Generally, the hides are left in these tubs eight days, the position being changed every day or two. Some manufacturers leave them a longer time in winter, but no difference need be made in this respect between the seasons.

Fig. 153.

CHAPTER CXLV.

SECOND ALUMING.

The skins being removed from the tubs and well shaken to remove the folds, they are subjected to the same series of operations as in the first aluming. Steep them twenty-four hours in the same alum water, take them out and leave them to drain on planks arranged in a slanting position, so that the liquor escaping from the hides runs back into the vats.

CHAPTER CXLVI.

DRYING AND STRETCHING.

When the hides are perfectly drained, make four holes in each strip, and thrust a stick through them; the stick is supported by its two ends upon poles near the ceiling of the drying room. Suspend the hides and leave them till nearly dried. Take them down, lay them upon the floor, being folded double with the hair side within; a workman stretches all their parts and takes out the wrinkles, which have formed in them by forcibly drawing a stick 2 ft. long and about ⅜ of an inch in diameter, in every direction over the surfaces. Then pile up the hides, leave them a day or two in this state, suspend them upon the poles until thoroughly dried.

During cold weather hang the hides for a time on the poles in the store-room, heated with charcoal. When sufficiently warm stretch and pile them one upon the

TREADING OUT THE HIDES.

other, and cover them with cloths to protect them from the cold. Thus prepared, this leather keeps as well as tanned leather, and it is only necessary to have dry winds, to avoid exposure to a hot sun, in order that it may not become so dry as to be worked afterwards with difficulty.

CHAPTER CXLVII.

TREADING OUT THE HIDES.

The leather being dried, is softened and prepared to receive the tallow, by a peculiar method of stamping. Erect a platform with planks slanting in one direction,

Fig. 154.

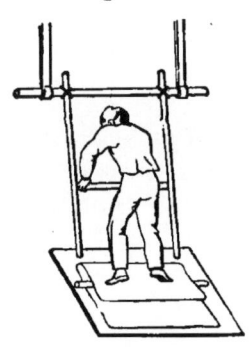

and supported upon cross pieces 12 to 13 inches a part. The hide to be worked is folded, double, with the hair side in contact, and a smooth stick of hard wood, 26 inches long and ¾ of an inch in diameter, is passed through.

Fig. 155.

The workman wears thick soled shoes without heels, and stands upon the folded strip, laid upon the upper part of the platform; and, holding on to a railing, he proceeds to roll the stick by repeated stamping and shuffling movements of his feet from its first position to the edge of the strip. He repeats again and again, changing the position of the stick, and the hide is turned until every part is well tramped. He folds the leather in the opposite direction, so that the flesh side is in contact, and it is exposed again to the stamping process. He continues the operations until the pores become as soft and supple as it is possible to make them. Then he piles the strips upon each other for a time, and if not sufficiently dry, he exposes them to a hot sun or to the heat of the drying room; then he treads them out a second time precisely in the same manner as before.

CHAPTER CXLVIII.

TALLOWING.

The hides are impregnated with tallow in the storeroom, and the tallow is melted in a boiler capable of containing 170 lbs. This boiler is 20 inches deep and

Fig. 156.

35 inches in diameter, and is imbedded in the masonry of the furnace.

In the middle of the store-room is a stove, massive, square, and large enough to put on it an iron grate 3 feet square; the object of this grate is to support the lighted coal destined to heat the room.

Fig. 157.

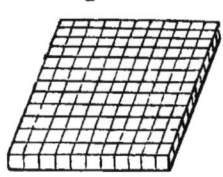

A heating apparatus has been proposed by Mr. Curandeau. It consists of an oval shaped stove 2 feet high and 3 feet in diameter. The interior consists of a cast-iron hearth, paved at the bottom with bricks, and adapted for burning wood. The smoke and heat ascend through a pipe 2 feet long and 5 inches in diameter, and are conducted into a vertical pipe 3 feet high and 11 inches diameter. From the top of this two smaller pipes diverge, and are connected with two other vertical columns, each two feet ten inches high and nine inches in diameter, which are placed at the side of the main column; and with the lower ends of these two pipes a fourth horizontal one, placed two inches above the top of the stove, is connected, and into this the smoke and heat finally enter; the former to escape through a chimney, and the latter to be given off to the air of the room.

In the oven you suspend poles on which you put the leathers to warm them. On both sides are two large tables used to spread the hides when you tallow them.

When the hides are ready to be greased, fill the boiler three-quarters full with tallow and heat it until melted.

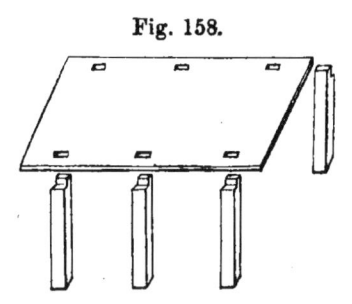

Fig. 158.

When it has attained a degree of heat a little above the melting point, it is ready for use. If the heat is too great, the draught must be lessened and lumps of cold tallow must be thrown in. While the tallow is being melted, kindle a fire upon the grate with a basketful of charcoal.

As soon as the charcoal is kindled, fold double 24 to 38 strips of hide according to the size, stretch them across the poles below the ceiling of the room, placing the largest and thickest the nearest to the fire. Then the workmen leave the stove-room, closing the door tightly behind them, in order to escape from the stifling vapors proceeding from the hides and the charcoal, and do not return until they are assured that the heating has been carried far enough. Then they air the room a little by opening the door, enter in with no clothing but short aprons, and examine the leather. When sufficiently warm they observe a white appearance, beginning at the extremities and extending over the whole surface of the hides. As soon as this is the case, they remove the strips from the poles, and stretch them out upon each other, with the flesh side uppermost, on the table near the boiler. The thickest parts of the hides are placed nearest to the boiler, and the smallest and thinnest strips are made to occupy the lowest position in the pile.

Two men are employed in tallowing the hides. One, the nearest to the boiler, takes off the uppermost strip of the pile and folds it double, with the flesh side out, and the head placed upon the table, assures himself that the tallow is heated to the proper point. Then he takes a tallowing cloth or mop made with pieces of rags or blanket stuffs, a foot long, and tightly tied around a wooden handle six inches long, and, having immersed it in the boiler long enough for it to become saturated with the melted fat, rubs it over the head part of the flesh side until the half of the surface is sufficiently *fed*.

Fig. 159.

He is assisted by other workmen with a similar mop, and when half of the leather is properly greased it is extended out at full length by the two workmen, and the whole of the flesh side is saturated with grease. Then the strip is turned over, and the hair side is greased with the tallow still adhering to the mops, which are not dipped again in the boiler, for fear of injuring the surface by the heat of the melted tallow. When greased throughout, lay the strip upon the table upon the opposite side of the room, with the flesh side up. The skins are in like manner successively greased and piled upon each other on the table until the end of the operation.

It takes one hour to prepare thirty strips. Grease of inferior quality, such as the residuum of melted tallow and kitchen stuff, may be employed, and about 3 lbs. of it are required for each piece of leather. In the country they use sometimes 10 lbs. of tallow for one leather, *i. e.*, 5 lbs. for each strip, but it is useless, as the skin does not absorb it all.

There is no art in which the workmen are exposed to

more fatigue and danger than those they are compelled to encounter while conducting the operations in the stove-room. They constantly inhale the suffocating vapors of the skins and melted tallow, and the dangerous oxide of carbon given off from the combustion of the charcoal; they are exposed to the risk of suffocation or at least to great irritation in the lungs, while the profuse perspiration of the body predisposes them to take cold. Precautions must be taken for them to leave the room immediately after the charcoal fire is lighted, and not re-enter it until the atmosphere has become changed by a current of fresh air entering through the open door.

They should not go into the room with full stomachs, but commence the operation three or four hours after a meal, and in quitting work should rub themselves down with a coarse towel before resuming their dress. Buzzing or tinkling noises in the ear, giddiness and headache, are regarded as premonitors of the dangerous effects of the inhalation of oxide of carbon, and upon the occurrence of this the men should immediately leave their work and go into the fresh air.

CHAPTER CXLIX.

FLAMING.

LEAVE the hides for a time to absorb the tallow with which they have been impregnated, and cover them with cloth in order to prevent the unequal action of the fire upon them. Then kindle a fire upon the grate with a basket full of charcoal, leave the room, and after a lapse of half an hour, open the door to allow the gas to escape. The charcoal being in full combustion, two men enter, take the uppermost strip off the pile, one by the head, the other by the tail, stretch it in every direc-

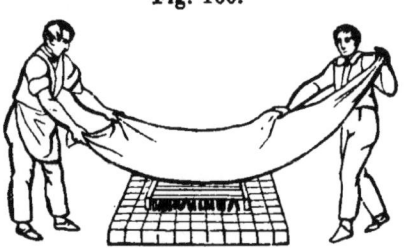

Fig. 160.

tion over the fire with the flesh side down, and continue this for about one minute. They extend the strip upon the empty table, the flesh side up, and repeat the same operation with the other strips. When the flaming is finished, they cover the new pile of hides with a cloth, and leave it so half an hour in summer, and three hours in winter. This operation is necessary for the complete penetration of the hides by tallow. Some manufacturers light a large fire in the room and keep the skins exposed to its heat with the door closed for half an hour or more.

CHAPTER CL.

EXPOSURE TO THE AIR.

AFTER the hides have remained in piles for about three-quarters of an hour, they are wiped on both sides with a dry rag or mop, to remove the excess of grease, and are hung in the air upon poles, the flesh sides up, and the heads and tails depending. They become firm if they are not exposed to the direct influence of the sun.

In summer they should be tallowed shortly before sun down, so that when they are aired, they need not be exposed to the heat, but may be cooled by the night air. In winter this precaution is unnecessary. It is sufficient to air during the night in summer, and thirty hours in winter.

CHAPTER CLI.

WEIGHING.—MARKING.—PILING.

The last operation consists in weighing, marking, and piling the leather. When dry, which takes place in one night in summer and in twenty-four or thirty hours in winter, they are piled and left so for a few days. A hide thus manufactured loses about half of its original weight, some less; some lose three-fifths, so that a hide which from the butcher weighed 50 lbs. is sometimes reduced to 20 lbs.

When the leather is weighed, mark the weight in Roman characters on the tail, pile them up, and a few days after they are ready for the consumer. The room in which they are piled must not be too damp or too dry. This leather can be kept nine or ten months without alteration in the quality, but at last it will lose of its weight and suppleness and become dry and hard.

In the summer season a hide of leather can be manufactured in fifteen days; but in winter it requires from three weeks to one month.

Fine Hungarian leather is worth, in France, from twenty to twenty-two cents a pound; a fine strip weighs from twenty-six to twenty-eight pounds, and measures nine feet by three.

Alumed hides which have been dried can be kept a long time without alteration, and it is in that state that they must be kept when it is necessary to preserve them a long time in store after their manufacture.

CHAPTER CLII.

HUNGARY LEATHER MADE OF COW AND CALF-SKINS.

OCCASIONALLY cow-skins are prepared by the Hungarian method, but they are depilated by liming instead of scraping. They are left in the lime-pits until the hair is ready to come off, when it is removed, and the skins being washed and scraped until the last remaining portions of lime have been separated, are prepared in the same manner as thick hides, excepting that before being tallowed they are not exposed for so long a time in the stove-room.

The liming renders them spongy, and disposes them to absorb a larger quantity of alum and salt than ox-hides, in proportion to their weight.

Calf-skins are prepared in the same manner, but absorb much less quantities of the materials used; a large calf-skin requires about 1 lb. of alum, 8 ounces of salt, and 1 lb. of tallow.

CHAPTER CLIII.

HUNGARY LEATHER MADE OF HORSE-HIDES.

THESE hides are worked in the green state, and to prevent the inequalities of surface which would otherwise be found upon them, they are not thoroughly fleshed, but a part of the membranous substance is left upon their flesh sides. A horse-hide, thus prepared, weighs 30 lbs. and used to be sold for $1.20; it is now worth from $2.40, to $3.00.

The hides are first cut in half and put to soak for 12 hours, then they are fleshed with a sickle-shaped knife, and depilated by means of lime, first for one day in an old pit, then they are withdrawn and piled up for two or three days, when they are put in a second and third lime-pit for three days.

When depilated, soak them 12 hours in summer and 24 hours in winter, occasionally stirring in order to remove the lime. When clean, scrape them with the stone, and dress them upon the hair side with the round knife. Then roll them up from head to tail, and put them aside to drain six hours.

They are trodden out in the vats, like other hides, with three alum waters, the tails and manes being beaten more forcibly than the other parts. A large horse-hide requires about 5 lbs. of alum and 2¼ lbs. of salt.

After being stamped, place them in the tubs with alum water, let them remain in from two to eight days, and tramp them again in the same liquors.

Drain and partially dry them, stretch them out with the hands, dry them entirely, and work them upon the platform as ox-hides, heat them upon the poles in the stove-room for from a quarter to half an hour, according to their degree of dryness; when they are thus heated, they give off a vapor so offensive as to be scarcely endurable.

Tallow and finish them in the usual manner. They require half the quantity of grease which is used for ox-hides. The ordinary weight of a horse-hide thus prepared is 30 lbs., but they run from 14 to 60 lbs.

This leather is often mistaken and sold with that

prepared from ox-hides, but it is much inferior to the latter, being apt to harden and shrink and being much less firm and strong.

A few donkey-hides are also prepared, but they give a bad leather, hard, brittle, horny, and difficult to work. Their preparation is the same as that of other hides, but they take very little tallow. Such a hide is generally sold for 80 cents, and, when prepared, weighs from 6 to 8 lbs., and is sold from 15 to 16 cents a pound.

CHAPTER CLIV.

M. KRESSE'S PROCESS OF PREPARING BLACK HUNGARY LEATHER.

Mr. Kresse took a patent in 1836 for preparing black Hungary leather in the following manner:—

Take, when fresh, the hides intended to be blackened, and spread over the flesh side a mixture of orpiment and lime, and leave in contact for two hours. Then take the hair off, and pass for some days the hides in baths of tan, alum, and salt. Dry them partially; soften; supple, and dry them. Grease them with boiling tallow; soak them in water; stretch them upon the table, and apply the color on the hair side. Rub over at first the surfaces twice with stale urine. The third and fourth applications consist of a color made with decoctions of three parts of logwood and one part of fustic; the fifth and sixth of alder bark, iron rust, and nutgalls, mixed with lemon-juice. Being thus coated, dry the skins, and smooth them by stretching upon the table.

To make the color of the last two applications: Squeeze 100 spoiled lemons into a bucketful of broken pieces of alder bark, mixed with 10 lbs. of scraps of rusty iron and 1 lb. of bruised nutgalls. Stir up the contents of the bucket, and leave for fifteen days, at the end of which time the liquid is poured out and ready for use. Sometimes the skins become mouldy before being colored if they are piled in a moist place; and, in order to prevent this occurrence, prepare them in the following manner:—

Wash them in the river, and, before being alumed, place them in a vat, and cover them with warm water, with which a bushel of bran and four ounces of ferment have been previously mixed, steep them three days in this bath, and alum them; tread them out three times in warm water to remove the salt, and dry them.

To give the skins a brown color, similar to that of tanned leather, steep them for a few days in tan liquor. If it is desired to blacken them, they may then, after receiving the four first dressings mentioned above, be brushed over twice on the hair side with a solution of copperas instead of the mixture prepared with lemon-juice.

CHAPTER CLV.

DEFECTS IN THE QUALITY OF HUNGARY LEATHER.

THE causes of these defects have several different springs. Generally a bad skin will not make a good leather, whatever is the process. In the art of tanning we have indicated the signs to recognize a skin of bad quality, and the cuts made by butchers are the greatest trouble in the preparation of this kind of leather.

We have said before that horse-hides must be used

immediately after the animal has been killed; and this precaution must not be neglected, for if the skins experience a beginning of fermentation the hair side loses its consistency.

Leather imperfectly tramped during the aluming process, or which has been treated only with two or three waters, cannot be properly worked upon the platforms. It will not absorb as much tallow as is necessary, and is apt to contain *horny* and hard portions, which diminish its strength. The hides, which have spots of extravasated blood upon their surfaces, should be rejected as being weak and of bad quality.

CHAPTER CLVI.

USES OF HUNGARY LEATHER.

This leather is particularly used by collar and harness-makers, who employ it for harness and main braces of coaches. For the latter, according to Dessables, they take the strongest leather and put five or six strips one on the other. After being sewed together, they are covered with curried cow-hide. Hungarian leather is the only one to which, in France, suppleness is given by tallow, but in some parts of Italy they tallow leathers even destined for soles.

The tallowing is the most difficult operation. Too much heat renders the leather brittle; not enough, it does not absorb the tallow well. If the tallow is too hot, it burns the leather; if not, it does not penetrate. The difficulty is to operate at the right time.

The tallowing is very important, for if it has not succeeded, it cannot be done over, for the tallow will not penetrate well, and the leather takes a blackish color.

CHAPTER CLVII.

IMPROVEMENT OF M. CURANDEAU.[1]

Curandeau, believing that the change experienced by the skins in the bath of alum and salt is due chiefly to the excess of sulphuric acid, proposed the substitution of this acid for alum. Consequently he prepares the following bath:—

Water	25 gallons
Salt	20 pounds

to which he adds

Sulphuric acid	4 lbs.

The skins, after passing through the preliminary processes, are macerated in this bath, and after a maceration of twenty-four hours they are withdrawn and dried. As much progress is made by the skins in this bath in twenty-four hours as by those which are exposed for a much longer time in the bath previously given, and they possess all the best qualities of Hungary leather.

The advantages of this process are the following:—

1. It requires only two parts of acid, the price of which is lower than alum.

2. This bath does not require to be as warm as alum.

3. The manipulations are much shorter than by the use of the salt bath.

[1] Mémoire de l'Académie des Sciences.

PART V.

GUT DRESSING.

The art of the gut dresser consists in separating the middling or muscular coat of the intestines of certain animals from its external or peritoneal covering, and from its internal lining or mucous membrane, and may be divided into two distinct branches: the preparation of the intestine of oxen and cows for the preparation of alimentary substances, and that of the intestines of sheep for the manufacture of cords for various purposes.

SECTION XIII.

PREPARATION OF THE INTESTINES OF CATTLE.

The intestines are submitted to the eleven following operations, which will be described in the order as below:—

1. Scouring.
2. Turning over.
3. Putrid fermentation.
4. Scraping.
5. Washing.
6. Insufflation.
7. Desiccation.
8. Disinsufflation.
9. Measuring.
10. Sulphuration.
11. Folding.

CHAPTER CLVIII.

OPERATIONS FOLLOWED IN THE PREPARATION OF INTESTINES OF CATTLE.

Description of the Workshop.

THE workshop of the gut dresser consists of a room twenty feet long, sixteen feet wide, and twelve feet high, with four windows; these windows are opened or shut according to the seasons. Around the sides of the room are ranged casks of about sixty gallons capacity, and in the middle of the ground are fixed wooden stakes for attaching hooks. The remnants of the intestines are usually allowed to lie about the floor, and they exhale an odor which, with that from the putrefying intestines in the tubs, is the most disgusting that can be conceived, and is so permanent that the clothes of the workmen remain for a long time impregnated with it. Usually a well is sunk in a yard attached to the building for receiving the waste matters of the factory.

I. OPERATION.—*Scouring.*

As soon as the small intestines of oxen and cows are brought from the slaughter-house to the workshop they are steeped in water, in order to moisten and smooth the surfaces, so that the knife may slide easily over them. When this is done, an end of one of the intestines is attached, by tying it in a kind of knot around a hook, to one of the stakes in the centre of the room at a height of six or seven feet above the ground. The workman then grasps the depending portion between the thumb and first finger of the left hand, and gradually slides the hand down along the whole length of the intestine, follows its motion by passing a knife, held in the right hand, over the surface, so as to separate the fat and as much as possible of the outer or peritoneal coat.

Another portion of gut is then treated in the same way, and the operation is continued until all the contents of the casks have been cleaned.

If any parts of the intestines have been scratched or divided by the butchers in separating the fat, these are cut off and thrown aside.

The fat falling to the ground is separated from the feculent and other matters, and, after being washed a number of times, is dried, melted, and rendered.

II. OPERATION.—*Turning Over.*

The intestines are next washed in a large cask half full of water, and the workman proceeds to turn them inside out, by introducing a thumb into the interior of each, and working the gut upon it with the fingers until the whole is inverted.

A number of the pieces are then tied together at their ends with a cord which is attached to the edge of the cask, and when a sufficient number of inverted intestines are thus fastened, they are left with only their original contents of water to undergo the next operation.

III. OPERATION.—*Putrid Fermentation.*

Experience alone can guide the workman in determining when putrefaction is sufficiently established. It should be carried only far enough to disorganize the mucous membrane and other parts which are to be separated from the middle coat of the intestines, and, if allowed to advance too far, the whole tissue will be softened and rendered useless.

In summer, two or three days of exposure are sufficient, and it requires from five to eight in winter. The putrefaction is known to have reached the proper stage when bubbles of gas begin to escape from the surface of the intestines. This operation is a most disgusting one, but it does not seem to be injurious to the health of those working in the room.

IV. Operation.—*Scraping*.

When sufficiently rolled, the pieces are untied, soaked in a cask half full of water, and the next operation consists in separating the disorganized mucous lining, which is now upon the outside. This the workman proceeds to effect by scraping it off with his thumb-nails until it is entirely detached. The operation is facilitated by frequently dipping the pieces in water.

V. Operation.—*Washing*.

The intestines are introduced into tubs full of pure water, and they are stirred several times every day. The water is changed two or three times a day, and the operation is continued until the water comes from them unclouded and free from taint.

VI. Operation.—*Insufflation*.

When the intestines are perfectly cleaned, one end of each piece is tied with a string, and the workman introduces into the other orifice a hollow cylinder of cane, angle, or reed, about five inches long, and after making the joint air-tight by pressing the rim of the gut tightly around it, applies his mouth to the end, and expands the gut by blowing into it, and then closes the orifice, tying it tightly with a cord. If holes are found, the intestine is cut off at the place where they occur, and tied again with a cord.

VII. Operation.—*Desiccation.*

When all the pieces are thus filled with air, they are carried to the drying place, and are laid out, so as not to be in contact with each other, upon horizontal poles placed about five feet from the ground, and left until dried.

VIII. Operation.—*Disinsufflation.*

When perfectly dry, the pieces are taken down, cut across with scissors as near the ligatures as possible, then they are pressed and flattened with the hand so as to expel all the air contained in them.

IX. Operation.—*Measuring.*

They are then assorted into different sizes, according to the purpose for which they are intended; they are collected into bundles and hung in a damp place preparatory to be sulphuretted.

X. Operation.—*Sulphuration.*

After being kept in a damp place for some time, the intestines are exposed to the vapors of sulphur in a room five feet square and 6½ feet high. For this purpose they are strung on sticks, and if not sufficiently moist when introduced into it, they are sprinkled over with water from a brush, and are then suspended across the upper part of the chamber to the number of a hundred bundles. A pound or more of flowers of sulphur is then put in an earthen dish on the floor of the room, and ignited by burning coals thrown upon it. The door is immediately closed, and the further precaution to prevent the escape of vapors being taken of luting it around the edges, and of gluing stout pieces of paper upon any apertures which exist in the room.

XI. Operation.—*Folding*.

At the end of some hours, open the door of the room and allow the vapors to escape. The intestines which have been thus exposed are bleached, deprived of their bad odor, and are protected against the attacks of insects.

While still damp they are twisted into hanks, packed with camphor and sent to market.

CHAPTER CLIX.

DISINFECTION OF THE WORK-SHOPS. MODE OF SUPPRESSING PUTREFACTION.

In order to prevent the offensive smell arising from the putrefaction of intestines, the following process of separating the mucous membrane has been devised by Labarraque.

The small intestines of fifty cattle which have been cleaned and turned inside out are mixed in a cask with two pailfuls of water, each containing 1½ lb. of chloride of potash at 12 or 13°, and if there is not enough liquid to cover them, another pailful of fresh water is added.

The whole is stirred about, well mixed, and left over night. The membrane can be detached as easily the next day, as after many days of putrefaction in the usual method, and the unpleasant odor is entirely avoided.

The succeeding operations are performed in the same manner.

CHAPTER CLX.

GOLD-BEATER'S SKIN.

This skin is prepared from the external or peritoneal coat of the cæcum or blind gut of neat cattle. The workman separates and turns over the portion which encircles the junction of this pouch with the rest of the intestines, and draws it off inverted from the other coats to the length of 25 or 30 inches. It is then immersed a short time in a weak solution of potash, and is cleaned by scraping upon a board with a knife. When thus well cleaned, and by soaking in water, the piece is stretched upon a kind of frame from 40 to 50 inches in length and 11 inches wide, and made of two uprights held together by two cross-pieces having longitudinal grooves, two and a half lines in width. The surface of the membrane, which was outside in the animal, is placed in contact with the upper part of the frame; it is stretched in every direction, and is glued to its rim. Another membrane is then stretched above the first with its external surface placed upwards and is attached to it by gluing around the edges. When dry, the membranes are separated by running a sharp knife along the grooves. Each strip is then glued upon a frame similar to the first one, but without a groove, and is washed over with a solution composed of—

    Alum, 1 ounce.
    Water, 2 quarts.

When the surface is dried, pass over it a sponge dipped in a concentrated solution of fish-glue in white wine, rendered aromatic by cloves, nutmegs, or camphor. When this coating is dried, cover it with a coat of white of eggs, and the strip is cut into pieces 5¼ inches square, which are then smoothed out under a press, and made up into leaves.

CHAPTER CLXI.

LATHE-CORDS.

These cords are made of intestines of horses, cleaned and prepared by the separation of the mucous membrane in the manner before described. A wooden ball, armed in its lower part with four cutting blades, at equal distances from each other, is fixed by an upright piece of wood to a bench. The end of an intestine is then drawn over this ball, and as the gut is pulled downwards it is divided into four equal bands or strips.

Four or eight of these strips, according to the thickness which it is intended to give to the cord, are tied with a peculiar knot to one end of a thick piece of cord. The end is passed around a peg introduced into a hole in a solid post, to the side of which a number of pegs are attached. At a distance of ten or eleven yards from the first one, another post is fixed, similarly provided with pegs, and over one of these latter the middle of the assemblage of strips is passed, the other end being brought back, and attached to the first peg by means of another knotted cord. The tied ends of the strips are then attached to the wheel by a hook connected with the *whirl*, which is made to revolve until the strips are sufficiently twisted. The twisted end is then kept stretched by attaching it to the peg, and any projecting filaments are cut off. After being stretched for some time, the cords are then twisted again, and a third and a fourth time are twisted by hand, being each time rubbed with and drawn through a bunch of moistened horse-hair after the twisting, and again stretched out between the two posts. If the cord is not smooth and even after the twisting is completed, it is made so by rubbing with a piece of dog-skin. It is then dried, and by some makers is exposed to the vapors of sulphur. At last the ends are cut off, and the cord is rolled in a coil.

In order to avoid the putrid emanations from the intestines, which are generally in an incipient state of decomposition, Labarraque recommends to clean them at once; turn the inside out, and put to soak over night in a cask containing, for fifteen or twenty intestines—

Chloride of potash at 13 or 18°, 1 lb.
Water, 4 galls.

The mucous membrane is ready to be detached the next day; and after its removal, and a thorough washing, the intestines can at once be prepared as has been already described.

CHAPTER CLXII.

MANUFACTURE OF CORDS FROM THE INTESTINES OF SHEEP.

REMOVE the intestines from the body of the animal when warm, clean and free them from fecal matter, and carry them to the workshop. If they are not perfectly clean, and if decomposition has been allowed to commence, they are stained so as to be unfit for most of the purposes for which they are intended.

They are unravelled and deprived of adhering fat while soaking in a tub of water; then they are placed in fresh water, and the small ends of the intestines are tied together, and laid on the edges of the tub, while their bodies are left to steep for two or three days in water which is frequently changed. The removal of the mucous and peritoneal coats is facilitated. After this, the intestines are placed upon a bench, which slopes down towards the edge of the tub, and the surface is scraped with the back of a knife blade in order to separate and remove the external membranes, in breadth of about half of the circumference. The *filandre* (the coating) can only be freely removed in pieces of the proper size and length by pulling it off in the direction from the small to the large end of the intestine. It is employed as thread to sew intestines, and to make the cords of rackets and battledores. In the event of its breaking, the separated pieces must be tied together, and they are laid aside with the others for use.

The guts are then soaked in fresh water for twenty-four hours, and are taken out and scraped clean upon the bench with the back of a round-bladed knife. About eight feet of the larger ends are now cut off and sold to the sausage makers. The rest are then cut of a proper length, and are imbedded, as it were, between layers of salt. Alternating heaps of intestines and layers of salt are packed in until all the intestines have been salted. Some days after, remove and pack them with a small quantity of salt, so as to be ready at any time for the following process.

After the *curing* process is completed, take out the intestines, and soak them over night in fresh water, and deposit them the following day in a lye made with—

Pearlash	8 ounces
Water	4 galls.

The strength of the lye is determined by the experience of the workman. Pour the lye in successive quantities upon the intestines, and pour it off again every two or three hours until they have been sufficiently acted upon. Then draw them two or three times through an open brass thimble, and press against it with the nail in order to scrape off unnecessary and projecting parts from the surfaces, after which they are selected for different purposes according to their size.

CHAPTER CLXIII.

DIFFERENT CORDS.

Cords for Rackets.

These cords are generally made of intestines of inferior quality, or which have been stained by commencing putrefaction. The pieces, while still moist, are sewed together with strips of the outer membranes or *filandre*, each junction being cut aslant so as to make it smooth and strong.

Three or four of these intestines are thus attached by strings to the whirl, and are twisted in the usual way; after which the cord is smoothed and deprived of moisture by the hand of the workman, and is left stretched for a time. It is again twisted and rubbed with a bunch of horse-hair. The inferior kinds of cords are made by twisting one gut along with two or three pieces of the filandre.

Whip-cords are made of intestines of good quality, prepared, cut, and sewed as described. Each end is twisted separately, as whip-cords are seldom made of two intestines sewed together. Sulphur the cord once or twice, and dye it black with common ink, or of a rose color with red ink, which the sulphurous acid turns to a pink color, or with a green dye. Dry and smooth the cords, and coil them up into suitable sizes for sale.

Hatter's Cords for Bowstrings.

These cords are usually from sixteen to twenty-eight feet long; they are made by twisting the longest and largest intestines of sheep, four, six, eight, ten, twelve being put together according to the intended size.

Their preparation requires more care than that of those which have been described before, and it must be perfectly free from seams and knots. Twist them with the wheel in the usual way, and stretch them well and smooth them after each operation. When partially dried expose them twice to the vapors of burning sulphur, then rub them well with a bunch of horse-hair rope dipped in potash lye; dry them while in a state of tension, cut off, and coil.

Clock-Maker's Cord.

This kind differs from the other in being extremely thin. It is made of intestines of the smallest size, or of stripes made by dividing each gut into two pieces by drawing it down over a kind of lancet mounted upon a leaden or wooden ball, which guides the blade, the two sections of the gut falling into a vessel placed beneath. Sometimes clock-makers use cords of larger diameter made of two or more intestines.

CHAPTER CLXIV.

CORDS FOR MUSICAL INSTRUMENT STRINGS.

These strings should be of uniform diameter, perfectly smooth, round, and free from shreds and filaments. They should be as little liable as possible to stretch or break, and should preserve their polish and transparency during all the changes of weather. Their manufacture requires great experience and dexterity. The best strings have been made from time immemorial in Italy, and although some of superior quality are manufactured in France, the preparation of treble strings is confined to Naples. The membranes of lean animals are well known to be much more tough than those of animals in high condition, and the superior quality of the strings made at Naples is attributed in a measure to the smallness and leanness of the sheep in its vicinity.

The guts intended for these strings are first very carefully scraped. Then dissolve in six pailfuls of water three pounds of potash, and mix with the same quantity of water five pounds of pearlash, clarify the solution by adding to it a little alum. Keep the two solutions in stoneware vessels. Then half fill stoneware pans with the intestines, and pour in the potash liquor, mixed with an equal quantity of water, until the vessels are full.

Steep the intestines three or four days, and even longer, changing the solutions twice daily, and making them progressively stronger by adding each time some of the ash lye and diminishing the quantity of water mixed with it. Each time that the solution is changed, the intestines are removed from the vessel and are replaced, after draining upon a sloping table, and after being passed through a thimble in the manner before described. The effect of the alkaline solution is to bleach and swell the intestines, and they must be removed from it at the first appearance of little bubbles of gas escaping from them, or they will be rendered unfit for use. This occurs oftener in summer than in winter.

After being passed through the thimble so as to smooth and equalize their surface, and washed in fresh water, the intestines are attached to the frame in order to be twisted. This frame is five feet three inches long and twenty-five inches broad. A number of pegs are fixed in one of its sides, and a double number of holes are bored through the other side, so that the cords passed through them are kept in place when pegs are introduced. The ends of the intestines are first placed together upon the edge of the tub in which they have been soaked, and two or three or more of the same diameter and length are selected and fixed to one of the double holes by means of a peg, and the bodies of the intestines are then drawn out exactly of the same length and brought over the corresponding large pegs on the opposite side of the frame, the ends being carried back and fixed in the other one of the two holes. If some of the intestines are not sufficiently long to stretch across, they are sewed to other pieces as near as possible to the end of the cord, so that the points may be near the extremity of the string, and may not interfere with the uniformity of surface of its main part. The intestines are then twisted on the hooked wheel in the ordinary manner, and are exposed for two or three hours in the sulphuring room, after which they are forcibly rubbed with the horse-hair rope and twisted and rubbed again. They are again exposed to the vapor of burning sulphur, twisted once more and sulphuretted for a third time, after which they are left to dry in a state of tension.

The strings are known to be sufficiently dried when one of the strands, upon being removed from its peg, shows no tendency to turn, but remains in the straight position in which it is held. When the strings have arrived at this degree, they are rubbed over with olive oil, cut off at the ends, and coiled up.

The fourth strings of violins, which are wrapped in wire, are neither sulphuretted nor oiled. The string intended to be wrapped is cut off the length of one and a quarter yards, and one of its ends is attached to the hook of the wheel, and the other to the ring of a whirl, which keeps the string stretched by means of a weight at the end of a cord fastened to it and passing over a pulley. The wire is then fastened around the string close to the whirl, and as the wheel is made to revolve, the string and the whirl turn with it. The workman supports the string with his left hand, and the wire passing through his right hand is made to revolve around it in close spiral turns until it is entirely and equally covered.

As has been before observed, the utmost care and skill, on the part of the workman, are required for the manufacture of harp or violin strings of good quality. His experience alone will enable the workman to conduct the different operations with the requisite dexterity.

PART VI.

DIFFERENT KINDS OF APPARATUS USED BY LEATHER MANUFACTURERS.

CHAPTER CLXV.

IMPROVED MACHINE FOR ROLLING GREEN OR WET LEATHER.*

MR. J. WHITNEY, of Winchester, Mass., has invented a new and useful improvement in machinery for treating green or wet leather, so as to express the water or tanning liquor from the same, and not discolor the surface thereof. The following is an explanation of his patented machinery.

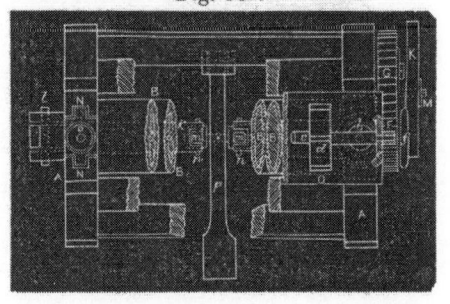

Fig. 161.

Fig. 161 is a plan with a portion of the frame and rollers broken away at the centre to show the treadle.

* Patented by J. Whitney, of Winchester, Mass., March 24, 1863.

654   APPARATUS USED BY LEATHER MANUFACTURERS.

Fig. 162 is a vertical longitudinal section through the centre of the rollers, showing an arrangement of levers for relieving the pressure.

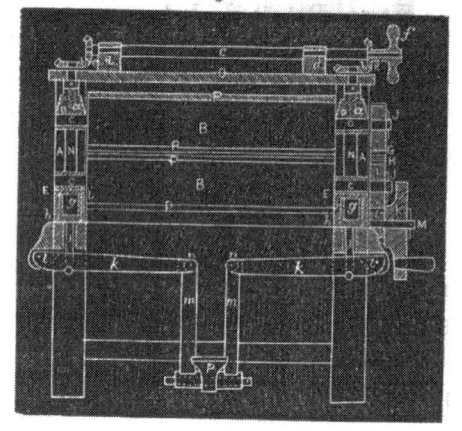

Fig. 162.

Fig. 163, an end elevation of the machine.

Fig. 163.

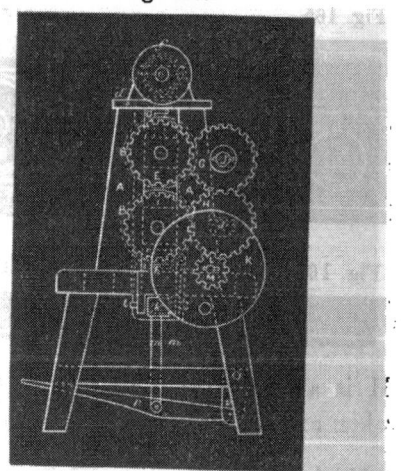

IMPROVED MACHINE FOR ROLLING LEATHER. 655

Fig. 164.

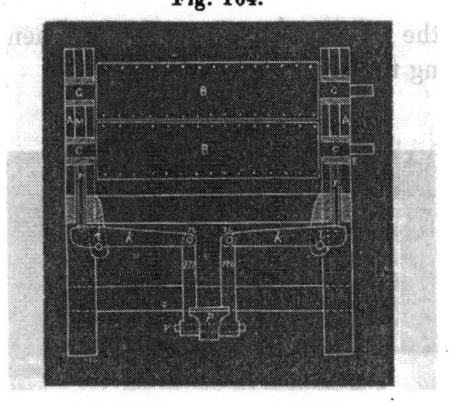

Fig. 164 is a modification of the lever arrangement.

Figs. 165, 166, 167, 168, 169, 170 are details of the machine. Similar letters of reference in the figures indicate corresponding parts.

In the process of tanning skins of which thick leather is made, it is necessary to split the leather in order to reduce the thickness; and in order to accomplish the

Fig. 165.

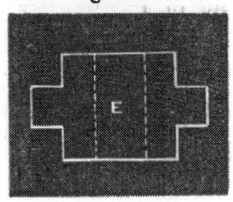

Fig. 166.

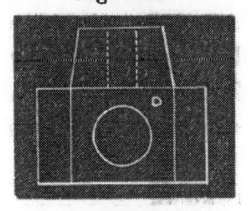

Fig. 167.

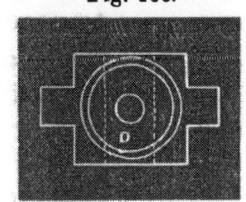

Fig. 168.

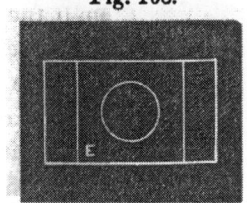

Fig. 169. Fig. 170.

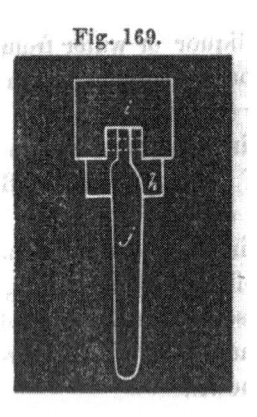

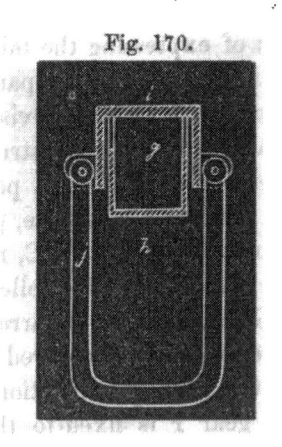

splitting at certain stages of the tanning process, the tanning liquor or water must be expressed from it before commencing the splitting operation, and in the expressing operation, means such as will not discolor the surface of the leather must be employed because the market value is greatly affected by the color.

If iron rollers are used, the tannic acid causes a corrosion of the metal and the rust is imparted to the surface of the leather, and besides this the leather is but imperfectly operated upon, as the surface of the rollers cannot conform to the irregularity of thickness of the leather, nor is it desirable at this stage of the tanning process to so compress the leather as to close its pores, therefore it is impracticable to overcome the irregularity in thickness by making the leather conform to the rollers. The latter difficulty obtains with all other hard surfaced rollers, even though the discoloring of the leather from corrosion might not be experienced.

Many machines have been devised for splitting and rolling leather at one operation. But this process of Mr. Whitney's is especially designed for the use of the tanner; and the only office it is intended to perform is

IMPROVED MACHINE FOR ROLLING LEATHER. 657

that of expressing the tanning liquor or water from the leather in order to prepare it for the action of such machines as have been devised for splitting leather.

AA is a frame constructed in a suitable manner to receive the component parts of the machine. B B are two rollers of equal size, placed one above another, and, with their journals C C, revolving in boxes D D and E. The revolution of the rollers is effected by means of gears F, G, H, I, which are arranged so as to allow the rollers to be set at any required distance apart without breaking the gearing connection as shown.

A gear F is fixed to the upper roller, and a corresponding gear to the lower roller outside of the journals; these gears F and I are both of the same size, and their diameter being less than the diameter of the rollers, the teeth of one never come in contact with the teeth of the other. The intermediate gears G and H are both of a size, but a little larger than the roller gears F and I; they are placed back of the roller gears, and fitted to revolve on studs J, J, attached to the frame. The lower intermediate gear H meshes into and drives the roller gear I; it also meshes into and drives the upper intermediate gear G, and the upper intermediate gear G meshes into and drives the upper roller gear E.

Motion is given to the rollers through the gears by a driving wheel K, with a pinion L attached thereto, which meshes into and drives the lower intermediate gear H; the pinion L is made fast to the driving wheel K, and is fitted to revolve on a stud M, set in the frame below the lower intermediate gear H. The roller boxes, D D and E E, have a tongue at each end, as represented in Figs. 165, 166, 167, 168, and are made to slide up and down in grooves N N, formed in the frame A A. At each end of the upper roller, directly over the journals C C, there is a gear screw a, hung to the cap piece O of the frame, and made to revolve in holes formed therein, and fitted to screw in the upper roller box D, for the purpose of elevating or depressing the upper roller. These screws a, a stand in a vertical position, and have a collar above and below the cap piece O, to prevent them from sliding up or down, and each screw has a fixed level gear b on the upper end above the cap piece O. A horizontal shaft c is placed above the cap piece O, running lengthways of the machine, and fitted to revolve in boxes $d\ d$ on the cap piece O, with a fixed level wheel $e\ e$ on each, and corresponding with those of the screws, and fitted to mesh therein. On one end of this shaft c, outside of the level gear, there is a fixed hand-wheel f, by which the shaft may be turned at pleasure. A rubber spring g, or its equivalent, is confined in a box h, and placed directly under each of the lower roller boxes E E, of sufficient power to give the required pressure. Over each rubber spring g there is an oil protecting cap i, on which the roller boxes E E rest. This cap i projects down on all sides outside of the box n, and is fitted to slide freely up and down thereon, and made to cover the spring g, and keep the oil used in lubricating the journals from coming in contact with it; the cap i also has a stirrup j attached to it, as represented in Figs. 169 and 170. There are two horizontal levers k, k, one at each end of the machine, extending longitudinally directly under the centre of the roller B. Each of these levers k extend through and rest on the stirrup j, and are hung at the outer end of the pins $l\ l$ for their fulcra outside of the frames. There are two connecting links m, m, one attached to the inner end of each lever k, by a pin n, and extending downwards; both of them are connected by a pin o, to a horizontal treadle p, running transversely through the lower part of the machine at the centre of its length. The treadle p is hung at its rear, and on a pin g, in the back part of the frame and the forward, and extends out beyond the front of the frame, so as to give a convenient chance to place the foot upon it. Thus it will be readily seen that by giving a gentle downward pressure with the foot on the treadle, the combined action of the levers k, k, on the stirrups j, j, will cause a depression of the oil protecting caps i, i, together with the lower roller B.

When the pressure on the rollers is not given by the use of springs, this combination of levers may be applied to give the pressure by extending the stirrups up, and attaching them to the upper roller boxes D, D, and attaching the geared screws $a\ a$ to the lower boxes E E; in that case the pressure would be given by the foot on the treadle. This combination of levers may also be used to give the pressure in another form, as represented in Fig. 164; the only change necessary to be made is to place the fulcra pins l, l, of the levers k, k, inside of the frame instead of outside, and stand an upright rod r, Fig. 164, on the outer end of each lever k, extending up centrally to the under side of the lower roller boxes E E. Thus, by giving a gentle downward pressure with the foot on the treadle p, the combined action of the levers $k\ k$ will cause an upward pressure to the lower roller B; in this case the geared screws would be attached to the upper roller boxes, as shown in Figs. 161 and 162.

Operation.

Wet leather to be deprived of water or tanning liquor, is introduced between the two rollers after the same have been adjusted apart to the proper degree; this adjustment being effected by depressing the treadle or raising the upper roller with the geared screws. The leather having been introduced, the rollers are adjusted together by withdrawing the foot from the treadle and lowering the boxes of the upper roller with the geared screws. Now by operating the gearing the rollers B have a uniform rotary motion imparted to them, and the leather is carried through under a pressure due to the rubber surfaces and to the geared screws and to the springs g g. This action upon the leather causes a thorough expression of the water or tanning liquor therefrom. The amount of the pressure is graduated by depressing the springs g, g, and operating the geared screws. It is obvious that the rubber surfaces of the rollers accommodate themselves to the irregular surface of the leather, and thus a uniform action is obtained. It is also obvious that the rubber surfaces protect the leather from discoloration as the tanning liquor cannot get to the iron of the rollers so as to cause a corrosion thereof. It is also obvious that the pores of the leather will not be closed by hardening or flattening down the leather, as the leather is between elastic surfaces.

CHAPTER CLXVI.

MACHINES FOR FINISHING LEATHER.

S. P. Cobb, of South Danvers, Mass., patented, in 1860, a machine for finishing leather, of which the following is a description.

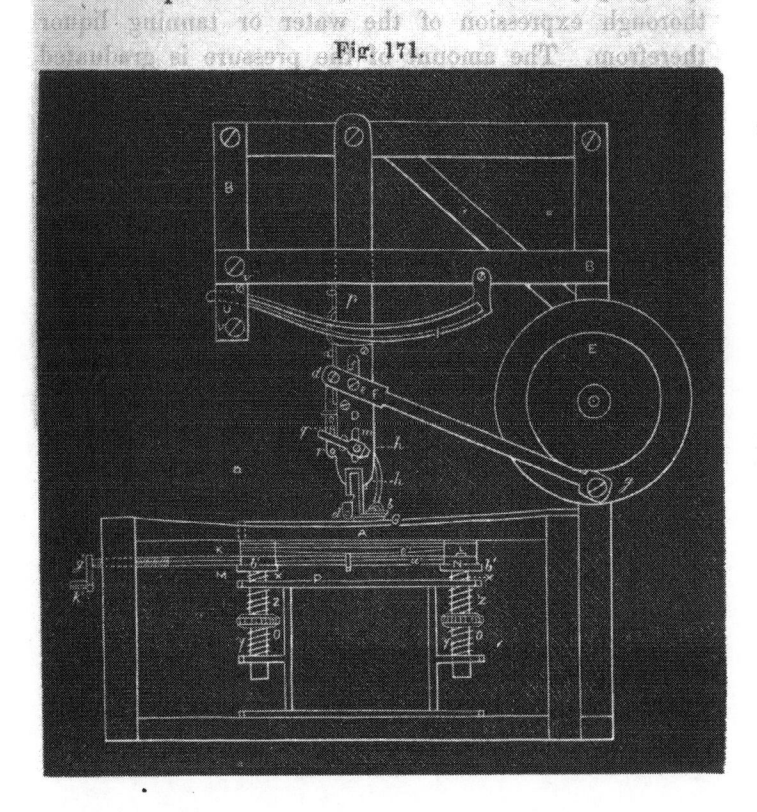

Fig. 171.

Fig. 171 is a side elevation.

Fig. 172.

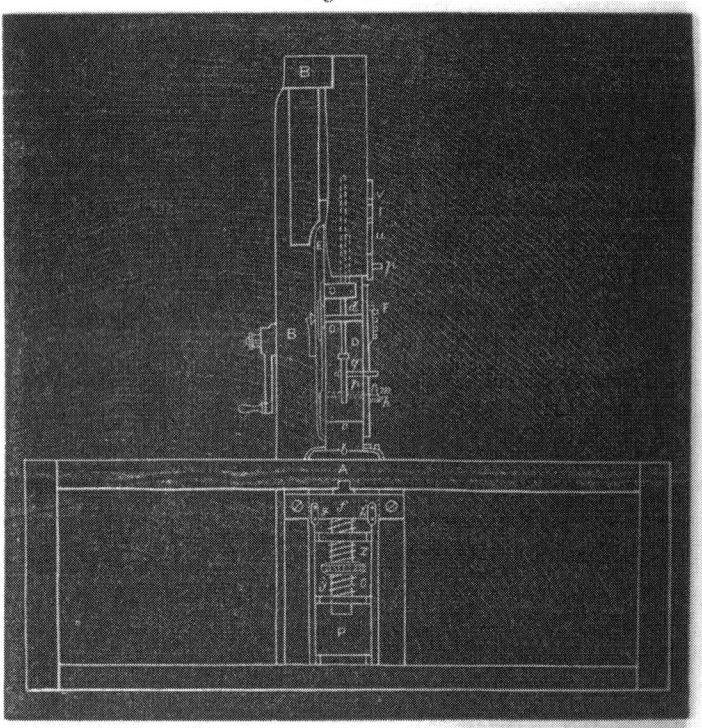

Fig. 172 is a front elevation.

Fig. 173 is a transverse and central section of the machine.

Fig. 174, rear view of the vibrator and parts at its foot.

Fig. 175, top view of the bed cams, their connection and operating screws.

In the drawings, A exhibits a table, from and above which a frame B extends and serves to support a vibrator or vibratory arm D and a fly-wheel E. This arm supports the sleeker or finishing tool *a*, which in

MACHINES FOR FINISHING LEATHER.

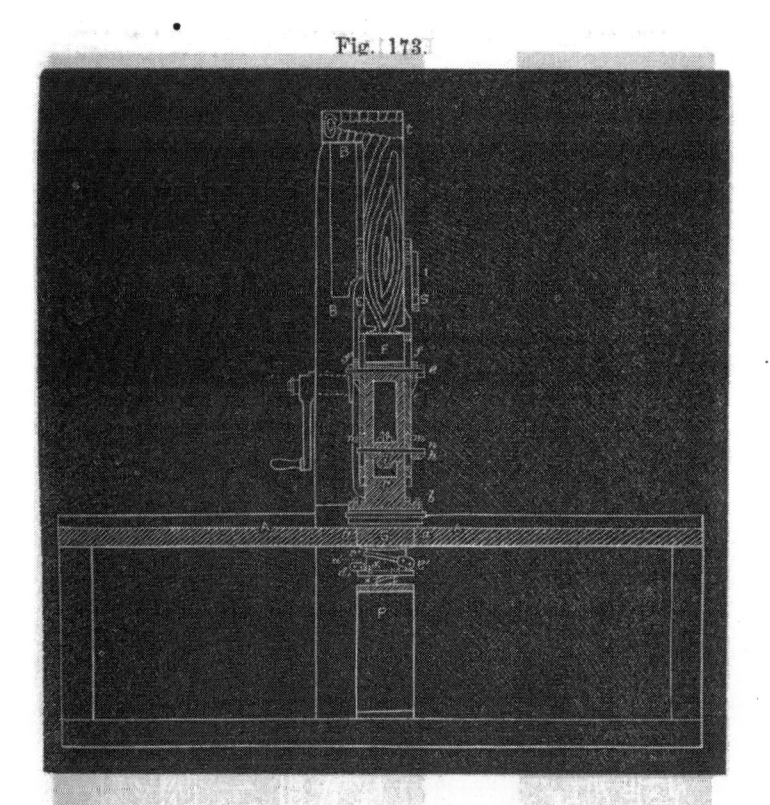

Fig. 173.

this machine is fastened to a tilting plate or frame *b*, which at its front edge is hinged to what is termed the carrier *o*. This carrier slides freely in a longitudinal direction within the vibrator D, and at or near its upper end is jointed to a forked connecting rod F, which straddles the vibrator, and is jointed to the front side thereof, as shown at *d*. Each joint pin *e* of the carrier *c* projects through a slod *f* made in the vibrator, as shown in figure 171; the near end of the connecting rod being applied to, and so as to turn on a crank pin *g* extending from the side of the wheel. By revolving the wheel the vibrator

664 APPARATUS USED BY LEATHER MANUFACTURERS.

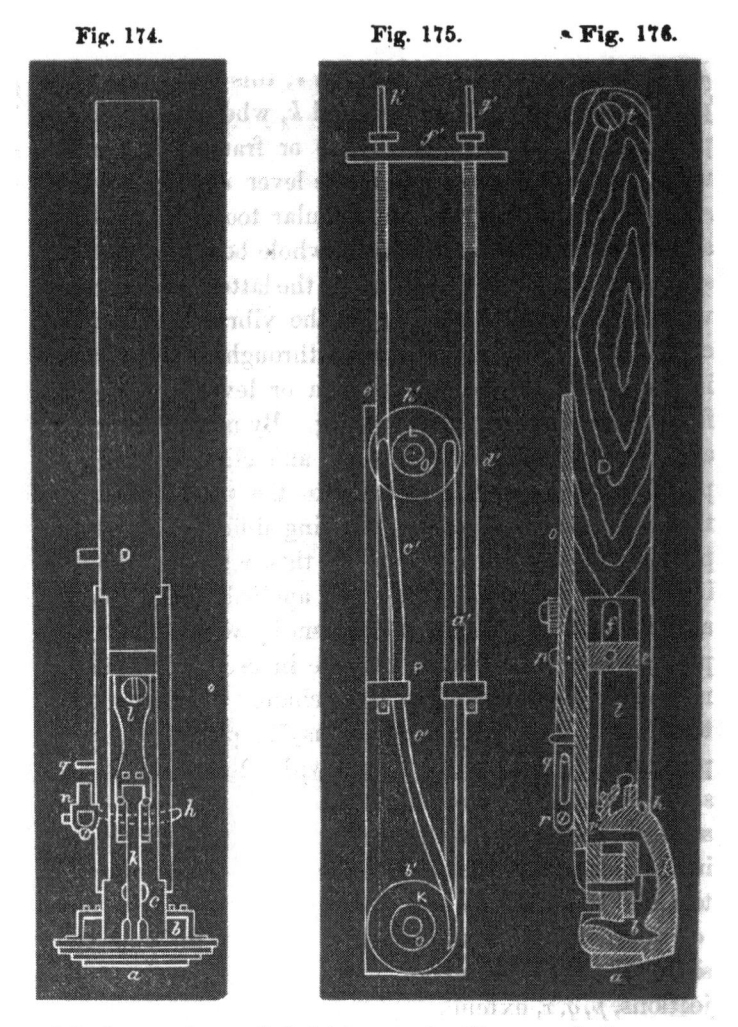

Fig. 174. Fig. 175. Fig. 176.

with the carrier and finishing tool will not only have an oscillating motion imparted to them; but the carrier c will be raised so as to lift thereon during the movement of the vibrator away from the fly-wheel, the tool being forced down upon the skin during the return movement of the vibrator.

Within the carrier c there is a short horizontal shaft h, which supports a sectoral lever i; this lever has its tail part jointed to a connecting rod k, whose lower hinder part hinges to the tilting plate or frame b. Furthermore, the toothed section of the lever i engages with a spring click l, carrying the angular tooth l', and being supported by the carrier c, the whole being arranged as shown in Figures 173, 174, 176, the latter being a transverse and vertical section of the vibrator D and the carrier c. The shaft h extends through a slat m (made in the vibrator) and has an arm or lever n projecting from it, as shown in the drawing. By means of such an arm n, shaft h, sectoral lever i and click, the angular position of the tool, relatively to the upper surface of the bed, may be varied; it being difficult, if not impossible, however, to accomplish this, when the vibrator is in rapid motion. It has been applied to the vibrator and its tilting plate, a mechanism by which the tilting plate, while the vibrator may be in oscillation, may be moved in its fulcrum, so as to change the angle of the tool to the bed while the tool may be passing over any portion of a skin. As a skin will often be thicker in some parts than in others, it becomes desirable to have some means by which the pressure or action of the finishing tool may be equalized on the surface, and this while the said tool may be in movement.

In order to accomplish this, apply to the vibrator a slider D to slide thereon. From this slider three projections, p, q, r, extend, as shown in Figs. 171, 172. The lever n, before described, extends between the projections q, r, while the other projection p is extended into the slot S of a long lever I, whose fulcrum t is supported by the frame B. The said lever, near its opposite end, is pressed against the frame by a friction-plate u, held in place by screws *v v*. By laying hold of the slatted lever, and forcing it either downward or upward, one of the pins *q r* will be made to so act on the lever or arm *n* as to move the same and steadily change the angular position of the tilting-plate or its tool relatively to the bed.

Furthermore, the said bed, as in various other leather or morocco-finishing machines, plays vertically within the table A, and rests on the tops of two cams, K, L, which, in their turn, are respectively supported on two other cams M N. These latter cams are upheld by two vertical rods O', O', each cam turning freely on its rod, but being supported on a shoulder X, formed on the rod. The two rods play vertically within a frame P, which supports springs Y, Y, through which the rods respectively pass, and on which they are sustained by means of screw-nuts Z, Z, screwed on the rods, the whole being as shown in the drawings. In this way the bed C may be said to be supported on springs.

The touching surfaces of the two cams K, M, or L, N, are helical in form. The two lower cams are connected on the same side each by a rod *a'*, whose ends, by means of joint-pins, are connected to projections or flanches *b'*, *b'*, of the lower cams, the same being such as to enable the two cams to move or turn simultaneously in the same direction, while the rod *a'* may be moving lengthwise.

The other two cams are similarly connected by a rod *c'*, but the rod extends from one side of one cam to the opposite side of the other. Screw rods *d' e'* are connected with the two rods *a' c'* respectively, and screwed throughout a stationary plate *f'*, and have cranks *g' h'* on their outer ends, the whole being so that, by turning either crank, a longitudinal movement

MACHINES FOR FINISHING LEATHER. 667

shall be imparted to the rod a' or c', with which the screw-rod of the crank may be directly connected. By revolving one crank, a vertical movement of the bed will be produced. By revolving the other, the bed may be tipped as occasion may require. Thus, by means of the mechanism directly below the bed, the vertical adjustment of opposite ends of the bed may be varied so as to either raise or depress both ends equally at the same time, or unequally, as circumstances may require.

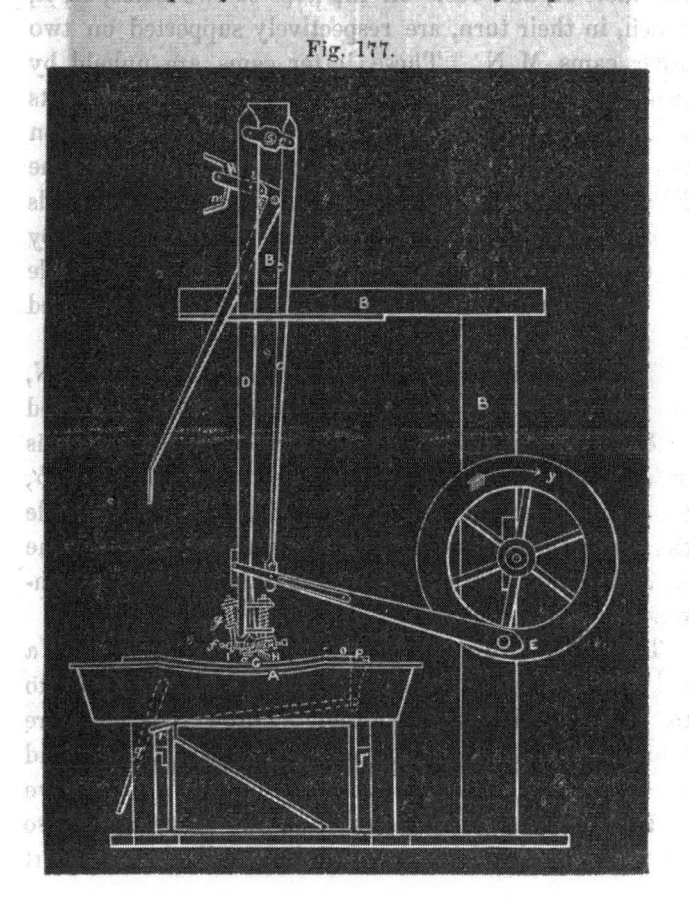

Fig. 177.

668 APPARATUS USED BY LEATHER MANUFACTURERS.

In 1863, Mr. S. P. Cobb invented and patented another machine for dicing, polishing, or finishing leather, a description of which will, we think, interest our readers.

Fig. 177 is a side elevation of the machine.

Fig. 178 is a front elevation of the machine.

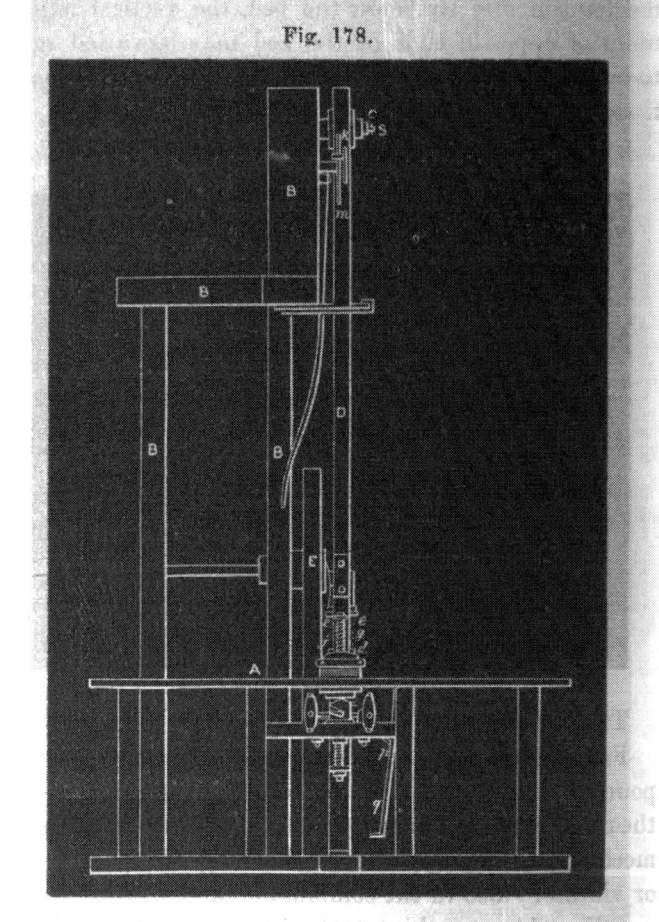

Fig. 178.

Fig. 179 is a vertical section of the machine.

Fig. 179.

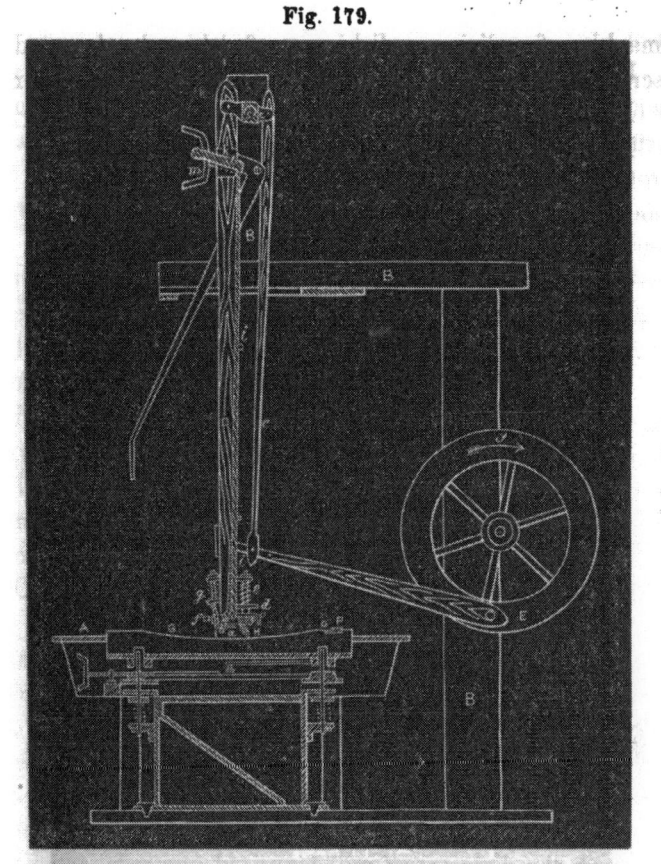

The nature of his invention consists as follows:—

First, in a peculiar mechanism for obtaining the compound movement of the vibrator or dicing staff; also in the combination and arrangement of a brush or cleansing mechanism, with the dicer or finishing tool and its staff or vibrator; also in the combination and arrangement of an adjustable smoothing tool with its dicer and its staff; also in the combination and arrangement of a dicer cleansing mechanism, with the dicer, its staff, and curved bed.

In the drawings, A exhibits a table from and above which a frame B extends, and serves to support the fulcrum S of a rocker lever c, which is arranged as shown in the figures. The dicing staff or vibrator D is jointed to one arm of the said rocker lever, and at its lower end supports the sleeker dicer, or finishing tool a, which is fastened to a tilting plate or frame b, hinged to the lower end of the vibrator or dicing staff D. A forked connecting rod straddles the vibrator, is jointed to it and to the crank pin of a fly-wheel E. Furthermore there is jointed to the connecting rod within its fork, and at a short distance from the dicer staff, a pitman c, which extends upwards, and at or near its upper end is jointed to the rocker lever c hereinbefore described, the arrangement of the said pitman with respect to the dicing staff and rocker lever being as shown in Figs. 177 and 179. On revolving the fly-wheel in the direction of the arrow (y) marked thereon, the dicer staff will not only be vibrated with a pendulous motion, but while moving towards the fly-wheel, the said dicing staff will be moved or pressed downwards towards the bed, in a manner to keep the dicing or finishing tool in contact with a piece of leather when on the bed. So while moving away from the bed, the dicing staff will be raised upwards, so as to elevate the dicer or polishing tool entirely off and keep it out of contact with the leather.

In advance of the polisher or dicing tool, there is arranged a brush H held by a suitable supporting frame d, having one or more springs e so arranged and applied to it and the dicer staff as to press the brush in a downward direction and upon the leather, while such leather may be resting on the bed G. This brush moves with the dicer and its staff, and is for the purpose of removing from the surface of the leather, and in advance of the dicer, any dirt, grit, or any extraneous matter that may collect on the leather, and be likely to cause injury to its surface from the action of the dicer. There is also placed to the rear of the dicer a smoothing tool I, it being carried by a clamp f, attached to the dicer staff. A spring g suitably applied to the smoothing tool serves to depress it, as occasion may require. The object of the smoothing tool is to remove from the surface of the leather, while the machine may be at work, more or less of the graining made by the dicing tool, or in other words, to low down the graining as may be desirable. The said smoothing tool may also be employed irrespective of the dicing tool, and either one or both may be used as occasion may require; a rod i, jointed to the tilting plate b of the dicing tool, extends upwards along the dicer staff, the said rod at its upper end being jointed to the shorter arm of a lever k, whose fulcrum t is supported by the dicer staff. This lever projects from the dicer staff, and has projecting from its longer arm a pin or stud which goes between the prongs of a forked lever m, formed and arranged as shown in the figures. By laying hold of the longer arm of said forked lever, and moving the same, the dicer tilting frame may be either raised or lowered, as circumstances may require.

At the front end of the curved bed G, there is arranged a dicer cleaning tool or scraper o, which is supported by a vibratory lever p, to which vibrating movements may be imparted by means of a foot lever q, and a connecting rod r. The same being arranged as shown in Figs. 177 and 179. By elevating the scraper previous to the expiration of any advance movement of the dicer, the said dicer in the continuation of its movement will be carried in contact with the scraper in such manner as to be cleaned or scraped thereby. In this way the grease or dirt which may collect on the dicer or polishing tool may be removed therefrom.

The advantages of this machine are the following:—

1st. It is noiseless comparatively, and adapted to all the different kinds of work of all others combined with much more convenience.

2d. The tools are carried in an oblique position, which may be varied so as to make a sharp or flat angle in relation to the bed, which is done by the rod i, i, encased in the pendulum and connected at or near b, to the tilting plate b, and operated by the long armed forked lever $m\ m$ acting on the pin of the short lever at I, which is connected with the encased rod i, i, etc., all done while the machine is at work.

3d. The bed may be adjusted (by means of the cams and rods) by the workman without leaving his place or stopping his work.

4th. The tools may be cleaned from dirt or any extraneous matters which may chance to stick to them while at work, without stopping the machine by means of a scraper at the back end of the bed and operated by the foot rod q and its connection at the front end.

Any kind of tool may be used, either stone, glass, or steel. There is also an apparatus for pebbling, which can be attached at pleasure; and further, a brush which can be used in connection with the other tools, or without, and is nicely adapted to belt, cord leather, etc.

CHAPTER CLXVII.

LEATHER POLISHING MACHINE.

The highly-finished surface of fine leather is usually imparted by hand labor. In the following we present a view of the machine for accomplishing this object, which does work in a superior manner, and effects a great saving in time and labor. This machine was invented by Messrs. R. and C. Smith, of Stockport, New York. The construction and operation of this machine is as follows:

The framing A carries a vertical shaft B, which works between two parallel bars C at the top, and is connected at D to a bar sliding between two rollers at E and F. This vertical shaft B is jointed to the connecting rod G, which, in turn, is fixed to a cross-head sliding on guides between the timbers H; from this cross-head proceeds the pitman I to the crank wheel J, which is turned by power of any kind, either steam, water, or by hand when neither of the other two is available; the bar B has a metallic roller K, fastened at its lowest extremity, so that it can be adjusted to suit the nature of the work, and the skin to be polished rests upon a metallic plate underneath it. At one side of the skin may be seen a clamp L; the skin is attached to this, as shown, and the clamp is then fed over the surface of the table, the roller, which is the polisher, acting on it continually. The belt which drives the feed gear is seen at M. There is also an arrangement for raising the tool-stock so that the operator can place another skin underneath the roller or tool when the first one is completed. This

674　APPARATUS USED BY LEATHER MANUFACTURERS.

Fig. 180.

arrangement consists in applying a lever at one side of the frame so that the workman can press upon it with his foot, and then accomplish the object. The frame slides through mortises N at the bottom. The stroke of this machine may be altered at will by simply turning the hand wheel O. This wheel is on a shaft that runs through the main driving shaft, and the pinion P is secured to it. There is a rack Q, on one side of the crank, which elevates or depresses the pin when the pinion is turned; suitable means are provided for keeping the pin stationary, except when it is necessary to move it. These are the principal parts. It is obvious that when the tool stock B is put in motion that the sliding action of the wheel K will impart a high finish to the leather in a manner apparent to every one without any further explanations. These machines are said to work exceedingly well. Several of them have already been put in operation.

CHAPTER CLXVIII.

JACOB PERKINS'S MACHINE FOR POMMELLING AND GRAINING LEATHER.

Fig. 181, side view.
Fig. 182, front view.
Fig. 183, plan.

a. Framework held together by bolts with nuts.

b. Large horizontal wooden shaft, its iron pivot c turning in the copper collars d.

e. Four wooden arms radiating from the middle of the shaft b, and curved at their bases.

f. Four fluted or grooved cylinders of lignum vitæ wood, in the ends of the wooden arms. The grooves are near or far from each other, according to the grain intended to be given to the leather.

Fig. 181.

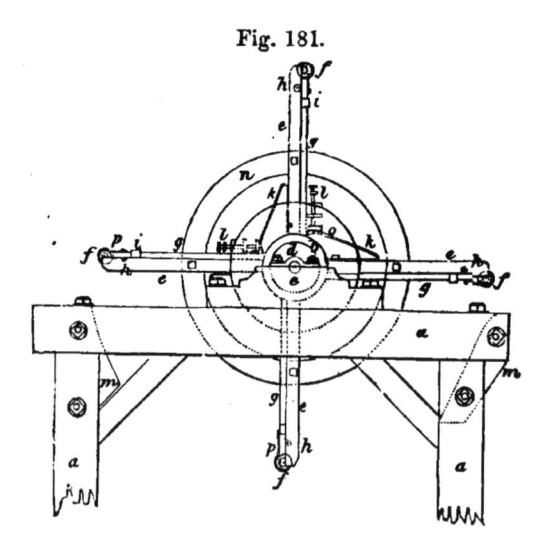

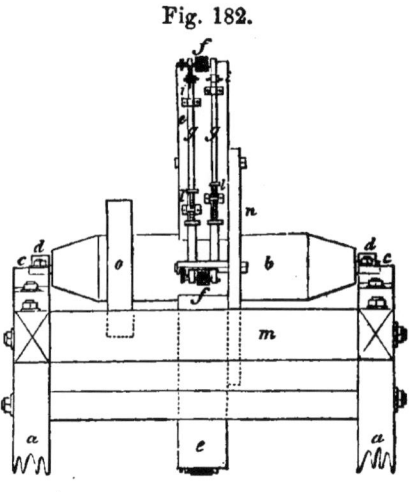

Fig. 182.

g. Two iron grooves attached to each of the arms, and receiving the pivots of the cylinders *f* in their extremities; these grooves are kept in place by the guides *i*, and slide against the blocks *h*, Fig. 181.

k, Fig. 181. Springs resting against the lower part of the base of the grooves *g*, and by their elasticity tending to push these grooves away from the shaft *b*.

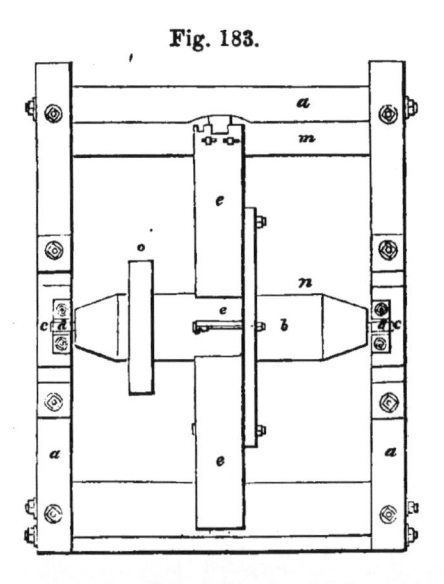

Fig. 183.

l. Screw and nut, the end of which presses to the required extent upon the lower end of the groove *g*. When this screw is tightened, the groove presses down the spring, and approaches the shaft; when loosened the opposite movement takes place.

m. Pieces forming a support or frame, and curved in the form of arcs of the circle of which the shaft is the centre, so as to allow the arms to revolve freely. This frame should be very firm, and supplied with a surface of hard wood for the cylinders to rotate upon.

n. Circle attached by bolts to the arms, and serving to strengthen them.

o. Pulley upon the shaft *b*, intended to receive the motive power by means of a band.

678 APPARATUS USED BY LEATHER MANUFACTURERS.

The leather, when prepared in the ordinary way, and ready to be grained and polished, is placed upon the wooden table or frame *m*, and the shaft *b* is turned. The grooved cylinders *f*, stamp furrowed surfaces upon the leather, and owing to the resiliency of the springs, adapt themselves to its variations of surface and thickness. The skin is moved about by the workman so that the different portions shall all be grained in the required directions, and during the process, the surface of hard wood *m* is from time to time moistened with water or oil, to prevent it from becoming heated.

The cylinders *f*, in the course of their revolution, press against brushes which keep them clean. Upon each of their axles is a ratchet-wheel with a catch *p*, Fig. 181, the object of which is to prevent them from revolving. When the grooves of the cylinder are worn out at one point, they can be renewed by turning the cylinder round, so as to present a new part of its circumference.

The shaft, the pulley, the arms, and the circular support can all be made of cast-iron in one piece.

CHAPTER CLXIX.

NISBET'S GROUNDING AND PUMICING MACHINE.

MR. JOHN NISBET, of England, recommends the substitution of machinery for the hand in the laborious process of grounding, or frizing, and has invented for that purpose a very ingeniously constructed apparatus. He employs knives and pumice stones, or other sufficiently rough materials, set into revolving cylinders which are made to turn in contact with the surfaces of leather. Fig. 184 represents a side view; and Fig. 185 a longitudinal section of one of these machines; *a a*, framework, *b*, axle turning in the supports *c c*, and made to revolve

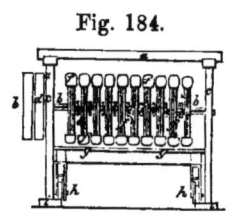

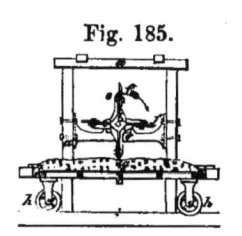

Fig. 184.　　　　　Fig. 185.

by means of a strap around the pulley *d*; *e e*, series of cross-pieces, or arms, each of which is provided with a paring-knife *f*, which, by the revolution of the shaft, is brought in contact with and made to pare the surface of the skin or portion of skin placed on the mattress *g*. This mattress is stuffed with hay or other suitable material, and is covered with oiled leather. It is placed upon the top or table of a car mounted on four grooved wheels *h h*, which run on the railroad *i i*.

The arms which carry the knives are made to revolve at least 360 times in a minute, and the rapidity of motion can be increased if it is desirable to do so.

The workman places the skin, or portion of skin, upon the mattress, and pushes the car forwards, so that the end of the piece shall be under one of the series of blades. These latter, by their revolution, then draw the leather away from the workman, and pare its surface while he retains the extremity in his hands and retards its progress more or less, according to the amount of action to which it is desired to expose it. When one side is thus pared throughout, the band is slipped off from the pulley, so as to stop the revolution of the axle; the car is drawn back, the leather turned, and the strap being replaced, the other side is made to undergo the same treatment. Besides great rapidity, this operation secures a uniform paring of the leather.

When light and thin skins are treated in this manner,

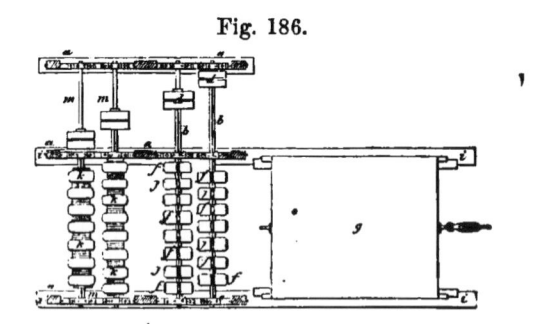

Fig. 186.

the intervals between the knives are filled up with wooden blocks, or wedges, so that the axle is surrounded by a compact cylinder of wood, beyond which the knives project only to a slight extent. Fig. 186 shows the plan, and Fig. 187 the side view of the machine so modi-

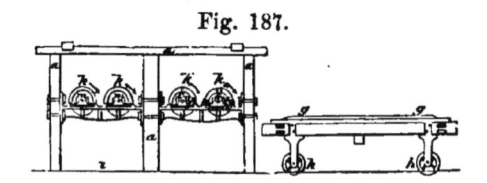

Fig. 187.

fied; and Figs. 188, 189, 190, and 191, exhibit a front view of the arms and knives from between which the

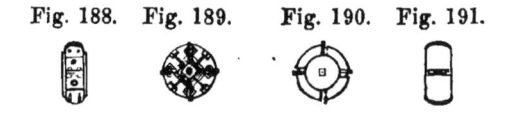

Fig. 188. Fig. 189. Fig. 190. Fig. 191.

wooden wedges have been removed; a section; a side view; and front view of the series of knives f, and of the wedges j.

Figs. 186 and 187 also represent the apparatus for *pumicing* leather. The pumice stones *k*, or other suitable rough substances, are attached to the shafts *m*, which are made to revolve by the ordinary means. In other respects, the machine resembles the preceding one, the same letters indicating corresponding parts of both.

The leather submitted to the action of this machine, is first pared by means of two sets of knives *f*, which are represented in the figure as turning upon two shafts, and it then passes under the *pumicing* cylinders, which

Fig. 192. Fig. 193. Fig. 194.

act progressively upon every part of the surface. Figs. 192, 193, and 194 exhibit, the first section, the second

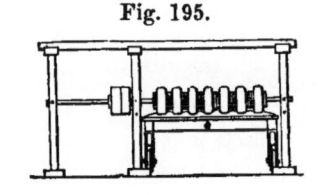

Fig. 195.

a side view, and the third, a front view of these cylinders and stones. Figures 195 and 196 show, the one a

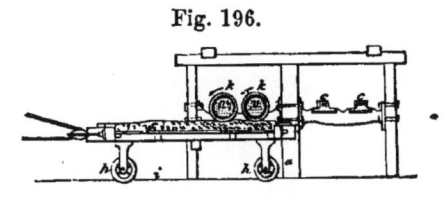

Fig. 196.

cross section, and the other a longitudinal section of the pumicing machine while in action.

CHAPTER CLXX.

EMBOSSING OF LEATHER.

This is a method of manufacturing ornamental leather intended for furniture, hangings, bookbinding, and other uses.

Bernheim and Labouriau's Process.

The plates, by means of which the figures in relief are stamped upon the leather, in this process, are made of type-metal, or fusible alloy, cast in plaster moulds, on which the reverse of the figures has been designed. The type-metal plates are used for stamping leather without the assistance of a press, by which they would be broken to pieces, and those of fusible alloy are employed for large single designs in panel upon hangings, or for the repetition of the same figures, by associating a number of plates together. For this latter purpose, as many plates as are necessary for the whole design are placed together upon a level surface, in their proper places, and their edges are then joined together, first by running a hot iron along them, and then by filling up the interstices with melted fusible metal. The projecting veins of metal are then cut and scraped off, and the whole presents the appearance of a single plate.

The large plates thus prepared will not bear the force of a press, but are used with the assistance of heat. The ingredients of which the alloy is composed are not in the proportion to make the most fusible metal, the quantity of lead being somewhat greater than in the ordinary alloy. Those plates which are intended to be subjected to the action of the press, also, have a smaller quantity of tin in their composition than is usual, so as not to be rendered brittle by an excess of it. These latter should be perfectly smooth below, and should be of considerable thickness. They are prepared of the proper thickness in the following manner: A fine thin sheet of tin-foil is first pressed into all the cavities of the original plaster mould, so as to give a reversed copy of it, and a plate of softened wax of the desired thickness of the metal plate, is forced into it so as to take its form. A plaster mould is then taken of this wax impression, covered with tin-foil, and the model and the mould, placed parallel to each other, are separated by little leaden tubes, which are equal in height to the thickness of the wax-plate before used.

In order that the casting should be successful, the plaster models and moulds must be perfectly dry, and heated to the temperature of the fused alloy, and when filled must be placed in a position to cool rapidly.

The large compound plates are exposed, in stamping, to the action of heat by means of pipes conveying steam, placed below them.

Two means of stamping leather with figures in relief are resorted to, that by use of the press, and that in which the stamping is effected by hand or the chisel, with the assistance of heat. The leather is first fulled in tepid water, until it becomes as soft as it is possible to make it. In this condition it is placed upon the plate without being stretched, and is made to enter all the depressions of the figures by pressing and squeezing it in every direction with the fingers, while the projections and folds upon the edges of the design are smoothed down by a wooden instrument like the chisel used by sculptors. When the leather is in contact with all parts of the mould or plate, if the character of the figures is such as to admit of perpendicular pressure, the frame is filled up with warm sawdust, and the gentle force of a press is applied above, so as to keep the leather and metal surfaces in contact. After a time, the screw is loosened, the moistened sawdust is removed, and replaced with fresh, the press is again brought to bear, and this process is repeated once more. At the end of the third operation, the leather will generally have acquired enough consistency to retain the form impressed upon it, and it may then be removed from the plate and dried in the stove-room.

If the plate be too large for the press, or if there are many projections on its surface, having slight or narrow bases, the pressure must be conducted entirely by hand. For this purpose the plate is warmed by placing it upon the tubes conveying hot air or steam, and the moistened leather is laid upon it, and forced down into all the depressions and grooves of the plate by means of paper-hangers' paste, which is thrust and pressed down into them with the end of the wooden instrument or chisel, and when the chief cavities are filled in this way, the rest of the surface is worked so as to bring the leather in contact with the plate in every part. The folds which form at the borders and corners are then smoothed out with the chisel, first longitudinally, and then across, until they are made to disappear. The whole surface of the leather is then rubbed with a dry sponge so as to remove the excess of moisture, and the workman then continues forcing it down into the depressions with a chisel, until it is perfectly dry, when the rest of the paste is removed from the hollows. The elasticity of the leather, when dry, allows of its removal from the plates even when the elevations on the latter are larger at top than at bottom.

If it is intended to stamp a design, or series of designs, the dimensions of which require the use of a number of skins, the latter are first cut into parallelograms, and their edges are pared and thinned down. One of them in the softened state is then placed at an angle or edge of the plate, and is impressed with the figures in the manner before described. A second skin is then placed alongside of the first, with one edge projecting about an inch over its border, and is printed in the same way; a third is placed next to and partly over the second, and so on, even if a number of rows of skins are required, until the whole extent of the plate is occupied. After the skins have all been pressed, sponged, worked with the chisel, and dried, their overlying edges are gently raised, covered with strong glue, carefully replaced, and retained in their original position, by covering the whole with sawdust and weighted planks, until it dries and forms a continuous sheet.

By these two processes, leather beautifully ornamented in relief, and suitable for many purposes of luxury, may be manufactured. These ornaments may be allowed to retain, in a slight degree, the suppleness and elasticity of the leather, or may be rendered perfectly firm and hard, by pouring into them, while still warm upon the castings, a solution of gum-lac in alcohol, or a watery solution of glue, and filling up all the depressions with paste, sawdust, or, what is still better, the raspings of cork mixed with glue. Their surfaces may be made impervious to moisture, by the penetration of the gum-lac or of other resinous material, and may be painted, gilded, and varnished.

F. W. East's Process.

This invention, patented in 1851, differs from the usual method in being exclusively applicable to the flesh side of leather, and thus producing an effect superior to that obtained by embossing the grain side. It is adapted to all tanned skins except those which are oil-tanned.

The skins, just sufficiently shaved to remove flaws and give them uniform thickness, are to be immersed in water of 120° F., and brushed on the flesh side to remove dirt and open the fibre. They are then to be folded grain-side inwards and the edges sewed together in bag form, so as to prevent the intrusion of the dye. The dyeing succeeds "scouring" and "sweetening," and is effected with much weaker liquors than are used for dyeing the grain side of skins; but requires a longer time, as the process must be several times repeated in order that the color may penetrate the fibres, and appear uniform. They are then rinsed, opened, and dried.

When dry, they are to be "perched" on the flesh side with a moderately sharp knife, so as to soften the fibres, and nap the surface without cutting the flesh off. Each skin is to be again folded as before, and passed through a glutinous solution of one part, by measure, of size in three parts of water; then stretched on boards to dry, trimmed around the edges, and bruised on the surfaces with cork, to render them soft, the flesh side being kept outwards.

The skins, just previous to being embossed, are moistened on the grain sides with clean water, and then laid together, with the grain sides in contact, and under cover in order to prevent access of air, and thus to promote the thorough penetration of the water through the hide, thereby making the gelatinous matter auxiliary to the production of a gloss upon the embossed parts. The embossing is done with engraved rollers, previously heated to 250°, and exactly in the same manner as is employed for embossing velvet, cloth, &c.

CHAPTER CLXXI.

DEGRAND'S MACHINE FOR SPLITTING AND SHAVING LEATHER.

A TRANSVERSE section of Degrand's machine is shown in Fig. 197. A horizontal knife a, longer than the

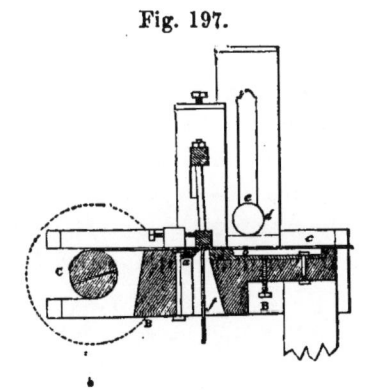

Fig. 197.

greatest width of a skin, is fixed upon a wooden table B. A cast-iron plate b is set in the table in front of the knife-blade, and is intended to support the leather c at the desired elevation, its position being regulated by screws and nuts. It is movable in every direction, being supported upon four springs. Above it, a little wooden shelf d, which is pressed upon by a roller e, maintains the leather in close contact with the plate, so as to flatten and stretch it thoroughly before it is exposed to the blade. One of the separated surfaces of the leather, as it rises over the knife, is attached to a wedge-shaped tongue, which projects from the whole length of the wooden roller C, and is wound up upon the latter as it advances.

The leather is seen in the figure as split by the blade of the knife, the upper portion of it being already rolled upon the cylinder c. The lower half passes down under the knife through a slit in the table, and the uncut portion, which is about to be exposed to the action of the blade, is seen resting upon the table, and pressed down by the upper plate d. The movement of revolution is given to the cylinder by a winch which turns a pinion gearing with a toothed wheel at one of its ends. Two operations are required to split the leather, one-half of it being first separated, the skin being then unrolled from the cylinder, turned, and the split part attached to it, so that the other half may be in like manner divided.*

CHAPTER CLXXII.

GIRAUDON'S MACHINE FOR SPLITTING AND SHAVING LEATHER.

THIS interesting invention has been described by M. Armengaud, in the *Publication Industrielle des Machines, outils et appareils*, t. vi. liv. 9. The machine is simple

---

* The author has omitted to explain the mode of forcing the edge of the leather upon the knife-blade, by which the first part of the incision is effected. The process can only be rationally understood by supposing that a longitudinal incision is first made down the centre of the skin extending half through in thickness, and that, while one edge of the skin is attached to the roller, the knife is accurately engaged in the bottom of the cut previously made.

in construction, operating rapidly and continuously upon the skins exposed to its action, and can be employed either for the purpose of dividing the leather into thin sheets or leaves, or for that of diminishing and equalizing its thickness.

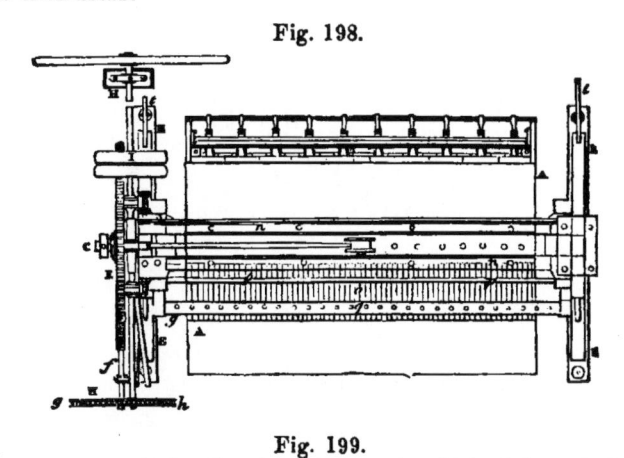

Fig. 198.

Fig. 199.

The hide or skin which is to be cut is placed upon the circumference of a large drum or cylinder A (Figs. 198,

690   APPARATUS USED BY LEATHER MANUFACTURERS.

199, and 200), carefully turned and attached to three crosspieces with six branches or spokes B, which are con-

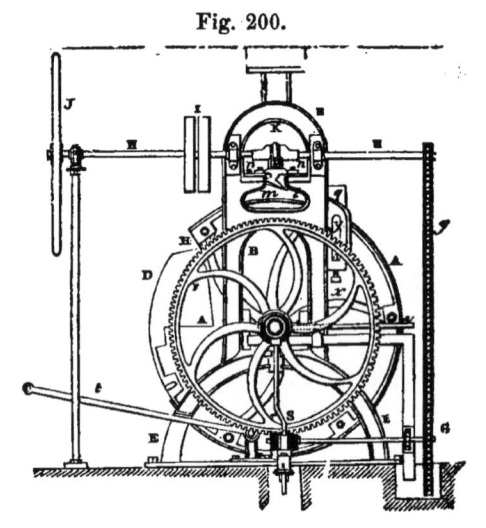

Fig. 200.

nected with the cast-iron horizontal shaft C. This cylinder is hollowed out, as seen in the section shown in Fig.

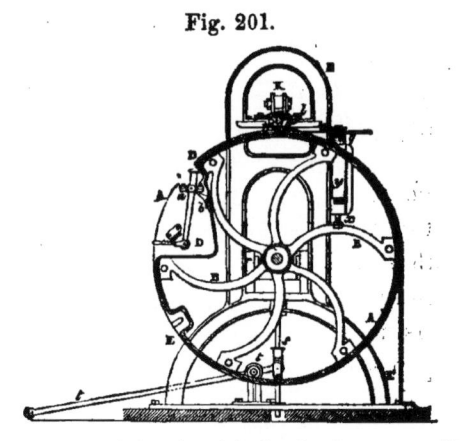

Fig. 201.

201, for the reception of a kind of pincers D (Fig. 207), which serve to support the extremity of one of the detached portions of skin against the edge of the cylinder. For this purpose, these pincers are all mounted upon the same iron axle a, which rests upon small supports b, fastened to the cylinder, and they are kept in place by a flat, angular regulator.

The horizontal shaft c, which extends on each side beyond the cast framework E, carries at one end the

Fig. 202.   Fig. 203.

larger cog-wheel F, which is geared with the endless screw e (Figs. 202 and 203), situated at the lower part

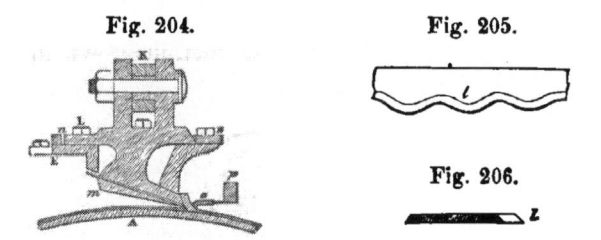

Fig. 204.   Fig. 205.

Fig. 206.

of the machine, and revolving upon the axle f, the slow movement of which is produced by means of the wheel G, the endless chain g, and the pinion h. This pinion turns upon the cast-iron shaft H, which is made to revolve by means of a strap passed over one of the pulleys I; a fly-wheel J giving the necessary uniformity to the motion. A roller i, at the end of a counterpoised lever j,

Fig. 207.

presses against the endless chain, and gives it the proper amount of tension.

The shaft H is elbowed in the middle, so as to form a crank for the head of the cast-iron rod K, which is articulated at its other end with the middle of the movable rabbit or carriage L (Figs. 201 and 204). At the base of this is attached the long cutting steel blade which is inclined a little in direction to the horizon, and touches the exterior of the cylinder when made to approach it. It is very thin and of an undulating form, as shown in the plan (Fig. 205), so as to act upon the leather like a saw, the teeth of which are rounded off; by which arrangement it cuts more easily and with less wear of edge. This knife-blade is attached to the base of the rabbit by means of an iron plate m, the position of which can be accurately adjusted with a screw.

The movable rabbit or carriage is dove-tailed into the tops of two cast-iron supports E, which compose the framework. The grooved plates n above it prevent any deviation from the reciprocating rectilinear movement produced by its connection with the crank. Thus the shame shaft H which moves the crank causes the revolution of the lower axle f, and of the endless screw, by means of which the drum upon which the skin is wound is also turned; but with a motion exceedingly slow, when compared with that of the crank above, and the knife connected with it. The ratio of size between the pinion h and the wheel G being as one to eight, and the large wheel F having 244 teeth, it follows that the cylinder only turns once while the axle f and the endless screw are making 244 revolutions, and the main shaft H is making 1952. By causing the main shaft to revolve 75 times in a minute, the knife is made to cut the leather 150 times, so that a skin 78.74 inches in length will be split in 15½ minutes.

The leather is maintained in close contact with the cylinder in front of the knife-blade by the pressure of a series of flexible spring-keys which adapt themselves to its irregularities of surface, and keep its uncut edge firmly pressed down by means of a crosspiece extending along its whole breadth and supported by projections upon the inside of the framework. A strong bar g serves to support the other ends of the springs, and also assists in keeping the leather applied to the surface of the cylinder. Two grooved uprights y are adjusted in rectangular vertical mortises of the framework, and the screws x, in their lower parts, regulate the height of the bar.

The lower separated portion of the split leather remains in contact with the cylinder while it revolves, and the upper part may be rolled off, if desired, upon a roller placed above the machine.

When a skin is divided throughout, in order to replace it by a fresh one, it is necessary to lower the cylinder from its position, in order to disengage the knife from the surfaces. For this purpose, the cushions r of its axle are adjusted in movable collars supported upon uprights s and s', which can be elevated or lowered by means of iron swipes t, which are supported upon the base of the framework E, and are connected by a crossbar, or treadle, which the workman can lower by a pressure of his foot, the collars and uprights being only movable in a vertical direction. In order that the cog-wheel and the screw may continue in gear during this change of position, the cushions which support the axle of the latter are connected with the crossbar between the two uprights.

694 APPARATUS USED BY LEATHER MANUFACTURERS.

The revolution of the cylinder can be stopped at pleasure by ungearing the wheel E, which can be moved upon its axle by the handle u and fork v.

Thirty-six raw hides can be readily divided by this machine in a day of twelve hours.

CHAPTER CLXXIII.

MACHINES FOR SPLITTING AND SHAVING LEATHER.

RICHARDSON'S MACHINE, invented by Alpha Richardson, of Massachusetts, is generally used throughout the United States. It serves for splitting either green or tanned hides. There are two modifications, that shown in perspective, by Fig. 208, is intended for splitting

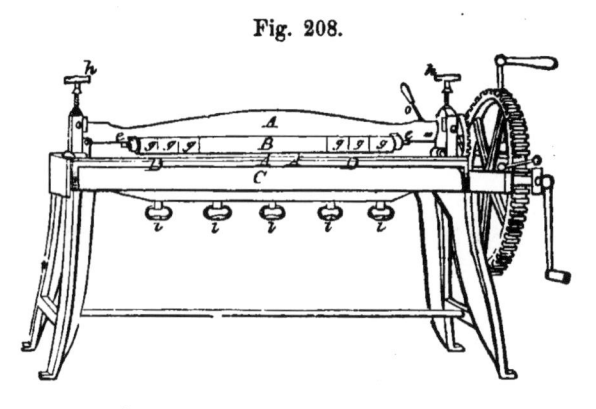

Fig. 208.

upper leather, which is drawn between the knife and roller by means of a crank and windlass. This is styled the Tanner and Curriers' Machine. A is the cast-iron piece connected with the gauge-roller B, which revolves on the centres $e\ e$, and is turned up by the lever o, to allow the placing of the leather upon the top of the knife and back-spring $A\,A$. The skin being in right position, the gauge is then turned back, and forms the gauge for the thickness of the skins which may be regulated at will, by means of the screws $h\,h$. B is the roller with the sectional tubes $g\,g\,g$, which are arranged to turn on its end, and to serve as friction-rollers when the shanks and loose part of the skin are being drawn through. The knife D is bolted, firmly, to the bed by the screws $i\,i\,i$. The leather is placed upon the cylinder C, and drawn through against the knife D by the aid of the crank at the end of the machine.

The leather is prepared for splitting by being only partially dried. In New England and in the middle States it is generally split before it is wholly tanned, as the quality of the leather is thought to be improved by finishing the tanning after it has been thinned or divided by the machine.

The other modification of the machine is constructed for splitting and skinning sole leather, welt leather, and stiffenings for boot and shoemaker's use. It is represented by Fig. 209, and works by means of rollers which

Fig. 209.

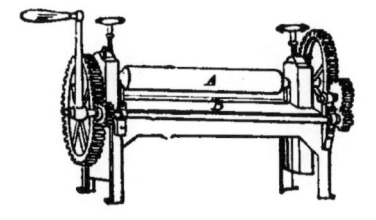

force the leather against the edge of the knife. A is the gauge-roller, which is regulated by screws according to the thickness it is desired to split the skin. B is the lower roller, which forces the leather, or hide, against the knife, and the two are put in motion by the crank, &c., at the end. The leather must be damped through before being placed in the machine.

SEGUIN'S SHAVING AND SMOOTHING MACHINE.—This machine consists of two metallic rollers, each six feet six inches long; one of them five and nine-tenth inches in diameter, having a cutting-blade set spirally into its surface, and intended to pare the skin wrapped around the other roller, which is two feet five inches in diameter. A longitudinal groove in the surface of the lower roller receives the end of the hide, which is kept in place by means of wedges. The cutting-blade begins to form a spiral at the middle of the upper roller, and makes the entire circuit on both sides before reaching the ends. The pivots of the lower roller turn in two fixed supports, and those of the upper one in two levers, by means of which it can be lowered upon, or raised from the surface of the first one. These rollers turn in opposite directions, and their motion is so adjusted that the lower one turns completely around once, while the upper is making twelve revolutions.

The end of the leather having been engaged in the groove, it is gradually wound upon the roller, while the

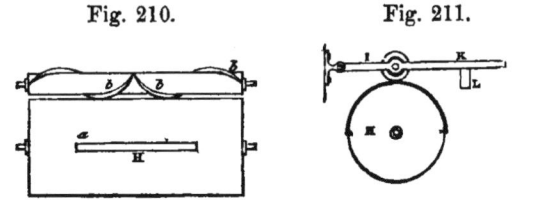

Fig. 210.   Fig. 211.

levers upon which the upper roller turns being charged with smaller or greater weights, as the case requires, the skin, with its grain side up, is shaved from the centre to the sides, throughout its whole extent. Fig. 208 is a front view, and Fig. 209 a side view of this machine. H, the lower roller, with the horizontal groove a for the end of the leather; I, upper roller, with the blade b, curving spirally from the centre; K, lever carrying the roller, and supported by the crosspiece L.

Chapman's Improved Leather Splitting Machine.

The annexed engraving represents an improvement for getting the most possible surface out of a given weight of leather, and splitting the thick hides into two thinner sheets.

A thin circular knife C (Fig. 213), made dishing with the convex side uppermost, is made to revolve by suitable machinery, with its sharp edge just above a horizontal table D, and the leather to be split is drawn over this table against the edge of the revolving knife. The lower sheet O of the split leather passes down below the knife around the feed roller F, to which it is secured by the clamping bar f. The leather is drawn along and pressed against the edge of the knife by the rotation of the feed roller F, which is turned by the machinery at the proper speed for this purpose. The upper sheet P passes above the knife and is removed by hand. A series of springs G, with their ends curved to fit near the cutting edge of the knife, are placed above the leather to hold it down close to the table. The shaft which carries the knife rests upon a stiff spring at the bottom, and is pressed down by a set screw at the top, by which means its distance above the table may be regulated and the thickness of the lower sheet of leather varied at pleasure. The table has racks d secured to its lower side, which racks mesh into pinions I, the shaft of the pinions having a crank upon its end. By this means the table

698 APPARATUS USED BY LEATHER MANUFACTURERS.

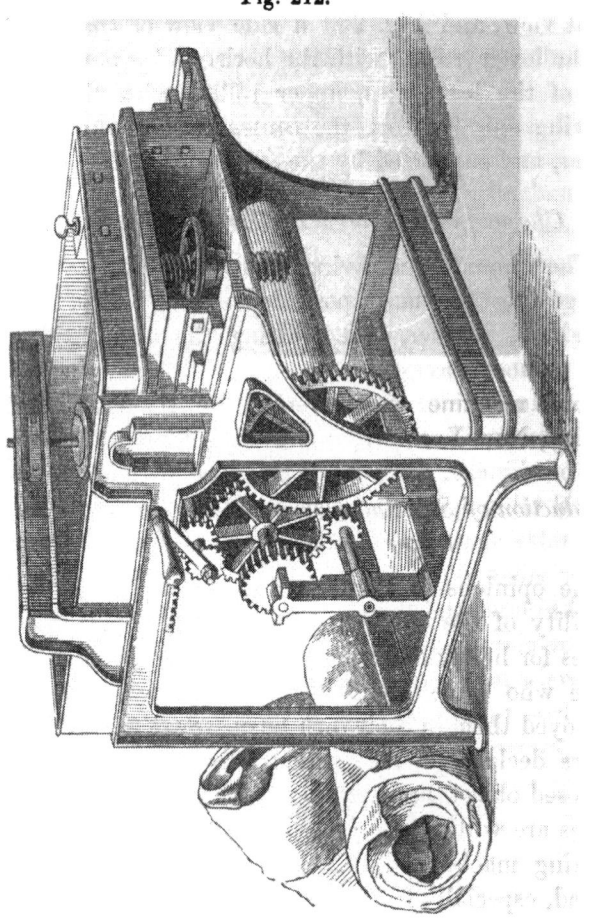

Fig. 212.

may be drawn back from the edge of the knife, for the purpose of placing the sheet of leather to be split upon it. After the leather is placed, with one end secured to the feed roller, the table is carried up to the knife, the machine started, and the operation proceeds. This in-

Fig. 213.

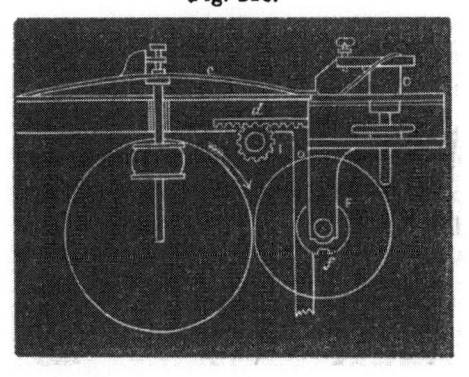

genious machine was invented by H. E. Chapman, Albany, New York.

*Introduction of Splitting Machines into German heavy and upper Leather Tanneries.**

The opinions of tanners in Germany upon the desirability of the employment of leather splitting machines for heavy and upper leather are widely different. Some who have seen them in operation or actually employed them in their own business are satisfied, while others declare them in advance to be unsuited to the proposed object, and many who have bought such machines are willing to dispose of them at a loss. These splitting machines have either been introduced from abroad, especially from America, or they have been constructed at home chiefly after the American models, but not much has hitherto been made public concerning the practical working of the same. The reason of this, after allowing for the strong antipathy leather-makers have to writing, lies partly in the fact that those who after much

* By P. A. Gunther. Gerber Zeitung.

pains have at last become satisfied with the execution of the splitting machine, do not desire, from motives easy to be understood, to promote its spreading by their indorsement, and again in this that such as are not content with the machine and its execution, although they confess to themselves their errors in judgment, will not publicly admit it in a report, fearing to write that they have deceived themselves. The meetings of union German tanners have already several times afforded opportunities to see machines of German make in operation. We first saw such a one at the general meeting at Dresden constructed by M. Wilsdorf upon an American model. The second was one exhibited by the Wamosy tannery at the Hamburg meeting, and at the meeting recently held at Eisenach we saw another of Wilsdorf's American machine, having many improvements of his devising; but owing to the late date at which it was sent to the exhibition, only a few saw it in operation. In our opinion, however, a couple of hours' experimenting is not enough to form an accurate judgment of the worth or working capacity of a machine like this, which is always so complicated and so difficult to manage. The operator must understand thoroughly the working of the machine in order to produce satisfactory results. The best machine, unless worked by an adept, will give imperfect results. The manifold inquiries that have been addressed to us by members of the trade, we could only reply to in this inefficient manner; for the goods sent to our leather establishment for split goods showed only too clearly the great importance of the proper working of these machines, and we have remarked with interest how, through greater practice, the goods of the same shippers have gradually grown better and better, until they finally thoroughly answered the requirements of consumers. From the purchaser of the splitting machine exhibited at Eisenach, M. J. Dritzen, a Rhenish white leather tanner, we recently received a communication regarding the operation of his splitting machine which may be of interest to our readers.

"I first became acquainted with the splitting machine in America, in 1849, at which time I was with Schafer & Co., in Pittsburg, Pa. They use it there to split large heavy ox-hides into three parts. The grain was used for carriage-tops, and it was lacquered; the middle portion, also lacquered, was employed for various purposes, and the last third, the fleshy part, was dressed for upper leather. Since then other business took my attention from tanning, until the summer of 1861, when personal matters induced me to return to it.

"As a tanner having in mind the great lever of industry, the division of labor, I decided upon upper leather tanning, without on this account removing the advantages offered to me in my position by the small leather trade, with the consumers of the neighborhood. I purchase the various descriptions of leather necessary for the latter branch of my business at the large markets, while I appear at the same time upon the same markets with my own manufacture as a seller. And thus I am in a position to restrict myself to one single article as a manufacturer, to perfect my means of producing the same, and to concentrate my labor and attention upon one single point.

"My object consists, by selecting the best possible raw material, and by working the same in the most suitable manner, in producing a prime article which will leave me a clear profit at any large market. In this connection I recollected the American splitting machine which appeared the more suitable to me as the hides in my section possess very compact layers. I became acquainted with the constructor of the splitting machine, and from him I got the machine exhibited at Eisenach. The maker gave me instructions on the spot in the manipulation of the machine, using a single hide for the purpose, and in the same time he agreed, in case I should not be able to work it readily, to give me more thorough instructions upon a few dozen of hides. But the necessity for this did not occur. I put up the machine myself, and gradually have acquired the necessary dexterity in splitting, although not without paying for it, that is, after having damaged a dozen hides more or less. Its manipulation is not difficult, but it requires practice, and much of it before one attains to proficiency; still I must not omit to mention that with a little precaution, the damage done by the machine, except to the grain side, leather is not essentially injurious. When the splitter lets the knife cut the hide improperly small hollows or *noses* as they are called are made, and sometimes also, but rarely, holes; but by skilful handling the machine gives splendid results.

"I work into upper leather generally hides weighing 35 lbs. green weight. Such a hide split, so that brisket and butt are of equal solidity, yields me from 13 to 14 lbs. of well-tanned, well-dried, and slightly fatty leather, and a split weighing two or three pounds which I hitherto sold at the best price. My customers are quite satisfied with the durability of the new sort of leather. The only thing that the leather, especially the split, loses, is the grain and consequently the softness, and on this account it is particularly suitable for the hinder parts of boots. The advantage in my opinion consists principally in this, that I can split white leather thin, and thus obtain a more valuable article, without its being essentially injured, for as I work my leather strongly I gain a more valuable split. I split my leather during the process of tanning, after the hide has received half of the tan liquor. The more the leather is tanned the easier the splitting knife cuts, and the finer and smoother is the bisection. M. Knoderer, of Strasburg, to whom I made known my intention of buying a splitting machine, advised me to select one with which I could cut my hides in the beginning while they were yet in the lime. He assured me that all the great manufacturers of France bought such machines only; but the matter of expense restrained me from following this counsel, as such a machine cost $720.

"However, they possess important advantages over others. By their employment the process of tanning is accelerated and a considerable economy in tanning material is effected. A large amount of hide cutting, which is now useless to me, being only half tanned, could be turned to account as glue. But, as I have said, my financial position did not allow me to procure such a machine.

"In conclusion, I would call special attention to the following in answer to the erroneous opinion that splitting machines are only adapted to large establishments. My business is a very small one. I tan yearly only from 400 to 600 pieces of white dressed skins, but I hold that a limited trade is better than an extensive, that, therefore, a tanner had better devote one-half of his capital to the procurement of suitable apparatus and keep an inn with the other half than to avoid machines and other suitable apparatus, and only produce goods in large quantities."

INDEX.

A

Age of trees relatively to the richness of their bark in tannin, 113
Albumen, 169, 172
Aldrich's apparatus, 403
Alumed skins, 564
Aluming hides, 619
Animal oils, 615
Apparatus used by leather manufacturers, 653
Ash bark, 104

B

Barks, 96, 98
Bark, ash, 104
    birch, 103
    beech, 103
    black-thorn, 103
    chestnut, 103
    chopping machine, 146
        Birely's, 159
        Bourgeois's, 150
        Farcot's, 146
        Lespinasse's, 153
        Wiltse's, 155
    cinchona, 104
    cinnamon, 101
    containing the most tannin, parts of the, 112
    elm, 104
    estimation of the value of, 123
        chemical process, 123
            Bell Stephens', 125
            Davy's, 125
            Gerland's, 131
            Muller's, 126
            Warrington's, 124
    hemlock, 107
    horse-chestnut, 103
    Lombardy poplar, 103
    oak, 107
        American, 110

Bark—*continued.*
    oak, black, 110
        European, 108
        white, 110
    poison-oak, 104
    pomegranate, 103
    proportions used, 252
    sassafras, 102
    sumach, 104
    tamarisk, 107
    wild olive, 104
    willow, 106
Barking of trees, 112
    most convenient time, 113
    influence of the season and place at the time of, 115
Baron's process, 481
Beam, marking on the, 237
Beating of leather, 257
    and rolling by machinery, 257
    Bell's process, 480
Berendorf's machine, 270
Berenger & Sterlingue's process, 371
Bernheim and Labouriau's process of embossing, 682
Blet's process, 481
Bunting's process, 476
Burbidge's process, 393

C

Calf-skins called alumed skins, 564
    classification of, 295
    currying of, 522
    English, 525
    grained, 556
    leather for belts, 557
    oiled, 522
    tallowed, 524
    tanning of, 291
    waxed, 293, 526
Catechu, 78, 82
Chapman's improved leather-splitting machine, 697

INDEX.

Chestnut bark, 103
Cinchona bark, 104
Cinnamon bark, 101
Cochran's process, 475
Color of red Russia leather, 584
Common russet, 521
Cordovan leather, 333
Cords from intestines of sheep, manufacture of, 645
    clock-makers', 648
    different, 647
    hatters', 648
    musical instruments, 643
    rackets, 647
Corniquet's process, 379
Cox's machine, 275
Cuirs a muron leather, 425
Currying, 487
    calf-skins, 522
    goat-skins, 571

D

Daniel's process, 478
Danish process, 339
D'Arcet's process, 366
Decrease in weight of bark when exposed to the air, 115
Degrand's machine for splitting and shaving leather, 687
Depilation by caustic soda, 204
    steam, 203
    sulphuret of calcium and soda, 204
Desmond's process, 393
Dietz's process, 477
Dipping, 488
Disinfection of workshops, 642
Distillation of the empyreumatic oil of the birch-tree bark, 578
Divi-divi, 93
Drake's process, 398
Dressing, bran, 225
    decomposition of the white, 226
    method of working the, 223
    rye, 227
Drying hides, 622
    leather, 253
Dunseith's process, 473

E

East's process of embossing, 686
Eggleston's process, 476
Ellagic acid, 65, 71
Elm bark, 104
Embossing of leather, 682

English calf-skins, 525
    hides, 518
    process, 391, 443
Epidermis and cutis, with reagents, behavior of the, 167
Excrescences containing tannin, 86
Exposure to the air, 629
Extractive, 73

F

Fibrin, 169
Flaming, 628
Flint hides, 368
Flotard & Delbut's machine, 269
Flowers, 88, 91
    and flower tops, list of, 94
Fruits, 88, 91

G

Gallic acid, 65
    chemical properties of, 65, 68
    composition of, 65
    preparation, 65, 66
        Braconnot's, 66
        Fiedler's, 66
        Scheele's, 66
        Ure's, 67
Gelatin, 169, 171
Giraudon's machine for splitting and shaving leather, 688
Glossed leather, process to prepare, 354
Goat-skins, bleaching, 326
    currying, 571
    tanning, 322
Goldbeater's-skin, 643
Grain black, 506
Grained calf-skins, 556
Greases, 615
Greasing tanned hides, 557
Guiot's process, 483
Gut-dressing, 637

H

Halvorson's process, 461
Hannoye's process, 433
Harness-makers, leather for, 569
Harper's process, 479
Hatch's process, 420
Heald's apparatus for tanning hides, 247
Hemlock bark, 107
    tanning, 456
Hibbard's process, 454

INDEX.

Hides, aluming, 619
   English, 518
   greasing tanned, 557
   hippopotamus, 181
   horse, 178
   ox, 177
   proper treatment of, 173
   raising, 195
   salting, 173, 181
   soaking of foreign, 186
   stacking, 198
   tallowing, 624
   treading, 623
Hill's process, 480
Horse-chestnut bark, 103
Horse-hides, tanning of, 335
Hungary leather, 613
   defects in the quantity of, 634
   improvements by Curandeau, 636
   Kresse's process of preparing black, 633
   made of cow and calf-skins, 631
      horse-hides, 631
   uses, 635

I

Indian method of preparing elk-hides, 419
Introduction, 17
Importation of hides at Boston for 1863, 24, 25
   at New York for 1863, 22, 23
   at Philadelphia for 1863, 26
   at Salem for 1863, 26
   for the past sixteen years, 21
Irish process, 425

J

Jahkel's process, 569
Jennings's process, 370, 611
Johnson's process, 447

K

Kalmucks' process, 427
Kennedy's process, 474
Kid, imitation, 466
Kino, 78
Kips, 178
Kleman's process, 394
Knowlis's process, 402

L

Lacker for shoes and leather belts, black, 604
Lamb-skins, method of coloring small, 467
Lathe-cords, 644
   from intestines of sheep, 645
Lard, 615
Leather, 165
   action of frost on, 282
   beating, 257
      and rolling, 259
   belt, 284
   bottles, 338
   Cordovan, 333
   cow, 288
   cuir a muron, 425
   defects of the, 280
   drying of the, 253
   with grease, saturation of, 563
   harness-makers', 562
   Hungary, 613
   machine for finishing, 661
      for rolling green, 653
   method of coloring white tawed, 469
   morocco, 329
   oil, 510, 515
   patent, 600
   preparation of stretched, 498
      of sleeked, 499
   process to prepare glossed, 354
   proximate principles of, 165
   quality of, 280
   red, 339, 590
   Russia, 575, 583
   tallowed or grained, 504
   Transylvania, 227
   Turkey, 429
   Wallachia, 219
   water, 510
   water-proof, 610
   waxed, 518
   white, 521
Leaves, 88
   list of tanning, 89
Leprieur's process, 360
Lime process, inconveniences of the, 201
Lombardy-poplar bark, 103

M

Machine, Chapman's improved leather-splitting, 647
   Cox's, 275
   for chopping barks, 138

708 INDEX.

Machine—*continued.*
    for rolling green leather, 653
    finishing leather, 661
    Flotard & Delbut's, 264
    pressing, 270
    Richardson's, 694
    Seguin's, 279
        for shaving, 696
    Wiltse's, 277
Male fern, 96
Marsh rosemary, 97
Marking, 630
Method of estimating the tanning power of astringent substances, 123
    of making leather water-proof, 611
Mill for grinding oak-bark, 143
Morocco leather, 329
Mutton suet, 615
Myrobalans, 93

N

Needham's process, 479
Nenory's preparation to render leather water-proof, 607
Newton's process, 367
Nisbet's grounding and pumicing machine, 678
Nossiter's process, 438
Nuessley's process, 480
Nutgalls, 86

O

Oak-barks, 107
    American, 110
    black, 110
    European, 108
    poison, 104
    white, 110
Odoriferous substance of the birch-tree bark, nature of, 582
Ogereau's process, 390
Oiled calf-skins, 522
Oils, dolphin, 617
    fish, 616, 618
    porpoise, 617
    process to give to a mixture of different oils the properties of fish, 618
    process for rendering vegetable oils to take the place of fish, 618

P

Parchment, 592, 595

Patent leather, 600
Perkins's machine for pommelling and graining leather, 675
Piling, 630
Plants containing tannin used as a substitute for oak-bark, 117
Poison-oak bark, 104
Pomegranate bark, 103
Pommelling, 493
Preparation of the intestines of cattle, 637
    operation, 638
Process, American, 391
    D'Arcet's, 366
    Baron's, 481
    Bell's, 480
    Bletz's, 481
    Berenger & Sterlingue's, 371
    Bunting's, 476
    Burbidge's, 393
    Cochran's, 475
    Corniguet's, 379
    Daniel's, 478
    Danish, 339
    Desmond's, 393
    Dietz's, 477
    Drake's, 398
    Dunseith's, 473
    Eggleston's, 476
    English, 391, 443
    Guiot's, 483
    Halvorson's, 461
    Hannoye's, 433
    Harper's, 479
    Hatch's, 420
    hemlock, 456
    Hibbard's, 454
    Hill's, 480
    improved, 352
    Indian, 419
    Irish, 425
    Jahkel's, 569
    Jennings's, 370, 611
    Johnson's, 447
    Kalmucks', 427
    Kennedy's, 474
    Kleman's, 394
    Knowlis's, 402
    Leprieur's, 360
    Needham's, 479
    Newton's, 367
    Nossiter's, 438
    Nuessley's, 480
    Ogereau's, 390
    quick, 482
    Robinson's, 476
    Rotch's, 399
    Seguin's, 352
    Shakers', 458

INDEX. 709

Process—*continued.*
   Smith & Thomas's, 606
   Spilsbury's, 396
   Squire's, 442
   Snyder's, 452
   to tan with decoction of oak-bark, 391
   tanning leather in Russia, 586
   Thompson's, 476
   Turnbull's, 447
   Vauquelin's, 380
   Webster's, 475
   Wells's, 475

Q

Quick process, 482
   tanning, 471

R

Raising by acids, 202
   by barley, 210
   by sour tan-liquor, 228
   by yeast, 236
Red leather, 339, 590
Residues and products of tanneries, 484
Rhatany, 97
Richardson's machine, 694
River work, 618
Robinson's process, 476
Roots, 96
Rotch's process, 399
Russet, common, 521

S

Sassafras bark, 102
Seeds, 88, 95
Seguin's machines, 279, 696
   process, 352
Shagreen, 592
Shakers' process, 458
Shaving, 492
   improved machine, 696
Sheep-skins, tanning of, 322
   coloring of, 327
Skin, 165
   calf, 178
   composition of the, 169
   constituents of the, 169
   deer, 181
   goat, 180
   gold-beater's, 643
   pig, 181
   porpoise, 181

Skin—*continued.*
   preliminary treatment of, 183
   seal, 181
   sheep, 179
   structure of the, 165, 166
   suitable for tanning, 173, 176
   treatment of, 173
   washing, 183
Smith & Thomas's process, 606
Smith's leather polishing machine, 673
Spilsbury's process, 396
Splitting machine, 694
   in Germany, 697, 699
Squire's process, 442
Stretching, 494
   hides, 622
Sumach bark, 104
Sweating process, 208
Synder's process, 452

T

Tallow, 616
Tallowed calf-skins, 624
Tallowing, 624
Tamarisk bark, 107
Tan, 41, 137
   liquor, preparation of the, 233
   vats, 239
Tannin, 41, 44
   artificial, 61
      composition, 61, 62
      first variety, 61, 62
      properties, 61
      second variety, 61, 63
      third variety, 61, 63
      turf, 61, 63
   of bark of trees, 59
   black precipitate in sesqui-salts of iron, 60
   catechu, 59
   chemical properties, 44
   composition, 44, 50
   contained in principal tanning substances, 134
   green precipitate in sesqui-salts of iron, 60
   impure, 53
      chemical properties, 53
      preparation, 53, 55, 56, 57, 58
      varieties, 53, 58
   from various sources, 64
Tanning, 183
   Aldrich's apparatus, 403
   calf-skins, 291, 444
   chemical researches on the art of, 344
   chemistry of, 41

Tanning—*continued.*
   with decoction of oak-bark, 391
   different skins, 337
   extracts, 161
      Connel's, 161
      Steers's, 162
   goat and sheep-skins, 322
   with grape skins, 357
   hemlock, 456
   hides, Heald's apparatus for, 247
   horse-hides, 335
   juices, 78
   lamb-skins, method of, 467
   materials, 76
      table, 77
   with myrtle, 356
   origin and development of the art of, 31
   processes, 239
      of Leprieur, 360
   quick, 471
   saps, 78
   sheep-legs, 337
   with statice, 358
   substances necessary to tan an equal quantity of leather, comparative quantities of different, 136
   with tar and soot, 417
   theory of, 340
   time necessary for, 251
   wheel, 413

Tawed leather, method of coloring, 469
Tawing, 463
Tea, 88, 90
Thompson's process, 476
Transylvania leather, 227
Treading hides, 623
Turkey leather, 429

V

Valonia, 91
Vauquelin's process, 380
Varnishing leather for belts, 605

W

Wallachia leather, 219
Water, 192, 193
   upon the quality of the leather, influence of, 191
Water-proof leather, 606
Webster's process, 475
Weighing, 630
Wells's process, 475
Wild-olive bark, 104
Willow bark, 106
Wiltse's machine, 277
Woods, 96
Working on the beam, 237
   with the round knife, 496

Printed in Great Britain
by Amazon